Football and the Law

Football and the Law

Nick De Marco QC, Blackstone Chambers

Bloomsbury Professional

LONDON • DUBLIN • EDINBURGH • NEW YORK • NEW DELHI • SYDNEY

BLOOMSBURY PROFESSIONAL
Bloomsbury Publishing Plc
41–43 Boltro Road, Haywards Heath, RH16 1BJ, UK

BLOOMSBURY and the Diana logo are trademarks of Bloomsbury Publishing Plc

First published in Great Britain 2018

British Library Cataloguing-in-Publication Data

A catalogue record for this book is available from the British Library.

ISBN:	PB:	978 1 84766 882 0
	ePDF:	978 1 78451 236 1
	ePub:	978 1 78451 235 4

Typeset by Compuscript Ltd, Shannon
Printed and bound by CPI Group (UK) Ltd, Croydon, CR0 4YY

To find out more about our authors and books visit
www.bloomsburyprofessional.com. Here you will find extracts, author information,
details of forthcoming events and the option to sign up for our newsletters

Reviews of Football and the Law

'*Football is big business. Increasingly we find the need to consult specialist lawyers in relation to commercial and regulatory issues arising in our work. This book covers the full spectrum of issues that we and our clients often have to deal with. It is a must have resource for anyone in the football business.*'

Jonathan Barnett, leading football agent and chairman of the Stellar Group

'*If you want to understand legal issues in football, this book, written by some of the best lawyers in the field, should give you all you need to know.*'

Joey Barton, professional footballer and broadcaster

'Football and the Law *is a comprehensive and well-written book that provides a helpful guide to the legal principles and procedures that arise within the football industry. The authors of the book have done a great job in breaking down many of the opaque legal areas within football including the international governance and regulatory frameworks, all the way through to players' contracts, taxation and youth development.*

This book will not only be of great value to students, junior lawyers and those wishing to develop a legal or commercial career in football, but also those who are well-established lawyers, executives, agents and professionals, working within football, who will find the analysis and practical guidance in the book a useful reminder, or as a cause for reflection on current practices and structures.

I congratulate Nick De Marco QC, and the contributors to this book, for producing a body of work that is clearly a labour of love, with contributions from leading professionals with both a personal and professional enthusiasm for football, sport and law.'

Sean Cottrell, CEO Law in Sport

'*This comprehensive and accessible book, in which Nick De Marco QC and his specialist contributors focus in detail on the particular legal issues faced by those regulating, participating in, and financing the world's most popular sport, is a welcome addition to the available texts. It should not only form a part of every sports lawyer's library, but also be of great use to governing bodies, football clubs, players' representatives and the sport's financial partners.*'

Adam Lewis QC, author of *Sport: Law and Practice* and barrister, Blackstone Chambers

'*A unique, comprehensive work that provides guidance on virtually every legal aspect of football. As useful to the legal practitioner as it is to the executive or administrator working in football.*'

Lee Hoos, chief executive officer of QPR, former CEO of Burnley, Southampton, Leicester City and Fulham

'*An informative and well-written guide to the legal issues thrown up by football on a daily basis, from player contracts and transfers, discipline and arbitration to TPO and agent regulation. A must-read for those working in the industry and curious fans.*'

Matt Hughes, Deputy Football Correspondent, The Times

'Football and the Law *provides you with the best experts and legal minds in the football industry all at your fingertips. Given all the domestic and international legal complexities in football today, together with the risk of litigation, this becomes an essential legal reference book for every Football Club Executive.*'

Jeff Mostyn, Chairman AFC Bournemouth and FA Council Member.

'*This is quite simply a stunning book. It will become an automatic classic and is a must have for any practitioner serious about wanting to work in the field of football.*'

Nick Randall QC, Chairman Nottingham Forest FC and sports lawyer

'*This book makes out a strong case for the existence of a body of "football law" justifying a work dedicated to the subject. By its expert, detailed and wide-ranging coverage of the relevant legal issues, it represents the fine execution of an excellent idea.*'

The Rt. Hon. Sir Stephen Richards, Former Lord Justice of Appeal and judge in the seminal *Bradley v Jockey Club* case.

'*The Laws of the Game for professional football and all its regulations need to mirror and reflect both civil and criminal law in their letter and spirit, both on and off the field. This book provides that reflection for all students of both the game and the law, pertaining to the world's greatest spectator and participant sport. In an ever changing litigious world this is a must read for all players, spectators and administrators to keep ahead of the game!*'

Gordon Taylor OBE, Chief Executive of the Professional Footballers' Association and former professional football player.

'*At a time when there has never been a greater need for clarity as to the legal and regulatory aspects of the modern game,* Football and the Law *provides the reader with access to a one-stop-shop of expert commentary and analysis of the highest quality in all of the key areas.*'

Howard Wilkinson, Chairman of the League Managers Association, former manager of Notts County, Sheffield Wednesday, Leeds United and Sunderland and former Technical Director of The FA.

Preface

This book has been many years in the planning. It was originally the brainchild of Nick Randall QC, one of the foremost lawyers practising in football disputes in England. It was Nick's concept, and he was responsible for bringing together many of its outstanding contributing authors. In the summer of 2017 Nick moved on to bigger and better things – from being a frequent advocate for football clients in legal disputes to becoming the Chairman of one of the most prestigious football clubs in English (and European) football history, Nottingham Forest FC. Nick Randall QC is not only an expert in all things football (the law, as well as the game), but he has a special generosity of character not always found in either the legal or football industries. Many of those of us who have contributed to this book owe much to Nick, and so it is fitting that this book is dedicated to him.

My most grateful thanks go to all of the 53 contributing authors of this book. Amongst them are most of the leading practitioners in legal disputes in football, and we are most fortunate to have them share their considerable expertise over the many chapters in this book. It is their years of specialist expertise, across a wide span of areas, that provides the real value to this work. It is not often that so many leading solicitors and barristers from competitor firms and sets of chambers can collaborate together on one project, and it is testament to the commitment of them to this subject area. Thanks to them, I am confident this book brings a wholly unique breadth and depth to the subject. I am also grateful to many others, especially those working for the football regulators, many mentioned in the footnotes, for providing particularly useful and unique information for us to draw on.

As explained in the Introduction, it has been the commercialisation of the world's biggest game, leading to an increase in legal issues and disputes arising in the sport, that behoves a book dedicated to the topic of Football and the Law. This book is the first comprehensive review of legal issues arising in football to have been published in the world, but we are sure it shall not be the last. In the Introduction, the argument is made that there may now be a 'football law', and we hope this book provides a basis for the content of that law. The reminder of the Introduction explains the structure of this book to the reader.

Special thanks are also due to the publisher Bloomsbury Professional, and all its staff, especially Kiran Goss, for supporting the project from the start, stewarding it through all its difficult stages, and for having such patience with all of us who contributed to it.

Finally, my personal acknowledgements to my brilliant colleagues at Blackstone chambers, from whom I am always learning, and to the excellent clerking team, for allowing me to spend my time practising in this exciting area and for the occasional freedom from fee-paying work to dedicate to this project.

Nick De Marco QC
Blackstone Chambers, London

March 2018

Contents

List of Contributors

Kieron Beal QC is a member of Blackstone Chambers. He was called to the Bar in 1995 and took silk in 2012. His practice covers all areas of commercial and civil work, especially European law, competition law, telecommunications, judicial review and human rights, VAT, customs and excise duties. He regularly appears before the Court of Justice of the European Union and General Court, as well as all levels of domestic courts. He is a regular contributor to a number of practitioner texts, including Luis Ortiz Blanco's EU Competition Procedure, now entering its fourth edition.

The Hon Michael Beloff QC is a barrister at Blackstone Chambers, Former President Trinity College, Oxford, Treasurer of Gray's Inn; and Senior Ordinary Appeal Judge of Jersey and Guernsey. Member of the Court of Arbitration for Sport from 1996 and served on ad hoc Divisions at five Olympic Games from, Atlanta to Rio. Ethics Commissioner London Olympic Games 2012. President, British Association of Sport and Law (2004–2012). Hon Legal Adviser to London 2017 IAAF World Championships. Chair, IAAF Ethics Board and the IAAF Disciplinary Tribunal. Chair ICC Code of Conduct Commission and Dispute Resolution Committee. Former Member FIA International Appeal Panel.

Nick Bitel is Head of Sport at Kerman & Co and has been the Chief Executive of London Marathon Events since July 1995. Since April 2013 he has also been Chair of Sport England and a Board Member of UK Sport. He is a previous Chair of the Sports Rights Owners Coalition and of the British Association for Sport and Law. He lectures in Sports Law at Universities in the UK and USA.

Karim Bouzidi is a partner in Clintons' Litigation and Dispute Resolution team. His practice covers a broad range of disputes in the sports, media and entertainment industries including intellectual property and contractual disputes, as well as regulatory and disciplinary proceedings. He acts for and advises prominent individuals, as well as leading corporate entities. Karim has a Masters in UK, US and EU Law of Copyright from King's College.

Alice Bricogne is a barrister and associate tenant of 2 Bedford Row specialising in regulatory, criminal, human rights, sports, and health and safety law. She has appeared in two appeals to the Court of Arbitration for Sport, one involving an allegation of match-fixing in tennis and the other arising out of a contractual dispute between a football player and his agent. She has also appeared before the National Anti-Doping Panel. Alice is also a Senior Associate at Ogier in Guernsey.

Richard Bush is a Senior Associate at international law firm Bird & Bird LLP. He advises on a range of sports-related issues including challenges to regulatory decisions, rules and regulations, disciplinary matters, child protection/safeguarding, and commercial dispute resolution. He has represented clients before a range of dispute resolution forums, including the English courts, FA Rule K arbitration, the Court of Arbitration for Sport, and the FIFA Dispute Resolution Chamber. Richard regularly chairs FA Anti-Discrimination Disciplinary Commissions, and was previously employed by The FA as an in-house solicitor.

Liz Coley is a Senior Associate in the Walker Morris Sports Group who specialises in advising football clubs, intermediaries and players in contractual, transfer, regulatory and disciplinary matters. Prior to joining Walker Morris, Liz worked for four Premier League/EFL clubs and for The Football Association.

Nick Cusack is Assistant Chief Executive of the PFA. He joined Leicester City in 1987 after leaving university and graduating in politics. He was a professional footballer for 15 years making 535 league appearances and scoring 90 goals. Nick was a member of Motherwell's 1990 Scottish Cup winning squad. He also captained Swansea City to the Division 3 championship in 2000 and as Vice-Captain played in every game but one in Fulham's promotion season 1996/1997. In addition to his Degree in Politics, Nick has a Degree in Law and recently completed the Postgraduate Diploma in Legal Studies gaining a Distinction. Nick is currently undertaking his training contract with Mills and Reeve in conjunction with carrying out his role at the PFA.

Anita Davies is a barrister at Matrix Chambers with a broad practice encompassing public law, regulation, competition and telecoms. She regularly advises companies, broadcasters and regulators on the application of EU and competition law. Anita was involved in *BT v Ofcom* 2016 CAT 3 and contributed to 'UK Competition Law: The New Framework' (OUP).

Nick De Marco QC of Blackstone Chambers is ranked as one of the leading sports law barristers and the foremost practitioner in football disputes. He acts for football clubs, federations, players, and agents in commercial and regulatory disputes before FIFA, CAS and various domestic forums. He has appeared in most recent high-profile cases in football in the UK and has a significant international sports practice. In cricket, boxing and sailing he acts for the regulator, and, in other sports, sits as an arbitrator. He writes and lectures on sports law and is an author of *Challenging Sports Governing Bodies* (Bloomsbury).

James Eighteen is a founding partner of Northridge who specialises in dispute resolution, governance and regulation in the sport and gambling sectors. His experience of football includes acting for The FA, Premier League and European clubs and high profile players. James is ranked in Chambers and recognised as a Next Generation Lawyer in Legal 500, who describe him as 'impressive', as someone who provides 'quick, reasoned and sensible advice' and a person 'to turn to in a crisis'. He lectures on the BASL/DMU postgraduate certificate in sports law.

Jonathan Ellis is a founding partner of Northridge. He is a trusted advisor to some of the biggest names in sport, with clients describing him as 'an exceptional litigator, who is superb when the stakes are highest' and as being 'one of the leading sports regulatory lawyers in the industry'. His experience in football includes acting for The FA, Premier League and European clubs, the Scottish FA and leading players. Jonathan is ranked as a 'Leading Individual' in Chambers (Band 1), Legal 500 and in the International Who's Who of Sports & Entertainment Lawyers.

Leon Farr is an associate at Onside Law. Leon's practice focuses on commercial, corporate and regulatory matters for clients in a range of sports, including the commercial exploitation of media rights, sponsorship rights and personal endorsement programmes; player transactions and image rights; governance reform; and the delivery and protection of major sporting events. Leon has advised Paris Saint-Germain, West Ham United and Leeds United on issues relating to player transactions. Leon is currently based at Lord's Cricket Ground, advising the England and Wales Cricket Board on the delivery of the ICC Cricket World Cup 2019.

Pedro Fida is partner and head of the Sports and Entertainment Law Department of Bichara e Motta Advogados in São Paulo, Brazil, and former Counsel to the Court of Arbitration for Sport. He specialises in sports law, intellectual property and dispute resolution, and advises clients in sports-related litigation and transactional matters, especially those involving football, transfers of players, anti-doping, eligibility, governance, integrity, regulatory, and disciplinary matters. He is also a Member of the Disciplinary Tribunal of the IAAF, Member of the Disciplinary Panel of the e-Sports Integrity Coalition (ESIC) and arbitrator at the Brazilian Center of Mediation and Arbitration (CBMA).

Paul Fletcher is the senior solicitor at boutique Sports law firm, Adelphi Sports Law. Paul has a wealth of experience advising sporting clients including Premier League, Championship and League One football clubs, rugby clubs, international sports brands, high profile international footballers, cricket, rugby, darts and snooker players, media personalities and a number of leading football agents from the UK and around the world. Paul's practice is primarily focused on football, in particular sponsorship and endorsement contracts, dispute resolution, intellectual property contracts, commercial contracts and regulatory matters. Paul has provided legal analysis for Sky Sports News and several national newspapers.

Daniel Geey is a Partner in the Sheridans Sports Group. Daniel's practice focuses on helping clients in the sports sector, including rights holders, leagues, governing bodies, clubs, agencies, athletes, sports technology companies, broadcasters and financial institutions. Daniel has significant experience in the football industry and has worked on a variety of club takeovers, high profile transfers, commercial endorsement deals and disputes. Daniel also works in the wider entertainment industry advising on competition and anti-trust matters.

Paul Gilroy QC of Littleton and 9 St John Street Chambers is renowned for his football work, having been retained as Counsel to the League Managers Association since 2009. He has acted for a stellar list of clients from domestic and international football, appearing in most of the high-profile manager dismissal cases over the last decade. He holds a number of sitting appointments with The FA, and has conducted cases before FIFA and the Court of Arbitration for Sport. His sports practice also covers rugby, cricket, tennis, cycling, boxing, athletics, weightlifting, and gymnastics. He has extensive experience of selection issues, anti-doping and safeguarding in sport.

Edwin Glasgow CBE QC is a barrister, mediator and arbitrator at 39 Essex Chambers. After nearly 50 years in practice at the Bar, Edwin now concentrates at sitting as an arbitrator and mediator – working principally on international commercial and sporting disputes. He is Chairman of Sports Resolutions, co-Chairman of the Singapore International Mediation Centre, President of the FIA International Tribunal and a member of many dispute resolution panels.

Paul Goulding QC is a barrister at Blackstone Chambers specialising in sports, employment and commercial law. He has appeared in many sports cases involving football (including *Sheff Utd v FAPL* (the *Tevez* case), *Fulham FC v Tigana*, *Jones v Southampton FC*), rugby, athletics (*Modahl v BAF*), tennis (*Korda v ITF*), Formula One, and snooker (*Hendry v WPBSA*). He is a Specialist Member of the Football Association Judicial Panel, a Member of the Chairmen's Panel of Sports Resolutions, and a former qualified FA football coach. He is also the General Editor of *Employee Competition: Covenants, Confidentiality, and Garden Leave* (OUP).

Tom Grant is a solicitor at Adelphi Sports Law and advises high profile footballers, managers, agents and brands on a wide range of legal issues. On a day-to-day basis, Tom handles both contentious and non-contentious matters ranging from advising on agency disputes to reviewing commercial, sponsorship or endorsement agreements for athletes.

Mark Hovell is a partner at Mills & Reeve and leading Court of Arbitration for Sport arbitrator. Over the last decade, he has been involved in over 250 arbitrations. In 2016, he was appointed to the CAS's Olympic ad hoc Division in Rio. He is also an arbitrator on the UK Sport Resolutions' Chairpersons Panel, the National Anti-Doping Panel and the Saudi Sports Arbitration Centre. He acts for various sports union organisations including The PFA, some Sports Governing Bodies and Professional Leagues, as well as for a number of football clubs. He is a lecturer/visiting professor on Sports Law and finance at Universities in Madrid and New York; for other Colleges in London and Timisoara.

Oliver Hunt is a founding partner of Onside Law, a specialist sports and media practice, having previously qualified at Nabarro and served as a senior in-house lawyer at IMG. Oliver Heads up the firm's football practice and his clients include Paris St Germain, Tottenham Hotspur, West Ham United, Southampton, Leeds United, Eden Hazard, Eric Dier, Patrick Vieira and Alan Pardew. Oliver is a commercial lawyer and also has extensive experience in golf and across all other sports such as rugby and cricket. Other notable clients include Sir Steve Redgrave, Red Bull Racing and Ryder Cup Europe.

Christopher Jeans QC is a leading silk at 11 KBW Chambers who has appeared in many of the major employment law cases of the last 30 years. His football-related work has involved acting for or against many famous managers, players, officials and football institutions and sitting on arbitral panels connected with the game.

James Kitching is Managing Director of Kitching Sports, based in Australia and Malaysia, the first specialist firm consulting on international sports regulations and business in the Asia-Pacific region. He is the former Head of Sports Legal Services at the Asian Football Confederation. Among other appointments, he is the Chairman of the Saudi Arabian Football Federation Disciplinary and Ethics Committee, a Member of the Badminton World Federation External Judicial Experts Panel, and a Member of the Disciplinary Panel of the e-Sports Integrity Coalition.

Daniel Lowen is an experienced sports lawyer, recognised as a leading adviser in the football industry. He acts for players, intermediaries and clubs on a wide range of issues, from player transfers and intermediaries' arrangements to disputes, disciplinary matters and all manner of commercial opportunities. Dan's clients include numerous talent management agencies and he advises international athletes throughout the sports industry, from talented young stars of the future through to global icons. In late 2017, Dan co-founded LEVEL, an innovative new sports, media and entertainment law firm.

Ian Lynam is a Founding Partner of Northridge with wide experience across corporate, commercial and regulatory matters in the sports industry. Ian is a contributing author to a number of other leading textbooks including *Sport: Law and Practice*, The Sports Law Review and *The Negotiator's Desk Reference*. He is ranked as a 'Leading Individual' in Sport by Chambers and Legal 500 and as a 'Thought Leader' in European Sports Law by Who's Who Legal. He is admitted to practise in England & Wales, Ireland and New York.

Sara Mansoori is barrister practising in Media and Information law at Matrix Chambers. She has acted for many footballers, and others connected with football, in privacy and libel claims, including Rio Ferdinand, David Beckham, Karl Oyston and Tony Adams. She has represented them in both litigation and in arbitration. She is a co-author of *Online Publications: A Practical Guide* (Matrix, 2017). She is an ADR accredited mediator.

Emma Mason was, at the time of writing, an Associate in the Sports Group at Squire Patton Boggs. Her work involved a range of sports dispute resolution and regulatory matters for a variety of high profile sports clients. Emma is a graduate of UK Sport's International Leadership Programme and a WeAreTheCity Rising Star in Sport. Away from law, Emma is a former international badminton player who represented Scotland at European, Commonwealth and World Championship level. She is now a Council Member of the World Badminton Federation and its Deputy Chair of Communications. Emma is also a Director of Badminton Europe.

Alistair McHenry is a director in the Walker Morris Sports Group. He advises clubs, owners and players on a range of contentious issues. He has acted on numerous football arbitrations and his high profile cases include acting for Crystal Palace in the club's successful claim against its former manager Tony Pulis, during both the Premier League Managers' Arbitration Tribunal and then in the High Court.

Ian Mill QC is a member of Blackstone Chambers. He practises in the fields of commercial, media and sports law. As a sports lawyer he has acquired specialist knowledge of a wide range of issues, having acted for many participants, teams organisers, managers, intermediaries, governing bodies and broadcasters. As well as acting as an advocate, he has established himself as an experienced decision-maker in sporting disputes (both commercial and disciplinary) in football, tennis, rugby, golf, cricket, boxing and snooker. He is co-author of the Arbitration chapter in Lewis and Taylor, *Sport and the Law*, 3rd Edition (Bloomsbury).

Gavin Millar QC of Matrix Chambers specialises in all areas of media law, including libel and privacy. He often acts in cases involving elite sportspeople and news outlets. He is the co-author of *Media Law and Human Rights* (OUP 2010) and *Newsgathering – Law, Regulation and the Public Interest* (OUP 2010). He sits part-time as a criminal judge in the Crown Court.

George Molyneaux is a barrister at Blackstone Chambers, where he has a broad practice. He has worked on a variety of football cases, including disciplinary proceedings, contractual disputes, and litigation on the extent to which police forces can charge clubs for the cost of match day policing.

Tom Mountford is a barrister at Blackstone Chambers. He is Legal Secretary to the International Association of Athletics Federation's Ethics Board. He has acted in a broad range of sports disputes including player agent disputes, transfer disputes, challenges to decisions of sports governing bodies, discrimination, anti-doping and ethics, in football, rugby, cricket, athletics, sailing, cycling and other sports. Tom speaks Chinese and French and has a keen interest in sport and sports governance internationally. Burnishing his credentials, he recently took up skiing and looks forward to the time when he can outclass the five year-olds on the blue runs.

Jane Mulcahy QC is a barrister at Blackstone Chambers who specialises in sport and employment law. A large part of her sports law practice revolves around football: she acts for players, clubs, managers and agents in relation to contractual disputes, regulatory issues, disciplinaries and general employment issues.

Tim Owen QC is a founder member of Matrix chambers and specialises in business crime, regulatory law, civil fraud, sports and public law. In addition to his practice at the Bar, he sits as a Deputy High Court Judge in the Administrative Court, as a Recorder of the Crown Court and as an Acting Judge of the Grand Court of the Cayman Islands.

Ariel Reck is a lawyer based in Buenos Aires, Argentina focused exclusively on the sports sector, mainly football. He has broad experience as an advisor in football-related deals, including player transfers, employment contracts, investment, intermediary and agency agreements and also acts regularly as counsel in disputes before National Federations, Continental Confederations, FIFA and CAS. On an academic level, he is a visiting lecturer on several masters and postgraduate programmes in Argentina and other countries and a regular contributor to various publications worldwide.

Tom Richards is a barrister at Blackstone Chambers, specialising in commercial, competition and public law as well as sports law. He has acted in a number of the major football cases of recent years, including the challenge to the award of the Olympic Stadium concession to West Ham United FC and an arbitral challenge by Queens Park Rangers FC to a fine imposed by the Football League for breach of Financial Fair Play rules.

Stephen Sampson is the Head of the Sports & Entertainment Group at the global law firm Squire Patton Boggs. He specialises in regulatory and contentious work for clients in the sports, media, advertising and marketing services sectors. He has over 20 years' experience in sports law and has been recognised by Chambers and Partners and the Legal 500 as a top tier sports law practitioner for a decade. He has particular expertise in structuring player transfers, in advising on national and international regulatory issues and in handling disputes for governing bodies, clubs, players and agents before courts, national arbitration tribunals, FIFA bodies and the Court of Arbitration for Sport.

James Segan is recognised as a leading sport law barrister by Chambers and Partners, Legal 500 and Who's Who Legal. Having practised from Blackstone Chambers since mid-2005, he is a veteran of numerous well-known sporting cases including *RFU v Viagogo*, *Ohuruogu v BOA* and *QPR v EFL*. He practises in the full range of sports work, from disciplinary and doping cases through to commercial and regulatory disputes. He is an author of *Challenging Sports Governing Bodies* (Bloomsbury).

Diya Sen Gupta is a barrister at Blackstone Chambers specialising in sports, employment and commercial law. Diya is often instructed in cases in which employment law issues arise in a sporting context, particularly football. Recently she has appeared for a Championship football club in the employment tribunal, and has advised a Premier League club on player issues. Diya was named Employment Junior of the Year at the Chambers UK Bar Awards 2016.

Graham Shear has been an internationally recognised sports law expert for over 25 years, acting for EPL, La Liga, Bundesliga, FFF, MLS and South American clubs and athletes in relation to TPO, tax, financing, player transfers, reputation and regulatory matters. He acted for Ashley Cole and Gareth Bale, acted in Rio Ferdinand's missed drugs test and transfers and TPO issues relating to Tevez and Mascherano. As a sport finance expert in broadcast rights and receivables he structures over €500m of transactions each year. He has acted for 14 EPL clubs in tribunals concerning transfers and other issues including tax enquiries.

Zane Shihab is a Partner in the Sport Department at Kerman & Co and the sole In-house Legal Counsel at Wimbledon, advising all departments across the organisation. He specialises in intellectual property, data protection and contract law and provides practical commercial advice to global brands, international sporting bodies and events and high-profile individuals. Zane has negotiated numerous lucrative event related contracts on behalf of rights-holders and governing bodies including the PGA European Tour, Ryder Cup, World Marathon Majors, London Marathon, RideLondon, Racehorse Owners Association and Wimbledon. Zane has been named as a recognised Sports lawyer in the 2016 and 2017 editions of the Legal 500.

Supinder Sian is a partner in Squire Patton Boggs's corporate immigration team. He specialises in sport, corporate and private-client immigration matters. Supinder acts for a wide range of multinational enterprises including a number of leading Football Clubs, sportspersons and high net worth individuals. Supinder frequently advises clubs in respect of Tier 2 & 5 Certificates of Sponsorship, visa and extension applications. He has successfully challenged GBE refusals and civil penalties for alleged illegal working and supported clubs with complicated Home Office Sponsor Licence notifications post acquisition.

Shane Sibbel is a tenant at Blackstone Chambers. He has a broad commercial litigation and sports law practice. He has been instructed by the Football Association on a number of Rule K arbitrations, and recently acted as sole counsel for the English Football League intervening in *Ipswich Town FC v Chief Constable of Suffolk Constabulary* [2017] EWCA Civ 1484, a landmark decision of the Court of Appeal concerning the charging of football clubs for policing on match days.

Jamie Singer is a founding partner of Onside Law and advises on a wide range of commercial, intellectual property and regulatory matters across the sports and entertainment industries. Recently his practice has ranged from advising on high profile sponsorships for the England Cricket team and Team Sky to appearing before the Court of Arbitration for Sport in Lausanne to secure successful match fixing prosecutions. Jamie regularly speaks at conferences, writes articles and appears on television as a sports law expert. Chambers and Legal 500 recommend him as a leading sports law practitioner. They describe him as 'providing an amazingly efficient, straightforward service' and being a 'knowledgeable and comforting presence to work with'. He also sits as an independent advisor to the ECB's Anti Corruption Commission and as a Non- Executive Director on the Board of England Squash.

Andrew Smith of Matrix Chambers is ranked by Chambers & Partners as a leading junior barrister in the field of sport law. With regard to football disputes, Andrew's clients include UEFA, FIFPro, clubs, players, managers and intermediaries. He is regularly instructed to appear in domestic football arbitrations. In addition to his football practice, Andrew has experience of doping, selection and funding disputes involving elite athletes. With regard to international sports arbitration, Andrew has been appointed as the ad hoc clerk to the Court of Arbitration for Sport on several cases, as well as regularly working on cases before the Basketball Arbitral Tribunal.

Peter Stockwell is a solicitor and a CEDR accredited mediator with a particular interest in sport-related ADR and discipline. He is an Independent Panelist for Sport Resolutions and an Honorary Bencher of Gray's Inn.

Andrew Street is an associate within BCLP's Litigation and Dispute Resolution team. He has advised clients in the football industry on a range of contentious and regulatory issues such as contractual disputes (relating to representation, playing and endorsement agreements), defamation, privacy injunctions, compliance with FIFA, UEFA and National FA Regulations and financing receivables transactions. He acted on cases relating to Premier League, FFF, La Liga, Serie A and South American clubs, and for high profile international players and various leading intermediaries in proceedings in the High Court, at FA level (Rule K Arbitrations) and under FIFA's dispute resolution channel (DRC Arbitrations).

Jim Sturman QC was called to the Bar in 1982 and took silk in 2002. He is Deputy Head of Chambers at 2 Bedford Row. Ranked in all the Legal Directories in the top tier for Sports Law, Crime and Fraud. He has appeared in sports tribunals in the UK and all over the world, advising on all aspects of Sports law (including doping) and has a particular niche practice in cases where there are both sports and criminal law issues.

Rhodri Thompson QC is a specialist silk at Matrix Chambers practising in EU law, regulatory law and competition law, with extensive experience of their application to sports broadcasters, clubs and associations, including state aid, collective selling and purchasing, restraint of trade, freedom of movement, and pricing and licensing of exclusive rights.

James Thorndyke is a Senior Associate in the Sport department at Kerman and Co. He has acted for athletes as well as sporting bodies and event organisers such as the London Marathon, Wimbledon, the RFU and the WRU, and has extensive experience in resolving contractual disputes in a variety of sports. James also has particular experience in advising on regulatory and disciplinary issues involving The FA, the BHA, the Motor Sports Association and the EFL. James has a substantial IP practice within which he advises clients on claims relating to copyright and trade mark infringement as well for passing off.

Victoria Wakefield is a barrister at Brick Court Chambers. She specialises in competition/EU law, public law and commercial law, and has acted in various sports cases (from horseracing to tennis). Having been instructed as junior counsel in QPR's challenge to Championship Financial Fair Play rules, she has now been bitten by the football law bug.

Chris Walsh is a Partner and Head of Dispute Resolution at Onside Law, specialising in regulatory, contentious and commercial matters in the sport sector, both nationally and internationally. His long-term clients include the England and Wales Cricket Board and a number of other national and international governing bodies, rights-holders, clubs, sports agencies and prominent individuals operating across all the major sports. He is recommended as a leading sports law practitioner in all of the independent legal directories.

Table of Legislation

Table of Football Regulations

UNION OF EUROPEAN FOOTBALL ASSOCIATIONS (UEFA)

Table of Cases

D

F

G

xlviii   Table of Cases

H

Halsey v Milton Keynes NHS Trust [2004] EWCA Civ 576, [2004] 1 WLR
3002, [2004] 4 All ER 920, [2004] CP Rep 34, [2004] 3 Costs LR 393,
(2005) 81 BMLR 108, (2004) 101(22) LSG 31, (2004) 154 NLJ 769, (2004) 148
SJLB 629... 27.13
Hamed v Mills [2015] EWHC 298 (QB) 17.34
Harrigan v Jones [2001] NSWSC 623 .... 22.67
Harris v Sheffield United Football Club Ltd [1988] QB 77, [1987] 3 WLR 305,
[1987] 2 All ER 838, 85 LGR 696, (1987) 151 LG Rev 810, (1987) 84 LSG
1327 .... 19.25, 19.26, 19.28,
19.32, 19.37
Haslam (Nathan) v Football Association, FA Appeal Board (Ch Mr Stewart QC)
17 July 2017, para 15.. 12.59
Hendry v World Professional Billiards & Snooker Association Ltd [2002] UKCLR 5,
[2002] ECC 8, [2001] Eu LR 770.. 4.48
Hoeppner v Dunkirk Printing 227 NYAD 130 (1929).. 22.67
Hoffmann-La Roche & Co AG v Commission (Case 85/76) [1979] ECR 461, [1979]
3 CMLR 211, [1980] FSR 13 .... 20.58
Horan v Express Newspapers [2015] EWHC 3550 (QB)... 22.67
Horrocks v Lowe [1975] AC 135, [1974] 2 WLR 282, [1974] 1 All ER 662, 72 LGR
251, (1974) 118 SJ 149, HL... 22.79
Hosking v Marathon Asset Management LLP [2016] EWHC 2418 (Ch), [2017]
Ch. 157, [2017] 2 WLR 746 .... 25.44
Hull City AFC (Tigers) Ltd v Football Association, 23 February 2015 .... 1.19, 23.9
Hull City AFC (Tigers) Ltd v HMRC [2017] UKFTT 629 (TC)................................... 14.31
Hussaney v Chester City Football Club (No EAT/203/98) 15 January 2001.......... 5.54, 5.58
Hutcheson v News Group Newspapers Ltd & Others [2011] EWCA Civ 808, [2012]
EMLR 2, [2011] UKHRR 1329... 22.17, 22.44

I

Imageview Management Ltd v Jack [2009] EWCA Civ 63, [2009] 2 All ER 666,
[2009] 1 All ER (Comm) 921, [2009] Bus LR 1034, [2009] 1 Lloyd's Rep 436,
[2009] 1 BCLC 724 .... 1.17,
12.89, 25.44
Inntrepreneur Pub Co v Crehan [2006] UKHL 38, [2007] 1 AC 333, [2006] 3 WLR
148, [2006] 4 All ER 465, [2006] UKCLR 1232, [2007] ECC 2, [2006] Eu LR
1189, [2006] ICR 1344, [2006] 30 EG 103 (CS), (2006) 150 SJLB 983, [2006]
NPC 85.. 4.59
Ipswich Town Football Club Co Ltd v Chief Constable of Suffolk Constabulary [2017]
EWHC 375 (QB), [2017] EWCA Civ 1484, [2017] 4 WLR 195................. 1.17, 19.20,
19.23, 19.25, 19.28–19.30,
19.36, 19.37, 19.39
Irvine (Eddie) v Talksport Ltd [2003] EWCA Civ 423, [2003] 2 All ER 881, [2003]
2 All ER (Comm) 141 [2003] EMLR 26, [2003] FSR 35, (2003) 26(5) IPD 26029,
(2003) 147 SJLB 421... 13.9–13.13

J

JIH v News Group Newspapers Ltd [2010] EWHC 2818 (QB), [2011] EMLR 9,
(2010) 154(43) SJLB 34 .... 22.4
John v MGN Ltd [1997] QB 586, [1996] 3 WLR 593, [1996] 2 All ER 35, [1996]
EMLR 229, (1996) 146 NLJ 13, CA 22.86
Johnson v MGN Ltd [2009] EWHC 1481 (QB)... 22.69
Jones v Ricoh UK Ltd [2010] EWHC 1743 (Ch), [2010] UKCLR 1335...................... 4.64

K

K v News Group Newspapers Ltd [2011] EWCA Civ 439, [2011] 1 WLR 1827, [2011]
EMLR 22, (2011) 108(18) LSG 18 .... 22.47

N

T

EUROPEAN COMMISSION DECISIONS

FIFA DISCIPLINARY COMMITTEE

UEFA

List of Abbreviations

ADV	Anti-Doping Violation
ADR	Anti-Doping Rules
AFA	The Association of Football Agents
AFC	The Asian Football Confederation
CAF	The Confédération Africaine de Football (the African Football Confederation)
CAS	The Court of Arbitration in Sport
CEDB	The UEFA Control, Ethics and Disciplinary Body
CFCB	The UEFA Club Financial Control Body
CONCACAF	The Confederation of North, Central American and Caribbean Association Football
CONMEBOL	The Confederación Sudamericana de Fútbol (the South American Football Federation)
DCMS	Department of Culture, Media and Sport
ECA	The European Club Association
EFL	The English Football League
EPFL	The Association of European Professional Football Leagues
DRC	The FIFA Dispute Resolution Chamber
FAPL	The Football Association Premier League
FDC	FIFA Disciplinary Code
FIFPro	The Fédération Internationale des Associations de Footballeurs Professionnels (the International Association of Professional Football players)
FIFA	Fédération Internationale de Football Association (the International Football Association Federation)
FIFA ADR	FIFA Anti-Doping Regulations
FIFA RWI	FIFA Regulations on Working with Intermediaries
FRA	The FA's Football Regulatory Authority
FSS	FIFA Standard Statutes
GBE	Governing Body Endorsement
IFAB	International Football Association Board
IFMA	The Institute of Football Management and Administration
ITC	International Transfer Certificate
LMA	The League Managers Association
LOTG	Laws of the Game
MA	FIFA Member Association
ODT	Owners' and Directors' Test
OFC	The Oceania Football Confederation
PFA	The Professional Footballers' Association
PFAA	The Professional Football Administrators Association
PFCA	The Professional Coaches Association
PFSC	The UEFA Professional Football Strategy Council
PSC	The FIFA Players Status Committee
RA	The Referees' Association
RSTP	The FIFA Regulations on the Status and Transfer of Players
Rule K	FA Rule K, the rule governing FA arbitration
SDPR	The FA's Social Drugs Policy Regulations
The FA	The English Football Association

TMS	FIFA's Transfer Matching System, matching data relating to every international transaction
TPI	Third Party Investment
TPO	Third Party Ownership
UEFA	Union of European Football Associations
WADA	World Anti-Doping Agency

CHAPTER 1

Introduction

Nick De Marco QC (Blackstone Chambers)

A FOOTBALL: THE BIGGEST GAME IN THE WORLD

1.1 There are many good books that are now available about sports law. Why have a book just about 'Football and the Law'?

1.2 Football is the biggest game in the world, and the richest. This has led to a growth of legal issues in football and, as discussed below, perhaps we can now even speak of 'football law' in the same way that we have spoken of 'sports law'. Having considered these points, this introduction sets out a brief outline of the scheme of this book, the first of its kind – a book focusing entirely on legal issues in football.

1.3 Football is the world's biggest sport, by every margin and by a long way. It is the most popular game in the world, the one that is played by the most people throughout the globe, and the sport that is watched by more people than any other. It takes centre stage, as the main sport, in more nations and continents than any other. It is also the richest game. There is more money in football than in any other sport.[1]

---

1 All indicators show football to be the world's number one sport. The website *sporteology.com* states that football 'is played by 250 million players in over 200 countries, making it the world's most popular sport' and has an estimated 3.5 billion fans internationally, mostly in Europe, Africa, Asia, and America; followed by cricket with 2.5 billion fans (mostly in Asia, Australia, UK); basketball (2.2 billion fans mostly in the US, Canada, China and Philippines); hockey (2 billion fans in Europe, Africa, Asia, Australia) and tennis (1 billion fans in Europe, Americas, and Asia) (https://sporteology. com/top-10-popular-sports-world (accessed March 2018)). Worldatlas.com ranks football as the biggest sport by a wide margin, with 4 billion fans 'globally'; followed by cricket (2.5 billion in 'the UK and Commonwealth'); hockey (2 billion in Europe, Africa, Asia, and Australia); tennis (1 billion globally); and then volleyball (900 Million in Western Europe and North America) (https://www.worldatlas.com/articles/what-are-the-most-popular-sports-in-the-world.html (accessed March 2018)). Another website, *totalsportek.com*, used 13 factors to develop its list of 'most popular sports' in the world (global base and audience, TV viewership, number of professional leagues, TV rights deals, endorsement and sponsorship deals, average athlete salary in top league, biggest competition (and number of countries represented), social media presence, prominence in sports headlines on media outlets. relevancy through the year, regional dominance, gender equality and accessibility to general public worldwide). Again football was way out in front: 'With over 4 billion followers of football, it is by far the most popular sport in the world. Considering all of our criteria factors football top most of them we have discussed … which makes football's popularity unmatched.' It was the most watched competition in the world: 3.9 billion people tuned in at some point during the FIFA World Cup 2014 making it by far the biggest sport competition; had the highest paying sports competitions: $1.5 billion being awarded in prize money and bonuses every year in UEFA Champions league; had the most expensive sports TV rights deal (the English Premier League deal); had the most professional leagues; had the biggest sport kit deals; the highest paid athletes; as well as the richest sports team in the world, with around 30 football clubs featuring in the top 50 list of most valuable sports teams in the world. Applying its criteria basketball came second, followed

1.4   An estimated 4 billion people watch football in every region and just about every country in the world. It is the only *truly* international sport – other sports such as cricket, basketball and tennis, while very popular in some regions in the world are virtually unwatched or hardly played in others. Football is played in more countries than any other sport and is considered the *national game* in more countries than any other game.

1.5   Football is also the richest game. Year on year commercial activity in football has dramatically increased, both in terms of investment into football, the size of broadcasting deals and the revenues earned and amounts spent.

1.6   The largest revenues derive from broadcasting rights deals. In the 2016/17 season, broadcasting deals for European football leagues alone were worth nearly €12 billion (the largest deal being for the English Premier League then worth over €4 billion; followed by the UEFA Champions League and Europa League, worth nearly €2 billion; Spanish La Liga worth €1.7 billion; Italian Serie at €1.7 billion; the German Bundesliga at €800 million; and French Ligue 1 at €770 million).[2]

1.7   The English Premier League's broadcasting rights deal for 2016–19 was worth an incredible £5.136 billion, a 71% increase on the previous deal (with Sky paying £4.2 billion and BT Sport paying £960 million). Averaged out it equated to £10.19 million per Premier League game.[3] Specific market factors meant the rights deal for 2019–22 was slightly less, yet still massive, at a combined £4.464 billion[4] – but the innovation in the rights sale (more goal clips packages aimed at non-traditional broadcasters such as Amazon, google etc) suggest that the Premier League will continue to bring in substantial revenues.[5]

1.8   The English Premier League is watched in nearly every corner of the globe: the December 2017 Manchester derby between Manchester United v Manchester City was expected to be the world's most watched league game ever, with over 4 billion viewers worldwide. Incredibly, the game was broadcast in every country but four in the whole world.[6]

1.9   2017 saw a new record set in the transfer market. 15,624 international player transfers took place, 6.8% more than in 2016 and spending was up, reaching US$6.37 billion, 32.7% more than the previous year.[7]

---

by cricket, tennis and then athletics (http://www.totalsportek.com/most-popular-sports/ (accessed March 2018)). Whatever criteria is used, and whatever the rest of the rankings, football always comes out clearly in the lead.

2   See TV Sports Markets report, September 2013: https://www.sportbusiness.com/tv-sports-markets/ media-rights-value-top-european-football-leagues-2016-17 (accessed March 2018).

3   'Premier League in record £5.14bn TV rights deal', *BBC*, 10 February 2015 (http://www.bbc.co.uk/ news/business-31379128 (accessed March 2018)).

4   See, 'Sky and BT Sport retain grip on Premier League rights but TV frenzy cools', *The Guardian*, 13 February 2018, https://www.theguardian.com/football/2018/feb/13/sky-bt-sport-premier-league-tv-rights (accessed March 2018).

5   See eg https://www.theguardian.com/football/2018/feb/18/sky-premier-league-tv-rights-deal-amazon-on-sidelines (accessed March 2018): 'Sky netted a sweet Premier League deal but the TV rights bubble isn't over', *The Guardian*, 18 February 2018.

6   'Manchester derby poised to become most expensive and most watched Premier League game in history,' *The Telegraph*, 7 December 2017 (http://www.telegraph.co.uk/football/2017/12/07/ manchester-derby-poised-become-expensive-watched-premier-league/ (accessed March 2018)). The only countries in the entire world that did not broadcast the match were North Korea, Cuba, Saint Kitts & Nevis and Moldova.

7   Global Transfer Market Report 2018, FIFA TMS, pp 6–7.

1.10   As shown in Table 1, below, spending is dominated by the so called 'big 5' European nations (England, Spain, France, Germany and Italy). During the summer 2017 transfer window the big 5 accounted for nearly 80% of the spending on transfers.[8] Looking at figures for the whole of 2017, England remains by far the biggest spender in the world: US$1.653.6 billion being almost double the amount spent by any other country (France, no doubt bolstered by the spending of Paris Saint Gremain, came in second with US$859.6 billion). Spending also increased outside of the 'big 5' in 2017, with Turkey, the Netherlands and the USA all seeing over 100% increases in their spending on previous years. While China's spending was significantly down (by nearly 37%) it still came in the sixth highest spender in the world with US$285.9 million being spent on transfer fees.

Table 1: Top 15 FIFA member associations by club spending on incoming transfers in 2017 and % change from 2016[9]

Engaging association	Spending (US$ million)
England	1,643.6 (+19.7%)
France	859.8 (+314.0%)
Spain	730.3 (+43.2%)
Germany	721.8 (+25.2%)
Italy	654.0 (+28.6%)
China PR	285.9 (−36.7%)
Turkey	159.4 (+141.5%)
Russia	150.0 (+30.7%)
Belgium	128.0 (+28.3%)
Netherlands	96.7 (+187.6%)
Portugal	95.8 (−46.2%)
Wales	89.8 (+51.2%)
Mexico	83.7 (+7.4%)
Brazil	71.9 (−15.7%)
USA	68.7 (+156.5%)

1.11   Investment, revenue and spending in football has been increasing internationally in every area: shirt sponsorship deals, player salaries, broadcasting revenues, transfer and intermediaries' fees and the amount owners spend on buying and investing in football clubs. While it is important not to become carried away with the high spending of the super-rich clubs, as it remains the case that most player transfers are for free, most player salaries in the world are low, most clubs run at a loss, and the huge spoils of the fantastic broadcasting rights deals are shared by a tiny minority of the sport's elite, it is nevertheless this growth in the commercialisation of football that has been the main driving force for the development of law in football.

---

8   The big 5 accounted for 1,608 incoming transfers in the 2017 summer window, spending USD 3.67 billion, or 77.9% of the global total (Big 5 Transfer Window Analysis, Summer 2017, FIFA TMS, p 2). The figures shown in Table 1, above, show a larger picture, including all transfer activity in 2017, but the dominance of the big 5 remains.

9   Global Transfer Market Report 2018, FIFA TMS, p 21.

B   THE GROWTH OF LAW IN FOOTBALL

1.12   This confluence of factors – the popularity of football, its international nature and, in particular, the large sums of money involved – contribute to the growth of legal issues and disputes in football and to an increasingly specialised legal services market in football. As with any other sector of cultural or economic activity, law follows the money.

1.13   Since 2002, approximately half of all sports disputes before the Court of Arbitration in Sport (CAS) have been in football.[10] In other words, despite the CAS having a popular association with Olympic sports and regulatory issues such as doping, there are in fact as many disputes determined by sport's highest international court in football as there are in every other sport put together. Many, perhaps most, of these disputes are not what an outsider, or even some lawyers, might at first think of when they think about legal issues in sport. They are mostly not about doping, player discipline, match-fixing or other cheating, though some of course are; they are most often about issues of contract – disputes between players and clubs, or clubs with each other relating to transfers.

1.14   Before reaching the CAS, many disputes are dealt with by FIFA, or the regional confederations or national associations. Many of those disputes are what one might describe as purely *disciplinary* (which includes everything from doping, match-fixing and player eligibility to issues relating to the payment of football agents, now called intermediaries, financial 'overspending', or the racist behaviour of a club's supporters). Many other disputes are purely *commercial* and dealt with through private arbitration, though often held under the umbrella of these regulatory bodies (for example FA Rule K arbitration, player transfer disputes before FIFA, or arbitrations before the CAS).

1.15   A snapshot of the various disputes (see Table 2) considered by FIFA over the last three years demonstrates a significant increase over those years in the number of disputes considered and highlights the types of dispute considered at the international level.

Table 2: Disputes considered by FIFA 2015–24 August 2017[11]

	2015	2016	2017 (until 24.8.2017)	Total
Players' Status cases	451	539	535	1525
TMS (compliance with Annexe 3 of RSTP, TPO, protection of minors etc.)	78	67	99	244
FIFA International Matches Approval	43	32	4	79
FIFA competitions (yellow and red cards, eligibility, other incidents etc)	192	330	172	694
Extensions of decisions taken at national level by the member associations	127	178	102	407
FIFA doping	0	1	3	4
Others	94	59	22	175

10   See Chapter 29, International Disputes and the CAS, at para **29.26**.
11   I am particularly grateful to Omar Ongaro, the Football Regulatory Director of the Legal & Integrity Division of FIFA, and his colleagues from the FIFA Players' Status and Disciplinary Departments for compiling these statistics and this table for us.

1.16   The vast majority of disputes (nearly 50%) concern 'player status'; broadly speaking these are mostly disputes between players and clubs in relation to the employment contract and transfers – they are thus largely contractual disputes.[12] Field of play disciplinary disputes, including eligibility issues, ie largely more traditional disciplinary disputes, account for about 25% of all disputes determined by FIFA. The remaining disputes will fall relatively evenly between contractual and disciplinary disputes, with often some overlap.

1.17   Within England, football disputes arise in many areas and are determined in a variety of different forums. Disputes in the civil courts are perhaps the least common, yet important recent cases concerning, for example, payments to intermediaries,[13] or who pays for policing on closed roads outside football stadia[14] have been determined in national courts, while others have been determined in the European Court.[15]

1.18   But most disputes in English football are determined either by arbitration, held under the auspices of FA Rule K or of the various leagues, independent of the regulators and subject to the requirements of the Arbitration Act 1996, or they are disciplinary/ regulatory disputes determined by various bodies of The FA and/or the leagues.

Table 3: Number of FA Rule K arbitrations 2014–17[16]

2014	2015	2016	2017
20	18	22	24

1.19   Table 3 shows a steady rise in the number of FA Rule K arbitrations, in the last two years at least. FA Rule K arbitrations are confidential to the parties and, unless the regulator is a party,[17] the decisions are therefore not published. However, anecdotally,[18] most recent Rule K arbitrations have been essentially commercial disputes arising out of player contracts or transfers, the parties generally being clubs, intermediaries, players, or all three. There are no statistics on the average value or cost of these arbitrations, but again anecdotally recent arbitrations have usually been for damages of between £200,000–£300,000 to over £1 million, and costs on either side can often eclipse those sums.

---

12   See Chapter 3, International Federations, Status and transfer of players, paras **3.47–3.53** below and, see further, Chapter 8, Player Transfers.

13   *Imageview Management Ltd v Jack* [2009] EWCA Civ 63, [2009] 2 All ER 666; *Anthony McGill v The Sports and Entertainment Media Group ('SEM')* [2016] EWCA Civ 1063, [2017] 1 WLR 989; for a brief commentary on the two cases see, Chapter 12, Football Intermediaries, Regulation and Legal Disputes, paras **12.86–12.89** below.

14   See eg *Ipswich Town Football Club Company Ltd v Chief Constable of Suffolk Constabulary* [2017] EWCA Civ 1484, [2017] 4 WLR 195 and Chapter 19, Stadia, Hillsborough, Health & Safety and Policing, paras **19.23–19.39**.

15   See, eg in relation to broadcasting Joined Cases C-403/08 and C-429/08: *Football Association Premier League Ltd v QC Leisure* and *Karen Murphy v Media Protection Services Ltd* [2011] ECR I-9083, ECLI:EU:C:2011:631 ('*FAPL*') and Chapter 18, Broadcasting, para **18.29** below and, of course, the seminal case on player transfers: Case C-415/93: *Bosman* [1995] ECR I-4921, CJEU; see Chapter 4, European Law in relation to Football, paras **4.117–4.119** below.

16   I am particularly grateful to Bryan Faulkner, Head of Legal (Football Regulation and Litigation) at The FA for compiling these statistics and this table for us.

17   See eg *Hull City Tigers v The FA*, 23 February 2015, FA Rule K arbitral panel (Ch. Sir Stanley Burnton QC); see further Chapter 23, Discipline, n 13.

18   The author of this chapter appeared as counsel in at least 10 FA Rule arbitrations in the last year, and other authors of other chapters of this work have appeared in many of the others.

1.20   There are also arbitrations held under the auspices of the various leagues ranging from, most commonly, disputes between players and clubs in relation to the employment contract (which are usually by contract to be determined by league arbitration), to other matters falling under the jurisdiction of the league as opposed to the FA, such as *QPR v The English Football League*[19] arbitration concerning the legality of the English Football League's Financial Fair Play Rules, which may be one of the longest running and most expensive sports disputes nationally, but remains confidential at the time of writing. Chapter 28 of this book considers arbitration in football in greater detail.

1.21   Most *disciplinary* disputes are determined by a separate system of football tribunals operated by the regulators, especially The FA, but also including at FIFA and UEFA level, and under the rules of the leagues. Chapter 23 of this book considers discipline in detail. The FA Regulatory Commissions (and the FA Appeal Boards) determine by far the largest number of disciplinings in English football.

Table 4: Number of FA disciplinary proceedings 2014–17[20]

Year	2014	2015	2016	2017
FA Regulatory Commissions	230	240	207	249
FA Appeal Boards	14	18	10	20

1.22   Table 4 shows the very large number of disciplinary cases the English FA considers every year, reaching a high of on average nearly five cases every week in 2017. It is important to note that most of these cases are for minor infractions by often lower or non-league clubs or players, with relatively low penalties, often taking place without an oral hearing, and usually without legal representatives. Only the most serious cases, or those involving elite level professional clubs and players, will normally involve lawyers on both sides in contested oral hearings.

1.23   A breakdown of the types of disciplinary cases most commonly determined by The FA is not available, but from a review of the useful FA database of written reasons on its website[21] for the 2017/18 football season (conducted by the author), summarised in Table 5, below, we can see that most of the cases lead to short suspensions (usually of players, and usually for a few matches only) or small fines (of less than £100). Unless the case involves a top Premier League player, the suspension of whom for even one match might be significant, or a manager or club at the top level, likely to face a higher fine, or unless the case involves a breach of the Intermediaries Regulations which, for some unexplained reason usually leads to an intermediary being banned from working for many months, then these cases are unlikely to justify the costs of legal assistance, at least on the part of the accused.

1.24   Of the 100 records of a search of the FA website's written reasons, the vast majority (59%) of offences relate to FA Rule E3(2): improper conduct aggravated by some form of discrimination.[22] These typically involve lower league or non-league

19   See Chapter 16, Financial Regulation and Financial Fair Play, para **16.79** below.
20   I am particularly grateful to Mark Ives, Head of Judicial Services at The FA for compiling these statistics and this table for us.
21   The database of written reasons for decisions of The FA's Regulatory Commissions and Appeal Boards can be accessed and searched here: http://www.thefa.com/football-rules-governance/discipline/written-reasons (accessed March 2018).
22   FA Rule E3(2) provides that: 'A breach of Rule E3(1) is an "Aggravated Breach" where it includes a reference, whether express or implied, to any one or more of the following:– ethnic origin, colour, race, nationality, religion or belief, gender, gender reassignment, sexual orientation or disability.'

Table 5: Breakdown of 100 FA disciplinary decisions with written reasons
for season 2017/18

Type of offence	%
E3(2) Aggravated misconduct	59
Serious foul play	10
E20 Club failure to control supporters	6
E3 Improper conduct	5
E1 Misconduct in relation to Intermediaries Regs	5
E3 Successful deception of a match official	4
E3 Use of abusive/insulting words/gestures	3
Denial of goal scoring opportunity	2
E8 Breach of betting rules	1

Suspension period	%	Fine	%
Not proven	8	Not proven	8
Proven, no suspension	9	Proven, no fine	20
1–2 matches	11	£1–99	52
3–4 matches	20	£100–249	7
5 matches	35	£250–499	6
6–10 matches	8	£1,000–1,999	2
35 days	2	£2,000–4,999	3
42 days	2	£5,000–9,999	1
2–3 months	2	£40,000–49,999	1
4–6 months	2		
10 months	1		

players most commonly ending in a 5-match suspension and a fine of up to £99 (higher-profile players will usually be banned for the same period but fined a higher amount). Only one case (improper conduct against Arsenal manager, Arsene Wenger – relating to an altercation with referee Mike Dean) led to a fine of over £40,000 – no doubt because of the experience, profile and income of Mr Wenger, and the fact it was his second similar offence in a short period.[23] The lengthy periods of suspension imposed (four months and above) were all imposed on intermediaries for breaches of the FA Intermediaries Regulations.[24] It will thus be in only a handful of FA disciplinary hearings that the accused (whom statistics demonstrate is invariably found guilty) will be able to justify the costs of legal representation.[25]

---

23   *FA v Arsene Wenger*, FA Regulatory Commission, 10 January 2018 (Ch. G. Farrelly).
24   See, Chapter 12, Football Intermediaries, Regulation and Legal Disputes.
25   For example, during 2017, the author of this chapter acted in three FA disciplinary hearings in which QCs and junior barristers, as well as solicitors, were involved: *FA v Joey Barton* (Regulatory Commission (Ch. Mr C. Quinlan QC) 21 April 2017; Appeal Board (Ch. Mr D Casement QC) 25 July, 2017, which led to an 18-month ban being reduced to a 13-month ban, and a £30,000 fine, see further: Chapter 25, Corruption and Match-Fixing, paras **25.137–25.141** below; *FA v Massimo Cellino* which led to a ban of 18 months being reduced to 12 months, and a combined fine of £500,000 being reduced to £300,000, see further, Chapter 12: Football Intermediaries, Regulation

1.25   Law in football is not only about disputes. Much of the work of lawyers in football is advisory, or involves the drafting of contracts. The demand for legal assistance in the non-contentious area, just as in relation to disputes, has grown in proportion to the commercialisation of football and its increased revenue and spending. Unlike 10 years ago, most Premier League clubs (and many Championship clubs) now employ full-time in-house legal counsel and many of the big clubs have a whole team of full-time in-house lawyers working for them, dealing with everything from advice on regulatory requirements to employment contracts, player transfers, contracts with commercial partners and property development.

C   TOWARDS A 'FOOTBALL LAW'

1.26   So far as we know, this book is the first comprehensive guide to legal issues in football to be published in the world. We can perhaps describe the body of law explained in these pages as 'football law' as others have popularly coined the term 'sports law' for the wider field of legal issues across many sports. The use of the term sports law remains controversial with some, though has become increasingly accepted as a practical description at least. Some still debate whether there is such a thing as 'sports law' or whether this is just a convenient term to describe the application of other areas of law (eg the law of contract, tort, employment, principles of fairness borrowed from public law, competition law etc) to sport. Beloff *et al* argue there is such a thing as sports law,[26] postulating that sports law has many of the incidents of an autonomous legal area: there are specialist sports tribunals, nationally and internationally, which deliver judgments on sporting disputes themselves sometimes reported in specialist law reports; professional bodies whose members proclaim themselves to be sport lawyers; books and journals devoted to the subject; courses in sports law taught at an increasing number of universities; sports specific legislation; sporting regulators, both national and international, that promulgate rules to which those who participate in sport are subject which again must be interpreted by regulatory bodies and may be subject to challenge in sports tribunals.

1.27   What, then, is this *football law* and does it really exist? The scope and content of this work suggest it may indeed do so. First, the specificity of football means there are standard approaches to such fundamental issues as the regulation of employment and agency contracts, the regulation of the most significant commercial transactions that football clubs usually ever enter (player transfers) as well as highly regulated rules concerning the resolution of disputes between those participating in football – almost all of which are subject to football specific arbitration. These rules not only create a powerful regulatory regime, they also shape (and are in turn shaped by) the commercial transactions in football. Not only are there generally standard rules applying to all clubs and players and other participants in English football, for example, but many of those are international rules that create a body of regulation and dispute resolution and, arguably, a system of law and regulation that is international.[27] Many of the other incidents identified by Beloff *et al* also apply to football law: there are specialist football tribunals, nationally (ie the FA Regulatory Commissions or Rule K arbitral tribunals) and internationally (the FIFA

and Legal Disputes, para **12.55** below; and one other confidential case involving a Premier League club. These cases are the exception.

26   Beloff, Kerr, Demetriou and Beloff, *Sports Law*, 2nd Edition (2012), pp 1–7.
27   Consider, in particular, the FIFA Regulations on the Status and Transfer of Players (RSTP) which regulate player contracts and transfers on an international scale, or the FIFA Regulations on Working with Intermediaries that regulate the use by players and clubs of intermediaries (agents), and the various case law developed with reference to those regulations.

Dispute Resolution Chamber (DRC) and Players Status Committee (PSC), and the CAS 'football list') which deliver judgments on disputes in football; an increasing number of sports lawyers work primarily or exclusively in football; there is now at least one book devoted to the subject of football law, and there are bound to be more in the future; an increasing number of courses on sports law taught internationally are focused on football; there is football specific legislation;[28] and football regulators, both national and international, that make rules applying to all those involved in football, that are in turn subject to interpretation and challenge in football specific tribunals.

1.28   The second thing that the chapters in this book reveal is that this 'football law' embodies within it legal principles from an incredibly wide spectrum of law in general. Football law is both highly specialised and remarkably wide. It includes everything from the fundamental principles of commercial and contract law, trusts, fiduciary duties and the law of agency, to employment law, discrimination and human rights, privacy and defamation, personal injury and intellectual property, criminal approaches to evidence and commercial arbitration law, the conflicts between national and international systems of law, doping and regulatory law, tax, European and competition law. There is hardly an area of law that is not relevant to football.

1.29   This book aims to embody the main legal principles and procedures that arise in football law. The 53 experts that have contributed to the various chapters are amongst the leading experts in the world not only in football-related disputes but also in the individual areas of law in which they also practise.

1.30   Football law, as a distinct area of law, may or may not exist, or be widely recognised as such. But the practical need for lawyers with a specialist understanding of the issues specific to football certainly does exist; as does the need for football associations, clubs, owners, directors, players, agents and sponsors to have access to advice from and representation by lawyers with a comprehensive understanding of the legal issues arising in football. This necessity is the cause of this book which, in turn, we hope may well help to mark out the parameters of football law.

D   USING THIS BOOK

1.31   *Football and the Law* is a guide to the entire framework of potential legal issues and disputes in football as well as a reference work that can be consulted in relation to individual problems and issues as they arise for those involved in the industry, whether as lawyers, football club officers, players and their unions, intermediaries or anyone else involved in the football business. It can be read by those, including students, wishing to have a complete knowledge of football law, from cover to cover, but is also intended to be a valuable resource for those who need to dip in and out in relation to a specific issue they are faced with.

1.32   The authors of the book come from all around the world, but most are practitioners in England. The chapters relate to common issues that arise in football internationally, and much of the governing law and regulation discussed shall have universal or at least wide application (such as the law of the FIFA Regulations, or to a certain extent, European law); however, as most of the contributing practitioners are English lawyers, and because the English football market, being the largest commercially in the world, is also the largest market for legal services in football,

---

28   See eg the Football Spectators Act 1989, see further para **19.14** below.

there is an inevitable English law and regulatory focus to this book. It will obviously be of use to anyone involved in English football, or transactions with English clubs, but the basic principles discussed are likely to be of use to those involved in football worldwide.

1.33   The scheme of the book starts with the international federations and confederations that regulate football and postulate the fundamental regulations of universal application. Chapters 2, Institutions and 3, International Federations, provide a helpful explanation of the pyramid structure of international football and the various relative competencies of the different institutions regulating the sport. Chapter 4, European Law in Relation to Football, provides a review of the influence of European Union law on football, from the famous *Bosman* ruling[29] with its fundamental effect on FIFA's main international regulation of player contracts, to competition law.

1.34   Chapters 5–7 focus on the fundamental contractual issues in football. Chapter 5, Employment law and Football, provides an overview of the key aspects of employment law in the football context. Chapter 6, Contracts – Players, considers the specific issues that arise in standardised professional football player contracts; and Chapter 7, Contracts – Managers, those that arise in relation to football managers' contracts and their disputes. Chapter 8, Player Transfers, considers the regulation of football transfers and the legal issues that arise.

1.35   Chapters 9–22 consider a number of important distinct specific legal and regulatory areas arising in football. Chapters: 9, Immigration and GBEs; 10, Academies and Youth Issues; 11, Third Party Investment; and 12, Football Intermediaries, Regulation and Legal Disputes, all deal with important specific regulatory issues arising in football. Chapters 13, Image Rights; 14, Taxation; and 15, Sponsorship and Commercial Rights, consider various legal issues arising in relation to common commercial issues in football; while Chapter 16, Financial Regulation and Financial Fair Play, considers football's regulation of how clubs spend their money. Chapters 17, Personal Injury; and 18, Broadcasting; as well as Chapter 22, Privacy, Defamation and Football, consider the application of other important areas of law to football. Chapters 19, Stadia, Hillsborough, Health & Safety and Policing; and 20, Ticketing, look at important legal issues arising from the ownership and use of football stadia. Chapter 21, Ownership Issues and the Fit and Proper Person Test, considers the regulation of those who own and control football clubs.

1.36   Finally, Chapters 23–29 consider the various disciplinary issues and arbitral dispute resolution mechanisms, principles and forums in football. Chapter 23, Discipline, considers the principles of fairness in football disciplinary hearings and has a summary review of league and international disciplinary procedures before considering in detail The FA's various disciplinary and appeal rules and procedures. Chapters 24, Doping; and 25, Corruption and Match-Fixing, consider two key disciplinary areas; whereas Chapter 26, Players' Representation, the PFA and FIFPro, explains the role of the player's union in representing its members in relation to disputes and more broadly. Chapters 27, Mediation; 28, Arbitration in Football; and 29, International Disputes and the CAS, consider the other key forums for the resolution of disputes in football and the various core legal principles applying to and flowing from them.

---

29   Case C-415/93: *Bosman* [1995] ECR I-4921, CJEU.

1.37   Readers should find the index and the tables of statutes, football regulations and cases useful when looking up a specific issue. The glossary of abbreviations describes the various acronyms and initials most commonly used in football.

1.38   The law and regulations in this book are as stated in March 2018. It is important to note that every football season The FA and the various leagues bring out new rules. The majority of the content is the same each year, as often is the various regulation numbering and so on. However, for football season 2018/19 and each season thereafter the practitioner or student is well advised to check the rules then current, all of which are published online and free.

CHAPTER 2

Institutions

Andrew Smith (Matrix Chambers) and **Richard Bush** (Bird & Bird LLP)

A   INTRODUCTION

2.1   Football, like many sports, is governed via a pyramid structure. At the top of football's pyramid is the international governing body, the Fédération Internationale de Football Association (FIFA), under which sit six continental federations: (i) the Asian Football Confederation (AFC); (ii) the Confédération Africaine de Football (CAF); (iii) the Confederation of North, Central American and Caribbean Association Football (CONCACAF); (iv) the Confederación Sudamericana de Fútbol (CONMEBOL); (v) the Oceania Football Confederation (OFC); and (vi) the Union of European Football Associations (UEFA).[1] In turn, each of the six continental federations oversees the national associations in its territory. There are currently 211 national associations affiliated to FIFA in this way, each of which is responsible for the governance of football in their territory.

Figure 2.1: Football's pyramid of governing bodies

2.2   Operating under this structure are a number of participant stakeholders, including leagues, clubs, league and club officials, managers, players, match officials, agents/intermediaries etc. There are also a number of other stakeholders in football who, whilst they do not participate in the same manner (in the sense that they are not directly subject to the regulatory authority of football's governing bodies), are

---

1   Chapter 3, International Federations, considers in greater detail the various competencies of FIFA and its confederations, and their relationship to each other.

still very much part of the football 'ecosystem'. These include stakeholders such as government and public authorities, fans, the media, commercial partners (including broadcasters and sponsors), and pressure groups. Many of these participant and non-participant stakeholders have a powerful influence on the governance and organisation of football, often through organised unions/federations.

Figure 2.2: Basic football stakeholder map (from perspective of national football association)

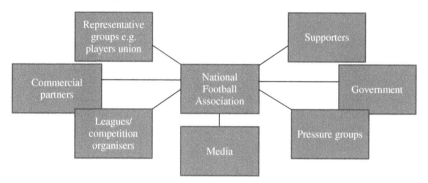

2.3   This chapter outlines the role of a number of key institutions in football, and seeks to provide a general introductory overview of the landscape from the perspective of English football in particular.

B   GOVERNING BODIES

(a)   FIFA

2.4   FIFA is the international governing body of world football, founded in Paris in 1904 by seven national associations (France, Belgium, Denmark, Netherlands, Spain, Sweden, and Switzerland). Its headquarters are in Zurich, Switzerland. It has 211 member associations across six continental federations. As is well documented, FIFA's recent history has been plagued by corruption scandals. The current (April 2016) version of the FIFA Statutes – which provide the foundation of the laws for world football – was ratified in the context of reforms seeking to rebuild and restore trust in FIFA.

2.5   As set out in the FIFA Statutes, FIFA's objectives include (not exhaustively):[2]

(a) promoting the game of football globally, particularly through youth and development programmes;
(b) organising its own international competitions (including the FIFA World Cup, FIFA Women's World Cup, FIFA Futsal World Cup, and the Olympic Football Tournaments);[3]
(c) drawing up regulations and provisions governing the game of football and related matters and to ensure their enforcement; and
(d) promoting integrity, ethics and fair play.

2   FIFA's objectives are set out in full at FIFA Statutes, Article 2.
3   A full list of FIFA's tournaments is available on FIFA's website at http://www.fifa.com/fifa-tournaments/index.html (accessed February 2018).

2.6   FIFA's organisational structure is, in summary, as follows:[4]

(a) *FIFA Congress*.[5] The FIFA Congress is FIFA's supreme and legislative body. It ordinarily meets once a year, but can also meet on an extraordinary basis (such as it did in February 2016 when it approved various reforms). Amongst other things, the FIFA Congress is responsible for: (i) the admission, suspension and expulsion of members; (ii) votes on proposals for adopting and amending the Statutes; and (iii) the election or dismissal of the FIFA President (whose role, broadly, is to represent FIFA generally and chair meetings of the Congress and the Council)[6] and various committee chairpersons and members. Each member association has one vote in the FIFA Congress and only the member associations are entitled to vote.

(b) *FIFA Council*.[7] The FIFA Council is a non-executive, supervisory and strategic body, which defines FIFA's mission, strategic direction, policies and values. It consists of 37 members: the FIFA President; eight Vice-Presidents; and 28 other members elected by the member associations (with a minimum of one female representative per confederation). The FIFA Council replaced the FIFA Executive Committee as part of the 2016 reforms (various members of the FIFA Executive Committee having been complicit in the corruption scandals).

(c) *The General Secretariat*.[8] The General Secretariat is FIFA's executive function, headed by the FIFA Secretary General (ie FIFA's CEO). It is essentially responsible for the day-to-day business of FIFA. The General Secretariat is supervised by, and accountable to, the FIFA Council.

(d) *Standing and ad-hoc committees*.[9] There are nine standing committees covering various aspects of FIFA's work. Standing (and, when appointed from time to time, ad-hoc) committees advise and assist the FIFA Council and the general secretariat in fulfilling their duties. Of particular note in the context of this book, they include the Players' Status Committee (PSC). The PSC's purpose is to set up and monitor compliance with the FIFA Regulations on the Status and Transfer of Players and determine the status of players for various FIFA competitions. The PSC is also responsible for the work of the FIFA Dispute Resolution Chamber, which is competent for employment-related disputes between clubs and players that have an international dimension, as well as for disputes between clubs (for example regarding disputed transfers).

(e) *Independent committees*.[10] The independent committees include the Audit and Compliance Committee and the FIFA Judicial Bodies. Members of these committees are elected by the Congress, must have appropriate expertise (ie financial and/or regulatory and legal matters) and cannot be members of any other FIFA body. The FIFA Judicial Bodies include:

  (i) *FIFA Disciplinary Committee*, which may hear cases and impose sanctions, as prescribed by the FIFA Statutes and the FIFA Disciplinary Code. Its function is governed by the FIFA Disciplinary Code.

  (ii) *FIFA Ethics Committee*, which may hear cases and impose sanctions, as prescribed by the FIFA Statutes, the FIFA Code of Ethics and the FIFA

---

4   The FIFA bodies are listed at FIFA Statutes, Article 24.
5   Provisions in the FIFA Statutes relating to the operation of the FIFA Congress are set out at FIFA Statutes, Articles 25–32.
6   The role of the FIFA President is detailed at FIFA Statutes, Article 35.
7   Provisions in the FIFA Statutes relating to the operation of the FIFA Council are set out at FIFA Statutes, Articles 33 and 34.
8   Provisions in the FIFA Statutes relating to the operation of the FIFA General Secretariat and General Secretary are set out at FIFA Statutes, Articles 36 and 37.
9   Provisions in the FIFA Statutes relating to the operation of these committees are set out at FIFA Statutes, Articles 39–48.
10   Provisions in the FIFA Statutes relating to the operation of the independent committees are set out at FIFA Statutes, Articles 50–55.

Disciplinary Code. It is divided into an investigatory and adjudicatory chamber and its function is governed by the FIFA Code of Ethics.

(iii) *FIFA Appeal Committee*, which is responsible for hearing appeals against decisions from the Disciplinary Committee and the Ethics Committee that are not declared final by the relevant FIFA regulations. Its function is governed by the FIFA Disciplinary Code and the FIFA Code of Ethics.

Certain decisions of the FIFA Judicial Bodies may be appealed before the Court of Arbitration for Sport (CAS).[11]

2.7   It is to be noted however that, whilst FIFA is the international governing body, it is not, itself, responsible for the Laws of the Game. That responsibility rests with a separate body – the International Football Association Board.[12]

(b) UEFA

2.8   UEFA is the governing body of football at the European level. It was founded in 1954 and its headquarters are in Nyon, Switzerland. It is one of FIFA's six continental federations (alongside the AFC, CAF, CONCACAF, CONMEBOL and OFC), and its membership currently includes 55 national associations.

2.9   The current version of the UEFA Statutes was adopted by the UEFA Congress in February 2018, a number of measures aimed at improving UEFA's governance having been made in a previous version of April 2017.

2.10   As set out in the UEFA Statutes, UEFA's objectives include (not exhaustively):[13]

(a) dealing with all questions relating to European football;
(b) promoting football in a spirit of unity, solidarity, peace, understanding and fair play, without any discrimination on the part of politics, race, religion, gender or any other reason;
(c) organising and conducting international football competitions and tournaments at the European level (these include competitions such as the UEFA European Championship (also known as 'the Euros'), the UEFA Champions League, and the UEFA Europa League);
(d) promoting and protecting ethical standards and good governance in European football; and
(e) ensuring that the needs of different stakeholders in European football (leagues, clubs, players, supporters) are properly taken into account.

2.11   UEFA's organisational structure is not entirely dissimilar to FIFA's and, in summary, is as follows:[14]

(a) *UEFA Congress.*[15] The UEFA Congress is UEFA's supreme and legislative body. An Ordinary UEFA Congress is held every year, and a second Ordinary Congress may be called by the UEFA Executive Committee to deal with financial matters

---

11 See, in general, FIFA Statutes, Articles 57 and 58.
12 FIFA Statutes, Article 7. General information about the International Football Association Board is available on its website, at http://www.theifab.com/home (accessed February 2018).
13 UEFA's objectives are set out in full at UEFA Statutes, Article 2.
14 The UEFA bodies (or 'organs') are listed at UEFA Statutes, Article 11.
15 Provisions in the UEFA Statutes relating to the operation of the FIFA Congress are set out at UEFA Statutes, Articles 12–20.

and/or matters of particular significance. Matters within the power of the UEFA Congress include (not exhaustively): (i) amendments to the UEFA Statutes; (ii) elections to the positions of President (whose role, broadly, is to represent UEFA generally and chair meetings of the UEFA Congress and UEFA Executive Committee),[16] the UEFA Executive Committee, and the European members of the FIFA Council; and (iii) consideration of membership applications and the suspension and exclusion of member associations. Each member association has one vote in the Congress and only the member associations are entitled to vote. An Extraordinary UEFA Congress may be convened by the UEFA Executive Committee, or at the written request of one-fifth or more of the UEFA member associations.

(b) *UEFA Executive Committee.*[17] The UEFA Executive Committee is UEFA's supreme executive body. It comprises the UEFA President and 16 other members (including at least one female member) elected by the UEFA Congress, and two members elected by the European Club Association. The UEFA Executive Committee is empowered to adopt regulations and make decisions on all matters that do not fall within the legal or statutory jurisdiction of the UEFA Congress or another UEFA body. The UEFA Executive Committee manages UEFA, except to the extent that it has delegated such management, or unless such management has been delegated by the UEFA Statutes to the UEFA President or the UEFA administration.

(c) *UEFA Administration.*[18] UEFA's business and administrative affairs are run by the UEFA Administration. The UEFA General Secretary is responsible for the organisation, management and direction of the administration, and is appointed by the UEFA Executive Committee.[19]

(d) *UEFA Professional Football Strategy Council* (PFSC).[20] The PFSC is composed of four UEFA vice-presidents, four representatives elected by the Association of European Professional Football Leagues, four representatives elected by the group recognised by UEFA as representing the interests of the clubs participating in the UEFA competitions (ie the ECA), and four representatives elected by FIFPro (Division Europe). Its purpose is to bring together the main stakeholders in European football to work together to find common solutions on major topical issues affecting the game.

(e) *UEFA Committees and Panels.*[21] UEFA currently has nineteen standing committees and six expert panels, dealing with a wide range of issues affecting European football. The committees and expert panels have an advisory function, unless the UEFA Executive Committee grants them decision-making powers.

(f) *UEFA Disciplinary Bodies.*[22] UEFA has three independent disciplinary bodies – the Control, Ethics and Disciplinary Body (CEDB), the Appeals Body, and the Club Financial Control Body (CFCB). The CEDB deals with on-field and off-field disciplinary cases, and the Appeals Body handles appeals against the decisions of the CEDB. The CFCB oversees the application of the UEFA Club Licensing and Financial Fair Play Regulations. It may impose disciplinary

---

16   The role of the UEFA President is detailed at UEFA Statutes, Article 29.
17   Provisions in the UEFA Statutes relating to the operation of the UEFA Executive Committee are set out at UEFA Statutes, Articles 21–28.
18   Provisions in the UEFA Statutes relating to the operation of the UEFA Administration are set out at UEFA Statutes, Articles 39–41.
19   The role of the UEFA General Secretary is detailed at UEFA Statutes, Article 30.
20   Provisions in the UEFA Statutes relating to the operation of the PFSC are set out at UEFA Statutes, Article 35.
21   Provisions in the UEFA Statutes relating to the operation of these committees and panels are set out at UEFA Statutes, Articles 35bis–38.
22   Provisions in the UEFA Statutes relating to the operation of the UEFA Disciplinary Bodies are set out at UEFA Statutes, Articles 32–34ter.

measures in the event of non-fulfilment of the requirements of those regulations, and its final decisions may only be appealed before CAS.

(g) Save for limited exceptions, any decision taken by a UEFA body may be disputed exclusively before CAS. Likewise, CAS has exclusive jurisdiction in relation to any disputes between UEFA and associations, leagues, clubs, players and officials, or disputes of a European dimension between associations, leagues, clubs, players and officials.[23]

(c)   The Football Association (The FA)

2.12   The FA is the governing body of English football. It was founded in 1863 in London and its headquarters are at Wembley Stadium. The FA is responsible for the governance of all affiliated football in England, from the professional game to the grass roots. It is a not-for-profit organisation (it re-invests over £100m back into football each year), which oversees some 12 million players, 400,000 volunteers, 300,000 coaches and 27,000 qualified referees. It runs 24 England teams across men's, women's, youth and disability football and organises a number of competitions, of which The FA Cup is the most famous.[24] The FA Group (ie The FA and its subsidiary companies) also owns and operates Wembley Stadium and St George's Park (ie the National Football Centre). At the local level, the work of The FA is supported by a network of County FAs, which govern and develop the game at the local (predominantly grass roots) level.

2.13   The FA's Articles of Association, Rules, and Regulations are published annually in The FA Handbook, which is a lengthy publication that governs a very wide range of matters (reflecting the FA's broad remit).

2.14   There are two main bodies of The FA that are concerned with its governance: The FA Board and The FA Council. The day-to-day operation of The FA is overseen by The FA's staff and led by a Senior Management Team (who work together with The FA Board and The FA Council):

(a) *The FA Board*.[25] The FA Board is responsible for The FA's overall strategy, and its financial and operating performance. The FA Board comprises ten directors, including The FA's Chief Executive Officer, three independent non-executive directors (including The FA Chairman), three non-executive directors from the 'Professional Game' (appointed by the Premier League and the English Football League), and three non-executive directors from the 'National Game' (put broadly, all football played below the English Football League).[26] The FA Board has a number of standing committees and is empowered to appoint further committees as it considers appropriate.[27]

(b) *The FA Council*.[28] The role of The FA Council is to regulate football matters including disciplinary matters, referees and match and competition sanctioning.

---

23   See, in general, UEFA Statutes, Articles 61–63.
24   Factual information in relation to The FA is sourced from its 2016 Report and Financial Statements, available at http://www.thefa.com/about-football-association/what-we-do/financial-statements (accessed February 2018).
25   The powers of The FA Board are set out in The FA's Articles of Association 2017–2018, Article 96.
26   The FA Articles of Association 2017–2018, Article 77.
27   Ibid, Articles 98 and 99.
28   The powers of The FA Council are set out in The FA's Articles of Association 2017–2018, Article 147.

The FA Council comprises representatives from different stakeholder groups, including County FAs, the Premier League and English Football League, various leagues within the National League System, managers, players and supporters.[29] The FA Council delegates areas of responsibility to numerous standing committees, which have various sub-committees and working groups. Two important bodies are also established under the auspices of The FA Council:

(i)   *The Football Regulatory Authority (FRA).*[30] The FRA is the regulatory, disciplinary and rule-making authority of The FA. Membership of the FRA consists of four representatives from each of the National Game and Professional Game and a further four independent members.

(ii) *The FA Judicial Panel.*[31] The FA Judicial Panel is a group of individuals from which FA Regulatory Commissions and Appeal Boards are drawn. This includes members of The FA Council, individuals with relevant football experience and professionally qualified members such as barristers and solicitors. The Regulatory Commissions have the authority to impose penalties or other sanctions for breach of The FA's Rules, with the Appeal Boards established to hear cases and appeals in prescribed circumstances.

2.15   The governance of The FA has long been subject to criticism, particularly in relation to difficulties in keeping it to modern standards and a lack of diversity in membership of The FA Board and The FA Council. The Articles and Rules of The FA may only be amended by a binding decision of shareholders,[32] some of which – notably members of The FA Council (often disparagingly referred to as 'blazers') – have been historically reticent to approve change. However, in May 2017, The FA's shareholders ratified a number of new corporate governance proposals, aimed at modernising the organisation (a number of which came into effect in July 2017).[33]

C   THE ENGLISH LEAGUE SYSTEM

2.16   The English league system also operates through a pyramid structure, via promotion and relegation of clubs between leagues. There are four divisions in professional English (men's) football, being (in descending order): the Premier League, the English Football League (EFL) Championship, EFL League One, and EFL League Two. The Premier League and the English Football League are traditionally referred to as 'league' football, whereas football played below (as part of the largely semi-professional 'National League System') is commonly referred to as 'non-league' football (and anything below that is likely to be purely amateur).

---

29   Ibid, Article 123.
30   See terms of reference for the composition and operation of the FRA, at pp 43 *et seq* of The FA Handbook 2017–2018.
31   See terms of reference for the composition and operation of the Judicial Panel, at pp 50 *et seq* of The FA Handbook 2017–2018.
32   The shareholders include the FA Premier League, the English Football League, voting members of The FA Council, 'Full Member' Clubs, County FAs, and The FA company secretary. The FA Articles of Association 2017–2018, Article 12.
33   See TheFA.com, 'A significant moment for The FA, as governance reforms confirmed by shareholders', 18 May 2017, available at http://www.thefa.com/news/2017/may/18/fa-governance-reforms-180517 (accessed February 2018).

Figure 2.3: The English league pyramid (simplified) (men's)

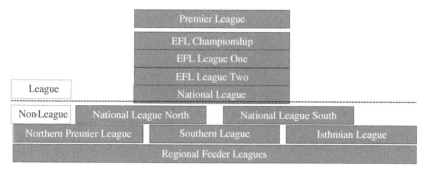

(a) The Premier League

2.17   The Premier League is the top flight of English football. It is organised by the Football Association Premier League Limited (FAPL), which was incorporated in May 1992. It was established following the resignation of clubs from the First Division of the Football League (which was then the top flight of English football), primarily as a result of a desire by those clubs to extract more value from broadcasting rights. Its inaugural season was the 1992/1993 season and, since then, the Premier League has been phenomenally successful.

2.18   One of the key objects of the FAPL includes making, adopting, varying and publishing rules, regulations and conditions for the management of the Premier League. It does this via the annually published Premier League Handbook. Like The FA's Handbook, the Premier League Handbook is a lengthy publication reflecting the large number of governance, commercial, operational and other matters it addresses. It contains various disciplinary and dispute resolution provisions and procedures in relation to matters arising between the FAPL, member clubs and other participants in the Premier League (see further Chapter 28, Arbitration in Football).

(b) The English Football League (EFL)

2.19   The EFL consists of three divisions (with 24 teams in each): the EFL Championship, EFL League One and EFL League Two, with promotion and relegation between each division (and into the Premier League and the National League). The EFL is organised by the Football League Limited, which also organises the EFL Cup (commonly known as 'the League Cup') and EFL Trophy. The first Football League competition was formed in 1888 and it is the world's oldest league football competition.

2.20   Like The FA and the FAPL, the Football League Limited publishes an annual Handbook, including the regulations which govern the various EFL competitions, and disciplinary and dispute resolution procedures.

(c) The National League System

2.21   Below the professional level,[34] the National League (formerly the Football Conference) is the top division of the National League System, which is divided

---

34 Though increasingly many clubs playing at the top level of the National League System are now professional or include professional players.

into seven 'steps' stretching down into the 'Northern', 'Southern' and 'Isthmian' Leagues, and then into various county 'feeder' leagues (and then down in to the purely amateur game).

2.22   The operation of the National League System is governed by FA regulations,[35] and each league will have its own rules. For leagues in steps 1–6 these will be based on The FA's Standardised Rules,[36] and for all leagues in step 7 and below, rules will be based on The FA's Standard Code of Rules.[37]

(d) The women's game

2.23   The women's game has its own league pyramid, with – as at the 2017/18 season – two divisions of The FA Women's Super League at the top (with matches taking place during the summer),[38] and The FA Women's Premier League, and its various 'feeder' regional and county leagues below (with matches taking place during the winter). The FA Women's Super League and The FA Women's Premier League are (unsurprisingly) organised by The FA, and are governed by the regulations contained within The FA Handbook.[39] The women's league pyramid will be restructured from the beginning of the 2018/19 season.[40]

D   REPRESENTATIVE BODIES

(a) The Association of European Professional Football Leagues (EPFL)

2.24   The EPFL is the representative body for professional football leagues across Europe. Its membership includes 32 professional football leagues (including the Premier League and EFL). It was founded in Nyon, Switzerland, in 2005, and works in cooperation with FIFA, UEFA, national associations, and other stakeholders.[41] As a result of amendments to the UEFA Statutes in September 2017, it occupies one seat on the UEFA Executive Committee.

---

35 See Regulations for the operation of the National League System, at pp 180 *et seq* of The FA Handbook 2017–2018.
36 See Standardised Rules, at pp 517 *et seq* of The FA Handbook 2017–2018.
37 See Standard Code of Rules, at pp 477 *et seq* of The FA Handbook 2017–2018.
38 It was recently reported that a consultation process is underway between The FA and the 20 Women's Super League clubs, in respect of a proposal that from 2018/2019 the Women's Super League shall operate as a one-tier league strictly for clubs that can sustain full-time players, with 'WSL 2', which started in 2014, being rebranded and becoming a part-time league: see http://www.bbc.co.uk/sport/football/41127545, 'Women's Super League: FA considers one-tier full-time league from 2018–19', BBC Sport, Tom Garry, 7 September 2017 (accessed February 2018).
39 See Regulations for the establishment and operation of the women's football pyramid, and girls' football, at pp 192 *et seq* of The FA Handbook 2017–2018.
40 On 27 September 2017 The FA announced that, from the start of the 2018/2019 season, the top tier of The FA Women's Super League would be expanded to include 14 teams with full-time professional players, with a new semi-professional national league to be established at the second tier to include 12 teams. The leagues below will maintain a regional structure with promotion and relegation. See http://www.thefa.com/news/2017/sep/26/fa-restructure-womens-football-pyramid-wsl-wpl-270917 (accessed February 2018).
41 General information about the EPFL is available on its website, at https://epfl-europeanleagues.com/ (accessed February 2018).

(b)   European Club Association (ECA)

2.25   The ECA, formed in 2008, represents professional football clubs at the European level. It has some 220 member clubs (including nine English Clubs). The ECA has a Memorandum of Understanding with UEFA (and, as above, elects two members to UEFA's Executive Committee) and a 'collaboration agreement' with FIFA.[42]

(c)   FIFPro

2.26   FIFPro[43] is the worldwide representative body for professional footballers, representing more than 65,000 players (across the men's and women's game). It was established in 1965 in Paris, and advocates for the interests of players in relation to a wide range of issues, including seeking to ensure fair dispute resolution procedures for players, seeking fair and uniform player contracts, opposing transfer systems and concepts such as third party ownership, and educating players in relation to such matters as doping, corruption and life after football. It is recognised by FIFA and operates four divisions in Europe, Asia/Oceania, Africa and the Americas. Its members consist of national player associations.[44]

(d)   The Professional Footballers' Association (PFA)

2.27   The PFA was established in 1907 and is the world's longest established union for professional sportspeople. Its primary aims are to protect, improve and negotiate the conditions, rights and status of all professional players in the English game through collective bargaining agreements. It offers a wide range of services to its members, including negotiating with Clubs on behalf of players, providing personal, financial and legal support to players, and education in relation to matters such as doping, betting and the use of social media. It is the English member of FIFPro.[45]

(e)   League Managers Association (LMA)

2.28   The LMA, established in 1992, represents and promotes the views and interests of managers in English professional football (specifically, the Premier League, EFL and The FA Women's Super League). Amongst other things, the LMA represents the interests of professional football managers to The FA, leagues and other governing bodies and stakeholders, and provides a range of support services to its members (including legal, finance, health and media services).[46] The LMA has three constitutional associations, namely the Institute of Football Management

---

42   General information about the ECA is available on its website, at http://www.ecaeurope.com/ (accessed February 2018).
43   The Fédération Internationale des Associations de Footballeurs Professionnels (the International Association of Professional Football players).
44   See further, Chapter 26, Players' Representation, the PFA and FIFPro; General information about FIFPro is available on its website, at https://www.fifpro.org/en/ (accessed February 2018).
45   See further, Chapter 26, Players' Representation, the PFA and FIFPro; General information about the PFA is available on its website, at https://www.thepfa.com/ (accessed February 2018).
46   General information about the LMA is available on its website, at http://www.leaguemanagers.com/ (accessed February 2018).

and Administration (IFMA), the Professional Football Administrators Association (PFAA), and the Professional Coaches Association (PFCA).

(f)   Referees' Association (RA)

2.29   The RA, founded in 1908, is a membership organisation for match officials in England, and represents the interests of its members to the governing bodies of football. It seeks to support and protect its members from unfair treatment in matters relating to refereeing, and operates a network of local associations across the country.[47]

(g)   Association of Football Agents (AFA)

2.30   Founded in 2005, the AFA promotes the collective interests of its member agents/intermediaries in the UK. This includes lobbying governing bodies in relation to regulations that affect the business of agents/intermediaries. It also offers continuing professional development for its members with a view to ensuring high standards in the industry, and operates a code of conduct for its members.[48]

E   GOVERNMENT AND PUBLIC AUTHORITIES

2.31   As the national game, football often comes under close scrutiny from government. The government department that oversees football is the Department for Digital, Culture, Media & Sport (DCMS). Its stated aim is to work closely with football (as with other professional sports) to – amongst other things – advise on government policy, to encourage better governance, to increase participation, and to contribute funding to improve grass roots sports facilities. In relation to funding specifically, The FA, Premier League and DCMS contribute to the Football Foundation, which is the UK's largest sports' charity and directs £30m every year into grass roots sport.

2.32   Whilst any number of public authorities may from time to time take an interest in matters relating to football, one that is worthy of particular note is the Sports Ground Safety Authority, which is an executive non-departmental public body funded by the government to carry out three main functions: (i) to issue annual licences to football grounds; (ii) to supervise local authorities in relation to Safety of Sports Grounds legislation and safety certification; and (iii) to provide general advice and guidance on spectator safety.

F   PRESSURE GROUPS

2.33   There are a number of pressure groups operating in English football, in relation to a variety of causes. Notable examples include:

(a)   The Football Supporters' Federation, which is an organisation representing the rights of football supporters in England and Wales. It was founded in 2002 and

---

47   General information about the RA is available on its website, https://www.the-ra.org/ (accessed February 2018).
48   General information about the AFA is available on its website, http://theafa.uk/ (accessed February 2018).

has over 500,000 members. It lobbies on issues such as safe standing, diversity and inclusion, and the treatment of away fans.

(b) *Kick It Out*, which is a campaigning organisation that seeks to tackle all forms of discrimination within football (having been established in 1993 by the then Commission for Racial Equality and the PFA to combat racism).

(c) *Football v Homophobia*, which exists to challenge discrimination based on sexual orientation, gender identity and expression at all levels in football (launched in 2010).

G   THE COURT OF ARBITRATION FOR SPORT

2.34   The CAS was created in 1984. It is an institution that is independent of any sports organisation and provides services to facilitate the settlement of sports-related disputes through arbitration or mediation, by means of procedural rules adapted to the specific needs of sport.

2.35   Two types of dispute may be submitted to the CAS: those of a commercial nature (governed by the 'Ordinary Arbitration' procedure), and those of a disciplinary nature (governed by the 'Appeal Arbitration' procedure). CAS is also able to establish ad-hoc tribunals for major events to take into account the circumstances of such events (and such tribunals have been established for the FIFA World Cup and the UEFA European Football Championship).

2.36   The importance of CAS to the law relating to football is enshrined within both the FIFA and UEFA (and other confederation) Statutes, and it is football's ultimate appeal body at the international level. However, it should be noted that within the domestic game, legal challenges to regulatory decisions by The FA or the domestic professional leagues are generally addressed by domestic arbitral tribunals.

2.37   The role of the CAS is considered in more detail in Chapter 29, International Disputes and the CAS.

CHAPTER 3

International Federations

James Kitching (Kitching Sports) and **Pedro Fida** (Bichara & Motta – Brazil)

A   INTRODUCTION

3.1   This chapter examines the governance model of international football and the key principles through which the game is managed on a global basis. It deciphers how that governance model translates into regulatory authority at an international, regional, and national level.

3.2   The governance structure of each international sport is generally organised in a top-down, 'pyramid' model. The international federation, at the top of the pyramid, is usually a member-based organisation, with those members being the regional federations (if they exist) and national federations for the sport within a specific territory or country. All sports governing bodies commonly undertake three core functions: organisation of competitions; development of their sport, both from a technical and infrastructure perspective; and regulation of their sport.

3.3   As set out in the previous chapter, global football governance by and large follows the defined international model. The three core functions form part of the constitutional documents of the international federation, the Fédération Internationale de Football Association (FIFA), and the six regional confederations: (i) the Asian Football Confederation (AFC); (ii) the Confédération Africaine de Football (CAF); (iii) the Confederation of North, Central American, and Caribbean Association Football (CONCACAF); (iv) the Confederación Sudamericana de Fútbol (CONMEBOL); (v) the Oceania Football Confederation (OFC); and (vi) the Union of European Football Associations (UEFA).

3.4   FIFA and the confederations utilise several key control mechanisms to govern football internationally. Nationally, FIFA and the confederations require FIFA Member Associations (MAs) to adopt constitutions which respect the principles set out in the FIFA Standard Statutes ('FIFA Statutes'), a 'model constitution' formulated by FIFA.[1] This ensures that the core functions and key control mechanisms are codified and practised at national level.

B   GOVERNANCE OF INTERNATIONAL FOOTBALL

3.5   Regulating football, futsal, and beach soccer is a significant challenge. As most MAs represent sovereign nations, geopolitical complexities often manifest

1   FIFA Statutes, Article 14.

themselves in matters both on and off the field of play. Bridging the differences between economies, political systems, religions, ethnicities, and culture when forming a global regulatory framework is thus an unenviable task.

(a)   Pyramid model

3.6   The seminal *White Paper on Sport* (2007) published by the European Commission aptly described international sports governance as: 'a pyramid structure of competitions from grassroots to elite level and organised solidarity mechanisms between the different levels and operators, the organisation of sport on a national basis, and the principle of a single federation per sport'.[2]

3.7   In this context, the *White Paper on Sport* went on to state:

'The case law of the European courts and decisions of the European Commission show that the specificity of sport has been recognised and taken into account … there are organisational sporting rules that – based on their legitimate objectives – are likely not to breach the anti-trust provisions of the EC Treaty, provided that their anti-competitive effects, if any, are inherent and proportionate to the objectives pursued. Examples of such rules would be "rules of the game" (e.g. rules fixing the length of matches or the number of players on the field), rules concerning selection criteria for sport competitions, "at home and away from home" rules, rules preventing multiple ownership in club competitions, rules concerning the composition of national teams, anti-doping rules and rules concerning transfer periods. However, in respect of the regulatory aspects of sport, the assessment whether a certain sporting rule is compatible with EU competition law can only be made on a case-by-case basis …'[3]

3.8   Although this 'pyramid model' has recently been the subject of significant scrutiny by European Union competition authorities,[4] it remains the preferred governance model of international sports governing bodies.

3.9   Football practises a unique take on the pyramid, with an overlapping 'dual pyramid' model:

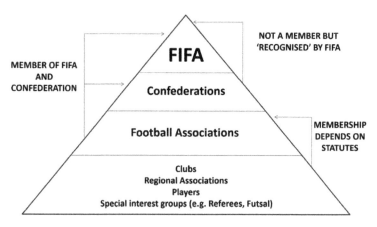

2   *White Paper on Sport* (European Commission, 2007), at [4.1].
3   *White Paper on Sport* (European Commission, 2007), at [4.1].
4   See for example: *Antitrust: Commission sends Statement of Objections to International Skating Union on its eligibility rules* (27 September 2017), available at http://europa.eu/rapid/press-release_IP-16-3201_en.htm (accessed February 2018); *Why sports federations are under increasing scrutiny from competition authorities* (19 December 2017), available at https://www.lawinsport.com/topics/articles/item/why-sports-federations-are-under-increasing-scrutiny-from-competition-authorities (accessed February 2018).

3.10   At the top of the pyramid, FIFA is a private association established pursuant to Article 60 of the Swiss Civil Code. Under Swiss law, an association is an organised group of persons that pursues a non-economic purpose, and has legal personality. Associations are not subject to state approval or supervision and, in general, no registration is required. Associations are free to include a strict regulation in their statutes pertaining to the admission of members. This rule is fundamental to ensuring the proper functioning of sporting competition on the international and continental level through a single regulatory authority. The membership of FIFA is comprised (at the time of writing) of the football associations of 211 countries or territories. Such membership is restricted, *inter alia*, to football associations that are already members of confederations.[5]

3.11   Except for the President, who is directly elected by the MAs at the FIFA Congress, the FIFA Council, the executive and strategic body of FIFA, is directly elected by the confederations at their respective congresses.[6] The confederations, however, are *not* members of FIFA but instead are *recognised* constitutionally by FIFA.[7] The MAs are also separately members of their respective regional confederation within an autonomous governance structure; hence the overlapping 'dual pyramid'.

3.12   The FIFA Statutes contain several constitutional objectives through which FIFA asserts global authority over the control and management of football, the most relevant being:

> 'to control every type of association football by taking appropriate steps to prevent infringements of the Statutes, regulations or decisions of FIFA or of the Laws of the Game';

and

> 'to draw up regulations and provisions governing the game of football and related matters and to ensure their enforcement'.[8]

3.13   The confederations within their own constitutional documents express similar statutory objectives, albeit limited to their regional territory. While all MAs are both FIFA and confederation members, some confederation members either do not meet the requirements for FIFA membership or have not yet applied for FIFA membership. The confederations are therefore *prima facie* autonomous of FIFA: running their own regional competitions, managing their own development programmes, and regulating football within their regional territories.

(b) Control

(i) FIFA and the MAs

3.14   The relationship between FIFA and the MAs is formally one of contract. The MAs pay a subscription fee to FIFA which confirms their membership on an annual basis.[9] In exchange for the payment of such fee, the MAs receive various rights, including *inter alia* participation in FIFA competitions and having a vote at the FIFA Congress.[10]

5   FIFA Statutes, Article 11.
6   FIFA Statutes, Article 37.
7   FIFA Statutes, Article 23.
8   FIFA Statutes, Article 2.
9   FIFA Statutes, Article 64.
10   FIFA Statutes, Article 13.

3.15   Simultaneously, the MAs have several statutory obligations, including the requirement to 'comply fully with the Statutes, regulations, directives, and decisions of FIFA bodies at any time as well as the decisions of the Court of Arbitration for Sport (CAS) passed on appeal on the basis of art. 51 par. 1 of the FIFA Statutes'.[11] They must ensure that their own affiliates are similarly compliant, and adopt the principles set out in the FSS in their own constitutional documents.[12]

3.16   The largest concession to FIFA by the MAs is authority over their executive affairs. The FIFA Statutes permit FIFA, in 'exceptional circumstances' and after consultation with the relevant confederation, to remove the executive body of an MA and replace it for a specific period with a 'normalisation committee'.[13] In recent years, such action has been implemented by FIFA against the football associations of, *inter alia*, Argentina, Cameroon, Greece, Guinea, the Maldives and Thailand.

(ii)   FIFA and the confederations

3.17   Given that the confederations are not members but rather are 'recognised' constitutionally by FIFA, their legal relationship is indirect. UEFA is the only confederation which contains a specific statutory provision which permits it to enter into a contract with FIFA to delineate the nature of their relationship.[14] All other confederations contain clauses in their constitutional documents which cede regulatory authority over various issues to FIFA, as well as agreeing to comply with all decisions and regulations of FIFA.[15] UEFA, on the other hand, very simply sets out in the UEFA Statutes that 'UEFA shall be a confederation recognised by FIFA'.[16]

3.18   Despite appearing to have limited regulatory authority over the confederations due to the indirect nature of their relationship, the FIFA Statutes impose numerous obligations on the confederations. In a similar manner to the MAs, confederations must 'comply with and enforce compliance with the Statutes, regulations, and decisions of FIFA' and submit their constitutions and regulations to FIFA for approval.[17] Confederation constitutions must comply with principles of good governance and contain provisions, *inter alia*, relating to political and religious neutrality; a prohibition on discrimination; independence of their judicial bodies; recognition of the Court of Arbitration for Sport (CAS); and constituting their legislative bodies in accordance with the principles of representative democracy and gender equality in football.[18]

3.19   As such, although the confederations are *prima facie* autonomous in the pyramid structure, in practice, it is very rare for a confederation to deliberately fail to comply with a decision or regulation of FIFA.

(iii)   Confederations and their members

3.20   The legal relationship between the confederations and their members is also contractual – the annual payment of a fee in exchange for membership – and operates in an identical manner as the relationship between FIFA and its MAs.

11   FIFA Statutes, Article 14.1(a).
12   FIFA Statutes, Articles 14.1(d) and (f).
13   FIFA Statutes, Article 8.2.
14   UEFA Statutes, Article 3.
15   AFC Statutes, Articles 2 and 6; CAF Statutes, Article 2; CONCACAF Statutes, Articles 2 and 12; OFC Statutes, Articles 2 and 7.
16   UEFA Statutes, Article 3.
17   FIFA Statutes, Article 22.
18   FIFA Statutes, Article 23.

(iv)   FIFA/Confederations and the affiliates of the MAs and confederation members

3.21   The legal relationship between FIFA, the confederations and the affiliates of the MAs and confederation members (ie their constituent clubs, players, officials, leagues, regional associations etc) is indirect. FIFA asserts authority to regulate and sanction these constituents within the FIFA Statutes: 'Every person and organisation involved in the game of football is obliged to observe the Statutes and regulations of FIFA as well as the principles of fair play.'[19]

3.22   Similar language exists in the confederation constitutions, but also incorporates an obligation to comply with the confederation constitution and regulations. Where an affiliate of an MA or confederation member is not a direct member of that association, the obligation and recognition of FIFA (and confederation) jurisdiction to regulate and sanction those affiliates is generally founded through participation agreements entered into prior to competing in national, regional, or international competitions.

3.23   This indirect relationship has been described by the CAS as follows:

'[55].   In this respect, the Sole Arbitrator notes that the Appellant is, as a member of the NFV, affiliated to the DFB and bound by the latter's rules and regulations (cf. para. 3 of the Statutes of the NFV). The DFB, in turn, is a member of FIFA and therefore bound by FIFA's rules and regulations (art. 13 para. 1 lit. a of the FIFA Statutes). In addition, as a member of FIFA, the DFB has the obligation to ensure that its own (direct or indirect) members, i.e., inter alia, the Appellant, comply with the Statutes, regulations, directives and decisions of FIFA bodies (art. 13 para. 1 lit. d of the FIFA Statutes). Accordingly, pursuant to § 3 para. 1 of the Statutes of the DFB, the latter's members are bound by the regulatory provisions enacted by FIFA. This concept is generally known, on the one hand, as an "indirect reference" to the rules and regulations of an international federation: a club is a member of its national (or regional) federation and therefore bound by the applicable national regulations, while these regulations, inter alia, refer to the applicable international regulations and declare these regulations equally binding on a club at national level. As a result, the club is, on the basis of its (direct or indirect) membership with the national federation, also bound to the applicable international regulations (see HAAS/MARTENS, Sportrecht – Eine Einführung in die Praxis, p. 67 et seq.).

[56].   On the other hand, another aspect of this concept is generally known as a "dynamic reference": the applicable regulations generally refer to higher-ranking (or international) regulations in their currently applicable version, so that all athletes and clubs are always and equally bound to the most current version of the respective regulations (cf. CAS 2009/A/1931, para. 8.8).

[57].   The Sole Arbitrator is of the view that these concepts constitute one of the main pillars of sport in a structure based on the pyramid structure of regional, national and international sports federations, and that both the indirect and dynamic reference are necessary to ensure that all participants to national and international sports are bound to the same set of rules. As a consequence, these principles, not least, safeguard the equal regulatory treatment of all participants in sporting competitions (cf. CAS 2007/A/1370 & 1376; CAS 2008/A/1575 & 1627; CAS 2009/A/1817 & 1844; see also Circular n° 1080 issued by FIFA on 13 February 2007).'[20]

---

19   FIFA Statutes, Article 8.
20   CAS 2012/A/3032 *SV Wilhelmshaven v Club Atlético Excursionistas* at [55]–[57].

(c)   Key governance mechanisms

3.24   The cessation of autonomy by the MAs to FIFA and the confederations is underpinned by several governance mechanisms which delineate the decision-making power of the international bodies within the 'dual pyramid' system.

3.25   The failure of an MA to comply with or abide by these principles may, in exceptional circumstances or extreme cases, lead to the suspension or expulsion of the MA from FIFA or their confederation. MAs are prohibited to maintain 'sporting contact' with any MA that has been suspended;[21] effectively isolating any suspended football association from participation and engagement in international football activity until it effectively 'falls in to line' and becomes compliant.

(i)   One controlling body

3.26   FIFA and the confederations require that only one football association exists in each country or territory.[22] This ensures, *inter alia*, clarity as to the controlling and authoritative body for football in each geographical area and provides stability to the 'dual pyramid' system, allowing the international bodies to establish global and regional regulatory frameworks which can be effectively enforced through the MAs.

3.27   In mid-2015, FIFA suspended the Football Association of Indonesia for, *inter alia*, failing to adhere to this principle.[23] In late 2011, a rival football association was formed in Indonesia following a political struggle within the domestic game. After years of negotiations and failed mergers, suspension by FIFA was undertaken as a final resort. The primary consequence was the Indonesian representative team was not eligible to enter the qualification stages of the FIFA World Cup 2018 and AFC Asian Cup 2019, effectively losing four years of competitive international matches.

(ii)   Structural subordination

3.28   FIFA and the confederations practise the principal of 'structural subordination': all relevant stakeholders in a country or territory (eg clubs, leagues, regional associations, player associations or other groups of stakeholders) must both be subordinate to and recognised by the relevant MA.[24]

3.29   This ensures – or attempts to ensure – that organised football within a geographical territory, particularly each (professional) national top division league, is organised and operated consistent with a single global regulatory standard. This principle also provides for the 'indirect' relationship between FIFA, confederations, and affiliated members of the MAs and confederation members.

---

21   FIFA Statutes, Article 16.
22   FIFA Statutes, Article 11.
23   Asian Football Confederation, *Impact of Football Association of Indonesia Suspension* (3 June 2015), available at http://www.the-afc.com/media-releases/impact-of-football-association-of-indonesia-suspension-25854 (accessed February 2018).
24   FIFA Statutes, Article 20.

(iii)   Democratic process

3.30   The executive bodies of the MAs must be directly elected or appointed by the members of the association in an independent and democratic manner.[25] Failure to undertake a democratic election shall result in that executive body and its decisions not being recognised internationally.[26]

(iv)   Mandatory national regulations

3.31   Aside from compliance with the FSS, MAs must adopt national-level regulations containing mandatory clauses that mirror their FIFA counterparts. This ensures quasi-uniformity in the international, regional, and national regulatory frameworks.

3.32   By way of example, MAs are obliged to adopt mandatory clauses in their national regulations derived from the FIFA Disciplinary Code (FDC), FIFA Anti-Doping Regulations (FIFA ADR), FIFA Regulations on the Status and Transfer of Players (RSTP), and the FIFA Regulations on Working with Intermediaries (FIFA RWI).[27]

(v)   Third-party influence

3.33   MAs must ensure that no natural or legal person is able to exercise third party control over more than one club or group which may impact upon the integrity of any match or competition.[28] Prohibition against such 'cross-ownership' is also directly regulated by the confederations in their eligibility rules to participate in competitions.[29]

(vi)   Prohibition on state courts

3.34   The prohibition on recourse to state courts and the primacy of arbitration to resolve sports-related disputes is fundamental to the stability of the 'dual pyramid' system.[30]

3.35   Arbitration is viewed as a justifiable alternative to state courts given the many elements that differentiate sport from traditional business activity, such as: the competing adversaries are interdependent; uncertainty as to sporting results, which requires some form of equality within the competition; the pyramid structure; athletes having limited professional careers and earning opportunities; and its economic, educational, recreational, and cultural value.[31]

---

25   FIFA Statutes, Article 19.
26   FIFA Statutes, Article 19.
27   FIFA Disciplinary Code, Article 146; FIFA Anti-Doping Regulations, Article 2; FIFA Regulations on the Status and Transfer of Players, Article 1; FIFA Regulations on Working with Intermediaries, Article 1.
28   FIFA Statutes, Article 20. See also, Chapter 11, Third Party Investment.
29   See eg Entry Manual to AFC Club Competitions 2017–2020, Article 12; Regulations of the UEFA Champions League 2015–2018 Cycle, Article 5.01.
30   FIFA Statutes, Article 59.
31   *White Paper on Sport* (European Commission, 2007), part 3.

3.36 State judges generally do not possess the expertise to acknowledge these specificities, which has been recognised by the Swiss Federal Tribunal: '[i]n competitive sport [...] it is vital both for athletes and for the smooth running of events that disputes are resolved quickly, simply, flexibly and inexpensively by experts familiar with both legal and sports related issues'.[32]

3.37 Arbitration provides other advantages. Appeals against decisions of FIFA and the confederations generally require fast adjudication due to the ongoing nature of competitions. Faster legal procedures are generally less expensive; state courts cannot provide similar expedition of proceedings or cost-savings. The jurisdiction of FIFA and the confederations also generally exceeds the territorial limits of state courts. Finally, if state judges applied international sport regulations, it is inevitable that they would be interpreted and applied differently in the various countries.[33]

3.38 Arbitration is thus essential in providing a degree of uniformity in the application and enforcement of international regulations; a principle consistently recognised by the CAS.[34]

(vii) Prohibition on third party interference

3.39 The most controversial mechanism is the prohibition on 'third party interference' in MA affairs. Colloquially, this is referred to as 'government interference'.[35] MAs whose affairs are deemed to have been interfered with are routinely suspended by FIFA. However, neither FIFA nor the confederations have constitutionally defined the meaning of 'third party interference', leaving them open to criticism regarding the perceived selective enforcement of this principle.

3.40 In recent years, MAs have been suspended where their government or a national court has passed national sporting laws which impact upon the democratic election process of the MA executive body; vacated elections approved by FIFA and confederation; appointed a government official as administrator over MA affairs; ordered the removal of the MA President and installed its own executive leadership; and dissolved the executive body of the MA.

3.41 By contrast, executive body positions within numerous MAs have been historically or are currently filled by royal family members, state politicians, or public servants. At the time of writing, persons holding such titles are also members of the FIFA Council and confederation executive bodies.

C AREAS OF REGULATORY AUTHORITY

3.42 The 'dual pyramid' system provides for independent and interdependent regulatory authority for FIFA and the confederations. The distribution of twelve key

---

32 *A. & B. v IOC and FIS* (ATF 129 III 445) Judgement of 27 May 2003 (*Lazutina*), excerpt of the judgment published in *Digest of CAS Awards III 2001–2003* (The Hague: Kluwer Law International, 2004), 674–695.

33 See further, Chapter 28, Arbitration.

34 CAS 2012/A/3032 *SV Wilhelmshaven v Club Atlético Excursionistas* at [57]; CAS 2006/A/1180 *Galatasaray SK v Frank Ribéry & Olympique de Marseille* at [11]–[12].

35 FIFA Statutes, Article 19.

areas of regulatory authority between the bodies can be found in the graphic below:

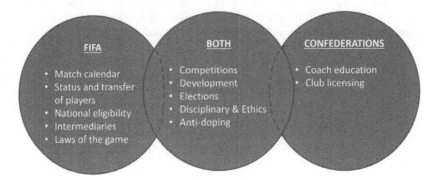

(a)   FIFA

3.43   FIFA has exclusive authority to regulate areas which are global in nature.

(i)   International match calendar

3.44   The international match calendar is approved by the FIFA Council through the compilation of dates in which official matches and competitions involving representative teams may take place. This compilation of dates is undertaken in direct negotiation with, *inter alia*, the European Clubs Association, the World League Forum and FIFPro. The dates set forth in this calendar are binding and must be observed by the confederations, MAs and leagues.[36]

3.45   FIFA has introduced strict rules relating to the call-up by MAs of players to participate in representative teams. It is mandatory for clubs, as employers, to release their players to MAs for matches which are played on the defined dates or in the defined competitions in the international match calendar.[37] Outside of these defined dates and competitions, it is not compulsory for clubs to release their employees to MAs; a principle which has been confirmed by the CAS.[38]

3.46   The organisation of non-official international matches and competitions are regulated by the FIFA Regulations Governing International Matches.[39] Such matches must be authorised by (where applicable) FIFA, the confederation or MA to which the participating teams are affiliated, and the MA on whose territory the match is to be played.[40] The confederations have also established similar regulations to complement the FIFA rules.

(ii)   Status and transfer of players

3.47   The FIFA RSTP establishes global and binding rules concerning the status of players, their eligibility to participate in organised football, and their transfer

36   FIFA Statutes, Article 70.
37   FIFA Regulations on the Status and Transfer of Players, Annexe 1.
38   CAS 2008/A/1622 *FC Schalke 04 v FIFA;* CAS 2008/A/1623 *SV Werder Bremen v FIFA*; CAS 2008/A/1624 *FC Barcelona v FIFA.*
39   FIFA Statutes, Article 71.
40   FIFA Regulations Governing International Matches, Article 6.

between clubs belonging to different MAs.[41] They effectively act as the international 'labour law', providing basic minimum standards and protections for players who participate in professional football outside of their country of origin.[42]

3.48   To properly participate in amateur and professional football, a player must be registered at an MA. This registration must occur within a registration period (colloquially known as 'transfer windows'), which occur twice a year. As an exception, a professional whose contract has expired prior to the end of a registration period may be registered outside that registration period (ie a 'free transfer'). Any player not registered at an MA who participates for a club in an official match is considered ineligible. Once registered, professional players and clubs must sign an employment contract, which shall be valid from its effective date until (at least) the end of the season. The maximum permissible length of a contract is five years or three years for players under the age of 18. Contracts of any other length shall only be permitted if consistent with national laws.[43]

3.49   Employment contracts may only be terminated upon expiry or mutual agreement, unless either party has 'just cause' to terminate. The RSTP set forth the consequences of terminating a contract with and without just cause, and stipulate special conditions that must be observed when a contract is terminated (ie the amount of compensation, specificity of sport, sporting sanctions, the concept of a 'protected period').[44]

3.50   The international transfer of players is governed through an electronic administrative process called the FIFA Transfer Matching System (TMS). Should a player sign a new employment contract with a club affiliated to a different MA, his new club (and its MA) and former club (and its MA) are required to disclose certain documents to FIFA to facilitate the transfer of an International Transfer Certificate (ITC) from the former MA to the new MA. Only after the transfer of the ITC is a player eligible to participate in football.[45] ITC-related disputes may occur when the former club asserts that it still has a contractual relationship with a player seeking to transfer, or when the transfer is not processed within the registration window and blocked by the FIFA TMS system. Such matters are resolved by the FIFA Players' Status Committee.[46]

3.51   The RSTP also regulate the international transfer and registration of minors.[47] As a threshold rule, international transfers are only permitted if a player is over the age of 18. Certain regulatory exceptions apply where: (i) the player's parents move to the country in which the new club is located for reasons not linked to football; (ii) the transfer takes place within the territory of the EU or European Economic Area (EEA) and the player is aged between 16 and 18; (iii) the player lives no further than 50km from a national border and the club with which the player wishes to be registered in the neighbouring association is also within 50km of that border; and (iv) where the player has lived in the country for five years and his move to the country was for reasons not linked to football. Various other unwritten exceptions exist (eg in cases of international students, for refugees). Decisions regarding

41   FIFA Regulations on the Status and Transfer of Players, Article 1.
42   See further, Chapter 5, Employment Law in Football; and Chapter 6, Contracts – Players.
43   See generally, FIFA Regulations on the Status and Transfer of Players.
44   FIFA Regulations on the Status and Transfer of the Players, Articles 14–17.
45   See generally, FIFA Regulations on the Status and Transfer of Players, Annexe 3.
46   FIFA Regulations on the Status and Transfer of Players, Article 22.
47   FIFA Regulations on the Status and Transfer of Players, Article 19. See, further, Chapter 10, Academies and Youth Issues.

the international transfer and registration of minors are made by a specialised Sub-Committee of the FIFA Players' Status Committee.

3.52   In May 2015, FIFA specifically prohibited third party ownership of players' economic rights.[48] No club or player shall enter into an agreement with a third party whereby a third party is entitled to receive, either in full or part, compensation in relation to the future transfer of a player from one club to another, or is being assigned any rights in relation to a future transfer or transfer compensation.

3.53   The FIFA Regulations Governing the Application of the Statutes govern the rules regarding the eligibility of players to participate for representative teams of MAs in international competitions. They also provide a mechanism for players, in limited circumstances, to change their 'sporting nationality' if they have previously participated for a representative team of an MA in an official match or competition. Such decisions are made by the FIFA Players' Status Committee;[49] the relevant regulations have been upheld under challenge at the CAS.[50]

(iii)   Intermediaries

3.54   Prior to 1 April 2015, player agents were subject to the FIFA Player's Agents Regulations (Edition 2008) which implemented a licensing system providing specific standards and requirements. MAs were obliged to implement and enforce these regulations at national level. However, FIFA found it increasingly difficult to enforce its regulations, taking note that many international transfers were concluded without the use of licensed agents.

3.55   On 1 April 2015, the FIFA RWI introduced a new approach based on the broader concept of 'intermediaries', effectively delegating the regulation of intermediaries' activities to the MAs by establishing minimum standards to be implemented at national level. An intermediary is now defined as a 'natural or legal person who, for a fee or free of charge, represents players and/or clubs in negotiations with a view to concluding an employment contract or represents clubs in negotiations with a view to concluding a transfer agreement'.[51]

3.56   Along with establishing standards for advising on the conclusion of employment and transfer agreements, the FIFA RWI also set standards for registration of intermediaries, drafting representation contracts, remunerating intermediaries, disclosure of payments, and avoiding conflicts of interest.[52]

(iv)   Laws of the Game

3.57   The laws of association football, popularly known as the Laws of the Game (LOTG), are issued by the International Football Association Board (IFAB), a Swiss association based in Zurich, with a membership composed of FIFA and the four British football associations of the UK.[53] The IFAB has its own organisation,

---

48   FIFA Regulations on the Status and Transfer of Players, Article 18ter. See further, Chapter 11, Third Party Investment.
49   FIFA Regulations Governing the Application of the Statutes, Articles 5–8.
50   CAS 2010/A/2071 *Irish Football Association v Football Association of Ireland, Daniel Kearns and FIFA.*
51   FIFA Regulations on Working with Intermediaries, Definitions.
52   See further, Chapter 12, Football Intermediaries, Regulation and Legal Disputes.
53   FIFA Statutes, Article 7.

duties and responsibilities which are set out in its statutes. Serving as the guardian of the LOTG, IFAB together with FIFA ensures that the confederations and every MA are obliged to follow and implement the LOTG within their respective jurisdiction.[54]

3.58   Only IFAB is competent to alter and lay down the LOTG, which are annually reviewed to improve and develop the game for players, match officials and fans. It also assesses the implementation of new technology which can improve football. The LOTG vary from, among others, regulating the field of play, to the players' equipment, the referees, the other match officials, the duration of the match, the start and restart of play.[55]

3.59   A long-established rule in football (and sports law in general) relates to the principle that 'purely sporting rules' or 'field-of-play decisions' cannot be subject to external control or revision to protect the integrity and the uninterrupted flow of the game. This prohibition is reflected in the FIFA Statutes (and confederation constitutions) where it forbids CAS from dealing with appeals arising from violations of the LOTG.[56] The question of whether such rules were justiciable was answered by the CAS in a landmark case involving UEFA:

> 'This result follows in particular from the intent and purpose of the provision of Art. 63 (1) (a) of the UEFA Statutes. The latter can be inferred from, inter alia, the Minutes of the XXXth UEFA Congress in Budapest of 23 March 2006. It was said at Congress that it was decided to introduce Art. 63 of the UEFA Statutes in order to protect the integrity and the uninterrupted flow of the game. According to the Minutes, UEFA's internal lawmaker wanted to avoid that "the game would be constantly interrupted" and that the competition would be "paralysed" by the control by the state courts or the arbitration courts. According to CAS precedents (see CAS 98/199 *Real Madrid Club de Futbol v/ UEFA*), such minutes are to be taken into account when interpreting federation rules as they do reflect the (historical) intent of the federation's internal lawmaker. If one now uses this understanding of the rule as a basis, one cannot help but localise the focus of the present case as being in the breach of a "purely sporting rule". The consequence of this is that CAS does not have jurisdiction.'[57]

(b)   Overlapping areas of authority

3.60   FIFA and the confederations have overlapping regulatory authority in various areas.

(i)   Competitions

3.61   Competitions are an integral part of association football, and FIFA, together with the confederations, host and coordinate several international competitions each year.[58] Confederations, for example, organise their own international competitions and interclub competitions in compliance with the international match calendar. They apply, among others, the LOTG and FIFA regulations relating to sporting nationality and the international transfer of players, as well as their own licensing and eligibility rules governing entry into such competitions.

---

54   FIFA Statutes, Article 7.
55   Laws of the Game, Laws 1–17.
56   FIFA Statutes, Article 58.3(a).
57   CAS 2006/A/1176 *Belarus Football Federation v UEFA & FAI*.
58   FIFA Statutes, Article 22.2.

(ii)   Development

3.62   As described at the outset, the development of sport is one of the three key functions of all sports governing bodies. The FIFA Statutes provide that FIFA has the objective of 'improv[ing] the game of football constantly and promote it globally in the light of its unifying, educational, cultural and humanitarian values, particularly through youth and development programmes'.[59] To meet this statutory objective, FIFA has established development programmes which redistribute income earned from its competitions to the MAs for technical programmes and infrastructure investment.

3.63   Following recent scandals relating to the misappropriation of funds, these development programmes are now underpinned by robust regulations which provide minimum due diligence and governance standards which must be met for funds to be allocated. These include quarterly reporting requirements; separate bank accounts; annual auditing requirements; minimum technical persons appointed within an MA; and publishing of financial statements online.[60]

3.64   The confederations have comparable programmes and statutory objectives with similarly robust regulatory frameworks. By way of example, the AFC has passed the AFC Development Regulations to govern its development programmes.[61] These regulations go further than the various FIFA regulations and provide the AFC with regulatory power to halt fund allocation due to MA inactivity[62] and take whatever action deemed necessary (ie additional audits or initiating a disciplinary investigation) should it believe that funds or other benefits provided through development programmes have been 'misused or not utilised in accordance' with the regulations or relevant internal policy.[63]

(iii)   Elections

3.65   FIFA has drawn up several regulations to ensure transparent and democratic processes for the elections to the FIFA Council and for FIFA President. FIFA has also drawn up Regulations on Standard Electoral Code to be applied to elections held by confederations and MAs.[64]

3.66   FIFA carries out its electoral procedures independently and prohibits third-party interference (including government interference) of any kind. All elections are organised and supervised by an Electoral Committee responsible for all election-related decisions and observation of all FIFA regulations.[65] The majority of confederations have also implemented their own codes governing elections to their executive bodies and engage in similar practices.

3.67   The Review Committee, which is a sub-committee of the Governance Committee, undertakes an eligibility check on every candidate for a position on the FIFA Council.[66] Any individual that fails the eligibility check is declared ineligible

---

59   FIFA Statutes, Article 2.
60   See eg FIFA Forward Development Programme Regulations, Article 8.
61   With the exception of the AFC Financial Assistance Programme which is governed by its own set of regulations.
62   AFC Development Regulations, Article 10.
63   AFC Development Regulations, Article 11.
64   Regulations on Standard Electoral Code, Article 1.
65   Regulations on Standard Electoral Code, Article 3.
66   FIFA Governance Regulations, Article 4 and Annexe 1.

for election; this authority has been upheld on several occasions by the CAS.[67] The AFC has introduced a similar integrity check into its electoral procedure.[68]

(iv) Disciplinary and ethics

3.68   FIFA and the confederations have introduced disciplinary rules which regulate the conduct of their direct and indirect members and provide for sanctions for any regulatory violations committed by those parties. For FIFA or a confederation to discipline any natural or legal person, it must have jurisdiction to do so. As such, FIFA and the confederations have authority to discipline MAs due to their direct relationship as members, while they also have authority to discipline affiliates of MAs and confederation members through their indirect relationship described above.

3.69   The various disciplinary regulations provide substantial rules (ie offences) with applicable penalties, as well as procedural rules which provide various rights to parties alleged to have violated any relevant regulations. The substantial rules contain a number of different types of 'sporting sanctions', which range from match suspensions and bans from participating in football-related activity, to the forfeiture of prize money and prohibition on playing home matches with spectators.

3.70   The most common disciplinary cases in football relate to breach of rules prohibiting specific actions, such as doping; misconduct on the pitch (eg red card offences); misconduct off the pitch (eg corrupt behaviour); spectator misconduct; and eligibility of players.

(v) Anti-doping

3.71   FIFA governs anti-doping procedures under its jurisdiction through the FDC and FIFA ADRs. The confederations and MAs are obliged to implement either the FIFA ADRs by reference or to establish their own anti-doping regulations which are consistent with the FIFA ADRs and the World Anti-Doping Agency (WADA) Code.

3.72   The FIFA Statutes as well as the confederation constitutions contain express provisions permitting both FIFA and the WADA the authority to directly appeal any doping related decision made by a confederation or an MA to CAS.[69]

(c) Confederation areas of authority

3.73   The confederations have exclusive authority to regulate matters specific to their operations.

(i) Coaching education

3.74   Raising technical standards of coaches is oft-forgotten when discussion turns to the development of football. The confederations, on their own initiative,

---

67   CAS 2015/A/4311 *Musa Hassan Bility v FIFA*; CAS 2016/A/4579 *Gordon Derrick v FIFA*.
68   AFC Statutes, Articles 31.11 and 31.12.
69   FIFA Statutes, Article 58.5.

have rolled-out coach education and licensing regimes which aim to facilitate the improvement of coaching globally.

3.75   UEFA led this initiative with the establishment of the UEFA Coaching Convention ('Convention') in 1997. By 2008, all UEFA members had become members of the Convention. The Convention regulates and governs the minimum standards of UEFA-branded coach education workshops and their instructors, as well as the issuing and eligibility criteria for attaining UEFA coaching licences.[70]

3.76   Through licensing, the confederations control the quality of coaches which participate in their national and club competitions. The AFC, for instance, has minimum licensing requirements for Head Coaches, Assistant Coaches, Goalkeeping Coaches, and Fitness Coaches. At present, Head Coaches for international 'A' men and women's teams must hold an AFC 'A' licence or equivalent; by 2019, that minimum licence requirement will increase to an AFC 'Pro' licence or equivalent.[71]

(ii)   Club licensing

3.77   UEFA and AFC have established club licensing regimes which govern the minimum standards expected of clubs which participate in their competitions. Although FIFA has also passed the FIFA Club Licensing Regulations as a minimum standard for the confederations to meet, they ultimately have limited authority in determining which clubs can participate in confederation competitions.

3.78   The UEFA and AFC regimes could form a chapter on their own in this volume. In simple terms, they provide five categories of criteria of which must be met by clubs entering their competitions: (i) technical; (ii) personnel; (iii) infrastructure; (iv) legal; and (v) financial. Failure of a club to meet any 'A' level criterion within those categories shall result in the club being denied entry.[72] The majority of cases litigated are when clubs fail to meet either of the 'overdue payables' criteria; such criteria require certain types of debts to be cleared before participation in continental competitions is permitted.[73]

3.79   Both regimes require their members to establish national club licensing regulations and a decision-making framework which assesses compliance vis-à-vis the licensing criteria. Both UEFA and AFC have established independent bodies with the authority to withdraw licences incorrectly granted by their members: the UEFA Club Financial Control Body and the AFC Entry Control Body. Decisions of both bodies are appealable to the CAS.[74]

D   CHALLENGING DECISIONS OF FIFA AND THE CONFEDERATIONS

3.80   It is clear that FIFA and the confederations regulate and control numerous facets of the football industry and must regularly make decisions which directly

70   UEFA Coaching Convention 2015.
71   AFC Competition Operations Manual, Appendix 5.
72   See generally, UEFA Club Licensing and Financial Fair Play Regulations; AFC Club Licensing Regulations.
73   See eg CAS 2013/A/3067 *Malaga CF SAD v UEFA*; CAS 2013/A/3233 *PAS Giannina v UEFA*; CAS 2014/A/3533 *Metallurg v UEFA*; CAS 2014/A/3970 *Bursaspor Kulubu Dernegi v UEFA*. See further, Chapter 16, Financial Regulation and Financial Fair Play.
74   Procedural Rules governing the UEFA Club Financial Control Body, Article 34; Procedural Rules governing the AFC Entry Control Body, Article 5.

affect the legal and sporting rights of their direct and indirect members. As described above, the use of arbitration to resolve disputes is one of the key governance mechanisms within international football. The CAS is generally the arbitration institution preferred by FIFA and the confederations.

3.81 In accordance with Article R47 of the Code of Sports-related Arbitration, an appeal 'against the decision of a federation, association or sports-related body may be filed with CAS if the statutes or regulations of the said body so provide or if the parties have concluded a specific arbitration agreement and if the Appellant has exhausted the legal remedies available to it prior to the appeal, in accordance with the statutes or regulations of that body'.[75] The FIFA Statutes and confederation constitutions all provide the possibility of appeal to CAS in similar terms.

3.82 The FIFA Statutes state that any final decision by FIFA may be challenged at the CAS within 21 days of notification.[76] Appeals in recent years have been made against decisions of the FIFA Congress, FIFA Council, General Secretariat, Appeal Committee (for appeals from the Disciplinary Committee and Ethics Committee), Competitions Committee, Dispute Resolution Chamber, Players' Status Committee, Sub-Committee for Minors, Review Committee and Electoral Committee.

3.83 The FIFA Statutes also limit the types of matters that may be arbitrated. Appeals are not permitted against decisions arising from: violations of the Laws of the Game; suspensions of up to four matches or up to three months (with the exception of doping decisions); and decisions against which an appeal to an independent and duly constituted arbitration tribunal recognised under the rules of an association or confederation may be made.[77]

3.84 Various FIFA regulations state that certain decisions made by a FIFA body are 'final and binding and not appealable', despite such matter not falling within those categories of decisions set out in the FIFA Statutes as being expressly excluded from CAS jurisdiction. In a recent decision, the CAS found that this type of provision was unenforceable and that CAS had jurisdiction to hear appeals against such decisions.[78]

3.85 In a similar manner, confederation decisions may also be appealed to the CAS subject to the arbitration clauses founded within their constitutional documents. UEFA, for instance, has defended decisions at CAS in recent years made by its Congress, Executive Committee, Appeals Body (on appeal from its Control, Ethics, and Disciplinary Body) and Club Financial Control Body. The question of whether a non-member of UEFA 'directly affected' by a decision of its bodies may appeal such decision to CAS was answered positively in a recent case; such party being found to not be expressly prohibited by the UEFA Statutes from appealing.[79] In response to the FIFA decision described above, the AFC recently enacted a prohibition in the AFC Statutes specifically against arbitrating 'decisions which any Regulations declare as final and binding and not appealable';[80] this has yet to be tested at the CAS.

75   Code of Sports-related Arbitration, Article R47.
76   FIFA Statutes, Article 58.1.
77   FIFA Statutes, Article 58.3.
78   CAS 2016/A/4654 *Saudi Arabian Football Federation v FIFA*.
79   CAS 2016/A/4787 *Jersey Football Association v UEFA*.
80   AFC Statutes, Article 65.3(c).

3.86   UEFA and the AFC both also recognise the capacity of the CAS to deal with disputes as an ordinary (as opposed to appeal) arbitration tribunal. By way of example, the UEFA Statutes provide that the CAS may resolve disputes in its ordinary chamber if the dispute does not fall within the competence of a UEFA organ in cases of 'a) disputes between UEFA and associations, leagues, clubs, players or officials; and b) disputes of European dimension between associations, leagues, clubs, players or officials'.[81] Similar language exists in the AFC Statutes.[82]

E   CONCLUSION

3.87   The governance model of international football depends on the implementation of key control mechanisms which MAs willingly accept as a condition of their membership of FIFA and the confederations. These principles are predominantly founded within the *FIFA Statutes* and confederation constitutions. The 'dual pyramid' system which is underpinned by these key control mechanisms provides for independent and interdependent areas of regulatory authority between FIFA and the confederations and ensures a uniform approach to governing football internationally.

---

81   UEFA Statutes, Article 61.
82   AFC Statutes, Article 64.

CHAPTER 4

European Law in Relation to Football

Kieron Beal QC (Blackstone Chambers) and **Daniel Geey** (Sheridans)

A INTRODUCTION

4.1 This chapter explores the influence of European Union (EU) law on football. It has direct relevance for the ability of football players (and their agents) to play for clubs (and conduct business) in any of the 28 Member States of the EU. The famous *Bosman* ruling[1] is one of a number of judgments of the Court of Justice of the European Union (CJEU) which have had a profound effect on the game. In addition, there has been an increasing tendency for persons dissatisfied with aspects of the regulation of the game to challenge regulatory decisions by relying on EU rules on free movement of workers, competition law and/or the English doctrine of restraint of trade.[2]

4.2 The CJEU ruling in the *Walrave* case[3] established that EU law applies to sports, insofar as their practice constitutes an economic activity within the EU within the meaning of what is now Article 3 of the Treaty on the European Union (TEU).[4] Thus rules providing for the payment of fees for the transfer of professional players between clubs (transfer clauses); or limiting the number of professional players who are nationals of other Member States which those clubs may field in matches (rules on the composition of club teams); or fixing different transfer deadlines for players coming from other Member States, without objective reasons concerning only the sport or justified by differences in the circumstances between players (clauses on transfer deadlines), fall within the scope of the Treaty on the Functioning of the European Union (TFEU).[5]

4.3 More generally, where a sporting activity takes the form of gainful employment or the provision of services for remuneration, which is true of the

---

1 Case C-415/93 *Bosman* [1995] ECR I-4921, CJEU.
2 Indeed, in the *Olympique Lyonnais* case, Advocate General Sharpston even cited Bill Shankley's observation that football was not a matter of life and death, it was 'much, much more important than that'. See Case C-325/08 *Olympique Lyonnais v Bernard and Newcastle United* [2010] ECR I-2177, Advocate General's Opinion at endnote 2.
3 Case 36/74 *Walrave and Koch* [1974] ECR 1405, para 4.
4 Case 36/74 *Walrave and Koch* (above), para 4; Case 13/76 *Donà* [1976] ECR 1333, para 12; Case C-415/93 *Bosman* (above), para 73; Cases C-51/96 and C-191/97 *Deliège* [2000] ECR I-2549, para 41; Case C-176/96 *Lehtonen and Castors Braine* [2000] ECR I-2681, para 32; and Case C-519/04 P *Meca-Medina and Majcen* [2006] ECR I-6991, para 22.
5 The *Bosman* case, paras 114 and 137; the *Lehtonen* case, para 60; and Case C-438/00 *Deutscher Handballbund* ('*Kolpak*') [2003] ECR I-4135, paras 56–58.

activities of semi-professional or professional sportsmen, it falls, more specifically, within the scope of EU law rules on the free movement of workers (Article 45 TFEU *et seq*); or the freedom to provide services (Article 56 TFEU).[6]

4.4   Most football league bodies have a framework of rules, commonly incorporated into the employee's contract of employment, that provide for the suspension of a sportsman from competing in competitions, and therefore carrying out his employment, for various disciplinary or doping offences. Whilst the principles governing the applicability and enforceability of these rules largely reflect those found within the disciplinary and regulatory framework of other professions, the frequency and scale of their application has led to a number of challenges to their legality on restraint of trade or competition law grounds. Regulatory rules in football and the actions of regulatory bodies have also been assessed for compatibility with the rules on competition law (Articles 101 and102 TFEU) by the EU Commission and the courts.[7]

4.5   On the other hand, EU law does not apply to purely sporting rules: that is to say, rules concerning questions of purely sporting interest and, as such, having nothing to do with economic activity (see the *Walrave* case, para 8). In fact, such regulations, which relate to the particular nature and context of sporting events, are inherent in the organisation and proper conduct of sporting competition and cannot be regarded as constituting a restriction on the EU rules on the freedom of movement of workers and the freedom to provide services. In that context, it has been held that the rules on the composition of national teams (the *Walrave* case, para 8, and the *Donà* case, para 4), or the rules relating to the selection by sports federations of those of their members who may participate in high-level international competitions (the *Deliège* case, para 64), constitute purely sporting rules which therefore, by their nature, fall outside the scope of Articles 45 and 56 TFEU.

4.6   Also among such rules are 'the Laws of the Game' in the strict sense, such as, for example, the rules fixing the length of matches or the number of players on the field, given that sport can exist and be practised only in accordance with specific rules. That restriction on the scope of the above provisions of the Treaty must, however, remain limited to its proper objective.[8]

4.7   Football players have been found by the CJEU to be engaged in economic activity, either in a self-employed or an employed capacity.[9] If, however, they are employees of a football club, the employment relationship between club and player will fall outside the scope of the EU competition rules. As a general proposition, competition law does not apply to relations between an employer and an employee, since an employee is not treated as an economic undertaking distinct from the company or firm for which he or she works.[10] The CJEU has recognised that the

---

6   Case C-325/08 *Olympique Lyonnais v Bernard and Newcastle United* [2010] ECR I-2177, para 28.
7   Case T-193/02 *Laurent Piau v Commission* [2005] ECR II-209, GCEU, paras 45–53. An appeal was dismissed by the CJEU in Case C-171/05 P *Piau v Commission* [2006] ECR I-37. See also Case T-46/92 *Scottish Football Association v Commission* [1994] ECR II-1039, GCEU, paras 29–33.
8   *Walrave*, para 9; *Donà*, para 15; *Bosman*, paras 76, 127; *Deliège*, para 43; and *Lehtonen*, para 34 (for all cases, see n 4 above).
9   See Case C-325/08 *Olympique Lyonnais v Bernard and Newcastle United* (n 2 above), para 28. If a football player is self-employed, he could be considered as an 'undertaking' for competition law purposes. The concept of an undertaking encompasses every entity engaged in an economic activity, regardless of the legal status of the entity and the way in which it is financed: Case C-67/96 *Albany* [1999] ECR I-5751, CJEU, para 77. See also the EU Commission decision in *Re UNITEL* [1978] 3 CMLR 306, where an opera singer was found to be an undertaking.
10   Case C-22/98 *Jean Claude Becu* [1999] ECR I-5665, CJEU, paras 24–26. Similarly, agreements concluded in the context of collective bargaining between employers and employees and aimed at

employment relationship between workers and the undertakings employing them is characterised by the fact that they perform the work in question for and under the direction of each of those undertakings. Generally, therefore, while employees are categorised as workers for the purposes of Article 45 TFEU, their arrangements with employers fall outside the scope of Article 101 TFEU.[11]

4.8   However, the nature of professional sport means that the employment relationship can often contain some unusual features. For example, a professional football player is generally not free to walk out of his employment and join another club during the period of his contract, unless a 'transfer fee' is paid.[12] Such transfers of employment can only occur during specific periods, and are often strictly regulated, further restraining the freedom of the player's ability to move between clubs as he chooses.

4.9   This chapter looks initially at the EU competition provisions and the case law on the restraint of trade as applied to regulatory football rules. It will then explore the different considerations that arise under the free movement of workers and services provisions found in the TFEU. These provisions are likely to be of greater relevance for an exploration of the mutual rights and duties owed by clubs and their players.

B   THE BASIC COMPETITION LAW PROVISIONS

4.10   The basic prohibitions in EU competition law are set out in Articles 101 and 102 TFEU (formerly Articles 81 and 82 of the EC Treaty).[13] Article 101(1) TFEU prohibits, as incompatible with the internal market, all agreements between undertakings, decisions by associations of undertakings, and concerted practices which may affect trade between Member States and which have as their object or effect the prevention, restriction, or distortion of competition within the internal market. This prohibition applies to agreements or concerted practices in particular which:[14]

(a)   directly or indirectly fix purchase or selling prices or any other trading conditions;
(b)   limit or control production, markets, technical development, or investment;
(c)   share markets or sources of supply; apply dissimilar conditions to equivalent transactions with other trading parties, thereby placing them at a competitive disadvantage;
(d)   make the conclusion of contracts subject to acceptance by other parties of supplementary obligations which, by their nature or according to commercial usage, have no connection with the subject of such contracts.

4.11   Article 102 TFEU provides that any abuse by one or more undertakings of a dominant position within the internal market or in a substantial part of it is

---

improving employment conditions are not, by reason of their nature and purpose, to be regarded as falling within the scope of Art 101(1) TFEU: Joined Cases C-180/98 to C-184/98 *Pavlov* [2000] ECR I-6451, CJEU, para 67.

11   Case C-22/98 *Jean Claude Becu* [1999] ECR I-5665, CJEU, paras 24–26.

12   Although see, CAS/A/12398, 1299 & 1300 *Heart of Midlothian plc v Webster and Wigan AFC Ltd* for an examination of the compensation he must pay where he is able to leave during his contract after the so-called 'protected period' in football.

13   The changes from Articles 81 and 82 EC to Articles 101 and 102 TFEU took effect with the entry into force of the Lisbon Treaty on 1 December 2009. Articles 81 and 82 EC were themselves formerly known, prior to the renumbering introduced by the Treaty of Amsterdam, as Articles 85 and 86 of the Treaty of Rome.

14   This non-exhaustive list is found in Article 101(1)(a)–(e) TFEU.

prohibited as incompatible with the internal market insofar as it may affect trade between Member States.

4.12   Section 2 of the Competition Act 1998 (CA 1998) (the Chapter I prohibition) is in materially the same terms as Article 101(1) TFEU; and s 18 of CA 1998 (the Chapter II prohibition) is in materially the same terms as Article 102 TFEU, save for a threshold jurisdictional issue. While the EU competition provisions require that the anti-competitive conduct should produce an actual or potential effect on trade between Member States or in a substantial part of the EU, the UK's domestic competition provisions require an equivalent effect on trade in the UK or a substantial part of it.

4.13   The case law from the EU courts[15] is presently of direct relevance to the application of domestic competition law because s 60 of the CA 1998 requires consistency (so far as possible) between the domestic principles and the case law of the EU courts. UK courts and regulators must also have regard to decisions of the EU Commission in this field.[16]

(a)   Article 101 TFEU and the Chapter I prohibition

4.14   The rules of the game by which football clubs agree to compete with one another also represent agreements of undertakings or associations of undertakings which fall within the scope of competition law. They therefore are capable of being caught by Article 101 TFEU (and the Chapter I prohibition under the CA 1998) unless they are 'pure' rules of the game; or unless they either do not restrict competition appreciably; or they benefit from exemption from Article 101(1) TFEU by fulfilling the criteria in Article 101(3) TFEU (or a like exemption granted under CA 1998, ss 6 to 11).

4.15   But the application of the competition provisions is not restricted to express agreements between football clubs or under the auspices of a league. Some forms of concerted behaviour may be capable of classification under more than one of the descriptions 'agreement', 'decision', or 'concerted practice'. If parties cooperate so as to bring about a restriction of competition, little will turn on the precise form that the cooperation takes. The Commission, the General Court of the European Union (GCEU), and CJEU have each given a broad definition to the concept of agreement. In *Tate & Lyle v Commission*,[17] the GCEU confirmed that an agreement to substitute interdependent conduct for competition would be made out when one only of the participants revealed its proposed pricing plans for the future, with the intention that the other participants would follow its lead. It was held that the requirement of independence did not deprive economic operators of the right to adapt intelligently to the existing and anticipated conduct of their competitors. Nonetheless it did strictly preclude any direct or indirect contact between such operators, where the object or effect was either to influence the conduct on the market of an actual or potential competitor or to disclose to such a competitor the course of conduct which they themselves had decided to adopt or contemplated adopting on the market.

---

15   The principal courts are the CJEU and the General Court of the European Union (GCEU) (formerly the Court of First Instance or CFI).
16   See also Case C-344/98 *Masterfoods* [2000] ECR I-11369, CJEU.
17   Joined Cases T-202/98, T-204/98, and T-207/98 *Tate & Lyle v Commission* [2001] ECR II-2035, GCEU, paras 54–61. The appeal by British Sugar in Case C-359/01 P *British Sugar plc v Commission* [2004] ECR I-4933, CJEU, did not address this point.

(b)   An object or effect of an agreement

4.16   The requirement for an 'object or effect' of restricting competition is alternative and not cumulative.[18] The words are to be read disjunctively. In applying Article 101 TFEU, the first step is to consider the object of the agreement in the light of its economic context in order to see whether its intended effect is appreciably to restrict competition. 'Competition' means the competition which would exist in the absence of the agreement.[19]

4.17   It is not necessary at this stage to consider what the effects of the agreement actually are.[20] An agreement may therefore be caught by Article 101 TFEU before it has come into effect.[21] An agreement can be contrary to Article 101(1), whether or not the restrictive provision is complied with (*Trefileurope Sales v Commission*)[22] or enforced (*Dunlop Slazenger v Commission*),[23] or whether or not the attempt to restrict competition succeeds (*Compagnie Royale Asturienne des Mines SA and Rheinzink GmbH v Commission*).[24] The liability of a particular undertaking is established where it participates in a collaborative meeting with knowledge of its object, even if it did not proceed to implement any of the measures agreed at those meetings.[25]

4.18   Nonetheless, a finding of an 'object restriction' is not lightly made. It is usually reserved for those agreements whose natural and ordinary effect would constrain competition, without it being necessary therefore to show that they do in fact do so.[26] As the CJEU has stated, the very nature of the coordination may be considered so likely to have '… negative effects, in particular on the price, quantity or quality of the goods and services, that it may be considered redundant, for the purposes of applying art. [101(1) TFEU], to prove that they have actual effects on the market' (*Groupement des Cartes Bancaires v Commission*).[27] If the analysis of the intended effects of the agreement does not disclose an appreciable restriction of competition, the actual effects of the agreement or practice should then be considered in order to see whether the agreement or practice in fact appreciably restricts competition (*Delimitis v Henninger Bräu AG*).[28]

---

18   Case C-8/08 *T-Mobile and others* [2009] ECR I-4529, CJEU, paras 28–30.
19   Case 56/65 *Société Technique Minière v Maschinenbau Ulm GmbH* [1966] ECR 235, CJEU; Case 99/79 *Lancôme SA v Etos BV* [1980] ECR 2511, CJEU; Cases T-374, 375, 384, and 388/94 *European Night Services v Commission* [1998] ECR II-3141, GCEU, para 136.
20   Joined Cases 56, 58/64 *Consten and Grundig v Commission* [1966] ECR 299, CJEU; Case 123/83 *BNIC v Clair* [1985] ECR 391, CJEU; Case 45/85 *Verband der Sachversicherer eV v Commission* [1987] ECR 405, CJEU. See also more recently Case C-510/06 P *Archer Daniels Midland Co v Commission* [2009] ECR I-1843, CJEU, para 140.
21   Commission Decision (EEC) 72/480 [1972] OJ L308/52, [1973] CMLR D43 (*WEA-Filipacchi Music SA*); Commission Decision (EEC) 74/634 [1974] OJ L343/19, [1975] 1 CMLR D8 (*Franco-Japanese Ballbearings Agreement*).
22   Case T-141/89 [1995] ECR II-791.
23   Case T-43/92 [1994] ECR II-441, [1994] 5 CMLR 201, para 61.
24   Joined Cases 29, 30/83 [1984] ECR 1679.
25   See Joined Cases C-238/99 P, C-244/99 P, C-245/99 P, C-247/99 P, C–250/99 P to C–252/99 P, and C-254/99 P *Limburgse Vinyl Maatschappij v Commission* [2002] ECR I-8375, paras 508–510; Joined Cases C-189/02 P, C-202/02 P, C-205/02 P to C-208/02 P, and C-213/02 P *Dansk Rørindustri A/S v Commission* [2005] ECR I-5425, CJEU, para 145. See also Case T-99/04 *AC-Treuhand AG v Commission* [2008] ECR II-1501, GCEU.
26   The Commission has indicated that an object restriction is one which has '… such a high potential for negative effects on competition that it is unnecessary for the purposes of applying Article [101(1)] to demonstrate any actual effects on the market': see the Commission Guidelines on the application of Article 81(3) of the Treaty, [2004] OJ C101/8, at para 21.
27   Case C-67/13 *Groupement des Cartes Bancaires v Commission* [2014] 5 CMLR 22, paras 49–51.
28   Case C-234/89 [1991] ECR I-935, CJEU.

4.19   The question of whether an agreement has the object of preventing, restricting, or distorting competition is a question of interpretation of the foreseeable effects of the agreement, not of the subjective intentions of the parties. Thus, the CJEU has held that it is not necessary to enquire which of the two contracting parties took the initiative in inserting any particular clause or to verify that the parties had a common intent at the time when the agreement was concluded. It is rather a question of examining the aims pursued by the agreement as such, in the light of the economic context in which the agreement is to be applied (*Compagnie Royale Asturienne des Mines SA and Rheinzink GmbH v Commission*).[29] Article 101 will apply whether or not the parties had a common purpose or one or more of them was apathetic or unwilling (*Trefileurope Sales v Commission*).[30]

4.20   The competition rules also apply to the rules of professional associations and sports bodies which restrict the freedom of individuals or athletes to negotiate or contract with different undertakings, organisations, or clubs.[31]

(c)   The prevention, restriction or distortion of competition

4.21   An agreement may prevent, restrict, or distort competition within the meaning of Article 101(1) TFEU not only as between the parties to the agreement but also as between one of them and third persons (*Etablissements Consten SARL and Grundig-Verkaufs-GmbH v Commission*).[32] Article 101(1) thus applies both to agreements between actual or potential competitors, referred to as 'horizontal' agreements;[33] and to agreements between a supplier and an acquirer of goods or services, referred to as 'vertical' agreements.[34]

4.22   Article 101(1) is not infringed unless competition is 'appreciably' prevented, restricted, or distorted.[35] Similarly, Article 101(1) is not infringed where there would be no possibility of any appreciable competition even in the absence of the agreement. This may be the case, for example, where owing to extensive government regulation the scope for competition is minimal or non-existent (*Suiker Unie*).[36] In order to assess whether there is an appreciable restriction of competition in the relevant market, it is customary to analyse the relevant product market and the relevant geographical market.[37]

---

29   Joined Cases 29, 30/83 [1984] ECR 1679, 1703, 1704.
30   Case T-141/89 [1995] ECR II-791, GCEU.
31   Case C-519/04 P *Meca-Medina and Majcen* [2006] ECR I-6991, CJEU, paras 22–31. The distinction to be drawn is less about whether or not a rule is a 'sporting rule' and more about whether or not a particular rule has an effect on the pursuit of an economic activity. See also Case C-49/07 *Motosykletistiki Omospondia Ellados NPID (MOTOE) v Greece* [2008] ECR I-4863, CJEU, para 51 and Commission Press Release IP/17/5184 of 8 December 2017 in relation to the Commission's decision that International Skating Union (ISU) rules imposing sanctions on speed skating athletes participating in competitions not authorised by the ISU are in breach of Article 101 of the TFEU.
32   Joined Cases 56, 58/64 [1966] ECR 299, CJEU. See also Case 31/85 *ETA Fabriques d'Ebauches SA v DK Investment SA* [1985] ECR 3933, 3944, CJEU.
33   Commission Notice: Guidelines on the applicability of Article 101 TFEU to horizontal cooperation agreements: [2011] OJ C11/1, 14.1.2011.
34   See Commission Regulation (EU) No 330/2010 of 20 April 2010 on the application of Article 101(3) of the Treaty on the Functioning of the European Union to categories of vertical agreements and concerted practices, [2010] OJ L102/1 (the 'Vertical Restraints Block Exemption'). See also the Commission Guidelines on Vertical Restraints [2010] OJ C130/1.
35   Case C-226/11 *Expedia Inc v Autorité de la concurrence* [2013] Bus LR 705, CJEU, para 16.
36   Joined Cases 40–48/73, 50/73, 54–56/73, 111/73, 113/73, 114/73 *Cooperatieve vereniging Suiker Unie UA v Commission* [1975] ECR 1663, CJEU.
37   Commission Notice on the definition of relevant market for the purposes of Community competition law, [1997] OJ C372/3.

4.23 In assessing the effects of an agreement upon competition, the agreement must be viewed in its economic and legal context taking into account all relevant facts.[38] An agreement may have the object or effect of distorting competition, both where the parties are actual competitors and where they are potential competitors. The EU courts have stressed the importance of looking at the 'counterfactual' of what would have happened but for the agreement or practice.[39] In *MasterCard Inc v Commission*,[40] the CJEU emphasised the need to consider the actual context in which the relevant coordination arrangements take place, in particular the economic and legal context in which the undertakings concerned operate, the nature of the goods or services affected, as well as the real conditions of the functioning and the structure of the market or markets in question. Courts will analyse what could be expected to have occurred in the relevant market absent the allegedly restrictive agreement, decision or concerted practice.

4.24 But this poses complex challenges in a football context. These are explored in more detail in section D below. The economics of professional football is not easy to analyse through the prism of 'ordinary' competition between businesses. Unlike companies selling competing products, football teams need each other to co-exist in order to hold a sporting spectacle. Driving all of ones' rivals out of business in a football context would mark the end of the game. The sporting competition usually runs over dimensions far longer than a single match or game, taking place over a whole season or even longer. If the professional sporting spectacle is to be worth paying for, then there must be a substantial number of economically viable and financially stable participants.[41]

(d) Restrictions necessary for the promotion of competition or to promote legitimate commercial interests

4.25 The EU courts have recognised that not every restriction on commercial freedoms will amount to a restriction on competition for the purposes of Article 101 TFEU. This will be the case where the restrictions imposed by contract are ancillary to a contractual term imposed to protect a legitimate commercial interest. This concept is often referred to as an 'ancillary restraint'. However, the case law has not always been consistent in its approach.[42]

4.26 The CJEU's practice has developed over time, so that it now examines the nature and scope of any putative restriction on competition in its full legal and economic context. In some cases, it has found that a restriction may fall outside the scope of application of Article 101(1) TFEU altogether. In others, it has considered that a restriction may be caught by the prohibition but benefit from an exemption

---

38 Case C-399/93 *Oude Littikhuis* [1995] ECR I-4515, CJEU, para 10.
39 Case T-328/03 *O2 (Germany) GmbH and Co v Commission* [2006] ECR II-1231, GCEU, paras 68–71.
40 Case C-382/12 P *MasterCard Inc v Commission* [2014] 5 CMLR 23, CJEU, paras 161–165.
41 As the European Commission observed in its 2007 Staff Working Document (COM(2007)391) accompanying the Commission's 2007 White Paper on Sport, para 3.4(a), indent 2, 'Sport teams, clubs and athletes have a direct interest not only in there being other teams, clubs and athletes, but also in their economic viability as competitors.'
42 Compare the approaches adopted in Case 56/65 *Société Technique Minière* [1966] ECR 235, CJEU; Case 56/64 *Grundig* [1966] ECR 299, CJEU, at 342; Case 161/84 *Pronuptia de Paris GmbH, Frankfurt am Main v Pronuptia de Paris Irmgard Schillgalis* [1986] ECR 353, CJEU; Case 258/78 *LC Nungesser KG v Commission* [1982] ECR 2015, 2069; and Case C-234/89 *Delimitis v Henninger Bräu AG* [1991] ECR I-935, CJEU.

under Article 101(3) where the overall pro-competitive benefit of an agreement or practice justifies it.[43]

4.27   Guidance as to the application of this case law may be derived from the GCEU's treatment of ancillary restraints in *Métropole Télévision (M6)*.[44] If a restraint is a minor part of a major operation and is directly related and necessary to it, then that restraint may fall outside the scope of Article 101, if the main operation itself falls outside Article 101. The CJEU has also held that Article 101 TFEU does not cut across legitimate interests held by an undertaking in other areas, such as selective distribution systems,[45] exclusive copyright licences,[46] and plant breeders' rights.[47]

4.28   The EU courts and Commission have also considered whether legitimate commercial or business interests may be protected by means of restrictive covenants following the sale of a business from the perspective of EU competition law. Such covenants usually contain non-competition or non-solicitation clauses. In its decision in *Reuter/BASF*,[48] the Commission approved a non-competition clause found in an agreement governing the sale of a business. Having examined the reasons for the clause and the objective necessity to protect the goodwill of the business, the Commission concluded that Article 101(1) would not, in principle, be infringed by a proportionate non-competition clause in such a context. However, the protection conferred had to be limited to the period required for the purchaser to take over undiminished the vendor's market position. Similar restrictions on the free movement of players are examined below, under the restraint of trade doctrine.

(e)   The rise and fall of the sporting exemption

4.29   A topic that is closely related to the concept of 'ancillary restraint' is that of the exemption for sporting rules.[49] The *Meca-Medina* case[50] is the leading case on the dividing line between purely sporting rules, which escape the application of EU law, and rules ostensibly sporting but which are sufficiently linked to economic activity to engage EU law, including the EU competition rules.

4.30   The athletes in *Meca-Medina* challenged the rejection by the Commission of their complaint against the International Olympic Committee (IOC). The athletes sought a declaration that certain doping rules adopted by the IOC and implemented by the Fédération Internationale de Natation (International Swimming Federation, 'FINA') were incompatible with the EU rules on competition and freedom to provide

---

43   See the approach of the CJEU in Case C-309/99 *Wouters* [2002] ECR I-1577, CJEU where at para 97 the Court observed that not every agreement between undertakings which restricts the freedom of the parties necessarily falls within the prohibition laid down in Article 101(1), so that the rules governing the operation of the Netherlands legal profession did not fall within it. Contrast that with the judgment of the GCEU in Case T-112/99 *Métropole Télévision (M6) v Commission* [2001] ECR II-2459, para 72, where the Court rejected the suggestion that any express 'rule of reason' fell to be applied at the Article 101(1) stage.
44   See Case T-112/99 *Métropole Télévision (M6) v Commission* above, paras 103–106.
45   Case 26/76 *Metro SB-Grossmärkte v Commission* [1977] ECR 1875, CJEU.
46   Case 262/81 *Coditel* [1982] ECR 3381, CJEU.
47   Case 258/78 *Nungesser v Commission* [1982] ECR 2015, CJEU.
48   [1976] OJ L254/40, [1976] 2 CMLR D44.
49   This is not strictly the same as the 'ancillary restraints' doctrine in a commercial case: see eg Bellamy & Child, *European Union Law of Competition*, 7th Edition (2013), para 6.117; Whish & Bailey, *Competition Law*, 8th Edition (2015), pp 136–142. The *Meca-Medina* case lays down an analytical framework specifically directed to ascertaining whether a sports regulatory rule is compatible with EU competition law.
50   Case C-519/04 P *Meca-Medina and Majcen* [2006] ECR I-6991, CJEU.

services (*Meca-Medina and Majcen/IOC*).[51] In Case T-313/02 *Meca-Medina*,[52] the GCEU at para 45 held that 'sport is essentially a gratuitous and not an economic act, even when the athlete performs it in the course of professional sport'. It followed that it was not necessary to subject the contested anti-doping rules to an analysis under competition law, since the rules were 'purely sporting' in nature (para 64).

4.31   On appeal, the CJEU held, as a starting point, that the competition rules 'do not affect rules concerning questions which are of purely sporting interest and, as such, have nothing to do with economic activity' (para 25). It also held (at para 26) that the competition rules 'do not preclude rules or practices justified on non-economic grounds which relate to the particular nature and context of certain sporting events'. The CJEU stressed, however, that 'such a restriction on the scope of the provisions in question must remain limited to its proper objective. It cannot, therefore, be relied upon to exclude the whole of a sporting activity from the scope of the Treaty.' Critically, the CJEU held that 'the mere fact that a rule is purely sporting in nature does not have the effect of removing from the scope of the Treaty the person engaging in the activity governed by that rule or the body which has laid it down' (para 27). Thus, even purely sporting rules are required to be justified.

4.32   The CJEU thereby overturned the decision of the GCEU on the basis that it was an error to hold that once a sporting decision could be shown to be 'purely sporting' for the purposes of the freedom of movement and provision of services rules under Articles 45 and 56 TFEU, it automatically fell outside the scope of the competition rules. The CJEU proceeded to conduct a detailed analysis of the anti-doping rules, the legality of which it ultimately upheld.

4.33   This is a significant decision in a number of respects. First, it throws doubt on whether a genuine 'sporting exemption' exists since, under the terms of the *Meca-Medina* case, even a purely sporting rule must be shown to be 'limited to its proper objective'. It must legitimately pursue that objective in a proportionate manner. Secondly, it demonstrates that the EU courts (and national courts applying the same competition rules) will conduct a detailed analysis of the necessity and proportionality of the rule since 'the compatibility of rules with the [EU] rules on competition cannot be assessed in the abstract' (para 42). Thirdly, however, the CJEU also confirmed (again at para 42) that '[n]ot every agreement between undertakings or every decision of an association of undertakings which restricts the freedom of action of the parties or of one of them necessarily falls within the prohibition laid down in Article [101(1)]'. The analysis would turn on whether the consequential effects restrictive of competition were inherent in the pursuit of legitimate objectives and were proportionate to them.

4.34   A national court may also confer a margin of discretion on a sport's regulatory body in its assessment of the legitimacy of the objective pursued and in the proportionality of measures adopted in response.[53] The appropriate margin

---

51   Case COMP/38158.
52   [2004] ECR II-3291, GCEU.
53   The CJEU's reasoning in *Meca-Medina* was in part based on its judgment in Case C-309/99 *Wouters* [2002] ECR I-1577, where the CJEU considered whether a regulatory body '... could reasonably have considered that that regulation, despite the effects restrictive of competition that are inherent in it, is necessary for the proper practice of the legal profession, as organised in the Member State concerned' (paras 107, 110); and whether that regulatory body was '... entitled to consider that the objectives pursued by the 1993 Regulation cannot, having regard in particular to the legal regimes by which members of the Bar and accountants are respectively governed in the Netherlands, be attained by less restrictive means' (para 108). See also *Flaherty v National Greyhound Racing Club Ltd* [2005] EWCA Civ 1117, para 21 per Scott Baker LJ.

of discretion in a sports context was considered in *London Welsh RFC v RFU*.[54] In that case, London Welsh argued that the margin of discretion in a competition law challenge to the RFU's 'primacy of tenure' rule was narrow because that rule was in reality commercial in nature, being concerned with maximising broadcasting revenue (para 44). The RFU argued (para 45) that the rule was sporting in nature, being aimed at the organisation, health and popularity of the sport, so that the margin was wide in the same way as it was wide in *Wouters* and *Meca-Medina* itself. The panel concluded (paras 47 and 48) that the rule was a hybrid, and that the RFU '... was entitled to a substantial margin of appreciation'.

4.35   The *Meca-Medina* case is likely to increase the ability of footballers to challenge decisions of their employers and sports governing bodies which they regard as restrictive of their right to 'ply their trade'. The test for justification under competition law is not identical to that under the restraint of trade doctrine. Where, for example, Ashley Cole challenged his inability to communicate with a new club without his current club's permission (under FA Rule K5) on restraint of trade grounds, it is possible that a claim would also now incorporate a challenge to that restriction under Article 101 TFEU.[55] The inter-relationship between EU competition provisions and the common law doctrine of restraint of trade is considered further in section C below.

(f)   The need to show an actual or potential effect on trade

4.36   An agreement, decision, or concerted practice must exercise an effect, direct or indirect, actual or potential, on the flow of trade between Member States.[56] This is the case even if the actual effect of the agreement may well be to increase trade flows between Member States.[57] The CJEU has interpreted the test widely, so that even agreements between two undertakings in a single Member State do not fall outside it.[58] Similarly the threshold is met even if an actual effect on trade between Member States is unlikely.[59] Under the CA 1998, in contrast, only an actual or potential effect on trade within the UK need be shown.

4.37   In practice, the potentially wide ambit of the EU competition provisions is reduced by the operation of the *de minimis* doctrine. The CJEU has held that an agreement falls outside the prohibition in Article 101(1) where it has only an insignificant effect on the markets, taking into account the weak position which the parties have in the product market in question (*Parker Pen v Commission*).[60] Article 101(1) does not apply to an agreement unless its effects, both upon competition and upon inter-state trade, are 'appreciable', ie not *de minimis*.[61]

---

54   Decision of 20 June 2012, Panel: James Dingemans QC, Ian Mill QC, Tim Ward QC.
55   It may be necessary to examine, however, the extent to which any rules were the product of a collective bargaining agreement between employers and employees, since such agreements generally fall outside the scope of application of Article 101: see Case C-67/96 *Albany* [1999] ECR I-5751, CJEU.
56   Case 56/65 *Société Technique Minière v Maschinenbau Ulm GmbH* [1966] ECR 234, CJEU.
57   Cases 56 and 58/64 *Consten & Grundig* [1966] ECR 299, CJEU.
58   See Case 23/67 *Brasserie de Haecht v Wilkin (No 1)* [1967] ECR 407, CJEU; Case C-234/89 *Delimitis v Henninger Braü* [1991] ECR I-935 (foreclosure or compartmentalisation of the national market may be sufficient to satisfy this threshold requirement).
59   Case 161/84 *Pronuptia* [1986] ECR 353, CJEU.
60   Case T-77/92 [1994] ECR II-549, GCEU.
61   See Commission Notice on Agreements of Minor Importance which do not appreciably restrict competition under Article 101(1), [2014] OJ C291/1; and Commission Notice on Guidelines on the effect on trade concept contained in Articles 81 and 82, [2004] OJ C101/81. See also Case 5/69 *Völk v Vervaecke* [1969] ECR 295, CJEU.

The *de minimis* doctrine will not be applied to agreements containing 'hardcore' restrictions, including price and output fixing and market allocation.

4.38   Nonetheless, if an agreement affects competition, it is no defence for an individual participant to say that his own position made no difference (*Ferrière Nord SpA v Commission*).[62] If market share is only slightly above the relevant threshold set out in the Notice on Agreements of Minor Importance, there is a heavier onus to show that the agreement in question has an appreciable effect on competition and trade (*European Night Services v Commission*).[63]

(g) Article 101(2) and s 2(4) of the Competition Act 1998

4.39   Article 101(2) TFEU provides that agreements or decisions prohibited pursuant to Article 101[64] are automatically void (*Robert Bosch GmbH*).[65] It has, however, been held that as a matter of EU law only those elements of an agreement which infringe Article 101 are void, unless it is impossible to sever them from the rest. The consequences for other provisions of the agreement are a matter for national law.[66] Further, just as the prohibition under Article 101(1) is itself of transient application, in play only so long as an agreement offends the provision, so too the nullity under Article 101(2) can be transient. Thus, if circumstances change and the agreement in question ceases to offend Article 101(1), it will cease to be void under Article 101(2) (*Passmore v Morland plc*).[67] Section 2(4) of CA 1998 similarly provides that 'any agreement or decision which is prohibited by subsection (1) is void'.

(h) Exemption

4.40   Article 101(3) TFEU provides that Article 101(1) may be declared inapplicable in the case of any agreement or category of agreements between undertakings, any decision or category of decisions by associations of undertakings, or any concerted practice or category of concerted practices which contributes to improving the production or distribution of goods or to promoting technical or economic progress while allowing consumers a fair share of the resulting benefit and which does not impose on the undertakings concerned restrictions which are not indispensable to the attainment of these objectives or afford such undertakings the possibility of eliminating competition in respect of a substantial part of the products in question.

4.41   Sections 6 to 11 of CA 1998 make provision for exemptions in similar terms to the relevant EU provisions.

---

62   Case T-143/89 [1995] ECR II-917, GCEU.
63   Cases T-374, 375, 384, and 388/94 [1998] ECR II-3141, GCEU.
64   Article 101(2) applies to an agreement or decision which is prohibited by Article 101(1) and not 'exempted' pursuant to Article 101(3). Article 101(2) does not provide that a concerted practice is void, presumably because concerted practices do not generally purport to give rise to legally binding obligations.
65   Case 13/61 *Kiedinguerkoopbedrijf de Geus en Uitdenbogerd v Robert Bosch GmbH* [1962] ECR 45.
66   Case 56/65 *Société Technique Minière v Maschinenbau Ulm GmbH* [1966] ECR 235. See also Case 319/82 *Société de Vente de Ciments et Betons de l'Est SA v Kerpen and Kerpen GmbH & Co KG* [1983] ECR 4173, CJEU; Case 10/86 *VAG France SA v Etablissements Magne SA* [1986] ECR 4071, CJEU.
67   [1999] 1 CMLR 1129, CA, paras 26–27 per Chadwick LJ.

4.42   Until 2004, an exemption under Article 101(3) could be granted either individually by a decision of the Commission; or in the form of a 'block exemption' in respect of a category of agreements, decisions, or concerted practices by Regulation. Nonetheless, under Article 9(1) of Regulation 17/62, only the Commission was able to grant an individual exemption. While national courts and national competition authorities could apply a Block Exemption Regulation, they could not grant individual exemptions for agreements. Furthermore, any agreement which had not been notified to the Commission could not benefit from an individual exemption under Article 101(3).

4.43   Since 1 May 2004, however, and the entry into force of the Modernisation Regulation,[68] the power to grant exemptions has been de-centralised. The notification requirement has been swept away. Article 101(3) now operates as an 'exception' to Article 101(1). Exemption under Article 101(3) on an individual basis may be obtained by a ruling from a national court or national competition authority on an individual basis. This change was intended, amongst other objectives, to free the Commission to pursue more serious cases of infringement of the competition rules, as well as to encourage more private enforcement of the competition rules.[69] The Regulation seeks to replace the system of individual notification with a system where 'undertakings would have to make their own assessment of the compatibility of their restrictive practices with Community law, in the light of the legislation in force and the case law'.[70]

(i) The potential application of Article 102 TFEU and the Chapter II prohibition

4.44   Article 102 TFEU prohibits an abuse by one or more undertakings of a dominant position within the internal market or a substantial part of it. The Article contains a non-exhaustive list of abusive practices, such as imposing unfair purchase or selling prices or other trading conditions.

4.45   The CJEU has recognised that the list of particular abuses found in Article 102 TFEU is not exhaustive.[71] New types of abuse may (and no doubt will) emerge over time. In *Compagnie Maritime Belge*,[72] the court recognised that abuse may occur if an undertaking in a dominant position strengthens that position in such a way that the degree of dominance reached substantially fetters competition. In that case, the practice of operating 'fighting ships' in a liner conference, through selective price cuts timed deliberately to match those of a competitor, was held to be an abuse.

4.46   Furthermore, the CJEU has held that Article 102 TFEU prohibits a dominant undertaking from eliminating a competitor and thereby strengthening its position by using methods other than those which come within the scope of competition on the

---

68   Council Regulation (EC) No 1/2003 of 16 December 2002 on the implementation of the rules on competition laid down in Articles 81 and 82 of the Treaty ([2003] OJ L1/1), as amended by Council Regulation (EC) No 411/2004 amending Regulation (EC) No 1/2003 ([2004] OJ L68/1).
69   See the Commission White Paper on modernisation of the rules implementing Articles 81 and 82 of the EC Treaty, [1999] OJ C132/1, [1999] 5 CMLR 208; and the White Paper of 2 April 2008 on damages actions for breach of the EC antitrust rules (COM(2008)165 final).
70   The Modernisation White Paper, above, para 77.
71   Case C-333/94 P *Tetra Pak v Commission* [1996] ECR I-5951, CJEU, para 37.
72   Joined Cases C-395 and 396/96 P *Compagnie Maritime Belge Transports v Commission* [2000] ECR I-1365, CJEU, paras 112 and 113.

merits.[73] Similarly, an intention to resort to practices falling outside the scope of competition on the merits cannot be said to be entirely irrelevant, since that intention can still be taken into account to support the conclusion that the undertaking concerned abused a dominant position, even if that conclusion should primarily be based on an objective finding that the abusive conduct actually took place (*Astra Zeneca v Commission*).[74] Whilst the fact that an undertaking is in a dominant position cannot deprive it of its entitlement to protect its own commercial interests when they are attacked,[75] it cannot use regulatory procedures in such a way as to prevent or make more difficult the entry of competitors into the market, in the absence of grounds relating to the defence of the legitimate interests of an undertaking engaged in competition on the merits or in the absence of objective justification.[76]

4.47   In *Atlantic Container Line*,[77] the GCEU found that an abuse consisted of the outright prohibition of individual service contracts in 1994 and 1995 and, where they were authorised with effect from 1996, the application of certain terms and conditions collectively agreed by the liner organisation. The court found that the enforcement of such contractual terms (even if agreed with the parties themselves) resulted in a dominant undertaking weakening the competitive structure of the market to the detriment of consumers.

4.48   It is accordingly arguable that conduct by a dominant undertaking that consciously seeks to drive a competitor from the market or exclude effective competition through non-price means might constitute an abuse in certain, exceptional circumstances. The Commission has, for example, indicated that a sporting organisation might infringe Article 102 if it refused properly to certify, other than on legitimately objective grounds, a competing organiser or a market player meeting requisite quality and safety criteria.[78] In addition in the *MOTOE* case,[79] the CJEU noted that Article 102 TFEU would preclude a national rule which conferred on a national organiser of a sport (motorcycling) the power to give consent to applications for authorisation to organise such competitions, when the organiser itself entered into its own sponsorship, advertising and insurance contracts when running competitions. Any such power had to be subject to appropriate restrictions, obligations and review procedures.[80]

C   THE COMMON LAW 'RESTRAINT OF TRADE' DOCTRINE

(a)   The restraint of trade doctrine and the *Bradley* case

4.49   In a sporting context, challenges relying upon the restraint of trade doctrine usually involve challenges to the enforceability of the rules of sports governing bodies

---

73   Case C-457/10 P *Astra Zeneca v Commission* [2012] ECLI:EU:C:2012:770, CJEU, paras 74–75.
74   Case T-321/05 *Astra Zeneca v Commission* [2010] ECR II-2805, GCEU, paras 354 and 359. This finding was referred to on appeal by the CJEU at para 63 and not subjected to any criticism.
75   Case T-65/89 *BPB Industries and British Gypsum v Commission* [1993] ECR II-389, GCEU, para 69.
76   Case T-321/05 *Astra Zeneca v Commission* [2010] ECR II-2805, GCEU, para 672; Case C-457/10 P *Astra Zeneca v Commission* [2012] ECLI:EU:C:2012:770, para 93.
77   Joined Cases T-191, 212–214/98 *Atlantic Container Line v Commission* [2003] ECR II-3275, para 1106.
78   Commission Press Release IP/99/133 of 24 February 1999, [1999] 4 CMLR 596.
79   Case C-49/07 *Motosykletistiki Omospondia Ellados NPID (MOTOE) v Greece* [2008] ECR I-4863, CJEU, paras 51–53.
80   See also *Hendry v World Professional Billiards & Snooker Association Ltd* [2002] UKCLR 5, Lloyd J, for the application of Article 102 TFEU to the competitive organisation of snooker. A rule

which restrict participants' ability to earn a living from their sport. In addition, the common law doctrine has been applied to sports' disciplinary issues in the seminal case of *Bradley v Jockey Club*.[81] In that case, a jockey challenged a disqualification order imposed by the Jockey Club which prevented him from working as a bloodstock agent for five years. Richards J held that the court had jurisdiction to grant declarations and injunctions in respect of a decision of domestic tribunals that affected a person's right to work. The basis for the jurisdiction was the common law doctrine of restraint of trade (paras 35 and 36 and 38 and 39). The court upheld the decision of the Jockey Club, finding that it had been entitled to conclude that the disqualification order imposed was proportionate. It was for the primary decision maker to strike the balance in determining whether the penalty was proportionate. The court's role was to determine whether the decision reached fell within the limits of the decision maker's discretionary area of judgment.[82]

4.50   The essential concern in a *Bradley* review should therefore be with the lawfulness of the decision taken. That is whether the procedure was fair, whether there was any error of law, whether any exercise of judgment or discretion fell within the limits open to the decision maker, and so forth.[83] This was the approach adopted by The FA Premier League (FAPL) Arbitral Panel (Sir Philip Otton, David Pannick QC and Nicholas Randall) in *Sheffield United Football Club Ltd v FAPL*.[84] In that case, Sheffield United FC complained that West Ham United FC acted in breach of FAPL rules in respect of its registration of the players Carlos Tevez and Javier Mascherano. The Panel observed that had it been reaching a decision of its own, it would have upheld the complaint. Since, however, it was exercising a supervisory role, it declined to interfere with the decision reached by the Disciplinary Commission.

(b)   Examples of restraint of trade cases in a sporting context

4.51   Examples of successful challenges based on the restraint of trade doctrine include *Eastham v Newcastle United FC*[85] (football transfer rules and the 'retention' system); *Greig v Insole*[86] (rules banning participants in a breakaway series from playing test and county cricket); and *Stevenage Borough FC v Football League Ltd*[87] (qualifications for winner of Conference to be promoted to Football League – although the challenge failed on grounds of delay). An example of an unsuccessful challenge is *Gasser v Stinson* (athletics doping rules in restraint of trade but reasonable).[88] In *Dwain Chambers v British Olympic Association*,[89] the effect of anti-doping rules on an athlete's ability to 'ply his trade' was considered by the courts. Once a rule is held to be in restraint of trade because it affects the claimant's ability to earn a living to a sufficient extent, the application of the reasonableness test requires consideration of

restricting the ability of competing events to hold snooker tournaments was struck down as an abuse of a dominant position.

81   [2004] EWHC 2164, [2007] LLR 543, QBD; see further Chapter 23, Discipline, para **23.6** for the use of *Bradley* in disciplinary proceedings.
82   But this should not be equated with 'unthinkingly servile obeisance' to the decision maker: *McKeown v British Horseracing Authority* [2010] EWHC 508 (QB) per Stadlen J at paras 35–37.
83   *Bradley v Jockey Club* [2004] EWHC 2164 (QB) per Richards J at para 37, approved by the Court of Appeal [2005] EWCA Civ 1056.
84   [2007] ISLR 77, paras 25–26.
85   [1964] Ch 413.
86   [1978] 1 WLR 302.
87   The Times, 1 August 1996, affirmed (1997) 9 Admin LR 109, CA.
88   15 June 1988.
89   [2008] EWHC 2028 (QB).

the legitimacy of the governing body's aims and the proportionality of the means it has adopted to achieve them.

4.52   These cases also highlight the ability of claimants to challenge restrictions other than the terms of contracts to which they are party, including individual decisions of governing bodies – see, for example, *Newport AFC v Football Association of Wales Ltd*.[90] In that case, certain Welsh clubs playing in the English leagues secured a declaration that the decision preventing them playing their home games at their own grounds was void as being in unreasonable restraint of trade.

4.53   Restraint of trade challenges have also been brought against restrictions on the ability of a sports player to transfer between clubs or within different branches of a sporting competition. *Leeds Rugby Ltd v Iestyn Harris*[91] was an unsuccessful challenge to an option in a release contract, which permitted Leeds Rugby club to have first option on the player's services in the event that he switched back to rugby league from rugby union. Gray J held that although the option was a restriction on the ability of Mr Harris to 'ply his trade', nonetheless it was a reasonable one for the parties to have agreed.

4.54   In *Watson v Prager*[92] the court held that although it would not usually intervene in matters relating to the terms of a commercial contract or a contract of service freely entered into by the parties, the terms of the boxer-manager agreement were prescribed by the British Boxing Board of Control as a sport's governing body. They were the only terms a licensed boxer and licensed manager could enter into. It was not a normal commercial contract and public policy required judicial supervision to ensure the restrictions imposed were reasonable and not in undue restraint of trade. The agreement contained many restrictions on the boxer, and whilst a three-year contract with an option to renew on the boxer becoming a champion was reasonable, the option to renew for a period as long as a further three years was unreasonable.

4.55   The decision in *Watson v Prager* raises two significant points. First, as many employment contracts within professional sports are required to contain the standard terms of the governing body, there may be more justification for judicial intervention than in 'normal' employment contracts more freely negotiated. Secondly, the case has led to a suggestion that even in freely negotiated contracts, the courts may be prepared to intervene on restraint of trade grounds where the duration of the contract is for a particularly long period.[93]

(c)   The interaction between the common law doctrine and the EU competition provisions

4.56   There is a note of warning to be sounded, however, about the interaction between the common law doctrine of restraint of trade and EU competition law. The doctrine of restraint of trade has been recognised as being a form of domestic competition law.[94] That has practical consequences which are analysed below,

---

90   [1995] 2 All ER 87, Ch D. The decision was declared void at trial by Blackburne J in an unreported decision dated 12 April 1995.
91   [2005] EWHC 1591 (QB), [2005] SLR 91.
92   [1991] 1 WLR 726, Ch D.
93   See eg Lewis and Taylor, *Sport: Law and Practice*, 3rd Edition (Bloomsbury Professional, 2014), para H1.24 and the footnote citing *Instone v Shroeder Music Publishing Ltd* [1974] 1 WLR 1308.
94   See *Days Medical Aids Ltd v Pihsiang Machinery Manufacturing Co* [2004] EWHC 44, [2004] 1 All ER (Comm) 991, para 265.

but it is still worth bearing in mind that the principles and policy underlying the competition rules are different from those of the restraint of trade doctrine. First, while the restraint of trade doctrine is largely concerned with the effect of the restriction between the parties, competition law is concerned with the object or effect of the restriction on competition in the market generally. The latter normally requires an economic analysis of the relevant product and geographical markets.

4.57   Secondly, the *effect* of an agreement may change with circumstances and thus fall within or without Article 101(1) according to those circumstances. There is therefore a possibility that an agreement might initially be considered to be void as infringing Article 101 TFEU, but later be redeemed as circumstances change.[95] Conversely, an innocuous agreement might become pernicious if the factual and economic matrix changes. An example might be where, over time, the parties achieved a market share which provided the power to operate anti-competitively. This, as Nicholls LJ noted in *Apple Corps Ltd v Apple Computer Inc*,[96] contrasts with the common law of restraint of trade. The relevant time at which reasonableness of the agreement is to be considered under the restraint of trade doctrine is the time of entering into the contract which contains the restraint.[97] The court is concerned to see how an agreement is capable of operating viewed at the time the agreement is made, not to see how it has in fact operated viewed with the benefit of hindsight. The courts have refused to accept that supervening events can render an initially reasonable covenant unenforceable (and vice versa).[98] It would appear that the reason for this is that to hold otherwise would be to give rise to an unacceptable degree of legal uncertainty (*Gledhow Autoparts Ltd v Delaney*).[99] In *Shell UK Ltd v Lostock Garage*,[100] Ormrod LJ expressed some concern about the possibility that a restrictive covenant might initially be enforceable but become voidable as being in restraint of trade through subsequent conduct post-dating the conclusion of the contract. In *Passmore v Morland plc*,[101] Chadwick LJ nonetheless accepted that this concern at common law about 'a wholly novel doctrine' was now 'enshrined in Community competition law'.

4.58   Thirdly, a contract that offends Article 101(1) and is not exempt under Article 101(3) is 'automatically void' (see Article 101(2) TFEU). In contrast, a contract that is in restraint of trade is *prima facie* unenforceable if either party to the contract chooses not to abide by the contract and to invoke the doctrine.[102]

4.59   Fourthly, when an agreement infringes Article 101 TFEU, both parties to the agreement and third parties may bring actions for damages for loss arising from its operation.[103] In contrast, third parties may not bring a claim for damages in respect

---

95   See *Passmore v Morland plc* [1999] 1 CMLR 1129, CA, paras 26–27; and Joined Cases T-125/97 and T-127/97 *Coca-Cola v Commission* [2000] ECR II-1733, GCEU, paras 81, 82, and 85. 'Automatic invalidity' under Article 101(2) is, as noted by Chadwick LJ in *Passmore v Morland*, paras 28–34, only effective for as long as the prohibition in Article 101 was infringed. An agreement could accordingly return Lazarus-like to full binding effect as soon as the anti-competitive effect ceased. It is difficult to see how this reasoning could be applied to an agreement that is void because it has an anti-competitive object.

96   [1991] 3 CMLR 49, CA, para 113.

97   *Schroeder Music Publishing Co Ltd v Macaulay* [1974] 1 WLR 1308, 1309 per Lord Reid; *Watson v Prager* [1991] 1 WLR 726, 738 per Scott J.

98   *Shell UK Ltd v Lostock Garage Ltd* [1976] 1 WLR 1187, CA, 1202 per Ormrod LJ.

99   [1965] 1 WLR 1366, CA, 1377.

100   [1976] 1 WLR 1187, CA.

101   [1999] 1 CMLR 1129, CA, para 54.

102   *Esso Petroleum Co Ltd v Harper's Garage (Southport) Ltd* [1968] AC 269, HL, 297.

103   See Case C-453/99 *Courage Ltd v Crehan* [2001] ECR I-6297, paras 25–27; and *Inntrepreneur Pub Co v Crehan* [2006] UKHL 38, [2006] 3 WLR 148.

of a contract that is void as being in restraint of trade,[104] although they may obtain declaratory[105] or injunctive relief.[106]

4.60   The differences between the application of the competition law rules and the restraint of trade doctrine are also very significant in practice because of the supremacy of EU law rules. If there is a conflict of result, EU competition rules will prevail. The CJEU held in *Walt Wilhelm*[107] (at paras 4 to 7) that the parallel application of national and EU rules 'can only be allowed in so far as it does not prejudice the uniform application throughout the Common Market of the Community rules on cartels and the full effect of the measures adopted in implementation of those rules'. It stated that conflicts between EU rules and national rules in the matter of the law on cartels must be resolved by applying the principle that EU law takes precedence.

4.61   In *BMW*,[108] Advocate General Tesauro took the view (although the issue was not ultimately resolved by the CJEU) that an exempt agreement under Article 101(3) TFEU could not be prohibited under national competition legislation (paras 38 and 39) since 'the exemption granted to them cannot but prevent the national authorities from ignoring the positive assessment put on them by the Community authorities'. This applied whether the agreements were protected by individual exemption or an exempting regulation. In *Bundeskartellamt v Volkswagen and VAG Leasing*,[109] Advocate General Tesauro addressed the separate question of a conflict between EU and national competition law 'not only where an exemption is granted ... but also where the conduct at issue does not fall within the prohibition laid down in [then] Article 85(1)' (now Article 101(1)). In paras 58 and 59 of his Opinion, Advocate General Tesauro considered, on the basis of the judgment in *Walt Wilhelm*, that where conduct was permitted by EU law as falling outside the scope of Article 101(1) it could not be prohibited under national competition rules.

4.62   In respect of the period after 1 May 2004, Article 3 of the Modernisation Regulation[110] provides for the dual application of EU and domestic competition law by national courts in any situation where domestic competition law is to be applied. In this regard, Article 3(2) states that:

> 'the application of national competition law may not lead to the prohibition of agreements, decisions by associations of undertakings or concerted practices which may affect trade between Member States but which do not restrict competition within the meaning of Article [101(1)] of the Treaty, or which fulfil the conditions of Article [101(3)] of the Treaty, or which are covered by a Regulation for the application of Article [101(3)] of the Treaty.'[111]

Article 3(3) of the Modernisation Regulation confirms that neither Article 3(1) nor 3(2) 'preclude the application of provisions of national law that predominantly pursue an objective different from that pursued by Articles [101] and [102] of the Treaty'.

4.63   In the *Days Medical Aids* case,[112] Langley J held that the qualification in Article 3(3) was aimed at consumer protection laws relating to unfair contract terms

---

104 *Mogul Steamship Co Ltd v McGregor, Gow & Co* [1892] AC 25, HL at 39, 42–48.
105 *Eastham v Newcastle United FC* [1964] Ch 413, 440 per Wilberforce J.
106 *Nagle v Feilden* [1966] 2 QB 633, CA, 646 per Lord Denning MR.
107 Case 14/68 *Walt Wilhelm* [1969] ECR 1, CJEU.
108 Case C-70/93 *BMW* [1995] ECR I-3439, CJEU.
109 Case C-266/93 [1995] ECR I-3477, CJEU.
110 Regulation 1/2003, see n 68 above.
111 Article 3(2) nonetheless also confirms that Member States shall not under this Regulation be precluded from adopting and applying on their territory stricter national laws which prohibit or sanction unilateral conduct engaged in by undertakings.
112 [2004] EWHC 44 (Comm), [2004] 1 All ER (Comm) 991.

and the like. The judge found that the common law doctrine of restraint of trade did not predominantly pursue different objectives to Articles 101 and 102. Langley J noted that there was a close relationship between the two sets of legal rules and referred in this regard to *WWF v World Wrestling Foundation*[113] and *Apple Corps Ltd v Apple Computer Inc*.[114] He accordingly found that the common law doctrine of restraint of trade was a species of domestic competition law.[115] The judge went on to find that, to the extent that there was a conflict between the application of the doctrine of restraint of trade and the application of Article 101 TFEU, the court was 'precluded by Community law from applying the restraint of trade doctrine'.[116]

4.64   While that conclusion may be somewhat controversial, it has been followed.[117] Accordingly, where an agreement falls within the potential scope of application of Article 101 TFEU,[118] but is either not prohibited by it,[119] or benefits from the application of the exemption conferred by Article 101(3) TFEU or a block exemption,[120] then the common law doctrine of restraint of trade cannot be applied. Langley J acknowledged that this may have significant repercussions in practice and warned that:

> 'It would, I suspect, come as something of a surprise to many practitioners if it were the case that the common law doctrine of restraint of trade even in the non-employment field had been emasculated let alone trumped by Community competition law.'[121]

D   PRACTICAL APPLICATION OF COMPETITION RULES IN FOOTBALL

(a)   General considerations

4.65   The potential application of competition rules in the context of sport was considered in the Commission's Staff Working Document (SWD).[122] The following summary of the steps to be taken into account when considering the potential application of the competition rules comes from section 3.4 of the SWD.

4.66   *Step 1.* Is the sports association that adopted the rule to be considered an 'undertaking' or an 'association of undertakings'?

(a)   The sports association is an 'undertaking' to the extent it carries out an 'economic activity' itself (eg the selling of broadcasting rights).

(b)   The sports association is an 'association of undertakings' if its members carry out an economic activity. In this respect, the question will become relevant to what extent the sport in which the members (usually clubs/teams or athletes) are

---

113   [2002] EWCA Civ 196, paras 64, 66 per Carnwath LJ.
114   See n 96 above, paras 109–113 per Nicholls LJ.
115   See n 112 above, para 265.
116   See n 112 above, para 266.
117   The reasoning in *Days Medical Aids* was followed by Roth J in *Jones v Ricoh Manufacturing* [2010] EWHC 1743 (Ch) at para 49.
118   Because, eg, it is an agreement that actually or potentially has an effect on trade between Member States or in a substantial part of the EU.
119   *Days Medical Aids*, para 263 and Article 3(2) of the Modernisation Regulation.
120   *Days Medical Aids*, para 262 and Article 3(2) of the Modernisation Regulation.
121   *Days Medical Aids*, para 254. The observations of Roth J in *Jones v Ricoh Manufacturing* indicate that the warning was justified.
122   Commission Staff Working Document, *The EU and Sport: Background and Context - Accompanying document to the White Paper on Sport*, COM(2007) 391 final.

active can be considered an economic activity and to what extent the members exercise economic activity.

(c) In the absence of 'economic activity', Articles 101 and 102 TFEU do not apply.

4.67   *Step 2.* Does the rule in question restrict competition within the meaning of Article 101(1) TFEU or constitute an abuse of a dominant position under Article 102 TFEU? This will depend, applying the principles established in the *Wouters* judgment,[123] on the following factors:

(a) the overall context in which the rule was adopted or produces its effects, and its objectives;
(b) whether the restrictions caused by the rule are inherent in the pursuit of the objectives; and
(c) whether the rule is proportionate in light of the objective pursued.

4.68   *Step 3.* Is trade between Member States affected?

4.69   *Step 4.* Does the rule fulfil the conditions of Article 101(3) TFEU?

4.70   In a football context, some of the most difficult issues concern market definition. The European Commission's Notice on Market Definition[124] observes (at para 4) that: 'The definition of the relevant market in both its product and its geographic dimensions often has a decisive influence on the assessment of a competition case.' The Notice confirms that market definition is a tool. It requires the relevant product market and relevant geographic market to be defined. This is necessary to enable a competition authority or court to ascertain whether there has been an appreciable effect on competition under Article 101(1) TFEU and to define the market for the purposes of Article 102 TFEU. In doing so, it is common to look at sources of competitive constraints derived from demand substitution, supply substitution and potential competition (para 13). Expert economists normally examine whether a small but non-transitory increase in price would cause customers to switch to a competing product. That necessarily requires a product market to be defined (para 15).

4.71   One of the difficulties in a football case is to know how that particular market should be defined. There are a series of economic markets in football which could be relevant: stadium attendances, broadcasting rights, the market for players' or agents' services, advertising and hospitality services and so on. For any given market, the analysis may well be complex. For example, attendances at football stadia may in some respects be inherently 'local' to a given area.[125] It is possible that attendance at a football match is in competition, at least from a consumer's perspective, with other leisure activities (cinema, rugby matches etc). Moreover, it may be doubted whether a Plymouth Argyle fan would be interested in attending a match (not involving his team) featuring Newcastle at St James' Park, for example. But both sets of fans might have a shared interest in watching a televised match not involving either of their teams. A properly conducted market definition exercise may well require a lengthy,

---

123 The *Wouters* principles were explicitly referred to in the Third Party Ownership (TPO) case TAS 2016/A/4490 *RFC Seraing v FIFA* where the CAS, when assessing the compatibility of the FIFA TPO ban, for example in para 143, emphasised that the ban had a number of legitimate objectives (including according to FIFA, the prevention of conflicts of interests). There was no breach of Article 101 or 102 TFEU. See http://www.tas-cas.org/fileadmin/user_upload/Sentence_4490__FINALE__internet.pdf (accessed February 2018).
124 Commission Notice on the definition of relevant market for the purposes of Community competition law, [1997] OJ C372/5.
125 See for instance *Burgess v OFT* [2005] CAT 25 (crematorium and funeral services) and *Chester City Council v Arriva Plc* [2007] EWHC 1373 (Ch) (local bus services).

careful and detailed analysis of substitutability by reference to evidence on consumer preferences, pricing, supply constraints, evidence of shifting and the suchlike.

4.72   Official studies into the relevant market have largely focused on the television broadcasting market. In 1999, the Monopolies and Mergers Commission (MMC) published a report on the proposed acquisition of Manchester United FC by British Sky Broadcasting Group. It conducted a detailed analysis of the broadcasting market for live football matches. The MMC found evidence that FAPL and FA Cup football were more important for broadcasting rights than other football competitions. Insofar as it considered the market for stadium attendances, the MMC considered it arguable that Manchester United's home matches were in a market of their own, but ultimately found it unnecessary to reach a concluded view because its overall analysis did not depend upon the question (paras 2.18–2.21).

4.73   Subsequently, in a decision taken in 2006, the EU Commission examined the compatibility with Article 101 TFEU of joint selling of TV rights for FAPL football.[126] The Commission accepted commitments given by FAPL as to the rights' auctions to be conducted, bringing the competition investigation to an end. In doing so, it defined the relevant upstream market as that for the sale of live broadcasting rights of FAPL matches. It identified a series of downstream markets in the media sector, including that for the sale of television programmes to consumers and associated advertising services.

4.74   The Office for Communications (Ofcom) conducted a substantial investigation into the UK Pay TV market as part of its decision to impose a 'wholesale must offer' obligation on Sky in 2010.[127] Ofcom examined the market for the wholesale of television sports channels. It did not analyse the market in relation to stadium attendances. Ofcom emphasised that stadium attendances were not a close substitute for watching matches on television, stating (at para 5.7) that '[f]or football fans, going to watch an event live at a stadium is an attractive alternative to viewing at home on TV, but given the cost of purchasing tickets and travelling to see events, and the limited capacity of sports stadiums, watching events live is not a close substitute for subscribing to [core TV channels].'

4.75   In terms of competition between clubs for fans, no detailed study has been conducted which has reached any definitive conclusions based on empirical data. Professor S Szymanski and R Smith have observed in an article that '[c]ompetition between clubs on ticket prices is not likely to be a general phenomenon',[128] given fan loyalty and geographical constraints on travelling to matches. Evidence of fans switching between clubs based on the success of the clubs is very limited. Szymanski and Smith suggest that the demand for attendances at a particular club shows a price inelasticity of demand. Clubs generally are unable to turn this inelastic demand into monopolistic profits because even if other clubs are not a good substitute for attendance at their own stadia, other leisure activities constrain demand.

4.76   The SWD (in section 3.4) also gives a summary of rules which are not likely to raise competition concerns in a football context and those which may pose

---

126 Commission Decision of 22/3/2006 on *Joint Selling of Media Rights to the FA Premier League* (COMP C-2/38.173).
127 Ofcom's *Pay TV Statement*, 31 March 2010.
128 'The English Football Industry: Profit, performance and industrial structure', (1997) 11(1) *Journal of Applied Economics* 149.

a greater risk of doing so. In terms of those rules unlikely to be problematic, it states:

> 'The following types of rules constitute examples of organisational sporting rules that – based on their legitimate objectives – are likely not to breach Articles [101] and/or [102 TFEU] provided the restrictions contained in such rules are inherent and proportionate to the objectives pursued:
>
> – "Rules of the game" (e.g., the rules fixing the length of matches or the number of players on the field);
> – Rules concerning selection criteria for sport competitions;
> – "At home and away from home" rules;
> – Rules preventing multiple ownership in club competitions;
> – Rules concerning the composition of national teams;
> – Anti-doping rules;
> – Rules concerning transfer periods ("transfer windows").'

4.77   In terms of those presenting a greater risk, the SWD states:

> 'The following rules represent a higher likelihood of problems concerning compliance with Articles [101] and/or [102 TFEU], although some of them could be justified under certain conditions under Article [101(3)] or Article [102 TFEU]:
>
> – Rules protecting sports associations from competition.
> – Rules excluding legal challenges of decisions by sports associations before national courts if the denial of access to ordinary courts facilitates anti-competitive agreements or conduct.
> – Rules concerning nationality clauses for sport clubs/teams.
> – Rules regulating the transfer of athletes between clubs (except transfer windows).
> – Rules regulating professions ancillary to sport (e.g. football players' agents).'

4.78   The SWD confirms that this list is tentative only and an individual analysis of every challenged organisational sporting rule on a case-by-case basis is indispensable. This chapter now looks at certain aspects of the rules governing football which have, in practice, generated challenges on competition law grounds.

(b)   Restrictions on club ownership and grounds

4.79   In *AEK PAE and SK Slavia Praha v UEFA*,[129] the Court of Arbitration for Sport (CAS) rejected a challenge by the majority owner of certain clubs (ENIC) to a UEFA rule which prevented substantial common ownership for clubs competing in the UEFA competitions. CAS held that the UEFA rule was an essential feature for the organisation of a professional football competition. It was not more extensive than necessary to serve the fundamental goal of preventing conflicts of interest which would be publicly perceived as affecting the authenticity, and then the uncertainty, of results in UEFA competitions.

4.80   ENIC then complained about the UEFA rule to the EU Commission. In its decision in *ENIC*,[130] the Commission considered that the UEFA rules could be assessed for their compatibility with EU competition law. UEFA was an association of associations of undertakings, prescribing rules which governed in large measure a form of economic activity. The Commission accepted that the rule against dual ownership, despite some inherently negative competitive effects, was nonetheless indispensable as a means of maintaining public confidence in the football market and

129 CAS 98/2000, 20 August 1999.
130 COMP/37 806, *ENIC/UEFA*, 27 June 2002.

ensuring that games would be fair and honest and not at risk of being subverted by commercial interests. Such a rule therefore fell outside the scope of Article 101(1) TFEU in its entirety. The Commission accordingly rejected ENIC's complaint.

4.81   The *Mouscron* case[131] saw the EU Commission reject a complaint that a UEFA rule requiring home and away ties to be played in separate countries was an infringement of Article 102 TFEU. The Commission in fact analysed the competition issues under Article 101 TFEU, but concluded the objective of the rule was not to distort competition, but to protect the integrity of UEFA competitions. The Commission left open the question of whether or not UEFA was dominant in the market for organising football competitions.

(c)   Promotion and relegation issues

4.82   A number of cases have seen promotion or relegation decisions challenged on competition law or restraint of trade grounds. The doctrine of restraint of trade was considered in *Stevenage Borough Football Club Ltd v The Football League Limited*.[132] Stevenage were refused promotion to the Football League because their ground failed to meet certain criteria required for promoted clubs. Carnwath J drew a broad distinction between expulsion cases, where an existing status is taken away, and application cases, where a future status is refused. The application of the common law doctrine where there was no contractual nexus between the parties was harder to achieve. He nonetheless accepted that, in principle, a refusal to permit admission to a league could be challenged as being an unreasonable restraint of trade notwithstanding the fact that Stevenage could carry on playing football in the Conference. He concluded that if entry criteria were arbitrary or capricious, they would be open to challenge, with due weight being given to the regulatory function of the sporting body. On the facts, he found certain requirements to be unreasonable, but declined to grant the relief sought. His decision was upheld on appeal.[133] The rules governing admission to the league were a contract, but they were also regulatory in nature. The court's assessment of those rules would be supervisory in nature.

4.83   In *London Welsh v RFU*,[134] London Welsh were refused promotion to the Premiership by the RFU on the basis of the primacy of tenure rule for the club's ground. This required a newly promoted club to satisfy the RFU that it was the 'primary' tenant at its ground, even though three premiership clubs already in that league were not. In the light of concessions made by the RFU, there was no dispute about market definition, the RFU's dominance or the fact that the rules represented a *prima facie* restriction of competition. The sole question was whether the RFU could justify the restrictive effects of the rule as being 'inherent in the pursuit' of legitimate sporting objectives and proportionate to them. The arbitral panel ruled that the primacy of tenure rule infringed Article 101 TFEU and the Chapter I prohibition, did not fall within the scope of a 'pure sporting rule' (holding it was hybrid in nature), and could not be subject to any exemption under Article 101(3). While the rule included exceptions for three particular Premiership clubs, there was insufficient justification for the narrowness of that exception. It could have been wider, given its restrictive effect on aspirant Championship clubs. London Welsh's appeal was therefore allowed.

---

131 COMP/E3/36.85 *Lille/UEFA*, 3 December 1999.
132 23 July 1996, Carnwath J, reported in The Times, 1 August 1996.
133 (1997) 9 Admin LR 109, CA per Millett LJ at pp 115–116.
134 RFU Appeal Panel 29/6/12.

4.84 Mark Warby QC issued a Rule K arbitration award in relation to the challenge by Handsworth FC on 6 July 2012.[135] The club challenged a refusal by the FA Appeal Board to allow its continued stay in the premier division of the Northern Counties East league, in the light of the ground's grading conditions. The club proposed a ground sharing arrangement to avoid relegation. The FA declined to allow it to do so, citing an FA rule which generally permitted ground sharing, but prohibited it when seeking promotion or seeking to avoid relegation. The arbitral panel rejected a belated challenge to that rule as being an unreasonable restraint of trade. It refused to entertain a very belated competition law challenge, raised only on the basis of the *London Welsh* decision.

(d)   Player transfers and controls on agents

4.85 The CJEU in the *Bosman* case[136] declined to give a ruling on the competition law implications of restrictions on player transfers. But Advocate General Lenz in the same case did provide some guidance. He concluded (paras 255–256) that clubs were undertakings for competition law purposes, and the UEFA and national football associations would be associations of undertakings to whom the competition provisions applied. Having concluded that the rules on transfers were capable of affecting trade between Member States (para 261), he also found that they represented an appreciable restriction on competition (paras 262–263). The transfer rules restricted the ability of clubs to compete between themselves for players' services. At para 270, the Advocate General recognised that the fact that football clubs were mutually dependent on each other distinguished football from other market sectors. That fact might justify restrictions on competition aimed at the proper functioning of the game. But he rejected the suggestion that transfer restrictions were one such rule. The Advocate General also mooted the possibility that there might be cases where UEFA or a national association were in a dominant position, or where the clubs in a particular competition occupied a position of collective dominance, for the purposes of Article 102 TFEU. But the Advocate General considered that no concluded view needed to be reached on those issues, since the relevant market was between clubs and players where neither was dominant.[137]

4.86 The restraint of trade doctrine has also featured in cases concerning the transfer of players between different clubs. The ability of a football player to leave his employment with one club and move to another is complicated by the fact that the previous employing club holds the player's registration (with the football authorities), without which the player is not entitled to play. A player cannot simply walk out of one club and join another. Unless he does so in accordance with the rules, he will be prevented from playing for the new club.

4.87 Historically, the common law did little to assist the player. Even if the player's contract had expired, and he was thus no longer playing for, or paid by, his former club, the player could be 'retained' by his previous club and could not transfer to another club without the consent of his previous club – which usually meant the payment of a fee. This situation was challenged by the player in *Eastham v Newcastle United FC*,[138] and the system was declared illegal and unenforceable as a restraint of trade. The position has now been relaxed yet further as a result of the

---

135 Available on www.thefa.com (accessed February 2018).
136 Case C-415/93 *Bosman* [1995] ECR I-4921, CJEU.
137 Paras 281 to 296 of the Opinion.
138 [1964] Ch 413.

important decision of the CJEU in *Bosman*[139] (considered below). After *Bosman*, it is no longer possible for a club to demand the payment of a 'transfer fee' to transfer the registration of a player who is out of contract.

4.88   In *Cooke v Football Association*,[140] the court held that a football player who wished to transfer from an Irish club to an English club could challenge the FIFA rules that prevented him doing so and the English FA's decision to apply the FIFA rules, on the basis that they acted unreasonably to restrain the player's trade.

4.89   Nevertheless, there remain restrictions on a player's ability to 'ply his trade' where he sees fit as a result of the transfer rules. For example, under the rules, a player can only move between clubs during a specified 'transfer window' (usually during the closed part of the season in the summer up until the end of August, and during the month of January). In addition, a player cannot approach another club to try and arrange a new contract for the period after his current contract ends, except in certain prescribed circumstances.

4.90   This latter restriction was challenged in the *Ashley Cole* case. The former Arsenal player was disciplined by FAPL for meeting Chelsea's manager and Chief Executive. FAPL applied Rule K5 which states that a 'Contract player, either by himself or by any other Person on his behalf, shall not directly or indirectly make any such approach as is referred to in Rule K5 without having obtained the prior written consent of his Club'. An approach referred to in Rule K5 was 'an approach to a Club … with a view to negotiating a contract with such Club'. Mr Cole argued that Rule K5 was a restraint of trade. It prevented a footballer from engaging in merely preliminary discussions regarding a possible move, even to the extent of discussing potential employment in the period after the termination of his existing employment. The club, on the other hand, was free to discuss the future employment of the player without restriction. The FAPL disciplinary commission held that Rule K5 was in restraint of trade but nevertheless found that it was reasonable. As regards the parties' interests, the restriction was not imposed unilaterally but was the result of a process of collective bargaining involving the Professional Footballers' Association. As regards the public interest, it found that 'we cannot escape the conclusion that if the restraint were removed, the number of transfers would increase and the balance between players' agents and the Premiership clubs would tilt significantly in favour of the agents (and their incomes). We consider that this is a potent consideration'.

4.91   The FAPL disciplinary commission was guided by authorities such as *McInnes v Onslow Fane*,[141] which indicate that a court should be slow to interfere with the manner in which a sporting body governs its own sport. The FAPL Appeals Board, on Mr Cole's appeal, declined to follow the *McInnes v Onslow Fane* approach, since it considered that it applied to courts only (as an expression of non-expert judicial deference to the expert professional body) and not to the operation of discipline by the sporting authority itself. The Appeals Board upheld the finding that the restraint was reasonable since 'overall the Rule in fact works to the benefit of the great majority of players' and it was also in the public interest. A further appeal to the Court of Arbitration for Sport was rejected for lack of jurisdiction.

4.92   EU competition law has also been prayed in aid by a French football agent who complained about agents' regulations introduced by FIFA to the EU Commission.

---

139   Case C-415/93 *Bosman* [1995] ECR I-4921, CJEU.
140   The Times, 24 March 1972, Foster J.
141   [1978] 1 WLR 1520.

When the Commission rejected the complaint, the agent brought a challenge to that decision before the GCEU. In *Piau v Commission*,[142] the GCEU noted that FIFA was an association governed by Swiss law whose members were national associations of amateur or professional football clubs. FIFA was recognised to be an association of undertakings, formed of football clubs (both professional and amateur) (paras 69–70). FIFA, as holder of exclusive broadcasting and transmission rights for the sporting events in question, carried on an economic activity (paras 71–72).[143] At paras 112 to 116, the GCEU concluded that FIFA, the national associations and the groups of football clubs collectively held a dominant position in the market for players' agents' services. The buyers in the market were both football players and clubs. The sellers were the football agents. FIFA was considered to be acting on behalf of the clubs, since it was an 'emanation of those clubs as a second-level association of undertakings formed by the clubs'. By adopting the FIFA Players' Agents Regulations, the clubs had collectively adopted a common approach to their treatment of agents. The Regulations were binding on national associations and clubs forming part of them, with sanctions for non-compliance. They were the product of a collectively dominant position.

4.93   The GCEU nonetheless considered that there had not been any abuse. The Regulations did not impose quantitative restrictions on access to the occupation of players' agent that could be detrimental to competition. They imposed qualitative restrictions, but ones which were justified. The Regulations would have benefited from an exemption under Article 101(3) TFEU and accordingly there was no EU interest in the complaint being allowed to proceed by the Commission.

(e) Salary caps

4.94   The direct interest of sport teams, clubs and athletes in the economic viability of their sporting competitors, at its most powerful, has led organisers of some sports to impose direct constraints on the amount that teams can spend on players. In other words, a salary cap, with a view to ensuring competitive balance on the field.[144] Salary caps, ie limits on the amount permitted to be paid to the playing staff of a particular club over a given period, exist in many sports, and in the United Kingdom in rugby league and rugby union (although, significantly, not yet in football at any level).[145]

4.95   The potential vulnerability of salary caps to competition law challenges has been debated over a lengthy period. A salary cap risks being characterised as a horizontal agreement between competitors which restricts the amount of money that they spend on a key input, or raw material. Trade is affected in that the salary cap controls how clubs allocate their resources between players' remuneration and other economic activities. The markets which are likely to be relevant for these purposes include the market for players' services and the market for the rights to players' services.

142 Case T-193/02 *Piau v Commission of the European Communities* [2005] ECR II-209, GCEU. An appeal to the CJEU in Case C-171/05 was dismissed as being partly inadmissible and partly unfounded: [2006] ECR I-37, CJEU.
143 See also Case T-46/92 *Scottish Football v Commission* [1994] ECR II-1039, GCEU.
144 Salary caps exist in English, Australian, French and New Zealand club rugby union; North American hockey, football and baseball; and certain cricket leagues.
145 Salary caps are either 'hard' or 'soft' caps. 'Hard' caps impose a limit of a fixed sum on spending on players; 'soft' caps limit clubs to spending a proportion of their individual revenues on players. Salary caps may be a basis for preserving competitive balance between clubs and, in difficult economic conditions, may be necessary to preserve the existence of poorer clubs.

4.96   In the *Bosman* case, UEFA argued that despite the restriction in the transfer market created by the rule in that case, the 'downstream' markets benefited from the restriction, for example the market for tickets to attend matches. UEFA argued that the popularity of the sport was assisted by the rule in question. The CJEU rejected this argument since the restriction imposed by the rule was disproportionate. But the need to sustain both 'upstream' and 'downstream' markets is relied upon by supporters of the legality of the salary cap. They claim that restrictions in the 'upstream' market (for players' services) may be justified on the basis of beneficial effects in 'downstream markets' (entertainment, ticket sales, etc).

4.97   The effect of the judgment in *Meca-Medina* and earlier Commission decisions such as *ENIC/UEFA*[146] is that any rule such as a salary cap which has as its object a restriction on commercial freedom designed to ensure the long-term survival of the sport may escape the competition rules if: (i) it is inherent in the pursuit of the very existence of credible competitions; and (ii) its absence would, in the long term, render any competition impossible; and (iii) it is proportionate.

4.98   A further factor to consider is the extent to which any salary caps are imposed as a result of a collective bargaining procedure. In the *Albany* case,[147] the CJEU held that Article 101(1) TFEU would not apply to collective agreements between employees and employers which had the effect of distorting competition if such agreements were the result of negotiations between management and labour, and had the effect of improving players' working conditions, for example their remuneration (paras 59 et seq). Such collective agreements 'by virtue of their nature and purpose' fall outside the Article 81(1) prohibition. The CJEU recognised that such agreements were likely to restrict competition but decided that the social policy objectives of collective agreements would be seriously undermined if subjected to the application of Article 101(1).[148]

(f) Financial fair play rules

4.99   Similarly, competition law provisions have been invoked by clubs or agents disgruntled with the financial fair play (FFP) rules which are now applied at domestic and UEFA levels of competitions. On 27 May 2010, the UEFA Executive Committee approved the UEFA FFP Regulations 2010. Under those regulations, any club competing in a UEFA competition would have to move towards a 'break-even model',[149] designed to reduce the level of debt which a club could permissibly sustain on a rolling basis. A failure to comply with the regulations would lead to a range of sanctions, including fines and disqualification from European competition.

4.100   The FFP rules were challenged by a club in *Galatasaray v UEFA*.[150] The CAS held that the UEFA FFP Regulations did not have as their object the restriction or distortion of competition. It held (para 63) that their object was the financial conduct of clubs wishing to participate in UEFA competitions. The Panel did not find sufficient evidence that the object was to favour or disfavour certain clubs, as

---

146 Case COMP/37 806.
147 Case C-67/96 [1999] ECR I-5751.
148 This reasoning was restated by the CJEU in Joint Cases C-115/97 to 117/97 *Brentjens* [1999] ECR I-6025, paras 56–60 and in Case C-219/97 *Bokken* [1999] ECR I-6121, para 47.
149 The UEFA FFP Regulations had a three-year rolling monitoring period, with a reducing level of 'Acceptable Deviation' from a break-even result (£45m equity plus £5m losses initially, £30m equity plus £5m losses thereafter, and lower levels into the future).
150 CAS 2016/A/4492.

opposed to preventing clubs from trading at levels beyond their resources. It did not consider that the evidence showed that the 'break even' requirement was likely to have negative effects in the market or appreciably constrain competition. The club failed to substantiate the alleged impact of the FFP regime on the relevant market (para 74). They had a limited impact and made an overall positive contribution to the sporting competition (para 76). By reference to the *Wouters* criteria, the CAS then observed that the UEFA rules were inherently and objectively necessary. The fact that they evolved over time did not impact on their proportionality (paras 77–79).

4.101 There have also been a series of challenges by football clubs in the Championship to penalties imposed under the English Football League's FFP rules, but few details of the challenges are yet in the public domain.

(g) Doping

4.102 The case of *Meca-Medina*, considered above, demonstrates that anti-doping rules may be subjected to challenges on competition law grounds. This topic is addressed separately in Chapter 24.

(h) Marketing: tickets, advertising and TV rights

4.103 There have been numerous instances of the competition rules forming the basis for a complaint about the distribution or allocation of tickets, hospitality packages and TV or broadcasting rights. In *UEFA Champions League*,[151] the Commission granted a conditional exemption under Article 101(3) TFEU for the rules governing the collective selling of television rights to the Champions League. This was done after modifications were made to meet the Commission's concerns. Other challenges have been brought in respect of ticket allocations in *Italia 90*[152] and the *World Cup 1998*,[153] where exclusivity arrangements in relation to ticket sales were found to infringe Articles 101 and 102 TFEU respectively.

E FREE MOVEMENT OF WORKERS AND FREEDOM TO PROVIDE SERVICES

(a) Introduction

4.104 The remaining part of this chapter focuses on topical and long-standing footballing issues arising from EU rules on the free movement of persons and the freedom to provide services, including the iconic *Bosman* ruling which, in 1995, fundamentally reshaped the European and global footballing landscape. This section provides an overview of the Treaty principles; outlines their application and context; and finally highlights a variety of practical contemporary examples.

---

151 OJ [2003] L 291/15.
152 Commission Decision 92/521/EEC of 27 October 1992 relating to a proceeding under Article 85 of the EEC Treaty (IV/33.384 and IV/33.378 – *Distribution of package tours during the 1990 World Cup*).
153 Commission Decision 2000/12/EC: Commission Decision of 20 July 1999 relating to a proceeding under Article 82 of the EC Treaty and Article 54 of the EEA Agreement (Case IV/36.888 – *1998 Football World Cup*).

4.105   The fundamental, underlying principle underpinning this section is best articulated in the SWD:[154]

> 'EU law prohibits (with some exceptions based on public policy, public health and public security) any discrimination on grounds of nationality. It establishes the right for any citizen of the Union to move and reside freely in the territory of the Member States. The Treaty also aims to abolish any discrimination based on nationality between workers of the Member States as regards employment, remuneration and other conditions of work and employment. The same prohibitions apply to discrimination based on nationality in the provision of services.'

4.106   While this fundamental principle may need to be reviewed in the light of any final agreement reached with the EU in the Brexit negotiations and the final terms of the European Union (Withdrawal) Act, the prohibition on discrimination on the grounds of nationality will remain applicable for existing cases until that time. Until that point, EU law will continue to provide protection for any citizen of the Union to move and reside in another Member State territory. Accordingly, various direct and indirect forms of discrimination based on nationality between workers of Member States as regards employment or the provision of services are likely to remain outlawed for several years to come. Post-Brexit, there is the possibility for existed prohibitions to be reversed by governmental legislative action. One such example is the issue of player quotas, as discussed below at para **4.122** et seq.

(b)   The basic free movement of people and services provisions

4.107   In the area of sport, the CJEU has primarily focused on two fundamental internal market freedoms: namely the freedom of movement of workers and freedom to provide services. Article 45 TFEU governs the free movement of persons and Article 56 TFEU governs the freedom to provide services. These two Treaty freedoms have consistently featured in court and Commission decisions relating to sportsmen and women wishing to become employed or provide services in another Member State.

4.108   Article 45 TFEU states that 'freedom of movement for workers shall be secured within the Union'. Pursuant to Article 45(2), this shall 'entail the abolition of any discrimination based on nationality between workers of the Member States as regards employment, remuneration and other conditions of work and employment.' Article 45(3) TFEU then sets down the specific incidents of such rights, including the right to accept offers of employment, to move freely within the EU for this purpose, to stay in a Member State while employed and to remain thereafter, subject to conditions for doing so established by EU law. These rights may be subject to limitations justified on grounds of public policy, public security or public health (Article 45(3) TFEU).

4.109   Article 56 TFEU prohibits restrictions on freedom to provide services within the Union for service providers established in a Member State other than that of the service recipient. The second indent of Article 56 permits the European Parliament and the Council to adopt EU legislation to extend the scope of this prohibition to services from third country nationals.

(c)   The specific treatment of sport

4.110   As explained in paras **4.1–4.9** and **4.29–4.35** above, the case law of the EU courts and decisions of the Commission illustrate the degree to which: (i) purely

---

154   See n 122 above.

sporting rules fall outside the scope of the Treaty provisions; and (ii) the specificity of sport has been taken into account and accepted in circumstances where such restrictions can be objectively justified and are proportionate to the objectives pursued.

4.111 For example, when assessing sporting rules in the context of EU law, the EU Commission has acknowledged that:[155]

> 'Sport events are a product of the contest between a number of clubs/teams or at least two athletes. This interdependence between competing adversaries is a feature specific to sport and one which distinguishes it from other industry or service sectors.
>
> – If sport events are to be of interest to the spectator, they must involve uncertainty as to the result. There must therefore be a certain degree of equality in competitions. This sets the sport sector apart from other industry or service sectors, where competition between firms serves the purpose of eliminating inefficient firms from the market. Sport teams, clubs and athletes have a direct interest not only in there being other teams, clubs and athletes, but also in their economic viability as competitors.
> – The organisational level of sport in Europe is characterised by a monopolistic pyramid structure. Traditionally, there is a single national sport association per sport and Member State, which operates under the umbrella of a single European association and a single worldwide association. The pyramid structure results from the fact that the organisation of national championships and the selection of national athletes and national teams for international competitions often require the existence of one umbrella federation. The Community courts and the Commission have both recognized the importance of the freedom of internal organization of sport associations.
> – Sport fulfils important educational, public health, social, cultural and recreational functions. The preservation of some of these essential social and cultural benefits of sport which contribute to stimulating production and economic development is supported through arrangements which provide for a redistribution of financial resources from professional to amateur levels of sport (principle of solidarity).'

4.112 The developing case law of the EU courts and of the Commission has recognised the need to balance the application of the Treaty freedoms to a form of economic activity, while continuing to pay due regard to the specific (and often unique) aspects of sporting competitions and their organisation.

(d) The general approach to the application of free movement principles in football

(i) The three-stage test

4.113 The application of the free movement rules in a sporting context was considered in detail in the SWD. The approach of the Commission and the EU courts has been, on the whole,[156] to set out a three-stage test:[157]

(a) Is there a restriction?
(b) Is the existence justified on the basis of a legitimate objective?
(c) Are the restrictions proportionate?

---

155 Section 3.4 of the SWD.
156 Some commentators have suggested that Cases C-51/96 and C-191/97 *Deliège* [2000] ECR I-2549 pursued a more purposive 'rule of reason' approach rather than the structured three-stage test. See: Lewis and Taylor, *Sport: Law and Practice*, EU Free Movement Rules and Sport Chapter, 3rd Edition (Bloomsbury Professional, 2014) paras F3.78–F3.79.
157 See, for example, the test as set out in Case C-176/96 *Jyri Lehtonen* [2000] ECR I-2681, CJEU.

4.114   Across a range of sports a number of restrictions in cycling, judo, basketball, and a variety of international and national football associations have been previously found to be unlawful. Other restrictions, as illustrated below, have been found to be objectively justifiable and proportionate. The SWD provides a useful overview of the types of restrictions that are more likely to be upheld as objectively justifiable and proportionate. Section 4.2.1 states:

> 'Limited and proportionate restrictions to the principle of free movement, in line with Treaty provisions and ECJ rulings, can thus be accepted as regards:
>
> – The right to select national athletes for national team competitions;
> – The need to limit the number of participants in a competition;
> – The setting of deadlines for transfers of players in team sports.'

4.115   In addition, section 4.7 of the SWD recognises the beneficial impact of a licensing system (like UEFA's Financial Fair Play regime) for financial management and transparency reasons, but in each individual case the regulations 'must be compatible with competition and Internal Market provisions and may not go beyond what is necessary for the pursuit of a legitimate objective relating to the proper organisation and conduct of sport. The principle of proportionality must be respected.'

(ii)   Direct and indirect discrimination

4.116   There are a number of examples where a sporting regulation or restriction directly discriminates against a player because of his nationality. There are other examples where the discriminatory impact is indirect, perhaps because although there is no explicit nationality requirement, in practice the restriction has the same discriminatory effect, or makes it more difficult or less attractive for a player to move or provide services between football clubs established in different Member States.

4.117   A rather blatant example of a restriction which was directly discriminatory on nationality grounds was the 'foreign player' quota system imposed by UEFA, which was struck down by the CJEU in *Bosman*.[158] The UEFA rule provided for no more than three 'foreign players' and two 'assimilated'[159] players to be fielded by a team participating in a UEFA club competition. This restriction, along with the proposed FIFA 6+5 rule[160] (detailed in para **4.141** below), directly discriminated against football players from a Member State other than that of the club. For that reason, the CJEU found that the quota system was incompatible with Article 45 TFEU.

4.118   The court in *Bosman* also found that other rules, while not directly discriminatory, were nonetheless indirectly discriminatory on the grounds of nationality. It ruled that the requirement for a transfer fee to be demanded even after the expiry of a player's contract constituted an indirect obstacle to that player's free movement rights across the EU even though the restriction itself made no express reference to nationality.[161]

---

158 See n 1 above.
159 Defined as foreign players that had played for five years in the country in question, three of which were in the youth team.
160 By this proposed rule, six of the eleven football players on the pitch were required to be of the nationality of the country of the football club.
161 See *Bosman* paras 96–101.

(iii)   Objective justification and proportionality

4.119   *Bosman* is again the seminal case from an objective justification and proportionality perspective. The court agreed that free movement restrictions had the potential to be objectively justifiable because of the need to maintain competitive balance, uncertainty of outcome and the recruitment and investment in youth development. Nonetheless, the court concluded that the restrictions were not proportionate as the aims of the restriction could have been achieved through less restrictive means. In this case, redistribution of income between competing clubs would have been a less restrictive alternative. Therefore UEFA's restrictions failed the *Bosman* proportionality test.

4.120   In *Bernard*,[162] a French football association rule required youth players to sign their first professional contract at the club they had previously trained with, otherwise the training club could claim compensation from the player in question. The rule did not detail how compensation should be assessed. The questions referred to the CJEU asked whether the requirement to pay compensation was a restriction on the free movement of workers; and, if so, whether it could be justified. The player and his new club (Newcastle United) argued that the rule was contrary to Article 45 TFEU because it made it more difficult for a player to move between Member States. His training club, Olympique Lyonnais, argued that as Bernard was still able to move between clubs, the rule did not limit his free movement rights. In addition, they submitted that the compensation payable reflected the club's costs in training and educating the player over his years at the club.

4.121   The CJEU held that the rule was contrary to Article 45 TFEU. The player's right to move was less attractive since he was at risk of being sued for compensation in the event that he decided not to join his training club as a professional player. Whilst the court agreed that a legitimate objective justification for the restriction could be to encourage the training and recruitment of young football players[163] and that a scheme providing compensation for the actual training costs incurred by a club would likely be proportionate, on the facts of this case the compensation claimed appeared 'unrelated to the real training costs incurred by the club'.[164] The proportionality requirement was not fulfilled and the rule fell foul of Article 45 TFEU.

(e)   The practical application of these principles to football and footballers

(i)   Player transfer rules and quotas

4.122   *Bosman*[165] is seen by many commentators as the most significant sports case in EU law. The challenge by Jean-Marc Bosman brought into question the legality of the football transfer system and, in particular, the legality of transfer fees for 'out of contract' footballers. Bosman was a footballer who played for the Belgium club FC Liége. His playing contract expired in 1990. A French club, Dunkerque, wished to buy him but did not offer a large enough transfer fee to Liége. As a result, Liége kept his registration and refused to let him leave the club. Bosman argued that this refusal

---

162   Case C-325/08 *Olympique Lyonnais v Bernard and Newcastle United* [2010] ECR I-2177.
163   *Bernard*, para 39.
164   *Bernard*, para 46.
165   See n 1 above.

infringed his right to work freely in another Member State. He also argued that the restriction was in breach of EU competition law. The club and the national football association argued that transfer fees benefit smaller clubs through money 'trickling' down the traditional football pyramid structure. They contended that the requirement for a transfer of the registration of an out of contract player promoted competitive balance in football.

4.123   The CJEU found there was a breach of Article 45 TFEU. While both sets of justifications were recognised as being available in principle, the court was not persuaded that the transfer rules did in fact promote 'competitive balance' or 'trickle down' compensation. Nor could they show that the transfer rules were the least restrictive way of pursuing those legitimate aims. The second facet of the *Bosman* ruling has already been addressed in para **4.116** et seq above, namely that nationality quotas were also contrary to Article 45 TFEU on the grounds of direct discrimination on grounds of nationality.

4.124   The following consequences arose from *Bosman*:

(a) Footballers at the end of their contract can leave their club and join another without payment of a transfer fee. Such a player is free to sign for a club in another Member State. It is now unlawful for a club to retain his playing registration documentation in order to forestall a free transfer.

(b) UEFA quotas which had previously allowed for a limit of three 'foreign' players and two 'assimilated' players in a team squad are also illegal. No restrictions can be imposed on clubs by FIFA or UEFA that discriminate against players on grounds of nationality. The UEFA Home Grown Player Rule (HGPR), which is based on where a player trains rather than where the player was born, is seen by many as a consequence of the *Bosman* decision. The HGPR can lead to outcomes which on their face seem anomalous. Spanish born Chelsea player Cesc Fabregas qualifies as an English 'home grown' player for UEFA club competitions, because he trained with Arsenal, but he also qualifies to play for the Spanish national team.

(c) The *Bosman* ruling sparked a new trend in the late 1990s for football players departing clubs on free transfers at the expiry of their contracts. Some of the highest profile *Bosman* transfers over the years have included Sol Campbell from arch rivals Tottenham to Arsenal and Steve McManaman from Liverpool to Real Madrid. The summer before McManaman moved to Madrid, Barcelona bid £12m for him, but the transfer fell through. Less than a year later, in 1999, he had joined Madrid on a free transfer. Michael Ballack, Robert Lewandowksi, Andrea Pirlo, Fernando Llorente and James Milner are all more recent examples of high profile *Bosman* transfers.

(d) Players are said to be in a stronger position in negotiating a new more lucrative contract when their existing contracts begin to run down (usually when entering the final two years of their contract) because clubs would not wish to lose the player on a free transfer. Conversely, buying clubs will pay higher wages and signing on fees because there is no transfer fee to pay.

4.125   Following the *Bosman* ruling, the Commission commenced formal infringement proceedings against FIFA and UEFA. It nonetheless entered into dialogue with FIFA and UEFA to put in place a new set of international transfer rules in the late 1990s. A set of broad proposals were agreed between the Commission, FIFA and UEFA. But FIFPro, the football player's union, objected to them and in around 2001 threatened to challenge the rules in a number of Member State courts. A suitable compromise was reached and FIFPro's legal challenge was withdrawn.

The following principles were agreed (which formed the basis for the revised Regulations on the Status and Transfer of Players (RSTP)):

-   'For players under 23, a system of training compensation should be in place to encourage and reward the training effort of clubs, in particular small clubs.
-   The creation of solidarity mechanisms to compensate clubs, including amateur clubs, for training costs.
-   International transfers of players under 18 should be allowed subject to agreed conditions. The football authorities will establish and enforce a code of conduct to guarantee that sporting, training and academic education is provided to such players.
-   The creation of one transfer period per season, and a further limited mid-season window, with a limit of one transfer per player per season.
-   Minimum and maximum duration of contracts of respectively 1 and 5 years.
-   Contracts are protected for a period of 3 years up to the age of 28; 2 years thereafter.
-   A system of sanctions to be installed to protect the integrity of sport competitions so that unilateral breach of contract is only possible at the end of a season.
-   Financial compensation can be paid if a contract is breached unilaterally, whether by the player or the club.
-   Proportionate sporting sanctions are to be applied to players, clubs or agents in the case of unilateral breaches of contract without just cause in the protected period.'[166]

4.126   In 2002, the Commission considered the above approach to be acceptable and closed its investigation.[167]

4.127   However, matters did not end there. In 2015, FIFPro made a formal complaint to the Commission. It complained that the above RSTP principles had impacted negatively on footballers and as such the rules needed to be redrafted. FIFPro published an executive summary of their complaint.[168] FIFPro contended that more needed to be done:

(a)   to safeguard players' contracts. FIFPro wanted to ensure a player could not be unilaterally fired without good cause. FIFPro objected to the fact that players could be required to pay millions of euros to former clubs when breaching their contracts because of their high transfer market value;
(b)   to maintain competition stability so that players could not move clubs on a monthly basis;
(c)   for clubs to be financially stable (ie to ensure players are paid on time and do not have to forgo wages). One of FIFPro's main complaints related to players not getting paid;[169]
(d)   to promote competitive balance (ie to maximise uncertainty of outcome and have results like Leicester City winning the Premier League). FIFPro also contended that national disciplinary procedures were not fit for purpose; and
(e)   to promote solidarity (ie so that a trickle-down effect through the traditional football pyramid structure occurs with money flowing down to the grass roots level). FIFPro complained that the 'trickle-down effect' was something of a fallacy because most of the transfer spending involved big clubs paying

---

166   Section 4.3 of the SWD.
167   See http://europa.eu/rapid/press-release_IP-02-824_en.htm (accessed February 2018).
168   See https://www.fifpro.org/attachments/article/6156/FIFPro%20Complaint%20Executive%20Summary. pdf (accessed February 2018).
169   A FIFPro survey of more than 3,000 players in 12 countries revealed 42% of players confirmed they had not been paid on time and 14% said they were consistently paid three months late. See heading 4 https://www.fifpro.org/attachments/article/6242/Embargoed%20Stefan%20Szymanski%20Transfer% 20System%20Analysis.pdf (accessed February 2018).

astronomical sums to each other rather than re-circulating monies to a wider set of clubs by way of true solidarity payments.

4.128   Over two years after the complaint was lodged, it was announced in November 2017 that FIFPro and FIFA had reached a cooperation agreement. FIFPro agreed to withdraw its complaint and FIFA agreed to set up a taskforce in order conduct a broader review of the transfer system. The taskforce will examine areas for reform perhaps including speedier resolution for players who are owed wages and new guidelines on the financial and sporting penalties which can be imposed if a player breaches his contract, with or without just cause.[170] The agreement is part of a six-year cooperation plan to 'strengthen relationships and improve the governance of professional football'.[171] Ultimately it appears that the FIFPro claims, including the legitimate objectives of the transfer system not being met and the restrictions being disproportionate, will not be substantively assessed now a compromise has been reached.

(ii)   Transfer windows and registration deadlines

4.129   Transfer deadlines were one of the structural changes brought about by the cooperation agreement between UEFA, FIFA, the Commission and FIFPro. The windows (for the majority of European leagues) are during the summer (June to August) and the winter (in January).[172] In principle the transfer windows only affect players under contract, but in practice squad lists must be submitted by many leagues at the end of each window. A *Bosman* player signed outside the window will usually be unable to play in the relevant league or cup competition if he is not registered on the squad list by a stipulated cut-off date.

4.130   Transfer windows and registration deadlines clearly restrict the ability of players under contract to move. It stops players transferring between clubs except at the identified times. Some, including FIFPro, have questioned why football should receive such differential treatment from other industrial sectors. There has not yet been any formal challenge to the football transfer window system. Potential grounds of justification for the system are likely to focus on the integrity of the game and the maintenance of sporting competition:

(a) Anything which allows teams to buy and sell players during crucial parts of the season may disrupt the level playing field and ultimately the competition itself.
(b) Late transfers in a season could change the sporting strength of one team over another. This could distort the proper functioning of a full league season. So, for example, clubs, with only a few games left to play, should not be able to buy players from a team that has nothing to play for, if, say, they are trying to win the league, qualify for the Champions League or avoid relegation.
(c) An open transfer window would also make it easier for other clubs to unsettle players. This longer-term instability may lead to greater player turnover, less connection between the fans and players and less player continuity throughout a season.

170 See Chapter 6, Contracts – Players, and paras **6.7** and **6.62–6.69** on the RSTP and just cause in particular.
171 See http://www.fifa.com/governance/news/y=2017/m=11/news=fifa-and-fifpro-sign-landmark-agreement-and-announce-measures-to-enhan-2918747.html (accessed February 2018).
172 See the FIFA TMS website for the transfer window periods for particular leagues https://www.fifatms.com/itms/worldwide-transfer-windows-calendar/ (accessed February 2018).

4.131   In 2000, the CJEU in *Lehtonen*[173] (in the context of basketball) found that the setting of deadlines for transfers of players may meet the objective of ensuring the regularity of sporting competitions. Late transfers might be liable to change substantially the sporting strength of one or other team in the course of the championship. This might affect the comparability of results between the teams taking part in that championship, which in turn might impact on the integrity of the competition as a whole.

4.132   The SWD expressly notes that transfer windows and registration deadlines may be justified in particular instances,[174] even if it fundamentally restricts the periods when footballers can move between clubs. Ultimately, the findings of the 'transfer system taskforce' (considered at para **4.128** above) will be important in balancing the need to maintain the integrity and stability of a sports league, on the one hand, and the desire to improve the mobility of football players on the other.

4.133   As for the Football Association Premier League, in early September 2017 its clubs voted in favour of closing their transfer window in the days before the start of the season. Previously, the FAPL transfer window had remained open until the end of August. As from 9 August 2018 at 5pm, FAPL clubs will not be able to register new players in the summer window. This puts FAPL clubs at a disadvantage, as clubs in other Member States will still be able to buy and register players up until 31 August. The FAPL Chief Executive, Richard Scudamore, believed that other leagues may follow its lead. He explained that the decision was taken, in part, to prevent the possibility of a player playing for one FAPL team before the window closes, then transferring to a team and playing against his original team soon after.[175] Italy's Serie A clubs are reported to be considering a 31 July transfer window cut off. It remains to be seen whether a coordinated approach to transfer deadlines will emerge at European level.

4.134   Another aspect to consider is the further detrimental impact of a shortened window on player transfer mobility. So far, the Professional Footballers Association (the PFA) has not publicly stated its position on the shortened window but a challenge to the FAPL window closing three weeks earlier than previously is a possibility.

(iii)   The Home Grown Player Rule

4.135   The UEFA HGPR was introduced for the 2006/07 season. It now requires each team entering UEFA European club competitions to name eight home grown players in their 25-man squad. Four of the designated squad players must be 'club-trained' and four must also be 'association-trained'. A club-trained player is defined as a player who, regardless of his place of birth, has been registered between the ages of 15 and 21 with his current club for a period of three entire seasons or 36 months. An 'association-trained' player fulfils the same criteria but with another club in the same association.

4.136   FAPL introduced its own HGPR in time for the start of the 2010/11 season. The FAPL HGPR does not distinguish between association and club-trained players. 'Home grown' is defined as anyone registered with the English or Welsh Football Associations for three seasons or 36 months before a player's 21st birthday.

---

173   See Case C-176/96 *Jyri Lehtonen* [2000] ECR I-2681, CJEU.
174   Section 2.4 of the SWD.
175   That scenario did in fact occur with Alex Oxlade Chamberlain moving from Arsenal to Liverpool for around £35m on summer transfer deadline day 2017. He had previously played for Arsenal against Liverpool before the transfer and played for Liverpool against Arsenal in late December 2017.

FAPL clubs submit a squad of 25 players to the league after the transfer window has closed. Those players will then be eligible to compete in that season's competition. Changes to the list can only be made in the January transfer window, unless special permission is granted. The UEFA and Premier League rules permit an unlimited number of under-21 year old players (regardless of nationality) to supplement each 25-man squad.

4.137   Importantly, there is no UEFA nor FAPL restriction on how many home grown players must be selected in any starting team. Indeed, it would be possible for no home grown players to be in the match day squad of 18 and for a FAPL team having 17 non-home grown players and one foreign born under-21 player in their match day squad.

4.138   In a recent report on the HGPR,[176] Dalziel, Parrish et al explain that the HGPR was justified by UEFA as, among other things, encouraging youth development and competitive balance. It was envisaged that developing a talented youth development structure could counter the perceived lack of opportunity for domestic young players to play in the first team. It would also save clubs significant sums on transfers or provide significant sums when one of a club's players was subsequently sold. Similarly, competitive balance is said to be maintained and/or strengthened because the squad size only allows a certain number of established players to be registered for a particular competition. This has the additional potential effect of preventing the wealthiest clubs from hoarding the most talented players.

4.139   Since the HGPR is based on where a player trained rather than where he was born, it is not directly discriminatory. But by parity of reasoning, the rationale that the HGPR is beneficial for developing a nation's next generation of players that can represent their country may prove to be misplaced. It is possible that the HGPR may give rise to a risk of indirect discrimination, since it may be easier for young national players to have access to training facilities in a club in a Member State than for players arriving from other Member States.[177] On the other hand, some have argued that the unintended side-effect of the HGPR has been to encourage clubs to recruit even younger players from across the globe so that they subsequently qualify as a HGP. That would then provide less opportunity for domestically born youth players to play.

4.140   The objectives of training youth players and maintaining competitive balance are likely to be seen by a court as legitimate justifications for any restriction on the free movement of workers. As for proportionality, because a club can field a squad without any home grown players at all (ie 17 non-HGP and an under-21 player), it would appear that the restrictions are less likely to go beyond what is necessary for the attainment of the legitimate objective.

4.141   It should be noted that FIFA did propose selection criteria which appeared directly to discriminate between football players on the basis of nationality. In February 2008,[178] FIFA announced a proposed rule whereby every team must field at least six players who would be eligible for the national team of the country in which the club was domiciled. FIFA considered that such requirements were needed to

---

176 See http://ec.europa.eu/assets/eac/sport/library/studies/final-rpt-april2013-homegrownplayer.pdf (accessed February 2018).

177 See n 176 above, executive summary paragraph 6 of http://ec.europa.eu/assets/eac/sport/library/ studies/final-rpt-april2013-homegrownplayer.pdf (accessed February 2018).

178 See   http://www.fifa.com/about-fifa/news/y=2008/m=2/news=yes-principle-rule-684707.html (accessed February 2018).

protect domestic players and encourage them to break through into particular national leagues. FIFA sought to justify the proposal as necessary to maintain the integrity of the sporting competition. This type of nationality requirement has already been found to be unlawful as a matter of EU law in *Dona*,[179] *Walrave*[180] and in *Bosman*. It was clear that the Commission was unlikely to react favourably. Commissioner Vladimír Špidla made clear what the concerns were:

> 'Concerning FIFA's 6+5 rule which proposes that 6 of the 11 football players on the pitch have to be of the nationality of the country of the football club: The Commission is showing a red card to the 6+5 rule. Professional football players are workers, therefore the principle of non-discrimination and the right to free movement apply to them. The *Bosman* case was very clear on this issue. The 6+5 rule would constitute direct discrimination on the basis of nationality, which is unacceptable to the Commission. If Member States allowed the application of the 6+5 rule they would be in breach of the Treaty and the Commission would have to take the Member States to court.'[181]

4.142   FIFA's proposals were dropped by 2010 and, to date, no further substantive proposals have been proposed.

(iv) Post-Brexit quotas

4.143   Following Brexit, when EU law principles of non-discrimination will possibly no longer apply, nationality restrictions may be resurrected. The former Football Association (FA) Chairman Greg Dyke explained that:

> 'Fewer home-grown players than ever started matches in the Premier League last year. Although I was not a supporter of Brexit, it could be that by leaving the EU this problem could be solved. If the FA and the government were to have the determination to restrict the flow of European players coming to play in Britain to the very best and introduce quotas on the number of British players in Premier League sides it could be changed quickly.'[182]

4.144   It is therefore possible that the FA might seek to introduce quotas for English players. Mr Dyke also stated that: 'At the moment many very average European players are increasingly taking the slots which could be going to talented young English players from clubs' academies.'[183] The FA might wish more English players to be exposed to top level football. But the FAPL clubs are unlikely to be in favour, since such a rule might well diminish their ability to recruit top class European players. While nationality quotas might prove difficult to implement in the higher football leagues, the FA might consider such rules for its own FA Cup competition. At the time of writing it is unclear how the government will control the ability of skilled EU workers, including footballers, to play in the UK post-Brexit.

(v) Non-EU player rights

4.145   A number of issues also arise in relation to non-EU football players wishing to play in the EU. The first relates to the ability to obtain a work permit under FA

---

179 Case 13/76 *Donà* (n 4 above).
180 Case 36/74 *Walrave and Koch* (n 3 above).
181 European Commission Press Release: *The Commission shows a red card to the 6+5 rule proposed by FIFA*, 28 May 2008.
182 See   http://www.skysports.com/football/news/12016/10508845/greg-dyke-hopes-brexit-gives-young-english-players-a-chance-in-parting-letter-to-fa-board (accessed February 2018).
183 See n 182 above.

regulations. The second concerns particular Association Agreements entered into between the EU and third countries which include non-discrimination provisions. In *Kolpak*[184] and in *Simutenkov*,[185] the CJEU applied the principle of equal treatment to sportsmen from third countries having an Association Agreement with the EU. The non-discrimination provisions found in those Agreements were treated as being as applicable as the general principle of non-discrimination in EU law. The requirement for equal treatment extended to working conditions, remuneration and dismissal. A critical distinction was that '[t]hese clauses however, do not allow a right to free movement within the European Economic Area'.[186] The position remains therefore that for non-EU football players to qualify to play in the UK, they must meet FA published criteria.

(vi)   FFP and Financial Regulations[187]

4.146   As set out in para **4.99** above, the FFP rules were intended to help clubs achieve financial self-sustainability by introducing break-even requirements in the medium to long term. UEFA, FAPL, the EFL Championship and a variety of other leagues all have different regulations setting out spending restrictions that participating clubs must adhere to. Sanctions vary depending on the regulations, but include transfer embargos and financial penalties in the Championship, and points deductions in the FAPL. For UEFA competitions, a more comprehensive list of sanctions includes a warning, a fine, withholding of prize monies, points deductions, refusal to register players for UEFA competition, reducing a club's squad size, disqualification from competitions in progress and/or exclusion from future competitions. In 2015, UEFA banned Dynamo Moscow from future competitions. It more recently banned Galatasaray (see para **4.100** above). Clubs like Manchester City, PSG, Monaco, Inter Milan and others have received significant sanctions including fines, squad size reductions and future spending restrictions.

4.147   For example, Manchester City in a settlement agreement with UEFA was given a €20m fine and a €60m transfer spending restriction on transfers in the 2014/15 summer transfer window.[188] The settlement agreement had a significant impact on the club's ability to sign players, specifically because transfer and wage spending was to be substantively curtailed. It does not appear that any challenge was brought against the penalties imposed on free movement grounds. Whilst the wider FFP rules may well produce some restrictions on the free movement of players, UEFA would no doubt have sought to justify the rules on the basis that they were necessary to ensure the integrity of the competition, promoted good financial governance, safeguarded the financial stability of clubs and leagues and encouraged longer term infrastructure investment. Moreover, in order for the rules to have sufficient deterrent effect, the sanctions needed to be substantive, significant and enforced. Clubs are more likely to adhere to a regulatory regime that punishes non-compliance.

4.148   There is one other aspect of the sanction imposed on Manchester City which merits comment. Manchester City's squad size for Champions League competition was reduced to 21 players from 25. It was assumed by many that the club would still be required to submit eight HGPs even though their squad size had been reduced

---

184 Case C-438/00 *Kolpak* [2003] ECR I-4153.
185 Case C-265/03 *Simutenkov* [2005] ECR I – 2579.
186 Section 4.2.2 of the SWD.
187 See further, Chapter 16, Financial Regulation and Financial Fair Play.
188 See, http://www.uefa.com/insideuefa/disciplinary/club-financial-controlling-body/cases/index. html?redirectFromOrg=true (accessed February 2018).

(ie 21 squad players minus eight HGPs would have left only 13 non-HGP squad slots available). However, following an intervention from FIFPro, UEFA permitted Manchester City (and others) to submit their 21-man squad with only five HGPs.[189] FIFPro were willing to intervene to protect the interests of their player members in the light of the significant impact removal from a squad would have on a player's ability to attract other clubs. This is because playing in the elite European club competitions showcases the player's talents. It also has a significant financial impact on potential bonus payments too.

(vii)   Selection and release for national team competition

4.149   Whilst the above topical matters are more contemporary examples of free movement issues arising in sport, issues relating to the composition of national teams go back as far as the 1970s. In its *Walrave* and *Donà* rulings,[190] the CJEU held that the principle of non-discrimination did not prevent a requirement for national teams to be selected on the basis of the sports person's nationality. That was a question of 'purely sporting interest' which had 'nothing to do with' economic activity. In *Deliège*,[191] the CJEU explained that the selection of a judoka based on a limited set of places for those individuals to compete in international judo competitions did not constitute a restriction on that individual's freedom of movement so long as it was justified on the grounds of protecting the integrity and make-up of the competition. Evidently having unlimited places for national participants would be practically impossible.

4.150   The SWD explicitly set out in section 4.2.2 that:

> 'The composition of national teams is inherent in the organisation of competitions opposing national teams. Rules concerning the composition of national teams, in particular rules that exclude non-national sportspeople from national teams, have been considered as rules that do not infringe the Treaty's free movement provisions.'

4.151   More recently, in the *Charleroi*[192] case brought against FIFA, there were a number of potentially interesting free movement issues raised by the then G-14 clubs in relation to a mandatory requirement to release players for international competition (when historically compensation was not forthcoming from a national football association for the loss of the players' services whilst away on international duty or if the player returned injured). The matter was resolved in 2008 after an agreement was reached by FIFA, UEFA and the reformed G-14 clubs under the remodelled European Club Association (ECA). Before such resolution, the national court had gone as far as to refer to the CJEU particular questions of EU law, including whether the mandatory release and lack of compensation provisions were contrary to EU free movement rules. No formal ruling was given in the light of the compromise reached by the parties. FIFA and UEFA have put in place compensation for clubs whose players play in their international competitions, as well as an insurance policy should players be injured whilst on international duty.

---

189 This decrease is not in line with the overall reduction of the squad and appears rather *ad hoc.*
190 See nn 3 and 4 above.
191 See n 4 above.
192 Case C-243/06 *SA Sporting du Pays de Charleroi and Groupement des clubs de football européens* [2008] ECLI:EU:C:2008:649, CJEU.

CHAPTER 5

Employment Law and Football

Paul Goulding QC and **Diya Sen Gupta** (Blackstone Chambers)

A INTRODUCTION

5.1   The performance of football clubs, football players, and football managers is rarely out of the press. The vast sums of money paid to highly sought-after football players, the great demands placed on football managers to ensure their teams perform well each season, and the pressure on clubs to have the right players and coaching staff in place all combine to create a pressurised environment in which things frequently go wrong, off the pitch as well as on it.

5.2   Employment disputes in football are on the increase and can lead to a wide range of interesting legal issues, particularly in the context of player transfers and the termination of managers' contracts. Discrimination allegations are also more prevalent, as seen in The Football Association's ('The FA') investigation into allegations against the former England Women's manager Mark Sampson, and Dr Eva Carneiro's sex discrimination claim against Chelsea Football Club and José Mourinho.

5.3   This chapter provides an overview of the key aspects of employment law in the football context. Whereas Chapters 6 and 7 consider more specific issues in relation to players' and managers' contracts respectively, this chapter considers the following fundamental topics: (i) the employment relationship; (ii) termination of employment; (iii) restrictions on an employee leaving to join a competitor; (iv) discrimination; and (v) whistleblowing provisions.

B THE EMPLOYMENT RELATIONSHIP

5.4   Like other businesses, football clubs employ or otherwise engage a host of individuals for different types of work.

5.5   As well as employing players and coaching staff, including a first team manager and an assistant manager, a football club is likely to employ or otherwise engage a variety of other people such as academy staff, medical staff and catering staff.

5.6   All those individuals will be engaged on different contractual terms. Some of them will be employees but some of them will not.

(a)   Contract of employment

5.7   A contract of employment is a 'contract of service', as distinct from a 'contract for services' or engagement as an independent contractor.

5.8   Whether an individual is an employee, a worker or independent contractor is a mixed question of fact and law and depends on a detailed consideration of various factors which can include: the responsibilities of the individual, the nature of their work, the degree of control exercised over the individual, the extent to which they are part of the organisation and the economic reality of their relationship.

5.9   Employees have greater statutory rights than workers. For example, an employee has the right to bring an unfair dismissal claim (only after two years' continuous service) whereas a worker or independent contractor does not have the entitlement to bring such a claim.[1]

5.10   In the case of *Lawrie Sanchez v Barnet Football Club*,[2] Mr Sanchez claimed that his dismissal from the role of football manager was unfair. However, the employment tribunal found that he did not have the requisite 12 months' service (as was then required) for such claim since, for the initial period of his engagement, he had negotiated a consultancy agreement as a self-employed independent football consultant.

(b)   Terms of the contract of employment

5.11   This section contains a summary of the key terms which are included in a contract of employment, with some references to particular cases involving football clubs.

(i)   Express terms

5.12   The express terms of a contract are those specifically agreed by the parties. Such agreement may be in writing, or oral, or a mixture of the two. The express terms in an employment contract will usually include the duration of the contract, the employee's duties, the employee's salary, any bonus entitlement, the notice period, any garden leave term, and any restrictive covenants. We consider below some of the express contractual terms which have been the subject of dispute.

Residence clause and termination clause

5.13   The issue in *Macari v Celtic Football & Athletic Co Ltd*[3] was whether the club was entitled to terminate its manager's employment contract for his failure to comply with the express residence clause. The residence clause provided: 'The manager, during the duration of this contract, shall not, without the written permission of the board, reside at an address which is outwith the radius of 45 miles from George Square, Glasgow'. Mr Macari's claim for damages was dismissed by the Lord Ordinary and by the Court of Session (Inner House). The Court of Session

---

1   *Harvey on Industrial Relations and Employment Law*, Division AI.
2   (Unreported, 10 December 2012, Case No. 3302270/2012).
3   [1999] IRLR 787.

held that Mr Macari was in material breach of his contract of employment in failing to comply with lawful and legitimate instructions to abide by the contractual residence clause, to attend more regularly at the club's ground and to report to the managing director on a weekly basis. It held that, under the normal application of the law of contract, the club was entitled to treat his conduct as a repudiation of the contract and to accept that repudiation by dismissing him without notice or pay in lieu of notice. The termination clause contained in Macari's employment contract is discussed in para **5.32** below.

Early termination payment clause

5.14   Henning Berg was engaged by Blackburn Rovers as manager under a fixed-term contract. Before the end of the fixed period, Blackburn terminated its agreement with Mr Berg. He brought a claim for £2.25 million which he asserted was due to him under clause 15.3 of the contract following the early termination of the agreement. The club initially admitted liability but later sought to withdraw its admission. In *Berg v Blackburn Rovers Football Club & Athletics Plc*,[4] the High Court dismissed Blackburn's application to withdraw the admission. As part of its judgment it considered the nature of clause 15.3 of the service agreement. That clause provided:

> 'In the event that the Club shall at any time wish to terminate this Agreement with immediate effect it shall be entitled to do so upon written notice to the Manager and provided that it shall pay to the Manager a compensation payment by way of liquidated damages in a sum equal to the Manager's gross basic salary for the unexpired balance of the Fixed Period assuming an annual salary of £900,000.'

It was held that a sum of money payable under a contract on the occurrence of an event other than a breach of a contractual duty owed by the paying party to the receiving party is not an unenforceable penalty. The termination of Mr Berg's employment prior to the expiry of the fixed term did not constitute a breach of contract – to the contrary, early termination was permitted as of right – whereupon a sum of money became payable by Blackburn to Mr Berg. The law relating to penalty clauses was not engaged.

(ii)   Implied terms

5.15   In addition to the express terms of a contract, certain terms are implied into every contract of employment:

Employee's duties:

- duty of good faith and fidelity;
- duty to obey reasonable instructions.

Employer's duties:

- duty to take care of the employee's health and safety;
- duty to provide redress for grievances.

Duties on employers and employees:

- duty to give a reasonable period of notice of termination (where no specific notice period has been agreed);

---

4   [2013] IRLR 537; see para **7.69**.

- mutual duty of trust and confidence. This is generally expressed as a duty not, without reasonable and proper cause, to act in a manner calculated or likely to destroy or seriously damage the relationship of trust and confidence between employer and employee.

5.16   In addition to the terms specified, other terms may be implied into a contract of employment either if such a term is so obvious that both parties would have regarded it as a term even though it was not expressly stated or if it is necessary to imply the term in order to give the contract business efficacy.

Examples of breaches of implied terms

5.17   Breach of the duty of trust and confidence by a football club amounts to a repudiatory breach of contract which entitles the employee to terminate the contract without notice and claim constructive dismissal. Likewise, breach of the duty of trust and confidence by an employee entitles the club to summarily dismiss.

5.18   In *Williams v Leeds United Football Club*,[5] the club's technical director, Evan Williams, was summarily dismissed following the discovery that he had forwarded pornographic emails to a junior female employee and to friends at other clubs five years earlier. The emails had only come to light because the club had decided to make Mr Williams redundant and wished to find evidence to justify a dismissal for gross misconduct. Mr Williams claimed that he had been wrongfully dismissed. He argued that, given that he had worked for the club for over five years after sending the emails, their discovery would not have been likely to have destroyed the relationship of trust and confidence. His claim was rejected. The High Court held that the club was entitled to rely on acts of misconduct by Mr Williams, which it discovered after he had been given notice of termination, to justify his subsequent summary dismissal, and that Mr Williams' conduct in emailing the pornographic images had been a repudiatory breach of contract such that he was not entitled to damages.

5.19   By contrast, in *Farnan v Sunderland Association Football Club Ltd*,[6] Whipple J held that Michael Farnan, marketing director of Sunderland Association Football Club, had not acted in breach of contract by sending a lewd Christmas card using his SAFC email address. The judge held that: (i) cards like this were on sale openly in shops on the high street and could not be reasonably classified as 'indecent' or 'obscene'; and (ii) the SAFC work environment displayed a relaxed attitude towards offensive communications by senior football executives such that the club would not have taken further action had they discovered the emails at the time they had been sent rather than subsequent to Mr Farnan's dismissal. *Williams v Leeds United Football Club* was distinguished on the basis that 'those images were markedly more extreme in their offensive content than the single image forwarded by Mr Farnan'. Another possible basis for distinction was that Mr Farnan's Christmas card was not sent to any employees of the club, whereas the recipient of the pornographic emails sent by Mr Williams included a junior female employee, leaving the club vulnerable to a claim for harassment.[7]

---

5   [2015] IRLR 383.
6   [2016] IRLR 185.
7   [2015] IRLR 383, at [57]–[58].

5.20   More recently, in *Milanese v Leyton Orient Football Club Limited*,[8] the High Court considered the claim by a director of football for the sums due pursuant to his employment contract on termination without notice or, alternatively, damages for wrongful termination. Leyton Orient argued that it had grounds to summarily dismiss Mr Milanese for his misconduct. Five of the six grounds relied on by the club, such as overspending on players, were rejected. The sixth ground, which concerned Mr Milanese's conduct in relation to a youth player at the club's academy, was upheld. In particular, it was held that Mr Milanese had abused his position as the club's director of football to introduce his friend to the youth's father in order to get the father to sign an agent agreement. This amounted to a very serious breach of the implied term of mutual trust and confidence and constituted gross misconduct which entitled Leyton Orient to summarily dismiss Mr Milanese.

5.21   Three examples of successful constructive dismissal claims brought by football managers against their former clubs are summarised below. In each case, the manager resigned after their position at the club had been undermined, in breach of an implied term in their employment contract.

5.22   Kevin Keegan, then manager of Newcastle United, resigned and claimed constructive dismissal when the club signed a player despite his objections. His contract provided that he would 'perform such duties as may be usually associated with the position of a manager of a Premier League football team (including but not limited to those specific duties set out in Schedule 1) together with such other duties as may from time to time be reasonably assigned to him by the board'. Paragraph 1 of Schedule 1 provided that he would be responsible for 'the training, coaching, selection and motivation of the team'. The club had a director of football, Dennis Wise, who had a seat on the board and to whom the manager reported.

5.23   Mr Wise told Mr Keegan that he had a great player for the club to sign: Ignacio Gonzalez. Although Mr Keegan made it clear that he very strongly objected to the signing of Mr Gonzalez, the club proceeded with the deal, signing the player on loan with an option to purchase. Mr Keegan considered that he, as manager, should have the final say over transfers, and he resigned. He commenced arbitration proceedings before the Premier League Managers' Arbitration Tribunal. His claim succeeded: *Keegan v Newcastle United Football Club Ltd*.[9] The arbitration tribunal held that it was an implied term of the contract that Mr Keegan would have the final say as to transfers into the club. The club had sought to impose upon him a player whom he did not want, in fundamental breach of contract. Accordingly, he had been constructively dismissed.

5.24   James McBride was the manager of Falkirk Football Club's under-19 team. He resigned when he was told, without any discussion or consultation, that a newly-appointed academy director would be responsible for picking the under-19 team, which would have significantly diminished Mr McBride's role. He claimed constructive dismissal but was unsuccessful before the tribunal. The tribunal had accepted the club's argument that 'this style of communication is not unusual within football, an autocratic style of management being the norm'. Mr McBride successfully overturned this conclusion on appeal to the Employment Appeal Tribunal (EAT).

5.25   In *McBride v Falkirk Football & Athletic Club*,[10] the EAT held that the tribunal accepted that 'the claimant should have been consulted, that the failure

---

8   [2016] IRLR 601.
9   [2010] IRLR 94.
10   [2012] IRLR 22.

to consult was bound to have an adverse effect on him and it seems that, had the claimant not had the misfortune to be working in the world of football, a finding of breach of the trust and confidence term would have followed'. Lady Smith said: 'The Tribunal's reason for refraining from making such a finding is that an autocratic style of management is the norm in football but ... that is not a good reason at all. An employer cannot pray in aid that he and others in his industry treat all employees badly and therefore treating an employee badly cannot amount to a breach of the duty of maintain trust and confidence.' The conduct to be expected of the employer is to be judged by an objective standard, and the duty of trust and confidence is a mutual one. Excusing bad behaviour by the employer by reference to industry standards would make it a one-way duty. The EAT held that imposing the change on Mr McBride 'without prior notice, consultation or discussion was a plain breach of the duty of trust and confidence. It was indicative of a wholesale lack of respect for the claimant and for his views not only on the change itself but, if it was to happen, on the means of its implementation.' This approach might be contrasted with the reasoning of Whipple J in *Farnan v Sunderland Association Football Club Ltd*,[11] finding that SAFC's 'tolerant attitude towards offensive behaviour' was relevant to concluding that Mr Farnan had not breached his contract by sending a lewd Christmas card using his SAFC email address (see para **5.19** above). Of course, in the latter, the judge took account of the club's relaxed attitude towards offensive communications by senior football executives as informing the likely context in which Mr Farnan's behaviour would be received, rather than as a justification for the club's own conduct. The EAT in *McBride* held that the club could not rely on the poor treatment of employees by the profession to justify further unacceptable conduct by the club.

5.26   *Gibbs v Leeds United Football Club Ltd*[12] concerned a constructive dismissal claim by the assistant manager, Nigel Gibbs. Mr Gibbs had been employed by the club at the suggestion of Brian McDermott, manager of Leeds United, with whom he had worked at Reading Football Club. In early 2014, a company controlled by the chairman of Leeds United, Massimo Cellino, acquired a majority interest in Leeds United and McDermott agreed terms of departure from the club. David Hockaday was appointed to replace McDermott. Mr Gibbs was then 'excluded from taking any meaningful part in the training of the first team players by the actions of Mr Hockaday'. He resigned by letter dated 26 July 2014 and claimed constructive dismissal. Langstaff J held that although the precise duties of an assistant manager were not spelt out in the contract of employment between Mr Gibbs and Leeds United, the evidence was all one way as to the duties to be expected of someone whose job was described as 'assistant manager' of a football league club. Such a person was to be involved in the selection, tactics and training of the first team. In that context, requiring a manager and coach who had previously worked with the first team to have no contact with the first team thereafter but instead to work only with the under-18s and the under-21s could not be said to be a reasonable direction. The loss of status would be plain, not only to the parties, but to others with whom Mr Gibbs had to deal. In short, to require Mr Gibbs to work in this way was to show an intention thereafter to refuse to perform the contract as it had originally been made. A breach is repudiatory where, objectively viewed, one party to a contract shows by their conduct that they no longer intend to be bound by its essential terms. Mr Gibbs' resignation in those circumstances was what one would expect a self-respecting person to do. Leeds United had breached Mr Gibbs' contract and he had been entitled to accept such a breach.

---

11   [2016] IRLR 185.
12   [2016] IRLR 493.

5.27   In contrast to the three cases above, in *Macari v Celtic Football &
Athletic Co Ltd* the manager unsuccessfully sought to rely on an earlier breach of the
implied duty and trust and confidence without having terminated his employment.
This case is discussed more fully in paras **5.32** and **5.33** below.

(c)   Fiduciary duties

5.28   In addition to contractual duties, some employees owe fiduciary duties to
their employers due to the nature of their duties.

5.29   *Milanese v Leyton Orient Football Club Limited*[13] is an example of a case
in which the existence of such fiduciary duties was alleged. The club had brought a
counterclaim against Mr Milanese, arguing that he was a fiduciary because he was
trusted to spend Leyton Orient's money on transfers. Mr Milanese claimed that the
club was simply attempting to improve the nature or extent of the remedy available
to the club in contract in circumstances where: (i) the totality of Mr Milanese's
obligations were contractual and covered by the service agreement with the club; and
(ii) there were no specific contractual obligations undertaken within that employment
relationship which were capable of making Mr Milanese a fiduciary. Whipple J
described the counterclaim based on the existence of a fiduciary duty as 'tenuous'.[14]
She held that there was no additional fiduciary obligation owed by Milanese above
and beyond the contractual obligations (express and implied) under the service
agreement.

C   TERMINATION OF EMPLOYMENT

(a)   Termination provisions

5.30   A contract of employment may only lawfully be terminated in accordance
with its terms. The contract is generally either a fixed-term contract (for example,
in the case of a football player) or expressly stated to be terminable by either party
giving to the other written notice of termination of a specified duration (typically,
six or twelve months in the case of a senior employee). Where the contract is not
for a fixed term, and does not contain an express notice provision, a term is implied
that it is terminable on *reasonable* notice. What is reasonable is judged according to
all relevant circumstances, including the seniority of the employee, and custom and
practice.

5.31   In addition to notice provisions, it is common for a contract to provide that
it may be terminated by the employer in certain specified circumstances such as the
employee's gross misconduct, serious or persistent material breach of contract, or
other conduct bringing the employer into disrepute.

5.32   Apart from express termination provisions contained in the contract,
where one party acts in fundamental breach of the contract (also referred to as a
repudiatory breach), it is open to the other party to accept the breach and terminate
the contract. The relationship between express termination provisions and the
common law right to terminate in response to the other party's repudiatory breach

13   [2016] IRLR 601.
14   [2016] IRLR 601, at [141].

was the subject of consideration by the courts when Lou Macari was sacked by Celtic: *Macari v Celtic Football & Athletic Co Ltd.*[15] Mr Macari's contract contained a provision for termination on not less than two years' notice and an express term that Celtic could terminate the employment if 'in the opinion of the board' any of a number of specified events occurred, including that the manager shall have committed any material or repeated breach of the obligations of the manager in terms of the agreement. Following a takeover of the club, Mr Macari was instructed to comply with the residence clause and attend full-time to the performance of his duties. He failed to do so and was summarily dismissed (see para **5.13** above). Under the normal application of the law of contract, therefore, the club was entitled to treat his conduct as a repudiation of the contract and to accept that repudiation by dismissing him. The club was entitled under the general law of contract to dismiss Mr Macari, notwithstanding the existence of a contractual provision which gave the club the power to terminate Mr Macari's employment summarily in the event that, 'in the opinion of the board', any of a number of specified events had occurred. That provision supplemented, rather than excluded, the club's rights and powers of dismissal under the general law of contract.

5.33   It is also worth noting that the court found that Mr Macari was not entitled to withhold performance of his obligations under the contract on the ground that the club was in breach of the implied term of trust and confidence. There was conduct on the part of the club's managing director which was calculated or likely to cause serious damage to the relationship of trust and confidence between employer and employee, and the club was therefore in breach of the implied term of trust and confidence. That was a material breach of contract which Mr Macari would have been entitled to accept by leaving his employment and suing the club for damages. However, he did not do so: he remained and drew his salary under his contract but failed to comply with the instructions given to him by the managing director. Mr Macari was obliged to comply with those instructions and his persistent failures to do so were not only breaches but material breaches of his contract with the club.

(b)   Unlawful termination

5.34   An employer unlawfully terminates a contract of employment where it deliberately brings a contract to an end without lawful grounds for doing so, or where the employee resigns in response to the employer's repudiatory breach. This is what happened when Kevin Keegan resigned as manager of Newcastle United: *Keegan v Newcastle United Football Company Ltd.*[16] The Premier League Managers' Arbitration Tribunal upheld Mr Keegan's claim that he had been constructively dismissed by the club. It held that it is settled law that if one party to a contract is in fundamental breach of that contract, that breach can amount to a repudiation of the contract entitling the other party to resign. In the present case, it was a term of the contract that Mr Keegan would have the final say as to transfers into Newcastle. It was not implicit in the structure of the club that the director of football would have the final say. The duties usually associated with the position of a manager of a Premier League football team included the right, indeed the duty, to have the final say as to the transfers into the club. A similar decision was reached in *McBride v Falkirk Football & Athletic Club,*[17] discussed above in paras **5.24** and **5.25**.

---

15   [1999] IRLR 787.
16   [2010] IRLR 94.
17   [2012] IRLR 22.

(c)   Remedies for unlawful termination

5.35   Where a party unlawfully terminates a contract of employment in the world of football, there are generally three forums in which the wronged party may seek remedies: (i) arbitration; (ii) an employment tribunal; and (iii) the High Court.

5.36   There are standard provisions in the contracts of employment of football managers and football players that provide for arbitration in the event of disputes, including termination of employment. Examples of the arbitration procedures are found in a number of the football employment cases discussed in this chapter, including *Keegan v Newcastle United* as well as others such as *Wise v Leicester City Football Club*[18] and *Chelsea v Mutu*.[19] These arbitration procedures are discussed in detail elsewhere in this book.[20]

5.37   Arbitration clauses contained in contracts of employment cannot, however, exclude the right of an employee to make statutory employment claims to an employment tribunal.[21] Generally an employee must lodge an employment tribunal claim within three months of the act complained of. Compensation awards are capped for certain claims (such as unfair dismissal), but uncapped for others (such as discrimination, whistleblowing and unpaid wages).

5.38   Absent an effective agreement to arbitrate, employment claims can also be brought in the High Court. These, typically, will include claims for wrongful dismissal (where an employer has terminated the employment in breach of contract). An example of a High Court claim arose from the dismissal of Jean Tigana as manager of Fulham football club: *Fulham Football Club (1987) Ltd v Tigana*.[22] Fulham purported to dismiss Mr Tigana for gross misconduct relating to player transfers. The effect of the dismissal, rather than the fixed-term contract expiring through effluxion of time, was to deprive Mr Tigana of share options worth £2.1m and other sums that would otherwise have been payable. Fulham's allegations against Mr Tigana were dismissed by the court, and he recovered damages representing the value of his share options and other sums payable.

D   RESTRICTIONS ON LEAVING

5.39   An employee who changes jobs will often move to a competitor where he may be seen as a threat to his former employer. A football manager, for example, may be appointed as manager at another club and may try and sign players from his former club. A director of football may leave to take up a similar position at another club and may try and use his knowledge of the former club's transfer targets for the benefit of his new employer. What are the restrictions on competitive activity by employees, and what remedies are available to prevent unlawful competition?

(a)   Garden leave

5.40   An employee may attempt to resign without providing the notice required by his contract in order to take up a new job. This has happened with football

---

18   UKEAT/0660/03/RN.
19   CAS 2006/A/1192.
20   See Chapter 6, Contracts – Players and Chapter 7, Contracts – Managers; and also Chapter 28, Arbitration in Football.
21   Employment Rights Act 1996, s 203.
22   [2004] EWHC 2585 (QB), [2005] EWCA Civ 895.

managers, directors of football and other executives. Whilst the parties (including the new employer) may come to an agreed settlement, often involving the payment of compensation, this will not always be the case. The first employer may need to take legal action to stop the employee from walking out. Another not uncommon situation is where an employee resigns on notice to join a competitor but the employer does not want the employee to work his notice because, if he does, he would continue to have access to confidential information about his employer's business, and could unsettle other employees or harm relationships with third parties.

5.41   It is important that the contract of employment contains appropriate terms to deal with situations such as these. The contract should contain terms that, during the employment:

(a) the employee will well and faithfully serve the club to the best of his ability, exercise best professional judgment in performing the required work and carry out his duties in a proper and efficient manner;

(b) the employee will not be interested in any business other than the business of the club;

(c) the employee will not disclose any confidential information relating to the club's affairs other than in the performance of his duties for the club;

(d) the club shall not be under any obligation to provide the employee with work and may during any period of notice amend the employee's duties or suspend him from the performance of his duties and may exclude him from the club's premises and require him not to communicate with the club's employees and require him to work from home (a 'garden leave' clause).

Even in the absence of express terms requiring the employee to faithfully serve his employer during employment, the law will imply into the contract a duty that the employee will act with good faith and fidelity towards his employer. This implied duty will prevent the employee working for a competitor for so long as his employment continues.

5.42   A practice has developed whereby an employer may prevent an employee from leaving to join a competitor, without giving proper notice, by placing him on garden leave and, if necessary, applying to the court for an injunction to prevent the employee working for the competitor until the expiry of his contractual notice period. This is known as a garden leave injunction. This practice was successfully adopted by Crystal Palace FC against its manager, Steve Bruce, when he tried to leave to become manager of Birmingham City: *Crystal Palace FC (2000) Ltd v Bruce*.[23] Mr Bruce resigned after Palace refused to allow him to talk to Birmingham. Palace sought an injunction to hold Mr Bruce to nine months' garden leave. Mr Bruce had already given undertakings to Palace not to solicit or endeavour to entice away other employees, including players, at the club. But that was not sufficient to prevent the court granting an injunction, at least until a speedy trial could take place in a matter of weeks. The court noted the concern that the mere fact of Mr Bruce leaving would be sufficient to destabilise the workforce.

5.43   Reading Football Club claimed that it had a similar interest in preventing its manager, Alan Pardew, from joining West Ham United Football Club in September 2003. Reading refused to accept Mr Pardew's resignation and sought a garden leave injunction to hold Mr Pardew to his contract for the balance of the season. The case settled at the door of the court on the basis of the following

---

23   [2002] SLR 81.

undertakings: (i) West Ham would not solicit or employ any of Reading's coaching staff or players until the end of the season; (ii) Mr Pardew would remain on garden leave for a further month and not use or disclose Reading's confidential information; and (iii) Reading would receive £380,000 in compensation.[24]

(b)   Restrictive covenants

5.44   Garden leave applies before employment comes to an end. After termination of employment, it is possible to protect a business by means of restrictive covenants. These are often found in the contractual arrangements between football clubs and managers or other senior executives (such as directors of football or chief executives), and may be included in settlement agreements reached when clubs sack their managers. Restrictive covenants may take various forms: for example, for a limited period of time after termination of employment, restricting an employee from:

(a)   working for a competitor, such as (in the case of a premiership manager) managing another premier league club (a 'non-competition covenant');
(b)   soliciting other employees from leaving to join the competitor (a 'non-poaching covenant'); and
(c)   soliciting or dealing with clients of the employer (a 'non-solicitation/dealing covenant').

5.45   Given that such restrictions are in 'restraint of trade', they will only be enforceable if they satisfy two conditions. First, they must protect a legitimate business interest. An employer cannot simply restrain a former employee from competing. The restriction must be designed to protect some asset of the business. Whilst the categories of interests that can be protected in this way are not closed, they generally take one of three forms: (i) the protection of confidential information (which can be protected by a non-competition covenant); (ii) the stability of the workforce (for which a non-poaching covenant may be apt); and (iii) client relationships (which a non-solicitation/dealing covenant is designed for). The second condition of enforceability is that the covenant is reasonable. This means that it should go no further than reasonably necessary to protect the interest that it is intended to protect. Reasonableness is judged according to all the circumstances, including the scope and duration of the covenant. It is also important to remember that the enforceability of the covenant is to be judged at the time that it was entered into rather than at the time when it is sought to be enforced.

5.46   An example of an enforceable covenant was found in Kevin Keegan's contract of employment as manager of Newcastle United: *Keegan v Newcastle United Football Club Ltd*.[25] Mr Keegan's contract provided that if the club terminated his contract during its term, other than where the club had grounds to dismiss him, the club would pay Mr Keegan £2 million in consideration for which Keegan agreed that he would 'not work nor be employed in any capacity for any other premier league football club for a period of six months from the date of termination'. Mr Keegan argued that the covenant was too wide because it would prevent him from working or being employed for such a club *in any capacity*, for example, it would prevent him from carrying out any journalistic, administrative or corporate hospitality work for any such club. A Premier League Managers' Arbitration Tribunal

---

24   James Goudie QC and Simon Devonshire, 'Garden leave injunctions in the sporting arena' (2004) 1 ISLR 15.
25   [2010] IRLR 94.

disagreed and decided that the covenant was not unreasonable in the circumstances. Mr Keegan might have been of value to another Premier League club to the detriment of Newcastle in some capacity other than manager, coach or director of football. He would have taken with him his knowledge of Newcastle United: its players, their salaries and contract details, and their position at Newcastle United, all of which might have been of value to the other club. Even his association in some capacity with another club might have given that club a boost which might be reflected by the performance of its team on the pitch. The restriction was limited to premier league football clubs, and it applied only for six months. It did not prevent him from looking for another job as a premier league club manager during those six months, only from taking up such employment.

E DISCRIMINATION

5.47   The FA has various initiatives to promote inclusion and anti-discrimination. However, discrimination issues still arise in the world of football. Compensation for a discriminatory dismissal, as distinct from an ordinary unfair or wrongful dismissal, is uncapped and damages can be substantial. Discrimination claims can also cause significant reputational damage. This section provides a brief outline of aspects of discrimination law which may be particularly relevant in the context of football, by reference to specific examples of reported cases and allegations which are in the public domain. A detailed analysis of discrimination law is outside the scope of this work.

(a) Protected characteristics

5.48   The Equality Act 2010 (EA 2010) prohibits discrimination based on nine protected characteristics: age; disability; gender reassignment; marriage and civil partnership; pregnancy and maternity; race; religion or belief; sex; and sexual orientation (s 4).

(b) Liability

5.49   An employer must not discriminate against applicants or employees (s 39 of the EA 2010) or former employees (s 108). Employers and principals are liable for the conduct of their employees and agents (s 109). Claims can also be brought against individual employees and agents since they can be personally liable for their conduct (s 110). For example, club doctor Dr Eva Carneiro brought a sex discrimination claim against both Chelsea Football Club and its then manager, José Mourinho, following her departure from the Club in 2015.

(c) Prohibited conduct

5.50   Below is a broad outline of some of the main forms of conduct prohibited by the EA 2010.

5.51   **Direct discrimination** occurs when a person (A) discriminates against another person (B) by treating them less favourably than they treat, or would treat, others because of a protected characteristic (s 13).

5.52 **Indirect discrimination** occurs where employees are all treated in the same way by the employer but this causes a particular disadvantage to those with a specific protected characteristic. If a person (A) applies, or would apply, a provision, criterion or practice (PCP) which puts persons with a protected characteristic including (B) at a particular disadvantage and A cannot show it to be a proportionate means of achieving a legitimate aim then that amounts to indirect discrimination (s 19).

5.53 **Harassment** occurs when a person (A) engages in unwanted conduct related to a relevant protected characteristic and that conduct has the purpose or effect of violating B's dignity, or creating an intimidating, hostile, degrading, humiliating or offensive environment for B (section 26). Sexist, racist or homophobic remarks can amount to harassment within this definition.

5.54 In *Hussaney v Chester City Football Club*,[26] a member of the club's youth squad, who complained that the manager had referred to him as a 'black cunt', succeeded before the employment tribunal in his claims against the club and the manager for the racial abuse. He was awarded £2,500 compensation for injury to feelings.

5.55 As part of a culture review by The FA, the England player Eniola Aluko alleged that the then England women's team manager, Mark Sampson, told her to be careful her Nigerian relatives did not bring ebola to an England game at Wembley in 2014, and that in 2015 at the China Cup he had asked the mixed-race midfielder, Drew Spence, how many times she had been arrested. The manager denied the allegations. An FA inquiry concluded that the manager made 'ill-judged attempts at humour which, as a matter of law, were discriminatory on grounds of race within the meaning of the Equality Act 2010'. The report recommended that all employees of the FA, regardless of their position and no matter how senior, be trained in equal opportunities and diversity matters.

5.56 **Victimisation** occurs when an employer retaliates against an employee: A subjects B to a detriment because B does a protected act or A believes that B has done, or may do, a protected act (s 27). An example of a protected act is making an allegation of discrimination (s 27(2)(d)).

5.57 In *McCammon v Gillingham Football Club*,[27] the dismissal of a professional footballer after he had made allegations of race discrimination against the manager and assistant manager was held to be victimisation by the club. The player was awarded £68,278 by way of remedy.

5.58 In *Hussaney v Chester City Football Club* (referred to at para **5.54** above), when the club dropped Mr Hussaney he claimed that this was a result of him complaining about racial abuse and amounted to victimisation. The employment tribunal initially dismissed Mr Hussaney's victimisation claim but the EAT upheld his appeal against that decision and remitted the claim to a differently constituted tribunal.

F   WHISTLEBLOWING

5.59 There is little by way of domestic reported cases of whistleblowing in the context of football. However, this is likely to be a developing area given the

26   January 2001, EAT 203/98.
27   UKEAT/0559/12/DM and UKEAT/0560/12/DM.

substantial compensation which is available for successful whistleblowing claims and publicity about allegations of match-fixing and corruption in football.

5.60 The Employment Rights Act 1996 (ERA 1996) provides employees and workers with a right to claim compensation if they are dismissed or subjected to a detriment for having made a protected disclosure, colloquially known as 'whistleblowing'. No qualifying period of employment is necessary to bring a claim.

5.61 Section 103A of the ERA 1996 provides that an employee who is dismissed shall be regarded as unfairly dismissed if the reason (or, if more than one, the principal reason) for the dismissal is that the employee made a protected disclosure. Compensation for such a dismissal is uncapped.

5.62 Section 47B(1) of the ERA 1996 provides that a worker has the right not to be subjected to any detriment by any act, or any deliberate failure to act, by his employer done on the ground that the worker has made a protected disclosure.

5.63 Section 47B(1A) of the ERA 1996 provides that workers and agents can be personally liable for subjecting a worker to a detriment on the ground that they have made a protected disclosure.

5.64 Protected disclosures are defined by ss 43A and 43B of the ERA 1996. A 'protected disclosure' means a qualifying disclosure which is made by a worker in accordance with any of ss 43C to 43H (s 43A). Section 43B provides that a 'qualifying disclosure' means any disclosure of information which, in the reasonable belief of the worker making the disclosure, is made in the public interest and tends to show one or more of the following:

(a) that a criminal offence has been committed, is being committed, or is likely to be committed;
(b) that a person has failed, is failing or is likely to fail to comply with any legal obligation to which he is subject;
(c) that a miscarriage of justice has occurred, is occurring or is likely to occur;
(d) that the health or safety of an individual has been, is being or is likely to be endangered;
(e) that the environment has been, is being or is likely to be damaged; or
(f) that information tending to show any matter failing within one of the preceding paragraphs has been, is being or is likely to be deliberately concealed.

Section 43C provides that a qualifying disclosure is made in accordance with this section if the worker makes the disclosure to his employer 'or other responsible person'.

5.65 Previously, it was necessary for a protected disclosure to have been made in good faith. The Enterprise and Regulatory Reform Act 2013 introduced two key reforms to the whistleblowing provisions in the ERA 1996. First, s 17 inserted an express condition that the disclosure, in the reasonable belief of the worker, must be made in the public interest. Secondly, s 18 removed the 'good faith' requirement in ss 43C, 43E, 43F, 43G and 43H of the ERA 1996. However, this element is re-introduced into the remedy stage. Sections 49 and 123 of the ERA 1996 allow a tribunal to reduce compensation in a successful whistleblowing claim by up to 25% if it appears that the protected disclosure was not made in good faith. The reforms shift the focus away from the motives of the worker making the disclosure towards the content of that disclosure.

CHAPTER 6

Contracts – Players

Jane Mulcahy QC (Blackstone Chambers), Ian Lynam (Northridge)
and Liz Coley (Walker Morris)

A   INTRODUCTION

6.1   An employment contract for a footballer differs in material respects from the general run-of-the-mill employment agreement. This is because of the oddity of a footballer's lot: he or she is not just an employee but also an asset, with a registration capable of being sold on football's open market (albeit only at specified times of the year).

6.2   In addition, football, both at home and abroad, is circumscribed by rules emanating from the various international and national regulators, spanning the world governing body FIFA down to the particular league.[1]

6.3   It is this strange landscape that leads, for example, to footballers being potentially fined for misconduct[2] (in a way that never happens in any other industry) or to invoking 'sporting just cause' for walking away from a club.

6.4   In this chapter we consider the oddity of the football framework as well as the specifics of the relatively standardised playing contracts that subsist within the leagues.

B   FOOTBALL FRAMEWORK

6.5   When starting to draft a professional player's contract, the regulations of the national association, the relevant league and FIFA must all be taken into consideration. A number of FIFA's Regulations on the Status and Transfer of Players (RSTP)[3] are stated to be binding at national level without modification[4] and therefore these regulations will be considered first.[5]

(a)   FIFA RSTP

6.6   The RSTP are based on Article 5 of the FIFA Statutes which state that FIFA's Executive Committee 'shall regulate the status of players and the provisions

1   See para **6.73** et seq below.
2   See para **6.86**, below.
3   See paras **6.6–6.17**, below.
4   RSTP, Article 1.3.
5   The current version at the time of writing is from March 2016.

for their transfer, as well as questions relating to these matters, in particular the encouragement of player training by clubs and the protection of representative teams, in special regulations'. Hence, although the main focus of the RSTP is transfer activity, the issue of player contracts is also covered.

6.7   The purpose of the RSTP is to lay down global and binding rules concerning the status of players, their eligibility to participate in organised football, and their transfer between clubs belonging to different associations. As regards player contracts, Article 1 of the RSTP places an obligation on domestic associations to protect contractual stability, paying due respect to mandatory national law and collective bargaining agreements. It sets out a number of key principles which shall be incorporated into the regulations of domestic associations, ie that:

(a) contracts must be respected;
(b) contracts may be terminated by either party without consequence where there is 'just cause';
(c) contracts may be terminated by professionals with 'sporting just cause';
(d) contracts cannot be terminated during the course of the season;
(e) in the event of termination of contract without just cause, compensation shall be payable and such compensation may be stipulated in the contract;
(f) in the event of termination of contract without just cause, sporting sanctions shall be imposed on the party in breach.

6.8   It therefore follows that FIFA seeks to establish certain principles as regards the contracts between players and clubs which protect the integrity of both the sport and the principle of respect for contractual relations. Furthermore, these principles are expressly stated to take into account the relevant domestic legal provisions relating to employment.

6.9   Article 2 of the RSTP is of fundamental importance as it defines the difference in status between a professional player and an amateur. It states: 'A professional is a player who has a written contract with a club and is paid more for his footballing activity than the expenses he effectively incurs. All other players are considered to be amateurs. It follows that the existence of a written contract is crucial to the existence of a professional relationship.'

6.10   Article 5.1 provides that all players must be registered as amateur or professional. The widely coined phrase in the UK of a 'semi-professional' player is not recognised by FIFA.

6.11   The classification of a player's status is also important when determining the level of training compensation that is to be paid to a player's former club(s) after an international move in accordance with Article 20. (Training compensation is dealt with in detail in Chapter 10, Academies and Youth Issues).

6.12   In the early years of the RSTP, the English scholarship contract had been deemed to be an amateur registration and therefore did not trigger compensation to be payable to all of a player's former clubs between the ages of 12 and 16 years old on a first registration in England. However, the Court of Arbitration for Sport (CAS) in 2007[6] stated: 'The only relevant criterion chosen by FIFA to differentiate between an amateur and a non-amateur player is the remuneration. The receipt by the player of any remuneration "other than for the actual expenses incurred during the course of their participation in or for any activity connected with association football"

---

6   CAS 2006/A/1177 *Aston Villa FC v B.93 Copenhagen* at p 4.

is what alone distinguishes an amateur from a non-amateur player.' A scholarship registration was therefore deemed to give a player professional status.

6.13   However, recent CAS jurisprudence[7] casts doubt on this principle. In the *Cercle Brugge* case the Sole Arbitrator reviewed the payment the player in Belgium received under his scholarship arrangement and compared it to living expenses: in the specific circumstances of the case 'a flat-rate for football-related expenses therefore has to be admitted [as an amateur contract] as long as it broadly reflects the average football related expenses of a player'.[8] As a result, the player should 'be considered as an amateur during the duration of the 'scholarship contract'[9] and the claims for training compensation failed.

6.14   Whether this judgment opens the floodgates for clubs to challenge the status of the scholarship agreement in England remains to be seen; however it does demonstrate that the CAS is prepared to consider each case on its individual merits.

6.15   Article 5 of the RSTP provides that players may be registered with a maximum of three clubs during one season but are only eligible to play official matches for two clubs. As an exception, a player who moves between two clubs belonging to associations with different seasons (ie start of the season in summer/autumn rather than winter/spring) may be eligible to play in official matches for a third club during the relevant season, provided he has fully complied with his obligations towards his previous clubs. It is key to monitor this regulation at domestic level especially in mid-season transfers. Registrations on a standard loan count towards this calculation.

6.16   Article 18 of the RSTP sets out a number of specific provisions which must be considered when entering into professional playing contracts. These are as follows:

(a) If an intermediary has been involved in the negotiation of a contract he shall be named in the contract. The regulations relating to intermediaries are considered further at Chapter 12.
(b) The minimum length of contract shall be from its effective date until the end of the season. This is varied domestically, however, with week-by-week and monthly contracts, see para **6.28** below.
(c) The maximum length of a contract shall be five years. Contracts of any other length shall only be permitted if consistent with national laws. Players under the age of 18 may not sign a professional contract for a term longer than three years. Notwithstanding this, under English law there is no limitation on the length of an employment contract.
(d) A club intending to conclude a contract with a professional must inform the player's existing club in writing before entering into negotiations. A professional shall only be free to conclude a contract with another club if his contract with his present club has expired or is due to expire within six months. This is more permissive than the position domestically.
(e) The validity of a player contract may not be made subject to a successful medical examination and/or the grant of a work permit.

6.17   It can therefore be seen that the basic structure relating to player contracts is set down by FIFA. However the practical implementation of these broad principles

---

7   CAS 2014/A/3659 & 3660 & 3661 KSV *Cercle Brugge v Clube Linda-A-Velha & Club Uniao Desportiva e Recreativa de Alges & Sport Club Praiense.*
8   Ibid, p 85.
9   Ibid, p 89.

is left primarily to the national associations. In the case of the domestic game, whilst some rules are sourced by The FA, it is largely left to the leagues to monitor the terms of the contracts submitted to them.

(b) Domestic rules

6.18   As of the 2017/18 season, player contracts are dealt with in the Premier League Rules at Section T and by the English Football League (EFL) at EFL Regulation 61. The FA Rules relating to players with professional contracts are dealt with at Rule C1. These are dealt with below by topic as the rules and regulations are in the main very similar, at least between the two leagues, although any significant differences are highlighted. The FA rules highlighted are those that relate to players playing in the Premier League and EFL only.

(i)   Form of contract

6.19   Premier League Rule T.10 dictates the form of professional contract to be adopted. It provides as follows: 'Save for any contract entered into by a Promoted Club before it became a member of the [Premier] League which are in Form 18, contracts between clubs and players shall be in Form 19'. A copy of Form 18 is at page 286 and a copy of Form 19 is at page 314 of the Premier League Handbook.[10] EFL Regulation 61.2 mirrors this regulation. The contents of these contracts are considered later in this chapter.

6.20   FA Rule C1(c)(i) states that all contracts must be in the full name of the club and, if the club is a corporate body, the contract should also include the company registration number.

6.21   Premier League Rule T.21 sets out some formalities for a player's contract to come into being. It requires the contract to be signed by the player and an authorised signatory on behalf of the club. If a player is under 18 (ie a minor) it must also be signed by the player's parent or guardian.

6.22   EFL Regulation 61.1 confirms the above in relation to players who are minors; however, EFL Regulation 61.3 is more prescriptive than the similar Premier League rule stating that the contract must be signed on behalf of the club by either the chairman alone or the club secretary or duly appointed signatory together with one director.

6.23   Premier League Rules T.23 and T.24 require the submission of contracts within five days as well as requiring a club to request that the player should complete Form 20 (the Player Ethnicity Monitoring Questionnaire) and submit the completed form at the same time. Both the Premier League and the EFL require original copies of contracts to be submitted, whereas The FA is happy to register a player after receiving scanned documentation only.

6.24   The above deadline for submission of paperwork is mirrored in EFL Regulation 61.5 and FA Rule C.1(f)(i).

---

10   Season 2017–2018, available online (along with updates) at: https://www.premierleague.com/ publications (accessed February 2018).

6.25   It should be remembered, however, that failure to submit the relevant contractual paperwork in accordance with the above deadlines will not invalidate the contract *per se*; although it will put the registering club in breach of the regulations.

(ii)   Contractual length/minimum age

6.26   Premier League Rules T.11 and T.12 deal with the length of player contracts. The general rule is that a contract may be for any period subject to a requirement that every contract must have an expiry date of 30 June. This is to ensure that contracts are in place until the end of the relevant season which provides for the stability of the relevant sporting competition.

6.27   The Professional Footballers' Association (PFA), the Premier League and the EFL have entered into a collective agreement in this respect which is detailed in the Code of Practice and Notes on Contract as follows:

> 'The Contract will always be for a fixed term until 30th June and is likely to be renewed from time to time for further fixed terms. For this to remain effective under the European Directive on Fixed Term Contracts which has been incorporated into English law there has to be a collective agreement acknowledging the importance and validity of this type of successful fixed term contract within football and setting out objective reasons justifying it'.[11]

6.28   However there are three exceptions to the contract expiring on 30 June, namely: (i) any contract for a player who is under 18 must not be capable of lasting more than three years; (ii) monthly contracts; and (iii) week-by-week contracts. These provisions are also subject to the overall requirement that a player under the age of 17 may not enter into a professional contract and may only be registered as an academy player, as defined in the Youth Development Rules.[12] It should be noted however that under FA Rule C1(e), outside of the Premier League and the EFL, contracts may finish on the first Saturday of May in a season or on the date of a club's last first team league or knockout match.

6.29   In the event that a young player signs a professional contract during the course of his scholarship agreement, EFL Regulation 61.8 provides that clubs must ensure that the player continues the educational aspect of his scholarship.

6.30   In addition, FA Rule C.1(a) prohibits a player in full-time education from entering into a professional contract with a club.

6.31   Options to extend the term of the player contract are relatively common in English football, in both bilateral (ie each of club and player have a right to extend, perhaps conditional on certain events) and unilateral (generally a club-only right to extend) form.

6.32   FA Rule C1(j)(xiii) provides that options to extend are permissible in principle provided the extension is on no less favourable terms and the period of extension is no longer than the initial period.

6.33   The legal enforceability of unilateral options to extend has been considered by the FIFA Dispute Resolution Chamber and CAS in a number of cases, with the key

---

11   Code of Practice and Notes on Contract, p 12.
12   See further, Chapter 10, Academies and Youth Issues.

factors to consider helpfully set out in the decision in *Gremio v Lopez*.[13] The majority of CAS decisions have found unilateral options to be unenforceable. National law has an important role to play, however, and there has yet to be a DRC or CAS case challenging the enforceability of a unilateral option under English law.

(iii) Remuneration

6.34 FA Rule C1(b)(iv) states that:

> '… all payments and/or benefits due and/or made to a Player must be set out in a written agreement between the Club and the Player. Any other payments and/or benefits whatsoever due and/or made on behalf of, or in relation to, a Player (not otherwise detailed in the written agreement between the Club and Player) must also be set out in a written agreement, to which the Club shall be a party. In each case a copy of any such agreement must be provided to The Association.'

6.35 Premier League Rules T.13 and T.14 deal with remuneration. The first requirement is that all remuneration of any description must be included in the contract. Rule T.14 obliges the club and the player to strictly adhere to the terms of the contract. These provisions are required not only to provide for good practice but also to ensure that side payments are not made which may result in breaches of the Financial Fair Play Rules (see Rule T.15). Remuneration is dealt with more fully later in this chapter.

6.36 EFL Regulation 61.6 also states that the full details of all payments or benefits whether in cash or in kind must be included in the playing contract. However it goes further than the Premier League regulations as it requires clubs to detail any changes to remuneration in the event the divisional status of the club changes during the term of the contract. It is also good practice to detail any changes to appearance money and other payments contained in the contract.

6.37 Premier League Rules T.16–T.18 deal with signing-on fees. Signing-on fees cannot be paid for a contract which lasts for a period of less than three months or for monthly, conditional or week by week contracts. In any contract lasting for more than one year the signing on fee must be paid in equal annual instalments. Furthermore the signing on fee must be paid if it is outstanding on the date of a transfer unless the underlying contract has been validly terminated, the player has waived the sums or the player has been transferred pursuant to a written transfer request made by him or otherwise provided for by the Premier League Board.

6.38 EFL Regulations relating to signing-on fees can be found at Regulations 61.14–61.18 and broadly replicate the above.

6.39 Premier League Rule T.19 prohibits lump sum payments other than signing-on fees or relocation expenses (which must comply with HMRC limits) being

---

13 CAS 2013/A/3260. They were: (i) taking extensions under the option(s) into account, the total duration of the contract must not be excessive; (ii) it should be necessary for the option to be exercised reasonably in advance of the contract's expiry date, so that there can be no eleventh hour extensions; (iii) the salary reward from the exercising of the option should be established in the contract so that the financial outcome for the player is clear; (iv) the terms of the contract should not put one party at the mercy of the other; (v) the option should be clearly identifiable so that the player is aware of it when signing the contract; (vi) the extension period should be in proportion to the 'basic' contract period; and (vii) multiple extensions are not recommended – a single extension is more likely to be considered enforceable.

paid in the first year of the player's employment with the club. EFL Regulation 61.13 mirrors the Premier League rule.

6.40   Premier League Rule T.20 and EFL Regulation 61.6 impose a requirement that any Image Contract Payment must be set out in the playing contract. Image rights are considered elsewhere in this work at Chapter 13.

6.41   Premier League Rule T.26 deals with amendments to the playing contract. The general principle is that the parties are free, at any time, to amend their contract. However if the amendments increase the player's remuneration and are agreed once the season has commenced, the amended contract must extend the contractual term by a minimum of one year. This provision is replicated in EFL Regulation 61.4.

6.42   Notwithstanding the relatively light regulatory restrictions, there is a large degree of uniformity as to how football clubs pay players. Most remuneration is paid on a fixed basis (with the majority paid as salary, and up to 20% under a separate image rights contract) with relatively limited variable amounts.

6.43   Comparing a typical contract from the start of the Premier League era and today, and notwithstanding the massive growth in individual remuneration, it is striking to note the lack of change in structure and approach. This is particularly the case when viewed in light of club revenues which have, similarly, increased greatly over the period but have, in contrast, become considerably more variable from year to year. The two key revenue variables are, at the top end, qualification for the Champions League and, at the lower end, the threat of relegation to the far less lucrative Championship.

6.44   To the extent variable amounts are used, the most common are bonuses and ratchets based on appearances, league position (including triggers based on qualification for Europe), avoiding relegation, goals and assists. In addition to bonuses included in individual contracts, most clubs still use a standard 'squad bonus schedule' which pays the players relatively modest amounts based on performances and the success of the team over the course of a season. Money paid under squad bonus schedules does not generally feature in player negotiations and has questionable impact on player motivation or satisfaction. Squad bonus schedules can cause unrest, however, as they are negotiated by the players on a collective basis (not by agents) and disputes are not uncommon.

(c)   Obligations of players and clubs

6.45   The essential obligations for players and clubs mirror those in the normal employment context, ie a player is obliged to be ready and willing to work[14] (train, play football, attend various public engagements and so on) while the club is obliged to remunerate him or her for that work. This mutuality of obligation is central to the relationship of employment.

(i)   Common law duties

6.46   Over and above that there are other duties that are implied by the common law into an employment contract. Commonly both parties will be considered to

---

14   *Cresswell v Inland Revenue Board* [1984] IRLR 190.

owe the other a duty of trust and confidence, meaning that an employer should not, without reasonable and proper cause, conduct itself in a manner calculated or likely to destroy or seriously damage the relationship of trust and confidence that subsists with an employee (and vice versa).[15]

6.47   An employer also owes an employee:

(a) A duty to take care. Pursuant to this, a club must select proper staff, provide adequate materials and provide a safe system of working. Failure to do so opens the club up to a claim in negligence.[16]
(b) Potentially, a duty to provide work. The traditional view was that an employer did not have to provide work: as master he or she had the power to ensure that an employee worked or stayed idle. But that concept has changed over the years[17] and, in the case of skilled workers,[18] courts are more inclined to find that an employer should not unreasonably withhold work having regard to an employee's interest in exercising and improving his or her skills. See also the concept of sporting just cause, above and below.[19]

6.48   As for the employee, he or she is expected to:

(a) Obey the lawful instruction of the employer.[20]
(b) Be loyal. This means, for example, behaving honestly, not making any secret profits, and keeping confidential information secret.

(ii)   Specific obligations in football

6.49   The standardised employment contracts within football also provide for express obligations on both players and clubs. By reference to Form 19 of the Premier League contract,[21] a player agrees, among other things, to:

(a) attend and participate in training and matches, as directed;
(b) play to the best of his skill and ability at all times;
(c) maintain a high standard of physical fitness and not endanger his ability to play or train;
(d) observe the Laws of the Game and the rules of the various regulators (see also above);
(e) not invalidate his insurance;
(f) not live anywhere the club reasonably deems unsuitable;

---

15 *Malik v Bank of Credit and Commerce International SA* [1997] IRLR 462, HL.
16 *Kieron Brady v Sunderland Football Club*, 17 November 1998, unreported, although the footballer's claim failed on the facts. See also *Michael Appleton v Medhat Mohammed el Safty* [2007] EWHC 631 (QB), in which a player retired from professional football following negligent treatment for an injury, and *Watson & Bradford City v Kevin Gray & Huddersfield Town*, 29 October 1998, concerning a broken leg sustained by a footballer.
17 See, for example, cases concerning garden leave in Chapter 5, Employment Law and Football, paras **5.40–5.43** in particular.
18 *Langston v Amalgamated Union of Engineering Workers* [1974] IRLR 15, CA; *William Hill v Tucker* [1998] IRLR 313, CA.
19 See paras **6.7** and **6.68–6.69**.
20 Football manager Lou Macari was lawfully dismissed for failing to comply with instructions to abide by a contractual residence clause; to attend Celtic's ground regularly, and to report to the managing director on a weekly basis: *Macari v Celtic Football Athletic Club Ltd* [1999] IRLR 787, Court of Session; see further Chapter 5, Employment Law and Football, paras **5.13**, **5.27** and **5.32–5.33**; and Chapter 7, Contracts – Managers, para **7.39**.
21 For the year 2017/18.

(g) participate in promotional, community and public relations activities for up to six hours each week and allow his image to be used to promote the club (and its sponsors) and the Premier League (and its sponsors).[22]

6.50   For its part the club agrees, among other things, to:

(a) observe the Rules and provide copies of the Rules to the player;
(b) promptly arrange medical treatment;
(c) maintain insurance for the player;
(d) support the player in undertaking education and training;
(e) release the player as required for fulfilling his obligations to his national team.

(d)   Release clauses and buy-out clauses

6.51   Release clauses have become somewhat more common in recent years.[23] A release clause is an undertaking from a club to accept a transfer offer for the player if it receives a bid over a certain amount (potentially with additional conditions such as the club having failed to qualify for the Champions League or having been relegated).

6.52   A buy-out clause is a provision stipulating an amount which the player can pay the club in order to terminate his contract. Buy-out clauses are mandatory in Spain[24] but not common in England. Many Premier League clubs do now, however, include language to confirm that 'market value' compensation will be due to the club if a player unilaterally terminates the contract, thereby enshrining into the contract the prevailing approach from CAS decisions interpreting Article 17 of the RSTP.[25]

C   TERMINATION

6.53   At common law a contract can be lawfully terminated in whatever way specified in the contract, most commonly by either the employer or the employee exercising their right to give notice pursuant to a contractual clause. Alternatively, if one party has behaved sufficiently badly – for example, a player committing gross misconduct – then the other party can accept that repudiatory breach and bring the contract to an end.

6.54   The complication in the field of employment is that any dismissal of an employee does not only have to be pursuant to the contract but also (if the employee has sufficient qualifying employment) has to be done fairly so as not to fall foul of the statutory tort (under the Employment Rights Act 1996) of unfair dismissal (see further as to unfair dismissal below). It must be remembered, also, that the end of a limited term contract, such as those commonly used in football, is treated as a dismissal for the purpose of the Employment Rights Act 1996.[26]

---

22   Note that this grant of image rights is in a club context only and is subject to limitations (eg cannot imply a personal endorsement and use must be spread equally amongst first team players). Separate image rights deals can be entered into to grant wider rights; see Chapter 13 for more on image rights.
23   Although there is no standardised drafting and some of the clauses used are of dubious enforceability.
24   Real Decreto 1006/1985.
25   As dealt with in Chapter 29, International Disputes and the CAS, at paras **29.106–29.121**.
26   Section 95(1)(b) of the Employment Rights Act 1996.

(a) Termination in football

6.55   In football a somewhat more elaborate procedure has been adopted on occasion of termination, no doubt to prevent clubs instantly having to offer up a player's registration on his dismissal/leaving and/or to regularise the release of that registration.

6.56   Hence a club is entitled, for example under the Premier League contract (at clause 10), to terminate the employment of a player[27] if the player is guilty of gross misconduct; has failed to heed any final written warning given under the disciplinary procedure (see below); or is convicted of any criminal offence where the punishment consists of a sentence of imprisonment of three months or more (which is not suspended).

6.57   However, the club has to terminate by giving 14 days' notice in writing to the player and has to notify the player, within seven days, of the full reasons for the actions taken. Such strictures are not requirements of the common law.

6.58   Further, a player can appeal if he gives notice in writing within 14 days of the written notice of the reasons, to be determined in accordance with the Premier League Rules. Pending the hearing and determination of the appeal the club can suspend the player for up to a maximum of six weeks. Various other provisions deal with the payment to the player but the contract is maintained pending the outcome of the appeal.

6.59   Only once the termination becomes operative, at the end of the process, is the player's registration released.

6.60   Similar provisions subsist if (pursuant to clause 11) a player terminates the contract on the basis that the club is guilty of serious or persistent breach of the terms and conditions of the contract or fails to pay any remuneration/provide benefits which are due for 14 days and has still failed to pay after the period of 14 days' notice.

6.61   A club can also terminate (pursuant to clause 8) where a player is long-term incapacitated from playing football, usually on 12 months' notice. The approach to this issue varies significantly from country to country with the Premier League provisions being towards the more player-friendly end of the spectrum. The EFL has similar provisions in its standard contract.[28]

6.62   The ability to terminate the contract for serious or persistent breach can be relied on by a player asserting 'just cause' or 'sporting just cause' under the FIFA RSTP. The former is somewhat at large and depends upon the conduct.

---

27   Examples of players being dismissed include Adam Johnson, sacked by Sunderland after he pleaded guilty to one count of sexual activity with a child and one charge of grooming; Marlon King, sacked by Wigan Athletic after he was convicted of assault; Dennis Wise, dismissed by Leicester City for breaking a team-mate's jaw (which dismissal was subsequently found to be unfair on procedural grounds, *Wise v Filbert Realisations (formerly Leicester City Football Club) (in administration)* UKEAT/0660/03/RN); and Adrian Mutu, fired by Chelsea after he tested positive for cocaine.
28   Both the Premier League and EFL provide for appeals arising out of termination to be determined by football appeal committees. See, for example, Premier League Rule T36.

6.63   Article 14.2 of the FIFA Commentary on the RSTP[29] states that:

> 'behaviour that is in violation of the terms of an employment contract still cannot justify the termination of a contract for just cause. However, should the violation persist for a long time or should many violations be cumulated over time, then it is most probable that the breach of contract has reached such a level that the party suffering the breach is entitled to terminate the contract unilaterally.'

6.64   In relation to CAS jurisprudence, it appears that just cause will exist where (i) the breach is so serious that the injured party can no longer, in good faith, be expected to continue the contractual relationship; and (ii) the injured party has given sufficient warning to the other party of its unacceptable conduct.[30]

6.65   For example, in *Honefoss Ballklubb v Heiner Mora Mora*,[31] two alleged breaches of the playing contract were held by CAS to be insufficient to establish just cause. The player had complained of delays in paying his salary (one month followed by two days) as well as his exclusion from the first team for a period of two weeks. In relation to the former CAS noted that the player had an express right to terminate for late payment under the terms of his contract, but that was nevertheless insufficient for him to rely on termination for just cause under the RSTP. As to the latter the player had failed to notify the club of the allegation it was in breach: rather he had handed in a letter of apology and had resumed training after his two week exclusion.

6.66   Conversely, in *Club Samsunspor v Aminu Umar*[32] the club failed to pay three consecutive months' salaries plus a lump sum, leaving an unpaid debt of €75,000. In addition, the player had sent a reminder to the club and had given a formal warning that he would terminate the contract in the event that the outstanding sums were not paid within seven days. In those circumstances, CAS held that the player did have just cause to terminate the contract.[33]

6.67   In relation to allegations of breach by clubs, inadequate sporting performance will not constitute just cause.[34] Nor will uncertainty about a player's employment status.[35]

6.68   'Sporting just cause' is defined under Article 15 of the RSTP (see para **6.6** et seq above) as where a professional player has, in the course of the season, appeared in fewer than 10% of the official matches in which his club has been involved. However, a player can terminate only in the 15 days following the last official match of the season.

6.69   One aim of 'sporting just cause' is to prevent clubs leaving players on the bench at the same time as refusing to sell them, alternatively to provide players with a way out should they be forced to stagnate.

---

29   See link at http://www.thefa.com/football-rules-governance/policies/player-registration/fifa-regulations-on-the-status-and-transfer-of-players (accessed February 2018).
30   See, for a clear exposition on just cause, an article by Andrew Smith of Matrix Chambers in World Sports Advocate, April 2017 at pp 11–14.
31   CAS 2015/A/4083.
32   CAS 2015/A/4220.
33   In *Qingdao Zhongneng FC v Blaz Sliskovic*, CAS 2015/A/4158 a 17-day delay in paying one-fifth of a coach's salary was, perhaps unsurprisingly, insufficient to constitute just cause.
34   *Al Shaab RC v Aymard Guirie*, CAS 2015/A/4122.
35   *Hapoel Beer Sheva FC v Razak*, CAS 2015/A/4209.

(b) Unfair dismissal

6.70   Although there is no attempt in football's standard agreements to make players contract out of their right to bring an unfair dismissal claim (which would be unlawful) provisions are included to make such claims unattractive.

6.71   For example, in the Premier League contract at clause 19, if a player desists from bringing a claim for unfair dismissal when his limited term contract ends (and he is not offered similarly favourable terms in a new agreement) he will instead receive a payment equal to his weekly basic wage for a period of one month or until he signs for another Club, whichever period is the shorter.

6.72   Crucially, the maximum amount payable under this clause is *double* the maximum sum which an Employment Tribunal could award as compensation (as compensatory awards for unfair dismissal are subject to a statutory cap which is increased once a year). Hence most players would rather receive a sum under clause 19 than take their chances at fighting an unfair dismissal claim.

D DISCIPLINARY PROCEDURE AND PENALTIES

(a) Disciplinary procedure

6.73   It is important to start from clause 3 in the standard playing contract which, at clause 3.1.9, requires a player to 'observe the Rules', the Rules being defined in clause 1.1 of the contract as 'the statutes and regulations of FIFA and UEFA the FA Rules the League Rules the Code of Practice and the Club Rules'. As a result, these various rules and regulations are incorporated into the playing contract.

6.74   The 'FA Rules' are defined as 'the rules and regulations from time to time in force of the FA and including those of FIFA and UEFA to the extent that they relate or apply to the Player or the Club'. The rules of The FA relating to conduct, which are often relied upon in disciplinary action against a player, are set out at Rule E.

6.75   FA Rule E3 (1) states:

> 'A Participant shall at all times act in the best interests of the game and shall not act in any manner which is improper or brings the game into disrepute or use any one, or a combination of, violent conduct, serious foul play, threatening, abusive, indecent or insulting words or behaviour.'

6.76   The rules of the league of which the club is a member are also incorporated into the playing contract and hence are referenced throughout this section where relevant. Also incorporated is the Code of Practice, which forms an essential part of the playing contract, the purpose of which is to 'explain and amplify the formal provisions in the Contract as well as to indicate what is considered good practice'.[36]

6.77   In addition, clause 3.1.9 of the playing contract provides that a player will observe the 'Club Rules', meaning the rules or regulations affecting the player from time to time in force and published by the club, to the extent that they do not conflict with or seek to vary the express terms of the playing contract. It is usual that the club's individual rules are introduced after negotiation between the senior representatives of the playing squad and the manager and are normally reviewed prior to the commencement of each season.

---

36   Code of Practice and Notes on Contract, p 1.

6.78   Clause 9 of the playing contract provides that the disciplinary procedure set out in Part 1 of Schedule 1 shall apply in respect of any breach or failure to observe the terms of the contract or the Rules.

6.79   The playing contract states that the:

> 'disciplinary procedure aims to ensure that a Club behaves fairly in investigating and dealing with allegation of unacceptable conduct with a view to helping and encouraging all employees of the Club to achieve and maintain appropriate standards of conduct and performance. The Club nevertheless reserves the right to depart from the precise requirements of its disciplinary procedure where the Club considers it expedient to do so and where the Player's resulting treatment is no less fair.'[37]

The intention is that the procedure adopted be far removed from the days when a manager fined a player two weeks' wages without explanation. These days, the PFA in particular will wish to ensure that its members are fairly treated.

6.80   The procedure provides for a 'proper' investigation to take place into the matter complained of, during which the club has the ability by written notice to suspend the player for a period of up to 14 days. The player will continue to receive all of his contractual benefits during any period of suspension. It should be made clear to the player that any period of suspension does not constitute disciplinary action nor does it imply any assumption that he is guilty of misconduct.

6.81   In the event that the club decides to hold a disciplinary hearing it shall notify the player in writing giving full details of the complaint and reasonable notice of the date and time of the hearing. In the event that the player does not attend the disciplinary hearing it may proceed in his absence if he has received proper notice.

6.82   Paragraph 3.2.1 of Schedule 1 Part 1 and clause 13 of the playing contract provide for the player to be accompanied or represented at a disciplinary hearing by his club captain, a PFA delegate or any officer of the PFA.

6.83   Further, the playing contract provides that no disciplinary penalty shall be imposed without first giving the player the opportunity to state his case to the manager or a director of the club or where the player requests the same without a disciplinary hearing.

6.84   The player shall have the right of appeal in writing against any disciplinary decision to the club's board of directors within 14 days of the notification of a decision and an appeal hearing should be held as soon as possible thereafter.

6.85   If the player remains dissatisfied, and the sanction imposed has been greater than an oral warning, then he has a further 14 days from receipt of the club board's decision to submit a further appeal to the relevant league.[38]

6.86   The potential disciplinary penalties are set out at para 4 of Schedule 1 Part 1 namely:

(a)   an oral warning;[39]
(b)   a formal written warning;

37   Schedule 1, Part 1, p 1.
38   Premier League Rule T.28 and EFL Regulation 61.10.
39   The ACAS code does not cover verbal warnings as conduct that warrants this type of first level warning may be best dealt with informally.

(c) after a previous warning or warnings, a final written warning;[40]

(d) a fine of two weeks' basic wage for a first offence (unless otherwise approved by the PFA) or of up to four weeks' basic wage for subsequent offences in any consecutive period of 12 months;[41]

(e) ordering the player not to attend the club for a period of up to 4 weeks; or

(f) in cases of gross misconduct, failing to heed any final written warning or conviction of a criminal offence where the punishments consists of a sentence of imprisonment for three months or more (which is not suspended):

    (i) dismissal; or

    (ii) the imposition of such other disciplinary action (including suspension of the player and/or a fine of up to six weeks' basic wage).

6.87   Termination of a player's contract for disciplinary reasons is dealt with above at para **6.56**.

6.88   The Professional Football Negotiating and Consultative Committee have negotiated and agreed a recommended tariff of maximum fines for on-field offences to help ensure that player discipline is dealt with in a consistent manner.

6.89   The Code of Practice elaborates on any monetary fine stating:

> 'the maximum fine under the Contract for a first offence is two weeks wages rising to a maximum of three weeks for a second offence and four weeks for a third or subsequent offence. If a Club believes that a first offence has been committed which is sufficiently serious to merit more than two weeks fine in order to preserve the integrity of the Club or its Players then it can raise the matter with the PFA and if it is agreed by them in writing a higher fine may be imposed.'[42]

6.90   A club is not expected to impose a fine of greater than two weeks' wages without also imposing a suspension at the same time.

6.91   Clauses 5.4–5.5 of the playing contract provide that any fine imposed on a player calculated by reference to his weekly wage must be treated as a forfeiture of wages and shall be deducted from the player's gross wage on the next monthly pay date following (i) the expiry of any appeal period (if an appeal is not made) or (ii) the outcome of an appeal. A fine shall be payable over a period of weeks equal to double the period of the fine.[43]

6.92   A copy of any decision which leads to a player being fined or suspended shall be provided to the relevant league and The FA.[44] The club must keep a record of all cases of disciplinary action. However any warning or sanction given must be deleted after 12 months.[45]

---

40 This is in contrast to the ACAS code at p 20 which states: 'If an employee's first misconduct … is sufficiently serious, it may be appropriate to move directly to a final written warning. This might occur where the employee's actions have had, or are liable to have, a serious or harmful impact on the organisation.'

41 Note the express provision in the playing contract for a monetary fine, which is extremely unusual when compared to the usual employment relationship outside of sport.

42 Code of Practice and Notes on Contract, p 11.

43 Ibid, p 11.

44 Premier League Rule T.22, EFL Regulation 61.9 and FA Rule C1(m)(ii).

45 Schedule 1 Part 1, p 2 and p 4.2.

(b) Grievances

6.93   In the event that a player has any grievance related to his employment contract the procedure set out in his playing contract under clause 12 and Schedule 1 Part 2 is for him to raise the issue informally first of all with his manager.

6.94   If the matter is not resolved to the player's satisfaction, he may then serve a formal written notice of the grievance to the club secretary to be determined by the club's chairman or board within four weeks of receipt of his written notice. The player is entitled to be accompanied or represented in such procedure by his club captain, a PFA delegate or any officer of the PFA.

CHAPTER 7

Contracts – Managers

Paul Gilroy QC (Littleton Chambers & 9 St John Street)
and **Christopher Jeans QC** (11 KBW)

A   INTRODUCTION

7.1   A football manager's contract determines more than the parameters of his[1] legal entitlements and obligations. It sets the dynamic for the whole relationship between manager and club from its inception. Never has it been more important for football clubs and their managers to determine and understand their contractual obligations to each other.

7.2   Perhaps most important of all, the contract will deal with the arrangements which will apply on dismissal. For the modern day football manager, the question is usually when, rather than whether, he will be dismissed.

7.3   A dismissal can of course occur at any time. Until recently, football industry dismissals tended to 'spike' at certain times of the year, the so-called 'sacking windows'. It was generally expected that hiring and firing would be concentrated:

(a) during the close season;
(b) around 10 games after the start of a new season;
(c) early in the New Year; and
(d) 6 to 10 games before the end of the season.

In the current era, however, it has become common for manager dismissals to occur throughout the year. This can be explained by a range of factors, many of them outside the manager's control. One phenomenon is the mid-season takeover: new owners may want to appoint their own man.

7.4   Given the lack of security of tenure of the modern day football manager, the contractual provisions which will govern upon the termination of employment are of crucial importance. A manager will typically be appointed in a flurry of activity when time is at a premium. There will be a press conference. The manager will need to introduce himself to the players and the wider support staff at the football club. Typically, there will be a game for which he must prepare. The time spent on considering the contract of employment and digesting its terms will undoubtedly

---

[1]   We use the masculine to include the feminine for ease of reference. Whereas Hope Powell managed the Senior England Women's side for many years, and there are female referees officiating in English professional football, there has never, as yet, been a female manager of a league club in the UK.

pay dividends, particularly if, as is statistically probable, the manager is ultimately dismissed. Even Sir Alex Ferguson once suffered this fate.[2]

7.5   In the modern era, the dismissal of a football manager rarely carries with it any great stigma. It is seen as an occupational hazard. At some clubs the frequent replacement of the manager has become routine. From 2013 to 2017, Leeds United made no fewer than 11 managerial appointments,[3] whilst Cardiff City appointed eight. The shortest managerial reign in English football history is understood to be that of Leroy Rosenior. He is said to have been dismissed by Torquay just 10 minutes after taking the job, following a takeover of the club.

7.6   Every season, the bare statistics reveal the precarious position of managers in English professional football. To take the statistics from the 2016/17 season:[4]

(a)   Across the four professional leagues in England, comprising 92 clubs, 44 managers were dismissed. Add to this the figure of 19 resignations and it can be seen that there was a 68% 'churn' during the 2016/17 season.

(b)   Seven of the 20 Premier League managers parted company with their clubs. As of the time of writing, six Premier League managers have moved on during the first half of the 2017/18 season.

(c)   The average tenure of all dismissed managers in English professional football is[5] 1.16 years (1.31 years in the Premier League).

(d)   As of the conclusion of the 2016/17 season, the average tenure of all then serving managers was 1.66 years (2.68 in the Premier League). Ignoring the three longest serving managers (as of the time of writing Arsène Wenger at Arsenal, Paul Tisdale at Exeter City, and Jim Bentley at Morecambe), the longest serving manager in English professional football (Gareth Ainsworth at Wycombe Wanderers) had been with his club for only 4.68 years.

(e)   Half of first time managers who are dismissed never get another job as a football manager.

No modern day manager can enter employment with a football club with a comfortable notion of implementing a three-year plan.

7.7   Managerial turnover has implications for the development of the modern game. For example, it serves as a disincentive to nurturing young players, as the demands for instant success become ever more prevalent, and managers are driven to acquiring proven talent on the transfer market.

7.8   Some football clubs have template agreements for their managers. On appointment, the relevant club's pro forma document is adapted according to the personal circumstances of the appointee. Some managers' contracts, especially at the elite level, are lengthy documents, incorporating, for example, club policies on matters such as player transfers, and media, etc. Some contracts, particularly towards the lower level of domestic professional football, are far shorter and less detailed. Some contracts contain a range of terms which have been collected from various sources over the years. Not all of these 'collected' terms are particularly apposite for the purposes of the appointment in question. Careful scrutiny of the contract at the draft stage is essential for both parties.

2   https://www.theguardian.com/football/2008/may/31/manchesterunited.stmirren (accessed February 2018).

3   Albeit, on three occasions, the appointee was the same person, Neil Redfearn, taking the reins for the second, third and fourth time.

4   End of Season Managers' Statistics (League Managers Association) May 2017.

5   As of 31 May 2017.

B MANDATORY CONTRACT TERMS FOR PREMIER LEAGUE MANAGERS

7.9   Every season, the FA Premier League publishes a Handbook containing the updated version of the Premier League Rules. Any major rule changes require the approval of at least 14 out of the 20 clubs which constitute the Premier League at any one time. Section P of the current Premier League Rules deals with 'Managers'.

7.10   It is obligatory under the Premier League Rules for managers to conduct themselves in accordance with the Code of Conduct for Managers set out in Appendix 5 to the Premier League Rules (Rule P1) and for clubs to conduct themselves in relation to managers in accordance with the Code of Conduct for Clubs (Rule P2). Any failure by managers or clubs to conduct themselves in accordance with their respective Codes of Conduct will constitute a breach of Rule P3.

7.11   Rule P4 sets out the minimum coaching qualifications a Premier League manager must hold. Each manager shall either hold, or have commenced and be actively engaged on the requisite course to obtain, a valid UEFA Pro Licence (Rule P4.1), or hold the FA Coaching Diploma (Rule P4.2), or hold, or have commenced and be actively engaged on the requisite course to obtain, a valid diploma of a similar standard issued by another national association (Rule P4.3). Under Rule P5, no club shall employ any person as a manager who does not hold a qualification listed in Rule P4. Some dispensation is given in relation to coaching qualifications under Rule P6, which provides that the above general prohibitions shall not apply to managers until the expiry of 12 weeks from the date of their appointment and that this period can be extended by the Board of the Premier League if it is satisfied that a manager is acting as a temporary replacement for another who is medically unfit to resume his duties.

7.12   When the Premier League introduced the minimum coaching qualification standards, certain of the more established managers (who had begun their careers in a less regulated era) were granted official dispensation in recognition of their coaching credentials. It is unlikely that such an amnesty would ever be granted again by the Premier League.

7.13   The terms of the manager's employment must be evidenced in a written contract and a copy of this must be submitted to the Premier League within seven days of it coming into effect (Rule P7). Managers' contracts must include standard clauses in accordance with Appendix 7 to Section P (Rule P8.1), and must clearly set out the circumstances in which the contract of employment may be determined by either party (Rule P8.2).

7.14   In the Premier League, any dispute arising between the parties to a manager's contract with his club must be resolved under a special procedure whereby the claim is determined by the Managers' Arbitration Tribunal (Rule P12). The procedure is set out under Section Y of the Rules.

7.15   A Panel is appointed for the purposes of determining disputes under Section Y. The Premier League holds a list of Panel Members (not all of whom are legally qualified) who may sit on the Managers' Arbitration Tribunal.

7.16   Each party to the dispute nominates one member of the Panel. The two Arbitrators so appointed then select a third Arbitrator who must be a legally qualified member of the Panel. The third arbitrator sits as chairman of the Tribunal assigned to deal with the case.

7.17   A Premier League Club which applies for a UEFA Club Licence must, in addition to employing a manager, employ an individual (such as an assistant manager or head coach) to assist the manager in all football matters relating to the first team (Rule P13).

7.18   The English Football League (EFL), which is made up of the clubs playing in the Championship and Leagues One and Two, maintains (very limited) standard clauses for inclusion in managers' contracts. These include the obligation to comply with FA and League rules and a requirement to comply with reasonable instructions and requests arising out of commercial contracts concluded with the EFL.

7.19   Football industry stakeholders have engaged in discussions about introducing a standard manager's contract. Such a model contract – or at least the use of individual model clauses on particular issues – would have some obvious benefits. It could potentially reduce the scope for disputes and ultimately, litigation. Players in the Premier League and the EFL already have model contracts.

7.20   The League Managers Association has a model agreement for managers. A number of clubs have adopted it. Some clubs prefer to remain free to negotiate their own terms with their managers. Frequently, EFL clubs will incorporate the LMA Managers' Code of Conduct. There is an ongoing dialogue between the Premier League, the EFL and the LMA on the potential adoption of model clauses.

7.21   Clubs with experience of fluctuating between the Premier League and the Championship – the so-called 'yo-yo' clubs – will frequently enter a manager's contract which provides that the standard Premier League terms will come into effect as and when the club is a member of the Premier League. Such clubs may also seek to include terms which allow for downward variations in remuneration in the event of relegation.

7.22   Surprisingly, it has been known for a manager to have no written contract. Sometimes he will have a contract but it will not contain all the terms which have been expressly agreed. Matters such as bonus payments or particular benefits might be covered in side letters or memoranda. Another perhaps surprising feature is that the actual identity of the club as employer is sometimes not precisely defined. The club's legal identity is frequently not the name which appears in the match day programme. 'Come on The Liverpool Football Club and Athletic Grounds Limited' is a chant rarely heard at Anfield.

7.23   Outside the Premier League, club/manager disputes are handled either through the civil courts or arbitration, and in the case of the latter, typically under Rule K of The FA Rules.[6]

(a)   The period or 'term' of the employment as manager

7.24   The appointment of a football manager will usually be heralded in the media as an appointment for a fixed term ('manager signs 5-year contract'). However, where there is an appointment for a fixed term, such a term will often be subject to the right of either party to end the contract sooner by serving or imposing a specified period of notice, typically 12 months. This has the effect of limiting the financial liability of the terminating party if the contract is terminated before the fixed term expires.

6   See Chapter 28, Arbitration in Football.

7.25 Where there is a fixed term which is subject to the option of either party to serve notice prior to the expiry of that term, the contract will typically provide that if the employment continues until the conclusion of the fixed term it is deemed to expire on the last day of that fixed term, without the need of either party to serve notice. Sometimes managers' contracts do terminate in this way. It is far more usual, however (as is the case with a valued player), for a club to try to negotiate the extension of his contract around 12 months prior to the expiration of the then current fixed term.

7.26 If the club does not seek to renew or extend the manager's contract and a fixed term expires, the club will not (in the absence of a special provision in the contract) be acting in breach of the contract by not renewing it. In those circumstances, therefore, it will not be exposed to a claim for *wrongful* dismissal, that is to say, for terminating the contract in breach.

7.27 If, however, the manager has the requisite continuous service,[7] it will be open to the manager to claim *unfair* dismissal.[8] This is a statutory complaint which must be brought in the employment tribunal. Broadly, the success of an unfair dismissal claim depends on whether the employer had a permissible reason for dismissal and acted reasonably in treating it as sufficient to justify dismissal. Whether an employing club had a permissible reason or acted reasonably does not depend on whether the club was acting in breach of contract. In many cases, however, the obligations set out in the contract will nonetheless be relevant to fairness.

7.28 Given the financial ceiling[9] upon compensatory awards for unfair dismissal, football managers rarely consider it cost effective[10] to pursue a claim against their former clubs in the employment tribunal.

(b) Scope of the manager's role and authority

7.29 It is highly advisable for the scope of the manager's role and authority to be clearly defined in his contract.

7.30 Lack of clarity can lead to disagreement on such fundamental matters as (i) the manager's authority in relation to the sale and purchase of players, and (ii) potentially overlapping issues concerning the manager's authority within the hierarchy of the club structure and the interplay between his roles and responsibilities and those of a 'Director of Football' or similar.

---

7   Currently two years. Note that a period of continuous service is not needed if the dismissal is for certain 'automatically unfair' reasons; see s 108 of the Employment Rights Act 1996 (ERA 1996).

8   The statute deems the non-renewal of the contract to be a 'dismissal' for the purposes of the law of unfair dismissal: see ERA 1996, s 95.

9   For cases where the effective date of termination falls on or after 6 April 2018, the statutory cap on the compensatory award for unfair dismissal is £83,682. This figure is uprated annually. Since July 2013 the maximum compensatory award for unfair dismissal has been the lower of the statutory cap or 52 weeks' pay (actual gross pay for the employee, calculated at the time of dismissal). This is subject to certain exceptions. Importantly the limit is inapplicable where the dismissal is on certain specially prohibited grounds: see ERA 1996, s 124. In addition to a compensatory award, successful unfair dismissal claimants typically receive a basic award, for all intents and purposes (and subject to minor exceptions) the equivalent of a statutory redundancy payment.

10 The cost-benefit test is rarely made out in such circumstances, and legal costs are not typically awarded to the successful party in the employment tribunal.

7.31   Such issues lay at the heart of two high profile cases before the Premier League Managers' Arbitration Tribunal, *Keegan v Newcastle United*[11] and *Curbishley v West Ham United*. Both cases concerned the transfer of players without the manager's approval: in the former case a purchase; in the latter a sale.

7.32   Kevin Keegan resigned from his post at Newcastle United in September 2008, less than eight months into his second managerial spell at that club. He successfully claimed that the club had acted in breach of his contract by signing the Uruguayan player, Ignacio Gonzalez, expressly against his wishes immediately before the summer transfer deadline. He asserted that, as the manager, he had the contractual right to have the final say on transfers. The written contract was silent on this issue. It provided that Keegan would 'perform such duties as may be usually associated with the position of Manager of a Premier League Team' but did not explain what these duties might cover in relation to transfers. The club had told the manager at interview that it was proposed to introduce a Director of Football at the club. The club contended that it was implicit in this structure that the club, and not the manager, would have the final say on transfers, although statements in the club programme appeared to contradict this. The club argued that it was nonetheless within the scope of its authority to sign a player without the manager's approval, at least where the deal was 'commercial'. Here, the club said, the deal was commercial: the signing of the player on loan would stand as a 'favour' to influential South American agents who would look favourably on the club in the future. The manager objected to the transaction, protesting that no-one at the club had seen Gonzalez play and that he was not prepared to agree to his acquisition on the basis of some clips from You Tube. The manager resigned, contending that the club's actions in ignoring his wishes amounted to a fundamental breach of contract entitling him to resign and claim constructive dismissal. The Managers' Arbitration Tribunal agreed with him and upheld his claim. It concluded that the 'duties usually associated with the position of Premier League manager' included 'the right, indeed the duty to have the final say as to transfers into the Club'. The manager's claim to 'stigma damages', for the effect of this matter on his future earning capacity, was dismissed. The Panel upheld a clause in his contract which limited compensation to £2 million following dismissal or resignation. It further concluded that the manager's reputation would be restored by the publication of the Tribunal's decision.

7.33   Hot on the heels of the Keegan case came the matter of *Curbishley v West Ham United*. In this case, the manager claimed that he was similarly entitled to resign after the club sold a player, George McCartney, to Sunderland, against his wishes. The manager had an express clause in his contract which provided that 'the manager alone' had final say on transfers. Whilst acknowledging the existence of the clause, the club argued that the provision had to be read subject to the right of the club to act in its best interests in the event that financial considerations dictated whether a transaction should take place. The club maintained that it was essential for this transaction to take place irrespective of the manager's wishes. Some months before the McCartney transfer, West Ham had sold Anton Ferdinand, also against the manager's wishes. On the occasion of the Ferdinand transfer, the manager had protested, referring to the relevant clause in his contract, and was given assurances that there would be no repetition of such a sale without his approval, only for the McCartney transfer to proceed without his input. The Managers' Arbitration Tribunal

11   The decisions of arbitrators and arbitration panels in football cases are rarely made public. Decisions of the Premier League Managers' Arbitration Tribunal are never published unless the parties consent. *Keegan* is a rare example of a published decision of the Tribunal: [2010] IRLR 94.

upheld the manager's claim, dismissing the club's argument that it was entitled to override the relevant clause in his contract because it faced impending financial crisis if the sale did not take place.

7.34   The *Keegan* and *Curbishley* cases demonstrate the need for clarity about lines of authority as between club and manager when it comes to player transfers.

7.35   Historically, football clubs in this country have adopted the 'traditional' English approach, whereby authority (or at least the final word) on transfers vests in the manager. There is nonetheless a discernible shift in the domestic game towards the 'Continental' structure, whereby the manager deals with football matters, whilst the financial side of the business is controlled by other executives and/or the board of directors. The Continental system will frequently involve the appointment of a director of football or similar,[12] and when a club adopts such a structure it is more than desirable (as the *Keegan* case illustrates) for the manager's contract to set out explicitly and carefully the respective roles and responsibilities of manager and director of football.

7.36   To state the obvious, it is not safe to assume that a manager's role (whether it relates to transfers or any other function at the club) can be derived from the tasks the club gives to others. In *McBride v Falkirk Football Club*,[13] James McBride was appointed 'manager/head coach' of the under-19 team. It was expressly agreed that he would have control of that team. At the time of his appointment, the position of youth academy director was vacant. When the club filled the vacant post, it decided that the new appointee would henceforth select the under 19 team and that Mr McBride's role would become more limited. He resigned and alleged that he had been constructively dismissed. The club argued that it was implicit that Mr McBride's role would change when the youth academy director post was filled. The argument was successful before the employment tribunal but the Employment Appeal Tribunal (EAT)[14] reversed the decision. It did not follow from the vacancy of the director post that Mr McBride's authority over team selection would cease when the role was filled. Referring to the reasoning in *Keegan*, the EAT held that in undermining his authority over the team the club had fundamentally breached the contract. Accordingly, the club had constructively dismissed him.

7.37   Similarly, Leeds United was held liable to an assistant manager for constructive dismissal when he resigned on being told by the club to cease working with the first team and to confine his role to youth and reserve players: *Gibbs v Leeds United FC*.[15] The contract contained no power to restrict his activities in that way.

7.38   It is advisable that the contract also makes express provision on:

(a) the extent to which the manager is responsible for the employment of other employees at the club, aside from playing staff;
(b) the extent to which the manager is required to (or is free to) speak to the media;
(c) the extent to which the manager has to engage in the club's commercial and community activities;

---

12   Eg 'sporting director'. Sometimes roles may be combined. In *Milanese v Leyton Orient* [2016] EWHC 1161 the claimant was appointed Director of Football, to act as 'sporting director' *and* 'caretaker manager'.
13   [2012] IRLR 22.
14   Employment Appeal Tribunal (Scotland).
15   [2016] EWHC 960 (QB); see para **5.26** above.

(d) the identity of the person to whom the manager reports and who reports to the manager, and

(e) whether the manager is responsible for the first team alone, or whether he has a wider remit.

All of the above issues have formed the basis of litigation between clubs and their managers over the last decade.

7.39   If there are particular issues of concern to either party about the circumstances of the other, it may be worth formulating a specific clause to deal with the matter rather than to rely on 'gentlemen's agreements' or 'understandings', the existence, substance and effect[16] of which can be hotly disputed in litigation. By way of example, a club concerned that the manager is living too far from the club's stadium or its training ground might consider inserting a requirement that the manager reside within a specified radius. Breach of such a requirement was found to justify summary dismissal in *Macari v Celtic Football and Athletic Club*.[17] Some clubs will be content with the manager maintaining a private residence within a set distance from the stadium or training ground. Others may seek a clause which provides that the manager's *main* private residence shall meet this criterion.

(c)   Remuneration

7.40   Unless there is some express provision about the matter, a manager's salary does not vary according to the success or failure of the team. However, it is common to include an express provision that the manager's salary will be reduced to a specified level if the team is relegated. The contract may also provide for an increase in the event of promotion. The date upon which the rate of salary changes following promotion or relegation in any given season can be of critical importance. It can, for example, affect the level of compensation the manager is entitled to in the event of dismissal.

7.41   The point is illustrated by *Manchester City Football Club plc v Royle*.[18] The case concerned the interpretation of ambiguous expressions in a liquidated damages clause. This provided for different termination payments to be made to the manager depending on whether the club was in the Premier League or the former First Division of the Football League (now the EFL Championship) at the date upon which his employment was terminated. The manager had been dismissed following the conclusion of the 2000/01 season after the club had completed its fixtures and been relegated – but not before the full season had ended. When the club's relegation from the Premier League was confirmed, the manager was paid compensation on the basis that he was a First Division manager. He claimed that, with the season incomplete, he was still a Premier League manager and was therefore entitled to a higher sum in liquidated damages.

7.42   The manager succeeded in the High Court but the Court of Appeal overturned the ruling, holding that, for the purposes of determining the appropriate

---

16   Some managers' contracts will contain an 'Entire Agreement' clause specifying that there are no terms outside the written agreement and that no pre-contract representations have been relied on by the other party. The effect of such clauses can be open to debate but their presence underscores the importance of reflecting important matters in the contract itself.

17   [1999] IRLR 787; see para 5.32 et seq.

18   [2005] EWCA Civ 195.

rate of liquidated damages, the club was a First Division club with the consequence that the lower rate was payable. A club which is relegated from the Premier League has to relinquish its share in the Premier League, essentially its membership card to the elite professional division in English football. The Court of Appeal approached the issue on the basis that a reasonable person with knowledge of the game would understand that relegation from a division is effective following the final game of the season – and not the moment when the club transfers its Premier League share.

(d)   Bonus payments

7.43   Managers' contracts typically contain provisions for the payment of performance-related bonuses. In the lower leagues this can take the form of the manager being entitled to the same 'win/draw' bonus as members of the first team squad. The more usual arrangement, however, especially further up the football pyramid, is to include a provision for a bonus which is payable by reference to the club's league position at the conclusion of the season, and separate bonuses to reflect cup success (or progress to particular rounds).

(e)   Accrual of the right to bonus

7.44   There is an important difference between the date upon which the entitlement to the finishing league position bonus *accrues* – the date when it has been *earned* – and the date upon which the manager *shall be paid* that bonus. Invariably, Premier League clubs require that finishing league position bonus payments are made towards the end of the summer as a means of assisting cash flow, by reference to the timing of the television payments clubs receive in the close season. From the manager's perspective, it is important that the entitlement is specified in the contract as accruing upon the achievement of the relevant event, regardless of the date upon which the payment is made.

7.45   The accrual date was central in *Crystal Palace FC Limited v Tony Pulis*, a case which came before the Premier League Managers' Arbitration Tribunal, and subsequently before the High Court, when the manager sought to challenge the Arbitration panel's conclusions, in 2016.[19]

7.46   In that case, a £2million bonus was payable to the manager if (i) the club avoided relegation in 2013/14 *and* (ii) the manager remained employed on 31 August 2014. The club duly avoided relegation in 2013/14. In early August 2014, the manager asked for early payment of his bonus, assuring the club that he remained committed to it but explaining that he needed the money to fund a land purchase for his children. The club paid the money on 12 August. The manager resigned on 14 August. The manager said that his commitment to the club had been affected by a heated meeting on that day. The club claimed it was entitled to repayment of the bonus money and succeeded. The Arbitration Tribunal found that the manager had acted dishonestly in procuring the early payment: the heated meeting had taken place on 8 August and had not precipitated any sudden loss of commitment on 12 August; and there was no imminent land purchase which the manager needed to fund. The Arbitral Tribunal's judgment was upheld by the High Court.

---

19   [2016] EWHC 2999 (Comm).

7.47   It need hardly be pointed out that whilst the facts are highly specific, the case illustrates the value to a club (and the disadvantages to a manager) of making a bonus dependent on his continuing to serve at a date within a future season. This type of provision, which is commonly found in the bonus clauses of city bankers, is likely to be upheld as valid in principle.[20]

(f)   Pro rata bonus

7.48   Given their lack of security of tenure, it is generally prudent for modern football managers to ensure that their contracts contain a pro rata bonus provision to cater for dismissal mid-season. By way of illustration, a manager may be entitled to a £1 million bonus for his club retaining Premier League status at the conclusion of a given season. Suppose the manager is dismissed after 19 games during the relevant season, ie after half of his club's first team league games, and the club goes on to retain its Premier League status at the end of the season. Unless the matter is expressly addressed in the contract of employment, the club is not likely to pay him a bonus to reflect his contribution to the retention of Premier League status, and it will be difficult to argue that any part of that bonus has in law been earned. Often the contract will positively stipulate that no finishing league position bonus will be payable in the event that the manager is not in the employment of the club when the last league game of the season is played. Such a provision is likely to be valid, though a manager who is wrongfully dismissed may succeed in recovering a proportion of the bonus as damages for wrongful dismissal to reflect the chance that he would have earned the bonus but for his dismissal.

7.49   Where there is an express provision for payment of pro rata bonus, it will typically stipulate that the relevant sum is to be calculated by reference to the number of points gained during the manager's tenure in the given season, expressed as a percentage of the club's final end of season points tally. It is a generally accepted practice for clubs to agree to some form of pro rata bonus mechanism to cater for this situation.

C   TERMINATION OF EMPLOYMENT

(a)   Summary termination

7.50   A manager's contract will normally contain an express provision specifying the circumstances in which the club can terminate it summarily, that is to say immediately and without awaiting the expiry of any fixed term, or of notice.

7.51   Whilst there may sometimes be provisions entitling the club to terminate summarily in very specific situations (such as where the manager is convicted of a crime, or becomes bankrupt) the principal grounds for summary termination by the club are often expressed in a very generalised way such as 'serious breach' or 'gross misconduct' or 'repeated failure' (perhaps 'after warning') 'to observe the terms of this Agreement'.

7.52   Grounds for summary termination by the manager (ie where the manager can treat himself as constructively dismissed) are not normally specified, but every

---

20   It will not, for example, be vulnerable to attack under the Unfair Contract Terms Act 1977: see *Commerzbank v Keen* [2007] ICR 623.

contract of employment contains an implied term of trust and confidence. The employer must not without reasonable and proper cause conduct itself in such a way as to destroy or seriously damage trust and confidence between the parties.[21] A breach of this term can entitle the manager to terminate summarily.[22] This term is widely invoked by managers in constructive dismissal cases, at least where there is any doubt as to whether the club has breached an express term or has breached it sufficiently seriously.

7.53   In the absence of an express power of termination a contract can always be terminated summarily if one party commits a 'repudiatory' breach – a fundamental breach going to the root of the contract – and the other party accepts the breach by ending the contract.

7.54   Subject to any special provisions in the contract, the right to terminate summarily will however be waived if the 'innocent' party fails to act promptly in bringing the contract to an end in response to the other side's wrongdoing. This applies equally to manager and club. There have been many cases where a club's decision to take no action over misconduct of which it has been aware has entailed a waiver of the right to terminate, or, as it is sometimes put 'an affirmation' of the contract by the club.[23] This is a workplace which is subject to significant public scrutiny and media coverage. A club's contention that the manager committed an act of gross misconduct so serious that it justified his immediate dismissal on a Wednesday can often be countered with television footage of the manager sitting in the dugout at the club's next match the following Saturday.[24]

7.55   Whether wrongdoing by club or manager (as the case may be) is sufficiently serious to justify termination by the other under an express clause or under the general principle of repudiatory breach is often said to be a question of fact and degree – a 'jury question' which the tribunal or court may sometimes answer in either direction without being wrong in law (and so without being liable to reversal on appeal). The same can be said for the question as to whether the right to terminate summarily has been waived, and/or the contract affirmed.

7.56   Where there has been a series of incidents, the last of which is not sufficiently serious to justify summary termination on its own, the innocent party may seek to contend that the final incident was a 'last straw'. When taken together with the earlier incidents, the argument will run, there is (cumulatively) a sufficiently serious breach to justify summary termination; and, it will be argued, delaying termination until that last straw does not involve a waiver of the right to terminate because it is the amalgam of incidents which creates the right of termination.

7.57   Whether such a case can be made out will again be largely a matter of fact and degree. But a club relying on a last straw may have difficulty if no action was taken (eg a warning) about the earlier incidents.[25] Equally a manager relying on a series of incidents to establish a constructive dismissal may also struggle to establish his case if he has not previously made clear his mounting objections to the incidents he is invoking in support of his right to terminate.

---

21   *Malik and Mahmud v BCCI* [1997] ICR 606.
22   See eg, *Morrow v Safeway Stores* [2002] IRLR 9.
23   By way of example only: *Welsh v Cowdenbeath* [2009] CSOH 16.
24   Evidence to prove that a manager had not resigned (ie that he was still managing the first team after the alleged date of resignation) was led in *Macari v Stoke City FC* [High Court 2006], and *O'Leary v Al Ahli FC* [FIFA 2013] and CAS 2014.
25   See eg *Welsh* (n 23 above).

(b)   Damages and mitigation

7.58   Frequently, a club with no sufficient grounds for summary dismissal will nonetheless dismiss the manager without the requisite notice and before the expiry of any fixed term.

7.59   The manager's normal[26] remedy for such a breach is damages. In the absence of a liquidated damages clause (see below) the starting point for calculating damages is to take the manager's contractual entitlements up to the earliest date when he could lawfully have been dismissed. So if there is a fixed term of three years (with no provision for earlier termination by notice) and he has served exactly a year, the starting point will be two years' entitlements; if the employment was terminable on one year's notice (and any fixed term would have expired later) the starting point will be one year's contractual entitlements.

7.60   Where a contractual entitlement such as a bonus is contingent on a future uncertain event (eg success in a cup or league) it may be necessary (in the absence of a clause regulating the position) to value that entitlement by reference to the 'loss of a chance', the damages being a proportion of the bonus reflecting the probability that it would have been achieved (ie awarding 30% of the bonus if there was a 30% chance of achieving it). A tribunal or court adjudicating on the value of a bonus payable for, say, Champions League qualification will then have to engage in a degree of football 'punditry': what is the probability that the team would have qualified for the Champions League if the manager had stayed in place for the contractual period? Even if the team's ultimate success or otherwise is known by the time of the hearing, this will not be conclusive: inevitably one side or the other will say that results would have been different if the manager had continued.

7.61   A claim for damages is based on proven loss. Accordingly, once the contractual entitlements have been calculated for the additional period of employment to which the manager was entitled, there must be deducted anything which he has earned *or ought reasonably to have earned* in mitigation of that loss ie sums from alternative employment[27] during the period.

7.62   The onus of proving that the dismissed manager has failed to make reasonable efforts (and of proving what he would have earned if he had made reasonable efforts) lies on the club. Because the club is the wrongdoer in this situation the sympathy of the tribunal or court is generally with the manager and the duty to mitigate is not especially exacting, in theory[28] or in practice. Moreover, the limited managerial vacancies at any one time (and the usual plethora of candidates) create real problems of proof for clubs. But difficult questions may nonetheless arise. Has the manager acted unreasonably, focusing only on jobs at the same level at which

---

26   Injunctions are not normally available to prolong contracts of employment, although there are limited circumstances when an injunction can be obtained, for example, to compel compliance with a disciplinary procedure if one has been incorporated. Following a recent decision of the Supreme Court (*Geys v Soc Gen* [2013] ICR 117) it may be possible in theory for a manager to delay the effectiveness of an unlawful dismissal by refusing to 'accept' it as terminating the contract. The courts have still to map out the scope and consequences of this phenomenon. Clubs have also been known to deploy the weapon of an interim injunction against a manager seeking to depart without serving due notice and/or before the 'old' club and the 'new' club have agreed on appropriate compensation to reflect the move (*Crystal Palace v Bruce and Birmingham City* [2002] SLR 81).

27   Including work other than as a manager (eg television work) so long as it is earned *instead* of his former earnings at the club (and would not have been earned if the manager had still been employed by the club).

28   See eg *Fyfe v ScientificFurnishings Ltd* [1989] ICR 648.

he was previously managing? Should he have lowered his sights more quickly? Should he have been open to offers in a distant location or a foreign country? These are yet further questions of 'fact and degree' for the tribunal or court to decide according to the particular facts.

7.63   Where it is the manager who has terminated the contract unlawfully, the club can in principle claim damages for its losses for the minimum period (fixed term or notice) the manager was obliged to serve. Those losses will often be minimal or difficult to prove. A club sacking its manager will rarely claim that he would have brought the club great success if he had remained. Provable loss can potentially include the costs of hiring a replacement at short notice[29] and any additional remuneration (above the departing manager's remuneration) the club has had to pay the replacement over the period the manager ought contractually to have remained.

7.64   The difficulty of showing loss if the manager departs early sometimes leads the club to introduce a clause specifying an amount to be paid by a manager if he leaves in breach of contract. Such clauses are potentially vulnerable to attack (see the discussion of liquidated damages and penalties below).

7.65   An alternative approach, would be for the club to place the manager on 'garden leave' (see paras **7.76–7.79** below) for a short period[30] and seek an injunction restraining him from accepting employment with another club, or at least with a club in the same league, in that period. Such garden leave injunctions are common in certain industries. But they are rare in football, where a clean break is usually preferred once relations have broken down. It is also questionable whether the conditions for obtaining such injunctions would often be satisfied: for example, the club would normally be expected to show that significant damage could ensue from the manager's working for another club. Unless, perhaps, the two clubs are about to meet in a crucial fixture, this may be difficult to show.

(c)   Liquidated damages

7.66   Across all four domestic professional leagues, many managers' contracts will contain 'liquidated damages' clauses, that is to say provisions which specify the amount of compensation payable either way in the event of the early termination of a fixed term where there are no grounds for summary termination.

7.67   It is frequently the case that the amount of compensation payable by the club in such circumstances will be substantially higher than the figure the manager is obliged to pay in the event that he wishes to terminate his contract early. The benefit of such a clause is that it is supposed to give certainty as to the level of compensation which will be payable in defined circumstances, thereby reducing the scope for dispute and, ultimately, litigation.

7.68   A liquidated damages clause will sometimes be attacked on the footing that the clause is a 'penalty' and therefore unenforceable.

---

29   There may be issues as to whether costs would nonetheless have been incurred in hiring the next manager even if due notice had been given by the outgoing manager.
30   Certainly not longer than the unexpired period of the contract and possibly for a significantly shorter period. In summary, lengthy garden leave may be unenforceable by injunction for reasons of public policy.

7.69   Such an attack was attempted in *Berg v Blackburn Rovers FC*.[31] Henning Berg was appointed as the manager of Blackburn on a three year fixed term contract in November 2012. He was dismissed after 57 days. His dismissal triggered a clause in his contract under which he became entitled to a payment of his basic salary for the balance of his fixed term, a sum equating to £2.25 million. The payment was based upon a formula contained in his service agreement which specified the sum payable in such circumstances. (It was, therefore, misleading for the media to report that his level of compensation amounted to 'almost £40,000 for every day he had worked'.) Initially the club admitted the claim and sought time to pay. It then applied to the High Court to withdraw its admission on two grounds, namely (i) that the managing director who had agreed the relevant term of the contract did not have the authority to do so, and (ii) that the term in question constituted a penalty. The High Court dismissed both arguments and ordered the club to pay the full amount. It was held that the law on penalties was not engaged because the trigger for payment was not itself a breach of contract. The court applied the well-established principle that the penalty doctrine is restricted to cases where the sum is payable for *breach* of contract; it does not apply where the triggering event is not a breach.[32]

7.70   Suppose, however, the sum is expressed to be payable in the event of a breach of contract? In this instance the clause imposing an excessive liability may be attacked as a penalty. Until recently, the courts distinguished penalties from liquidated damages clauses based on the tests set out by Lord Dunedin in *Dunlop Pneumatic Tyre Co Ltd v New Garage and Motor Co Ltd*,[33] which focused on establishing whether the clause involved a 'genuine pre-estimate' of the loss. In *Cavendish Square v El Makdessi*,[34] the Supreme Court has revised the approach. The real question is now whether the clause imposes a detriment on the contract breaker which is out of all proportion to the innocent party's legitimate interests.

7.71   Commentators have suggested that after *El Makdessi* it will be harder to succeed in arguing that a liquidated damages clause amounts to a penalty. The courts may well be more inclined to uphold clauses providing for payments on breach. *El Makdessi* supposes that the best judges of the commercial issues arising in circumstances such as early termination are the parties to the contract themselves. At least where there is some parity of bargaining power, there may now be a presumption that such clauses will be held valid.

(d)   PILON clauses

7.72   Sometimes a manager's contract will include a provision whereby the club has the option of terminating the contract by paying salary (and it may also be specified other benefits) in lieu of the notice it was obliged to give.

7.73   Since the club is in these circumstances terminating in accordance with the contract,[35] rather than in breach of it, there is no calculation of damages required and no issue of mitigation arises. Calculating the sum due is relatively straightforward. So achieving a clean break is all the simpler. Such a clause is not likely to be considered a penalty even if the notice period is lengthy.

---

31   [2013] EWCH 1070 (Ch); see para **5.14** above.
32   *Export Credits Guarantee Dept v Universal Oil Products* [1983] 1 WLR 399; *Cavendish Square v El Makdessi* [2015] UKSC 67.
33   [1915] AC 79.
34   [2015] UKSC 67.
35   See eg *Abrahams v Performing Rights Society* [1995] ICR 1028.

7.74   The end result may however be expensive for the club if the contract had a lengthy period to run since there will be no deduction for mitigation, whatever alternative employment is obtained, or could have been obtained, by the manager.

7.75   A halfway house sometimes adopted is a clause whereby salary continues for the contractual period only until alternative employment is in fact obtained. (This is reported to have applied to Sven Goran Eriksson's contract with The FA). Such a clause can be coupled with further provision that the manager is obliged to seek further employment and/or that he will be compensated for any shortfall as between his old and new remuneration.

(e) Garden leave

7.76   If a club inserts a garden leave provision in its manager's contract, this will enable the club to instruct the manager to 'down tools' on condition that he continues to receive his normal salary and other benefits. Under the general law, it is unlikely that a club will be entitled to impose garden leave if no express clause has been included in the contract (*William Hill Organisation Ltd v Tucker*).[36]

7.77   The concept of garden leave was originally created to protect an employer in circumstances where an employee was seeking to leave his or her employment in order to work for a competitor. In this guise, such clauses could be seen as a defensive mechanism to afford protection to an employer of its legitimate business interests.

7.78   In professional football, however, garden leave can often be used as a tool to focus the manager's mind on reaching a compromise to terminate the employment altogether.[37]

7.79   By way of illustration, a Premier League manager may earn a salary of, say £3m per annum. Suppose he has an entitlement to 12 months' notice of termination. His club elects to place him on garden leave. In such circumstances he will be entitled to continue to receive his salary and benefits for as long as the garden leave period continues or, if notice of termination has been served, for a period of 12 months. At some point during the garden leave there is a distinct likelihood that he will wish to secure an alternative managerial position. The alternative post may be at a lesser salary. If the manager wishes to take up the alternative position he will be losing out financially. In such circumstances, it makes sense for the manager and the outgoing club to reach agreement that he will accept the alternative position and receive from the outgoing club the payment of a lump sum approximating to the difference between his old and new salary until the end of his notice period. This gives the club the benefit of a discount from the overall liability it would have if the manager did not obtain alternative employment. At the same time the manager can progress his career.

36   [1998] EWCA Civ 615.
37   See further the discussion of garden leave in Chapter 5, Employment Law and Football, paras **5.40–5.43**.

CHAPTER 8

Player Transfers

Stephen Sampson (Squire Patton Boggs) and **Liz Coley** (Walker Morris)

A   THE NECESSITY OF REGISTRATION

8.1   In order to be eligible to participate for a club in 'organised football'[1] within the meaning of the FIFA Regulations on the Status and Transfer of Players (RSTP)[2] a player must be registered for that club at an association.[3] Similarly, in order to participate in a particular competition a player must be registered with the competition organiser.[4]

8.2   In professional football generally an employed player may be registered with one club only.[5] When a player ceases playing for one club in order to play for another club the registration must be transferred. From this process the 'transfer system' has developed.

B   WHAT THE TRANSFER SYSTEM IS

8.3   A registration is transferred when: (i) a player who is not currently employed but has previously been registered with an old club seeks registration for a new club, most commonly in conjunction with the player taking up employment with the new club[6] (an 'out of contract player'); (ii) when an employed player, his current club

---

1   Defined as 'association football organised under the auspices of FIFA, the confederations and the associations, or authorised by them'.
2   See https://resources.fifa.com/mm/document/affederation/administration/02/70/95/52/regulationson thestatusandtransferofplayersjune2016_e_neutral.pdf (accessed February 2018).
3   RSTP, Article 5.1; See FA Rule C1(b)(ii) 'All players under written contract must be registered with The Association'.
4   See eg Premier League Rule U.1 'A Player shall not play for a Club in a League Match unless that Club holds his registration …'. For the categories of registration permitted see Rule U.9. EFL Regulation 41.2 'No Player may play in any competition organised by The League unless and until his registration has been so approved.' For the categories or registration permitted see Regulation 43.1.
5   See FA Rule C1(i)(i), Premier League Rule U.25. The FA Rules C2(a) permit players who are not employed to be registered with more than one club.
6   See Premier League Rule V.15 and EFL Regulation 45.3.

and a new club agree that the player may cease employment with the current club and take up employment with the new club; and (iii) when an employed player, his current club and a new club agree that the player will go 'on loan' to a new club.[7]

8.4 In England and Wales there are no laws specifically enacted to govern the transfer system. Instead the governing bodies and competition organisers adopt rules to regulate certain aspects of the transfer system.[8] The rules applicable to the transfer system are those promulgated by The Football Association (The FA),[9] The Premier League or The English Football League (EFL) (as relevant)[10] and, for international transfers, the RSTP.[11]

8.5 Those aspects where regulation is deemed necessary or appropriate include, among other things:

- restrictions on when a club and player may communicate over a prospective transfer;
- notification of who at a club has authority to negotiate and approve transfers;
- the due diligence that a new club should undertake;
- the documents necessary to effect a transfer;
- the content of those documents;
- whether and which documents must be submitted to the governing body for pre-approval before execution;
- which documents must be lodged with the governing body;
- restrictions on when a player may be transferred;
- transparency over the payment of transfer fees;
- who may benefit from the transfer fees;
- a restriction over a third party having any influence in the transfer or employment of players;
- the transfer of minors; and
- compensation for the clubs involved in the training and development of the player.

Those rules seek to strike a balance between the interests of the governing bodies and competition organisers, clubs, players and fans and, in particular, the employment rights of the players and the objectives of competitive balance and the integrity of competition.[12]

---

7   Where a player is transferred temporarily (or 'loaned') within England, effectively the player is seconded to the new club as the current employment contract remains effective. On international loans, the employment contract is suspended and an employment contract with the new club is executed. See para **8.75** below on loan transfers.
8   Those rules have to be lawful otherwise they are susceptible to challenge. A review of the justifications for and legality of transfer rules can be found in Lewis & Taylor, *Sport: Law and Practice*, 3rd Edition (Bloomsbury Professional, 2013), Chapter H4.
9   See, *inter alia*, FA Rule C1(g), Premier League Rules Section V, EFL Regulations Section 6.
10   Transfers to or from clubs playing in other leagues are also subject to the rules of that particular league.
11   Note that on 6 November 2017, FIFA and FIFPro announced that they had signed a six-year cooperation agreement which included, *inter alia*, an agreement to establish a task force to study and conduct a review of the transfer system. See https://www.fifpro.org/news/fifa-and-fifpro-sign-landmark-agreement/en/ (accessed February 2018).
12   For a detailed review of the transfer rules in place in European sport in general see the KEA – CDES: Study on the economic and legal aspects of transfer of players available at http://ec.europa.eu/assets/eac/sport/library/documents/cons-study-transfers-final-rpt.pdf (accessed February 2018). Note that FIFPro considers that the operation of international transfer systems 'sustains increasing competitive and financial disparity, invites commercial abuse by third party owners and agents and fails to protect players against abuses of their labour contracts via systematic non-payment'. On 18 September 2015 FIFPro filed a complaint with DG Comp of the European Commission;

8.6   Transfers of registration between clubs both playing in England are domestic transfers and subject only to the rules of The FA and the relevant league(s).[13] Transfers of registration between a team playing in England and a team playing in the country or territory of another national association (including Scotland, Wales and Northern Ireland) are international transfers and subject, in addition, to the rules of FIFA.[14] Such international transfers require the issuance of an International Transfer Certificate (ITC) before the new national association may confirm the eligibility of the player[15] and are administered through the online FIFA Transfer Matching System (TMS).[16]

8.7   The transfer of registration of an out of contract player is the least regulated and procedurally simplest transaction. The transfer is necessary as the old club is the last registered holder of the registration. The old club may retain an entitlement to compensation from the new club (and other clubs with whom the player registers) arising from the fact that it held the registration of the player and assisted in the training and development of the player.[17] TMS reports that in 2016 of 14,591 international transfers, 66.2% concerned out of contract players.[18]

8.8   Where the transfer concerns a player who is changing employment prior to the expiry of his employment contract with his current club, the process is more complex. This scenario sees the player and the current club terminate their employment contract and the player and the new club enter into a new employment contract and request the transfer of the registration. Commonly in such a scenario a transfer fee will be paid by the new club to the current club, as compensation for the early termination of the employment contract between the player and the current club and the loss of the benefit of the services of such player during the otherwise unexpired term of the employment contract. These are the transfers which, in addition to being most complex, create the headlines around the transfer system. It is reported that in the 2015/16 season Premier League clubs spent £1.3 billion on transfer fees, with EFL clubs spending a further £187 million.[19]

C   APPROACHES TO PLAYERS

8.9   'We tapped more players in our time than the Severn Trent Water Authority', Brian Clough is reported to have said. Is this practice any less prevalent 40 years on?

8.10   A regular problem faced by football clubs of all levels worldwide is that of illegal approaches to their contracted players with a view to encouraging them to join a new club, known commonly as 'tapping up'. The regulations relating to approaches to players vary between domestic and international movements.

---

see further Chapter 4, European Law in relation to Football, paras **4.125–4.126**. FIFPro's complaint led to the agreement announced on 6 November 2017 (see n 11 above).

13   See, *inter alia*, FA Rule C1(g), Premier League Rules Section V; EFL Regulations Section 6.
14   See para **8.1** above.
15   See RSTP, Article 9(1). In some instances an ITC is not issued but the national association is authorised by FIFA to register the player, for example where the old club raises a contractual dispute with the player and the national association of the new club applies to the FIFA Player Status Committee for a provisional registration.
16   See para **8.41** below.
17   See Premier League Rule V.17; EFL Regulation 65.
18   https://www.fifatms.com/data-reports/reports/ (accessed February 2018).
19   https://edu.deloitte.cz/en/Content/DownloadPublication/footbal-finance-2017 (accessed February 2018).

8.11   The Premier League Rules deal with approaches to contracted players at T1-4. A club is permitted to approach an out of contract player, or any player, with the prior written permission of the club he is registered with at any time. After the third Saturday in May of a season, a club is permitted to approach a player who will be out of contract as at 1 July that year who has not received an offer of re-engagement from his current club which is on no less favourable terms than his existing agreement or who has received such offer but rejected it. The EFL Regulations broadly mirror the Premier League Rules in this respect.

8.12   For an approach to be deemed illegal, it does not have to have come from an official of another club; it can be a direct or indirect approach from a contracted player himself to a new club or an approach from an intermediary or third party on behalf of another club or the contracted player by any means whatsoever.

8.13   The position internationally is somewhat different. Under Article 18.3 of the RSTP, a club intending to conclude a contract with a professional player must inform the contracted player's current club in writing before entering into negotiations with him. A professional player shall only be free to conclude a contract with another club if his contract with his present club has expired or is due to expire within six months. This regulation is often used as a negotiating tool at domestic level by many intermediaries, as the threat to a club of losing a promising young player internationally for the much smaller levels of international training compensation under the RSTP may be enough to secure an earlier improved contract for the player.

8.14   The substantial fines and sanctions levied on clubs and individuals for breaching these regulations do not seem to have deterred this type of behaviour and no doubt what is actually reported to the football authorities is just the tip of the iceberg. The decisions of the Premier League and EFL disciplinary bodies are not always published; however, some have been reported in the media.

8.15   In June 2005, Chelsea was found guilty of illegally approaching Arsenal's Ashley Cole by the Premier League; the club received a £300,000 fine and a suspended three point deduction to be invoked if they were found guilty of similar conduct the following season.[20] The player was fined £100,000, and the then Chelsea manager, Jose Mourinho, was fined £200,000 for breaking the managers' code of conduct, both sums being reduced to £75,000 on appeal.[21] The player's intermediary, Jonathan Barnett, was sanctioned by The FA for his part in the tapping up.

8.16   Surprisingly, given the nature of how a club finds out that a player is interested in joining it and vice versa, there have been few recent high profile sanctions. Perhaps clubs resolve matters between themselves or a public apology suffices and is enough to deter a transfer from actually taking place.[22] However 2017 saw an increase in action being taken in this area, predominantly relating to academy age players and inducements being offered for them to join another club, after increased monitoring in this area by the Premier League.

8.17   In April 2017, Liverpool was sanctioned by the Premier League in respect of the club's approaches towards and offer of inducements to an 11-year-old academy player registered with Stoke City.[23] Liverpool admitted the rule breaches and were

20   https://www.theguardian.com/uk/2005/jun/02/football.mattscott (accessed February 2018).
21   https://www.theguardian.com/football/2005/aug/11/newsstory.sport1 (accessed February 2018).
22   http://www.mirror.co.uk/sport/football/news/what-is-tapping-up-transfers-10586182 (accessed February 2018).
23   https://www.premierleague.com/news/362197 (accessed February 2018).

fined £100,000 and prohibited from registering any academy players who had been registered with a Premier League or EFL club in the preceding 18 months for a period of two years, with the second year suspended for a three-year period (to be activated in the event of any further similar breach by the club).

8.18   Similarly, in May 2017 Manchester City was sanctioned by the Premier League in respect of approaches to two academy players, an 11-year-old registered with Everton and a 15-year-old registered with Wolverhampton Wanderers.[24] The Premier League found evidence of contact between Manchester City and members of each player's family while they were still registered with their previous clubs. Manchester City was fined £300,000 and prohibited from registering any academy players in the under-10 to under-18 age range who had been registered with a Premier League or EFL club in the preceding 18 months for a period of two years, with the second year suspended for a three-year period (to be activated in the event of any further similar breach by the club).

D   REGISTRATION PERIODS

8.19   FIFA introduced the requirements for national associations to implement two transfer windows per season in their revised RSTP which came into force on 1 September 2001 and the present system as we know it was implemented by the Premier League from the start of the 2002/03 season.[25]

8.20   RSTP Articles.6.1 and 6.2 state:

'Players may only be registered during one of the two annual registration periods fixed by the relevant association. As an exception to this rule, a professional whose contract has expired prior to the end of a registration period may be registered outside that registration period.

The first registration period shall begin after the completion of the season and shall normally end before the new season starts. This period may not exceed 12 weeks. The second registration period shall normally occur in the middle of the season and may not exceed four weeks.'

8.21   A player may only be registered to play within one national association at a time. If a player wishes to join a new club under the auspices of a different national association and is aged 10 or above, an ITC must be obtained prior to the player being registered.[26]

8.22   The transfer window of the national association of the club signing the player has to be open for the player to be registered; however it is not necessary for the window of the player's former club to also be open. This can lead to issues when a player goes on loan to a club in a national association with a completely different transfer window; clubs must ensure that their own transfer window is open when they want the player to return, otherwise he remains in limbo until the window reopens.

8.23   Premier League Rules V1–V4 refer to the domestic transfer windows as being the periods in which clubs can apply for a new registration of a player or

---

24   http://www.manchestereveningnews.co.uk/sport/football/football-news/why-were-man-city-fined-12994179 (accessed February 2018).

25   www.premierleague.com/news/60258 (accessed February 2018).

26   RSTP, Article 9.

the registration of a player transferred either permanently or temporarily to it. The domestic transfer window is longer than the English international transfer window, which is limited in length by RSTP Article 6.2 (see para **8.20**), with the summer window opening at midnight on the last day of the season and ending on 31 August or the next working day thereafter, and the winter transfer window opening at midnight on 31 December and closing on 31 January or the next working day thereafter. These rules are mirrored by those of the EFL.

8.24   National associations may decide upon the time their window closes, however in recent years the English window has closed at 11 pm, to coincide with European associations whose windows close at midnight. There had been criticism in previous seasons when the English window closed at 5 pm as clubs could still lose players that same evening whilst the windows for many European associations remained open until much later that day.

8.25   Both the Premier League and EFL have implemented measures to help clubs comply with the deadline. The Premier League permit their clubs to complete a deal sheet in the last two hours of the window, outlining the key terms that have been agreed between the parties. Lodging a fully signed deal sheet prior to the transfer deadline allows the clubs two hours grace after the window has closed to complete the formalities.

8.26   The EFL, on the other hand, states that a club will be deemed to have met the deadline if the EFL receives a completed copy of the appropriate registration form/loan form in advance of the deadline. A contract and/or transfer agreement can immediately follow; however it is expected that the contract or transfer agreement must have been agreed prior to the deadline and that any delay resulting in these being received immediately following the deadline is due to prioritising the transmission of the appropriate registration form or loan form.

8.27   In addition, clubs involved in an international transfer or loan will also be required to comply with the relevant TMS deadline.

8.28   Premier League Rule V4 and EFL Regulation 41.6 make it quite clear that outside of a transfer window the leagues may refuse an application to register a new player. In certain circumstances, the transfer of players outside of a transfer window may be permitted with the approval of the relevant league, for example the registration of a player who was out of contract at the expiry of the previous transfer window or a goalkeeper on a temporary basis in exceptional circumstances. The EFL Regulations expand this to also include a player whose previous club has ceased to trade.

8.29   However, at its shareholders meeting on 7 September 2017, Premier League clubs voted in favour of closing the transfer window at 5 pm on the Thursday prior to the first league game of the season commencing from the 2018/19 season. The Premier League chairman, Richard Scudamore, said there was an overwhelming sense that clubs wanted to begin the season with more certainty over their squad.

> 'Most important was the integrity of the competition between each other … When the 20 are playing each other [it was wrong] you could have a person in your team one week and be playing against him the next, or worse the player not playing because of speculation about him going to another Premier League team so he's not available for a week or two of the season while the window is open.'[27]

27   www.theguardian.com/football/2017/sep/07/premier-league-clubs-transfer-window-before-start-season (accessed February 2018).

8.30   This change only affects movements into the clubs and they will still face the uncertainty of potentially losing players to clubs in other countries whose windows remain open after the English window has closed. In February 2018, EFL clubs voted to follow suit but agreed to permit loan signings to take place until 31 August; however whether other European associations follow the English lead in this area remains to be seen.[28] The change appears to be backed by UEFA president Aleksander Ceferin who wrote: 'I am aware there are serious discussions around Europe regarding the shortening of the summer transfer window and we are following them closely. There is a lot of uncertainty for a long time. Therefore I would say that the window might be too long and I would support it being shorter.'[29]

8.31   After the closure of the transfer window each Premier League club must submit to the Premier League a squad list of up to 25 players containing at least eight home grown players. Under-21 players are not required to be included in the 25.

E   PRE-TRANSFER STEPS

8.32   When negotiating the prospective transfer of a player registration, the parties need to take account of several principles, as set out below.

8.33   **Restrictions on who may be involved in negotiations**: The FA Regulations on Working with Intermediaries provide that negotiations must take place directly with the player or club concerned or with an intermediary appointed by such party in accordance with those regulations.[30] For Premier League clubs, negotiations concerning the financial aspects of the transfer and/or employment of the player must be undertaken by a person named in their Transfer Policy, lodged with the Premier League.[31]

8.34   **Terms to be agreed with current club first**: The effect of the regulations concerning 'tapping up' is that the financial terms under which the current club will consent to the transfer of the player should be agreed between the clubs before the new club is given permission to discuss personal terms with the player. That is subject to the following comments:

(a)   A player is permitted to file a written transfer request. Such a request (i) indicates to the current club that the player wishes to leave the club; and (ii) where the player is transferred as a consequence, causes the player to lose his entitlement to any unpaid instalments of his signing on fee.[32]

(b)   A player may have negotiated that his employment contract contains a clause which provides that in the event that either a certain club or clubs make an offer for the player, or an offer is received at or exceeding a certain value, permission for the player to speak with that club is automatically granted, or deemed, and the receipt of such offer must be notified to the player.[33]

---

28   https://www.efl.com/news/2017/september/efl-club-meeting-clubs-indicate-support-for-early-closure-of-transfer-window/ (accessed February 2018).

29   www.thetimes.co.uk/article/uefa-backs-plan-to-shorten-summer-transfer-window-7739jr97f (accessed February 2018).

30   See Chapter 12, Football Intermediaries, Regulation and Legal Disputes.

31   See Premier League Rules H.1 and H.5.

32   See Premier League Rule T.18 and EFL Regulation 61.15.

33   Note that these so called 'release clauses' are different in nature to so called 'buy out clauses' of the type required under some legal systems, including Spain. In those cases, the player and the club agree an amount which the player will be required to pay to secure his release from his employment

(c) The current club may be subject to a contractually agreed restriction upon its ability to transfer the registration of the player if it has agreed to grant to another club an option to acquire the player or a matching right, ie the right to match the transfer offer made by a third club which would otherwise be accepted.

(d) The terms agreed between the clubs will be recorded in a transfer agreement.

8.35   New club to undertake appropriate due diligence: The warranties provided by the current club upon the transfer of the registration of the player will likely be very limited and, generally, it is for the new club to satisfy itself as to all relevant aspects about the circumstances of the player. In particular, and in addition to being satisfied as to the playing abilities of the player, the new club may:

(a) undertake a medical and physical examination of the player;

(b) obtain confirmation of the player's citizenship and whether he will require a work permit entitling him to work within the UK;[34]

(c) obtain details of the player's disciplinary record;

(d) obtain confirmation of whether the player is subject to any dispute or regulatory or statutory investigation that may affect his employment;

(e) obtain details of any default by the player of his obligations under any anti-doping regulations;

(f) consider whether there are any off-field issues concerning the player and perhaps obtain a due diligence report concerning the player's personal life; and

(g) for international transfers, seek a copy of the player passport,[35] which should disclose the identity of the clubs that are entitled to training compensation and solidarity contributions.

8.36   Terms to be agreed with the player and any intermediary: The player is likely to have appointed an intermediary[36] to negotiate his personal terms. Those personal terms may include the payment of sums under an image rights structure.[37] The club and intermediary will also need to agree the financial terms of the amount payable to the intermediary.

8.37   Obtain a governing body endorsement to secure a work permit: Once all due diligence is carried out and financial terms agreed between the two clubs and the new club and the player, if necessary due to the citizenship of the player, the new club will need to apply to The FA for a governing body endorsement in order that the player may secure a work permit to work for the club in the UK.[38] If the player will not or does not secure a work permit he may still execute an employment contract and become registered with the club but will then be loaned immediately to a club in a country where he is entitled to work.

---

contract. Recently, and most famously, this saw Neymar secure his release from FC Barcelona in order to take up employment with Paris St Germain for a fee of €222 million. In practice, while the buy out fee has to be lodged on behalf of the player with the La Liga the buy out fee is provided by the new club.

34   Note that under Article 18(4) of the RSTP, the validity of the employment contract may not made subject to a successful medical examination and/or the grant of a work permit.

35   See RSTP, Article 7.

36   See Chapter 12, Football Intermediaries, Regulation and Legal Disputes.

37   See Chapter 13, Image Rights.

38   See Chapter 9, Immigration and GBEs.

F   THE TRANSFER AGREEMENT

8.38   The transfer agreement sets out 'the full particulars of all financial and other arrangements agreed between the [clubs]'and must be lodged with the relevant league[39] and The FA,[40] and on international transfers uploaded onto TMS.[41]

8.39   The basic structure of a transfer agreement is commonly as follows:

(a) An agreement to transfer the registration of the player.
(b) The consideration (transfer fee) payable, including fixed consideration and contingent consideration.
(c) Any conditions precedent to the completion of the transfer or the obligation to pay the transfer fee. Generally, the transfer agreement will be executed once the preliminary steps are completed. If not the agreement may provide that the transfer is conditional upon completion of a medical to the satisfaction of the new club, obtaining a work permit, and/or execution of an employment contract between the new club and the player. The new club may seek to negotiate that further performance is conditional upon the registration being transferred and the player being confirmed as eligible to play by a certain date.
(d) A deadline for fulfilment of the conditions and completion of the transfer. Usually, the new club will require the registration to be transferred by a particular date or in a particular registration period. Problems arise when the transfer is not concluded by the required date or in the registration period, the deadlines for which are absolute and not subject to deviation or successful challenge. The parties need to agree what happens in the event that the transfer is not completed as required. Usually the transfer is aborted and, perhaps, the agreement will be treated as void *ab initio* or the agreement is deemed terminated by mutual consent but without prejudice to accrued rights. In the event of seeking registration within a particular registration period the risk may be allocated to the new club and it is left with a player who is employed but not registered, thereby completing the registration in the next registration period.
(e) Warranties from the selling club including appropriate warranties addressing the following:
  (i)   that it holds the player's registration absolutely and free from any other contractual obligation;
  (ii) that it will continue to hold the registration pending completion of the transfer and will not solicit or entertain further offers;
  (iii) that it shall, and shall procure that the player shall, take all actions within its power to transfer the registration in accordance with all applicable regulations;
  (iv) the agreement is in full and final settlement of any claim by the current club against the new club concerning the player;
  (v)   that it is not aware of any claim by any third party concerning the player or his registration;
  (vi) that it has no knowledge of any breach of any anti-doping regulation;
  (vii) that it has disclosed relevant medical and disciplinary records;
  (viii) the player is not subject to any disciplinary or criminal investigation, charge or sanction.
(f) On international transfers, dealing with any issues concerning training compensation or solidarity contributions. On training compensation a failure to state that the transfer fee is inclusive of training compensation determines that

---

39   Premier League Rule V.11.1. See also EFL Regulation 46.1.
40   FA Rule C1(g)(iv).
41   See para **8.45** below.

it may be held to be payable in addition. While the obligation to pay solidarity contributions rests with the buying club, the clubs are able to allocate who bears the value of the solidarity contributions payable on the transaction.

(g) Confidentiality and announcement provisions. Financial details of the transaction will be reported to TMS, The FA and the relevant leagues but the parties may decide that they do not want that information being disclosed to the public.

(h) Boiler plate clauses of the type and content considered appropriate by the clubs.

(i) Jurisdiction and choice of law. Note that the position on who has jurisdiction in relation to any dispute arising between two clubs may be complicated, especially if the player is a party. The rules of each of The FA, the Premier League, the EFL and FIFA provide for settlement of disputes by specific dispute resolution bodies, with determination by arbitrators or administrators with expertise in football related disputes. Disputes may proceed in the courts where a party does not successfully apply for a stay of proceedings in favour of arbitration, under s 9 of the Arbitration Act 1996, or for interim relief. Any dispute resolved before the FIFA PSC or FIFA DRC carries an automatic right of appeal to the Court of Arbitration for Sport (CAS). The jurisprudence of the CAS on football related disputes is substantial and is applicable whenever there is an international element to a transfer.[42] As for choice of law, the parties may by contract seek to determine the governing law of the contract. Any Premier League or EFL Tribunal is bound to respect that choice of law. Disputes resolved in accordance with FA Rule K are resolved in accordance with English law. Decisions of the FIFA Players' Status Committee (PSC) or FIFA Dispute Resolution Chamber (DRC) tend not to make a finding on applicable law. Decisions of the CAS are determined in accordance with the applicable regulations and, subsidiarily, the law chosen by the parties. As a matter of practice, that may mean that the CAS panel determines the dispute in accordance with Swiss law, as the applicable law of the RSTP or the governing law of the domicile of FIFA.

8.40 On occasion the permanent transfer of the player may follow from a loan and the terms of the loan, the option over the player's registration and the permanent transfer are all included in the same agreement. In such event the clubs need to give particular consideration to:

(a) the length of employment contract which the player is initially permitted to enter with the new club during the period of the loan;

(b) whether the option granted to the new club is exclusive or whether the old club may accept an offer from a third party club;

(c) the terms of the option granted to the new club including the deadline by which the option must be exercised and whether the occurrence of any one of certain events, such as participation in a number of matches, is deemed to trigger the exercise of the option;

(d) whether service of the option notice entitles the new club to seek to agree personal terms with the player or whether the player's acceptance of personal terms with the new club is a condition precedent to the valid exercise of the option;

(e) ensuring the player's consent to the terms of the agreement.

8.41 The rules of The FA,[43] the Premier League[44] and the EFL[45] provide that certain agreements are required to be submitted for prior approval before execution

---

42 See Chapter 29, International Disputes and the CAS.
43 See the FA's Third Party Investment in Players Regulations.
44 See Premier League Rules U.8 and U.38.
45 See EFL Regulations 44.3 and 48.1.

or, in the case of the FA Rules, approval over some contracts is deemed and the agreement must be lodged with The FA within five days of execution. When considering transfer agreements, these rules are most commonly engaged when a club either grants or receives an option or matching right in relation to the future transfer of a player, whether as part of the transfer agreement or as a separate option agreement. Such arrangements are commonplace but need careful consideration given Article 18bis of the RSTP[46] and, the authors understand, they may be refused by the relevant league or The FA in some circumstances. Note that the English governing bodies distinguish between a member club deriving the benefit of an option to acquire a player in the future and granting an option.[47] The authors understand that where a governing body refuses permission for a member club to grant an option to another club, the relevant player may agree a form of release clause with his employer, although that is susceptible to difficulties as the club has no direct right to enforce against the other club or the player and any new employment contract, concluded after a re-negotiation, may not include the clause.

G   PROCESS

8.42   The transfer of a player from one club to another terminates the employment contract between the player and his former club. He is required to enter into a playing contract with his employer and this shall be submitted to the football authorities at the same time as the transfer agreement, any agreement with an intermediary and other associated forms as required by the relevant league and The FA. As in the case of player contracts, this paperwork is accepted electronically by the registering bodies, with the relevant leagues also requiring original copies of the documentation to be submitted to them.

8.43   The club registering the player will submit the documentation to the football authorities; in the main the documentation varies very little between registration in the Premier League and the EFL; however the EFL still require The FA's H1 transfer form to be completed as well as a further form which clarifies whether the transfer is a permanent or a temporary one; these forms are not currently required by the Premier League.

8.44   In respect of an international transfer, there is a further hurdle for clubs to complete to ensure that the player's ITC is received prior to his registration.

(a)   FIFA Transfer Matching System (TMS)[48]

8.45   TMS was developed following a two-year study commissioned by FIFA in 2005 to address concerns over transparency in the transfer market and to control the integrity of club and national association behaviour in international transfers. Before TMS, there was a lack of reliable data on the transfer market; it was designed to ensure that football authorities have more details available to them on international player transfers.

---

46   Article 18bis: 'No club shall enter into a contract which enables the counter club/counter clubs, and vice versa, or any third party to acquire the ability to influence in employment and transfer-related matters its independence, its policies or the performance of its teams.'
47   See for example para 1.14 of the FA's Third Party Investment (TPI) Regulations.
48   RSTP, Annexe 3.

8.46   TMS became mandatory for all international transfers of professional male players in 11-a-side football in October 2010. However prior to this in 2009, the use of TMS became obligatory for an international transfer involving a minor in accordance with Article 19 of the RSTP.

8.47   Club users are required to input details of the transfer: the type of transaction; the player's details; the compensation or transfer fee payable; both fixed and contingent sums; together with any training compensation/solidarity payment; details of the player's new employment contract and remuneration; confirmation that there is no third party ownership of the player's economic rights (to be signed by the former club and the player), confirmation of whether an intermediary was used in the transaction; and also to upload a number of mandatory documents to verify the above information. Evidence of payments made must also be uploaded once they have been made.

8.48   If the player has not completed an international transfer before, it is likely that his details will not be found in TMS and therefore he will need to be created on the system with details of his nationality uploaded. The player's former national association will need to verify the player's details before the transaction can progress.

8.49   The other club in the transaction is also required to complete the information relating to the transfer and the two entries must then 'match' to enable the transaction to proceed to verification by the two national associations. Once this has been completed the player's ITC will be issued and registration by the new national association can take place. In reality, clubs often send a copy of their proposed TMS entry to the other club to ensure that matching happens at the first attempt.

8.50   The ITC request can only be rejected in two circumstances:

(a) the employment contract between the former club and the player has not expired; or
(b) there was no mutual agreement regarding the early termination of said employment contract.

8.51   TMS has a compliance department which educates, monitors and investigates transfer activity in the international transfer market, sanctioning breaches and improving stakeholder awareness of regulatory requirements.[49] Sanctions may be imposed by FIFA or TMS on any association or club found to have entered false data into the system or for having misused TMS for wrongful purposes.[50]

8.52   Separate provisions have been put in place by FIFA for the transfer of players for associations outside TMS, for amateur male players, female players and futsal players.[51]

8.53   The important role that TMS and the timely receipt of an ITC plays in any international transfer has recently been highlighted in respect of Adrien Silva's move from Sporting Lisbon to Leicester City. The transfer paperwork was reportedly submitted 14 seconds after the TMS deadline resulting in his ITC not being issued and the player being left in limbo. The decision not to permit the player's registration

---

49   https://www.fifatms.com/products-and-services/#row7 (accessed February 2018).
50   RSTP, Annexe 3, Article 9.
51   RSTP, Annexe 3a.

was appealed by the club and rejected by FIFA;[52] however without the ITC, the player could not play for Leicester City and a reportedly £25m asset remained watching the game from the stands.

(b)   Transfer fees

8.54   A transfer fee may be considered as the compensation paid by the new club to the old club as consideration for its early termination of the employment contract of the player and the incumbent loss of services from the player. The fee commonly contains fixed compensation and contingent compensation.

8.55   Generally, the old club will seek to provide in the transfer agreement that the transfer fee is conditional upon confirmation from the relevant league of receipt of the registration of the player and, on international transfers, release of the ITC within the relevant registration period. Some clubs have concern about the flow of funds on the sale of players into certain countries. In such event, the transfer agreement may provide that cleared funds be received by the old club before it commences the termination of the player's employment contract and the TMS process for the release of the ITC.

8.56   Commonly fixed transfer fees are split into instalments, over the length of the player's employment contract with the new club or such shorter period as is agreed between the clubs. Such instalments should be payable whether or not the player remains registered with the new club. In some instances clubs may need to structure instalment payments with financial fair play regulations in mind.

8.57   Common contingent fees may arise on the occurrence of:

(a) Appearance fees. Consideration needs to be given to whether the player has to be in the starting line up, play a certain number of minutes or simply enter onto the field of play, the number of appearances to trigger a payment and the pro-rating of such a fee in the event that the player ceases to be registered with the new club for any reason.
(b) Success fees. If the club achieves or betters a certain position in a league or tournament. Consideration needs to be given to the part played by the player, by reference to matches or minutes, or whether the obligation to pay the fee arises in any event.
(c) International recognition. Less commonly the old club may be entitled to an additional fee in the event that the player achieves an international debut at a particular level or reaches a particular number of international caps.
(d) Sell-on fee. See para **8.63** below.

8.58   In addition certain payments arise on the transfer of the player by the application of the RSTP or the Premier League and EFL Youth Development Rules,[53] or the obligation to pay the transfer levy.[54]

---

52   http://www.telegraph.co.uk/football/2017/10/04/adrien-silva-left-limbo-fifa-rejects-leicester-appeal-late-paperwork/ (accessed February 2018).
53   See Chapter 9 on Academies and Youth Issues concerning training compensation and solidarity contributions. Note that, although these rules are notionally of international application, they are not currently applicable in relation to clubs within the jurisdiction of the USSF that trained and developed players.
54   See Premier League Rule V.38 and EFL Regulation 49.2.9.

8.59 In order to ensure transparency over the flow of funds, the payment of transfer fees is subject to regulation. For domestic transfers, Premier League and EFL clubs are required to pay transfer fees into a bank account operated by the relevant league for onward transmission to the old club.[55] For international transfers, transfer fees are required to be paid to The FA for onward transmission to the old club.[56]

8.60 The English governing bodies have long prohibited third party ownership and third party influence[57] and restrict the type of payments or liability that are permissible as a result of or in connection with the proposed or actual registration, transfer of registration or employment of a player, without prior approval.[58] By FIFA Circular 1464, FIFA imposed an outright ban on the creation of new third party ownership arrangements with effect from 1 May 2015.[59] Clubs are not permitted to be party to any arrangement by which a third party owner has an interest in a player's registration or an entitlement to all or part of a transfer fee.[60] Consequently this practice should soon become obsolete. In the meantime, the English governing bodies require that where a player who is subject to third party ownership is to be registered with an English club, the rights of the third party owner be bought out, usually accompanied by further warranties provided by the acquiring club, player and any relevant intermediary that there has been full disclosure of the third party ownership (TPO) agreements that no such ownership will persist.[61]

8.61 The football governing bodies have enacted regulations aimed at, *inter alia*, ensuring that transfer fees that are agreed to be paid are paid.

8.62 At an international level:

(a) By Article 12bis of the RSTP, any club that is in default of payment of a transfer fee for 30 days and has had a written demand from the new club setting a final deadline for payment of at least ten days, is liable to be sanctioned by the FIFA Disciplinary Committee. The FIFA Disciplinary Committee proceeds relatively slowly but its jurisdiction is effective. The debtor club which remains in default will receive a fine and a final deadline to pay, with the amount of the fine and period to pay determined by the amount of the debt, and a suspended sanction within the terms provided by the FIFA Disciplinary Code, to become effective in the event that the debt is not settled within the period set and the further application of the creditor. Commonly the sanction is a points deduction or, for a repeat offender, relegation from the relevant division of the national league.

(b) For those clubs who seek to participate in UEFA competitions, Article 49 of the UEFA Club Licensing and Financial Fair Play Regulations states that a licence applicant (club) must prove as at 31 March preceding the licence season that

---

55 See Premier League Rule V.29 and EFL Regulation 49.1.
56 See FA Rule C1(b)(v), Premier League Rule V.35 and EFL Regulation 49.2.8.
57 For a detailed account of the *Tevez* and *Faurlin* disputes, encapsulating the concerns and chaos arising from TPO and TPI, see SLAP H4.197 et seq.
58 See Premier League Rule U.38, EFL Regulation 48 and FA Rule C1(b)(iii) and the FA TPI Regulations.
59 TPO agreements executed between 1 January and 30 April 2015 were limited to a duration of one year. For a detailed review of TPO prior to its prohibition see the KPMG Report 'Project TPO' dated August 2013 http://www.ecaeurope.com/Research/External%20Studies%20and%20Reports/KPMG%20TPO%20Report.pdf (accessed February 2018).
60 RSTP Article 18ter. See also Article 18bis regarding counterclub and third party influence.
61 See Premier League Rule U.39 and EFL Regulation 48.2. See also Chapter 11, Third Party Investment.

it has no overdue payables towards other football clubs as a result of transfers undertaken prior to the previous 31 December.[62] In the absence of an agreement with the creditor club or a bona fide dispute concerning the payment, a breach of this regulation (may) result in the club being refused a licence to participate in the UEFA competition.

(c)   Notwithstanding the regulatory provisions above, in some instances the old club may require that the fixed instalments of a transfer fee be installed by the provision of security such as a bank guarantee. Great care must be taken in ensuring that the terms of the guarantee are effective, the triggering event appropriate, and the bank on which the call will be made appropriate to the identity and domicile of the creditor club.

8.63   At a domestic level:

(a)   The Premier League and EFL operate overdue payable regulations. Premier League Rule E.9 states that each club must by 7 April in each season prove that, *inter alia*, no transfer fee preceding 31 December is overdue as at the preceding 31 March.[63] If the club cannot satisfy the board that this has been complied with, the board may require the club to submit, agree and adhere to a budget; provide such further information as the board shall determine and for such period as it wishes; and refuse any application by that club to register any player or any new contract of an existing player of that club if the board reasonably deems that this is necessary in order to ensure that the club complies with its obligations.[64] In addition, the Premier League provides in its rules that, under certain circumstances, it may retain from central fund payments due to a debtor club to meet a transfer fee due to a creditor club.[65]

(b)   The Premier League and EFL operate 'football creditor' rules unique to English football, which in the event of insolvency broadly entails payments to other 'football creditors', such as clubs owed transfer fees, before other creditors.[66]

(c)   Sell-on clause

8.64   One of the purposes of a sell-on clause has been set out in *Sekondi Hasaacas v Borussia Mönchengladbach*:[67]

'To agree on a sell-on clause … is a quite standard practice in the world of professional football … Such transfers of a fairly unknown player from a "small league" to a "top league" club give a chance to the player's talents to be put in evidence and to increase accordingly his market value. Under such circumstances transferring clubs are often willing to accept a rather small "fixed price", if they are given through a sell-on clause the possibility to benefit from a later increase in the value of the player. The sell-on clause also allows the receiving club not to pay at once a too high transfer fee in case the player gets injured or his talent does not develop as expected … But of course the parties of a transfer agreement are free to decide on a case by case basis on which terms a sell-on clause shall be triggered.'

---

62   This is reflected in Article 50, which states that the licence applicant must prove that as at 31 March preceding the licence season it has no overdue payables in respect of its employees as a result of contractual or legal obligations that arose prior to the previous 31 December. Employees include, *inter alia*, professional players.

63   The similar EFL regulation is at Regulation 16.14.

64   See Premier League Rule E.15.

65   See Premier League Rule E.26.

66   For an account of the rule, its principles and challenges to it by HMRC see the article at https://www.entsportslawjournal.com/articles/10.16997/eslj.203/ (accessed February 2018).

67   CAS 2007/A/1219 *Sekondi Hasaacas FC v Borussia Mönchengladbach*, para 15.

8.65   However, sell-on clauses are not only effective when there is no or only a small initial fee payable and may also take effect on any subsequent transfer for a fee; it is not necessarily a profit-sharing clause whereby it will only be triggered in the event that the player moves on in the future for an increased value. The CAS in *Al Ain v Sunderland*[68] agreed that a profit-sharing clause is one possible effect of a sell-on clause but highlighted that the wording of the clause may ensure that the selling club receives an additional payment regardless of the value of the subsequent transfer ie that it could be a transfer of a higher or lower value than the original transfer. The exact wording of the clause needs to be closely examined in each transaction. It is quite normal for a young player to be transferred for no initial transfer fee but with a large percentage sell-on clause if he is sold for any fee in the future.

8.66   The buying club will be keen to minimise their potential liability under the sell-on clause whereas the selling club will approach the clause from the opposite perspective. It should be considered whether the sell-on fee is to be a percentage of any future transfer fee received by the buying club or a percentage of the excess received over and above the fee which has already been paid to the selling club. If it is based on a percentage of the excess, it should be agreed whether the sell-on fee is calculated purely on the value of the transfer fee paid to the selling club or on the net costs of the transfer where an intermediary's fee may be added into the equation.

8.67   If it is not stated otherwise, the CAS in *Al Ain v Sunderland* determined that:[69]

> 'Where the clear wording of a sell-on clause speaks of "any transfer fee received", not of a net transfer fee, i.e. a sum received after deduction of the costs in direct connection with the transfer of the player, including the agent's costs or intermediary remuneration, no deduction should be made from the transfer fee received by the club selling the player to a third club regarding the payment of the sell-on fee to "old club" of the player transferred.'

8.68   In *Fulham v Metz*,[70] the CAS determined that when a sell-on clause refers to a percentage of the 'net transfer fee' received by the buying club, this can only refer to the net transfer fee paid for the acquisition of the player after the deduction of the costs of an intermediary in the transaction and that the costs and expenses associated with the employment of the player shall not be taken into account.

8.69   When drafting a sell-on clause, careful consideration must be given to whether a sell-on fee would be payable by the buying club on the next transfer only or if the registering club was to receive proceeds in respect of the player on any subsequent transfer. An example of this would be if Club A transferred the player to Club B and the terms included a sell-on fee and then Club B subsequently transferred the player on to Club C and the terms included a sell-on fee and so on.

8.70   Clubs should also consider whether a sell-on clause would be payable on a fee received for the loan of the player or just on the permanent transfer of the player. Clubs must ensure their drafting in this respect is clear to avoid potential disputes at a much later stage when the intention of the parties at the time of the original transfer may be difficult to ascertain. In *Sekondi Hasaacas v Borussia Mönchengladbach*[71]

---

68   CAS 2016/A/4379 *Al Ain FC v Sunderland AFC,* para 108.
69   CAS 2016/A/4379 *Al Ain FC v Sunderland AFC,* para 3.
70   CAS 2005/A/896 *Fulham FC (1987) Ltd v FC Metz,* para 3.
71   CAS 2007/A/1219 *Sekondi Hasaacas FC v Borussia Mönchengladbach,* para 3.

the CAS determined that a sell-on clause could be triggered in a loan agreement for a player that had all the appearances of a permanent transfer:

> 'When the sell-on clause inserted in a Transfer Agreement does not specify whether the transfer triggering the right of the former club to a certain sum is only a final transfer or not, it is hardly imaginable that the mutual consent of the parties is to limit such right to a final transfer and to exclude any transfer which was structured as a loan but was de facto in many ways similar and equivalent to a final transfer.'

8.71   A transfer agreement should always document when a sell-on clause would become payable to the selling club. In the event of a domestic transfer between clubs in the Premier League and EFL, the sell-on fee is automatically deducted by the relevant league and remitted to the selling club. However in overseas transfers or transfers between clubs outside of the Premier League and EFL it is usual to document that the sell-on fee will be payable in the same instalments as a guaranteed fee or contingent sum is received by the buying club and within a set number of days.

8.72   In order for the selling club to calculate what is due/potentially due to it, it would be practical to include in the transfer agreement a clause which states that the buying club agrees to notify the selling club in writing within a set number of days of the subsequent transfer of the nature of the compensation for the player, the amounts payable/potentially payable and the relevant payment dates.

8.73   Another area of drafting a sell-on clause which varies between what the selling club and the buying club want is whether the sell-on clause relates only to monetary consideration or whether non-monetary consideration, eg the value of a player swap or a pre-season friendly, should also be taken into account. The parties should agree to enter into good faith negotiations to agree a cash value to any subsequent transfer and, if they are unable to do so, should agree to refer such dispute to arbitration under the provisions of the relevant football authority.

8.74   Historically, an intermediary may have had a percentage interest in the player's future transfer fee; however this has now been prohibited by The FA[72] and by FIFA.[73]

H   LOANS

8.75   FIFA's regulations on international loans can be found at Article 10 of the RSTP and state that the loan must be in writing, and is subject to the same rules relating to the transfer of players as for a permanent international transfer which includes completion of TMS (see Annexe 3) and the payment of compensation in accordance with the provisions on training compensation and solidarity as detailed at Articles 20 and 21. They further provide that a loan must have the minimum duration of window to window. The loan player will be required to enter into an employment contract with his English club and this will be submitted to the football authorities, together with a written loan agreement and any agreement with an intermediary/IM1 form in order for the loan to be registered after his ITC has been issued, once TMS has been completed. The EFL will also require a form to be completed confirming that the transaction is a loan rather than a permanent transfer.

---

72   FA Regulations on Working with Intermediaries 2017–18, regulation E5.
73   RSTP, Article 18ter.1. See also Chapter 11, Third Party Investment, and Chapter 12, Football Intermediaries, Regulation and Legal Disputes.

8.76 The domestic loan regulations are more detailed.[74] Until the end of the 2015/16 season, clubs had been permitted to take players on short term loan for a period of between 28 and 93 days (as well as from window to window); however these arrangements had become under an increasing level of scrutiny from FIFA who felt that they affected the integrity of the competitions involved. The FA and EFL had argued for several years to protect the domestic loan system: it served to give young players an opportunity to develop whilst playing first team football that they might not otherwise have had with their own clubs, as well as assisting clubs who found themselves short of players due to injuries or suspensions. It was popular with larger clubs and smaller clubs alike, with the ability to insert a recall clause after the initial 28 days of the loan giving the former club some comfort in case they needed the player.

8.77 Currently, a domestic loan can only take place from window to window or for an entire season finishing no later than 30 June. In a season long loan, the provision to recall the player is only permitted during the January transfer window with the exception of the loan of a goalkeeper whereby the EFL permit a recall clause to be exercisable at any time in exceptional circumstances subject to (i) the approval of the league; and (ii) the club seeking to recall the player, only having one professional goalkeeper available. The Premier League attempt to avoid this issue by only permitting a club to loan one goalkeeper at a time, subject to the possibility of loaning one further goalkeeper in exceptional circumstances. The EFL Regulations cover in detail the emergency loan of a goalkeeper at Regulation 55.

8.78 The Premier League prohibits a player to play against his parent club[75] and this is also mirrored in the FA Cup rules.[76] However this is permitted by the EFL as long as prior written permission has been given.[77] Furthermore, the Premier League is explicit in prohibiting a player going out on loan domestically during the same window that he joined his parent club.

8.79 The Premier League further prohibits a club from taking more than four loan players per season (however only two at a time) which must be from different clubs; however this may be varied at the Premier League's discretion in the event of an emergency loan of a goalkeeper. The EFL restricts clubs to naming a maximum of five loan players on the team sheet at any one time, reducing to four when they have also listed a goalkeeper who is on an emergency loan on the sheet. EFL clubs are not restricted in the total number of loans that they can take; however a maximum of four can be from the same club of which not more than two shall be over the age of 23.

8.80 The documentation required to register a domestic loan includes a temporary transfer form signed by both clubs and the player, a copy of any loan agreement/appendix to the loan form, a copy of the new club's bonus schedule (if any) and any agreement with an intermediary/IM1 form. The loan form or supplementary agreement must state as a minimum the player's wage and what proportion of it is being paid by the new club; any other benefits he is to receive whilst on loan; whether the player is to remain on the private medical scheme of the old club or to join that of the new club; whether there has been a loan fee; and whether the player is entitled to play non-first team football for his old club during the loan period. Any supplemental terms between the two clubs must also be documented. Some clubs will charge a loan fee that reduces upon appearances to try to ensure that the player that they are

---

74   See Premier League Rules at V.5 onwards and EFL Regulations 52–55.
75   Premier League Rule V.7.2.
76   Rules of the FA Challenge Cup Competition at 15(j)(iv).
77   EFL Regulation 52.7.

loaning out will actually play for the club he is on loan to. If there is a loan fee it must be paid by 30 June at the end of the season of the loan and any fee is not subject to the league's levy unless the loan becomes permanent. The loan agreement may look quite similar to a transfer agreement containing guaranteed and contingent sums and may also provide for the permanent transfer of the player at a later point in time (which would be required to have the player's consent).

I MINORS

8.81   This section concentrates specifically on the process relating to the transfer of minors and any international movement of minors; see Chapter 10, Academies and Youth Issues for details relating to compensation payable for out of contract minor players.

8.82   Domestically, a parent or guardian is required to counter sign a scholarship agreement[78] or playing contract for a player under the age of 18. If the player is registered under a scholarship agreement, there is no explicit provision in the rules for the transfer from one scholarship agreement to one with another club. The scholar, however, has the right under clause 13.1 of that agreement to request the termination of his registration and, save in the situation whereby the player has already agreed in writing to enter into a professional contract with that same club on or before the expiry of his scholarship agreement,[79] the club is obliged to complete and sign a mutual termination of registration form. Upon this occurrence, the scholar shall not be permitted to sign for a new club for a period of two years unless his former club gives permission or has received compensation for his training and development. Prior to the exception mentioned above, a club was obliged to sign a mutual termination upon the request of the player which gave the ability for larger clubs to unsettle another club's promising scholarship player with the risk of compensation being settled by the Professional Football Compensation Committee (PFCC) if it could not be agreed between the two clubs.

8.83   FIFA's standard position is that international movements are only permitted once a player reaches the age of 18.[80] This applies to both amateur and professional players. FIFA sets out in detail the reasoning behind these rules on its website.[81] However, there are a number of exceptions to this rule:[82]

(a) the player's parents move to the country of the new club for reasons not associated with football;[83]

---

78   In the form of Youth Development Form 1.
79   Youth Development Rule 288.
80   RSTP, Article 19.1.
81   http://resources.fifa.com/mm/document/affederation/administration/02/83/14/23/faq_
      protectionofminors_august2016_en_english.pdf (accessed February 2018).
82   RSTP, Article 19.2. For a detailed review of the exceptions permitted by FIFA or the CAS see the
      article by Stephen Sampson and Emma Mason in Football Legal #7, June 2017, 'Article 19 and
      Article 19bis FIFA RSTP', droitdusport.com.
83   See CAS 2015/A/4312 *John Kenneth Hilton v FIFA*. Where the move of the family was motivated
      by a mixture of reasons, and where each one of the other proven reasons is legitimate *per se*, the
      application of the exception will be assessed and decided based on the weight of the 'football factor'
      within the whole range of reasons and the overall circumstances of the matter, such as: the other
      reasons, whether all the family moved, to what extent the specific location to which the family
      decided to move was chosen with consideration of the football activity of the minor, etc. If the move
      of the parents is based on reasons that are not totally independent from football that is sufficient to
      exclude the exception of Article 19.2(a).

(b) the player is aged between 16 and 18 and the transfer takes place within the EU/EEA; or

(c) the player lives *and* the new club is located within 50km of a national border.

8.84   These requirements also apply to any player who has never previously been registered with a club, is not a national of the country in which he wishes to be registered for the first time and has not lived continuously for at least the last five years in that country.

8.85   In FIFA's circular 1468 of 23 January 2015, it notified its member associations that its Executive Committee had approved a reduction in the age limit for which an ITC is required from 12 to 10 due to the increased number of international transfers of players under the age of 12 and the need to reinforce the protection of minors. However the absence of the requirement for an ITC for players below the age of 10 does not remove the obligation to observe the transfer ban for under-aged players.[84] FIFA also reiterated that that if a national association intends to register players under the age of 10 it is the responsibility of that association to ensure that the provisions established in Article 19.2 (see para **8.83** above) are met.

8.86   All of these exceptional registrations, as well as those for a minor player who has lived continuously for at least five years in the country where he wishes to register must be approved by a sub-committee of FIFA's Players' Status Committee (PSC) after the details have been submitted through TMS in accordance with Annexe 2 of the RSTP. The following mandatory documents (dependent upon the nature of the application) are required:

(a) Proof of identity and nationality – player and player's parents.
(b) Birth certificate – player.
(c) Employment contract – player and player's parents/other documents corroborating the application.
(d) Work permit – player and player's parents.
(e) Proof of residence – player and player's parents.
(f) Documentation of academic education.
(g) Documentation of football education.
(h) Documentation of accommodation/care.
(i) Parental authorisation.
(j) Proof of distance: 50km rule.
(k) Proof of consent of counterpart association.
(l) Request for approval of first registration/international transfer.

8.87   Further details of the facts required in the above documentation are listed in FIFA's Minor Player Application Guide.[85] In order to speed up the process and reduce the risk of incomplete applications or conflicting information, The FA, League Football Education (LFE) and Premier League Education agreed with FIFA standard template documentation to be completed which can be accessed via a club's CPS portal. FIFA also advised that a letter of support from LFE or Premier League Education would also strengthen an application. Documentation submitted should be clearly labelled, legible and in pdf format.

8.88   Once The FA has confirmed that the minor application has been submitted to FIFA, clubs must then initiate a transfer instruction within TMS and upload all

84   CAS 2014/A/3793 *Futbol Club Barcelona v FIFA*, para 4.
85   http://resources.fifa.com/mm/document/affederation/footballgovernance/02/86/35/28/protectionof minors%E2%80%93%E2%80%9Cminorplayerapplicationguide%E2%80%9D_neutral.pdf (accessed February 2018).

relevant documents and match with the former club's instructions (if any) prior to the closing of the transfer window if the player is to be registered as a professional (including as a scholar). Once the minor application has been approved by the PSC, the ITC can then be requested and processed. If the decision of PSC has not been reached until after the closure of transfer window, the ITC can still be requested provided the above process has been fully completed. If the registration requested is for an amateur player, the application does not need to be made during an open transfer window.

8.89   The national association(s) concerned shall be notified of the sub-committee's decision via TMS and they then have ten days from notification in which to request in writing via TMS the grounds of the decision, otherwise the decision becomes final and binding.

8.90   When the validity of Article 19 has been challenged at the CAS, it has determined that the restriction on international transfers of minors does not contradict public policy or EC law since the restriction has a legitimate interest, being the protection of young players, the restriction is proportionate to its aim and it has reasonable exceptions.[86] The CAS states that Article 19 aims to strike a balance between the requirement to train at a young age, and the risks of this when football is practised away from home, especially in a foreign country.[87]

8.91   FIFA has recently handed out severe sanctions to high profile clubs in respect of breaches of RSTP Article 19. In December 2014 the CAS dismissed the appeal of Barcelona against the decision of FIFA whereby it received a transfer ban for two consecutive windows after it was found to have breached FIFA's Articles 19 and 19bis.[88] More recently both Atletico Madrid and Real Madrid have been found guilty by FIFA of breaches of the same Articles and served transfer bans, which were upheld by the CAS on appeal, in whole or in part.

---

86   See CAS 2005/A/955 & 956, CAS 2008/A/1485 and CAS 2012/A/2862 by way of example.
87   CAS 2014/A/3793 *Futbol Club Barcelona v FIFA,* para 9.34.
88   http://www.bbc.co.uk/sport/football/40117879 (accessed February 2018).

CHAPTER 9

Immigration and GBEs

Supinder Sian (Squire Patton Boggs) and **Emma Mason**

A INTRODUCTION

9.1 Football is a global business. As at 1 January 2017, it was valued at over €29.9 billion and the top three European clubs were valued at between €2.8 and €3.1 million each.[1] As a result, there is significant movement of players, managers, coaches and other key performance staff between nations as football clubs seek to acquire the employment of the best available talents to improve team performance and increase their own share of the lucrative football market. Naturally, the most talented players are not necessarily those that are native to a football club's home nation and clubs invest significant sums in scouting international talents and purchasing their registrations from football clubs around the world.

9.2 An English football club and its players are subject to the same framework of employment and immigration law and regulation as any other English employer and employee.[2] Accordingly, football clubs seeking to employ international players and personnel must understand the legal and regulatory framework or risk a significant penalty and/or the loss of opportunity to employ that particular individual.

9.3 In this chapter, the authors set out the key aspects of the UK immigration system for football clubs. As with any legal or regulatory system, these are subject to change and, in particular and as further set out in this chapter, the Governing Body Endorsement criteria produced by The English Football Association

---

1 See p 6 of '*The European Elite* 2017', KPMG's Football Clubs' Valuation, stated that the Enterprise Value of the 32 most prominent European football clubs totalled approximately €29.9 billion https://assets.kpmg.com/content/dam/kpmg/xx/pdf/2017/05/football-clubs-valuation-the-european-elite-2017.pdf (accessed February 2018).
2 See, Chapter 5, Employment Law and Football, and Chapter 6, Contracts – Players.

('The FA') are updated on a seasonal basis. At the time of writing and as a result of uncertainty generated by Brexit negotiations, the risk of significant change to UK immigration law and regulation is high.

B   SPONSORSHIP – THE POINTS BASED SYSTEM (PBS)

9.4   The primary immigration routes of entry for professional non-European Economic Area (EEA) and Croatian national players and coaches[3] who wish to play/ work in the UK are Tier 2 (Sportsperson) and Tier 5 (Temporary Worker) Creative and Sporting visas. Accordingly, any reference to immigration rules and regulations that are applicable to non-EU/EEA players and coaches in this chapter are, at the time of writing, also applicable to Croatian players and coaches.

9.5   To obtain a Tier 2 or Tier 5 visa, non-EEA players and personnel must be sponsored by an eligible club that has successfully applied for a Governing Body Endorsement (GBE) from The FA and hold a Tier 2 (Sportsperson) and/or Tier 5 (Temporary Worker) Creative and Sporting sponsor licence. Sponsor licences and GBEs can only be applied for by clubs who are members of the English Premier League, Football League or Women's Super League.

9.6   Sponsors should note that it is not possible for players or coaches to be sponsored under the Tier 2 (General) or the Tier 2 (Intra-Company Transfer) sub-tiers, where they have been approved on the club's licence.

(a)   Applying for a sponsor licence

9.7   The criteria for a sponsor licence are set out in the Home Office's Tiers 2 and 5 Guidance for Sponsors, supplementary guidance and appendix.[4] To be eligible for a sponsor licence, clubs must be able to demonstrate that they:

(a) are operating or trading lawfully in the UK;
(b) do not represent a threat to immigration control; and
(c) are capable of complying with the sponsor duties and responsibilities.

9.8   The sponsor licence application must be initiated online.[5] Once the online form has been completed, submitted and paid for, a 'submission sheet' will be generated. The submission sheet must be signed[6] and sent to the Home Office together with the relevant supporting documentation. Licence applications must be supported with specified original/original certified documentation as set out in Appendix A: supporting documents for sponsor licence application.[7]

---

3   As Croatia joined the EU on 1 July 2013 Croatian nationals now no longer require entry clearance or a visa to enter and reside legally in the UK for up to three months. However, Croatian nationals do not yet have free right to work in the UK and still need to obtain authorisation to work before starting any employment, unless they are exempt from doing so: Accession of Croatia (Immigration and Worker Authorisation) Regulations 2013, SI 2013/1460. The current registration requirements for Croatian workers will expire on 30 June 2018 bringing their rights to work in Britain in line with other EU citizens.
4   Home Office sponsor and supplementary guidance is available at https://www.gov.uk/government/collections/sponsorship-information-for-employers-and-educators (accessed February 2017).
5   See for the Sponsor Licence application registration page https://www.gov.uk/apply-sponsor-licence (accessed February 2017).
6   By the proposed Authorising Officer.
7   https://www.gov.uk/government/uploads/system/uploads/attachment_data/file/605931/Appendix_A_04-2017.pdf (accessed February 2017).

9.9 Applications for a sponsor licence are generally processed within 4–12 weeks. Upon approval the sponsor will be added to the Home Offices 'Register of Sponsors'.[8] The sponsor will be given an 'A' or 'B' rating based on their risk profile. The majority of football club sponsors under Tiers 2 (Sportsperson) and Tier 5 (Temporary Worker) Creative and Sporting will start with an A rating, which will be reviewed when audited or at licence renewal stage. The licence will be valid for an initial period of four years and can be renewed in four year increments.

(b) Sponsor compliance

9.10 Tier 2 sponsorship is essentially a trust based system. As such the Home Office retains discretion to audit sponsors[9] to ensure they are complying with their sponsor and immigration compliance obligations. Where a club is found to be in breach of its sponsor compliance obligations the Home Office retains the power to:

(a) issue civil penalties of up to £20,000 per illegal worker in the event that a club is found to be employing staff without the right to work in the UK; and/or
(b) downgrade, suspend and ultimately revoke a sponsor licence. If a sponsor has its licence revoked, anyone sponsored via that licence would have their immigration permission curtailed.

9.11 The main types of sponsor obligation that the Home Office expects licensed sponsors to fulfil are:

(a) monitoring all employees' immigration status and preventing illegal working;
(b) maintaining sponsored employees' current and past contact details since entering the UK;
(c) retaining pertinent records in respect of the sponsored employees' employment and recruitment;
(d) tracking, monitoring and reporting sponsored employees' attendance, end of employment, changes to role and/or immigration status;
(e) reporting changes to the sponsor's own circumstance, eg change of location, name, acquisition.

In line with a club's sponsor licence reporting they have an obligation to report changes to their ownership structure to the Home Office. A sponsor licence is a non-transferable asset; where there is a change to a sponsor's immediate parent company the sponsor will be required to apply for a new sponsor licence and transfer existing sponsored migrants to the new licence.

(c) Premium sponsorship

9.12 The Home Office invites sponsors to apply for a 'Premium Customer Service Scheme', which gives sponsors access to priority visa services including access to premium appointments and faster passport returns for applications made within the UK.

9.13 To be eligible for the scheme, sponsors must:

(a) have had no civil penalties for employing illegal workers from the Home Office in the past three years and must have paid in full any penalties issued before that;

---

8   Available to view at https://www.gov.uk/government/publications/register-of-licensed-sponsors-workers (accessed February 2017).
9   With or without notice.

(b) hold an A rating in all tiers of their licence;
(c) have passed a Home Office compliance check, before or during the application process, to make sure they still qualify for an A rating

9.14   Sponsors should ensure prior to application that they are fully compliant with sponsorship and right to work checks as the sponsor will be audited as part of the application process. As such it would be prudent for the sponsor to audit employee personnel files and associated documents to establish level of compliance prior to applying for the scheme.

9.15   The Home Office charges an annual fee of £25,000[10] to join the scheme, and sponsors must apply to join via the online Sponsor Management System.

9.16   Whether or not a club makes an application for Premium Sponsorship is, of course, entirely at its discretion. However, in the authors' experience, the benefits afforded by Premium Sponsorship are significant and the priority treatment can be very beneficial for clubs who are under time pressure.

C   GOVERNING BODY ENDORSEMENT (GBE)

9.17   The Governing Body Endorsement:

(a) The Home Office, through its UK Visas and Immigration department, is the governmental body that is responsible for issuing UK work visas. As previously stated, the UK work visas that are relevant to footballers and football clubs are Tier 2 (Sportsperson) and Tier 5 (Temporary Worker) Creative and Sporting. The relevant Governing Body must endorse any application to the Home Office for such work visas and, at that time, the applicant must be able to confirm the endorsement by evidencing the issuance of a Certificate of Sponsorship.[11]
(b) For football clubs operating in England, The FA is the relevant Governing Body to endorse applications to the Home Office for Tier 2 and Tier 5 visas for non-EU/EEA employees.[12] Football clubs seeking to employ non-EU/EEA employees must therefore make an initial application to The FA for a GBE on that employee's behalf. If a club's application is successful, it may then issue a Certificate of Sponsorship[13] and make an application to the Home Office for the relevant UK work visa. In England, the only football clubs who may apply for a GBE are those that are members of the Premier League, the English Football League (EFL) and the Women's Super League (WSL).[14]
(c) A simplified flow chart of the process for a football club to obtain a work visa for non-EU/EEA players or personnel (and the relevant bodies involved) is set out below:

---

10   Subject to change.
11   See the Home Office's Immigration Rules Appendix M: sport governing bodies, available online at: https://www.gov.uk/guidance/immigration-rules/immigration-rules-appendix-m-sports-governing-bodies (accessed February 2018).
12   Immigration Rules, Appendix M (see n 11 above).
13   An English football club may only issue a Certificate of Sponsorship if it is a member of the relevant football league and has satisfied the Home Office's criteria to become a sponsor. See the UK visa sponsorship for employers, https://www.gov.uk/uk-visa-sponsorship-employers/apply-for-your-licence (accessed February 2018).
14   See The FA's Points Based System Governing Body Requirements for Players, Managers, Assistant Managers, Directors of Football, Performance Managers, Female Players and Managers in the Women's Super League, http://www.thefa.com/football-rules-governance/policies/player-registration/points-based-system (accessed February 2018).

Premier League, EFL or WSL football club

Identifies non-EU/EEA player, coach, manager, assistant manager, performance manager or director of football that it wishes to recruit or acquire the registration of

Completes and submits a Governing Body Endorsement application to The FA together with supporting documentation and the applicable fee

The FA

Reviews the Club's Governing Body Endorsement application against its Governing Body Endorsement criteria

Grants a Governing Body Endorsement for any player that meets the automatic criteria or, following a set procedure, exercises its discretion to decide whether to issue a Governing Body Endorsement for any player that fails to meet the automatic criteria

Premier League, EFL or WSL football club

If the Governing Body Endorsement was not granted, Club cannot recruit the non-playing member of staff. They may acquire the registration of player but cannot play him in the UK and must therefore send him out on loan. In either case, the Club cannot make a further application until four months have expired

If the Governing Body Endorsement was granted, Club issues a Certificate of Sponsorship and makes an application to the Home Office for a Tier 2 or Tier 5 work visa, each on behalf of the individual

The Home Office

Reviews the Club's application against set criteria

Grants the individual a Tier 2 or Tier 5 work visa or rejects the Club's application

Premier League, EFL or WSL football club

If Tier 2 or Tier 5 work visa granted, individual can be safely recruited

(a) The FA's Governing Body endorsement criteria

9.18 There are presently seven categories of employee[15] of an English football club that may be granted a GBE, five of which relate to football clubs in the Premier League or the EFL, two of which relate to football clubs in the WSL:

(a) Football clubs in the Premier League or the EFL:
   (i) male players;
   (ii) managers;
   (iii) assistant managers;
   (iv) directors of football; and
   (v) performance managers.
(b) Football clubs in the WSL:
   (i) female players; and
   (ii) managers.

15   Ibid.

9.19   Each category of football club employee listed above is subject to its own GBE criteria agreed by the Home Office with The FA and on consultation with the relevant leagues and representative bodies. For male players, the representative bodies are the Professional Footballers' Association and the Home Associations. For managers and assistant managers, the representative bodies are the League Managers Association and the Home Associations. For directors of football and performance managers, the representative bodies are the League Managers Association, the Professional Footballers' Association and the Home Associations. For female players, the representative body is the Professional Footballers' Association.[16]

9.20   In general, however, the overriding objective of the GBE criteria is to ensure that each football club employee is:

(a) of the highest calibre of employee in their employment category; and
(b) able to contribute significantly to the development of football at top level in England.[17]

9.21   The FA review and update their GBE criteria on a seasonal basis. Though the Home Office must agree to the GBE criteria, The FA and the relevant stakeholders are free to propose changes that they consider will satisfy the overriding objective. Football clubs must therefore be aware that significant changes to the GBE criteria, and, in particular, to the procedural steps, may be introduced prior to the start of a new season. The authors recommend that those responsible for football transfers and registrations set sufficient time aside prior to the start of the new season to ensure that they fully understand the practical or other consequences to the GBE critieria changes.

9.22   A club may apply for a GBE at any time during the season. If a GBE is granted, a club must make the application to the Home Office for a work visa, including the Certificate of Sponsorship as confirmation that the GBE has been granted, within three months of the Certificate of Sponsorship being issued. A club will need to reapply for a GBE if they fail to make the application within the specified time.[18]

9.23   For the purposes of this chapter, the authors will only examine the GBE criteria relating to male and female players in close detail.

(b)   Male player GBE criteria

9.24   The male player GBE criteria are the most stringent and complex of The FA's GBE criteria. The main circumstances in which an English club will need to apply for a GBE are:

(a) when it is purchasing a new non-EU/EEA player;
(b) when an existing non-EU/EEA player is switching from a Tier 5 to a Tier 2 visa;
(c) where it is purchasing a non-EU/EEA player who has previously been loaned to it by an English club; and
(d) where it is signing a non-EU/EEA loan player from a non-English club.[19]

---

16   The latest GBE criteria for Managers in the WSL was not set on consultation with any representative body. See the GBE Requirements for Managers in the WSL, http://www.thefa.com/football-rules-governance/policies/player-registration/points-based-system (accessed February 2018).
17   See The FA's Points Based System Governing Body Requirements for Players, Managers, Assistant Managers, Directors of Football, Performance Managers, Female Players and Managers in the Women's Super League (see n 14 above).
18   See The FA's Points Based System Governing Body Requirements for Players, para 1.4.
19   Ibid, paras 3.2–3.8 (which set out a number of other discrete circumstances in which a GBE may be required).

9.25   It is important to note that a GBE will not be issued to clubs for the purpose of trialists.

9.26   The GBE criteria for male players were strengthened following recommendations made in May 2014 in Greg Dyke's (the then FA Chairman) England Commission Report.[20] Those recommendations were made as a result of the fact that the previous GBE criteria (as part of the overall UK work visa system) was failing to achieve its stated aim of encouraging 'clubs to develop their own players, rather than importing them, and to ensure that only exceptional players from outside the EU are given permission to work in the UK'.[21] In summary, The FA sought to tighten the GBE criteria to increase the overall percentage of English players playing in the Premier League.

9.27   In order to be granted a GBE, a player must either satisfy the automatic criteria or satisfy an FA Exceptions Panel that his 'experience and value',[22] assessed against discretionary criteria, mean that a GBE should be granted in any event. An application is made by the club on behalf of the player it is seeking to sign (or retain).

(c) Automatic criteria

9.28   To satisfy the automatic criteria, a player must be able to demonstrate that he has participated in the required percentage of senior competitive international matches[23] played by his national association during the reference period, ending on the date of the application for a GBE. Where a player is over the age of 21, the reference period is 24 months; where a player is 21 or under, the reference period is 12 months,[24] a difference that the authors consider was included to account for the difficulty a young player faces in establishing himself in the nation's senior team shortly after leaving the junior ranks.

9.29   The required percentage of matches is calculated on a sliding scale that is linked to the Aggregated FIFA World Rankings:[25] players emanating from a national association higher up the Aggregated FIFA World Ranking have a lower required percentage than those players emanating from a national association lower down the Aggregated FIFA World Ranking. A difference that the authors consider was included to account for the fact that it is likely to be more difficult for a player to establish himself as a regular member of the senior first team if his national association is one of the world's top teams. The required percentage of matches for the 2017/18 season is as follows:

(a) national associations ranked between 1 and 10 of the Aggregated FIFA World Rankings, 30% and above;

(b) national associations ranked between 11 and 20 of the Aggregated FIFA World Rankings, 45% and above;

20 See The FA's press release dated 8 May 2014 including a link to The FA Chairman's England Commission Report, http://www.thefa.com/news/2014/may/08/fa-commission-report (accessed February 2018).
21 See Section 3.2 of The FA Chairman's England Commission Report, http://www.thefa.com/news/2014/may/08/fa-commission-report (accessed February 2018).
22 The FA's Points Based System Governing Body Requirements for Players, para 2.2.
23 For the 2017/18 season, competitive international matches are any matches played in the FIFA World Cup Finals, the FIFA World Cup Qualifying Groups, the FIFA Confederations Cup, and the Continental Cup Qualifiers and Finals: The FA's Points Based System Governing Body Requirements for Players, Glossary.
24 The FA's Points Based System Governing Body Requirements for Players, para 2.1.
25 Updated monthly and available on The FA website at http://www.thefa.com/football-rules-governance/policies/player-registration/points-based-system (accessed February 2018).

(c) national associations ranked between 21 and 30 of the Aggregated FIFA World Rankings, 60% and above; and

(d) national associations ranked between 31 and 50 of the Aggregated FIFA World Rankings, 75% and above.

9.30   If a player satisfies the required percentage over the applicable reference period, The FA will automatically grant him a GBE. Notwithstanding, applicant clubs must be aware that there are a number of evidential factors to consider when calculating a player's percentage participation:

(a) the onus is on the applicant club to provide, at the time of the application, written confirmation of all matches (competitive international matches, friendlies, and any other international matches) that the player's national association participated in during the reference period and in which the player:
   (i) took part;
   (ii) was unavailable for selection;[26] and
   (iii) did not take part but was not unavailable for selection;

(b) an applicant club must exclude any competitive international matches from the calculation of the required percentage that occurred during the reference period and at a time where that particular player was not available for selection; and

(c) an applicant club must include any international friendly matches in the calculation of the required percentage if less than 30% of that particular player's national association matches during the reference period were competitive international matches.[27]

(d) Discretionary criteria

9.31   An applicant club may apply to the Player Status Department at The FA for any player who does not meet the automatic criteria. The FA will then appoint an Exceptions Panel to consider the club's application. The Exceptions Panel is made up of three members, appointed by The FA, comprising:

(a) an independent and legally qualified chairperson; and

(b) two independent panel members having relevant experience at the top of the game.

9.32   No individual who would, objectively, be considered to have a current association with the applicant club will be appointed to the Exceptions Panel. Applicant clubs are informed of the composition of the Exceptions Panel 'at the earliest opportunity in advance' and are able to challenge the appointment of any panel member if 'circumstances exist which give rise to an actual or perceived conflict of interest on the part of the Panel Member'.[28] The chairperson (where the challenge relates to an independent panel member) or The FA (where the challenge relates to the chairperson) has the absolute discretion to determine whether the panel member should be excluded and replaced.[29]

---

26 A player who was injured or suspended at the time of the match. Written supporting evidence must be provided by the national association or club doctor. See The FA's Points Based System Governing Body Requirements for Players, para 2.1.

27 The FA's Points Based System Governing Body Requirements for Players, para 2.1.

28 The test for whether there has been procedural unfairness in the context of an appearance of a conflict of interest is 'whether the fair-minded and informed observer, having considered the facts, would conclude that there was a real possibility that the tribunal was biased' (*Flaherty v* NGRC [2005] EWCA Civ 1117 CA, at 26–31).

29 The FA's Points Based System Governing Body Requirements for Players, paras 2.2.3–2.2.7.

9.33   A club's right to challenge the appointment of a panel member was introduced in the 2016–2017 edition of the GBE criteria and, in the authors' opinion, offers an important additional protection for clubs. If an application is unsuccessful, a club must wait four months before they can submit another application on behalf of the same player.[30] Accordingly, it is in the club's interest to take time to ensure that the Exceptions Panel does not contain any individual who, in the club's reasonable opinion, would not be able to deal with an application fairly and impartially.

9.34   Generally, an Exceptions Panel will consider an application on the papers. An oral hearing may be requested but will only be granted in the 'most exceptional circumstances and for those cases in respect of which [the Exceptions Panel] is persuaded are complex …'.[31] An Exceptions Panel will determine an application on the basis of simple majority with all panel members being required to vote.

9.35   An Exceptions Panel will follow the procedures set out in Appendix 1 to The FA's GBE Requirements For Players and assess the application based on a mix of objective and subjective criteria as follows:

(a)   the application is reviewed against the objective Part A criteria;
(b)   if the player achieves four or more points, the Exceptions Panel will subjectively review of the application and the supporting information provided by the applicant club and 'any other information which it considers to be relevant in its absolute discretion in respect of the player'; or
(c)   if the player achieves less than four points, the Exceptions Panel will:
  (i)   consider the application against the objective Part B criteria; and
  (ii) subsequently, subjectively review of the application and the supporting information provided by the applicant club and 'any other information which it considers to be relevant in its absolute discretion in respect of the player'.[32]

9.36   It is important to note that, even if a player achieves four or more points in respect of the objective Part A criteria, the grant of a GBE is not guaranteed and whether one is granted is entirely at the Exceptions Panel's discretion.[33] Anonymised previous decisions, including the outcome, are available from The FA[34] and applicant clubs would be well advised to request copies. Though there is no requirement for Exceptions Panels to follow previous decisions they will provide useful guidance as to how an Exceptions Panel may react to particular arguments.

9.37   The Exceptions Panel may take into account the following factors when carrying out a subjective review:

(a)   the fact that a player has satisfied or partially satisfied certain of the automatic criteria and the extent to which he falls short of these criteria;

---

30   The FA's Points Based System Governing Body Requirements for Players, para 2.2.14.
31   Ibid.
32   Ibid, Appendix 1, para 2.
33   In *Aston Villa FC, Limited v The Football Association Limited* the club challenged in a Rule K arbitration the refusal of a GBE where the requisite points total had been achieved, under a previous iteration of the GBE criteria. Sitting as sole arbitrator, Charles Flint QC held that 'the power to decline to recommend a GBE … is framed as an unfettered discretion'. That the discretion is unfettered has been clarified in the more recent iterations of the criteria.
34   And certain other stakeholders as defined in the GBE criteria. The FA's Points Based System Governing Body Requirements for Players, para 2.2.14.

(b)   the reasons why the automatic criteria were not met;

(c)   against which objective criteria the player has been assessed and how many points have been scored; and

(d)   the extent to which he has satisfied or partially satisfied the objective criteria.

9.38   In the authors' experience, applicant clubs are well advised to include with their application evidence that:

(a)   supports why a particular player is of the highest calibre. For example, a SWOT analysis of his attributes as a player, a player CV, or press coverage of notable achievements not falling within the GBE criteria but that are demonstrative of his playing prowess nonetheless; and

(b)   addresses any clear gaps in that player's application. For example, a letter from a director of football or manager at his current club or national association explaining the underlying reasons why a player has failed to meet the required percentage and why the club is convinced that those reasons will no longer be applicable going forward.

9.39   The objective criteria seeks to ascribe a numerical value to a particular player's 'experience and value'[35] to provide guidance to the Exceptions Panel as to whether that player is in fact 'internationally established at the highest level and that his employment will make a significant contribution to the development of football at the highest level in England'.[36] The objective Part A and Part B criteria are assessed on a seasonal basis and focus on the following:

(a)   the transfer fee paid for the player;

(b)   the wages being paid to the player;

(c)   the national league that the player's club is currently playing in and the number of minutes that the player has played; and

(d)   the player's current club's record in continental competitions and the number of minutes that the player has played.[37]

9.40   Applicant clubs must pay a base fee for each GBE application and an additional fee where an application is required to go before an Exceptions Panel. At the time of writing, the base fee was £500 + VAT and the additional fee was £5,000 + VAT[38] meaning that a failed GBE application can be a costly exercise for whoever foots the bill which, in the authors' experience, is often not the applicant club.

(e)   Female player GBE criteria

9.41   The GBE criteria for female players are much shorter than those applicable to their male counterparts. The circumstances in which an application for a GBE is required (and the circumstances in which one is not required) to be made are broadly the same as those for male players.[39]

---

35   The FA's Points Based System Governing Body Requirements for Players, para 2.2.
36   Ibid, Appendix 1, para 5.
37   In addition, the objective part B criteria also looks at the results of a player's national association. The FA's Points Based System Governing Body Requirements for Players, Appendix 1, para 3.
38   The FA's Points Based System Governing Body Requirements for Players, para 4.
39   Governing Body Endorsement Requirements for Female Players, pp 2–4 (see n 14 above).

9.42   In order to be eligible for a GBE, an applicant club must demonstrate that:

(a) they are a member of the WSL;

(b) the player has played for her country in at least 75% of its competitive women's 'A' team matches[40] where she was available for selection, during the two years preceding the date of the application; and

(c) the player's country must be at or above 40th place in the official FIFA World Rankings when averaged over the two years preceding the date of the application.[41]

9.43   If a player does not meet the above criteria, a club may request an appeal panel to consider the player's skills and experience. The appeals panel is specified to be independent and subject to separate terms.[42] Applicant clubs are warned to provide all supporting evidence at the time of submitting their application as it is not possible to present it at a later date and, following an unsuccessful application, an applicant club may not make a further application for that same player within four months of the original application date.[43]

9.44   Arguably, the simple GBE criteria for Female Players are more flexible and provide applicant clubs with a greater opportunity to obtain a GBE for their target non-EU/EEA players. However, there are a number of procedural uncertainties created by the GBE criteria for female players such as:

(a) confirmation that if a player meets the GBE criteria they will be automatically be granted a GBE. In the authors' opinion that is an inference that can likely be made but the criteria only specify that satisfaction of the criteria will make a player '*eligible*' for a GBE and therefore, without further guidance from The FA, applicant clubs should not take this fact for granted;

(b) the lack of clear guidance as to the processes the independent panel will follow. In the authors' opinion, for transparency and clarity, the independent panel should follow and be subject to the Exceptions Panel rules, tailored for the WSL;

(c) the lack of clear guidance as to what criteria the independent panel will assess any players against if they fail to fulfil the criteria. Again, in the authors' opinion, it can be strongly argued that the criteria against which those applications should be assessed is the objective Part A and Part B criteria from the male player GBE criteria, tailored for the WSL. However, applicant clubs and their applications would benefit greatly from further guidance from The FA; and

(d) whether the decision of an independent panel is appealable. The GBE criteria refer to the decision being an 'appeal' but do not expressly state that such a decision is final and binding and not subject to appeal. In the authors' opinion, that leaves the door open for appeal under The FA's Rule K Arbitration proceedings. This is an aspect of the GBE process in which both The FA and the applicant club would benefit from further clarification.

---

40 Defined as a FIFA World Cup match, a FIFA Women's World Cup Qualifying group match, a UEFA Women's Championships and Qualifier, the African Championship for Women and Qualifiers; the Asian Women's Championships and Qualifiers, the CONCACAF Women's Gold Cup, the CONMEBOL Women's Championships and Qualifiers, and the Olympic Football Tournament Women's Finals. Governing Body Endorsement Requirements for Female Players, p 2.

41 Governing Body Endorsement Requirements for Female Players, pp 1 and 2.

42 At the time of writing, the authors had been unable to locate the terms of the independent panel in the section of The FA's website for Players Status – Registrations and the Points Based System.

43 The same restriction is applicable to male players. Governing Body Endorsement Requirements for Female Players, p 5 (see n 14 above).

9.45   Applicant clubs need not pay a base fee for a GBE application but must pay a fee if an application is referred to the independent panel. At the time of writing that fee was £480 + VAT. The lower fees presumably reflect the lower number of applications made in the WSL when compared to the Premier League and the EFL.

D   TIER 2 (SPORTSPERSON) AND TIER 5 (TEMPORARY WORKER) CREATIVE AND SPORTING

9.46   Licensed sponsors, who have successfully applied for a player or personnel GBE, will be in a position to assign a Tier 2 (Sportsperson) or Tier 5 (Temporary Worker) Creative and Sporting Certificate of Sponsorship to the player via the Sponsor Management System. The sponsored player will then be able to apply for a visa (subject to meeting eligibility criteria below) to enter the UK or for Further Leave to Remain in the UK if they are already sponsored and in the UK and switching/ extending their permission or permanently transferring to a new club.

(a)   Tier 2 (Sportsperson)

9.47   Players applying for a visa under this category, must score a total of 70 points:

(a)   50 points for holding a valid Tier 2 (Sportsperson) Certificate of Sponsorship;
(b)   10 points for meeting the English-language requirement;
(c)   10 points for meeting the maintenance requirement.

9.48   The player will score 50 points for holding a valid Tier 2 (Sportsperson) Certificate of Sponsorship, which the sponsoring club will assign (subject to the GBE criteria being met and issued).

9.49   Players must score 10 points for English language. The requirement is met by taking and passing a Home Office approved test[44] at Level A1 of the Council of Europe's Common European Framework for Language Learning. Nationals of majority English speaking countries[45] or those who hold a degree level qualification taught in English[46] will automatically meet this requirement.

9.50   In addition, the player must meet the maintenance requirement to show they have enough funds to maintain and accommodate themselves (and any eligible dependants) in the UK for the first month of their visa. They must have held at least £945 for the main applicant and £630 for each dependant accompanying them to the UK for the 90-day period immediately prior to their visa application. Sponsors who are A rated can certify this requirement on behalf of the player and their eligible dependant family members.

---

44   The list of approved English language tests is available at https://www.gov.uk/government/ publications/guidance-on-applying-for-uk-visa-approved-english-language-tests (accessed February 2018).
45   Antigua and Barbuda, Australia, The Bahamas, Barbados, Belize, Canada, Dominica, Grenada, Guyana, Jamaica, New Zealand, St Kitts and Nevis, St Lucia, St Vincent and the Grenadines, Trinidad and Tobago or the USA.
46   Independent verification that the degree is equivalent to a UK degree and that it was taught in English is required from UK NARIC (National Recognition Information Centre).

9.51 The duration of visa issued will be linked to the duration of the GBE. The FA will issue a GBE for the shorter of three years or the length of the player's contract. The sponsoring club should assign the Certificate of Sponsorship in line with this duration, which in turn will dictate the duration of leave granted to the player. The player may extend their permission from within the UK up to a maximum of six years as a Tier 2 (Sportsperson). The player may however be eligible for Indefinite Leave to Remain in the UK after five years continuous residence in the UK. After six years' continuous residence in the UK or visa expiration as a Tier 2 (Sportsperson) the player will be hit by a 12-month cooling off period, which will prohibit them from extending their Tier 2 status or returning to the UK for a period of 12 months. The cooling off period must be completed outside of the UK or if in the UK outside of the Tier 2 sponsorship category. The cooling off period can be avoided in certain circumstances such as being classed as a Tier 2 High Earner which is currently a guaranteed gross annual base salary of £159,600 (subject to change).

(b) Tier 5 (Temporary Worker) Creative and Sporting

9.52 The requirement for a visa is broadly the same as for the Tier 2 (Sportsperson) category with the exception that there is no requirement to demonstrate competency in English language. The visa can be granted for a maximum of 12 months and can be extended up to a maximum of 12 months from within the UK. Time spent in the UK under Tier 5 (Temporary Worker) Creative and Sporting does not count towards indefinite leave to remain in the UK. A rated sponsors will be able to certify the maintenance requirement for the player but will not be able to certify the maintenance requirement for the player's dependant family member's visa applications.

9.53 A unique characteristic of this visa category is that sports-related visitor visa holders can switch to Tier 5 (Temporary Worker) Creative and Sporting (but not Tier 2 (Sportsperson) from within the UK, provided the sponsoring club assigned the Tier 5 Certificate of Sponsorship before the player entered the UK.

(c) Switching from Tier 5 (Temporary Worker) Creative and Sporting to Tier 2 (Sportsperson)

9.54 A key consideration for clubs in utilising Tier 5 (Temporary Worker) Creative and Sporting over Tier 2 (Sportsperson) is that there is no English language requirement. Where a player enters the UK under Tier 5 and satisfies the English language requirement within the first 12 months they may switch/vary their visa to Tier 2 (Sportsperson). The sponsor will need to apply for a new GBE, assign new sponsorship and the player will need to make a further Leave to Remain application to vary their immigration permission.

E LOANS/TRANSFERS

9.55 For the purpose of the GBE and immigration requirements, loans are defined as temporary transfers which do not extend beyond the end of the season in which the registration is temporarily transferred. The loan will only be permissible within a player's current period of approval.

9.56   Where a sponsored player is moving to another club in the UK on a loan basis, the parent club (ie the sponsor) must notify the Home Office that the player has temporarily moved location. The loaning club retains overall responsibility for the player as his employer and sponsor. The player is granted permission to move temporarily under the provisions of his current leave and sponsorship. The receiving club does not need to hold a sponsor licence.

9.57   Where a player is moving to a club outside the UK on a temporary transfer basis, the parent club must inform the Home Office via the Sponsor Management System of the player's technical change of employment ie to whom the payer will be loaned, location and loan duration.

9.58   Players joining an English club on loan from an overseas club (outside the UK) must meet all the requirements of Tier 2 (Sportsperson) or Tier 5 (Temporary Worker) Creative and Sporting and therefore an application for a GBE must be submitted to The FA.

9.59   Where a club wishes to make significant changes to the terms and conditions of the player's contract, eg change of salary or length of contract, the sponsoring club must notify the Home Office of this change via the Sponsor Management System in line with their sponsor compliance obligations.

9.60   Where a Tier 2 (Sportsperson)[47] sponsored player is permanently transferred to another club, the current sponsoring club must inform the Home Office via the Sponsor Management System and withdraw their sponsorship (within ten working days of the player's last day of employment). The new club will be required to obtain a new GBE for the player (and a sponsor licence if it does not have one already), before it can issue a Certificate of Sponsorship to the player. The player must then apply and secure further Leave to Remain in the UK or entry clearance from abroad in line with the new Certificate of Sponsorship prior to playing for the new club.

F   INDEFINITE LEAVE TO REMAIN AND BRITISH CITIZENSHIP

9.61   A player who has resided in the UK for a continuous period of five years as a Tier 2 (Sportsperson) may qualify to permanently settle in the UK by applying for Indefinite Leave to Remain (ILR). Once a player holds ILR they are deemed free from UK immigration control and therefore do not require further GBE's or sponsorship to live and play in the UK. After having held ILR for at least 12 months, a player may then be eligible and wish to naturalise as a British citizen.

(a)   Indefinite leave to remain

9.62   Players sponsored under Tier 2 (Sportsperson) may be eligible to apply to permanently settle in the UK by applying for ILR. This means that the player will no longer have any time restrictions on their stay in the UK and will be able to live and

---

47   Tier 5 (Temporary Worker) Creative and Sporting sponsored players cannot permanently change club/sponsor (loans permitted) from within the UK. They will be required to leave the UK and apply for a new visa.

work in the UK without restriction. ILR status can be lost where the holder is absent from the UK for a period of two years or more.

9.63 Players sponsored under Tier 2 (Sportsperson) may be eligible to apply for ILR provided they:

(a) entered the UK lawfully;
(b) have spent a continuous period of five years lawfully in the UK as a Tier 2 (Sportsperson), and have not been absent from the UK for more than 180 days during any 12-month period preceding the date of application;
(c) are paid a gross annual salary which is at least equal to the appropriate rate for the job[48] and is at least £35,000;[49]
(d) will continue to be employed and paid by their current Tier 2 (Sportsperson) sponsoring club;
(e) meet the Knowledge of Language and Life in the UK requirements; and
(f) are not in the UK in breach of immigration laws.

(b) British citizenship

9.64 The current legal framework governing the criteria under which an application for naturalisation can be made is set out in the British Nationality Act 1981 (BNA 1981). For the purposes of this chapter, we have set out the naturalisation criteria under the five-year Tier 2 residence rules.

9.65 A player who has held ILR for at least 12 months, may be eligible to apply to naturalise as a British citizen.

9.66 The legal requirements[50] to be met prior to application are that the player:

(a) is aged 18 or over on the date of application;
(b) is of sound mind;
(c) intends to continue to live in the UK;
(d) has sufficient knowledge of life and language in the UK;
(e) is of good character;
(f) has lived in the UK for a minimum of five years prior to application.

And must usually have:

(a) lived in the UK for at least the five years before the date of application;[51]
(b) spent no more than 450 days outside the UK during those five years;
(c) spent no more than 90 days outside the UK in the 12-month period immediately preceding the date of application;
(d) be free of immigration time restrictions on the date of application, and have been free of immigration time restrictions for the 12-month period before making the application; and

---

48 As stated in the Codes of Practice set out in the Immigration Rules, Appendix J (see n 11 above) (note the sports-related SOC codes do not specify a minimum salary).
49 Must be paid at least: £35,000 if the date of application is on or after 6 April 2016; £35,500 if the date of application is on or after 6 April 2018; £35,800 if the date of application is on or after 6 April 2019; £36,200 if the date of application is on or after 6 April 2020; £36,900 if the date of application is on or after 6 April 2021; £37,900 if the date of application is on or after 6 April 2022.
50 BNA 1981, s 6(1).
51 Applicants must also have been physically present in the UK on the day five years before the application is received by the Home Office.

(e) not have been in breach of the Immigration Rules in the five-year period before making the application.

9.67   The Home Office retains a degree of discretion, which they may exercise over some of the residence (ie waive absences over the 450/90 days requirement) and Knowledge of Language and Life in the UK requirements where there are special circumstances.[52] The reader will note that the residence requirement is stricter than for ILR.

9.68   If the player can meet the qualifying criteria they must complete and file an application for Naturalisation as a British Citizen (Form AN).[53] Naturalisation applications can take up to six months to process and there is no fast track option. If applying via an eligible local authority 'check and send' scheme, an applicant may wish to include their application for a first passport at the same time.

9.69   Upon approval of the naturalisation application, the applicant will be issued a 'Citizenship Invitation' to attend a citizenship ceremony where they will be issued their certificate of naturalisation. Applicants can attend a public ceremony or opt for a private ceremony. At the ceremony the applicant will be required to say either an Oath or Affirmation of allegiance to Her Majesty the Queen and the Pledge of loyalty to the UK.

9.70   On receipt of the certificate of naturalisation, the applicant will then be able to apply for a British Passport via Her Majesty's Passport Office (unless submitted alongside the naturalisation application).

G   DUAL OR MULTIPLE NATIONALITY

9.71   The UK allows dual/multiple nationality; however some countries do not. Certain countries have procedural steps that must be adhered to prior to naturalising as British in order for the applicant to retain their existing citizenship. Therefore prior to naturalising as a British Citizen, applicants must first verify whether the acquisition of British citizenship may result in them forfeiting their existing citizenship, or what procedural steps they must follow to retain their existing citizenship.

H   VISITORS

9.72

(a) Foreign players, coaches and associated key personnel may visit the UK for up to six months to participate in specific sports-related events. Whether or not a visa is required prior to their arrival in the UK will depend on their nationality, which will define the applicant as a non-visa national (entry granted on arrival in the UK) or a visa national[54] (prior entry clearance application and visa endorsement required before travelling to the UK).

---

52 BNA 1981, Sch 1, paras 2(a)–(e), 4.
53 Available at https://www.gov.uk/government/publications/application-to-naturalise-as-a-british-citizen-form-an (accessed February 2018).
54 Visa national list available at https://www.gov.uk/guidance/immigration-rules/immigration-rules-appendix-v-visitor-rules#appendix-2-visa-national-list (accessed February 2018).

(b) Whilst in the UK, a visiting sportsperson must limit their activities to the following:
  (i) taking part in a sports tournament or sports event as an individual or part of a team;
  (ii) making personal appearances and taking part in promotional activities;
  (iii) taking part in trials provided they are not in front of a paying audience;
  (iv) take part in short periods of training provided they are not being paid by a UK sporting body;
  (v) joining an amateur team or club to gain experience in a particular sport if they are an amateur in that sport.
(c) Associated personal or technical staff of the sports visitor may also enter as a visitor provided they are attending the same event as the sports person.
(d) Visiting sportspersons can stay in the UK for up to six months in a 12-month period and must intend to leave the UK. However, an Immigration Officer may challenge a visitor's intention if they plan to stay for the full six-month duration and may request additional confirmation that the visitor's proposed activities are not in breach of those permitted under the visitor rules. Further, visiting sportspersons cannot receive remuneration/pay for the time they are in the UK, clubs must limit any payment to accommodation and/or travel expenses. Visiting sportspersons must also be able to demonstrate that they are able to maintain and accommodate themselves in the UK without recourse to public funds.
(e) A player may visit the UK to receive private medical treatment provided they have arranged their private medical treatment before they travel to the UK. They will require a letter from their doctor or consultant detailing the medical condition requiring consultation or treatment; the estimated costs and likely duration of any treatment (which must be of a finite duration); and where the consultation or treatment will take place.

(a) Alternative visa considerations

9.73 Certain players may qualify for a visa in their own right based on ancestry and marriage that may allow them to work in the UK and do not restrict them from taking up employment as a professional sportspersons. Where players qualify for immigration permission in their own right they will not require a GBE and sponsorship to play in the UK.

I ALTERNATIVE VISA OPTIONS

(a) UK ancestry

9.74

(a) Where a player has UK ancestry they may qualify for a UK ancestry visa. To qualify they must be at least 17 years old, a Commonwealth citizen, able to prove that one of their grandparents was born in the UK, they plan to and are able to work in the UK and to maintain and accommodate themselves in the UK.
(b) Successful applicants will be given leave valid for five years. As there is no restriction on employment they are able to change employer/club without requiring further immigration permission. After five continuous years' residence they may qualify for ILR. Eligible family members may also apply for a visa to accompany them to the UK.

(b)   Spouse or partner of a British national or settled person

9.75

(a) Where a player is married to or a partner of a British national or a person with settled status in the UK, they can apply to join them in the UK or travel to the UK with them as their spouse/partner. To qualify for a visa as the spouse/ partner of a British national or person present and settled in the UK the foreign player must satisfy the following requirements: applicant and their spouse/ partner must be 18 years old or over; they must have met each other and be legally married; they must intend to live together permanently; they must have enough money to support themselves (and any dependants) without claiming public funds; the British national/person with settled status in the UK must earn more than £18,600 per year or have enough savings to be able to maintain and accommodate the applicant. The minimum financial requirement increases per dependent child; there must be suitable accommodation available in the UK; and the foreign spouse must satisfy the English language requirement.

(b) Upon successful application the visa will be granted for a period of 2.5 years and may be extended from within the UK for a further 2.5 years. This visa would also afford the foreign player unrestricted work rights and they may apply for ILR after five years' residence in the UK.

(c)   Non-EEA national partner of an EEA national

9.76

(a) Where a non-EEA national player is married to or the partner of an EEA national they may apply for an EEA Family Permit. This permit will be valid for six months and allow the non-EEA national to join or travel to the UK with their EEA national partner. Where the couple are not married they must demonstrate they are in a durable relationship and are cohabiting. Once in the UK the non-EEA spouse/partner can then apply for a five-year Residence Card. The EEA Family Permit and Residence Card afford the non-EEA national unrestricted working rights in the UK for as long the EEA national spouse/partner exercises 'treaty rights' in the UK. After five years' lawful residence in the UK they may be eligible for permanent residence in the UK.

(b) It is important to note that not all visas allow unrestricted work rights in the UK. Clubs must check a prospective player's immigration permission carefully so as to ensure there are no restrictions on the player taking up employment in the UK as a professional sportsperson.

J   EU/EEA NATIONALS

9.77

(a) As at the time of publication, the UK remains a member of the European Union. As such and until such time as the UK exits the European Union (expected to be 29 March 2019), EEA and Swiss nationals benefit from 'freedom of movement' provided they are exercising a 'treaty right' ie as a worker, self-sufficient person, student or self-employed. Clubs employing EEA national players (with the exception of Croatian nationals[55]) are not required to sponsor them under

---

55 Note restrictions on Croatian nationals expire on 30 June 2018.

the Points Based System and the EEA national is not required to hold a visa/residence permit to lawfully live and play in the UK.

(b) There are separate provisions that apply to Croatian nationals. Clubs seeking to employ a Croatian national player will be subject to the GBE and Tier 2 Sportsperson requirements. Instead of applying for a visa they must apply for an accession worker card. They will become exempt from authorisation following 12 months' continuous lawful employment in the UK.

(c) This area will undoubtedly see significant change over the coming months and years. EEA nationals may wish to secure permanent residence or residence certificates evidencing their eligibility to live, work and remain in the UK.

(d) EEA nationals who have lawfully exercised 'treaty rights' and resided in the UK for a continuous period of five years will have automatically acquired permanent residence status. Whilst the acquisition of Permanent Residence is automatic, EEA nationals should apply to the Home Office for a document certifying this status. It has been suggested by the UK government, that application for permanent residence prior to the UK's exit will likely speed up/streamline the application process for any documentation the Home Office require EEA nationals to hold post the UK's exit from the EU.

(e) EEA nationals who have resided in the UK for a period of six years and who hold a document certifying permanent residence, may be eligible to naturalise as British citizens. Naturalisation applications are subject to stricter residence requirements and knowledge of life and language in the UK tests.

(f) It is important that prospective applicants first check that they are allowed to hold dual nationality. Note also that the acquisition of British citizenship by a national of a European Economic Area (EEA) state or Switzerland will in most cases have implications for the exercise of free movement rights for that person and their family members in the UK.

(g) EEA nationals who do not qualify for permanent residence should consider registering their residence in the UK and lawful exercise of 'treaty rights' by applying for a registration certificate. This will provide the player a certificate valid for five years.

K   CONCLUSION

9.78   As set out at the beginning of this chapter, football is big business and English football clubs seeking to improve performance on the pitch while also enhancing their commercial return are increasingly looking to recruit the best talents from abroad.

9.79   This chapter has provided a 'whistle-stop' tour to the UK's immigration system as relevant to English football clubs. Though the specific detail of the UK's immigration system may undergo significant change following Brexit, the authors nonetheless hope that this chapter will serve as a useful practical guide to the key regulatory bodies, steps and documents with which any club seeking to attract and retain international talent must be familiar.

CHAPTER 10

Academies and Youth Issues

Jonathan Ellis and **James Eighteen** (Northridge)

A   OVERVIEW OF YOUTH FOOTBALL IN ENGLAND

(a)   Early formats

10.1   Competitive top-level youth football began in 1997 with the introduction of the FA Premier Youth League. This competition replaced the regional youth leagues as the focal point for top-level youth football in England.

10.2   A year later in 1998, The Football Association (The FA) introduced an academy system and the competition was renamed the Premier Academy League. Academy teams competed in two age groups (under-17 and under-19) and in four regional conferences. The Premier Academy League was open to Premier League and English Football League (EFL) clubs.

10.3   In the 2004/05 season, the format of the Premier Academy League changed again to become a single under-18 competition. Under-16 teams played friendlies against one another.

(b)   The Elite Player Performance Plan (EPPP)

10.4   The Elite Player Performance Plan (EPPP), introduced in 2012, is the result of consultation between the Premier League and its clubs; representatives of the EFL; The FA and other key football stakeholders. The stated aim of the EPPP is to produce more, and better, home grown players. The four key functions of the EPPP are: the Games Programme; Education; Coaching and Elite Performance.

10.5   The Games Programme replaced the Premier Academy League format with several competitions aimed at aiding the transition between youth football and elite-level competitive football both domestically and internationally. The Games Programme includes competitions such as the Premier League 2, the Professional Development League and the Premier League Cup.

10.6   The result is a sophisticated development programme that is designed to nurture children from a young age. Football clubs seek to identify the best young players through employing scouts and running well-resourced academies and development centres. There can be strong competition amongst clubs to attract the most talented players.

B ACADEMIES

10.7   The academy system, operated as part of the EPPP, is governed by the Youth Development Rules (YDRs). Academies are operated by clubs and are the place at which young players are coached and educated.[1]

10.8   An academy must be licensed[2] and operate in accordance with the YDRs.[3] To be awarded a licence, the Professional Game Board[4] must be satisfied that the academy complies with a set of lengthy requirements called the Core Conditions.[5] The maximum term for a licence is three years.[6]

10.9   Each academy is assigned to one of four categories,[7] from Category 1 to Category 4 (with Category 1 being the most elite). The categorisation depends on factors such as the quality of the training facilities and the coaching, education and welfare provisions available to the players. A Category 1 academy is required, for example, to have one floodlit grass pitch enclosed with perimeter fencing.[8] Categorisation also impacts the level of EPPP central funding received by the academy, with Category 1 academies receiving the highest and Category 4 academies receiving the lowest.

10.10   Each club which operates an academy is required to produce and make available several strategic documents, called the Vision Statement, the Playing Philosophy, a Coaching Philosophy and an Academy Performance Plan.[9]

10.11   Each academy is required to measure and record all aspects of a player's progression, development and education using an online application called a Performance Clock.[10] This application records the player's progress throughout their development and provides a breakdown of time spent on each area of training (such as technical and practical development, matches played and education).[11] Academies are required to subject players to review at regular intervals.[12]

10.12   The YDRs set out in detail the staff that each academy is required to employ. Some positions are mandatory for all Academies, such as a full-time academy

---

1   Premier League YDRs 2017–18, Rule 1.1.
2   Premier League YDRs 2017–2018, Rule 3.1.
3   Premier League YDRs 2017–2018, Rule 3.2.
4   The Professional Game Board appoints an Independent Standards Organisation to advise it on licence applications and annual audits of academies.
5   Premier League YDRs 2017–2018, Rule 8. The Core Conditions are referenced at Rule 1.23.
6   Premier League YDRs 2017–2018, Rule 4.
7   Premier League YDRs 2017–2018, Rule 5.
8   Premier League YDRs 2017–2018, Rule 303.
9   Premier League YDRs 2017–2018, Rule 28. Vision Statement refers to a written statement containing the club's desired culture, values, ambitions and strategic aims and the activities which have been or will be adopted for the achievement of the above (see Rule 1.77). Playing Philosophy means a written statement including the principles, values, playing style and tactical approach of all the teams, as well as profiles setting out the club's desired technical, tactical, physical and psychological skills of each player (see Rule 1.59). Coaching Philosophy similarly refers to a written statement setting out the means by which the club will coach its players in each age group, in order to best develop the skills set out in the club's Playing Philosophy (see Rule 1.20). Academy Performance Plan is a document with the club's academy goals, strategy and performance targets which should be consistent with the three aforementioned documents (see Rule 1.6).
10   Premier League YDRs 2017–2018, Rule 41. The Performance Clock is an embedded application in the Performance Management Application (an online support service developed and maintained by the League and utilised by each club); see Premier League YDRs 2017–2018, Rule 1.58.
11   Premier League YDRs 2017–2018, Guidance Note 1 to Rule 41.
12   For more information on these reviews see the Premier League YDRs 2017–2018, Guidance Note 1 to Rules 42–50.

manager[13] and coaches.[14] Other positions depend on the categorisation of the academy in question. For example, only Category 1 and Category 2 Academies are required to employ a full-time lead sports scientist.[15]

10.13   Each academy must produce a Coaching Curriculum[16] and provide a minimum number of hours of coaching per week (which depends on the age of the player and the category of the academy).[17]

C   CONTRACTING WITH MINORS

10.14   A club can register a player as an academy player from the age of 9. The law of England and Wales and football's regulatory regime govern how a minor contracts with others. We examine the position in relation to each in this section of the chapter.

(a)   General position under English and Welsh law

10.15   The laws of England and Wales provide that a child reaches the age of capacity at the age of 18.[18] A person under the age of 18 is unable to enter into a binding contract save where the contract is (i) necessary or (ii) analogous to a contract for apprenticeship, education or service, and in each case beneficial to the minor. If one of these exceptions does not apply, the contract is voidable at the option of the minor (ie binding on the other party, but not the minor). If the minor does not void the contract, it is binding on the other party.[19]

10.16   The law seeks to protect children as they are considered vulnerable. However, it also recognises that a minor may benefit from certain contracts such as ones for apprenticeship, education or service. To be valid, the contract as a whole must be beneficial to the minor at the time that it is entered into. It cannot impose onerous terms (such as a provision that wages depend on the will of the employer) or place the minor in a position of subservience to the employer.[20]

10.17   In this context, the High Court considered a contract between a 15-year-old Wayne Rooney and his then agent. Mr Rooney's contract with Everton Football Club was not voidable because it provided the player with education and training. However, the representation agreement between Mr Rooney and his agent was held to be voidable as it was not considered to be necessary in those circumstances.[21] Important factors included the fact that Mr Rooney was already contracted to Everton Football Club at the time he entered into his contract with his agent and that he had no desire to leave the club at that time. Moreover, he could not sign a professional player contract until he was 17 years old (as this is prohibited by the

---

13   Premier League YDRs 2017–2018, Rule 59.
14   Premier League YDRs 2017–2018, Rules 70 and 71.
15   Premier League YDRs 2017–2018, Rule 94 (although note that Rule 52 does provide a discretion that allows a club not to employ certain mandatory staff if they can demonstrate that other staff have the same expertise).
16   Premier League YDRs 2017–2018, Rules 111–113.
17   Premier League YDRs 2017–2018, Rules 114–121.
18   Family Law Reform Act 1969, s 1(1).
19   *Proform Sports Management Ltd v Proactive Sports Management Ltd* [2006] EWHC 2903 (Ch).
20   *Chitty on Contracts*, 32nd Edition (2015), para 9-025.
21   *Proform Sports Management Ltd v Proactive Sports Management Ltd* [2006] EWHC 2903 (Ch).

Rules of The Association). These factors all weighed in favour of the conclusion that the representation contract did not provide him with an education or allow him to earn a living. The judge declined to decide whether the contract was beneficial to Mr Rooney (as he did not have to consider the second limb of the test).[22]

10.18   The law relating to minors is complex and a detailed review of the case law is not within the scope of this book. However, it is worth referencing some of the key cases cited in the Wayne Rooney case as they are a good illustration of the legal position. It has been held that a contract between a minor and the British Boxing Board of Control, in which the minor agreed to be bound by the rules of the Board, was binding.[23] A contract between a minor and publisher for the publication of a minor's biography (which was to be ghost-written) was also binding on the minor.[24] These two cases can be distinguished from the case involving Mr Rooney as they both allowed the minors in question to earn a living (whereas Mr Rooney was already contracted to Everton Football Club before he contracted with his agent). In contrast to these examples, a contract between a minor who boxed professionally and his manager was deemed to be a 'trading contract' and not one that was necessary and was therefore voidable.[25]

10.19   In a recent football case between Aylesbury FC and 16-year-old player Lee Hook, the parties entered into an employment contract which was principally designed to strengthen Aylesbury FC's bargaining position in any future contract negotiation for the player's sale. In such circumstances, the court held that Mr Hook could not be bound by the contract as there was no benefit to him.[26] It was also relevant that the player's wages depended on the will of the employer and that The FA prohibited such arrangements.

(b)   Domestic regulatory restrictions on minors

10.20   The domestic regulatory regime regulates how and when clubs can engage with minors. The key provisions are Rule C of the Rules of The Association (Rule C) and the YDRs (which were adopted wholesale by the EFL).

10.21   The starting point is that a club cannot employ a player on a professional contract if they are under the age of 17.[27] If the person is in full-time education,[28] the prohibition is extended to any person under the age of 18.[29]

10.22   Whilst a club cannot employ a younger player, they can engage with players at a younger age through an academy, but only subject to the strict limitations described below. Before a player can be coached at an academy or play matches for the club which operates the academy, they must be registered as an academy player.

22   Ibid.
23   *Doyle v White City Stadium Ltd* [1935] 1 KB 110.
24   *Chaplin v Leslie Frewin (Publishers) Ltd* [1966] Ch 71.
25   *Shears v Mendeloff* (1914) 30 TLR 342.
26   *Aylesbury Football Club (1997) Ltd v Watford Association Football Club Ltd* (12 June 2002, unreported).
27   Rules of The Association 2017–2018, Rule C(1)(a)(ii).
28   Full-time education means a child who is of compulsory school age within the meaning of the Education Acts applying in England or who is over the school leaving age but is for the time being attending a school or full-time education in an establishment of further education (see Rules of The Association 2017–2018, footnote Rule C(1)(a)(i)).
29   Rules of The Association 2017–2018, Rule C(1)(a)(i).

(i)   Registering with an academy

10.23   The under-9 age group is the youngest age group an academy is permitted to coach.[30] A key principle of the YDRs is that the child continues their education whilst they play football. To register a child, they must be in full-time education. When they reach the under-16 age group, they can leave full-time education and register with an academy, but only on a scholarship.[31]

10.24   A registration requires an application to the league which shall be determined by the Professional Game Board. The YDRs permit a player to undergo a trial for up to six consecutive weeks in any one season without being registered (which can be extended for up to 12 weeks in certain circumstances).[32]

10.25   A club is not permitted to pay an academy player unless they commence a scholarship.[33] A club may, however, reimburse a player's legitimately incurred expenses.[34]

10.26   The YDRs break a player's development down into three stages. As the child grows up the restrictions begin to relax and once a child reaches the under-16 age group, the academy is permitted to contract with a player on a more formal footing.

(ii)   The Foundation Phase

10.27   The Foundation Phase covers the under-9 to under-11 age groups.[35] An academy may only register a player of this age if they live within an hour's travel time of the club's principal venue for coaching and education.[36]

10.28   The registration can only last one year.[37] At the end of the season, the player may decide whether they wish to remain at the club (assuming the club opts to retain their registration), or register for another club.[38]

(iii)   Youth Development Phase

10.29   The Youth Development Phase covers the under-12 to under-16 age groups.[39]

---

30   Rules of The Association 2017–2018, Rule C(4)(B)(i). Note that no application to register any academy player in the under-9 age group may be signed by the academy player before the third Saturday in May immediately preceding their under-9 year (Premier League Youth Development Rules 2017–2018, Rule 264).

31   Premier League Youth Development Rules 2017–2018, Rule 261.

32   See Premier League YDRs 2017–2018, Rules 237 to 248 for a more detailed explanation of how trials work.

33   See Premier League YDRs 2017–2018, Rule 286.

34   See Premier League YDRs 2017–2018, Rule 324.

35   Premier League YDRs 2017–2018, Rule 1.35.

36   Premier League YDRs 2017–2018, Rule 236.

37   Premier League YDRs 2017–2018, Rule 254. This states that players in age groups under-9, under-10, under-11, under-12, under-14 and under-16 shall be registered for one year and those in age groups under-13 and under-15 for two years.

38   There is a process that has to be followed by both the player and the club – see Premier League YDRs 2017–2018, Rules 268–271.

39   Premier League YDRs 2017–2018, Rule 1.78.

10.30   The player must live within 90 minutes travel time of the club's principal venue for coaching and education, with one exception.[40] A Category 1 academy may register a player who lives further than 90 minutes away, but only if they are engaged in the Full-Time Training Model. The Full-Time Training Model is a set of minimum requirements detailed in the YDRs, which includes a minimum of 20 hours' education per week.[41]

10.31   There are again limitations on the duration of a player's registration which varies between one and two years depending on the age of the player.[42]

10.32   Once a player turns 14, it will start to become clear to them whether a career in football is a possibility. From 1 January in the year in which a child turns 14, the player's club may offer them a scholarship agreement[43] (although the scholarship agreement cannot commence until the end of the under-16 year).[44] A scholarship agreement entitles a player to be paid for the first time (albeit the amount they may be paid remains modest).[45]

10.33   If an academy player in the under-16 age group has not received an offer to enter into a Scholarship Agreement by 31 December, they may register as an academy player for another club.[46]

(iv) Professional Development Phase

10.34   The Professional Development Phase is defined as the under-17 to under-21 age groups inclusive.[47]

10.35   There are no travel restrictions on players of this age or any limitations on how long the player can be registered for (save that the under-21 age group is the oldest age group for an academy player).[48]

(v) Inducement

10.36   As stated above, a club cannot pay an academy player anything other than legitimately incurred expenses. This extends to a prohibition on seeking to induce prospective players to either enter into a scholarship or to register with the

---

40   Premier League YDRs 2017–2018, Rule 236.
41   See Premier League YDRs 2017–2018, Rule 1.39 for an explanation of what constitutes a Full Time Training Model.
42   Players in age groups under-12, under-14 and under-16 shall be registered for one year and those in age groups under-13 and under-15 shall be registered for two years (Premier League YDRs 2017–2018, Rule 254). At the end of the season, the under-12 and under-14 players may decide whether they wish to remain at the club for two more seasons (assuming the club opts to retain their registration) or register for another club (Premier League YDRs 2017–2018, Rules 268–271).
43   Premier League YDRs 2017–2018, Rule 278.
44   Premier League YDRs 2017–2018, Rule 285.4. Note the exact date is the last Friday in June in the academic year in which the academy player reaches the ages of 16.
45   Premier League YDRs 2017–2018, Rule 286. The sum permitted is defined as the such remuneration 'as shall be determined by the league from time to time'.
46   Premier League YDRs 2017–2018, Rule 271. Note that in such circumstances the club is not entitled to receive compensation from any club the player subsequently registers with for the training and development of that player (save where the remains in Full Time Education beyond his under-16 year).
47   Premier League YDRs 2017–2018, Rule 1.63.
48   Premier League YDRs 2017–2018, Rule 236.

academy, by offering a benefit of any kind (save that from 1 January in a player's under-16 year, an academy player may be offered a professional contract).[49] Moreover, an academy cannot approach or communicate with a player who has registered with, or agreed to be registered with, another club.[50] This includes making a public statement of interest in such players.[51]

10.37   Academy players are subject to the same restrictions and cannot approach another club (subject to certain exceptions, such as if their registration with their current club has been terminated at the end of the season).[52]

(vi)   Development centres

10.38   A club that operates a Category 1, 2 or 3 academy may operate one or more development centres.[53] However, a minor being coached at a club's development centre may not be registered for, or play for, that club. Development centres allow clubs to trial players for longer periods of time without having the administrative burden of registering those players. The downside to the club is that the player is free to register with another academy.

(c)   International regulation

10.39   Article 19 of FIFA's Regulations on the Status and Transfer of Players (RSTP) prohibits the international transfer of players unless they are over 18 years old (subject to the exceptions set out below).[54] The Court of Arbitration for Sport (CAS) has held that this restriction applies to amateurs and professionals.[55]

10.40   The legality of the Article 19 prohibition has been challenged many times before CAS on the grounds that it is not compliant with European law (such as the freedom of movement requirement) or Swiss public policy. CAS has taken the view that the protection of minors was a legitimate and proportionate objective and rejected each of these challenges,[56] save for one (see para **10.46** below).

10.41   There are several exceptions to the Article 19 prohibition, some of which are provided for in Article 19 itself and some of which FIFA have communicated separately (ie Article 19(2) is not exhaustive).

---

49   An academy cannot induce or attempt to induce a player to enter into a scholarship, or to become registered as an academy player, by offering a benefit, whether in cash or in kind (Premier League YDRs 2017–2018, Rule 300).
50   Premier League YDRs 2017–2018, Rule 297.
51   Premier League YDRs 2017–2018, Rule 298.
52   Premier League YDRs 2017–2018, Rule 299.
53   Premier League YDRs 2017–2018, Rule 122. Note that each Development Centre must be located within one hour's travelling time of the location of its principal venue for the provision of coaching and education to academy players.
54   To avoid the Article 19 prohibition being circumvented through the use of academies which were not affiliated with a national association, FIFA now requires all clubs that operate an academy with 'legal, financial or de facto' links to the club to report all minors who attend the academy to the relevant national association (Article 19bis(1) of the FIFA Regulations on the Status and Transfer of Players).
55   CAS 2008/A/1985 *FC Midtjylland A/S v FIFA*, paras 7.2.5–7.2.6. Article 2 RSTP contains a definition of what constitutes an amateur and a professional player. What constitutes a professional player has been interpreted broadly by CAS (see *Aston Villa FC v B.93 Copenhagen*, CAS 2006/A/1177, para 30).
56   CAS 2008/A/1985 *FC Midtjylland A/S v FIFA*, para 7.4.20.

(i) Article 19(2)(a): parents

10.42   Under this provision an international transfer is permitted where the player's parents move to the country in which the new club is located for reasons not linked to football. As the purpose of the rule is to protect young players, not the parents who follow the player, the test is to assess the true intention and motivation of the player's parents.

10.43   In this regard, CAS has in the past taken into account the following considerations:[57]

(a) the time line between the arrival of the player in a foreign country and the registration request;
(b) the extent to which the player has taken part in football activities prior to the move abroad;
(c) public declarations of the player or parents concerning the motivations for the family's move abroad;
(d) the cultural background of the player's family;
(e) the family's ability to support itself financially without the need to rely on the working activity of the parents or the professional evolution of the player;
(f) the time that the parents first took steps to prepare for a move abroad; and
(g) evidence that the club was interested in obtaining the services of the player prior to the move abroad.

10.44   To date it has been held that the exception must be the player's natural parent(s) who move(s), not another relative. Nevertheless, CAS appears to have demonstrated a willingness to accept that, in certain circumstances, the rule 'conceivably could cover situations beyond the natural parents'.[58]

(ii) Article 19(2)(b): EU/EEA

10.45   The Article 19 prohibition does not apply where the transfer takes place within the territory of the European Union (EU) or European Economic Area (EEA) and the player is aged between 16 and 18, provided that the new club fulfils certain minimum obligations, including providing the player with an adequate 'football education' and ensuring 'optimum living standards'.

10.46   CAS has confirmed that, due to the free movement of workers within the EU/EEA, this exception shall include a player who transfers from a club outside of the EU/EEA to a club within the EU/EEA,[59] provided that the player is a national of a EU/EEA territory.

(iii) Article 19(2)(c): 50km rule

10.47   An international transfer is permitted if both the player's domicile and the club's headquarters are on opposite sides of, but within, 50km of a national border. The player must live at home and the registering club must gain the consent of the two national associations involved.

57 CAS 2013/A/3140; *A v Club Atlético de Madrid SAD & RFEF & FIFA*, paras 8.30–8.31.
58 CAS 2011/A/2354 *E v FIFA*, para 18.
59 CAS 2012/A/2862 *FC Girondins de Bordeaux v FIFA*.

10.48 In addition to the Article 19(2) exceptions above, FIFA has stated that it will permit the international transfer of a minor if:

(a) The player can establish that they relocated to study, not play football. The fact that the player is being educated at a 'serious and recognised educational program' is not sufficient; the primary motivation of the player may still have been sporting reasons.[60]

(b) The national association which has jurisdiction over the player and the new club have signed an agreement 'within the scope of a development program for young players' which includes certain conditions relating to education.[61]

(c) The player has lived continuously for at least five years in the country where they wish to be registered for the first time. This exception was first created by the jurisprudence of the FIFA Players' Status Sub-committee and has since been enshrined in the RSTP Articles.[62]

10.49 In 2010, in response to growing fears about the exploitation of young players, FIFA required all professional clubs completing an international transfer to use an online database called the Transfer Matching System (TMS). The buying and selling club must enter certain data into the TMS and, if there are no discrepancies, the selling club's national association will issue the buying club's association with an International Transfer Certificate (ITC). Annex 3 to the RSTP contains a detailed procedure for how to use the TMS in these circumstances.

10.50 There has been some confusion as to how old a minor needed to be for the provisions of Article 19 to apply. FIFA has amended the rules and confirmed that the position is as follows:

(a) Article 19 applies to all people under the age of 18;

(b) if the person has reached the age of 10 years old, an ITC is required; and

(c) if the person is under the age of 10, an ITC is not required but the national association that is registering the player is still responsible for ensuring that the requirements of Article 19 are observed.[63]

(d) Intermediaries

10.51 The FIFA Regulations on Working with Intermediaries adopt a fairly liberal approach to the contractual arrangements between a minor and an intermediary. They permit an intermediary to contract with a minor at any age and do not limit the duration of such a contract[64] (provided that the representation contract is signed by the player's legal guardian in compliance with the national law where the player is domiciled).[65]

10.52 The FIFA Regulations on Working with Intermediaries are a set of minimum standards and FIFA permits each national association to add to them.[66] The FA has done so and introduced a regime that offers significantly more protection to minors.

---

60 CAS 2008/A/1985 *FC Midtjylland A/S v FIFA*, paras 7.3.3 and 7.3.7.
61 CAS 2008/A/1985 *FC Midtjylland A/S v FIFA*, para 7.3.3.
62 Regulations on the Status and Transfer of Players, Article 19(4).
63 FIFA's Circular no. 1468 dated 23 January 2015.
64 FIFA Regulations on Working with Intermediaries, Regualtion 5(2) (approved by the FIFA Executive Committee at its meeting on 21 March 2014, in force since 1 April 2015).
65 FIFA Regulations on Working with Intermediaries, Regulation 5(2).
66 The preamble to the FIFA Regulations on Working with Intermediaries.

10.53   The FA Regulations on Working with Intermediaries provide that an intermediary must not, either directly or indirectly, make any approach to, or enter into any agreement with a player before 1 January in the year the player turns 16.[67] Even then, the maximum duration of the representation contract is two years.[68] For players under 18, the contract must be countersigned by the player's parent or legal guardian with parental responsibility.[69]

10.54   Both FIFA and The FA prohibit any payments being made to an intermediary if the player concerned is a minor.[70]

D   COMPENSATION REGIME

10.55   A club can only register and retain minors for a limited amount of time. Even when a player reaches the age of 17, a club cannot enter into a contract with that player for more than three years.[71] As a result, clubs can invest a significant amount of resources in training a player, only for that player to leave to play for another club. However, football's regulatory regime recognises this potential unfairness and includes several mechanisms for compensating clubs which find themselves in this position.

10.56   The European Court of Justice has accepted that this principle is a legitimate restriction on a player's freedom of movement provided that the scheme does not go beyond what is necessary to compensate a club for the cost of training a player.[72] It is deemed to be acceptable because it encourages clubs to provide training for young players.

10.57   There is a separate compensation regime for domestic and international transfers. Each is considered below.

(a)   Domestic transfers

10.58   Compensation is payable in relation to domestic transfers in the following circumstances:

(a) If an academy player moves from the academy of Club A to the academy of Club B, the YDRs provide that, in certain circumstances, Club B must compensate Club A for training and developing that player.[73] This obligation primarily applies where Club A has attempted to keep the academy player by, for example, indicating that it wished to retain the academy player[74] or offering the academy player a scholarship agreement.[75] In other words, a club is typically not entitled to compensation where it opts to release the academy player.

---

67 FA Regulations on Working with Intermediaries 2017–2018, Regulation B8.
68 FA Regulations on Working with Intermediaries 2017–2018, Regulation B10.
69 FA Regulations on Working with Intermediaries 2017–2018, Regulation B9.
70 FIFA Regulations on Working with Intermediaries, Regulation 7(8), although The FA has indicated in guidance that an exception will apply if the player signs a professional contract at age 17, so long as the payment for services related to that signing is only made on or after the player's 18th birthday – see further Chapter 12, Football Intermediaries, Regulation and Legal Disputes, paras **12.65–12.74**.
71 RSTP, Article 18.2.
72 C-325/08 *Olympique Lyonnais v Olivier Bernard and Newcastle United FC* EU:C:2010:143 (ECJ).
73 Premier League YDRs 2017–2018, Rule 326.
74 Premier League YDRs 2017–2018, Rule 326.1.
75 Premier League YDRs 2017–2018, Rule 326.2.

(b) Compensation is payable by a club which registers a professional player under the age of 24 where the registration is a new registration.[76] A new registration is defined as one where there has been either (i) no previous application to register that player; or (ii) the previous registration has been cancelled, terminated or expired.[77] The compensation is only payable to the former club, and only then in limited circumstances, including where the former club held that player's registration as an academy player or offered them a scholarship agreement (which was refused).

(c) Compensation is payable by Club B where a professional player under the age of 24 registers with Club B, in circumstances where his contract of employment with Club A has expired and Club A has offered the player a new contract (on terms at least as favourable as those in the expired contract).[78]

(i)   Calculating compensation

10.59   If the player being registered is an academy player of the ages under-9 to under-15, or under-16 and has not been offered a scholarship agreement, the amount of compensation payable is determined by reference to a set, non-discretionary, formula. The formula has the following two elements:

(a) a number is allocated to each age group (which varies depending on the academy's category). This is multiplied by the number of years that the player was at the academy. This is referred to as the 'initial fee'. In addition, the club registering the academy player must pay the former club any 'initial fee' it paid when it registered the academy player;[79] and

(b) a sum of money that is contingent on what the academy player does in the future. This includes appearance fees for playing in the club's first team and a percentage of future transfer fees.[80]

10.60   In all other cases, the compensation fee in each case must be agreed between the two clubs, failing which either club may apply for a determination by the Professional Football Compensation Committee (PFCC) in accordance with paras **10.61–10.65** below.

(ii)   The Professional Football Compensation Committee (PFCC)

10.61   As stated above, if clubs cannot agree the compensation payable, it is determined by the PFCC. This committee is composed of an independent chairman (appointed by the Professional Football Negotiating and Consultative Committee (PNFCC)), a representative of each of the leagues of which the transferor and transferee are members (or a single representative if they are members of the same league), a representative of the Professional Footballers' Association and a representative of the League Managers Association.[81]

---

76   Premier League Rules, V17 and Premier League YDRs 2017–2018, Rule 342.
77   Premier League Rules 2017–2018, Rule U.14.
78   Premier League Rules 2017–2018, Rule V.17 and EFL Regulations, Regulation 65.
79   Premier League YDRs 2017–2018, Rules 330–333.
80   Premier League YDRs 2017–2018, Rule 334.
81   Regulations of the Professional Football Compensation Committee, Regulation 5. See Appendix 11 of the Premier League Rules 2017–18, or Appendix 4 of the EFL Regulations 2017–18 for a copy of these regulations.

10.62   In determining the compensation due to a club, the committee must take into account the following factors:

(a) Regulation 3: relevant criteria, including but not limited to, the status of the clubs, the age of the player, the training model adopted by the transferor, the playing record of the player, the terms of the new contract offered to the player, any other substantiated interest shown in the player.[82]
(b) Regulation 4: costs incurred, including but not limited to, costs of operating the academy during the relevant period (accommodation, training facilities, scouting and coaching, education costs, medical costs), and any other relevant costs directly attributable to the development of players.[83]

10.63   A club that wishes to commence proceedings must make an application in writing to the PFCC Secretary. There is no set format for the application, only guidelines.[84] The other club then has 14 days to respond. The PFCC Chairman may conduct the proceedings as they see fit. A one-off hearing in front of the PFCC will then be conducted to determine the compensation fee payable.[85]

10.64   The highest profile decisions of the PFCC, and indeed the most high-value, are those regarding Daniel Sturridge and Danny Ings. Despite the fact that the decisions of the PFCC are not published, the following headline facts have been reported:

(a) After Daniel Sturridge moved to Chelsea from Manchester City in 2009, Chelsea were ordered to pay an initial £3.5 million, potentially rising to £6.5 million for contingency fees based on appearances and international caps. The decision also included a 15% sell-on fee.
(b) After Danny Ings moved from Burnley to Liverpool in 2015, Liverpool were ordered to pay an initial £6.5 million, set to rise to £8 million on contingency payments. The decision also included a 20% sell-on fee.

10.65   An important point to note is that the two cases above, the highest value PFCC decisions, both pre-date the most recent Premier League television rights deal. The increased distribution of money has dramatically increased the sums invested in the recruitment and development of players. It is to be expected that the PFCC awards will similarly grow, so as to reflect the greater sums invested by clubs in their academies.

(b)   Compensation for non-domestic transfers

10.66   There are two compensation regimes that apply to non-domestic transfers: (i) training compensation and (ii) solidarity payments.[86]

(i)   Training compensation

10.67   Article 20 of RSTP provides that training compensation is payable when, before the end of the season in which the player turns 23, a player either

---

82   Ibid, Regulation 3.
83   Ibid, Regulation 4.
84   Ibid, Regualtion 10.
85   Ibid, Regulations 9–15.
86   RSTP, Article 1(2).

(i) transfers internationally[87] or (ii) registers as a professional for the first time.[88] In terms of the latter, whilst the compensation applies to players up to the age of 23, it only compensates for the cost of training the player up to the age of 21. If a player has finished his training at an earlier age, compensation will end at that point.

10.68   Training compensation does not need to be paid if (i) the former club terminates the player's contract without just cause; (ii) the player is transferred to a Category 4 club; or (iii) a professional reacquires amateur status on being transferred.[89]

10.69   Training compensation is due to every club with which the player has previously been registered and that has contributed to his training since the season in which the player turned 12,[90] including any club which trained the player whilst they were on loan.[91] The sum payable to each club is calculated on a pro rata basis according to how long the player has spent with each club.[92] The club registering the player is responsible for making the payments within 30 days of the player being registered with the new association.[93]

10.70   In order to calculate the sum due, the starting point is that a national association must classify its clubs into a maximum of four categories in accordance with the clubs' financial investment in training players. A training cost is then set for each category. This sum is the amount required to train one player for one year multiplied by what FIFA calls an average 'player factor', which is 'the ratio of players who need to be trained to produce one professional player'.[94] This categorisation of each club is then placed by the national association in question into FIFA's TMS system and must be reviewed annually.[95]

10.71   The training compensation payable is calculated by multiplying (i) the player's new club's training cost by (ii) the number of years of training in question (ie in principle from the season in which the player turned 12, to the season in which they turned 21).[96]

10.72   In the case of a further transfer, the compensation is calculated by reference to the number of years with the former club.

---

87   RSTP, Article 1(2). The new club must be affiliated to a national football association (CAS 2008/A/1751 *Brazilian Football Federation v Sport Lisboa e BenficaFutebol S.A.D*).

88   In CAS 2013/A/3303 *Bradford City Football Club v Falkirk Football Club*, CAS was asked to determine whether a transfer had taken place in the season of a player's 23rd birthday (given the player's birthday fell on 23 June, between seasons). On the facts, CAS decided that the birthday had fallen during the season of player's 23rd birthday, but went on to implore FIFA to clarify this position. CAS's decision was based on the season of the player's former club (that is, the dates the former club's association had recorded on FIFA's TMS). This approach is the current position applied to training compensation.

89   RSTP, Annex 4, para 2(2).

90   RSTP, Annex 4, para 3(1), provided that the club is affiliated to a national association (*Brazilian Football Federation v Sport Lisboa e Benefica-Futebol S.A.D.*, para 22).

91   RSTP, Article 10(1).

92   RSTP, Annex 4, para 3(1).

93   RSTP, Annex 4, para 3(2). Any payments from domestic clubs to other national associations in relation to training compensation or solidarity payments must be made via The FA Clearing House (http://www.thefa.com/football-rules-governance/policies/intermediaries/standard-forms (accessed February 2018)).

94   RSTP, Annex 4, para 4(1).

95   RSTP, Annex 4, para 4(2).

96   RSTP, Annex 4, para 5(2).

10.73 FIFA has limited the training compensation payable for very young players to make sure that the compensation is not 'unreasonably high'. For the four seasons from the season in which a player turns 12, the categorisation figure shall be that of a category 4 club.[97]

10.74 There are three additional provisions that apply to players moving from one association to another within the EU/EEA. In these circumstances:

(a) If the player moves from a lower to a higher category club, the calculation shall be based on the average training cost of the two clubs. If the player moves from a higher to a lower category club, the calculation shall be based on the training costs of the lower category club.[98]

(b) The final season in relation to which compensation is payable may be earlier than the season of the player's 21st birthday, if it can be established that the player completed his training earlier.[99] In determining when a player concluded their training, a number of factors can be taken into account, including whether or not the player is playing for the first team,[100] the value of the player and the player's ability.[101]

(c) For compensation to be automatically payable, the former club must have offered the player a contract, of equivalent value to the current one, in writing by registered post at least 60 days before the expiry of his current contract. If no contract was offered, compensation will only be payable if the former club can show that it is justified (ie the former club must show a bona fide interest in keeping the player).[102]

10.75 Any disputes about the amount of training compensation payable will be determined by the FIFA Dispute Resolution Chamber.

10.76 FIFA's system of calculating compensation applies to a huge number of member associations with significantly varying financial means. The result is a system that calculates compensation based on little more than the member association's categorisation, the player's birthday and the dates he joined and left the clubs in question. It is intended to compensate for the cost of training and no more; there is no ability to take the future value of the player into account.

(ii) Solidarity payments

10.77 In addition to training compensation, Article 21 of the RSTP provides for the payment of a solidarity contribution. If a professional footballer moves during the course of a contract, to a club of a different national association, 5% of the total compensation shall be distributed by the new club to the clubs involved in the player's training and education. The RSTP sets out how the sum is allocated to each club involved between the ages of 12 and 21.[103]

---

97 RSTP, Annex 4, para 5(3).
98 RSTP, Annex 4, para 6(1).
99 RSTP, Annex 4, para 6(2).
100 It has been held that playing 15 times for a team's A team was sufficient evidence of a player having completed their training (CAS 2003/O/527 *Hamburger Sport-Verein e.V v Odense Boldklub*, para 27).
101 CAS 2004/A/594 *Hapoel Beer-Sheva v. Real Racing Club de Santander S.A.D.*, para 42.
102 RSTP, Annex 4, para 6(3) (for a discussion of what constitutes justification, see paras 60–74 of CAS 2012/A/2890 *FC Nitra v FC Banik Ostrava*).
103 RSTP, Annex 5.

E   PROTECTION OF MINORS

(a)   Introduction

10.78   After a series of high profile cases of abuse of young athletes, in 2001 a partnership between the NSPCC, Sport England, Sport Northern Ireland and Sport Wales led to the formation of the Child Protection in Sport Unit (CPSU). The unit was founded to work with sports bodies to help minimise the risk of child abuse.

10.79   Sport England requires all national governing bodies to adhere to the CPSU's Standards for Safeguarding and Protecting Children in Sport.[104] These standards provide a framework for all those involved in sport to help them create a safe sporting environment. The CPSU has since produced a document called the 'Sports Safeguarding Framework – maintaining and embedding safeguarding for children in and through sport' which builds on the safeguarding standards and assists organisations in evaluating whether they meet those standards.[105]

10.80   The government has also published a guide to agencies working together to safeguard and promote the welfare of children, called 'Working Together to Safeguard Children'.[106] The guidance includes an overview of the legislative requirements and expectations on individual services to safeguard and promote the welfare of children. It applies to all agencies whether statutory or non-statutory (and includes sports bodies).

(b)   Statutory safeguarding framework

10.81   There is no legislation in England and Wales which specifically tackles child protection in sport; the applicable legislation deals with child protection issues more generally. A detailed consideration of this legislative framework is outside the scope of this book. However, set out below is an overview of some of the key provisions.

10.82   The Children Act 1989 provides a comprehensive framework for the care and protection of children. It defines a child as a person who is under 18 years of age.[107] It emphasises that a child's welfare is the paramount consideration. In addition, regard should be had to the wishes of the child concerned, their physical, emotional and educational needs[108] and the fact that statutory intervention should only occur if necessary.[109]

10.83   Every local authority has a general duty to safeguard and promote the welfare of children within their area who are in need and so far as is consistent with that duty, to promote the upbringing of such children by their families, by providing a range of appropriate services.[110] A child is considered to be in need when (i) they are unlikely to achieve or maintain, or to have the opportunity of achieving or maintaining, a reasonable standard of health or development without the support

104   https://thecpsu.org.uk/media/1040/english-standards.pdf (accessed February 2018).
105   https://thecpsu.org.uk/media/1098/sport-safeguarding-framework.pdf (accessed February 2018).
106   https://www.gov.uk/government/uploads/system/uploads/attachment_data/file/592101/Working_ Together_to_Safeguard_Children_20170213.pdf (accessed February 2018).
107   Children Act 1989, s 105(1).
108   Children Act 1989, s 1(3).
109   Children Act 1989, s 1(5).
110   Children Act 1989, s 17(1).

of the local authority; (ii) their health or development is likely to be significantly impaired, or further impaired, without that support; or (iii) if they are disabled.[111] If a child falls within this definition, an assessment will be carried out by a social worker.

10.84   A local authority has a duty to investigate where they have reasonable cause to suspect that a child who lives, or is found, in their area is suffering, or is likely to suffer, significant harm.[112] There is no law requiring participants in football to report concerns to the local authority. However, The FA's policies state that any concerns should be reported to the person with responsibility for safeguarding and if they are not available to the authorities.[113]

10.85   The Children Act 2004 preserves much of the Children Act 1989. Of note in this context is that the Act envisages a role for any 'persons or bodies of any nature who exercise functions or are engaged in activities in relation to children' (which would include sports bodies). A duty is imposed on such bodies to cooperate with local authorities and their partners to promote the well-being of children.[114]

10.86   The Working Together to Safeguard Children publication dated March 2015 gives the following guidance to sports organisations:

'Voluntary organisations and private sector providers play an important role in delivering services to children. They should have the arrangements described in paragraph 4 of this chapter in place in the same way as organisations in the public sector, and need to work effectively with the LSCB [Local Safeguarding Children Board]. Paid and volunteer staff need to be aware of their responsibilities for safeguarding and promoting the welfare of children, how they should respond to child protection concerns and make a referral to local authority children's social care or the police if necessary.'[115]

10.87   The Sexual Offences Act 2003 prohibits consensual activity between an adult in a position of trust[116] and a child under that person's care.[117] However, the crime only applies to adults working in the public sector and not to anyone working in the private sector. This means that the relationship between a coach and a child athlete is not covered (save, for example, where the coach is operating within a school). When the bill was being debated there was support in the House of Lords to include sports coaches within the ambit of this offence. However, the government refused to do so because it was of the view that sports coaches do not have a special influence over 16- and 17-year-olds.[118]

10.88   In 2015 the Department for Culture, Media and Sport[119] commissioned Baroness Tanni Grey-Thompson to produce an independent report into the duty of care that sports have towards their participants. One of the key findings of the report was that the government should review the Sexual Offences Act 2003 to include sports coaches within the definition of 'Positions of Trust', in order to provide

111 Children Act 1989, s 17(10).
112 Children Act 1989, s 47(1).
113 Further information can be found at p 34 of The FA's document, 'Grassroots Football Safeguarding Children'.
114 Children Act 2004, s 10(1), (2).
115 Working Together to Safeguard Children, p 63 (dated March 2015).
116 'Position of trust' is defined in s 21 of the Sexual Offences Act 2003.
117 Sexual Offences Act 2003, s 16.
118 http://hansard.millbanksystems.com/lords/2003/jun/17/sexual-offences-bill-hl (accessed February 2018).
119 Which, since 3 July 2017, is named the Department for Digital Culture Media and Sport.

additional safeguards for 16- and 17-year-olds.[120] As was noted by the NSPCC in their summary of the report, teachers fall within this definition and sports coaches should be subject to the same restrictions.[121]

10.89   The CPSU briefing dated January 2015 defines a position of trust as pertaining to any person in a position of authority over another person. It considers that there is a need to protect young people aged 16 and 17 as they may be dependent on their coach or other adults for their sporting development, success or position in a club. It concludes that sports bodies should, through regulation, prohibit such relationships with 16 and 17-year-olds and take disciplinary action should they occur.[122]

(c)   Football's safeguarding framework

10.90   As the game's governing body in England, The FA provides the regulatory framework for safeguarding. Two of the key documents are The Association's Safeguarding Children Policy (Safeguarding Policy)[123] and The Association's Safeguarding Children Regulations (Safeguarding Regulations).[124] These apply to everyone who works in football. The successful implementation of the framework requires significant collaboration between those bodies charged with ensuring that the environment in which children participate in football is safe and supportive.

10.91   The Safeguarding Children Policy sets out The FA's aim of ensuring that every child and young person who plays or participates in football should be able to take part in an enjoyable and safe environment and be protected from abuse. A child or young person is defined as anyone who has not yet reached their 18th birthday and abuse is defined as 'a violation of an individual's human or civil rights by any other person or persons and, for the purposes of safeguarding children, shall include physical abuse, emotional abuse, sexual abuse, neglect, bullying and hazing'.[125]

10.92   The Safeguarding Policy requires that every club and league with youth teams must appoint a welfare officer.[126] A club's welfare officer must sit on the management committee of that club. The policy then sets out who would be suitable for the role and a code of conduct to which the welfare officer is expected to adhere[127] (which includes attending The FA Safeguarding Children and Welfare Officer Workshops). In addition, every county FA has a designated safeguarding officer who assists and guides the club welfare officers.

10.93   The Safeguarding Regulations set out a Safeguarding Process. The FA has a broad discretion as to who must comply with the process, which includes those involved in a 'regulated activity' (as defined in Part V of the Protection of Freedoms

120 https://www.gov.uk/government/uploads/system/uploads/attachment_data/file/610130/Duty_of_
      Care_Review_-_April_2017__2.pdf (accessed February 2018).
121 https://www.nspcc.org.uk/what-we-do/news-opinion/duty-of-care-in-sport/ (accessed February 2018).
122 CPSU Briefing: Preventing Abuse of Positions of Trust in Sport (dated January 2015).
123 The FA's Handbook 2017–2018, p 210.
124 The FA's Handbook 2017–2018, pp 214–221.
125 The FA's Handbook 2017–2018, pp 210–213.
126 There are currently 8,500 welfare officers in place in England. Guidance on a Welfare Officer's key
      roles and responsibilities and how to appoint one can be found here: www.thefa.com/football-rules-
      governance/safeguarding/welfare-officers (accessed February 2018).
127 The FA's Handbook 2017–2018, pp 211–213.

Act 2012) and those who would otherwise fall within this definition save for the fact that their duties are supervised. This will include any individual whose duties frequently[128] or intensively[129] include training, teaching, instructing, caring for, supervising or providing guidance or advice on well-being to children, or driving a vehicle (on behalf of an organisation) only for children.[130]

10.94   Any individual who falls within this definition must obtain and provide to The FA a DBS[131] Enhanced Criminal Records Check with Children's Barred List. If the individual is supervised, the obligation is limited to a DBS Enhanced Criminal Records Check. The Safeguarding Process also requires such individuals assist in other ways such as complying with a risk assessment carried out by The FA and providing two references.[132]

10.95   Those required to be checked will include coaches, team managers, referees, first aiders and physiotherapists. Typically, club chairmen, treasurers or secretaries do not require a check if they are mainly administrative roles. However, if they are helping with coaching or at matches, they will need to carry be checked as well.

10.96   The FA has broad powers to suspend an individual from football activity in certain circumstances, including where an individual is investigated in relation to or charged with an offence, poses a risk of harm to children, is barred from regulated activity relating to children in accordance with s 3 of the Safeguarding Vulnerable Groups Act 2006 or is disqualified from working with children under s 35 of the Criminal Justice and Court Services Act 2000.[133] Any interim suspension will be subject to review by The FA's Safeguarding Review Panel.

10.97   In addition, The FA can impose risk management measures on individuals ranging from education, mentoring and supervision agreements, to interim and permanent suspensions.

10.98   To assist with this process, The FA has a whistleblowing policy in place. This allows any person with concerns about an adult in a position of trust in football to report those concerns to The FA, the CPSU or the NSPCC.[134]

10.99   Every club and league with youth football should have a safeguarding children policy and procedures and an anti-bullying policy in place.[135] Bullying is a form of child abuse and can include cyberbullying and trolling on social media.

---

128 Frequently is defined as once a week or more often (see The Association's Safeguarding Children Regulations, Regulation 2(i)(b)).
129 Intensively is defined as 4 or more days in a 30-day period or overnight (see The Association's Safeguarding Children Regulations, Regulation 2(i)(b)).
130 The Association's Safeguarding Children Regulations, Regulation 2.
131 DSB is short for the Disclosure and Barring Service (established pursuant to the Police Act 1997). The FA provides guidance on how to carry out such a check: http://www.thefa.com/football-rules-governance/safeguarding/criminal-record-checks (accessed February 2018).
132 The Association's Safeguarding Children Regulations, Regulation 2.
133 The Association's Safeguarding Children Regulations, Regulations 3 and 13.1.
134 Details about the policy can be found here: http://www.thefa.com/football-rules-governance/safeguarding/policy-downloads.
135 Templates are available on The FA's website: http://www.thefa.com/football-rules-governance/safeguarding/policy-downloads (accessed February 2018).

(d)   Premier League Rules and EFL Rules

10.100   Whilst the FA provides oversight across the game in England, the Premier League and EFL have responsibility to support and monitor their club's compliance with The FA's safeguarding policies.

10.101   The Premier League Rules have a section called The Safeguarding of Vulnerable Groups and Safer Recruitment (which apply to academies and development centres).[136] In addition, the Premier League's YDRs contain a relevant section called Education and Welfare.[137]

10.102   Each Premier League club is required to:

(a)   Take reasonable steps to ensure that it protects the welfare of each of its academy players and players under the age of 21 by offering support for their well-being and pastoral care generally.[138]

(b)   Implement and review regularly written policies and procedures for the safeguarding of children that meet NSPCC standards. They are obliged to have them reviewed by their local authority where it is prepared to do so.[139]

(c)   Designate a member of its board of directors to be its senior safeguarding lead to take leadership responsibility for the club's safeguarding provision (in consultation with the club's head of safeguarding) and actively champion safeguarding at board level.[140]

(d)   Employ a person full time who has the necessary expertise to be the club's head of safeguarding.[141] The rules impose an extensive set of responsibilities on the head of safeguarding which may be delegated to other members of staff provided that they are supervised by the head of safeguarding.[142] In addition, each club must appoint an academy safeguarding officer who shall undertake the responsibilities of the head of safeguarding as far as the academy is concerned.[143]

(e)   Designate a member of staff as its Lead Disclosure Officer to act as the principal point of contact with the League on all matters connected with safer recruitment and the use of the DBS, which the League will undertake for those clubs not registered with the DBS.[144]

10.103   The EFL imposes similar obligations to those outlined above. Each club must implement written policies and procedures for the safeguarding of children and appoint a designated safeguarding officer. The EFL has produced a guide, *Safeguarding Children and Young People*, outlining what is required of member clubs.[145]

---

136   Section S of the Premier League Rules. Academies and Development Centres are defined at pp 359 and 365 of the Premier League Handbook 2017/2018 respectively.

137   Premier League Handbook 2017/2018, pp 417–424.

138   Premier League YDRs, Rule 184.

139   Premier League Rules, Regulations S.1 and S.2.

140   Premier League Rules, Regulation S.3.

141   Premier League Rules, Regulation S.4.

142   Premier League Rules, Regulation S.5.

143   Premier League YDRs, Rule 186.

144   Premier League Rules, Regulation S.21.

145   https://www.efl.com/siteassets/efl-documents/efl-guidance-to-member-clubs--trusts---safeguarding-children-and-young-p....pdf (accessed February 2018).

CHAPTER 11

Third Party Investment

Nick De Marco QC (Blackstone Chambers), Ariel Reck (Reck Sports Law)
and Pedro Fida (Bichara & Motta – Brazil)

A   INTRODUCTION

11.1   The football transfer market grows every year. Since the FIFA Transfer
Matching System (TMS) started to measure the number of transfers and amounts
involved in the international market only, each year shows higher sums that its
precedent. While there is no accurate measure from that time, this expanding system
really kicked off with the European Court of Justice (ECJ) *Bosman* decision.[1]

11.2   The two questions answered by the ECJ in *Bosman*, (i) that EU citizen
players shall be considered as nationals for players' quotas, and (ii) that a training
compensation system based on subjective parameters is illegal under European law,
shaped the modern transfer market.

11.3   The 'demand' for talent grew; more clubs were acting in the market and also
each club was able to hire more foreign players. On the other side the 'supply' also
grew. It was not as easy as before to retain a player in a club without an employment
contract (this has escalated in South America since 2005, when the unilateral-options
system was held invalid by FIFA and the Court of Arbitration for Sport (CAS)).
Therefore a transfer for a fee was a way to, at least, make some income once a player
(tempted by the new pool of offers) was willing to abandon a club, or a contract
renewal was too difficult or too expensive.

11.4   This new trend was immediately understood by some agents in South
America. They came from the world of finance and quickly realised that the profit of
a potential transfer was a future event, tradeable in the same way as any other futures
market product.

11.5   In its origin, Third Party Investment (TPI) was a way for clubs to obtain
funds without the need to transfer a player and a chance to continue to use his
sporting services while obtaining a financial benefit from the transfer of his economic

---

1   Case C-415/93 *Bosman* [1995] ECR I-4921, CJEU; see Chapter 4, European Law in Relation to
    Football, for a full discussion of the case.

rights. The transaction is essentially the sale to a third party of a future transfer value in a player. The entity buying the share believes the player has the potential to be transferred for a higher fee than it paid for the transfer share. For the club employing the player, the sale of portions of the economic rights helps it to balance its books and find credit from alternative sources. While the risks are high (ie the player might not fulfil his potential or get injured) the potential gains can outweigh such risks.

11.6   The use of the tool expanded and was also adopted by 'buying' clubs as a way to reduce the burden or risk and the costs in acquiring a player. Instead of paying the 'full' price, new clubs offered the former club the chance to buy only part of the 'economic rights' while getting the federative registration right and signing an employment contract with the player. This strategy was working well with mid-size clubs in Europe. If the player proved to be good, a further transfer to a larger European club was likely, and in that event both current and former club shared the gain.

11.7   The participation of private companies in the market made things more complicated. First, these private entities acted on the side of the 'selling' club by buying economic rights when the player was young and making a profit in a subsequent federative transfer. Then these companies took the side of the 'buying' clubs, offering part of the transfer fee against a share in a future transfer. This practice evolved and companies started to invest in a big part or even the total amount of the transfer fee, placing players in clubs that were not in a position to afford such moves but were a good showcase for these players.

11.8   Due to the fact that these rights are inexorably linked with the contractual situation of the player,[2] from a commercial perspective, it seems obvious that these companies will try to minimise the risks and include contractual clauses limiting the independence of clubs. But, while commercially understandable, these clauses are controversial from a sporting, and broader employment rights' perspective.

11.9   Did the practice reduce players to commodities? Could third party investors have the ability to unduly influence clubs? Should there be limits? To what extent could a company protect its investment? These questions were discussed for over a decade with strong arguments on both sides and, in general, without consensus. Even the name given to the practice was in dispute and reflected the different views on the topic.

11.10   The detractors of this investment tool labelled it Third Party Ownership (TPO). In fact, no third party *owns* a player, but only a share of the 'economic right' attached to the player. Those defending the practice or at least trying to adopt a more objective approach named it Third Party Investment (TPI).

11.11   As van Maren and Duval explain:[3]

> 'Beyond this semantic debate, various types of contractual situations are included
> under the umbrella term TPO. What is common to all cases is that a company or
> an individual provides a football club or a player with money in return for being
> entitled to a share of a player's future transfer value. Thus, TPO is enshrined in

2   Because a termination of the contract will also constitute a termination of the TPI agreement, if an
     offer arrives but the club decides not to transfer the player the company cannot force the deal at the
     federative level.
3   'Debating FIFA's TPO ban: ASSER International Sports Law Blog symposium' (2016) 15(3–4)
     The International Sports Law Journal 233–252.

a separate private law contract between a third-party and a club or a player. The plurality of TPO situations derives from this contractual basis. The parties are free under national private law to creatively draft those contracts as they see fit, each one of them being a specific type of TPO in itself.'

11.12   The final evolution before FIFA decided to ban the practice (and probably one of the reasons for such decision) was for companies to eliminate the risks in TPI. The arrangement that was originally a risk-sharing agreement became a mere loan of money. If the player was transferred for the desired amount, then club and company would share the obtained fee but if the player was not transferred (for whatever reason, eg bad performances, injury, retirement) or the fee was lower than the minimum established in the contract, then the club was obliged to repay the money that was lent with interest.

11.13   The introduction of the UEFA Financial Fair Play Regulations (UEFA FFP)[4] was also a landmark in the history of TPI. TPI had meant that clubs were able to acquire players that they would otherwise be unable to afford, and this could in turn circumvent the regulatory restraints imposed on expenditure by the UEFA FFP Regulations. UEFA FFP created a further impetus for the prohibition of TPI.

11.14   It is easy to understand the controversy surrounding TPI and the arguments on both sides: for those in favour, it is a way to reduce the competitive imbalance between big and small clubs and also the gap between Europe and other regions (in particular South America and Africa). By using TPI, a club can retain the sporting services of a player for more time without the need to transfer him in order to obtain a profit, just as the Brazilian club Santos FC did with Neymar Jr who remained at the club for several years before he was finally transferred to Barcelona FC. In addition, with the aid of an investor, a club can acquire the services of a player who would otherwise be beyond the club's budget and allow it to compete with bigger opponents. Proper regulation of TPI should allow clubs to maintain these benefits while limiting the abuses that are likely to arise.

11.15   On the other hand, those against TPI consider the practice as a type of modern slavery that imposes a property right over players and creates an artificial short-term financial situation for clubs that is damaging in the long run. It also raises concerns about the integrity of the game and the manipulation of matches by third parties (who might, for example, have an interest in players of teams competing against each other). For many detractors, regulation of TPI is impossible because undue influence will always be present (either *de facto* or in secret agreements) because influence is seen as inherent to the business model.

B   SUMMARY OF THE FIFA REGULATIONS

11.16   Article 17.2 of the Regulations on the Status and Transfer of Players (RSTP) provides:

'Entitlement to compensation cannot be assigned to a third party.'

11.17   This rule refers only to compensation in case of breach and was never applied in any case, but is still an important precedent since it is the first rule in the RSTP dealing with the issue.

---

4   See further Chapter 16, Financial Regulation and Financial Fair Play.

11.18   Article 18bis of the RSTP was the first rule that specifically dealt with TPI.[5] The norm was introduced in 2008 as a response to the critics that the *Tevez* case[6] triggered in the football community.

11.19   In the seven years from the introduction of Article 18bis until 2015 just a couple of cases were reported or investigated and no serious sanction was imposed.[7] Only after the introduction of the TPI ban in 2015 – as will be discussed below – FIFA sanctioned several clubs for violation of Article 18bis, including Palmeiras FC and Santos FC from Brazil, as well as Sevilla FC from Spain, and the Dutch club FC Twente.[8]

11.20   FIFA introduced a worldwide prohibition on TPI in May 2015. Article 18ter RSTP now provides:

'**18ter Third-party ownership of players' economic rights**[9]

1. No club or player shall enter into an agreement with a third party whereby a third party is being entitled to participate, either in full or in part, in compensation payable in relation to the future transfer of a player from one club to another, or is being assigned any rights in relation to a future transfer or transfer compensation.
2. The interdiction as per paragraph 1 comes into force on 1 May 2015.
3. Agreements covered by paragraph 1 which predate 1 May 2015 may continue to be in place until their contractual expiration. However, their duration may not be extended.
4. The validity of any agreement covered by paragraph 1 signed between one January 2015 and 30 April 2015 may not have a contractual duration of more than 1 year beyond the effective date.
5. By the end of April 2015, all existing agreements covered by paragraph 1 need to be recorded within the Transfer Matching System (TMS). All clubs that have signed such agreements are required to upload them in their entirety, including possible annexes or amendments, in TMS, specifying the details of the third party concerned, the full name of the player as well as the duration of the agreement.
6. The FIFA Disciplinary Committee may impose disciplinary measures on clubs or players that do not observe the obligations set out in this article.'

11.21   In addition to the above-mentioned innovations, this new article directly addresses the issue of 'sell on clauses' as it builds on the definition of the third party,

---

5   Article 18bis of the RSTP has been slightly amended subsequently to read:

'1. No club shall enter into a contract which enables another party to that contract or any third party to acquire the ability to influence employment and transfer-related matters, its independence, its policies or the performance of its teams.
2. The FIFA Disciplinary Committee may impose disciplinary measures on clubs that do not observe the obligations set out in this article.'

6   See paras **11.85–11.87** and **11.111–11.112**, below.
7   CAS 2004/A/662 *RCD Mallorca, S.A.D v Club Atlético Lanús*; CAS 2004/A/635 *RCD Espanyol de Barcelona SAD v Club Atlético Velez Sarsfield*; CAS 2004/A/781 *Tacuary FBC v Club Atlético Cerro & Jorge Cyterszpiler & FIFA*; CAS 2004/A/701 *Sport Club Internacional v Galatasaray Spor Kulübü Dernegi*; CAS 2011/O/2580 *Investfootball GmbH v Vasco Herculano Salgado da Cunha Mango Fernandes.*
8   See FIFA Disciplinary Committee's cases 150315, 150522, 150946, 160096 and FIFA press releases: http://www.fifa.com/governance/news/y=2016/m=3/news=several-clubs-sanctioned-for-breach-of-third-party-influence-third-par-2772984.html; http://www.fifa.com/governance/news/y=2017/m=1/news=fifa-disciplinary-committee-passes-decisions-relating-to-third-party-i-2865316.html (accessed February 2018).
9   'Third party' is defined in the RSTP Definitions section as: 'a party other than the two clubs transferring a player from one to the other, or any previous club, with which the player has been registered'.

and states that no party other than the parties in negotiation are to receive any 'future transfer or training compensation', except for the solidarity mechanism (5%).

11.22 Moreover, by 30 April 2015 all contracts with a sell-on clause had to be registered with FIFA TMS ensuring a level of transparency on these issues. The TMS has to include (i) the third party concerned (the name of the club), (ii) the name of the player, and (iii) the duration of the agreement.

11.23 More importantly, Article 18ter of the RSTP also provided that the FIFA Disciplinary Committee shall have the authority to impose disciplinary measures on clubs or players that do not observe the obligations set out in the new regulations. Consequently, several cases arose after Article 18ter was enacted, aimed at regulating and controlling abuses (see Section C, below).

11.24 To reflect FIFA's prohibition on TPI, Circular letter 1502[10] was also passed, establishing the clubs' obligation to provide a declaration on third party interest in a player's economic rights (ie whether a TPI agreement exists or not) when creating an instruction in FIFA TMS. If no agreement exists, a document signed by the player and his former club declaring that there is no third party ownership of the player's economic rights shall be uploaded, or if it exists, a copy of the relevant agreement with the third party must be presented.

11.25 Agents' regulations also dealt with TPI. Article 29 of the FIFA Players' Agent's regulations in force from 2008 until 2015 established:

> **'Article 29 Payment restrictions and assignment of rights and claims**
>
> 1. No compensation payment, including transfer compensation, training compensation or solidarity contribution, that is payable in connection with a player's transfer between clubs, may be paid in full or part, by the debtor (club) to the players' agent, not even to clear an amount owed to the players' agent by the club by which he was engaged in its capacity as a creditor. This includes, but is not limited to, owning any interest in any transfer compensation or future transfer value of a player.
> 2. Within the scope of a player's transfer, players' agents are forbidden from receiving any remuneration other than in the cases provided under Chapter IV of the present regulations.'

11.26 Article 7.4 of the FIFA Regulations on Working with Intermediaries currently in force (and replacing the FIFA Players' Agents Regulations) contains an analogous (and even more clear) provision prohibiting agents to have any interest in the transfer or the future transfer of players.

> 'Clubs shall ensure that payments to be made by one club to another club in connection with a transfer, such as transfer compensation, training compensation or solidarity contributions, are not paid to intermediaries and that the payment is not made by intermediaries. This includes, but is not limited to, owning any interest in any transfer compensation or future transfer value of a player. The assignment of claims is also prohibited.'

11.27 Agents and clubs have been sanctioned on a few occasions for breaching these regulations, by signing contracts containing the right to influence a transfer or to obtain part of a transfer fee, or the total fee in transfers of free agents. Most of

---

10   FIFA Circular Letter 1502: https://resources.fifa.com/mm/document/affederation/administration/ 02/70/93/55/circularno.1502-regulationsonthestatusandtransferofplayersamendmentstoannexe3- transfermatchingsystem(tms)_neutral.pdf (accessed February 2018).

these cases started when the conflicting contract was not respected, a claim before FIFA was filed and it backfired because FIFA sent the documents to the Disciplinary Committee for an investigation.[11]

11.28   In summary, FIFA's position before 2015, when the ban was imposed, was quite passive. Article 18bis was almost unapplied. In FIFA's defence most of these deals were private and undisclosed (especially before the FIFA TMS was introduced) and FIFA only took notice of them if case claims were filed before its judicial bodies. With this in mind and considering that the standard of proof for the disciplinary committee is rather high ('comfortable satisfaction', meaning more than the simple 'balance of probabilities' but less than the criminal 'beyond reasonable doubt'), that scenario is understandable.

11.29   The downside of this situation was that no case law developed in relation to the notion of 'influence' in order to determine which clauses could be held valid and which not. This situation impacted negatively over those who were trying to develop a serious and legal business in the field.

11.30   When FIFA imposed the complete prohibition on TPI, it took a more active role with the benefit of the TMS:it is easier to prove whether the ban is breached or not than to define and prove 'influence' in a specific agreement.

C   SUMMARY OF CASES REGARDING BREACH OF FIFA REGULATIONS

(a)   Development of concepts in the case law: economic rights and third party investment

11.31   Every summary of cases relating to TPI includes a majority of cases where litigants are clubs and only a few when one of the parties is a 'pure' investor or 'third party'. The reason for this is that cases involving third parties are usually confidential and unreported. However, the main principles that define and shape this legal issue are clearly developed in the cases between clubs.

11.32   The leading case in relation to TPI is *RCD Espanyol de Barcelona SAD v Club Atlético Velez Sarsfield*.[12] When the Argentine club Veléz Sársfield transferred the player Posse to Espanyol, both clubs agreed to share 50% of the economic and federative rights in case of a future transfer and also a yearly loan fee while the player continued in Espanyol. Every season Velez 'loaned' the player to Espanyol for a negotiated fee. After a few seasons, Espanyol questioned the validity of the agreement and a case was initiated before FIFA. After a complicated procedural pathway the FIFA Players' Status Committee upheld Vélez's claim for US$ $750.000 qualifying the move as a series of consecutive loans.

11.33   The notion of owning a share of the profits of a future transfer was rejected at first by FIFA; it was perceived as an attempt to maintain 'federative rights' over a player, meaning control over his movement even after the end of the relevant labour

11   See, eg CAS 2012/A/2740 *Carracedo Marcelo v FIFA*, https://jurisprudence.tas-cas.org/Shared%20 Documents/2740.pdf (accessed February 2018).

12   CAS 2004/A/635 *RCD Espanyol de Barcelona SAD v Club Atlético Velez Sarsfield*, award of 27 January 2005: https://jurisprudence.tas-cas.org/Shared%20Documents/635.pdf (accessed February 2018).

contract. This was clearly against the very foundations of the RSTP (2001). At the beginning of the case, the single judge of the FIFA Players' Status Committee noted that both clubs violated the FIFA regulations by entering into this deal.

11.34   However, the CAS modified the decision on appeal and ruled *de novo* with a clear differentiation between what was called 'federative rights' or technically the registration of a player and the 'economic rights' or the right to share the profit of a player's transfer. In terms of monetary result the compensation was reduced from US$ 750,000 to US$ 500,000.

11.35   In the CAS Panel's own words:[13]

> 'The registration of a professional player with a club and with the pertinent national federation serves the administrative purpose of certifying within the federative system that solely that club is entitled to field that player during a given period; obviously, such federative registration is possible only if there is an employment contract between the club and the player.
>
> A club holding an employment contract with a player may assign, with the player's consent, the contract rights to another club in exchange for a given sum of money or other consideration, and those contract rights are the so-called "economic rights to the performances of a player"; this commercial transaction is legally possible only with regard to players who are under contract, since players who are free from contractual engagements – the so-called "free agents" – may be hired by any club freely, with no economic rights involved.
>
> In accordance with the basic legal distinction to be made between "registration" of a player and "economic rights" related to a player, while a player's registration may not be shared simultaneously among different clubs – FIFA rules require that a player be registered to play for only one club at any given time –, the economic rights, being ordinary contract rights, may be partially assigned and thus apportioned among different right holders.
>
> The notion of "federative rights" – insofar as such expression may be taken to mean that a club can bind and control a player without the player's explicit consent, merely by virtue of the rules of a federation – is unacceptable and unenforceable. Indeed, sports rules of this kind are contrary to universal basic principles of labour law and are thus unenforceable on grounds of public policy. In other terms, the player's consent is always indispensable whenever clubs effect transactions involving his employment and/or his transfer.
>
> From a player's perspective, a contract apportioning the economic rights related to him between two clubs and according to which, as a result of their reciprocal commitments, neither club is in a position to lawfully hire the player or trade him to a third club without the other club's consent, in addition to the requisite player's consent, is a kind of employment pre-contract with both clubs, which has to be implemented through specific employment contracts with either club and which, conversely, precludes him from lawfully entering into employment contracts with third clubs.
>
> In accordance with the FIFA rules, players' "financial contracts" with clubs must be "concluded for a predetermined period". Consequently, a player's commitment towards a club/several clubs cannot be open-ended.'

11.36   This understanding was further confirmed in several awards including among others: CAS 2004/A/662 *RCD Mallorca, S.A.D. v Club Atlético Lanús*; CAS 2004/A/781 *Tacuary FBC v Club Atlético Cerro & Jorge Cyterszpiler & FIFA*; and

---

13   Paragraphs 5–9 of the CAS summary published at CAS website (see n 12 above).

CAS 2004/A/701 *Sport Club Internacional v Galatasaray Spor Kulübü Dernegi*.[14] Not surprisingly, these cases were related to Argentine, Brazilian and Paraguayan clubs.

11.37   The Panel in *Sport Club Internacional v Galatasaray Spor Kulübü Dernegi*,[15] also entered into the rationale of such agreements, characterising them as joint ventures:

> 'the Co-ownership Agreement established a sort of joint venture between the two clubs, whereby they arranged to jointly hold title to the economic rights to the performances of the Player. As a result of their reciprocal commitments, both clubs had a duty of transparency and cooperation towards each other.'[16]

Consequently, practices such as terminating the player's contract or letting him go for free were considered to be against good faith and against these deals.

11.38   In 2007, in an ordinary arbitration *Play International BV v Real Club Celta de Vigo*,[17] the Panel in charge of the case confirmed that these principles were also applicable in cases where one of the parties was not a club but a commercial company.

11.39   When re-reading these cases today, we find it strange how the various panels ignored the fact that many of the contracts in dispute included clauses imposing severe influence or even absolute control over the players or the transfers. Putting this in a context, Article 18bis of the RSTP had not yet been enacted and in general, the counterparts of these cases did not claim the nullity of these clauses either.

11.40   The prevalent notion was that 'federative rights' and 'economic rights' were two concepts running in 'parallel' and clauses in TPI contracts were only internal agreements. In *M. & Football Club Wil 1900 v FIFA & Club PFC Naftex AC Bourgas*,[18] the acting Panel held that:

> 'The mere fact that there might be an existing contract between a player and a company on some personality rights of that player is not relevant and certainly does not make an employment contract concluded between that player and a club invalid or null and void. In international football sport, the concept of "federative rights" does not exist anymore and has been replaced by the notion – and value – of contractual stability. Therefore, contracts on personality rights between a player and a commercial company may have an "internal" validity and may have consequences in regard to the relations between the player and the company, but do not affect the power of such player to enter into an employment agreement with a football club and do not affect the validity of such employment contract even if the signing of the employment contract may be considered as a breach of the "internal obligation" between the player and the commercial company.'

11.41   This idea was further developed in *Genoa Cricket and Football Club SpA v Club Deportivo Maldonado*.[19] When the case was decided, Article 18bis of the RSTP was already in force but not applicable because the facts were prior to its entry into force. However, the appellant claimed that the existing TPI agreement in relation

---

14   https://jurisprudence.tas-cas.org/Shared%20Documents/701.pdf (accessed February 2018).
15   CAS 2004/A/701.
16   Paragraph 1 of CAS summary (see n 12 above).
17   CAS 2007/O/1391.
18   CAS 2008/A/1568 *M. & Football Club Wil 1900 v FIFA & Club PFC Naftex AC Bourgas*, award of 24 December 2008, https://arbitrationlaw.com/sites/default/files/free_pdfs/CAS%202008-A-1568%20M%20et%20al%20v%20FIFA%20et%20al%20Award.pdf (accessed February 2018).
19   CAS 2008/A/1482 *Genoa Cricket and Football Club SpA v Club Deportivo Maldonado*, https://jurisprudence.tas-cas.org/Shared%20Documents/1482.pdf (accessed February 2018).

to the transfer fee (including the player and a company as beneficiaries) made the transfer null and void and therefore no transfer fee was payable to Maldonado. The Panel concluded:[20]

> 'Appellant submits that it is under no obligation to pay the Transfer Fee to Respondent because the Transfer Agreement is null due to the fact that Respondent falsely represented owning the transfer rights over the Player and entered into an agreement for the transfer of the Player without having any rights in that regard. Appellant claims that the Assignees and not Respondent held the transfer rights over the Player. Alternatively, Appellant claims that even if the Panel found that Respondent held "federative rights" over the Player, these would not have been sufficient to confer economic rights over the Player.'

> To determine whether the Transfer Agreement was validly concluded, the Panel has to determine whether Respondent was entitled to transfer the player to Appellant. In this regard, the Panel analyzes the following provisions of the FIFA Regulations which govern the registration and transfer of players between associations.

> As a result, the Panel finds that Respondent was entitled to transfer Mr. Rimoldi to Appellant, due to the fact that Rimoldi was a registered player under contract with Maldonado at the time of conclusion of the Transfer Agreement.

> The Panel does not need to decide whether the July 9, 2003 Contract, was valid. Indeed, the existence itself of such a contract is irrelevant as with regard to the validity of a transfer agreement. For international registration purposes, it is only the club, as employer, that is able to transfer a player under an employment contract to another club. The fact whether further "internal" arrangements may exist between investors, the player and even the club itself, does not matter, as it does not have any legal impact on the validity of the Transfer Agreement.'

11.42   Based on this parallel concept, almost every TPI agreement was held valid by the CAS panels. Only in cases where the abuse was obvious and a company was trying to enforce a TPI contract signed with a player as free agent imposing heavy obligations and penalties on him did the CAS decide that the contracts were null or unenforceable (TAS 2011/O/2580 and TAS 2013/O/3056).[21]

(b) Additional clubs sanctioned for third party influence and breach of Articles 18bis and 18ter

11.43   From 2015, following the announcement of the worldwide ban against TPI, FIFA began to thoroughly investigate any violations against the new rules, and initiated disciplinary proceedings against several clubs around the world. Consequently, FIFA sanctioned several clubs that violated the Article 18bis and Article 18ter of the RSTP. Apart from the sanctioned clubs discussed below,[22] the most relevant cases are further developed in this Section.

11.44   In the case *Santos Futebol Clube of Brazil*,[23] the club entered into TPI contracts that authorised third parties to influence the club's independence in employment and transfer-related matters, and did not declare the required information in the TMS, also failing to cooperate with an investigation conducted by FIFA TMS. As a consequence, the club was sanctioned with a fine of CHF 75,000, a warning

---

20   Paragraphs 81, 82, 86 and 87.
21   CAS 2011/O/2580 *Investfootball GmbH v. Vasco Herculano Salgado da Cunha Mango Fernandes.*
22   http://www.fifa.com/governance/news/y=2016/m=3/news=several-clubs-sanctioned-for-breach-of-third-party-influence-third-par-2772984.html (accessed February 2018).
23   FIFA Disciplinary Committee Case Ref. Nr. 150315.

and a reprimand for breaching Article 18bis of the RSTP (2008 edition), as well as Annexe 3 of the regulations.

11.45   In addition, Sevilla FC of Spain was also investigated by the FIFA Disciplinary Committee and ended up sanctioned with a fine of CHF 55,000, a warning for breaching Article 18bis of the RSTP (2012 edition), as well as Annexe 3 of the regulations, as the club entered into TPI contracts that enabled a third party to influence the club's independence in employment and transfer-related matters and also failed to enter mandatory information into FIFA TMS.[24]

11.46   Another example of a sanctioned club was Club K St Truidense VV of Belgium, which was sanctioned with a fine of CHF 60,000, a warning and a reprimand for breaching Article 18bis and Article 18ter para 1 of the RSTP (2015 Edition). The club was found to be liable for entering into TPI contracts that enabled a third party to influence the club's independence in employment and transfer-related matters and entering into an agreement that assigned rights to a third party in relation to the future transfer of a player.[25]

(i)   Liga de Quito v Palmeiras

11.47   In January 2012 the Ecuadorian club Liga de Quito and Brazilian side Palmeiras entered into a transfer agreement for the Argentine striker Hernán Barcos. The contract stipulated that Liga de Quito was retaining 30% of the economic rights for a future transfer with several clauses regulating the co-ownership of economic rights. Among these stipulations, a minimum transfer price was set and the obligation of Palmeiras to have Liga's consent to proceed with the transfer, with a penalty of US$ 2 million in case of breach.

11.48   In March 2013 Palmeiras, without obtaining the prior consent of Liga, transferred the player to another Brazilian team, Gremio, for a fixed transfer amount of US$ 5 million. Liga sued, claiming 30% of the minimum transfer price agreed in the contract and the penalty for breaching the duty to require Liga's consent to proceed with the deal. Palmeiras argued that the transfer was fair according to the player's market value and that the club was forced to transfer him due to its difficult financial situation. As to the 'co-ownership clauses', Palmeiras argued they were null and void and against Article 18bis of the RSTP and that the penalty was abusive.

11.49   The Dispute Resolution Chamber (DRC) passed a decision on 9 March 2016[26] partially upholding Palmeiras' claim. In relation to the 30% of the player's future transfer and the minimum fee clause, the Chamber considered that such clause was indeed against Article 18bis of the RSTP (especially because a penalty clause for transferring the player without the other club's consent was also in the agreement) and therefore decided to admit the claim only for the 30% of the effective transfer price.

11.50   As to the penalty clause, the DRC considered it valid and not against Article 18bis. For the DRC, both clubs were professional and fully aware of the nature of the contract they were entering. As to the amount of the penalty, considering that the clause was bilateral, the chamber decided it was proportionate and fully upheld

24   FIFA Disciplinary Committee Case Ref. Nr. 150522.
25   FIFA Disciplinary Committee Case Ref. Nr. 150946.
26   Unreported.

the claim in that sense. An appeal to CAS was lodged but eventually both clubs settled the matter.

11.51　Following that claim, the issue was submitted to the FIFA Disciplinary Committee which decided that Palmeiras had violated Article 18bis of the RSTP. The club was found to be liable for entering into a contract that enabled the other party to the contract, Liga de Quito, to influence Palmeiras' independence in employment and transfer-related matters and a CHF 50,000 fine was imposed on the Brazilian club.[27] Although the procedure was conducted under the previous version of Article 18bis it is still controversial that FIFA imposed no sanction on Liga de Quito, the counterpart that imposed the clauses held invalid by the Disciplinary Committee.

11.52　The rationale of the previous version of Article 18bis was also to punish parties involved in third party influence agreements. The original wording considered that the 'third party' exercising the influence was outside FIFA's disciplinary reach (a company or private investor). However, if the influencing party is subject to the FIFA disciplinary code, a sanction is appropriate even under the former version of Article 18bis. Irrespective of this opinion, the matter is settled now with the current wording that explicitly includes both clubs as potentially liable for breaching the third party influence rule.

(ii)　FC Twente v FIFA[28]

11.53　Futball Club Twente ('FC Twente') is a major Dutch professional football club that was faced with significant financial issues. Doyen Sports Investments Ltd ('Doyen') is a sports company based in Malta whose activities include investing in football players and clubs. In January 2014, it entered into a TPI agreement with FC Twente in order to help with the club's financial situation. According to the agreement, Doyen would pay FC Twente €5 million and in exchange it would be entitled to certain percentages of future transfer fees of seven players at the club.

11.54　After the Licensing Committee of the Dutch Football Association ('KNVB Licensing Committee') was made aware of the agreement, it asked to examine the draft contracts to verify if they were in accordance to the KNVB Regulations. After this analysis, it concluded that Doyen had too much influence on the transfer policy of the club, making it almost impossible for FC Twente to reject transfer offers without the consent of Doyen. The KNVB Licensing Committee asked the club to make some amendments to the TPI agreement, after which it was approved.

11.55　Nevertheless, after the website Football Leaks published the agreement, the KNVB Licensing Committee discovered that FC Twente had actually not complied with the determinations and had failed to insert certain additions to the TPI agreement, which violated KNVB's Regulations. Due to this violation, FC Twente was banned from European football for three seasons and in March 2016, FIFA sanctioned FC Twente with a fine of CHF 185,000, a warning and a reprimand for breaching Article 18bis of the RSTP (2012 edition) and Article 18ter of the RSTP (2015 Edition), as well as Annex 3 of said regulations. FC Twente was found to be liable for entering into contracts that enable a third party to influence the club in employment and transfer-related matters, and failing to upload a TPI agreement into the TMS library.

27　http://www.fifa.com/governance/news/y=2017/m=1/news=fifa-disciplinary-committee-passes-decisions-relating-to-third-party-i-2865316.html (accessed February 2018).
28　FIFA Disciplinary Committee Case Ref Nr. 160096.

(iii)   Boca Juniors v Atletico Mineiro[29]

11.56   The case involved a transfer agreement between Boca Juniors from Argentina and Atletico Mineiro from Brazil for the Paraguayan defender Julio Cáceres. The transfer agreed in January 2010 for a fixed transfer fee granted Boca a 50% of the profits of a future transfer of the player and included a clause imposing Boca's consent to Mineiro in order to transfer the player to another club or to assign its share of the economic right to a third party.

11.57   Immediately after the transfer, Mineiro assigned – with Boca's consent – its share of the economic rights to a private company.

11.58   One year later, in January 2011, Mineiro wrote to Boca asking its consent to terminate the player's employment agreement or in the alternative to loan him to Olimpia in Paraguay. Boca refused. Mineiro argued that, since the loan was free of charge and since the player was transferred only on loan, Boca's consent was not necessary, and the penalty was not applicable. The FIFA Players' Status Committee rejected the claim.

11.59   CAS overturned the decision and imposed the penalty (it was however reduced from US$ 2 million to US$ 1.5 million). The panel held that the clause also covered loan agreements or temporary transfers and the fact that the loan was free of charge was irrelevant.

11.60   As to the validity of the clause under the scope of Article 18bis the panel held it was lawful based on three arguments:[30]

(a)   Mineiro was estopped from invoking its nullity, since both clubs agreed with the inclusion of such clause in the transfer contract.
(b)   The right included in Article 18bis 1 of the RSTP vests in players and not clubs. It seeks to protect players from conduct between clubs jeopardising their future employment and transfer. It does not forbid clubs from reaching agreements as to the transfer and the distribution of proceeds flowing therefrom.
(c)   Article 18bis(1) does not foreclose entering into agreement as to the transfer of players (particularly where there is a shared interest in them by two teams) but forecloses agreements seeking solely to influence transfers. The goal is avoiding meddling in other people´s business, a sports concept similar to the common law theory of 'tortious contractual interference'. This situation is not at issue in this case.

(iv)   FC Seraing v FIFA[31]

11.61   In 2015, after the new Article 18ter of the RSTP came into force, several claims arose regarding the validity of the ban in the TPI contracts, claiming that such provision breached competition law and the freedom of movement of capital, services and workers within the EU. These claims were brought before state courts and international sports bodies.

11.62   One of the major claims resulted in the cooperation agreement entered into by the Walloon Royal Football Club Seraing ('FC Seraing') and Doyen,[32]

29   CAS 2014/A/3646 Award issued 24 August 2015.
30   Paragraphs 73, 74 and 75 of the award.
31   CAS 2016/A/4490 *RFC Seraing v FIFA*.
32   Brussels Court of Appeal of 10 March 2016, 18th Chamber.

where the future funding of any players of FC Seraing would be chosen by mutual agreement between the two parties. It also stipulated that Doyen would be entitled to 30% of the financial value arising from the federative rights of three players of FC Seraing. However, due to the new RSTP, the parties applied to the Regional Court of Brussels for interim relief in order to obtain an injunction against FIFA, UEFA, and the Union Royale Belge des Sociétés de Football Association to prevent them from implementing the terms of the FIFA Circular regarding the ban on the TPI contracts.

11.63   The Regional Court of Brussels ruled that it had jurisdiction to examine the petitions brought against FIFA, which had a link with Belgian territory. Nevertheless, it ruled that an examination of the legal aspects of the case was not sufficient to conclude with the necessary force that there had been a breach of competition rules. Courts in Belgium, considering matters on an interim application, could only rule on aspects of law and not on the merits of the case. Moreover, 'the tribunal held that the applicants had failed to prove their allegations that upon initial examination, the ban contravened EU law or was disproportionate to the attainment of the legitimate objectives sought by the introduction of this new regulation, such as the protection of players and the integrity of the game'.[33]

11.64   This decision was appealed to the Brussels Court of Appeal which decided, among other things, that the matter needed an in-depth examination since the 'ban was a result of a collective discussion in which there were many participants – not just UEFA or a few of its members – and is the outcome of several findings [...]: opacity, absence of control of the phenomenon as it relates to the world market, environment open to corruption and fraudulent practice, the scale of the sums involved'.[34] Thus, since it was ruling in a summary proceedings, the Appeal Court refused to give an opinion on the legality of the ban on TPI contracts.

11.65   Alongside these proceedings, the FIFA Disciplinary Committee banned FC Seraing[35] from transferring players during four registration periods and had ordered it to pay a fine of CHF 150,000 for breaches relating to TPO and TPI. Due to this sanction, FC Seraing was prevented from signing two players who were taken on after the sanction. Therefore, FC Seraing appealed to the FIFA Appeals Committee in order to prevent major harms pending a decision on the legality of the ban on TPO contracts. The FIFA Appeals Committee rejected the appeal lodged by FC Seraing and confirmed in its entirety the decision rendered by the FIFA Disciplinary Committee sanctioning the club for breaches of the regulations relating to the prohibition of third party influence on clubs and to the ban on third-party ownership of player's economic rights.

11.66   FC Seraing further appealed to the CAS,[36] and the tribunal rejected most of its claims under Swiss Law, the European Convention of Human Rights and the EU Fundamental Rights Charter. In any event, the CAS decided to reduce the transfer ban originally imposed by FIFA from four to three consecutive and complete registration periods, and a fine in the total amount of CHF 150,000.

---

33   Regional Court of Brussels, Judgment of 24 July 2015, para 98.
34   Brussels Court of Appeal, 18th Chamber, Judgment of 10 March 2016, p 35.
35   http://www.fifa.com/governance/news/y=2015/m=9/news=belgian-club-fc-seraing-sanctioned-under-third-party-influence-and-thi-2678395.html (accessed February 2018).
36   See CAS 2016/A/4490 *RFC Seraing v FIFA* and http://www.fifa.com/governance/news/y=2017/m=3/news=fifa-welcomes-cas-award-recognising-compatibility-of-tpo-ban-with-eu-l-2875475.html (accessed February 2018).

(v)   Doyen v Sporting Club: Marcos Rojo Case[37]

11.67   At the end of the 2011/12 season, Sporting Club Portugal ('Sporting') and Doyen Sports Investments Ltd entered into a TPI agreement regarding the participation on the economic rights of the player Marcos Rojo, where Doyen would fund a portion of the transfer cost of the player from Spartak and in return be granted 75% of the player's economic rights in case he was transferred from Sporting. Mr Rojo signed a five-year working contract with Sporting, which was valid until June 2017. However, at the beginning of 2014, Sporting requested Doyen to search for clubs interested in Mr Rojo, since it was no longer interested in his services. Nevertheless, after watching the player's performance during the 2014 World Cup, Sporting decided that it would continue to employ Mr Rojo. Despite this, Doyen informed Sporting that Manchester United was interested in acquiring the player for €20 million. Since Sporting refused this offer, Doyen invoked the clause of the agreement that stated that if a party refused to accept a transfer, Doyen could issue an invoice equal to 75% of the offer proposed by the third party club.

11.68   On 14 August 2014, Sporting notified Doyen of its decision to terminate the agreement due to the breach of contract. After terminating the agreement, Sporting transferred Rojo to Manchester United. When Doyen was informed about this fact, it issued an invoice equivalent to 75% of the player's economic rights.

11.69   In October 2014, Sporting issued a claim before the CAS against Doyen and a few days later Doyen brought an action before the CAS against Sporting. After analysing the party's arguments, the CAS determined it was in no position to express an opinion on TPI mechanisms but to simply access the parties' legal situation under the applicable law on the date the agreement was executed, focusing solely on its validity. The CAS found no legal cause for its nullity and determined that none of the facts alleged by Sporting justified the termination of the TPI agreement. Thus, CAS recognised the validity of the agreement and considered Doyen's claims legitimate. In this sense, the TPI Agreement was considered legitimate under previous legal frameworks, provided that it did not conflict with the former Article 18bis of the RSTP.

(vi)   *South American case:* Iago Maidana[38]

11.70   On September 2015, the Brazilian player Iago Justen Maidana Martins (the 'player') was transferred from the club Criciúma Esporte Clube ('Criciúma'), to Monte Cristo Esporte Clube ('Monte Cristo'), and then to São Paulo Futebol Clube ('São Paulo FC') – all of them Brazilian clubs – all in less than ten days. The transfer from Criciúma was due to the early termination of the employment agreement ('Employment Agreement 1') by the company Gestão de Patrimonio Ltda. ('GA'), owner of all of the player's economic rights and Criciúma's partner since 2012, which received from another company, Itaquerão Soccer Ltda, the total amount of R$400,000 regarding the termination of Employment Agreement 1.

11.71   Five days later, on 9 September 2015 the player signed a new employment agreement with Monte Cristo ('Employment Agreement 2'), which would be the new

---

37   CAS 2014/O/3781 & 3782, *Sporting Clube de Portugal Futebol SAD v Doyen Sports Investment Limited*, Award of 21 December 2015.
38   Case Ref Nr. 320/2015 – *Criciúma, São Paulo FC, Monte Cristo & Iago Maidana*, STJD 1st Disciplinary Commission, 5 May 2016.

owner of the player's economic rights. Nevertheless, only two days after Employment Agreement 2 had been signed, it was terminated. The next day, Monte Cristo and São Paulo FC signed an agreement stipulating the conditions of the transfer of the player to São Paulo FC. Consequently, the player signed a new employment agreement with São Paulo FC ('Employment Agreement 3') where it agreed to pay Monte Cristo the total amount of R\$ 2 million in order to obtain 60% of the player's economic rights while Monte Cristo would keep the remaining 40%. This significant transfer fee alarmed the Brazilian Football Association (CBF), once São Paulo FC paid an indemnification fee much higher than the contractual stipulation under Employment Agreement 2, ie R\$ 50,000 in order to obtain only 60% of the player's economic rights. In any event, from São Paulo FC's point of view, such transfer operation made no sense, once it could have initially obtained the player's economic rights from Criciúma for the value of R\$1.6 million as stipulated in the indemnification clause of Employment Agreement 1.

11.72   In view of the foregoing, the Brazilian Sporting Justice Tribunal competent to adjudicate the matter understood that the parties had violated the Brazilian Code of Sports Law and the CBF's Regulations on the Status and Transfer of Players, which was the first football association in Latin America to update its regulations in accordance with Articles 18bis and 18ter of the RSTP.

11.73   In general terms, the three clubs and the player were accused of using an unregistered intermediary (Itaquerão Soccer Ltda) in order to conclude the player's transfer (Article 38 of the National Regulation of Intermediaries) and of failing to inform CBF of said transfer operation, which also constituted a violation of the CBF Intermediaries Regulations (Article 13 of the National Regulation of Intermediaries). Moreover, a third party, GA (Criciuma's partner), was involved in the termination of Employment Agreement 1, which is expressly forbidden not only by CBF but also by RSTP.

11.74   On 26 October 2015, the Appeals Tribunal of the Brazilian sporting justice body finally ruled on the case and held Monte Cristo liable for contributing to the termination of Employment Agreement 1, as it acted as a 'bridge club' between Criciúma and São Paulo, with the sole purpose of profit, once it still had 40% of the player's economic rights. Consequently, considering that these subsequent transfers comprised the purchase and sale of the player's economic rights, the said operations were prohibited under the CBF Transfer Regulations (Article 66 of the National Regulation of Registration and Transfer of Football Athletes). In light of all the above, on 27 October 2015, São Paulo, Criciúma and Monte Cristo were fined in the first instance R\$100,000 while the player was fined R\$10,000.

D   LEGAL CHALLENGES TO THE FIFA REGULATIONS

11.75   As early as December 2014, after publication of news that FIFA proposed to prohibit TPI, the international football market demonstrated concerns about the use of such a drastic measure in banning a long-standing practice adopted by small and large clubs from South America and Europe, especially in Spain and Portugal.[39]

11.76   In view of the increase of third parties' investment in football, the differentiation between the registration and economic rights has generated heated

---

39   Research on Third-Party Ownership of Players' Economic Rights (Part II), CDES and CIES (June 2014).

discussions, especially before FIFA judicial bodies, the CAS and other national associations. As seen in Spain, Portugal, South American countries and many others around Europe,[40] TPI worked as an alternative financing mechanism and usually allowed clubs to purchase and sell players' economic rights and thus facilitate the renewal of squads. Moreover, the sale of economic rights resulted in the immediate injection of revenues into clubs, and allowed them to count on a significant income with less bureaucracy than finance from banks.

11.77   By analysing Brazil as one of the main users of TPI, considering that it remains the largest exporter of football players around the world, as acknowledged by the FIFA TMS Report (2016 edition),[41] between 1 January 2015 and 26 April 2016, 2,323 transfers worldwide involved Brazilians – more than double any other nationality – which corresponded to 12% of all transfers worldwide. Alongside Brazilians, the Argentinians stand out as the second most transferred nationalities worldwide. As a result, these transfers inevitably provide a positive result to Brazilian and Argentinian clubs and a relevant source of income that cannot be ignored, especially because most of these transfers are concluded involving some mechanism of TPI.

11.78   In view of the foregoing, and in light of the ban implemented on TPI, the most affected clubs and countries have suffered considerable economic impact, especially in South America, where the revenues originated from the sale of economic rights are the second most lucrative source of income for clubs.[42]

11.79   As a reaction to the enactment of Article 18ter of the RSTP and the TPI ban, several stakeholders in the football industry took actions against FIFA, in different forums but based on similar grounds, including intermediaries and some professional football leagues, which contested the validity of such rules in light of EU and competition law.

11.80   In 2015, Doyen and FC Seraing filed an application for a temporary injunction against FIFA before the Brussels first-instance tribunal to suspend the implementation of the TPI worldwide ban, more precisely the effects of Article 18ter of the RSTP. FIFPro also intervened in these proceedings on the side of FIFA, holding that the TPI-related agreements and mechanisms are exclusively financial, but with consequences of a sporting nature.

11.81   The application was rejected by the Brussels first-instance tribunal in July 2015. The tribunal held that the applicants failed to prove their allegations that upon initial examination, the ban contravened EU law or was disproportionate to the attainment of the legitimate objectives sought by its introduction, such as the protection of players and the integrity of the game.[43]

11.82   The court referred to the specificity of sport and to the arguments presented for justifying the imposition of the TPI ban, holding that although the activity is of a financial nature, it primarily has consequences of a purely sporting nature.

---

40   Ibid.
41   See FIFA TMS 2016 Report on Player Nationalities in the Transfer Market.
42   See ITAÚ BBA Report on Financial Status of Football Clubs in Brazil.
43   FIFA's press release http://www.fifa.com/governance/news/y=2015/m=7/news=fifa-welcomes-brussels-court-s-decision-to-reject-suspension-of-tpo-ba-2668122.html (accessed February 2018). See also Antoine Duval, 'EU Law is not enough: Why FIFA's TPO ban survived its first challenge before the Brussels Court' http://www.asser.nl/SportsLaw/Blog/post/eu-law-is-not-enough-why-fifa-s-tpo-ban-survived-before-the-brussels-court1 (accessed February 2018).

11.83   Almost a year later, in March 2016, the Court of Appeal upheld the position of the first-instance tribunal, emphasising the opacity of TPI, the absence of control by governing bodies, the worldwide reach of this phenomenon, the money involved and the environment, which is prone to corruption and other fraudulent practices.[44]

11.84   In October 2017 the substance of the case was heard in the Court in Brussels and a decision is still pending.

E   SUMMARY OF REGULATIONS IN ENGLAND

(a)   Introduction

11.85   Although FIFA's Regulations prohibiting TPI have been in force since 2014, there has been an outright prohibition of the practice in England since 2008.[45] English football prohibited TPI after the highly publicised *Tevez* case in 2007.[46] Carlos Tevez and another Argentinian player, Javier Mascherano, were owned by third parties who facilitated their transfer to West Ham United FC in order to provide them with greater exposure in Europe, so as to later achieve higher transfer fees. The third parties continued to own rights over the players (as well as control their subsequent transfers), and both players ultimately ended up at bigger clubs (Mascherano went to Liverpool, Tevez to Manchester United and then Manchester City).

11.86   West Ham United were not in breach of rules prohibiting TPI in English football, because such rules did not exist at the time; rather, it was in breach of rules prohibiting third party influence[47] (something that was even then prohibited by FIFA), and also good faith, because it concealed from the Premier League the arrangements whereby the third parties retained control over the transfers of the players. West Ham were fined £5 million for the breach (a fine that remains the highest levied in English football to date) and narrowly escaped a points deduction. Subsequently, West Ham was ordered to pay many millions more as compensation to Sheffield United FC who had been relegated from the Premier League and who proved that had it not been for West Ham's rule breach of the Premier League Rules, in fielding Tevez to play during the 2006/07 season, West Ham would have achieved at least three fewer points and Sheffield United would have thus avoided relegation (it had three points less than West Ham but a better goal difference).[48]

11.87   The considerable controversy surrounding the Tevez affair led to The FA, the Premier League and the Football League all incorporating rules to prohibit any form of TPI in English football from 2008 onwards. The widespread view in English football was that if any form of TPI was permitted, then third party influence (as with Tevez) was inevitable.

11.88   Whilst today rules are required by FIFA to prevent a club from entering an agreement 'with a third party whereby a third party is being entitled to participate,

---

44   FIFA's press release http://www.fifa.com/governance/news/y=2016/m=3/news=fifa-welcomes-brussels-court-of-appeal-ruling-on-third-party-ownership-2770816.html (accessed February 2018). See also Antoine Duval, 'Doyen's Crusade Against FIFA's TPO Ban: The Ruling of the Appeal Court of Brussels' at http://www.asser.nl/SportsLaw/Blog/post/doyen-s-crusade-against-fifa-s-tpo-ban-the-ruling-of-the-appeal-court-of-brussels (accessed February 2018).
45   The football authorities in France and Poland also prohibited TPI before FIFA's worldwide ban.
46   *FAPL v West Ham United*, FAPL Disciplinary Commission, 27 April 2007.
47   Former Premier League Rule I.7, based on RSTP, Article 18bis.
48   See *Sheffield United FC v West Ham United FC*, FA Rule K Arbitration (Ch. Lord Griffiths) [2009] ISLR 25.

either in full or in part, in compensation payable in relation to the future transfer of a player from one club to another, or is being assigned any rights in relation to a future transfer or transfer compensation',[49] an examination of the various rules and cases in England show that the prohibition on TPI goes considerably further.

(b)   The FA rules

11.89   The FA prohibits TPI by its Third Party Interest in Players Regulations ('FA TPI Regulations').[50] These Regulations are substantively more comprehensive than the FIFA prohibition.[51] The main prohibition is contained in Regulation A1 which provides as follows:

'A. PROHIBITION ON THIRD PARTY INTEREST

Club Obligations

1.   No Club may enter into an Agreement which enables any party, other than the Club itself, to influence materially the Club's policies or the performance of its teams or Players in Matches and/or Competitions.
2.   No Club may enter into an Agreement with a party whereby that Club:
   * makes or receives a payment, whether directly or indirectly, or
   * assigns, novates, sells, grants, acquires or otherwise transacts in any rights or obligations whatsoever, or
   * incurs any liability to, or from that party as a result of, in connection with, or in relation to
   * the proposed or actual registration (whether permanent or temporary), or
   * the transfer of registration, or
   * the employment or continued employment

by the Club of a player, save where:
2.1   the Agreement is permitted pursuant to Regulation B ("Permitted Club Agreements"); or
2.2   The Association has provided its formal written approval of the Agreement in advance

pursuant to Regulation D ("Club or Player Agreements Requiring Prior Written Approval").

11.90   Regulation A3 provides a similar prohibition on players.

11.91   Whereas the FIFA prohibition prevents a club from entering into an agreement with a third party where that party is entitled to compensation from the future transfer of a player from one club to another, or is assigned any rights in relation to a future transfer or transfer compensation, The FA prohibition appears to go further. For example, Regulation A2 prevents a club from receiving payments or assigning rights with respect to the continued employment of a player, and not only his future transfer.

11.92   Regulation B deals with 'Permitted Club Agreements', whereby it is possible for an agreement to be reached that would otherwise breach Regulation A. Generally, it is permitted to receive or pay a transfer fee from another registering club, or to pay an intermediary, pay associated expenses, or pay training compensation.[52]

49   RSTP, Article 18ter.
50   The current version of the Regulations (2017–18) have been in force since 2015.
51   By way of example, the FA Regulations consist of over 51 paragraphs, and a lengthy definitions section, compared to six short paragraphs under RSTP, Article 18ter, and a further two under Article 18bis (prohibiting third party influence).
52   Regulation B1.1–1.6.

11.93 Regulations B1.7–B1.12 deal with certain permitted financial arrangements. Broadly speaking they permit a transferring club to receive or pay certain fees from or to a financial institution.[53] This allows clubs to borrow money against future transfer fees in certain circumstances.

11.94 Regulations B1.13–B.1.14 permit arrangements where players and clubs can acquire rights as to future employment, under certain conditions, so a club can agree to a 'pre-contract' with a player, for example, promising to enter a full employment contract with him on a future specified date.

11.95 Most of the permitted exceptions require that the club must lodge the completed agreement with The FA within five days of its completion,[54] and it will be a breach of the FA TPI Regulations if this is not done. Whilst a club in breach might argue that had it lodged the agreement in time it would not have been in breach, and that there is no actual substantive harm, it may still be charged and sanctioned for its breach; but it is suggested that any such sanction would have to be lenient to be fair and proportionate in the circumstances of a purely technical breach.

11.96 Permitted player agreements are dealt with in Regulation C. Players can enter into a contract of employment, a representation contract with an intermediary, an image rights agreement, a commercial agreement or an agreement to pay incidental expenses.[55]

11.97 Regulation D provides that a club or a player may enter into agreements that are otherwise prohibited by the FA TPI Regulations so long as they have obtained the prior written consent of The FA to do so. Thus, if a party is considering entering a novel financing agreement, for example, but is concerned that it might fall foul of the Regulations, the sensible course is for that party to consult openly with The FA and seek to have its proposal approved under this Regulation.

11.98 Regulation D4 provides that The FA shall have regard to and shall apply principles consistent with the purpose and intention of its Rules in considering approval under this head. Thus, whilst The FA has a broad discretion to grant or refuse such approval, it must do so not only in accordance with normal principles of fairness (it must not exercise it arbitrarily or capriciously) but also must consider whether the approval or refusal is in accordance with the purpose and intent of The FA Rules. In the circumstances, The FA ought to provide reasons for the exercise of its discretion under these Rules, and a failure to provide adequate reasons, or a failure to exercise that discretion lawfully, may be challenged by way of an arbitral claim against The FA pursuant to Rule K of its Rules.[56]

11.99 Regulation D5 sets out 'typical agreements requiring prior written approval'. The one example given is the most obvious circumstance in which a club may enter into an agreement with a third party with an interest in a player – where the buying club wishes to acquire the totality of the rights in the transferring player and buy out the TPI. The agreement must extinguish any TPI rights to the player; the club must

53 Basically, a UK regulated bank – though defined as a UK entity with permission to carry out the regulated activity of accepting deposits, but not including a building society or credit union.
54 Regulation B2.
55 Regulation C1.1–C1.5. A '*Commercial Agreement*' is defined in Regulation E as a sponsorship or marketing agreement whereby the player receives remuneration in consideration for his marketing/ advertising products, but only 'in circumstances which do not grant to any party the ability to materially influence that player's performance' in matches.
56 See Chapter 28, Arbitration in Football, paras **28.43–28.81**.

pay all sums due to the third party before the end of the player's initial employment contract with it; it must pay all sums through FA accounts; it must not grant any right or confer any benefit to any party in relation to the future sale of the player, except a sell-on fee granted to the transferring club; and the club must record every term of the agreement in writing and submit it to The FA within five working days of its completion. Even after FIFA's prohibition of TPI, there will be existing legitimate TPI contracts between third parties and players/clubs that have not expired – Regulation D5 of The FA's Third Party Interest in Players Regulations allows for a club to enter agreements with players subject to such unexpired TPI arrangements, so long as those new agreements extinguish all previous TPI rights and comply with the formalities of that regulation.

11.100   Regulation D6 deals with other financing agreements where a club proposes to borrow money secured against the value of one of its players. Such agreements may be approved by The FA from time to time and under certain conditions. Regulation D7 allows for the transferring club to assign its entitlement to a fee to a financial institution, group undertaking or permitted individual in certain circumstances.[57] Regulation D8 allows for a registering club to pay a party to which an overseas transferring club has assigned its entitlement to a fee. Regulations D7 and D8 thus allow for the arrangements set out in Regulation D6 and D5 respectively.

11.101   In each of these cases (and in any other case), The FA's prior written approval is required, and the failure to obtain it shall be a breach even if it would have been obtained had it been sought.

11.102   On a strict construction of the FA TPI Regulations it is arguable that an arrangement between a player and his employing club by which the player would be entitled to a percentage of the fee earned by the club in transferring that same player's registration to a new club would be prohibited – even though it is not a 'third party' interest in the player at all; it is the player's own interest in the player. Regulation A3 prohibits (amongst other things) a player receiving any payment from a party in relation to a transfer, save where the agreement is permitted pursuant to Regulation C or The FA has provided its prior written approval to the agreement pursuant to Regulation D. Regulation B1.3 does, however, permit a club to make a payment to a player it employs for the benefit of the player, subject to the requirements of FA Rule C.1(b)(iv) – which provides that all payments made to a player must be recorded in a written contract provided to The FA. Whilst it appears counter-intuitive that regulations prohibiting third party interests in players should prohibit the player's own interest in his future transfer, players and clubs would be well advised to consider obtaining The FA's prior written approval for any such arrangements whereby a player becomes entitled to a percentage of the transfer fee received by the club on his transfer, or at the very least to make sure such contractual arrangements are lodged with The FA when they are made.

11.103   A more obvious, previously quite common, arrangement that would fall foul of the Regulations is one whereby a manager or coach of a club has reached an agreement with that club that he be entitled to a percentage of transfer fees received on the sale of a player that manager or coach has previously identified, recruited

---

57   See n 53 above for the definition of 'financial institution'. 'Group undertaking' has the meaning set out in Companies Act 2006, s 1161(5) (ie a parent undertaking or subsidiary undertaking of that undertaking or a subsidiary undertaking of any parent undertaking of that undertaking). 'Permitted individual' means an Official or Officer of the relevant transferring club who is at the time of the assignment compliant with the requirements of the applicable Owners' and Directors' Test.

or coached. The manager/coach may not be a traditional 'third party' as he is an employee of the club that holds the player's registration, but the payment would be to a party not permitted under Regulation B, and would thus be a breach (unless, again, The FA's prior written approval has been granted). It is important to recall that it is not simply the payment that would be a breach, but the entering into the agreement with the manager/coach itself.

(c) The Premier League Rules

11.104   FAPL Rules U.38–U.39 prohibit TPI. Whilst less detailed than The FA TPI Regulations, the essential substance of the rules is similar.

11.105   Rule U.38 provides a general prohibition:

> 'Unless otherwise agreed by the Board and subject to Rule U.39, a Club may only make or receive a payment or incur any liability as a result of or in connection with the proposed or actual registration (whether permanent or temporary), transfer of registration or employment by it of a Player in the following circumstances:'

There follows a number of permitted circumstances such as payments of transfer fees, loan fees, sell-on fees, solidarity payments, remuneration to the player or to a registered intermediary, and assignments of entitlements to a fee to a financial institution.

11.106   Rule U.39 is similar to Regulation D5 of the FA TPI Regulations – it permits registering clubs to 'buy out' TPI in a player upon his registration under certain circumstances. A payment not dependent on the happening of a contingent event may be made either in one lump sum or in instalments provided that all such instalments are paid on or before the expiry date of the initial contract between the club and the player. A payment payable upon the happening of a contingent event must be payable within seven days of the happening of that event.

(d) The Football League (EFL) rules

11.107   Regulation 48 of the EFL Regulations prohibits TPI. The regulation provides that unless the Board of the Football League otherwise agrees, a club can only 'make or receive a payment or incur any liability as a result of or in connection with the proposed or actual registration (whether permanent or temporary), transfer of registration or employment by it of a Player' in circumstances then set out in the regulation. Those circumstances are the familiar predictable ones: transfer, loan fees, and sell-ons, payments to intermediaries, payments of tax, buying out a third party interest (with wording and timescales similar to those in the Premier League Rules) etc.

11.108   Though the prohibition on third party interests is dealt with in Regulation 48 other regulations of the EFL may be relevant. For example, Regulation 44.2 provides that any contract a club proposes to enter which provides another party to the proposed contract rights relating to the transfer of the registration of a player must be registered with the EFL and is subject to the EFL's prior approval.[58]

---

58   See *Football League v (1) Watford Association Football Club & (2) Laurence Bassini*, 10 February 2013. Football League Football Disciplinary Commission (Ch. Alexander Milne QC) – discussed in paras **11.120–11.124** below.

(e)   The National League

11.109   The National League does not have any specific regulation dealing with TPI but, of course, TPI is prohibited amongst all National League teams by virtue of the FA Regulations (which apply to all association football clubs).

11.110   TPI in lower league football is just as important as it is at the higher levels. TPI investors are often most likely to use the vehicle of a lower league club, or less experienced players, for their investments which may then bring greater rewards for those players who succeed and end up transferred to a club at a higher level.

F   SUMMARY OF CASES IN ENGLAND

11.111   The various English football regulations prohibiting TPI may affect clubs (as well as intermediaries, club directors and other participants) in a variety of different ways. It is not only the classic Tevez-type third party influence situation that has led to charges of misconduct; other less obvious breaches have led to serious sanctions against clubs and individuals in football. Breaches may involve a failure to disclose arrangements, even if those arrangements themselves do not provide for TPI; or they may involve clubs and club officials being sanctioned for borrowing monies against future transfer fees of players even after the club has sold that player; or intermediaries being sanctioned for receiving commissions from a club based on that club's income for a sell-on fee the intermediary negotiated.

11.112   To appreciate the extent and scope of the prohibition and how it may affect participants in football it is useful to consider the three main regulatory cases involving breaches of TPI and associated regulations since the prohibition of TPI following the *Tevez* case: (i) the *Faurlin* case involving QPR and Mr Paladini; (ii) the *Graham* case involving Watford and Mr Bassini; and (iii) the *Phillips* case involving Wycombe Wanderers and Phil Smith.

(a)   The *Faurlin* case

11.113   In *The FA v (1) Queens Park Rangers FC & (2) Gianni Paladini*,[59] an FA Regulatory Commission considered serious charges against QPR and its then Chairman, Mr Paladini, in relation to an alleged TPI agreement involving one of QPR's star players in the 2010/11 season, the Argentinian midfielder, Alejandro Faurlin. QPR were the subject of seven different charges, four of them alleging breaches of The FA's Third Party Interest in Players Regulations; Mr Paladini was charged with one charge of misconduct. All of the charges related to dealings in connection with the player Faurlin.

11.114   The case received considerable coverage in the media. QPR were poised for automatic promotion to the Premier League for the first time in 15 years. There was speculation that if QPR were found to be in breach it would be subjected to a points deduction which might lead to QPR missing out on promotion. The hearing took place near the end of the season and the decision, and sanction, was not announced until an hour or so before QPR's final game of the season, in which they

---

59   FA Regulatory Commission (Ch. Craig Moore) 20 May 2011.

were, as it turned out, presented with the Football League Championship winners' cup and promoted. It was one of the rare occasions when the decision of a legal case in football received a greater cheer from the fans than anything in the match itself.

11.115 A US/Argentinian company had owned 100% of Faurlin's economic, federative (ie player registration), intellectual and image rights. In July 2009, Faurlin signed a three-year contract with QPR. There was an oral agreement (recorded in a letter) between Mr Paladini on behalf of QPR and the third party owners by which the third party owners agreed to suspend all of their rights in relation to Faurlin for the duration of the QPR playing contract. Various documents relating to the registration of Faurlin were registered with the FA upon his signing, but there was no indication that Faurlin was the subject of any TPI arrangements, nor that there had been an oral agreement suspending the TPI agreement – though The FA's Third Party Interest in Players Regulations had only just been brought into force a few days earlier.

11.116 In August 2010, QPR were negotiating an improved and extended contract with Faurlin. It decided to buy-out the third party rights to the player in accordance with the FA TPI Regulations for the sum of US$ 1 million (then £615,000), and informed both the Football League and The FA of the buy-out agreement. The FA sanctioned the buy-out but initiated an investigation into QPR's previous failure to disclose the TPI arrangements.

11.117 The Commission rejected the main thrust of The FA's case: that the various arrangements breached the FA TPI Regulations. It found that during the period of the first contract the TPI had been suspended – there was no actual third party interest or influence. The oral agreement was an agreement entered into with a third party, but it was entered into before the FA TPI Regulations came into force, and those regulations could not have retrospective effect.

11.118 Whilst The FA's main case on TPI failed before the Commission it was successful on a lesser charge of general misconduct against the club for failing to disclose the oral agreement. The failure of disclosure was not acting 'in the best interests of the game' even if it was not in breach of the FA TPI Regulations. It was a negligent but not a dishonest failure. QPR had obtained some sporting advantage as a result but this was in relation to the previous 2009/10 season in which it was not promoted. There was an economic advantage obtained in obtaining the services of the player for a lower fee. Accordingly, the Commission determined that a fine of £800,000 reflected this benefit. QPR was also fined a further £75,000 for breach of one of the Football Agents Regulations.

11.119 The *Faurlin* case is instructive for various reasons. It is the first, and remains the only, serious case to be brought by The FA alleging actual TPI in relation to a player in England. It is apparent that in considering such a serious charge the Commission was careful to construe the regulations and wording of the charges strictly, and QPR was able to avoid liability for the more serious breach and the points' deduction that may have followed with potentially disastrous consequences. Finally, on the other hand, it is an important lesson for clubs about the risks of not disclosing documents or arrangements they believe do not suggest any wrongdoing – QPR paid a hefty price for the failure to disclose a document it did not believe it needed to disclosure at the time. Clubs would be well advised to always err on the side of caution in relation to disclosure to the regulator in future, in particular in relation to any dealings relating to potential TPI.

(b) The *Graham* case

11.120   The case of *Football League v (1) Watford Association Football Club &
(2) Laurence Bassini*[60] provides a good example of the wide scope of TPI and the
associated regulations and how they can impact arrangements that really have nothing
to do with TPI in the traditional sense at all.

11.121   In July 2011, Watford transferred the player Danny Graham to Swansea
City for an agreed fee of £3.5 million, to be paid in various instalments over the
following year. Watford, through its then Chairman and owner, Mr Bassini, reached
an agreement with a lending company specialising in football, LNOC, for 'forward
funding'. In short, LNOC would advance sums to Watford in exchange for being
assigned the rights to receive the future instalments from the Graham transfer – which
were guaranteed payments to be made through the Football League's accounts.

11.122   The arrangement was found to be in breach of Regulation 44.2 of the EFL:
it was a contract entered into by Watford which gave LNOC the right to receive
payments in respect of a transfer, and the Football League had not been informed of
it, nor had prior approval been sought or granted. The arrangement was also found to
be in breach of Regulation 48, the prohibition on TPI, because Watford was receiving
monies in connection with a transfer from LNOC, which was not a specified financial
institution, and again no approval had been sought or granted. The club was also
found to have breached Regualtion 19.

11.123   Watford were subjected to a transfer embargo for the summer transfer
window and Mr Bassini, who was found guilty of misconduct as the guiding hand
behind the arrangements – given he showed a 'reckless disregard of the Regulation' –
was banned from being in a position of authority in football for three years.

11.124   The purpose of the prohibition of TPI is generally understood to be
(i) preventing third parties from having any influence in football; and (ii) a disapproval
of the idea of their parties having 'ownership' of a player. The *Graham* case, however,
shows how far from those purposes strict regulations can travel. Watford had already
sold Danny Graham by the time it entered the funding agreement with LNOC. It was
guaranteed the payments of the remaining instalments of the fee in the same way
that it was guaranteed monies from the Football League in respect of broadcasting
revenues. There was no suggestion of LNOC having any influence over the transfer
of the player, and it did not have an interest in the player. Nevertheless, Watford was
found guilty of a serious breach and only escaped more stringent punishment (such
as a points' deduction and/or a fine) because it was able to persuade the Commission
that the loan was largely arranged by Mr Bassini without the Board's knowledge or
consent.

(c) The *Phillips* case

11.125   The last case in the trio involves an agreement to pay a football agent,
Phil Smith, a percentage of a sell-on fee received by Wycombe Wanderers FC in
respect to the transfer of Matt Phillips from Wycombe to Blackpool in August 2010.
Mr Smith acted as Wycombe's agent in the transfer, securing an initial fee of £325,000
for the player and negotiating a sell-on fee whereby Wycombe would receive 25%

---

60   10 February 2013. Football League Football Disciplinary Commission (Ch. Alexander Milne QC).

of any future transfer fee received by Blackpool. In consideration for Mr Smith's services, and instead of paying him a fee on the transfer, Wycombe agreed to pay him 10% of any net proceeds received as a result of the sell-on fee.

11.126 In August 2013, Wycombe, under new ownership, agreed to sell its entitlement to the sell-on fee from Blackpool to Blackpool for the sum of £200,000. Within a few weeks, Blackpool sold the player to QPR for a fee of £6 million. Had Wycombe not sold its entitlement it would have received from Blackpool 25% of that fee minus the initial fee paid, ie £1,175,000, and Mr Smith would have been entitled to 10% of that amount, being £117,500. Mr Smith was not told about Wycombe's sale of its entitlement and, on hearing the news of the player's transfer to QPR requested Wycombe pay him his fee. The new owners of Wycombe refused to pay Mr Smith any fee and reported him to The FA.

11.127 In *The FA v (1) Phil Smith & (2) Wycombe Wanderers FC*,[61] the parties were charged with various breaches of The FA's Agents Regulations in force at the time. In particular, they were charged with a breach of Regulation H11 of those Regulations which provided that an agent must not hold any interest in relation to a registration right including an interest in any transfer fee or future sale value of a player. They were also charged with failing to disclose and concealing the arrangement that was made.

11.128 Wycombe pleaded guilty to the charges, Mr Smith denied liability. The Commission found the breaches had been committed, finding, amongst other things, that there could be an interest for the purposes of Regulation H11 even if the contract entered into creating it was not legally binding.

11.129 Wycombe was fined £10,000 for the breach and issued with a warning; the fine was low given its cooperation with revealing the breach to The FA. Mr Smith, on the other hand, had his agent's licence suspended with immediate effect for a period of two years, 18 months of which was suspended[62] (albeit that suspension was then quashed on appeal for unrelated reasons).[63]

11.130 The case is another example of the scope of the various prohibitions on TPI. Regulation E5 of the FA Regulations on Working with Intermediaries replaced H11 of the Football Agents Regulations. It provides that:

> An Intermediary must not have, either directly or indirectly, any interest of any nature whatsoever in relation to a registration right or an economic right. This includes, but is not limited to, owning any interest in any transfer compensation or future transfer value of a Player. This does not prevent an Intermediary acting solely for a Club in a Transaction being remunerated by reference to the total amount of transfer compensation generated by this Transaction.

11.131 The new regulation appears to have clarified that an intermediary acting solely for the club can receive a percentage of the fee that club receives as a result of the transfer, but it is unclear whether 'the total amount of transfer compensation generated' would include sell-on fees agreed as part of the same transfer.

11.132 It is clear that the purpose and intent of the regulations is to prevent an intermediary having TPI in a player. However, this is somewhat of an anomaly. If an

61 FA Regulatory Commission (Ch. Craig Moore), 26 April 2014.
62 FA Regulatory Commission (Ch. Craig Moore), Decision on sanction, 23 May 2014.
63 *Phil Smith v The FA*, FA Appeal Board (Ch. R Smith QC) 11 July 2014.

intermediary acts for a club in a transfer of a player then it is customary, and makes commercial sense, for him or her to receive a percentage of the revenue his or her work for that club achieves, such as a percentage of the transfer fee received and any further sell-on fees received. If the intermediary acts for the player then he shall usually be remunerated by reference to a percentage of the new salary he negotiates for the player, often as a result of negotiating a new registration right (ie transfer or initial signing). In either case it could be argued that the intermediary has a direct interest in relation to a registration right and it is not surprising that The FA TPI Regulations exempt payments to intermediaries from the general prohibition. It is difficult in those circumstances to understand the justification for rules such as the old Agents Regulation H11 and new Intermediaries Regulation E5, or to understand how they can work in practice.

11.133   The *Phillips* case is also a further example (in line with the *Tevez*, *Faurlin* and *Graham* cases) of how the failure to disclose arrangements to the regulators is regarded as a serious offence in cases touching upon TPI.

G   CONCLUSION

(a)   Distinction between third party influence and investment

11.134   TPI remains a controversial subject in football. There are strong views on either side of the argument about the scope and extent of regulation, and whether or not TPI should be regulated or prohibited. FIFA's relatively recent decision to prefer prohibition to regulation may be more to do with its belief that it cannot regulate (similar to its decision to de-regulate agency activity) than it is to do with any argument of principle.

11.135   In considering the various policy arguments, the starting point is to understand the distinction between third party influence and TPI. The arguments against third party influence are easy to understand. If a third party can influence a football club because of its interest in one or more of its players the integrity of the sport can be fundamentally undermined. Clubs could be forced to sell players they do not want to sell to clubs they do not want to sell to for fees they would not otherwise accept. The third party investor who only makes a profit every time a player is transferred for a fee to another club and who has influence will inevitably pressurise clubs and players to move repeatedly for transfer fees rather than serve out their contract, thus undermining the stability of teams and damaging the confidence of football fans in their teams. Worse still, third party owners could interfere with team selection, making sure the players they had an interest in played certain games and not others. Third parties with control over a number of players could in turn influence the outcome of football games. Where football agents and those who invest in football clubs also have interests in players in different teams and have the consequential ability to influence the teams playing those players (or the players in the team as to whether they play), there is a real danger that the competition can be corrupted by powerful interests concerned about their own profits and not the fair outcome of the game.

11.136   The ability of third parties with an interest in players to influence the clubs who employ those players risks undermining the credibility and integrity of football, distorting competition between clubs, undermining stability and ultimately public confidence in the game. It is because of these serious and genuine concerns that third party influence is prohibited in world football, and that the prohibition of third party *influence* has long been accepted and is most likely to be lawful and proportionate so that it is justifiable from a legal standpoint.

11.137 The arguments about third party *investment* are far more evenly balanced however.

(b) Arguments against third party investment

11.138 Those who support the total prohibition of TPI argue that it is impossible to have TPI without third party influence. An investor in a player is unlikely to simply sit back and allow a club to employ the player until the end of his contract thereby liquidating the whole of their investment, they argue; investors are bound to try and influence clubs into transferring their assets, and clubs that rely on TPI may feel obliged to act in accordance with the wishes of their powerful investors.

11.139 Secondly, it is said that TPI takes money out of football. Often significant transfer fees, instead of going to the football club who transfers the player will go, at least in part, to businessmen or other investors outside football. Money that could have been used to strengthen a football team, develop young players or build a new football stadium is siphoned out of football never to return, so the argument goes.

11.140 Thirdly, many argue that TPI undermines financial regulation in football because an impecunious football club could develop a football team without spending money or significant money, simply by relying on third parties acquiring the players in return for a share of their later transfer fee.

11.141 Fourthly, there are important arguments about transparency. The public expect a football player to be committed to the team for which he plays. If someone else has an interest in his economic rights, and therefore how he plays and his consequential value, then at the very least people should know who holds that interest. Knowing the identity of third party investors is necessary to prevent any influence by them, and to satisfy the authorities and the public that there is no risk of corruption. But the historic practice of TPI in many countries has been to conceal the identity of the beneficial owners of the players' economic rights, and has raised questions about the risk of those involved in organised crime using the mechanism as a means to launder money or at least to avoid tax. The division in ownership of economic rights between different parties also raises the prospect of conflict and litigation between those parties.

11.142 Finally, there is the moral argument made that has equated TPI with a form of modern slavery, in that financial speculators are able to profit from trading people rather than inanimate commodities. Football players become commodities, it is argued, and the trade in them by business interests further undermines the integrity and morality of the sport.

(c) Arguments in favour of third party investment

11.143 On the other hand, there are many advantages to TPI and arguments in its favour. First, it is an obvious means by which a football club can raise finances to bring money into football. Borrowing from banks is increasingly difficult, especially for clubs undergoing difficult financial situations, such as many South American clubs and in Portugal and Spain. Raising money by means of a mortgage against the land on which the football stadium is located – another conventional mechanism by clubs to raise funds – may well have already been exhausted, and is in any event increasingly seen as inadequate security, not only because of the difficulty mortgage providers may face when trying to sell and change the use of the land, but also because it can lead to disastrous results for football clubs that default who can lose their ground, identity and even existence. Football clubs already regard the economic rights, ie in this context the future transfer value, of a player as an important financial asset. Why should the club not be able to seek investment by utilising often the most valuable assets it has, particularly if by doing so it can secure financial survival, or be able to expand and develop its team or other facilities?

11.144   TPI can also allow young, not yet established football players from lower league clubs or underdeveloped countries the chance to succeed at a higher level or on an international stage. Because an investor takes the risk in their future success they can have the opportunity to prove themselves at a higher level, or at a better club. This may be an opportunity they would otherwise not have. This in turn can benefit the football club and league to which the new player has transferred, increasing the quality of the players, the strength of the team and the competition generally.

11.145   There are numerous ways in which TPI can be regulated to prevent influence and the other risks associated with it. A league could insist on the registration and publication of the identity of third party investors, ensuring transparency. Limits could be placed on the number of players or the percentage of ownership of economic rights in a particular player that any one investor can have an interest in. Limits could also be placed on who is entitled to invest in a player, for example, so that an owner of Club A might be prohibited in having an investment in a player who played for Club B in the same national association. A uniform and clear definition of third party influence could be made and severe and harmonised sanctions could be imposed on any party seeking to or actually influencing a player or club – including a future absolute prohibition on investment being permitted from any third party who breached the rules prohibiting influence.

11.146   There are answers to the arguments about financial regulation and money leaving football too. TPI can be regarded in the same way as any other kind of investment or borrowing. A football club can still be required to balance its books by financial regulation with the money advanced by third party investors in a player's economic rights regarded in the same way as a loan from a bank. The fact that the club will have to pay back the investor if a player is sold is no different from a club paying back a bank loan and using the profits of a player sale to do so. If a football club decides to responsibly raise money in this way so it can spend that money when it needs to, why should that be prohibited? It is already not unusual for football clubs to be forced to sell a player for financial reasons, such that the income generated in selling the player leaves football, for example by being used to pay a tax demand.

11.147   Indeed, there are good arguments that TPI provides financial assistance, or the ability to acquire the services of top players, to football clubs who would not otherwise be able to afford those opportunities and this advances, rather than undermines competition. If only five or six clubs in the English Premier League, for example, are able to exploit the transfer market to build a team that can finish in the top six, preventing the other clubs from utilising TPI to compete against the top clubs does not encourage a level playing field, rather it acts to sustain an unlevel one. Most commentators accept that it would have been impossible for a club like Atlético Madrid to compete with the likes of Barcelona and Real Madrid at the highest levels of Spanish and European football without heavily utilising TPI to strengthen its team.

11.148   Advocates of TPI also claim the total prohibition of this form of raising money will only either force it underground, exploited by precisely the type of people who have given TPI a bad name and who will try and influence clubs, or will be replaced by even worse schemes to circumvent the bans. For example, it has now become quite common in Europe for owners of one football club in one national association to purchase a share in a club in another association. The owners of Club A in Italy, for example, then loan players out to Club B in the UK to increase their market value and profile. The owners of Club A can then decide when to sell them and club A profits from the scheme, such profits being returned to the shareholding owners. This type of arrangement must surely be just as much a threat to the integrity of football as TPI. This model brings with it a real danger of influence. The owners of Club A, who also own Club B, might insist Club B plays a certain player in every match not because it might help Club B win a game but because Club B is being used to showcase the player. Properly regulated TPI provides a far more straightforward and less risky way for football clubs to raise investment than the alternative schemes which are already manifesting themselves in Europe including in England.

11.149   In addition, most supporters of TPI advocate its controlled regulation instead of a complete ban. Despite the difficulties of implementing a specific set of regulations in this regard on an international level, it would allow a controlled and transparent use of this efficient funding alternative. For example, prior to the worldwide ban imposed by FIFA in December 2014, countries in Europe such as Spain tried to implement – unsuccessfully – specific rules to control TPI, by means of a draft regulation enacted by the Liga de Fútbol Profesional (LFP)[64] on financing alternatives and mechanisms to clubs. In general, as long as a regulated environment can control and sanction undue influence of third parties in football, advocates of TPI will be against all types of bans.

11.150   An interesting and less obvious consequence to clubs that used to depend on TPI will be the need to concentrate efforts and resources in developing their own youth and grassroots programmes, in order to develop and train potential new talents who may bring not only important titles in the future, but be later transferred for substantial transfer fees. Moreover, by developing effective grassroots programmes, an established club may reduce the need for frequent and colossal acquisition of players.

11.151   Finally so far as the 'slavery' argument is concerned, the buying and selling of the economic rights of a football player by a third party is no different from the buying and selling of those rights by a football club. The player is paid a salary for providing services to the club but the football club owns his economic rights and already regularly trades in those rights. The fact a third party may have an interest in that trade does not alter the relationship at all, let alone transfer employment into slavery. Either the transfer of a player's economic rights owned by a club or a third party cannot properly be described as slave trading at all, especially as the player is remunerated for his services by the club, or the whole concept of football transfers is slavery and should be banned, as the international player's union, FIFPro, effectively argued in their complaint against the football transfer system.[65] On this view, TPI is no better or worse than a club benefiting from the exchange of players. In any event, abuses eventually committed by investors shall be punished and brought to the competent dispute resolution bodies of football and, ultimately, to the CAS,[66]

---

64   *Proyecto de Regulación LFP sobre Operaciones Especiales de Financiación* (March 2014).
65   See Chapter 4, European Law in Relation to Football, paras **4.123–4.126**.
66   See CAS 2011/O/2580 *Investfootball GmbH v Vasco Herculano Salgado da Cunha Mango Fernandes*.

which ruled in favour of players that signed abusive and endless agreements in which investors unilaterally determined where one should play, amongst other abusive third party influence.

(d)   The current legal environment

11.152   Whatever the pros and cons of TPI, FIFA and English football are now at one in strictly prohibiting the practice. It is most unlikely, however, that TPI will disappear. The economic necessity for football clubs to compete to attract players and the profits to be made by those speculating on transfers that created the fertile conditions for TPI have only intensified since it has been prohibited. TPI is likely to continue, whether as an underground concealed practice or by morphing into new variations of the model that are not (as yet) prohibited by FIFA – such as, for example, the growing concept of 'Multiple Club Ownership' whereby a number of wealthy individuals own more than one club in different competitions and jurisdictions and are able to use their collective ownership to develop and trade players.[67] Such developments, along with the need for football clubs to devise creative new ways to raise investment, will continue to require the attention of lawyers in football.

---

67   See eg *Disneyfication of clubs like Manchester City keeps showing benefits*, Paul MacInnes, *The Guardian*, 31 August 2017: https://www.theguardian.com/football/2017/aug/31/disneyfication-clubs-manchester-city-red-bull?CMP=share_btn_tw (accessed February 2018).

CHAPTER 12

Football Intermediaries, Regulation and Legal Disputes

Nick De Marco QC (Blackstone Chambers) and **Daniel Lowen** (Level)

A INTRODUCTION

12.1　Football agents, now called *intermediaries* by the regulators, are one of the key components of the modern football industry in England and throughout the world. Their activity is fundamental to most of the significant commercial transactions that take place every year in football: clubs' signing and re-signing of football players.

12.2　When FIFA controversially decided to de-license and partially de-regulate agency activity in 2014[1] one of its main justifications was that only a small minority of international transfers were conducted by licensed football agents. The logic was that as FIFA's regulation of agents was not working, rather than improve it, FIFA would simply walk away from it. Whereas FIFA's argument was based on its finding that only around 20% of international transfers were conducted by licensed football agents, these figures create a misleading picture. According to FIFA's own Transfer Matching System (TMS) tracking system, whilst since 2013 only 19.7% of all international transfers have involved at least one agent or intermediary, when one considers only those transfers where a transfer fee was paid the percentage rises to 47.9%. In almost half of all transfers where any fee is paid an agent or intermediary was used.[2]

12.3　In the small percentage of transfers that make up the largest amount of spending (on fees and wages), it is even more likely an agent or intermediary was used. For example, in England (the country that spends by far the most on transfer fees, and also on agents' fees) nearly 40% of all transfers involved an agent or intermediary, but when one considers only those transfers where fees were paid the figure rises to 67%.[3] Italian clubs have very similar numbers.[4] In the highest

---

1　On 21 March 2014, the FIFA Executive Committee voted to replace its previous Players' Agents Regulations (and licensing system) which had been in force since 2007, and upon which The FA's Football Agents Regulations were based, with its new Regulations on Working with Intermediaries (FIFA RWI), which came into force on 1 April 2015. The FA followed course replacing its Agents Regulations with the FA Regulations on Working with Intermediaries, which also came into force on 1 April 2015.

2　*Intermediaries in International Transfers 2016*, FIFA TMS Report, p 2. See also *Intermediaries in International Transfers 2017*, FIFA TMS Report, p 2.

3　*Intermediaries in International Transfers 2016*, FIFA TMS Report, p 3; in the first 11 months of 2017 the figure stood at 66.6%, *Intermediaries in International Transfers 2017*, FIFA TMS Report, p 3.

4　From 2013 to 2016, intermediaries were involved in 35% of all transfers in Italy, and 64.1% of all transfers where a fee was paid (*Intermediaries in International Transfers 2016*, FIFA TMS

spending countries, two out of every three transfers for any fee at all involve an agent or intermediary. It is most likely that a higher percentage of transfers for the highest fees (of £1 million or above) involve agents or intermediaries. Thus, in those transactions that matter the most, in terms of the money spent and the associated risks of abuse, intermediaries are almost certain to be involved – and it is in relation to these high value transactions that the need for regulation is most important.

12.4 In addition, since FIFA's de-regulation, the use of intermediaries has increased. Engaging clubs employed intermediaries in 1,125 international transfers in the first 11 months of 2016. This was a 17.2% increase on the figures in 2015 and represented a new record.[5] By November 2017 the figure increased again: in the first 11 months of 2017, engaging clubs employed intermediaries in 1,190 international transfers, 4.9% higher than in 2016.[6]

12.5 In the four years between 2013 and 2017, USD $1.59 billion was spent by clubs alone on commissions to intermediaries. Of this amount, 97.2% (USD $1.54 billion) was paid by European clubs; the rest of the world accouted for less than 3% (USD $45 million).[7] Table 1, below, demonstrates that by far the highest spending is by clubs in England (USD 489.9 million, approximately 32% of world spending, and more than ten times what the rest of the world outside Europe spend), closely followed by Italy (USD $343.8 million, approximately 22% of world spending). The 'big 5' footballing countries (England, Spain, Germany, Italy and France) all feature within the top six of spending nations – this is not surprising given the same countries are responsible for most of the spending on transfer fees too.

Table 1. Club intermediary commissions 2013–17[8]

	US$ millions
England	489.9
Italy	343.8
Portugal	161.1
Germany	145.6
Spain	121.7
France	61.4
Belgium	31.4
Russia	30.7
Wales	29.3
Croatia	19.9

12.6 Another justification for FIFA's new approach, with which many may have sympathised at first, was that too much money was 'going out' of football to third parties such as agents. By shifting the focus of the regulations from tight controls over who could act as agents to purportedly requiring more transparency in an intermediary's activities, as well as proposing a 3% cap on intermediaries'

Report, p 3). This rose to 36% of all transfers, and 65.6% when considering transfers involving a fee (*Intermediaries in International Transfers 2016*, FIFA TMS Report, p 3).

5   *Intermediaries in International Transfers 2016*, FIFA TMS Report, p 3.
6   *Intermediaries in International Transfers 2017*, FIFA TMS Report, p 3.
7   *Intermediaries in International Transfers 2017*, FIFA TMS Report, p 5.
8   *Intermediaries in International Transfers 2017*, FIFA TMS Report, p 5.

fees,[9] more money would stay in football. Whatever the merits of that argument, as the figures above and the considerable controversy that has surrounded the colossal intermediary fees alleged to have been paid in relation to certain high profile transfers show, this has evidently not been the case. The 3% cap has been largely ignored by the market,[10] and de-regulation, if anything, appears to have led to more money disappearing from the game, with less certainty as to its final destination.

12.7   When The FA's agents' license was first abolished in 2015, the number of intermediaries registered with The FA was just over 770. In only two years it increased to over 1,737 individual registered intermediaries and around 120 registered intermediary companies.[11] As the number of football players, clubs and transfers have remained more or less the same in those two years, there are many more intermediaries chasing the same deals now as there were previously, yet most of the new intermediaries will have not received training or been subject to a licensing regime, and shall not have their own clients. This marked change has led to an inevitable increase in disputes.

12.8   Other particular features of FIFA's more 'light touch' approach to regulation in its Regulations on Working with Intermediaries (FIFA RWI) have led to an increase in precisely the type of unedifying and at times corrupt arrangements and payments in football that created the desire for regulation in the first place. In particular both FIFA's, and initially The FA's, decision to no longer prohibit 'tapping up' or 'poaching' by intermediaries led to a predictable rise in legal disputes between intermediaries and other football participants. The relaxation of regulation in relation to dealing with young footballers, as well as the increase in money in the game, led to a particular increase in abuses in this area. Some of these factors are considered further in section C of this chapter.

12.9   As this chapter demonstrates, the English FA have gone further than required by the FIFA RWI in regulating intermediary activity, and so have many other European countries. Most notably, in December 2017, the Italian parliament enacted a new regulatory scheme for all sports agents in Italy. The scheme requires that all sports agents be registered by the Italian National Olympic Committee – as well as paying an annual fee, being an Italian or EU citizen and being free from criminal conviction for five years, they must be in possession of a secondary school diploma or equivalent and pass a qualifying test aimed at ascertaining their suitability to be a sports agent. Not only do all intermediaries have to pass the exam and be licensed, but the same is required of a player's family members

---

9   Regulation 7(3) of FIFA's RWI is non-mandatory. It provides that clubs and agents 'may' adopt a 'benchmark' in their agreements that an intermediary shall not receive commission in excess of 3% of the player's basic gross income for the entire duration of the relevant employment contract. Whilst there was no cap previously (whether mandatory or indicative) 5% remuneration was (and remains) most common for English transactions, and remuneration of up to 10% is not especially unusual. These rates of commissions refer to 'intermediary activity' only, ie negotiating the terms of a player's contract or transfer, and are distinguished from commission on commercial agreements, where the intermediary is often remunerated in the sum of 20% of sponsorship and other deals he or she has brought to the player.

10   One of the authors of this chapter, Nick De Marco QC, was involved (along with Lord Pannick QC and Tom Richards, also of Blackstone Chambers) in a competition law complaint to the European Commission brought on behalf of the Association of Football Agents in England about the inclusion of the 3% indicative commission in The FA's Regulations. The complaint was ultimately compromised because it became clear the indication had no real impact on the market, either in England, where intermediary fees continue to be usually agreed at 5% (and sometimes more), or across Europe.

11   Figures from The FA's lists of registered intermediaries as at September 2017: http://www.thefa.com/ football-rules-governance/policies/intermediaries/fa-registered-intermediaries-list.

who seek to be involved in/paid for intermediary activity. The regulation (part of the Italian Budget Law) provides that 'professional athletes and companies affiliated to a professional sports federation are prohibited from using non-registered members on the grounds that contracts are null and void.' Thus, all sports agents must be registered, and if they are not the law shall regard as void any agreement to pay them. This is particularly important given that Italy is the second biggest spending country on football intermediaries, and Italy's key place in the EU means that we may see moves for further and tighter regulation across Europe.[12] Notably, the members of the EU Sectoral Social Dialogue Committee for Professional Football (UEFA, FIFAPro Division Europe, the European Club Association (ECA) and the European Professional Football Leagues (EPFL)) carried out extensive consultations in 2017 with a view to collecting information on the practical effects of the FIFA RWI. They found that the FIFA RWI failed to address serious concerns in relation to the activities of intermediaries and resolved that a more effective and sustainable regulatory framework is required to address the many challenges associated with the activities of intermediaries. Furthermore, they resolved that: '[A]dequate, stronger regulatory oversight is essential to guarantee an appropriate level of protection for players (in particular minors), clubs and other relevant stakeholders, including the intermediaries/agents themselves.'[13] They asserted that, 'a harmonized, uniform European approach should be considered ...'. The Final Report to the European Commission on the Football Transfer Market,[14] published in March 2018, made similar observations though also contained a recommendation for a 3% cap on intermediaries' fees, which many believe is both unnecessary and unlawful.[15]

12.10   There are various legal issues that involve intermediaries and those dealing with them in football, including commercial and regulatory issues and disputes of just about all types, many of which are the subject of further discussion in other chapters of this book.[16] However, broadly speaking, issues can be divided into regulatory and private law issues. Regulatory issues concern the The FA's and FIFA's regulation of intermediaries: what intermediaries are allowed to do, when and how clubs and players can engage their services, how and what they can be paid, and how the regulation is policed. Section B of this chapter contains a guide to the main sections of the applicable regulations.

12.11   However, intermediaries remain subject to the common law and not only regulation. Disputes involving intermediaries may be outside the scope of regulation, or even if a regulation provides that a club or player is not permitted to pay an intermediary, the common law (or the law of another country where that applies to the contract) may require the payment to be made in any event. There is a considerable overlap between the regulatory scheme and the situation in private law. For example,

12   See further: '*Italian parliament enacts new regulation of Football Agents*', Nick De Marco QC, *Blackstone Chambers Sports Law Bulletin*, January 2018 https://www.sportslawbulletin.org/italian-parliament-enacts-new-regulation-football-agents/ (accessed March 2018).

13   The Resolution of the EU Sectoral Social Dialogue Committee for Professional Football, January 2018: http://www.uefa.com/MultimediaFiles/Download/uefaorg/FinancialFairPlay/02/53/09/85/2530985_DOWNLOAD.pdf (accessed February 2018).

14   'An update on change drivers and economic and legal implications of transfers of players': https://ec.europa.eu/sport/sites/sport/files/report-transfer-of-players-2018-en.pdf (accessed April 2018).

15   See, eg, Nick De Marco QC, 'The 2018 report to the EC on the Football Transfer Market: Fascinating data but flawed conclusions' (2018) 16(4) *World Sports Advocate* 4–6.

16   In particular the issues discussed in Chapters 4, European Law in relation to Football; 5, Employment Law and Football; 6, Contracts – Players; 7, Contracts – Managers; 8, Player Transfers; 9, Immigration and GBEs; 10, Academies and Youth Issues; 11, Third Party Investment; 13, Image Rights; 14, Taxation; 15, Sponsorship and Commercial Rights; 23, Discipline; 24, Doping; 25, Corruption and Match-fixing; 28, Arbitration in Football; and 29, International Disputes and the CAS.

most private law disputes involving intermediary services are subject to FA Rule K arbitration by virtue of a mandatory provision to that effect being incorporated into the Representation Contract as a result of regulation. It is particularly important to understand the interplay between the regulatory schemes and the situation at law. Section C of this chapter explores some of the most common regulatory and legal issues arising with intermediaries.

B   GUIDE TO THE REGULATION OF INTERMEDIARIES

12.12   From 1 April 2015, the concept of the licensed football agent – an individual who passed an exam, was licensed for five years by a national association to conduct agency activity and took out professional liability insurance – was no more. Instead, the FIFA RWI ushered in a new concept in player and club representation: the intermediary – a person or entity that need not pass an exam, does not require a licence or insurance and may have no previous experience or knowledge of player/ club representation.

12.13   The FIFA RWI require national associations to implement and enforce its provisions. However, it expressly reserves associations' rights 'to go beyond these minimum standards/requirements'.[17] Accordingly, The FA implemented its own Regulations on Working with Intermediaries on 1 April 2015 (the 'FA Intermediaries Regulations'). The FA had developed its old Football Agents Regulations[18] over a number of years and it had become a considerably more detailed and sophisticated body of rules governing the activities of players' agents operating in (or in respect of a player moving to) England than the old FIFA Players' Agents Regulations. It was therefore not entirely surprising that many of the principles and much of the detail in the FA Intermediaries Regulations derive from the old Football Agents Regulations that they replaced.

(a)   Definitions

12.14   Before turning to the substantive regulations, the authors consider it helpful to set out a few key definitions[19] at the outset:

(a) An 'intermediary' is 'any natural or legal person who carries out or seeks to carry out Intermediary Activity and has registered with The FA …'. As per the FIFA RWI, companies can be intermediaries. In this chapter, the term 'intermediary' has not been capitalised, but references to intermediaries should be taken to be references to 'Intermediaries' as defined in the regulations, where appropriate in the context.
(b) The definition of 'intermediary activity' is extremely broad: 'acting in any way and at any time, either directly or indirectly, for or on behalf of a Player or a Club in relation to any matter relating to a Transaction. This includes, but is not limited to, entering into a Representation Contract with a Player or a Club.'
(c) 'Representation contract' means 'any agreement between an Intermediary (on the one hand), and a Player and/or Club (on the other), the purpose or effect of which is to cover the provision of Intermediary Activity. A Representation Contract must comply with the Obligatory Terms of the Standard Representation Contract.'

---

17   The FIFA RWI, Articles 1.2 and 1.3.
18   The FA Football Agents Regulations, which came into effect on 4 July 2009.
19   See Appendix 1 to the FA Intermediaries Regulations.

(d)   'Transaction' means 'any negotiation or other related activity, including any communication relating or preparatory to the same, the intention or effect of which is to create, terminate or vary the terms of a player's contract of employment with a Club, to facilitate or effect the registration of a player with a Club, or the transfer of the registration of a player from a club to a Club (whether on a temporary or permanent basis). A completed Transaction is one that has so achieved the creation, termination or variation of the terms of the player's contract of employment with a Club, the registration of the Player with a Club or the transfer of the registration from a club to a Club.'

(b)   General principles

12.15   The FA Intermediaries Regulations are stated to be 'binding on all Participants', which term is defined in The FA's Rules of the Association and includes intermediaries. Accordingly, intermediaries are subject to The FA's Rules (including, for example, the prohibitions on betting on football).

12.16   Within Regulation A, there are a number of general principles to which intermediaries, players and clubs are subject. Players and clubs may only use or pay intermediaries who are registered with The FA and with whom they have signed a representation contract in relation to intermediary activity. That said, it is open to players and clubs to represent themselves in matters relating to a transaction.[20] As will be explored further in section C of this chapter, an intermediary, club, player or any other person or entity under The FA's control must not arrange matters so as to conceal or misrepresent the reality or substance of any aspect of a transaction.[21] The breadth of this provision means it is open to The FA to rely on it in any instance where there is a lack of transparency in relation to a transaction.

12.17   Players are free to engage whoever they want to represent them – no party to a transaction can make it subject to or dependent upon a player's agreement to use a particular intermediary. Clubs are required to use reasonable endeavours to ensure that the manager and other officials comply with the regulations.

12.18   Intermediaries, clubs and players are required to ensure that all relevant contracts and documents contain the name, signature and registration number of every intermediary who carries out intermediary activity in relation to a transaction. If either a player or a club has not used the services of an intermediary in a transaction, this must be stated in all relevant documentation.

(c)   Registration of intermediaries

12.19   Any person or entity wishing to represent players or clubs on transfers or contract negotiations in England (regardless of whether they are a relative of the player, based overseas or a lawyer) will have to register as an intermediary and will be subject to the FA Intermediaries Regulations (except that lawyers can provide 'permitted legal advice' in relation to a transaction without registering).[22] However, the regulations expressly prevent a player or 'official' (as defined in the FIFA Statutes) from registering

---

20   See Regulations A.1 and A.2.
21   See Regulation A.3 and para **12.47** below.
22   The fee payable upon registration (whether for a natural or legal person) is £500 ex VAT. Registration lasts for one year, after which the intermediary will need to renew their registration on an annual basis (at a cost of £250 ex VAT per year) if they wish to continue conducting intermediary activity.

as an intermediary. An intermediary must be registered in order to sign a representation contract, as such act falls within the definition of intermediary activity.

12.20 Both natural and legal persons can be registered and conduct intermediary activity.[23] However, only a natural person already registered as an intermediary can register a legal person as an intermediary and, importantly, intermediary activity on behalf of a legal person can only be carried out by natural persons registered as intermediaries.

12.21 Registration occurs via The FA's online portal, which is also used for the submission of all relevant documentation, including the 'Declarations, Acknowledgements and Consents' that an applicant is required to make during the registration process. These include confirming that an applicant does not, and will not throughout the period of their registration, have any interest in a club; agreeing to disclose within ten days of registration any pre-existing contract or arrangement between the applicant and any club official or manager whereby he or she represents their interests; and acknowledging that he or she has been advised by The FA of the importance of obtaining adequate professional indemnity or liability insurance in respect of the intermediary's professional activities.[24]

12.22 An applicant will also be required to satisfy The FA that they have an impeccable reputation, by confirming in the online application process that they meet the requirements of The FA's Test of Good Character and Reputation for Intermediaries (which includes declaring that the applicant is not subject to a disqualifying condition).[25] If they are unable to make such declaration, they will not be permitted to proceed with their registration.[26]

(d) Representation contracts and the Intermediary Declaration Form

12.23 An intermediary may not carry out intermediary activity without first signing a representation contract with a player or club.[27] A representation contract and any variation of it, as well as any subcontract between intermediaries, must be lodged with The FA within ten days of signature (and by no later than the registration of the relevant transaction by The FA).

---

23 As noted in para **12.7** above, approximately 120 companies were registered as intermediaries at the time of writing.
24 However, whilst professional indemnity insurance was mandatory under the old Football Agents Regulations, it is not under the FA Intermediaries Regulations.
25 Disqualifying conditions include (with reference to the point at which the intermediary goes through the registration process): (i) having an unspent conviction for any offence anywhere in the world that The FA considers falls within the category of a violent and/or financial and/or dishonest crime; (ii) being prohibited by law from being a company director; (iii) being subject to a suspension or ban from involvement in the administration of a sport or participation in a sport for a duration of at least 6 months, or being subject to a prohibition from working as a sports agent/intermediary, in each case where such suspension or prohibition has been handed down by any ruling body of a sport that is registered with UK Sport and/or Sport England, or any equivalent national or international association; (iv) being subject to various bankruptcy orders or arrangements; (v) being subject to any form of suspension, disqualification or striking-off by a professional body (such as the Law Society or equivalent professional regulatory bodies in other jurisdictions); (vi) being required by law to notify personal information to the police as a result of previous sexual offences.
26 The requirements are on-going, so intermediaries will be required to notify The FA (within ten working days) of any change in circumstances relating to the requirements of the test.
27 See Regulation B.1.

12.24   A representation contract must contain the entire agreement between the parties in relation to the intermediary activity and incorporate at least certain 'obligatory terms'. Whilst those obligatory terms form the content of The FA's own standard representation contract template, The FA expressly acknowledges that intermediaries may be keen to amend or supplement the obligatory terms. Intermediaries would be well advised to enhance The FA's standard form representation contract template in most circumstances.

12.25   Unlike the position under the FIFA Intermediaries Regulations, the maximum duration of a representation contract with a player is two years.[28] On 9 August 2017, The FA made various amendments to the FA Intermediaries Regulations, one of which was the addition of the new Regulation B.11. This provides that an intermediary 'shall only enter into a single Representation Contract with the same Player at any one time' and it prevents an intermediary from entering into two (or multiple) representation contracts, each dated differently, and thereby extending the intermediary's appointment beyond the two-year maximum. If an intermediary and a player wish to extend the intermediary's appointment, they can do so, but only once an existing representation contract has expired or is terminated early by mutual agreement.

12.26   Further notable changes introduced by The FA on 9 August 2017 were new Regulations B.12 and B.13, which state:

> 'B.12 An Intermediary shall not enter into a Representation Contract with a Player under an exclusive Representation Contract with another Intermediary.'

> 'B.13 A Player shall not enter into a Representation Contract with an Intermediary whilst under an exclusive Representation Contract with another Intermediary.'

Prior to the introduction of these new provisions, the regulations did not expressly prohibit an intermediary approaching a player who was under contract with another intermediary (which was a departure from the position under the old Football Agents Regulations). Indeed in the period between the introduction of the FA Intermediaries Regulations and 9 August 2017, if conflicting representation contracts in respect of a player were lodged with The FA, it would merely inform the parties and leave it to them to resolve the issue (typically by way of FA Rule K arbitration). Equally, players were minded or induced to appoint two or even multiple intermediaries under conflicting representation contracts, potentially exposing the player to multiple claims for commission and liability to intermediaries considerably in excess of the industry standard 5% (or indeed the 3% recommended by the regulations).

12.27   That position was most unsatisfactory, as it resulted in unfettered attempts by intermediaries to 'poach' other intermediaries' clients in the expectation that, at worst, the new intermediary (or indeed the player) would merely pay the old intermediary the basic amount of commission on the next transaction involving the player. Alternatively, the new intermediary would offer to pay a share of the commission to the old intermediary or even offer nothing at all, in the knowledge that the old intermediary may not have the time, resources or inclination to pursue the player and/or new intermediary by way of FA Rule K arbitration. That said, there was a significant increase in the number of FA Rule K arbitrations brought by intermediaries against players and competitors for breach of contract/inducement to breach a contract. Some of the problems caused by the de-regulation

---

28   See para **12.66** below for a discussion of the issues concerning representation contracts with overseas players that extend beyond two years.

of the agents' system and the influx of hundreds of new intermediaries, some with little training or knowledge of the industry, were compounded by The FA's failure to make the 'poaching' of players a regulatory (and not merely a contractual) breach.

12.28   In Regulations B.12 and B.13, The FA has sought to rectify this problem. An intermediary is now prohibited from entering into a representation contract with a player who is under an exclusive representation contract with another intermediary. Furthermore, a player may not enter into a representation contract with an intermediary whilst he or she remains subject to an exclusive representation contract with another intermediary. In the authors' opinion, this is a welcome change – the threat of regulatory breach(es) should result in a greater degree of respect for contracts entered into and less poaching of players. However, the new Regulations B.12 and B.13 do not provide an alternative remedy for the intermediary whose client has decided to sign with another intermediary during the term of an existing representation contract – the regulatory deterrence and threat of sanction against the new intermediary and player does not change the fact that the original intermediary will be left with little option but to claim damages by way of FA Rule K arbitration.

12.29   Additionally, it is interesting to note that the duty on a new intermediary under Regulation B.12 appears greater than his or her duties at law. For an intermediary to be found at law to have induced a breach of another intermediary's representation contract, the intermediary must have known that the player was already under a representation contract (or at least have turned a blind eye to the fact). Regulation B.12 on the other hand suggests that such knowledge is not a necessary ingredient for an intermediary to be found to be in breach (though any such knowledge will no doubt be relevant to any sanction).

12.30   In terms of minors (ie any player under the age of 18), in order to enter into a representation contract with a minor or with a club in respect of a minor, an intermediary must obtain additional authorisation from The FA to deal with minors. The FA requires that an applicant provides an Enhanced Certificate from the Disclosure and Barring Service and The FA will undertake an 'assessment', in which it considers whether the individual should be permitted to conduct intermediary activity in relation to minors.[29] Any such additional authorisation granted by The FA will remain valid for three years (subject to the intermediary remaining registered with The FA). Notably, only natural persons (not legal persons) can seek and be granted additional authorisation to conduct intermediary activity in relation to minors.

12.31   Regardless of holding additional authorisation, an intermediary may not approach or contract with a minor before 1 January of the year of the player's 16th birthday.

12.32   At the time of a transaction, any intermediaries (as well as the player and clubs) involved are required to sign The FA's Intermediary Declaration Form – the IM1 – which discloses not only the intermediary's involvement in the transaction

---

29   It is open to The FA to require the applicant to provide additional information, including written explanations and character references. The FA is required to act fairly and proportionately in reaching its decision based on all matters of significance and relevance, holding the welfare of minors as the paramount consideration. Applicants based overseas who wish to obtain additional authorisation from The FA to deal with minors are required to provide an equivalent criminal record check from their country of domicile.

and the payment details, but also requires the intermediary to tick a box to confirm 'that he complies with the terms of the Test of Good Character and Reputation for Intermediaries and the Declarations, Acknowledgements and Consents for Intermediaries'. As noted above, satisfaction of The FA's requirements for registration as an intermediary must be re-confirmed by the intermediary at the time of each transaction in which he or she is involved.

(e) Remuneration

12.33 Regulation C.1 provides that an intermediary can be remunerated by the club or player for whom he or she acts either in accordance with the representation contract or, alternatively and as is often the case, the relevant paperwork submitted to The FA at the time of the transaction.

12.34 The manner in which a player can discharge his or her liability to an intermediary is set out in Regulation C.2 and is driven in part by tax law.[30] The options are: (i) a player can pay his intermediary directly; (ii) the club can make deduction(s) in periodic instalments (ie monthly, shown on the player's payslip) from the player's net salary and pay those deductions directly to the intermediary; or (iii) the club can pay the intermediary on the player's behalf as a taxable benefit to the player. All payments by clubs to intermediaries (other than deductions from a player's net salary which are paid directly to an intermediary, ie option (ii) above) must be made through The FA's designated account.

12.35 When acting for a player, an intermediary's commission is calculable on a player's basic gross salary (but not any bonuses that are conditional on the player's or club's performances). An intermediary will remain entitled to receive commission in respect of a transaction after expiry of the representation contract for as long as the relevant employment contract (signed during the term of the representation contract) remains in force. Where the intermediary is acting for a club, the representation contract should set out what the commission will be and whether payment is to be made by way of a lump sum payment or in periodic instalments. Except where an intermediary is subcontracted in accordance with the regulations, intermediaries are prohibited from passing any remuneration directly relating to intermediary activity to any other person.

12.36 The FA Intermediaries Regulations contain two provisions relating to remuneration that stem directly from the FIFA RWI and which have proved amongst the most controversial of the intermediaries regime. First, players or clubs are prohibited from making payments to an intermediary if the player concerned is a minor. Further discussion of this prohibition can be found at paras **12.70–12.73** below. Secondly, the FA Intermediaries Regulations implement FIFA's *recommendation* that players, clubs and intermediaries *may* adopt a commission rate of 3% of the player's basic gross income for the entire duration of the relevant employment contract (or 3% of the eventual transfer compensation paid if the intermediary is engaged to act on a club's behalf in order to conclude a transfer agreement) – described in the Regulations as 'benchmarks'. As noted in Sections A and C of this chapter, whilst the implementation of this recommended commission rate prompted outcry from certain quarters,[31] it has been largely ignored by the market and a commission rate of 5% (and in some cases higher) remains prevalent.

30 Income Tax (Earnings and Pensions) Act (ITEPA) 2003, Part 3, Chapter 10. The specific charging provisions around employment-related benefits commence at s 201.
31 See n 9 above.

(f) Conflicts of interest

12.37   The FA Intermediaries Regulations permits dual representation and, indeed, have gone further than the FIFA RWI by expressly allowing 'multiple representation' (whereby an intermediary undertakes intermediary activity for the selling club, the buying club and the player). In order for an intermediary to act for more than one party to a transaction, (i) the intermediary must have had a pre-existing representation contract with one party to the transaction; (ii) the intermediary must obtain all parties' prior written consent to his or her provision of services to any other party to the transaction; (iii) the intermediary must inform all parties of the proposed arrangements (including the fee to be paid by all parties); (iv) all parties must be given a reasonable opportunity to take independent legal advice; and (v) all parties must provide their express written consent for the intermediary to sign representation contract(s) with any other party on the proposed terms.[32] The aforementioned requirements also apply where connected intermediaries wish to act for more than one party to a transaction.[33]

12.38   Neither an intermediary nor his/her organisation can have an interest in a club (which under Regulation E.4 means owning more than 5% or being in a position to exercise significant influence over the affairs of a club); likewise a player, club, club official or manager cannot have an interest in the business or affairs of an intermediary or his/her organisation (which means owning more than 5% or being in a position to exercise significant influence). As was the case under the old Players Agents Regulations, an intermediary cannot have any interest in the registration right, transfer compensation or future transfer value of a player. An intermediary cannot give or offer any consideration of any kind, which either relates in any way to a transaction or which is in return for any benefit favour or preferential treatment (and clubs and their staff (including any player or manager) are may not accept any such consideration). Likewise, intermediaries cannot give or offer any consideration of any kind to a player (or any family member) in relation to entering into a representation contract (and the player may not accept any such consideration).

12.39   The FA Intermediaries Regulations prescribe fairly comprehensive duties of disclosure regarding conflicts of interest. Amongst them, players, clubs, club officials, managers and intermediaries are required to disclose to The FA any arrangement that exists whereby money is paid by an intermediary (or an intermediary's organisation) to any such player, club, club official or manager. Additionally, any actual or potential conflict of interest in relation to a transaction must be disclosed to The FA and the express written consent of all parties involved in a matter must be obtained.[34]

12.40   In terms of disclosure and publication of information relating to intermediary activity, The FA has wide-ranging powers of publication, including the entitlement to publish a list of every transaction in which an intermediary has been involved and the total consolidated amount of all payments made by all players and by each club to intermediaries.[35]

---

32   See Regulation E.2.
33   'Connected intermediary' means intermediaries who are (i) employed, retained by or owners or directors of shareholders in the same organisation; (ii) representative of a legal person registered as an intermediary; (iii) married, siblings or parent and child; or (iv) subject to any contractual or other arrangement (whether formal or informal) to cooperate in the provision of intermediary activity or to share any revenue or profits thereof.
34   The form on which such disclosure is made is required to be submitted to The FA within ten days of being completed and in any event by the time of the registration of a transaction by The FA.
35   See Regulation D.

(g) Disciplinary powers and sanctions

12.41   Any breach of the FA Intermediaries Regulations will amount to misconduct under The FA's Rules[36] and will be dealt with by The FA Regulatory Commission under The FA's Regulations for Football Association Disciplinary Action. The aforementioned regulations set out in detail the procedure for dealing with a charge of misconduct.

12.42   As noted above, upon registering as an intermediary, the intermediary must declare that he or she consents to The FA's powers of inquiry and the publication of any aspect of an inquiry and any decision it makes under the FA Intermediaries Regulations, including in relation to the suspension or withdrawal of an intermediary's registration.

12.43   Finally, a further change recently introduced by The FA (on 9 August 2017) is the new Regulation G.3, which states: 'An Intermediary should use all reasonable endeavours to ensure that the Organisation through which he operates shall comply fully with the requirements of the Rules of The Association and these Regulations in relation to any Intermediary Activity carried out by that Intermediary.' This change can be seen as creating a type of vicarious liability, in that an intermediary working through or for an agency has a duty to ensure that not only he or she, but also the agency (and thus others working through or for it) comply with the FA Intermediaries Regulations in relation to the activity in which the intermediary is engaged. It is also incumbent upon an intermediary to ensure that any employee or agent working in or on behalf of the intermediary's organisation, but who is not himself or herself registered as an intermediary, is prohibited from carrying out any intermediary activity.

C   COMMON LEGAL ISSUES ARISING WITH INTERMEDIARIES

12.44   As set out in section A of this chapter, the most common legal issues involving intermediaries can be broadly divided into regulatory and private law issues, whilst there is often a considerable interrelationship between these two areas.

(a) Regulatory disputes generally

12.45   In terms of regulatory issues, section B of this chapter (above) identifies the key regulations that apply to intermediaries and their engagement. Breach of these regulations may (and often does) lead to disciplinary proceedings being brought against intermediaries by The FA. Those shall be subject to the same basic procedures and rule of law discussed in Chapter 23, Discipline.

12.46   A number of recent high profile disciplinary cases brought by The FA demonstrate the pitfalls that can arise for intermediaries and other participants when serious breaches of the rules are proven to have occurred. Whilst many of these cases

---

36   Rule E.1(b) of The FA's Rules states: 'The Association may act against a Participant in respect of any "Misconduct", which is defined as being a breach of the following: ... (b) the Rules and regulations of The Association ...'. Those Rules, to which all participants must adhere and are subject, are broad and detailed and include rules on general behaviour ('A Participant ... shall not act in any manner which is improper or brings the game into disrepute'), compliance with The FA's decisions and reporting misconduct.

were decided under the old FA Football Agents Regulations, they involve breaches of similar provisions to those found in the current Intermediaries Regualtions, and indications from recent Regulatory Commissions are that the sanctions shall be broadly similar.

12.47   In *The FA v Phil Smith & Wycombe Wanderers Football Club* (2014),[37] a Commission sanctioned both the agent, Phil Smith, and the club for various breaches relating to an agreement that Mr Smith would be paid his commission on a transfer by way of a percentage of any sell-on fee for the player Matt Phillips that the club may receive in the future. This was considered to be in breach of regulations essentially prohibiting third party interests; but the most serious breach was considered to be the breach of previous Regulation C.2 of the FA Football Agents Regulations (that a party must not conceal from The FA the real nature of their arrangements).[38] The club was fined £10,000.[39] The sanction imposed against Mr Smith was much greater, being a two-year suspension of his agents' licence, the first 18 months of which was suspended.[40] The immediate six-month ban on Mr Smith, which would have covered the all-important summer transfer window, was, however, overturned by an FA Appeal Panel because the Regulatory Commission had not taken into account, in imposing its sanction on Mr Smith, the effect of the sanction on him in terms of 'pipeline income' he was already due from work he had previously done which he might lose if the ban was not overturned.[41]

12.48   In *The FA v Sunderland & Abu Mahfuz* (2014),[42] the agent, Mr Mahfuz, carried out agency activity on behalf of unauthorised agents, and the agent and club misrepresented the reality of the transaction to the FA. The Commission found the agent to have been involved in 'a serious case of misconduct', involving multiple breaches and a significant transfer fee (€4.5 million). Similar to Phil Smith, he was suspended from agency activity for two years, 18 months of which were suspended, six months of which were immediate. He was fined £500. Sunderland was not subject to any sporting sanction, but given the seriousness of the beach, its ability to pay and the fact Sunderland was a Premier league club, it was fined £100,000.

12.49   In *The FA v Kleinman & Levack* (2015),[43] a Regulatory Commission considered similar charges against a football club and licensed agents.[44] The case involved a number of false declarations made on various forms and agreements signed by Mr Rahnama (a solicitor and football agent) and the club in relation to a transaction. All parties were aware that it was the football agents Mr Levack and Mr Kleinman that were to receive the commission in relation to the transaction, but

---

37   (Decision on sanction) FA Regulatory Commission (Ch. Craig Moore), 23 May 2014.
38   See Regulation A.3 of the FA Intermediaries Regulations.
39   It was found it could rely on mitigating factors because previous owners were responsible for the breach, new owners helped bring it to light, it pleaded guilty at the first available opportunity, it cooperated with the investigation and gave honest and straightforward evidence, and it had no relevant antecedents – see para 2.6 of the decision.
40   The Commission explained its reasons for giving Mr Smith a harsher sanction was because they found he had fought the charges and not pleaded guilty, his evidence was rejected as unreliable and contradictory, and the Commission deplored the manner in which he proceeded to pursue payment from the new owners of the club; they also found that although Mr Smith had an unblemished disciplinary record, this was tempered by the fact he had lengthy experience as a football agent – see para 2.18 of the decision.
41   *Phil Smith v The FA*, FA Appeal Board (Ch. Richard Smith QC), 11 July 2014.
42   Regulatory Commission (Ch. Christopher Quinlan QC), 21 May 2014.
43   FA Regulatory Commission (Ch. David Casement QC), 16 February 2015.
44   Charges of breach of FA Football Agents Regulation C.2 against all parties, H.10 against all agents and F.1 against the club.

knowingly concealed this from The FA claiming it was Mr Rahnama (the 'front' in that case) who was to receive the commission when he did not.

12.50   All of the participants had pleaded guilty to the charges but the sanctions imposed were markedly different. Mr Kleinman and Mr Levack were suspended from all agency activity for 14 months, seven months being immediate and seven months suspended, and they were each fined £7,500. Mr Rahnama was suspended for nine months, three months immediate and six months suspended; he was not fined. The Club was fined £90,000. The differences between the sanctions imposed were explained as being because the credibility of Kleinman and Levack was undermined;[45] they were 'the main protagonists' who had 'planned and implemented' the breach;[46] and whilst Mr Rahnama should have known better as a (junior) solicitor, he naively allowed himself to become involved in the misconduct to gain experience and contacts in football, but never intended to gain anything else.

12.51   The Commission's decision on sanction was upheld by an FA Appeal Panel in *Kleinman & Levack v The FA*.[47] The Appeal Board noted the Commission had found Mr Kleinman and Mr Levack had the most responsibility for the breaches – even though it was Mr Rahnama who signed the false declarations. Mr Kleinman and Mr Levack were 'by far the more experienced agents and the prime movers' and the Appeal Board could easily see why the Commission imposed a shorter suspension on 'the relatively very inexperienced' Mr Rahnama in comparison.[48]

12.52   Despite The FA and its Regulatory Commissions often claiming that previous cases of different Regulatory Commissions and Appeal Boards are of no use in determining sanction,[49] the Chairman of the Appeal Board in *Kleinman & Levack v The FA*, Mr Nicholas Stewart QC, suggested a new standard sanction for these types of breaches by football agents. Whereas, in the dozens of cases before the three cases considered above it was unusual for an agent to be suspended from all agency activity (and so effectively prevented from earning a living) for a period as long as six months, Mr Stewart QC concluded his judgment with the following observations:[50]

(a) It can only be in the most exceptional circumstances (not applicable here) that an agent or intermediary that has sought to mislead the FA by a dishonest breach of the regulations will *not* receive an immediate sanction.
(b) In most cases, as in this case, to be realistically effective at all the suspension will need to be for at least several months and will usually need to cover at least one transfer window.
(c) The financial effects of the suspension are clearly relevant as part of the overall picture in working out the penalty, but a Regulatory Commission is *not* required to fine tune suspensions. It could and should adopt a fairly broad approach.
(d) Suspensions are bound to hurt – that is the point of them. If the financial damage from suspension is going to be unusually heavy in a particular case, then that is something that the agent or intermediary (who is after all best placed to know that) should think about before committing the breach.

---

45   Para 29 of the Decision.
46   Para 34 of the Decision.
47   FA Appeal Board (Ch. Nicholas Stewart QC), 19 May 2015.
48   Para 31 of the Decision.
49   This claim is usually made by The FA when it seeks (or is defending on appeal) a more punitive sanction than has previously been applied, and unfortunately some Regulatory Commissions and Appeal Boards have been content to follow it, unhelpfully for participants and the interests of consistency and fairness.
50   Paragraph 44 of the Decision.

12.53   The presumption that a sporting sanction (suspension) should be applied against agents and intermediaries who dishonestly breach the rules is not entirely consistent with previous cases or with The FA's rules themselves. Regulatory Commissions have a broad discretion to apply a range of sanctions, including warnings and fines; suspensions from sporting activity are an extreme and exceptional measure. The effect of such suspensions, whether against a player or an intermediary, is to prevent the participant from being able to earn a living. Such suspensions shall therefore be subject to particular scrutiny under the law. They must be proportionate to be legal. The suggestion that such sporting sanctions should be routinely applied in all these types of cases, when they are not applied against, for example, football clubs committing the same breaches, may not stand up to such scrutiny. In addition, the apparent lack of regard to the financial consequences of a sporting sanction suggested in the extract above appears at odds with the decision of the FA Appeal Board in the *Phil Smith* case – where the suspension was lifted precisely because the Regulatory Commission had failed to properly consider the financial consequences.

12.54   The standard suggested by Mr Stewart QC has not been automatically adopted by all other Regulatory Commissions. *FA v Arsenal & Alan Middleton* (2015),[51] was another 'fronting' case involving an experienced solicitor and intermediary (Mr Middleton) 'fronting' for an unauthorised agent. Mr Middleton was fined £30,000 and subject to a three-month suspended suspension (that is, no immediate sanction). The Commission took into account the fact that the level of the fine reflected the benefit that went to Mr Middleton as a result of his involvement in the transaction; and he was entitled to mitigation as, although he was a very experienced solicitor who had held a senior position in a football club, he had only conducted one transfer before, he had given straightforward evidence and tried to assist the Commission, and although he did not plead guilty, he had expressed regret. The Commission in *Middleton* appeared more comfortable in explaining Mr Middleton's conduct as mistaken rather than dishonest, but that may simply be because it was a differently constituted Commission.

12.55   However, another Regulatory Commission (also chaired by Mr Stewart QC) imposed a sanction of a similar period in the case of *FA v (1) Leeds United, (2) Massimo Cellino & (3) Derek Day*.[52] The case involved the payment of £250,000 to an unauthorised agent, Barry Hughes, related to the transfer of a player, through the vehicle of a sham scouting agreement with the intermediary, Mr Day. The Commission found all three participants knew of and took part in the sham. Mr Day was fined £75,000 and banned from all intermediary activity for an immediate period of seven months. He did not appeal the sanction, but both Leeds United and Mr Cellino did, and both had their respective fines and Mr Cellino's prohibition from all football activty substantially reduced: the combined fine against Leeds and Mr Cellino of £500,000 (£250,000 each) was reduced by more than a third to £300,000 (£200,000 against Leeds and £100,000 against Mr Cellino), and Mr Cellino's ban reduced from 18 months to 12 months.[53] Had a similar reduction been applied to Mr Day, his ban would have been about four and a half months instead of seven.

---

51   FA Regulatory Commission (Ch. Craig Moore), 22 October 2015.
52   5 December 2016.
53   For a link to the decisions of the Commission and Appeal Board and a discussion of the case, see: '*FA v Cellino – Behind the Headlines*', Nick De Marco, *Blackstone Chambers Sports Law Bulletin*, 7 November 2017: https://www.sportslawbulletin.org/fa-v-cellino-behind-headlines (accessed February 2018).

12.56   A number of cases involving breaches of the FA Intermediary Regulations' provisions relating to dealing with minors have led to significant periods of suspension. In *The FA v Paolo Vernazza*,[54] the intermediary, Mr Vernazza, had admitted to breaching Regulation 3.1 of Appendix II of the FA Intermediaries Regulations: he had sought to enter into a representation contract with two different minors without the 'additional authorisation' required to do so. The charge was aggravated by the fact that, in respect to one of the contracts, he had failed to obtain the player's parent/guardian countersignature on the representation contract, contrary to FA Intermediaries Regulation B.9. The commission found that Mr Vernazza was at all times aware that he did not have the required authorisation and that those he was engaging with would have been led to believe that he did have it. He was immediately suspended from all intermediary activity for the period of six months, fined the sum of £2,500 and warned as to his future conduct.

12.57   In *The FA v Niel Sexton*,[55] a Regulatory Commission imposed a particularly stringent sanction against the intermediary for dealing with four different minors without the required authorisation – Mr Sexton was banned from intermediary activity for a period of one year. The Commission found that the charge was aggravated due to the number of breaches and, in particular, because it represented a breach of what was essentially part of The FA's 'safeguarding' regime.[56] An Appeal Board upheld the lengthy sanction and, while noting that there were no guidelines or suggested tariffs for breaches of this sort, they found that the period of suspension of one year was 'within the reasonable range in the exercise of the Commission's discretion in arriving at a fair and proportionate penalty'.[57]

12.58   A Regulatory Commission presided over by the same Chairman imposed a similarly long sanction of ten months (and a fine of £400) for a similar offence in relation to only one player in *The FA v Kieran Bradbury*,[58] again citing the 'safeguarding' point.[59] With respect, the sanctions in *Sexton* and *Bradbury* do appear excessive in comparison with other similar cases, and indeed even with the dicta of Mr Stewart QC in *Kleinman & Levack v The FA* – suggesting a ban of around six months shall be routine for a 'dishonest' breach of the regulations.[60] No dishonesty or deliberate deception was found in either *Sexton* or *Bradbury*, but while the Commission correctly noted that ignorance of a rule is not a defence, they do not appear to have properly taken it into account in terms of determining sanction – on the contrary, they imposed sanctions almost double the length that have been previously been indicated to be appropriate for deliberate and dishonest breaches.

12.59   *The FA v Nathan Haslam*[61] involved another charge against an intermediary for not having the required authorisation to deal with minors. The breach related to only one minor, and the intermediary pleaded guilty on the basis that he did not know of the requirement for additional authorisation; once he did know it he applied for authorisation. Mr Haslam was banned for a period of three months which included the remainder of the summer transfer window. The Commission 'noted there was no guidance or guidelines document in terms of recommended sanctions for breach of

---

54   FA Regulatory Commission (Ch. Mr G Farrelly), 12 December 2016.
55   FA Regulatory Commission (Ch. Mr I Odogwu), 18 May 2017.
56   See paras 16–17 of the Commission's written reasons.
57   *Niel Sexton v The FA*, FA Appeal Board (Ch. Mr C Moore), 7 July 2017, at para 3.26.
58   FA Regulatory Commission (Ch. Mr I Odogwu), 21 November 2017.
59   Paragraph 25 of the written reasons.
60   See para **12.52** above.
61   FA Regulatory Commission (Ch. Mr BW Bright), 7 June 2017.

intermediary regulations'.[62] The sanction was upheld on appeal, the Appeal Board finding that a suspension which did not cover a whole transfer window has far fewer teeth and is likely to be inadequate to mark the seriousness of the breach.[63]

12.60   However, in *The FA v Lawrence Fisher*,[64] a differently constituted Regulatory Commission imposed an immediate ban of only seven days against an intermediary (not during a transfer window, and a further 21 days suspended) who had admitted two breaches of Regulation B.8 of the FA Intermediaries Regulations by entering into two separate agreements with two players in relation to intermediary activity before the first day of January of the year of each players' 16th birthday. Mr Fisher's mitigation that he was unaware of the rule was accepted. In *The FA v Danny Webber*,[65] an intermediary found to have committed a similar breach of the same Regualtion B.8 was banned for 28 days (with 84 days suspended) and fined £1,250.

12.61   *The FA v Glen Tweneboah*[66] involved another case of an intermediary carrying out activity with a minor without the relevant authorisation. Mr Tweneboah cited various technical reasons for his failure to obtain the authorisation and changed his plea from not guilty to guilty during the hearing. The charge related to only one player. He was banned for a period of three months and fined £200. Another intermediary was banned for the same period of three months and fined £250 in *The FA v Robert Codner* for a similar offence.[67]

12.62   These recent cases involving breaches of the FA Intermediaries Regulations in relation to minors, in particular, suggest there is a real risk of markedly different sanctions being imposed for similar offences, indeed as different as a seven-day ban in one case to a year-long ban in another. Such inconsistency is unsatisfactory in a disciplinary regime in sport, where equal and predictable treatment for similar offences should be expected. The various comments by some of the commissions involved that there was no guidance or recommended tariffs set out by The FA for these types of offences (contrary to quite detailed guidance offered by The FA in other cases) should be carefully considered by the regulator. The distinct difference in sanction can lead to a belief that the length of a sanction has as much to do with the constitution of a commission as it does with the nature of the breach – and such a perception inevitably undermines the integrity of the regulatory regime.

12.63   However, the various cases do suggest that an immediate suspension from all intermediary activity of approximately six months (including one transfer window) for any breach found to be dishonest should probably now be expected to be the norm, and that breaches of the FA Intermediaries Regulations concerning minors may also be treated particularly seriously, even in the absence of dishonesty. There is a risk that one consequence of the presumption of a sporting sanction (ie suspension) for certain breaches may be to encourage intermediaries in future to plead not guilty to misleading The FA and claim confusion, rather than accepting they had (innocently or otherwise) in fact misled The FA. But intermediaries, and those dealing with them, would be wise to take note of the serious consequences that may arise if they are found to have misled The FA, or breached the regulations concerning minors. It is often thought common in football that many of the forms submitted on a transfer by

62   See para 14 of the written reasons.
63   *Nathan Haslam v The FA*, FA Appeal Board (Ch. Mr Stewart QC), 17 July 2017, at para 15.
64   FA Regulatory Commission (Ch. Mr B Jones), 11 October 2016.
65   FA Regulatory Commission (Ch. Mr R Burden), 13 December 2016.
66   FA Regulatory Commission (Ch. Mr P Clayton), 21 November 2016.
67   FA Regulatory Commission (Ch. Major W Thomson), 19 October 2017.

all parties (including, principally by the club) do not disclose the complete picture regarding the relationship between the parties and the final destination of all the payments made. While such conduct may be the norm within football, if The FA decides to bring a case in relation to a particular transfer, the intermediaries involved, in particular, risk punitive sanctions for participating in an arrangement they believed was neither unusual nor harmful. Likewise, an intermediary who fails to comply with the rules in relation to minors, in particular, risks a suspension of some sort even if his or her breach was wholly innocent.

(b)   Legal scrutiny of the regulatory process

12.64   It is important to note that not only must The FA act in accordance with its own rules in relation to the regulation of intermediaries, but also its conduct must be in accordance with fundamental principles of law and, in particular, natural justice. The suspension or withdrawal of an intermediary's registration, for example, shall only be permissible following a fair process. The legal principles established in the seminal Court of Appeal decision in the *McInnes v Onslow Fane*[68] case (involving the application to a regulator for a boxing manager's licence) – creating a threefold categorisation of the rights that arise in forfeiture, expectation and application type cases – shall apply. It shall not be permissible for The FA to arbitrarily refuse an applicant a licence to be an intermediary; and an intermediary shall have a right to a fair hearing before The FA suspends or withdraws his or her licence.[69]

(c)   Length of representation contracts and young players

12.65   The FIFA RWI do not provide for any maximum duration of the representation contract between player and intermediary. This is likely to create contentious disputes. The nature of the player/intermediary relationship is precisely the kind of relationship where regulatory measures are sensible to protect young or inexperienced players, in particular, and avoid litigation.

12.66   The previous regulation, that no representation contract could continue for any term beyond two years unless the parties agreed a new contract, was a reasonable measure to avoid such conflict. Young and inexperienced players, in particular, might enter into representation contracts with intermediaries in order to obtain their first professional contract, or their first 'big' professional contract or transfer, only to substantially increase their value and thus bargaining power over the following two years. If they are bound to an intermediary on terms they could substantially improve on if free to negotiate a new contract, or bound to an intermediary not able to take their career forward, for a more prolonged period of time then it is inevitable conflicts shall arise. Two years is a relatively long time for a professional footballer, but it is reasonable in the context of the average length of a playing contract. To bind a player for a substantially longer period to an intermediary may seriously frustrate his career, and players bound in such a way will be tempted to just walk out and breach their representation contracts or to find ways of claiming the intermediary is in breach thus allowing them to be released from the contract – in either case increasing the likelihood of contentious disputes and litigation.

---

68   [1978] 1 WLR 1520.
69   See, generally, Chapter 23, Discipline, and Part B of that chapter, 'The Importance of Fairness', in particular.

12.67   The risk of conflict is increased under the FIFA RWI because it is possible for an intermediary to enter into a representation contract with a 'minor' (any player who has not reached the age of 18 under FIFA RWI), so long as it is signed also by his legal guardian (Regulation 5(2)) and no payments are made to the intermediary whilst the player remains a minor (Regulation 7(8)). Theoretically, intermediaries shall be able to sign representation contracts with promising schoolboy players for extended periods of time under the FIFA RWI in numerous countries. The intermediary would not be paid until the player turned 18 and might decide to sign large numbers of promising school boy players to long representation contracts in the hope that just a few might turn out to be gifted players with a lucrative professional future. But if the contract is longer than 10 years, for example, then once the player has turned 18 and is able to command large transfer fees and salaries, the intermediary can obtain a return on his investment. Restraint of trade issues are most likely to arise here.

12.68   It is ironic that just as FIFA decided to prohibit third party investment in players (TPI),[70] it created the circumstances for what could be a far more pernicious situation. Intermediaries in countries where they are able to sign long agreements with minors would not only have an investment in the player (as with TPI) through which they can only obtain a return when negotiating future employment contracts and transfers (also similar to TPI), but also intermediaries can have a direct influence over the player, in that they are negotiating the player's contracts and advising him on his transfer(s). It is precisely this kind of influence (ie third party influence) which was prohibited by FIFA rules even when TPI was permitted, and such influence is widely regarded as the real vice of TPI.

12.69   The FA Intermediaries Regulations, on the other hand, go beyond the FIFA RWI and provide (as did the previous FA Football Agents Regulations) that a representation contract with a player (although not a club) shall only be for a maximum duration of two years (see Regulation B.10). Whilst this is sensible, issues may arise where foreign intermediaries with much longer representation contracts with players do business with English clubs. The difference in the regulations may put such foreign intermediaries at an advantage as compared to intermediaries in the UK.

12.70   The FA Intermediaries Regulations further differ from the FIFA RWI in that they do not allow an intermediary to enter into any representation contract with a minor, or indeed even approach him or conduct any activity on his behalf, until the 1st day of January in the year of the player's 16th birthday.[71] Whilst this may be a reasonable measure to protect very young players from intermediaries, what is far less sensible is the fact, no doubt as a consequence of the FIFA RWI, that an intermediary cannot be paid any sum with respect to activity carried out in respect of a minor until he has reached his 18th birthday.[72] For example, if a 17-year-old player has the chance of entering a lucrative contract with a Premier League football club, the player may be unable to have the benefit of an intermediary negotiating the terms of such a contract on his behalf unless the intermediary is prepared to do so for no commission at all. This makes little sense. A 17-year-old player is allowed to sign

---

70   See Chapter 11, Third Party Investment.
71   See Regulation B.8.
72   See Regulation C.10: 'Players and/or Clubs that engage the services of an Intermediary when negotiating an employment contract and/or a transfer agreement are prohibited from making any payments to such Intermediary if the Player concerned is a Minor.' But see also, para **12.72** below, setting out the way around this prohibition.

a full professional playing contract with a club and is able to enter a representation contract with an intermediary to assist him in signing such a playing contract and negotiating his terms; but the intermediary is unable to charge any commission for such work.

12.71   Those representing intermediaries pointed out to The FA that this provision does not appear to be in the interest of either the player or the intermediary, and could be viewed as putting clubs at an unfair advantage in negotiating terms with young players. It was argued by Association of Football Agents (AFA) that the provision was open to potential challenge on restraint of trade and/or competition law grounds, and that a more sensible rule would allow intermediaries to enter representation contracts with 16–18-year-old players, so long as there is parental/guardian consent, but not (as FIFA does) allow such contracts to be entered before the player is 16; and would allow the intermediary to charge commission for any services provided during such a contract (as neither The FA nor FIFA allow) and limit the term of the representation contract to a two-year period (as The FA does but FIFA does not). Such a provision would strike a proper balance between protecting the interests of young players whilst at the same time incentivising intermediaries to advance those interests by assisting in negotiating contracts.

12.72   The FA appear to have heeded some of these points and issued guidance on the regulations setting out the way in which payments could be made in these circumstances. According to The FA's Intermediary Guidance[73] on Regualtion C.10:

> 'A Player or Club may pay an Intermediary in relation to a Transaction completed while the Player was a Minor only in the following circumstances:
>
> –   Where the Player has attained the age of 18 before any payment is made; and
> –   The result of the completed Transaction was that the Player signed a professional contract with the Club.
>
> For the avoidance of doubt, an Intermediary is prohibited from receiving any remuneration in relation to a Player entering into a Scholarship agreement.'

12.73   Thus, the guidance states it is permitted for a player or club to enter a representation contract with an intermediary representing a minor that provides for payment to be made to that intermediary (i) for work related to a player signing a professional contract (which he may do from the age of 17); and (ii) so long as the payment is not actually made until the player reaches the age of 18.

12.74   Legal issues may also otherwise arise where players, clubs and intermediaries seek to subvert the rules and make allowance for some commission, inevitably by some concealed route, to help facilitate the signing of a promising young player. Other issues may arise where a foreign young player who has entered into a representation contract with a foreign intermediary before the age of 16, for a period in excess of two years, is signed by an English football club. It is unclear what would happen after his 18th birthday when an intermediary could be paid. Under a strict (and it is submitted a proper) reading of the FA Intermediaries Regulations an intermediary would have to register a representation contract with the player that conforms with the FA rules – even if he already had a long-term contract with him. But what happens if the player refuses to sign a new FA-compliant representation contract with his existing intermediary and instead enters a valid representation contract with an English intermediary? The foreign intermediary is likely to sue the player for breach of contract (and/or the other intermediary for inducement to

---

73   Latest version (July 2017) available at: http://www.thefa.com/football-rules-governance/policies/intermediaries/regulation-and-forms (accessed February 2018).

breach), which he would be entitled to do at law even though the player was not obliged to enter a new contract with the foreign intermediary that was necessary to facilitate the payment of commission in England.

(d)   Tapping up and poaching

12.75   There was at first an increase in disputes with regard to 'tapping up' – approaching players under contract to a club in an attempt to induce them to leave the club and join another. This activity was prohibited by the FA Football Agents Regulations which contained a presumption that an agent of a player who unlawfully terminated his playing contract had induced a breach of contract, but was then omitted by The FA from its initial Intermediaries Regulations. In addition, unlike the previous Football Agents Regulations, the FA Intermediaries Regulations did not (until a change in August 2017) prohibit an intermediary approaching a player already under a representation contract with another intermediary. In the past, attempts by agents to 'poach' the clients of other agents could sometimes be swiftly rebuffed by making it clear to the poaching agent that he could not do so without breaching the Agents Regulations (and thus risk suspension of his licence by The FA) whilst the player already had a valid representation contract. This opportunity to protect against the poaching of their clients was at first lost to intermediaries in England, and remains lost to intermediaries working in numerous countries outside England.

12.76   As a consequence of the scrapping of the regulatory prohibition on poaching, the authors of this chapter have witnessed a dramatic increase in litigation between intermediaries.[74] The majority of these claims are determined in confidential FA Rule K arbitrations, most often between the initial intermediary as claimant and the previous player client as respondent, joining (if possible) the new intermediary as co-respondent responsible for inducement to breach the contract. The normal principles of English contract law, and the law relating to the tort of inducement to breach a contract, apply to the determination of such arbitral claims. The situation is more difficult in relation to international disputes between intermediaries. First, FIFA has not (as The FA now have) re-introduced the prohibition on poaching, meaning there remains no regulatory disincentive to poaching clients from other intermediaries. Secondly, there is no mandatory arbitration clause in international intermediary contracts, unlike the situation under The FA Rules. Many players and intermediaries agree to be bound by an arbitration clause that provides CAS with jurisdiction (and there is a special CAS procedure for such claims),[75] but they may equally appoint another tribunal as arbitrator or have no arbitration clause at all. Some claims will have to be determined in the courts, subject to the law of the country of the contract or, if the contract is silent on that, where the contract is to be performed. In an international transfer case this may be uncertain. Parties entering such contracts in the future would be wise to agree with certainty the governing law and jurisdiction of the contract.

12.77   It remains to be seen whether the re-introduction of the prohibition on tapping up and poaching by The FA shall have the effect of reducing the number of disputes between intermediaries. The authors of this chapter believe that, whilst the move may offer some welcome deterrent, it is unlikely to have a substantial effect.

---

74   See, for example, *Corruption in football – player transfers, agents and the 'privatisation of regulation'*, Nick De Marco, 4 July 2017 (https://www.sportslawbulletin.org/corruption-football-player-transfers-agents-and-privatisation-regulation/ (accessed February 2018)).

75   See Chapter 29, International Disputes and the CAS, paras **29.57–29.61**.

The FA has finite resources, many more intermediaries are registered than agents were licensed, and The FA is unlikely to investigate and prosecute every incident of alleged poaching between intermediaries. Most of these disputes will most likely continue to be resolved by the intermediaries themselves.

12.78   One interesting question that does arise is what remedy an intermediary may have against The FA for failing to take action against a player or intermediary who has breached a contract with him or her and, in the process, also breached the regulations. Whilst the private law remedy remains one available to the intermediary usually by way of commencing a Rule K arbitration, such a process may be long and costly. The intermediary must also have a contractual right, arising from his or her relationship with The FA, to expect The FA shall take reasonable action against those who breach its regulations to the detriment of the intermediary. If The FA unreasonably refuses to investigate or take action, it may be possible to bring a claim against The FA for breach of contract also. The FA Rules are a contract that bind not only the intermediaries to adhere to the regulations made by The FA, but also The FA to act reasonably and fairly in applying those regulations consistently and fairly across the board. Clubs may also have similar potential claims if The FA fails to take action against an intermediary alleged to have tapped up a player. With the amount of disputes arising in this area, and the value of some of them, this is likely to be an interesting new area of potential litigation.

(e)   Arbitration

12.79   As set out above, most disputes involving intermediaries in England are determined by arbitration subject to the rules and procedure set out in FA Rule K – not least because all regulated agreements in English football between players and/ or clubs on the one hand, and intermediaries on the other, are required to contain an 'obligatory term' that any disputes between the parties shall be subject to FA Rule K arbitration.[76] Other international agreements may include a term that another arbitral tribunal, such as CAS, shall determine disputes.

12.80   Chapter 28, Arbitration in Football, considers the various issues that arise in relation to football arbitration, but for the purposes of this discussion the following points are most important to consider. First, it is not uncommon for some football participants, and even occasionally some lawyers, to misunderstand FA Rule K arbitration to mean that The FA Intermediaries Regulations apply in Rule K disputes as if they were substantive law. This is not the case. FA Rule K is merely the procedural rule under which the arbitration shall be held. English common law applies as the substantive law, and takes precedent over The FA Regulations. The arbitral tribunal is not 'The FA' in any sense at all, it is constituted by any independent legally qualified panel appointed by the parties under the Rules set out in Rule K.

12.81   A common expression of this confusion is the argument, often raised in Rule K proceedings, that because a particular contract is contrary to the FA Intermediaries Regulations regarding intermediaries a claim under it cannot succeed.

---

76   Clause 7 of the FA Standard Representation Contract (containing all of the minimum 'obligatory terms') provides as follows:

'Any dispute between the parties arising out of or in connection with the Contract, including but not limited to any question regarding its existence, validity or termination, shall be referred to and finally resolved by arbitration under Rule K of the Rules of The FA (as amended from time to time).'

This argument will almost always be unsuccessful, because a claim may be good in contract law even if the contract would breach The FA regulations. The approach a Rule K tribunal should take is the same approach a court would take: to give effect to the contract even if it is not compliant with regulation.[77]

12.82   The second important point about Rule K arbitration and intermediaries concerns the reach of the arbitration clause itself. It had previously been assumed by many in football that because FA Rule K provides that 'any dispute or difference between any two or more Participants ... shall be referred to and finally resolved by arbitration under these Rules', and because all FA registered intermediaries were parties to The FA Rules as if they are a contract, the existence of Rule K may itself be enough to make any disputes between intermediaries and other parties subject to binding Rule K arbitration. There is now considerable uncertainty about this following two apparently contrasting decisions of the High Court. In *Davies v Nottingham Forest FC*,[78] the Manchester District Registry of the High Court found that Nottingham Forest's former manager, Billy Davies, was bound to bring his claim by way of Rule K arbitration even though his last employment contract failed to incorporate an express arbitration clause. The decision was reached essentially on the basis that, as Rule K makes clear that all disputes between participants are to be determined by arbitration under Rule K, and as both parties had agreed to be bound by Rule K (by virtue of being participants), they had agreed to the arbitration clause in disputes between each other. However, in *Bony v Kacou*,[79] decided by another judge sitting in the Manchester District Registry of the High Court at almost the same time, Mr Kacou, Wilfred Bony's former intermediary, did not succeed in showing that there was an implied arbitration clause between him and the player. While the court indicated that for Rule K to apply it is essential also that there be a separate contract between the intermediary and player/club that expressly incorporates the Rule K arbitration clause, the facts of *Bony* can be distinguished for a number of reasons, not least that some of the intermediaries were not necessarily participants in any event. Nevertheless, the two cases have led to some uncertainty, and it cannot now be necessarily assumed that a party can rely on Rule K merely by virtue of the fact that it is a participant and so is the other party to the dispute – *Davies* suggests that shall be the case, whereas *Bony* casts some doubt on it. A detailed discussion of these cases is contained in Chapter 28, Arbitration.

12.83   This uncertainty may lead to a change in The FA Rules in the future. FIFA requires that all football disputes are determined by arbitration without interference by national courts, and The FA may be subject to sanction by FIFA if, as a result of its rules not being drafted widely enough, the English courts start to exercise jurisdiction over football disputes. One potential way in which The FA might consider changing its Rules is to make them a contract not only between each participant and The FA (as they currently are), but also a contract between each participant with each other. This is the approach in the Premier League Rules. If that approach was adopted then simply by agreeing to be bound by The FA Rules the participant would be agreeing to the arbitration clause in Rule K.

12.84   Other potential problems intermediaries may face in relation to arbitration, like those related to how to join further parties (such as other respondent

---

77   For example, see *Anthony Mcgill v The Sports and Entertainment Media Group ('SEM')* [2016] EWCA Civ 1063; [2017] 1 WLR 989, and the discussion of the case at para **12.86** below.
78   [2017] EWHC 2095.
79   [2017] EWHC 2146 (Ch).

intermediaries alleged to have induced a breach of contract by a player), confidentiality and so on, are also considered in Chapter 28.

(f)   Breach of contract and inducement to breach contract

12.85   As explained above, most private law claims involving intermediaries, whether determined by FA Rule K arbitration or otherwise, shall be claims of breach of contract (ie breach of a representation contract between intermediary and player and/or club) and/or inducement to breach contract, most often against competitor intermediaries said to have poached the player (or club's business) from the claimant intermediary. Normal principles of contract and tort law apply to these claims.

12.86   Whilst most of these disputes are determined in confidential arbitrations, and thus the decisions never made public, one claim involving football agents determined by the courts provides useful guidance. In *Anthony McGill v The Sports and Entertainment Media Group ('SEM')*,[80] the claimant, intermediary, Mr McGill, claimed he had reached an oral contract to act as agent for the player in a transfer to Bolton Wanderers FC, but that another firm of intermediaries, SEM, and Bolton had induced the player to breach the contract. SEM had entered into an agency agreement with Bolton to find the player and received commission from Bolton. Mr McGill brought various claims (including inducement to breach contract and conspiracy) against both SEM and Bolton. The defendants argued, amongst other things, that Mr McGill had not reached a valid contract with the player as there was only an oral contract that he would act as agent – there was no executed written representation contract (that would have to be lodged with The FA) that would have entitled Mr McGill to act as agent in the deal and receive fees (that is one of the reasons the claim was not brought by way of FA Rule K arbitration).

12.87   At first instance, the judge accepted that there had been an oral contract but dismissed the claim, holding that Mr McGill had not demonstrated that the player would have entered into a written contract with him had it not been for the defendants' unlawful conduct. The Court of Appeal held that the judge had been entitled to find on the balance of probabilities that the player would not have entered into a written contract with Mr McGill, but that was not the end of the matter. Mr McGill was entitled to an award of damages on the basis of loss of the opportunity to earn a fee under a written agency agreement when the player's transfer to Bolton was completed. The correct approach was not (only) whether the player would or would not have signed a contract, but what percentage chance there was that he would have. As the judge had been entitled to find that the player would not have signed, the percentage could not be more than 50%, but the case was remitted to the judge to determine what percentage chance there was that the player would have signed with Mr McGill, and for that to then inform the damages due to Mr McGill.

(g)   Other claims

12.88   There are various other causes of action/defences that often arise in disputes involving intermediaries, including conspiracy (which any party should always be sure there is sufficient evidence to allege before pleading), breaches of confidentiality, quantum meruit, restitution and, in particular, breach of fiduciary duties. The latter is particularly important in intermediary contracts because the football intermediary is a fiduciary to the player (or club) and owes particularly important duties as a result of that relationship.

12.89   The leading case on the question is *Imageview Management Ltd v Jack*.[81] A football agent owes fiduciary duties to his client and the non-disclosure of a conflict of interest between the agent's own interest and those of his player client was a breach of the agent's duty of good faith to his client. In the circumstances of the case, the agent forfeited his right to the commission to which he was otherwise contractually entitled and the fee he earned in breach of the duty was a secret profit, recoverable by the player, subject to the possibility of an equitable allowance. *Imageview* is not only relevant to allegations of secret profits (though they are not unusual in football), but to any breach of fiduciary duty – the principle being that if a fiduciary (such as a football agent) acts dishonestly he will forfeit his right to fees by the principal (subject to that being inequitable).

---

81   [2009] EWCA Civ 63, [2009] 2 All ER 666.

CHAPTER 13

Image Rights

Paul Fletcher and **Tom Grant** (Adelphi Sports Law); **Oliver Hunt**
and **Leon Farr** (Onside Law)

A   INTRODUCTION

13.1   'Image rights' are proprietary rights that arise from the commercial exploitation of a sporting personality's name and image. A sporting personality's 'image' can encompass a wide range of identifiable or personal characteristics including their name, nickname, likeness, photograph, autograph, initials, statements, endorsements, physical details and voice. This chapter only deals with image rights issues that arise in England and accordingly under English law.

13.2   The emergence of image rights within football has coincided with the growth of the Premier League, as the world's best players began to come to England to showcase their talent, resulting in the Premier League becoming a global brand.

13.3   In today's modern sporting world, image rights can hold enormous commercial value to sportspeople. Although image rights *per se* are not recognised as an intellectual property right under English law, they can be exploited commercially via a nexus of permissions and contract, and many of them are generally protected by way of the common law tort of passing off. Particularly well-known talent may also register trademarks to protect certain specific elements of their image rights.

13.4   In order to exploit their image rights, many sporting personalities will set up an image rights structure. To justify this, it must be apparent that the individual has an image of commercial value to sponsors, or has the potential to do so.

13.5   If a sporting personality has an image of commercial value and wants to hold this in a separate entity in order to protect and separately manage those rights, the image rights must be formally transferred/assigned to a company and should be assessed for value.

B   WHAT ARE IMAGE RIGHTS?

13.6   A player's ability to prevent the unauthorised use of their image rights and seek compensation from an infringing party, depends heavily upon whether, and to what extent, the law of a country recognises and protects image rights.

13.7   In stark contrast to the laws of many overseas jurisdictions, English law does not offer a specific, statute-based law protection in relation to image rights.

In France for example, 'personality rights' are protected under Article 9 of the French civil code, whereas in the United States (although varying from state to state) the right of publicity underpins the protection which purports to protect against uncompensated commercial exploitation of a player's image. In English law, instead, there is a reliance on a framework of statutory and common law intellectual property rights to prevent unauthorised exploitation. Players/image rights companies are left to rely upon a mixture of trademark and copyright law and the common law doctrine of passing off.

(a) Passing off

13.8   To succeed in a passing off claim, sporting personalities must show that they actively exploit their image by licensing their name and likeness in relation to a range of goods and services, and that by a brand using their name and likeness without consent, the brand's actions would lead consumers to believe that the sporting personality is endorsing that brand.

(i)   Eddie Irvine v Talksport Ltd[1]

13.9   Arguably the most important case for sporting personalities who wish to protect their image rights involved the former Formula 1 racing driver, Eddie Irvine.

13.10   Following talkSPORT's acquisition of the broadcasting rights to the FIA Formula 1 World Championship, the radio station was rebranded from Talk Radio to talkSPORT. During this time, talkSPORT had their marketing company send out over 1,000 promotional leaflets bearing a photograph of Mr Irvine. The photograph had been 'photoshopped' so that instead of holding a mobile phone to his ear, Irvine was holding a portable radio to which the words 'Talk Radio' had been added.

13.11   It was held by the court that there was no requirement for the claimant and defendant to be engaged in a common field of activity. If the actions of the defendant produced a false message which would be understood by the consumer to mean that a brand's products or services have been endorsed or recommended by the personality, then the personality can succeed in a claim of passing off.

13.12   Mr Irvine was able to successfully argue that the distribution of the promotional leaflets bearing his 'photoshopped' image falsely implied that he endorsed talkSPORT and constituted passing off.

13.13   This was a landmark case for the protection of the image rights of sporting personalities because previous actions had failed on the basis that there was a lack of a common field of activity or no real possibility of confusion in the mind of the general public.[2]

(ii)   Robyn (Rihanna) Fenty v Arcadia Group[3]

13.14   Rihanna, the famous pop star and style icon, sued Topshop (a member of the Arcadia Group and a well-known high street fashion retailer), for selling a T-shirt

---

1   [2003] EWCA Civ 423, [2003] 2 All ER 881, [2003] EMLR 538.
2   *McCulloch v Lewis A May (Produce Distributors)* [1947] 2 All ER 845.
3   [2013] EWHC 2310 (Ch).

bearing her image. The image had been photographed by an independent photographer and Topshop had obtained a license to use the image from the photographer, but not from Rihanna herself.

13.15   Rihanna argued that the sale of the T-shirt bearing her image infringed her rights on the grounds of passing off, on the basis that the general public would assume that she had licensed the use of her image to Topshop.

13.16   By contrast, Topshop argued that customers would buy the shirt because they liked the product and the image for their own individual qualities and that there was nothing on the T-shirt which represented it as an item of Rihanna's official merchandise. Topshop contended that the T-shirt was a high-quality fashion-led garment that was very different from standard pop star merchandise.

13.17   It was held that Rihanna had sufficient goodwill to succeed in a passing off action as she was a world famous pop star who ran very large merchandising and endorsement operations, in addition to being regarded as a style icon by many (predominantly young) females who constituted Topshop's target market).

13.18   The judge considered the wider issues surrounding Topshop's misrepresentation to the general public that Rihanna had in fact endorsed the sale of the T-shirt. For example, Topshop failed to explicitly set out that the T-shirt was not in fact endorsed by Rihanna on their website and two weeks before the shirt went on sale, Topshop had tweeted to say that Rihanna would be making a personal appearance at their flagship store.

13.19   As a result, it was found that a large number of purchasers were likely to have been deceived by Topshop into purchasing the T-shirt as a result. Topshop were forced to withdraw from selling the T-shirts. The *Rihanna* case marked the first occasion in which a high-profile personality had succeeded in the English courts in preventing the unauthorised use of their image on items of clothing.

13.20   Following on from the cases of *Irvine* and *Rihanna*, high-profile sporting personalities and celebrities who wish to further commercialise their image would be advised to trademark their name, likeness, signature, logos and any other identifiable characteristics that they are seeking to exploit as early as possible because a trademark infringement action is a far easier action to bring than that of passing off.

(b)   Copyright

13.21   UK copyright law automatically confers a property right on the author of original 'works', which can include literary, dramatic, musical or artistic works. The scope of 'artistic works' includes photographs and other graphical representations of a person's image (such as a cartoon drawing of a footballer). Copyright may also subsist in a player's signature, but there can be no copyright in his face[4] or his name,[5] because these are not original works. It is also important to note that copyright belongs to the author of the work (unless there has been a contractual assignment). In other words, sports personalities do not automatically own the copyright in works which bear their image. The copyright in a photograph of David Beckham will belong to the

---

4   *Merchandising Corpn of America Inc v Harpbond Inc* [1983] FSR 32.
5   *Exxon Corpn v Exxon Insurance Consultants International Ltd* [1982] Ch 119, [1981] 2 All ER 495.

photographer (absent an assignment). Likewise, the copyright in an audio recording of a media interview will belong to the interviewer. As a result, the law of copyright is of limited use to sporting personalities seeking to control the exploitation of their image, and is more suited to situations where a sporting personality wishes to protect their own creative output (for example, to prevent unauthorised copying of their autobiography) or, of course, for sports' rights holders protecting their products.

(c) Trade marks

13.22   A trademark is a registrable intellectual property right which comprises any sign capable of being reproduced graphically and capable of distinguishing goods and services of one undertaking from those of another undertaking. In other words, trademarks denote the origin of particular products and services. Sporting personalities can apply to register trademarks comprising their name, slogans, logo (amongst others), but such signs will only qualify for registration in the UK if they are sufficiently distinctive as to be 'capable of distinguishing goods and services of one undertaking from those of another'. For example, the famous footballers Alan Shearer and Ryan Giggs successfully registered their names as trademarks, but Mark Hughes was unable to do so on the grounds that his name was not distinctive enough.

13.23   In practice, it is difficult for sporting personalities to use trademarks to guard against the unauthorised use of their name/image, because the unauthorised use in question is often purely descriptive and does not indicate trade origin (and therefore does not constitute a trademark infringement under UK law). For example, if a publisher used Ryan Giggs' name and image on the front cover of a football annual, this use would not constitute an infringement because it simply describes the contents of the football annual and does not indicate that the annual was produced or published by Ryan Giggs.

(d) Human rights

13.24   The Human Rights Act 1998 (HRA 1998) incorporates the provisions of the European Convention for the Protection of Human Rights and Fundamental Freedoms ('the Convention') into English law. The relevance of this is that English courts are now obliged to take into account the rights provided by the Convention, principally for our purposes, the right to privacy.

13.25   Section 8(1) of the HRA 1998 states that:

> 'Everyone has the right to respect for his private and family life, his home and his correspondence.'

In a footballing context, this means that there is a positive obligation on the courts to ensure that there is sufficient protection from any outside interference in a player's private life.

13.26   The key case used to support such protection is *Douglas v Hello! Ltd*,[6] in which actor Michael Douglas sued Hello! Magazine for the unauthorised publication of the photographs from his wedding to actress Catherine Zeta-Jones. Douglas and

---

6   *Douglas v Hello! Ltd* [2001] 2 WLR 992.

Zeta-Jones were extremely careful when planning their wedding so as to not let any photographers into the venue, save for those belonging to OK! Magazine who had paid £1 million for world-wide exclusivity over the coverage of the wedding. Despite their best efforts, however, paparazzi were able to infiltrate the venue and take photographs of the couple which were later sold to Hello! Magazine. When Douglas brought his breach of confidence claim against Hello! Magazine, the court placed particular emphasis on the fact that Douglas and Zeta-Jones had gone to extreme lengths to protect the privacy of their wedding, despite otherwise courting the spotlight of the media in their day-to-day lives.[7] The courts made it clear that those who court media publicity in respect of their private lives would be unable to prevent publication of photographs or stories in respect of the same. This point was subsequently emphasised in the judgment handed down by Lord Woolf CJ in the case of *A v B plc* who stated at paragraph 11 that 'if you have courted public attention then you have less ground to object to the intrusion which follows'.[8] Whether the court will find that there is a reasonable expectation of privacy will depend on the way in which an individual has interacted with the media to date.

(e) Conclusion

13.27   Laddie J, the judge who oversaw the *Irvine* case, gave an interview shortly before his retirement, in which he stated his belief that it was a matter of time before an image right emerged in English law 'if not by legislation then by gradual expansion of the current law of passing off, or the development of a form of unfair competition'.[9] At present however, it remains the case that lawyers will continue to have to rely upon a bundle of contractual rights, trademark law and passing off case law to protect their client's image.

13.28   On the other hand, and even in the absence of a specific image right law, a party is able to contract to license what they may describe as their image in any event and shall then be able to at least enforce those rights by way of a contractual claim against another party in the event that they are breached.

C   FOOTBALL CLUBS AND IMAGE RIGHTS

13.29   In the context of football, clubs are constantly looking for ways to monetise and grow their commercial revenue and will attempt to enter into commercial partnership agreements in different territories throughout the world, allowing brands to be associated with the club and their high-profile players.

13.30   For example, during the 2017/18 football season, Manchester City announced upwards of 30 global and regional commercial partners, all seeking to use the image of its players in their advertising. Manchester United equally boast in excess of 80 global and regional commercial partners, ranging from the traditional official beer supplier, through to the more obscure official tractor partner. The diversification of Premier League clubs' commercial partners demonstrates the increasing commercial value to brands, both home and abroad, in being associated with the biggest names in world football.

---

7   [2003] 3 All ER 996, para 196.
8   *A v B & C* [2002] EWCA Civ 337.
9   (2006) 14(1) Sport and the Law Journal 12.

13.31   Given the ever-increasing value of a leading international player's image rights, football clubs are no longer solely interested in buying a player simply for their ability on the pitch. Instead, clubs are now paying greater attention to how they can exploit the player's image to boost their global reach, especially through using a player's social media. To emphasise the point, Real Madrid and Portugal superstar, Cristiano Ronaldo, currently has over 110 million followers on his Instagram account alone. Contrast this to his parent club, which boasts 55 million Instagram followers, an impressive total but still only half the number of followers of Ronaldo himself.

13.32   The disparity between a club's social media following and that of its highest-profile players is commonplace in football, albeit not to the same extent as Ronaldo and Real Madrid. The result of this means that, when buying a player, clubs now often also look to take control of a player's social media accounts as well as their personal image rights because, if managed correctly, they can obtain instant access to millions of additional people from around the world.

13.33   Players from countries such as Japan, Korea and China can open clubs up to valuable commercial partnerships within these territories, in addition to creating an interest amongst the general public that may result in clubs arranging profit generating pre-season tours to such regions.

13.34   It has, therefore, become crucial for top players and clubs to be very clear as to who owns which commercial rights. Clubs will insert clauses into image rights agreements with a view to obtaining as much control of a player's image rights as possible. On the other hand, the player, or the company to which he may have assigned his image rights, will try and retain as much control as possible.

13.35   On a practical level, as players' social media obligations to their club and commercial partners increase, it is becoming far more commonplace for players to employ specialist social media management companies to manage their personal accounts. These companies ensure that the players comply with their contractual obligations to make the minimum number of posts, or to use the correct hashtag when posting, and may also assist with ensuring that all posts are fully compliant with the relevant consumer protection and advertising regulations.

13.36   At the outset of a player's career, image rights are owned by the player (insofar as they cannot be exploited, licensed or assigned without his prior consent). In general, elite international players will license their image rights to three broad categories of licensee: (i) their club; (ii) their personal sponsors; and (iii) their national association. This creates challenges which players and their representatives face in managing the interwoven commercial programmes and the often competing interests of each category of licensee.

13.37   To ensure that clubs have at least some rights to use the image of every player on their books (and to reflect that clubs need some rights to reasonably conduct their day-to-day business) and to avoid requiring each player's individual consent when they join the club, the Premier League and Football League standard playing contracts grant the clubs some limited rights to use the player's image to promote themselves and their commercial partners. The Premier League and Football League regulations stipulate[10] that all playing contracts must be in the form of the relevant

---

10   Rule T.10 of the Premier League Rules 2017/18 and Rule 61.2 of the Football League Rules 2017/18 state that playing contracts between players and clubs must be in the relevant standard form. The Premier League and Football League standard playing contracts are contained at Form 18 and Form 19 respectively of the Premier League Handbook 2017/18.

standard playing contract, so the rights contained at Clause 4 of both contracts set out a minimum bundle of image rights which clubs are entitled to exploit in respect of every player in their squad. Some of the key rights contained in Clause 4 of the Premier League standard playing contract are reproduced below:[11]

> '4.1 ... the Player shall make himself available for up to six hours per week of which approximately half shall be devoted to community and public relations activities of the Club'
>
> '4.3 ... [the Player] shall not ... at any time during the term of this contract do anything to promote, endorse or provide promotional marketing or advertising services ... to any brand ... which conflict[s] or compete[s] with any of the Club's club branded or football related products (including the Strip) or any products, brand or services of the Club's two main sponsors/commercial partners'
>
> '4.6 The Player hereby grants to the Club the right to photograph the Player both individually and as a member of a squad and to use such photographs and the Player's Image in a Club Context in connection with the promotion of the Club ... so long as the use of the ... Player's Image ... shall be limited to no greater usage than the average for all players regularly in the Club's first team'

13.38   Although Clause 4 gives the clubs some ability to use the player's image, it is easy to see why clubs might consider these rights to be insufficient, particularly in relation to their most high-profile players. The six hours per week commitment required from the player in Clause 4.1 must be split equally between commercial and community appearances – leaving the clubs with only three hours per week to arrange for the player to work with the club's numerous commercial partners and its own marketing team. Furthermore, Clause 4.6 stipulates that the club's use of the player's image is limited to 'the average for all players regularly in the Club's first team', which further prevents the club from focusing its promotional activities around one or more star players.

13.39   Clause 4.3 prevents players from entering into personal endorsement deals (with the exception of boot and goalkeeper glove deals, which are carved out at Clause 4.2.2) to promote products or services which compete with club-branded products and/or the club's two 'main sponsors'. Initially, the restriction on players promoting products which compete with 'club-branded products' seems rather wide when one considers the breadth of products comprising many Premier League clubs' official merchandise ranges. A quick glance at the Liverpool FC club shop shows club-branded aftershave, chocolate and Bluetooth speakers. But in reality, clubs would struggle to rely on Clause 4.3 to prevent a player from entering a particular personal deal because of the difficulty in showing that the products being promoted by the player truly compete with the club's sale of the corresponding club-branded products. The brands with the marketing budget to sponsor top-level footballers are generally too large and established to be considered a genuine competitor of club merchandise. For example, a club is unlikely to be able to use Clause 4.3 to prevent the player from endorsing Rolex on the basis that this would compete with the sale of club-branded watches in the club shop.

13.40   The non-compete obligation in Clause 4.3 is also limited to the club's two main sponsors. This begs the question of what 'main sponsors' means in this context and also the question of which party is responsible for determining the identity of the two main sponsors. In any event, Clause 4.3 offers no protection to the majority

---

11   See Form 19 of the Premier League Handbook 2017/18.

of the club's commercial partners, meaning that in negotiations with sponsors, clubs cannot guarantee that their star player will not enter into a personal endorsement deal to promote one of their competitors.

13.41   Given the problems set out above, it is clear to see why clubs might find it attractive to pay some or all of their players an additional fee in return for certain enhanced rights, such as access to their social media accounts and additional appearances over and above the three-hour commitment in the standard playing contract. Clause 4.11 of the standard contract specifically permits clubs to enter into separate image rights agreements with their players:

> 'Nothing in this clause 4 shall prevent the Club from entering into other arrangement additional or supplemental hereto or in variance hereof in relation to advertising, marketing and/or promotional services with the Player or with or for all or some of the Club's players (including the Player) from time to time.'

13.42   As the notion of image rights began to emerge, HM Revenue and Customs' (HMRC) initial stance was that image rights structures were unnecessary and that Clause 4 of the Premier League standard playing contract provided sufficient coverage for clubs to exploit a player's image rights. But as set out above, the limited nature of the rights granted to clubs under Clause 4 means that in practice, it can be very difficult for clubs to satisfy the demands of the majority of their commercial partners unless they enter into separate image rights contracts with their players.

13.43   In negotiating an image rights agreement, there is a natural conflict between, on the one hand, the interests of the player, who will seek to retain as much control over his image rights as possible, and on the other hand the club, which will seek to maximise the scope of its rights for use in its own promotional activities and those of its commercial partners. Throughout any negotiation, players, clubs and their representatives must ensure that the agreement is drafted carefully and with their other commercial partners in mind, so that the various licensees and packages of image rights co-exist harmoniously and do not conflict.

13.44   For example, a player may have a pre-existing personal deal with Coca Cola and then decide to join a new club who has a shirt sponsorship with Pepsi. In addition, the player's national team might have an official partnership with Lucozade. The player's representatives should anticipate such situations and ensure that they are managed properly in his image rights agreement with his club, his personal endorsement agreement with the brand, and in any collective or individual image rights agreement he might have with his national association. From time to time, the commercial conflicts are so stark that significant carve-outs are required in the image rights agreement to exclude the player from any obligation to promote a particular commercial partner of the club. For example, when Zlatan Ibrahimovic joined Manchester United, the player's pre-existing personal deal with Swedish car manufacturer Volvo meant that Manchester United were not able to utilise their talismanic striker on any club advertising for their sponsor Chevrolet.

13.45   In addition to the above, it is also worth noting that the Premier League Rules place obligations on clubs to ensure that their players comply with the requirements of broadcasters and other official partners of the league. For example, Premier League Rule K.121 requires clubs to ensure that the players make themselves available for a half-day period before the start of each season to enable television broadcasters to capture footage for use in their 'dynamic line-ups' before each match.

D   BENEFITS OF AN IMAGE RIGHTS STRUCTURE

(a)   Limited liability status

13.46   An image rights company enjoys limited liability status, and therefore offers better protection in the event of being sued for breach of contract. For example, if a player was to cause embarrassment to a brand then, unless the player has signed a personal guarantee or letter of inducement, the player will benefit from the brand only being able to sue the image rights company for the cash and assets it possesses. In a culture where there are no hiding places for the misdemeanours of sporting personalities, this alone can be enough of a reason for a player's image rights to be assigned to a company and exploited by the company.

(b)   Tax

13.47   Football players are taxed in the normal way through HMRC's pay as you earn scheme (PAYE) on any salary from their employer club. Tax is deducted at the time of payment by the club. If a player has an image rights structure in place, however, it is possible for the player, or his image rights company, to be taxed in a more tax advantageous way in relation to separate endorsement deals and to an extent in relation to separate image rights payments from the club to the image rights company.

13.48   In order to ensure that players and clubs do not exploit such structures, HMRC monitor the commercial income of clubs and the level of payments paid by clubs in relation to image rights.[12]

(c)   Contract management

13.49   Players at the highest level can often have a number of endorsement agreements in place with brands. This makes managing the player's personal appearance calendar and social media obligations, keeping a record of the rights granted in particular brand categories and chasing the licence fees and entitlements to bonus payments (for example in football boot deals, bonus payments based on appearances or goals) a full-time job. By having an image rights company in place it is possible for the image rights company to hire employees to undertake such activities, helping to ensure that neither the image rights company nor the player acts in breach of existing endorsement agreements and fulfils all obligations that are required.

E   KEY CLAUSES WITHIN AN IMAGE RIGHTS AGREEMENT

13.50   When it comes to image rights, there has recently been a change in focus from the previous player-driven position of trying to achieve a greater net salary whilst protecting a player's commercial rights as much as possible, to a position of most leading Premier League clubs now seeking to take as much control of the image rights of their players as possible in order to maximise commercial revenue.

---

12   For a more detailed discussion of tax and image rights, see Chapter 14, Taxation.

13.51   In order to best protect the club, there are a number of must-have inclusions in an image rights document, some of which are outlined below.

(a) Morality clause

13.52   Morality clauses usually cover a number of eventualities, including doping, gambling, alcohol misuse and general bad behaviour. This is a vital term across sponsorship and endorsement deals as well as in image rights contracts. A morality clause may be relied upon when sporting personalities act in such a way that their commercial value to a club or brand is seriously damaged, along with their own reputation. The clause will usually entitle the brand or club to suspend the agreement whilst investigations are carried out or terminate the agreement.

13.53   The most recent and high-profile examples of this happening to a sporting personality include Lance Armstrong, who lost seven sponsors including Nike, Trek Bicycles, Giro, and Oakley following his doping scandal; Tiger Woods, who reputedly lost in the region of $22 million in endorsement deals following his well-publicised extra martial affairs; and Maria Sharapova who lost Nike, Porsche and Tag Heuer the day after confessing to failing a drugs test. Sponsors withdrew their association with these athletes for commercial and moral reasons. As is the same with sponsors, football clubs ultimately have the final say as to whether they wish to rely on a morality clause to terminate an image rights contract. In practice, however, this is rarely done in football unless the misdemeanour is particularly serious. A typical morality clause may be structured as follows:

> 'Without prejudice to any rights arising as a matter of law, the [Club/brand] may terminate this Agreement with immediate effect by giving written notice to the [Company]/[Player] in the event that …
>
> the Player conducts himself in a manner that is considered by the [Club/brand] to offend against decency or morality or which materially reduces the value of the Image Rights or causes any licensee to be held in public ridicule, scorn or contempt …; or
>
> the Player receives a punishment from any competent body, including any governing body, in respect of any gambling, alcohol or drugs-relate matter; or
>
> the Player is [charged]/[convicted] of any criminal offence …'

13.54   With regards to criminal penalties, the club/brand will look to include a clause that allows them to terminate should the player be 'charged' with a criminal offence. By contrast, the player will want this watered down so that their contract can only be terminated in the event that they are 'convicted' of a criminal offence.

(b) Right of reduction

13.55   The club will, understandably, want to include a right of reduction clause in the event that the player acts in such a way that harms his commercial value, but does not obliterate it completely. A right of reduction arguably allows for the club to deduct a larger sum of money from the player than would otherwise be possible by way of a fine under the playing contract.

13.56   If such a clause is requested by a club, the player/image rights company should seek to include a mechanism whereby an independent third party expert is required to adjudicate, on an informal but binding basis, over the level of damage that has been done to the commercial value of the player. This will avoid clubs having carte blanche to reduce payments. Furthermore, if acting for the player, it is good practice to include wording that would prevent the retrospective application of a reduction to any payments already received by the image rights company.

13.57 The club usually seeks to suspend any image rights payments due to be made to the player during any period for which the player is on loan at another club. Equally, the player will want to resist the suspension of any payments during any loan period (although it is a difficult argument to make given the rights have little value during this period) and certainly should refuse to accept any termination right for the club which is triggered by the player going out on loan.

(c) Personal guarantee

13.58 Finally, the club may want to ensure that the player signs a personal guarantee or letter of inducement to stand behind the obligations with which the image rights company has agreed to comply. This means that in the event that the company fails to procure that the player fulfils his obligations to the club, the club has a possible cause of action against the player personally, instead of just the image rights company. For those advising the player, it is important to ensure that the personal guarantee or letter of inducement does not allow the club to circumvent the provision of the image rights agreement with the club and expose the player to liabilities which may otherwise be excluded or limited under the terms of the image rights licence.

13.59 In order to best protect the player in an image rights agreement, we have summarised some of the key clauses and issues to consider below:

(i) Limiting scope of use by 'context'

13.60 One well-established method which has developed in football image rights agreements to help manage some of the contractual challenges described in this chapter is the concept of using a player's image in a particular 'context'. The agreement will usually make a distinction between using a player's image in either: (i) a 'club context' (ie in connection with the name, colours, strip and/or other identifying characteristics of the club); or (ii) a 'personal context' (ie not in a 'club context'). Where the player has been called up to play for their national team, the 'international context' is also relevant. Some clubs will be limited to using the image rights in a club context, whilst others may be granted rights to use in a personal context.

(ii) Existing personal agreements and 'protected category' – boot deals and glove deals

13.61 Any obligations on the player to refrain from promoting products which compete with any club partner should contain a carve out to allow the player to fulfil his obligations under his existing personal deals (and any renewals or extensions of those contracts). It is also important that the player retains the right to enter into personal deals in a certain 'protected category' (which will usually cover 'tools of the trade' such as boots and gloves) and the right to use those products at all times – regardless of whether or not the suppliers compete with the club's official kit supplier. The challenge involves the inevitable conflict between the club's needs – to minimise the extent of the protected category – and the needs of the boot supplier, which would typically manufacture a huge range of products, and its desire to include as many of those products as possible in its deal with the player.

(iii)   *Future personal agreements outside the 'protected category'*

13.62   As a general rule, the player should seek to retain complete discretion over new personal deals (ie which use the player's image in a personal context) entered into during the term, but clubs will often seek to limit the type of personal deals which the player can execute and may also demand some degree of control or consent right over the player's choice of new personal sponsors.

13.63   The club's primary concern is to protect its own commercial operations and the relationship with its commercial partners, particularly its most lucrative sponsors. Therefore, clubs will seek to restrict the player's freedom to sign personal deals as much as possible to reduce the risk of the player promoting a product or service which competes with one of its commercial partners. A negotiation will be required whereby the player seeks to narrow that restriction, often by way of reference to sector or territory.

13.64   Some overseas players may wish to retain the ability to license their image freely for third parties to exploit in the player's home territory jurisdiction. This can become a battleground as his image in that territory may have enhanced value for the club, whilst the player may feel his team is better equipped to land personal deals there. However, territory-specific deals are rare in today's world of global internet access, as they can complicate the relationship between the club and its existing partners and hamper the club's ability to secure major new partners looking to exploit a 'clean' set of rights worldwide.

13.65   In lieu of, or in addition to, the various complicated carve-outs and exceptions which are commonly found in modern image rights agreements, some clubs may seek the simplicity and certainty of an approval right over some or all of the player's new personal deals. For some clubs, this might involve a relatively modest obligation on the player to keep the club informed about new personal deals he proposes to enter, on the condition that the club retains an absolute approval right over particular types of personal deals which risk harming its relationship with one or more important club partners.

13.66   On the other hand, some clubs take a more aggressive approach and effectively require the player to give up control of their personal sponsorship programme to the club for the duration of the term. Clubs may also seek to restrict and control the player's interactions with the media and/or prevent him from writing an autobiography during the term.

13.67   Increasingly, clubs are not only concerned with protecting their existing commercial partners but wish to actively leverage their commercial contacts to create new personal deals for the player and share in the commercial benefits of those deals, via a royalty split or revenue share mechanism contained in the image rights agreement. Clubs may also wish to control the commercial rights to any revenue in the player's digital channels (social media, website etc) and the right to influence and control the content circulated on those channels.

CHAPTER 14

Taxation

Graham Shear and **Andrew Street** (Bryan Cave Leighton Paisner)

A INTRODUCTION

14.1 As the football industry has become increasingly prosperous, for players, intermediaries and investors alike, greater scrutiny of its tax affairs has followed from both the general public and public authorities, including various tax and revenue authorities[1] and, ultimately, relevant courts and tax tribunals.

14.2 The recent regulatory and criminal investigatory focus on tax matters in football was provided with significant impetus by the 2016 Football Leaks publication[2] and appeared to reach critical mass in 2017 as two of the world's most famous players, Cristiano Ronaldo and Lionel Messi, found themselves subject to criminal proceedings in Spain for issues relating to their tax affairs. In respect of the latter, Messi and his father were found guilty of defrauding the Spanish Tax Agency (Hacienda) of €4.1 million in tax by diverting income into special purpose vehicles in Belize and Uruguay.[3]

14.3 While the player ultimately avoided a custodial sentence following conviction, the Messi case demonstrated the cross-jurisdictional scope of taxation issues arising from the contractual and financial affairs of international footballers, and somewhat inevitably therefore attracted the subsequent interest of the European Parliament Committee of Inquiry into Money laundering, tax avoidance and tax evasion (PANA).[4] Scrutiny of taxation in football is undoubtedly here to stay, and may accelerate further still, subject to the outcome of the Ronaldo case[5] and Her Majesty Revenue and Customs' (HMRC) 'Operation Loom'.[6]

---

1 By way of illustration, HM Revenue and Customs (HMRC) indicated to the House of Commons Public Accounts Committee (PAC) in December 2016 that, at that time, 43 players, 8 agents and 12 football clubs were under inquiry on the issue of image rights (see para **14.10** below). This had expanded to 90 players, 13 agents, and 38 clubs, by September 2017, per HM Treasury's Answer to the Written Question of Peter Dowd MP (*Written Question 6165*).
2 The Football Leaks project was the work of the European Investigative Collaborations (EIC), comprising Germany's *Der Spiegel*, the UK's *Sunday Times*, Spain's *El Mundo*, and the Netherlands' *NRC*.
3 The verdict was upheld on appeal by the Spanish Supreme Court Criminal Chamber in *Appeal No: 1729/2016/Judgment No: 374/2017.*
4 See the PANA Committee meeting for 26 September 2017, [during which representatives of FIFA and UEFA were subject to questioning by various European Members of Parliament.
5 The *Ronaldo* case remains pending as at the date of this text.
6 'Operation Loom' gave rise to HMRC's raids on West Ham United and Newcastle United in April 2017 relating to HMRC's investigation of possible tax evasion offences arising from agency fee payments.

14.4   Failure to obtain proper professional advice on taxation can have severely adverse implications for clubs and footballers. There can be no better illustration of the need for accurate and appropriate advice than the case of Glasgow Rangers Football Club, whose wrongful use of an employee benefit trust (EBT) for the purposes of paying its playing staff, incorrectly believing it would reduce the club's liability for income tax, ultimately led to the company's liquidation.[7] Players and those representing them will also be mindful of the censure faced by all of those associated with the Rangers EBT, including their professional advisers, and the requirement to obtain proper professional advice on taxation therefore cannot be overstated.

14.5   This chapter does not intend to provide a comprehensive guide to all forms of taxation issues which affect clubs and individuals within the football industry. As the Rangers case aptly demonstrated, specialist tax advice will often be required on the legal implications of bespoke tax structuring which individuals or organisations enter into and the consequences of getting it wrong can be grave. Moreover, there are a range of corporate tax issues which will affect clubs specifically (including land transactions entered into by clubs, clubs' application of various tax reliefs to their trading profits for the purposes of their corporation tax calculations, and the tax implications of the domicile of clubs' holding and operating companies), which are adequately covered by the range of existing texts on the subject of taxation and which are not specific to the football industry.

14.6   Instead, this chapter provides an outline of the common tax issues that sports law practitioners and their clients within the football industry can expect to encounter under UK tax law, and which are broadly specific to football, namely: the regulatory obligations imposed upon clubs under the Rules of the Football Association and its various professional leagues, and the tax implications of image rights structures, agents fees, and employee benefits in kind.

B   CLUB REGULATORY OBLIGATIONS

14.7   Under the FA's Rules, all payments made to players by clubs must be made by the club itself (and not any third party) and must be fully recorded in the club's accounts.[8] All salaried payments must be subject to PAYE and National Insurance Contributions (NICs).[9] Contracts of employment between the club and any of its employees, including players, must specify that all emoluments due are paid to the employee concerned and not to any third party entity acting on behalf of the player or employee.[10]

14.8   The broad effect of these provisions of the FA Rules is that footballers (in England at least) are required to be employees of the clubs to which they are contracted and the relevant provisions of the UK tax code relating to employment income will apply. Footballers cannot act in the capacity of self-employed contractors and clubs are required to make the necessary PAYE deductions from salary payments made to players and to account to HMRC for PAYE and NICs.

---

7   That the Rangers EBT scheme attracted income tax despite amounts being payable by the club to a third party trust rather than directly to the players was upheld by the Supreme Court in *RFC 2012 Plc (in liquidation) (formerly The Rangers Football Club Plc) v Advocate General for Scotland* [2017] UKSC 45.
8   Football Association Rules of Association Rule C1(b)(v).
9   FA Rule C1(b)(vi).
10   FA Rule C1(c)(ii).

14.9   Premier League clubs are also subject to further regulatory obligations pursuant to which they are required to provide ongoing reporting to the League that they are no more than 28 days in arrears with their payments to HMRC.[11] Failure to keep up to date with liabilities to HMRC may, in certain instances, lead to the Premier League imposing sanctions upon a club, which may include the imposition of a set budget or a ban upon new player registrations.[12] Particulars of payments made relating to the image rights of a player are also required to be expressly set out in the player's contract with the club under the Premier League Rules.[13] These obligations are broadly mirrored within the English Football League's Rules,[14] which also confer the right upon the Football League to impose a suspension from competition upon a club which fails to comply with its obligation to report its liabilities to HMRC to the League.[15]

C   IMAGE RIGHTS

14.10   'Image rights' structures form a key part of the contractual arrangements entered into between many football clubs and the players whom they employ.[16] Typically the agreements entered into between a club and player will distinguish between the elements of payment which are made by the club to the player in respect of his playing duties as salary and the elements of his remuneration which reflect the commercial exploitability of his image ('image rights payments').

14.11   In certain instances players may assign their image rights to third party image rights companies (IRCs) in order for them to be exploited by the IRC. While English law does not recognise any intellectual property in an individual's personal image *per se*,[17] 'image rights', as understood in the sporting context, refer to a bundle of intellectual property rights including contractual rights, registered trademarks, passing off goodwill and copyright.[18] It is these rights which may be assigned to an IRC. The issue of such arrangements, including the exploitation of a player's image rights by IRCs, was subject to notable judicial consideration in 2000 as described at para **14.12** below.

(a)   The decision in *Sports Club*

14.12   The leading case in respect of the tax treatment of image rights arrangements is *Sports Club plc v Inspector of Taxes*,[19] which was published in a form which anonymised the taxpayer parties but is widely understood and known to relate to a leading English football club.[20] Despite being nearly two decades old, during which

---

11   Premier League Rule E.23.
12   Premier League Rule E.25 (which incorporates Rule E.15 in instances of breach).
13   Premier League Rule T.20.
14   EFL Rule 17.
15   EFL Rule 17.6.
16   See Chapter 13, Image Rights for a more detailed discussion of how image rights are structured and transacted, including details of the benefit to Premier League clubs in entering into such arrangements, due to the structure of the standard Premier League Playing contract (particularly clause 4).
17   Per Lord Hoffman in *Douglas v Hello! Ltd* [2007] UKHL 21 at para 124; Kitchen LJ in *Fenty v Arcadia Group Brands Ltd* [2015] EWCA Civ 3 at para 29.
18   HMRC has recognised this approach in CG68405.
19   SpC253, [2000] STC (SCD) 443.
20   HMRC confirmed that the decision related to a football club in HMRC Employment Income Manual (EIM) 00734; and it was widely reported at the time to relate to Arsenal FC.

time the football industry has changed almost beyond recognition, *Sports Club* remains good law and is the definitive authority on the proper tax treatment of image rights.[21]

14.13 *Sports Club* concerned two individuals at the football club in question ('Sports'), referred to within the judgment as 'Evelyn' and 'Jocelyn', both of whom were high-profile players who entered into image rights arrangements with the club. Both Evelyn and Jocelyn had pre-existing arrangements through which they had assigned their image rights to IRCs during the course of their playing careers outside of the UK. The IRCs were actively involved in the marketing and promotion of both players with a range of third party commercial partners pursuant to underlying agreements between the players and IRCs, which required each player to provide his promotional services to the IRC in order to facilitate the IRC's exploitation of the rights.

14.14 Upon signing both players in 1995, Sports agreed to enter into employment contracts with either player and, at the same time, concurrent agreements with both IRCs to which the respective player had assigned his image rights. The concurrent promotional agreements allowed for the commercial exploitation of the image of the player in question by Sports with third party companies, for example in relation to endorsement deals.

14.15 The Revenue issued a notice of determination in April 1997 to Sports which estimated the amount of tax due from Sports in its capacity as the employer of the two players and taxed certain amounts of income of the two players as 'other emoluments', these amounts being the sums due to the IRCs under the various agreements. Sports and the two players appealed the notice issued by the Revenue.

14.16 The issues for determination in *Sports Club* were: (i) whether the payments made by Sports under the various agreements with the IRCs were emoluments from the employment of the players and so chargeable to income tax by virtue of s 19 of the Income and Corporation Taxes Act 1988 (ICTA 1988); (ii) if the payments to the IRCs were not emoluments from the employment of the players, whether they were benefits in kind pursuant to ICTA 1988, s 154; and (iii) in respect of Evelyn only, if the payments were neither emoluments from the player's employment nor benefits in kind, whether they amounted to a retirement benefits scheme within the meaning of ICTA 1988, s 595.[22]

14.17 While the types of rights assigned to the IRCs by Jocelyn and Evelyn continue to be referred to by the football industry (and its advisers) as 'image rights', the Special Commissioners noted that, as stated at para **14.11** above, English law does not recognise any property in a person's image, and accordingly referred to the various agreements as 'promotional agreements', which concerned 'promotion, publicity, marketing, and advertising'.[23]

14.18 Sports and the two players were successful in their appeal, which now provides the legal basis for image rights arrangements as they currently exist in football. The Special Commissioners held that each agreement entered into was a genuine commercial agreement with an independent value, which the parties

---

21 HMRC have accepted that *Sports Club* remains the leading authority on the issue of taxation of image rights: see PAC Thirty-sixth Report of Session 2016–17 q23 response from HMRC.
22 The relevant current legislation relating to emoluments of employment is the Income Tax (Earnings and Pensions) Act 2003, s 62(2) under which the law is broadly the same as pursuant to ICTA 1988.
23 At para 8.

could seek to enforce, and could not be considered a smokescreen for additional remuneration. The Revenue's contention that the promotional agreements were in effect little more than a smokescreen for payments to be made to the players by Sports in any event, and which did not have any independent value, was accordingly rejected.

14.19 In terms of the nature of the rights being acquired by Sports, and the legitimacy of the agreements founded upon those rights, the Special Commissioners held the following at paragraphs 78–79:

> 'We also adopt [the respondents' counsel's] suggestion that what in practice Sports was getting from the promotional agreements was a series of contractual obligations both positive and negative; positive in the sense that the player would, if called upon to do so, do certain things like endorsing products or going to photoshoots and negative in the sense that he could not undertake such activities for others. Again we accept the suggestion of the respondent's counsel that the promotional agreements were for the personal endorsement of products and the like.
>
> In our view the promotional agreements were agreements to provide promotional services. They were genuine commercial agreements which the parties could seek to enforce.'

14.20 The Special Commissioners therefore held that none of the payments passing under the promotional agreements entered into between Sports and the IRCs could be classified as payments for the employment of Jocelyn or Evelyn (ie emoluments), given they had independent value and were independently enforceable, and therefore were not chargeable to income tax and should not have been treated as appropriate income tax deductions by Sports from the payments made to Evelyn and Jocelyn.

(b) Developments following *Sports Club*

14.21 While *Sports Club* provided sufficient clarity, and comfort, that image rights arrangements could be held to have a value independent from a player's playing activities, the scope of the application of this principle has been subject to change, and indeed misuse, in the years since.

14.22 Whether or not the player's image rights have been assigned to an IRC may affect the tax liability which he incurs since receipts of monies by the IRC relating to 'image rights' will be taxed at the applicable corporation tax rate, while the individual will, in the absence of such an assignment, be subject to income tax in the usual course (albeit that the receipt will not be deemed an emolument of employment, in line with *Sports Club*).

14.23 While the principle in Sports Club established that 'image rights' were capable of being dealt with separately from a player's salaried remuneration, and could be assigned to IRCs, many clubs and players entered into agreements which allocated disproportionate amounts of a player's overall remuneration to image rights as opposed to playing salary.[24] Given the formation of IRCs, and the proportion of payments relating to image rights being subject to corporation tax rather than income tax, the effect of the decision in *Sports Club* was to provide an opportunity for players to reduce their overall tax liability, often without genuine or proper justification.

---

24   Manchester United admitted in the SEC prospectus for its 2010 bond issue that it was subject to HMRC investigation relating to image rights allocations.

14.24   HMRC reached a settlement with numerous Premier League clubs in 2012, following reports that numerous clubs had entered into agreements where an artificially high amount of player remuneration had been allocated to the image rights proportion of their agreements with their respective clubs.[25]

14.25   A further agreement was reached between HMRC and the Premier League in 2015, which provided guidance on the extent of remuneration which can reasonably be attributed to image rights by a club in total and in respect of each player. In relation to the former (often referred to as the Club Cap), clubs are limited in the total amount that they can pay under all the image rights arrangements they enter into with players to 15% of their commercial revenue. For each player subject to arrangements of this type, image rights payments should not exceed 20% of the player's total pay from the club (the Player Cap).[26]

14.26   In light of the House of Commons Public Affairs Committee's (PAC) scrutiny of image rights, and HMRC's agreement to the PAC's recommendation that government ministers be provided with its views on how to reform the law relating to such structures, this area is likely to be subject both to increasing HMRC enforcement action and/or reform.[27] Indeed, HMRC issued guidance on image rights and reporting obligation on 16 August 2017. In order to avoid potential litigation against HMRC, clubs, intermediaries and players will all need to keep abreast of the changing landscape.

(c)   Income tax issues relating to image rights

14.27   Receipts relating to image rights may not, following *Sports Club*, be emoluments of employment, but they may still be liable to incur income tax charges, since royalties and other income from intellectual property that have a source in the UK are liable to income tax.[28] Some or all of the intellectual property rights that make up the image rights assigned to an IRC are likely to meet the statutory definition of intellectual property.[29]

14.28   Should players based in the UK wish to set up IRCs and to enter into assignments of their 'image rights' to those IRCs, they have little choice but to use a UK company for the purposes of such assignment and arrangement. Assignment to an offshore vehicle may still attract income tax in the UK notwithstanding any intention that the local rate of corporation tax in the jurisdiction in which the offshore entity is resident should apply.[30]

---

25   http://www.telegraph.co.uk/sport/football/news/9082870/Premier-League-sides-forced-to-pay-back-millions-of-pounds-in-tax-after-crackdown-on-image-rights-deals.html (accessed February 2018).
26   The terms of the 2015 deal between HMRC and the Premier League have not ever been formally published by either party but have been widely reported since the Football Leaks publication. The guidelines have neither formal regulatory nor legislative status, but provide helpful guidance on the type of image rights structures which are presently likely to attract HMRC scrutiny.
27   In fact, the PAC specifically recommended in its 36th Report of the 2016/17 Parliamentary Session that the government should take urgent action to address image rights taxation and that such action should be included in the next Finance Bill. HMRC has subsequently issued further guidance under EIM00731 but no specific provision was made within the September 2017 Finance Bill for reform of image rights.
28   Part 5 of the Income Tax (Trading and Other Income) Act 2005 (ITTOIA 2005).
29   ITTOIA 2005, s 579(2) provides the definition of 'intellectual property'.
30   Income Tax Act 2007 (ITA 2007), s 720 and the general anti-avoidance provisions which follow. Note also the provisions of the Criminal Finances Act 2017, discussed at [**14.39**].

14.29   To the extent that image rights payments are made by a club either to a player individually or to the IRC to which he has assigned his image rights on an annual basis, that club may be under an obligation to deduct sums representing the income tax liability at source.[31] Such withholding tax obligations may also apply to image rights payments made to players who are non-UK residents (on which see para **14.35** below onwards). Clubs should therefore assess the nature of the payments being made to players or IRCs under image rights agreements to determine whether any withholding tax obligation arises. In particular, where payments are made by clubs in respect of image rights, those clubs should take steps to ensure that any payments made to players or IRCs are commensurate with the extent of a player's viable commercial image.[32]

14.30   To the extent that the terms of an image rights transaction do not reflect a player's genuine commercial profile, clubs may become subject to enforcement action by HMRC seeking repayment of sums which ought to have been withheld at source in respect of the income tax liability which was incurred. Such enforcement and litigation may involve allegations by HMRC that the terms of the relevant agreements are little more than a sham intended to obfuscate the true nature of the transaction and thereby to conceal the tax liability which was in fact incurred.

14.31   However, following the 2017 decision of the First-tier Tribunal Tax Chamber in *Hull City AFC (Tigers) Limited v HMRC*,[33] if HMRC wishes to allege that the express terms of an image rights transaction are a sham, the burden of proof will fall upon HMRC to make out that allegation rather than the taxpayer being required to prove the validity of the terms entered into. HMRC will usually be required to prove dishonesty or deceit in order to succeed in arguing sham[34] and tax tribunals may have little basis to ignore the express terms of an agreement absent evidence of dishonest or deceit.[35]

(d)   Capital gains tax issues relating to image rights

14.32   Any assignment of image rights by a player to an IRC needs to make clear precisely what rights are being assigned, given the position under English law relating to the recognition of property in an individual's image and HMRC's internal position that there needs to be a commercial justification for differentiating between payment for performance of duties of the employment and the promotional services (ie the image rights).[36]

14.33   To the extent it is required, the assignment of the image rights from the player to the IRC should seek to value those rights that may need to be valued, if

---

31   ITA 2007, Pt 15, Ch 6.
32   This is particularly the case given HMRC continues to take an active interest in the structure of such payments and whether the transaction reflects the commercial reality of the player's situation (see paras **14.23–14.25** below).
33   *Hull City AFC (Tigers) Ltd v The Commissioners for Her Majesty's Revenue and Customs* [2017] UKFTT 629 (TC). This case relates to the image rights deals entered into between Hull City and the Brazilian player Geovanni, who joined the club in 2008. The litigation has not yet reached final determination, and HMRC had not as at the date of the 2017 case management decision pleaded sham.
34   In line with the established test for sham in *Snook v London and West Riding Investments Ltd* [1967] 2 QB 786.
35   *Hull City v HMRC* at para 161.
36   Per HMRC EIM00738 consideration should be given to whether the player in question has a sufficiently prominent image which justifies the entering into of an 'image rights' arrangement.

applicable, for capital gains tax (CGT) purposes. HMRC's current position is that to the extent only a contractual right to call upon the player's promotional services is being assigned to the IRC (as was the case in *Sports Club*), this will often be a right which has been created only for the purposes of the formation of the IRC and will not have had a value as at the date of it being granted to the IRC by the player, although there may be a value to that contractual right if the company disposes of it to a third party.[37] Accordingly, subject to the nature of the contractual obligations that have been created, it is possible that no chargeable gain may have arisen if the contractual obligation is a new one created for the benefit of the IRC for the first time (although much will obviously turn on the specifics of the arrangement entered into).

14.34   HMRC also takes the position that if the right being transferred is goodwill, an assignment may be possible if the goodwill has vested in a business (by way of an established IRC having already undertaken activities to exploit the player's image). This transfer of business goodwill may attract a CGT charge.[38] To the extent trademarks are being transferred as part of the assignment to an IRC, these will need to be valued to assess whether a chargeable gain has in fact arisen.[39]

(e)   Non-UK domiciled players and image rights

14.35   While image rights are not recognised in English law per se (see para **14.11** above), they are in many jurisdictions outside of the UK, including Germany, France, and over 30 US States.[40] To the extent that a jurisdiction recognises image rights as a property right rather than a personal right, those rights may amounts to assets for the purposes of s 21 of the Taxation of Chargeable Gains Act 1992 (TCGA 1992), but the position will vary from jurisdiction to jurisdiction.

14.36   As such, the divestment of such rights by a non-UK domiciled player may in principle attract a tax liability for a chargeable gain, but much will depend on the location of the image rights asset itself and what is actually being transferred. If a non-UK image right is deemed to be a non-UK situs asset for the purposes of the rules that determine the location of an asset,[41] a disposal offshore by a non-UK domiciled individual to an offshore company is not within the charge to CGT, unless there is a remittance to the UK.[42] To the extent the rights actually relate to commercial exploitation of the player's image in the UK (for example, due to his playing for a Premier League club), the asset may be held to be UK based for the purposes of CGT. In practice, many non-UK national players may for this reason seek to set up both UK vehicles relating to their image within the UK and offshore vehicles relating to their global image, so that their image rights are 'carved up' for tax calculation purposes.

14.37   Clubs (or indeed sponsors) may also be subject to a duty to deduct tax at source when a payment for the use of image rights is made to a non-UK resident,[43] which may include either a player who has recently moved to an English club or where the player in question is a foreign national whose image rights structures are

---

37   HMRC Capital Gains Manual CG68465.
38   TCGA 1992, s 21(1).
39   HMRC Capital Gains Manual CG68465.
40   See HMRC Capital Gains Manual CG68435.
41   TCGA1992, s 275.
42   HMRC Capital Gains Manual CG68440.
43   ITA 2007, s 906.

incorporated in foreign jurisdictions.[44] Clubs or sponsors making payments under image rights agreements to foreign domiciled parties (whether individuals or IRCs) should therefore proceed with caution and specialist advice is likely to be required.[45]

14.38   The party making payment under an image rights contract, whether a football club or a boot sponsor, to an overseas individual or entity will therefore need to consider the nature of the payments being made and to ensure that there is no requirement to withhold tax.

(f)   Criminal Finances Act 2017

14.39   Parties making payments to IRCs also need to be aware of their obligations since 30 September 2017 under Part 3 of the Criminal Finances Act 2017 (CFA 2017), which imposes corporate criminal sanctions upon organisations which fail to prevent the facilitation of tax evasion by any employee or intermediary. Clubs may arguably be liable for such offences if, for example, they deliberately and dishonestly make payments in respect of image rights to offshore IRCs which have been wrongfully set up by UK domiciled players with the intention of evading tax.[46] Clubs will therefore need to conduct risk assessments to identify where the risks of facilitation lie and then implement reasonable procedures to prevent the facilitation of tax evasion, whether in relation to image rights arrangement or otherwise.

D   BENEFITS IN KIND – PI I D

14.40   Since players are required to be employees of the clubs to whom they are contracted (see para **14.8** above), they are liable to the provisions of the income tax code which affect employees. This includes income tax charges being incurred in respect of benefits in kind provided, rather than just salary paid, by employer to employee. Under s 203 of the Income Tax (Earnings and Pensions) Act 2003 (ITEPA 2003), a charge to tax will be incurred where an employment-related benefit is provided to an employee by reason of their employment.[47]

14.41   A benefit is defined in s 201(2) of ITEPA 2003 as a 'benefit or facility of any kind'. When a benefit is provided to an employee by reason of the employment, it is an 'employment-related benefit' and, following the enactment of the Finance Act 2016, it no longer matters whether the employee has received the benefits as a 'fair bargain' (ie at market rate).[48]

---

44   ITA 2007, s 907 defines intellectual property. ITA 2007, ss 906 and 907 were amended by the Finance Act 2016. In particular, the definition of intellectual property in s 907 was expanded to cover a wider range of payments. The revised definition follows the definition contained within the OECD model tax treaty, whose guidance may be followed in determining the proper tax treatment of royalty payments to non-UK parties.

45   Including in relation to double taxation agreements (DTAs), given the duty to deduct income tax at source is subject to ITA 2007, ss 911 and 914. These provisions modify the obligation to deduct tax if the payer reasonably believes that the recipient of the payment is entitled to relief under a DTA or ITTOIA 2005, s 758 (which enacts the provisions of the Interest and Royalties Directive (2009/49/EC)).

46   Both UK tax evasion offences (CFA 2017, s 45) and foreign tax evasion offences (CFA 2017, s 46) are within scope of the offence of failure to prevent tax evasion by associated persons, so failure to prevent a non-UK domiciled player from committing a tax evasion offence in another jurisdiction will also fall within scope.

47   Except for those benefits which are already chargeable to income tax by virtue of ITEPA 2003, Pt 3, Chs 3–9 or other legislation, or are specifically exempt from charge.

48   Finance Act 2016, s 7, which amended ITEPA 2003, Pt 3.

14.42   The practical impact of the various provisions of ITEPA 2003 is that football clubs, players, and intermediaries should be aware that any benefits in kind provided to a player by his club, which may include company cars, personal loan facilities, accommodation, and private medical provision, is likely to be subject to an income tax charge. Advisers to players, whether lawyers or intermediaries, should therefore take steps to make sure players are aware that where benefits in kind are provided by their club, a tax charge is likely to follow.

14.43   As is the case for all UK employers, football clubs are required to report to HMRC on a yearly basis, by way of a Form P11D, the taxable benefits which have been provided to its employees (including its players). This may, in certain circumstances include intermediary fees which have been paid on a player's behalf by his club. Premier League clubs are also required to report to the League on an annual basis the extent of benefits in kind paid to players.[49]

E   INTERMEDIARY FEES

14.44   Immediately prior to the global deregulation of the intermediary industry in 2015 (covered in greater detail in chapter 12, The Regulation of Intermediaries), football agents in England were prohibited from acting for a club in a transaction where that agent had acted in the previous two transfer windows for the player counterparty with whom the club was entering into the transaction.[50] This regulatory prohibition broadly prevented agents from purporting to have acted for a club in a transaction when in fact they were acting in the interests of the player and provided some safeguard against the practice of 'switching'.[51] 'Switching' is a prohibited practice by which an intermediary seeks to pass himself or herself off as acting for the club solely immediately prior to the completion of a transaction, when up to that point in negotiations they may have been providing intermediary services to the player (often under an oral agreement). The purpose of arrangements of this type, and the 'switch' from acting for the player to acting for the club, is usually to reduce the tax liability of the player for any benefit in kind where payment of the intermediary fee is to be made by the club, by purporting not to have provided services to the player but to the club alone.

14.45   The adoption of the FA's Regulations on Working with Intermediaries (the 'FA Intermediaries' Regulations') in April 2015, which were based on FIFA's own Regulations on Working with Intermediaries, removed this prohibition. Under the FA Intermediaries' Regulations, clubs, players, and intermediaries (and other participants, as defined) are obliged not to conceal or misrepresent the reality and/or substance of matters relating to a transaction on which an intermediary has acted[52] but there is no prohibition upon an intermediary acting for a club in a transaction relating to a player who has previously been subject to representation by that intermediary.

14.46   In practice, an intermediary may therefore be entitled to act for the club only (rather than for the club and the player under a dual representation agreement)

---

49   Premier League Rules, Rule E.21 requires that Form 3, which provides particulars of P11D Payments made, must be returned on or before 1 March each season.
50   FA Football Agents Regulation 9 (as in force from 4 July 2009).
51   For a description of, and notable recent case relating to, 'switching' see the judgment of HHJ Waksman QC in *McGill v The Sports and Entertainment Media Group* [2014] EWHC 3000 (QB) at 29.
52   Regulation A3 of the FA Intermediaries Regulations. See also, Chapter 12, Football Intermediaries, Regulation and Legal Disputes.

in relation to a transaction which affects a player who has been subject to a previous representation agreement with that intermediary with the player representing himself in negotiations. This practice is controversial, given its underlying intention may be to reduce the player's overall tax liability, and may be broadly analogous to 'switching' as described in the *McGill* case.[53] However, clubs should be aware that where intermediary services are in fact being supplied to the player by the intermediary in relation to the transaction, rather than the club, the club will be under the same CFA 2017 obligations to prevent the facilitation of tax evasion.[54]

14.47   As transfers become more complex, with money changing hands between more parties to a transaction, the risk of facilitating tax evasion will surely increase. Clubs should seek advice in order to ensure that they take all measures within their control to prevent any transaction or part of a transaction falling foul of CFA 2017. Whilst a club might be confident in the innocence of its own representatives, it must also be diligent in ensuring that its actions are not facilitating an intermediary's or player's tax evasion by the manner in which a transaction is structured and should put in place reasonable procedures to prevent this.

14.48   Under the FA Intermediaries Regulations, players are entitled to discharge their liabilities to their intermediary by requesting that their club discharges the liability as a taxable benefit.[55] At present this election is made by the player with the agreement of the club by way of an Intermediary Declaration Form, which declares that the player has requested the club to discharge the liability, acknowledges that such payment may be treated as a benefit in kind for tax purposes, that the player may consequently be liable to tax on the amount paid to the intermediary by the player, and that the player has had the opportunity to take independent advice. The agreement of the club to discharge the liability is also required, with a similar declaration that the player has had the opportunity to take adequate advice and that a tax liability may be incurred by both the club and player as a result of the club's agreement to discharge the liability.[56]

---

53   See n 51 above. HMRC have demonstrated an ongoing and specific interest in the practice of switching, by their 'Operation Loom' raids on West Ham United and Newcastle United in April 2017. NUFC unsuccessfully applied for permission to commence judicial review proceedings on the grounds that the warrants were unlawfully issued in *Newcastle United Football Club Ltd v HM Revenue & Customs* [2017] EWHC 2402.
54   To the extent services are in fact being provided to the club by the intermediary, a VAT liability may be incurred. Considerations relating to VAT fall outside of the scope of this chapter, but should be borne in mind whenever payments are made by clubs to intermediaries (or indeed to IRCs).
55   Regulation C2(b)(ii) of the FA Intermediaries' Regulations.
56   FA Form IM1.

CHAPTER 15

Sponsorship and Commercial Rights

Chris Walsh and **Jamie Singer** (Onside Law)

A   SPONSORSHIP AND COMMERCIAL RIGHTS

(a)   Introduction

15.1   In less than 30 years, football has transformed itself from a sport with declining attendances beset by hooliganism into a global business warranting a place on the agenda of government trade trips.

15.2   Dramatic increases in rights fees from broadcasters triggered the transformation. However, the importance of the packaging and marketing of the game, in particular by the English Premier League, is often underestimated. A large part of football's recent growth owes a debt to the marketeers and has been fuelled by brands' desire to associate themselves with the sport and the emergence of new ways to exploit the rights held by football property owners. These rights, principally sponsorship, can now command staggering rights fees. In turn, as fees have increased, the underlying contracts have become more complex and sophisticated. This chapter seeks to explain:

(a)   What are the key commercial rights available in football?
(b)   How is the exploitation of such rights effected and regulated?
(c)   What are the principal provisions in a football sponsorship contract?
(d)   What types of dispute typically arise from football sponsorship?

(b)   Key commercial rights available

(i)   Stadium sponsorship

15.3   For many football clubs, and to a certain extent national football teams, the stadium is at the heart of their commercial strategy. The Taylor Report, commissioned by the government in the aftermath of the 1989 Hillsborough Stadium Disaster, recommended that all major football stadia be converted to an all-seater model. This led to a surge of new and redeveloped stadiums in the UK (and globally) and a general increase in investment in stadium infrastructure. Improved facilities gave clubs more opportunities to deliver innovative rights packages. Clubs could now offer exposure on big screens, digital clocks, branding on seats and digital perimeter boards in addition to premium experiences through enhanced hospitality and use of the pitch on non-match days.

15.4   Another key commercial innovation as stadia have modernised, is WiFi. The introduction of WiFi-enabled stadia has led to a dramatic increase in the number of marketing and revenue generating opportunities available, including through the production of new digital and in-app content.[1]

15.5   The most important right for stadium owners is the right to name the stadium or incorporate the sponsor's brand into the name of the stadium. Indeed, stadium-naming deals often form a significant part of the funding for stadium development projects. With new-build stadiums, sponsors can benefit from a 'blank canvas' and associate their brand with the club's new home from the outset – for example, Arsenal's Emirates Stadium. Naming an existing stadium is generally a high risk strategy[2] and clubs and sponsors should give careful thought to the strength of loyalty to the existing name and use of the name in the media.[3]

(ii)   Shirt sponsorship

15.6   Shirt sponsorship is one of the most valuable football sponsorship properties due to the level of exposure that a shirt sponsor can receive through broadcast, match day attendance and the sale of replica shirts. Increasingly, football clubs are looking to carve up their shirt sponsorship rights in order to maximise revenues.[4] The scope for shirt sponsorship is regulated by the competition in which the team is competing. As of the 2017/18 season clubs in the Premier League are allowed to carry additional sponsorship on the arm of player's shirts for the first time with the advertising space being valued at roughly 20% of the value of the main kit sponsorship.

(iii)   Kit supplier sponsorship

15.7   In addition to promoting sponsors on shirts and kit, a football team may sell the right to exclusively supply the kit. The arrangement allows the supplier to promote its association with the team alongside other sponsors and to supply its products for the team to showcase. In addition, kit supply agreements allow both the team and sponsor to generate additional revenues through sales of replica kit.[5]

---

1   Celtic FC entered into a joint venture with Cisco generating new match day revenue opportunities via an exclusive app developed by Cisco. EE's exclusive supply and sponsorship for Wembley again generates new opportunities through bespoke apps and enhanced Wifi and connectivity.

2   Where the sponsor secures naming rights early enough and long enough, the association can remain even once the commercial deal has expired. Bolton Wanderers Macron Stadium is a good example. The stadium was built in 1997 and Reebok secured the naming rights on a long-term basis with their name attached to the stadium until 2014. Fans' initial opposition to Reebok's association with the ground lessened with time as fans became accustomed to, and even warmed to, the association with the local sports behemoth. Consequently, despite the Italian sportswear company Macron assuming the naming rights in 2014, many fans still refer to 'The Reebok' to this day.

3   Renaming historic stadia in favour of a brand is notoriously difficult. Mike Ashley's decision to rename St James' Park as the Sports Direct Arena, still remains unpopular and has antagonised fans and the media. This may be part of the reason why Manchester United have made the conscious decision not to sell naming rights to Old Trafford, despite these rights being potentially the most valuable in the Premier League.

4   Liverpool FC currently have a different sponsor for their training kit (Bet Victor) from their match day kit (Standard Chartered), and clubs may also agree additional short-term shirt sponsorship agreements for special events such as pre-season tours.

5   adidas' current kit deal with Manchester United, is worth £750m over 10 seasons but adidas expect to at least double their investment over the course of the deal, through shirt sales and sales of other merchandise with the Manchester United brand.

(iv) League or cup sponsorship

15.8   Competition organisers and governing bodies may also choose to sell naming rights to league and cup competitions. As with stadium-naming deals, long-term sponsors are rewarded through the development of an entrenched association between the brand and the competition. New or reworked competition formats represent a good opportunity for sponsors to develop an early association with a competition whilst associating with well-loved properties can be difficult.[6] Increasingly, high-profile competitions decide to develop their own brand and preserve their integrity by avoiding naming-rights deals entirely. The absence of a Premier League title sponsor for the first time since 1993 has helped a rebranding exercise by presenting a clean image to its global audience.

(v) Broadcast sponsorship

15.9   Broadcast sponsorship may include 'breakbumpers' (short advertising slots at the beginning and end of advertising breaks) as well as programme naming rights.

15.10   Broadcasters offset part of the rights fees paid to secure the broadcast of football matches by allowing commercial partners to sponsor the broadcast of matches.

(vi) Merchandising/licensing

15.11   Football clubs, national associations and their players have long lent their intellectual property to merchandise sold in official club stores or by third party retailers. The production of everything from mugs to novelty Christmas jumpers featuring football club logos is now commonplace. In addition to exploiting the rights themselves, third parties can be licensed to exploit intellectual property. Sticker albums used to be the most common example of this form of merchandising, but they are now being usurped by the video game sector.

(vii) Player endorsements

15.12   Individual football players commonly enter into agreements to endorse products and services. Endorsement agreements are split into two categories:

(a) general brands whose promotion will be entirely outside of the player's professional services for club and country; and
(b) technical products relating to football such as boot deals and sports drinks which will impinge on their role for club or country.

Players must be vigilant to ensure that the rights granted to their individual sponsors (in particular technical sponsors) and their obligations pursuant to such deals do not overlap or conflict with their contractual obligations to club and country (and their commercial partners).[7]

---

6   The FA Cup has gone through multiple sponsors but the recent deal with Emirates provided it with its first title sponsor. It remains to be seen how effective this will be.
7   For example David Beckham was at the centre of a clash between heavyweight drinks clients Coca-Cola and Pepsi in advance of the 2002 World Cup. Beckham was used by Pepsi in his personal capacity as a Pepsi ambassador whilst Coca-Cola chose an image of Beckham to adorn their bottles as part of their sponsorship with the England national team.

(viii)   Official supplier deals

15.13   Official supplier deals allow the club to grant a set of rights to a sponsor including the right to be an exclusive or preferred supplier to the club or the club's ground of their particular product or service.

15.14   The more sophisticated deals will include revenue shares. For example, the drinks manufacturer granted exclusive pourage rights at a stadium will generally be expected to share the revenues generated, as will an official betting partner in respect of revenues generated in stadia.

(c)   Restrictions on exploitation

15.15   The football sponsorship landscape is subject to a myriad of regulatory restrictions and third party concerns which rights-holders and sponsors must be able to navigate skilfully.

(i)   Tobacco

15.16   Following the implementation of legislation at European and national level in the UK, the EU Tobacco Advertising Directive (2003/33/EC) prohibits tobacco sponsorship of events with a cross-border element across Member States and dramatically limits tobacco advertising in print and in the non-television media. In the UK, the subsequent Tobacco Advertising and Promotion Act 2002 bans all tobacco advertising and sponsorship in the UK. The FA had already updated its regulations to ban tobacco sponsorship in football in 1986.

(ii)   Alcohol

15.17   Alcohol brands are free to sponsor football in the UK, but their number has generally declined in recent years (Budweiser's continued association with The FA Cup being a notable exception). When the Premier League started in 1992/93, a quarter of the clubs had beer logos on their shirts, but none do so in the 2017/18 season. The CAP Code, BCAP Code[8] and Portman Group Code lay down detailed rules to govern the promotion of alcohol sponsorship in sport. Key provisions in these codes to be aware of:

(a)   prohibit any suggestion that consumption of a drink can lead to social success or popularity;

(b)   prohibit any suggestion that the product enhances mental or physical capabilities; and

(c)   prohibit all advertising targeted at an audience below 18 years of age.[9]

(iii)   Gambling

15.18   Unlike in many other countries, gambling advertising and sponsorship are not prohibited in the UK and not subject to any specific regulation by the football

---

8   These are the two advertising codes in the UK, the Committee of Advertising Practice Code and the Broadcast Committee of Advertising Practice Code, that govern non-broadcast and broadcast advertising respectively. The Portman Group Code is a code of practice agreed by the leading alcohol producers and distributors.

9   Note Carlsberg's shirt sponsorship of Liverpool FC: From 2008 onwards the children's shirt replica kit was plain rather than featuring the Carlsberg logo.

authorities (note the Gambling Commission's voluntary code of practice suggests certain limitations that should apply to gambling advertising and children, such as not having gambling logos on children's replica shirts). However, sports governing bodies are facing growing pressure to curb the volume and intensity of gambling advertising in their sport. Gambling companies feature on the shirts of nine Premier League clubs in the 2017/18 season and gambling promotions dominate both in-stadia advertising and live football broadcasts. According to research by Nielsen, the gambling industry spent a total of £430 million on sports gambling advertising since 2012. In June 2017, The FA called an end to its partnership with Ladbrokes claiming it could not reconcile having a commercial gambling partner and properly regulating betting on football in accordance with its own rules. Although, the gambling industry constitutes one of the most lucrative sectors for football sponsorship, it seems inevitable that this sector will face further regulation and restrictions in the future.

(iv) Unhealthy food and drink: high in fat, salt or sugar ('HFSS')

15.19   Under the CAP Code, HFSS brands are prohibited from promoting their products in children's media – meaning media targeted at children or other media where children make up 25% or more of the audience. The CAP Code rules do not stop HFSS brands from sponsoring football, but brands must ensure that the activation of their sponsorship rights does not involve the exploitation of any children's media (for example, sections of a football club's website aimed at children).

(v) Clean branding requirements

15.20   When considering whether to sponsor a football property a sponsor must consider what the rights-holder can actually offer. English football clubs will be required to remove much of their marketing inventory from stadia if hosting matches organised by UEFA (such as Champions League or Europa Cup) or FIFA events such as World Cups.[10]

15.21   Similarly different competitions will have differing rules and regulations as to what branding teams may have on their kit.[11]

(d)   Principal provisions in a football sponsorship contract

15.22   As detailed earlier in this chapter, there are numerous packages of sponsorship rights available in football, each of which will be granted using a contract containing bespoke provisions reflecting the specific nature of the sponsorship (for example, a stadium naming rights contract is likely to be far more restrictive in relation to the other types of branding that may be placed inside the stadium than a contract between a club and its official soft drinks partner would be). There is not, therefore, a 'standard' football sponsorship contract, but this section seeks to illustrate some of the most important provisions generally found in football sponsorship contracts.

---

10   For example the UEFA regulations for Euro 2020 require 'Clean Sites' so that during the tournament 'each stadium must be free and clean of any contractual obligations of whatever nature in the areas specified by UEFA such as (without limitation) obligations binding to sponsorship and advertising agreements, naming rights agreements, leases, reserved seating arrangements, etc. that have not been authorised by UEFA in advance. For the avoidance of doubt, during that period, no commercial signage of any type should be visible within, or in the immediate vicinity of, the outer security zone unless it is expressly authorised by UEFA.'

11   For example, although the Premier League has moved to allow sleeve sponsors, such sponsors will not be allowed on club shirts in European Competitions such as the Champions League.

(i)   Initial considerations

15.23   The sponsored club will generally prepare the first draft of each of its sponsorship contracts. This helps the club to ensure that there is no overlap between rights granted to its various sponsors and to ensure that each of its sponsorship contracts operates on broadly similar terms. In addition, a club is likely to enter into several contracts each year in relation to its rights, so will be better placed to accurately document the available rights inventory than a sponsor, who may enter into sponsorship contracts less frequently.

15.24   In addition to the right to use the club's logo and place its branding on kit and within the stadium (and other areas controlled by the club), the sponsor may also be granted rights such as access to players, branding on digital inventory, tickets and hospitality, rights to supply products at matches, access to the club's databases, use of exclusive content and imagery, 'money can't buy' VIP experiences and many other types of rights. These will typically be set out in a standalone rights schedule and agreed between the commercial teams of the parties prior to the drafting of the contract.

(ii)   Fees

15.25   Along with the inventory of rights, the sponsorship fee is a fundamental point that is likely to have been agreed between the parties prior to the contract being drafted. Despite this initial agreement, the fee payment clauses of a sponsorship contract can raise a number of issues due to the parties' competing interests.

15.26   As a general rule, a club will wish to receive as much of the sponsorship fee as early as it possibly can. This is beneficial from a cash-flow perspective (although it should be noted that there are limits to this, as a single lump sum payment of the entire sponsorship fee for a five-year contract would cause issues for the club's finance team in terms of recognising the revenue prior to having delivered five years' worth of sponsorship rights) and also reduces the sponsor's leverage and capacity to withhold an instalment of the sponsorship fee in the event of a dispute during the term of the contract. Clubs may also look to protect themselves by including provisions which allow them to suspend the delivery of the rights if the sponsor is in arrears with its payment of the sponsorship fee.

15.27   Conversely, a sponsor will look to ensure that the payment schedule allows it to have enjoyed as many of its rights as possible prior to payment of a substantial portion of the fees, so payment in multiple instalments is a common request. A sponsor may also look to reduce the 'guaranteed' element of the fees by structuring the fee so that a lower base amount is paid, but extra conditional fees and performance bonuses are paid on the occurrence of certain events. Whilst this is typically not preferable for the club, as it will have less certainty over its annual income, if the club is confident in its team's abilities and/or the conditional or bonus elements of the payment structure opens the possibility that materially higher sums would be received by the club than if a flat sponsorship fee were paid, the club may be amenable to such a structure.

(iii)   Product category exclusivity

15.28   Some of the most important provisions in any football sponsorship contract are those which set out the sponsor's 'category exclusivity' or the club's 'competitor' restrictions. These clauses generally prevent the club from granting sponsorship rights during the term of the agreement to competitors of the sponsor, being those companies operating in a defined product category (or sometimes framed as a defined list of named competitor companies). This is often an area of intense negotiation, as a sponsor will want to prevent the club from granting sponsorship rights to any business which it considers might possibly compete with it, whereas a club needs to ensure that it does not unnecessarily 'close' product categories in which it might want to enter into a sponsorship in the future. For example, a bank wishing to sponsor a football club might want its exclusive product category to be 'financial services', which would conceivably include categories as wide as retail banking, corporate banking, insurance, investment, asset management, pensions, life products, financial consulting and many others. The sponsored club would be restricted from accessing many types of business that regularly sponsor sporting organisations if it were to accept this definition, so may argue that the excluded category should be limited to 'banking', or possibly even 'retail banking'. Ultimately, this is a commercial negotiation point for the parties and the agreed definition will depend on their bargaining power and the club's intentions for its future commercial programme.

(iv) Intellectual property

15.29   The primary exchange in a sponsorship contract is the sponsor's payment of a fee in consideration for the rights to display its logo on the club's inventory of advertising space and to use the club's logo and intellectual property on its own promotional and advertising materials. Football club sponsorship contracts therefore contain numerous protections and warranties relating to each party's use of the other's intellectual property.

15.30   First, the sponsor will generally be required to obtain the club's approval to any new uses of the club's intellectual property. This approval is usually obtained through the club's approvals process, which will be operated by its marketing team and look to strike a balance between ensuring the club retains control and oversight over how its intellectual property is being used by its sponsors, on the one hand, and allowing its sponsors sufficient flexibility and autonomy to run innovative and effective activations on the other (particularly in the fast-moving social media age).

15.31   The sponsor will also need to grant the club the right to use the sponsor's logo for the purposes of delivering the sponsorship rights, and the club will be expected to warrant that it will only use it in the exact format provided by the sponsor and shall not use other intellectual property rights of the sponsor without permission.

15.32   It is worth noting that, historically, sponsors and clubs sometimes worked together to create 'composite' logos, where each of their logos is merged into a single, entwined logo. However, this tended to cause additional complexity in terms of ownership and whether to register the new designs as trademarks, along with increased design expenses. This has led to a move away from such practice and today the majority of composite logos feature the respective logos of the club and sponsor side-by-side, rather than combined.

(v) Renewal and expiry

15.33   Whilst neither sponsor nor club will want to begin their relationship by discussing how it ends, the termination or expiry of a sponsorship contract is another key area within the contract.

15.34   Many sponsors will take the view that as they will have invested in the sponsorship during the term of the agreement, they should be entitled to the right to renew at the expiry of the term of the contract. This renewal right may take one of several forms, including:

(a) *unilateral option to extend*: where the sponsor is able to extend the agreement on the same (or pre-agreed) terms at its discretion by notifying the club;

(b) *right of first refusal*: where the sponsor must be offered the first option to renew the agreement before the club may discuss opportunities with potential replacement;

(c) *matching rights*: where the sponsor has the right to be notified of the key terms of any third party offer received to replace the sponsor and if the sponsor chooses to 'match' the third party offer then the club is obliged to appoint the sponsor in preference to the third party; and

(d) *right of negotiation*: where the parties agree to discuss the possible extension or renewal of their sponsorship during what is commonly-known as a negotiation window (which, depending on the length of the original contract, can occur anywhere from 3–18 months prior to the expiry of the contract). This right would not place an absolute obligation on the parties to enter into an agreement, but rather to discuss and negotiate in good faith. If the negotiation window expires then the club will be entitled to discuss a replacement for the sponsorship content with third parties.

15.35   The club should ensure it is not overly restricted in its future dealings and to avoid a situation where it is unable to accept a more valuable replacement offer from a third party because of the incumbent sponsor's rights of renewal. Given this, a club is likely to prefer to agree to a negotiation window, which should be as early in the term of the contract as possible to allow the club more time to find a replacement if a renewal is agreed, rather than affording a sponsor the unilateral option to extend or a right of first refusal. As a compromise, a matching right at least provides the club with comfort that it will not be financially less well-off than it would have been if it had been free to solicit third party offers for a renewal.

(vi)   Termination

15.36   As with any contract, the parties will wish to ensure that they have the right to terminate for material or repeated breach, insolvency events and other standard rights of termination. However, football sponsorship contracts may also include some specific termination rights, including:

(a) *break clauses*: these clauses allow one (or both parties by mutual agreement) to terminate the sponsorship at a defined point before the expiry of the term of the agreement. Such clauses would usually be requested by the sponsor and reasons given for inclusion may include the sponsorship being the sponsor's first foray into sport sponsorship or other external factors which may affect the sponsor's business and overall marketing budget. Additionally, break clauses may sometimes be triggered by a club's performance on the pitch, for example a failure to qualify for European competition;

(b) *'morality' or reputational clauses*: these clauses seek to protect the sponsor's reputation and can range from a right to terminate if the sponsor is criticised by the club or its players, through to a right of termination if an individual player is judged to have acted in a manner which is immoral or offends a section of the public. A club should try a limit the scope of the morality clause to statements made by key personnel, such as its directors and management, who it can control, rather than the actions of individual players. The club's argument for this approach is that, unlike an individual player endorsement deal where the sponsor has a direct relationship with the player, the sponsor's relationship is with the club as a whole and therefore the actions of an individual player should not be sufficient cause for termination. On the other hand, the sponsor will wish to ensure that the morality clause is as widely-drafted as possible to give itself discretion as to how to react to any scandal which may arise. It should also be noted that it is now not uncommon for clubs to seek so-called 'reverse morality' clauses which grant the club the right to terminate in the event of a scandal involving the sponsor. These types of clauses tend to be more common where the sponsor operates in an industry such as gambling or financial services;

(c) *relegation clauses*: many sponsors will insist upon a right to terminate in the event that the club is relegated. This is a reflection of the reduced exposure and value of the rights that relegation would bring. Although a club may try to resist this clause, it is often a significant point for sponsors and clubs may therefore have to at least offer some form of fee-reduction in order for the sponsor to accept that it should not be entitled to terminate upon relegation.

B DISPUTES

(a) Introduction

15.37   Given that one of the primary purposes of a brand sponsorship is to leverage positive public association with the sponsorship property in question, it is perhaps unsurprising that sponsors and rights-holders alike are reluctant to be drawn into public litigation which is likely to result in the benefits of the association being undone and wider public relations and other damage being caused to the brand and sponsorship property.

15.38   As a result, there are relatively few football (or other sport) sponsorship or endorsement cases which make it to court because, generally speaking, any such disputes are settled well before that stage.

15.39   The increasing quality and sophistication of the drafting of sponsorship agreements has also mitigated the risk of legal disputes in relation to them because, as a general rule, the parties' rights and obligations are now more clearly set out in detailed agreements, leaving less room for disagreement.

(b) Types of dispute

15.40   The sponsorship-related disputes which do occasionally arise typically span the following areas:

(i)   failure by the sponsored party to deliver specified contractual sponsorship rights;
(ii) breaches by the sponsored party of morality/reputation provisions;
(iii) breaches by the sponsored party of brand exclusivity provisions; and
(iv) disputes regarding renewal rights (including matching rights and rights of first refusal).

(c) Failure to deliver contractual sponsorship rights

15.41   A typical football governing body or football club sponsorship agreement will contain a wide variety of sponsorship rights ranging from naming/designation rights to advertising/branding rights at matches and events to brand/intellectual property licensing, hospitality/tickets and merchandising rights. Sponsors also now commonly want to be able to promote their association with the sponsored party to the sponsored party's fans via the relevant databases.

15.42   In that regard, in the 2011 case of *Playup Interactive Entertainment (UK) Pty Ltd v Givemefootball Ltd*,[12] the defendant company (being a joint venture between the Professional Footballers' Association and Sports News Media Ltd) was held to be in repudiatory breach of a sponsorship agreement with the sponsor claimant (an interactive gaming business) for failing to deliver SMS and email advertising of the sponsor to recipients collated on the sponsored party's online databases.

15.43   The court concluded that not more than 260,000 of the 1 million emails and 39,450 of the 250,000 SMS messages which the sponsored party was contractually obliged to send were in fact sent to qualifying participants. It held that this constituted a repudiatory breach for which the sponsor was entitled to terminate the sponsorship agreement.

15.44   The issue of quantifying the sponsor's loss was made fairly straightforward by virtue of an express provision in the sponsorship agreement which stipulated that in the event of a material breach, the sponsored party would repay the sponsor the portion of the sponsorship fee which had already been paid and which related to the unelapsed term. This led to a contractual payment to the sponsor of c. £340,000 plus VAT.

15.45   Further, the court held that additional damages were also payable to the sponsor. These were calculated by the court by taking into account the percentage of emails/SMS messages contractually due which the sponsored party had in fact sent (24%) and applying that percentage to the difference between the actual payments made by the sponsor and the amount due to be repaid to it by the sponsored party under the sponsorship agreement (being c. £350,000). That gave rise to a figure of c. £267,000. The court than apportioned a percentage of the sponsorship fee to the data rights in question (deemed to be 20%) and applied that percentage to the £267,000 figure giving rise to additional damages of £53,000.

15.46   It is notable that the sponsor still remained a net payor under the sponsorship agreement because the sponsored party had successfully delivered all the other contracted sponsorship rights.

15.47   A further example of failing to deliver contractual sponsorship rights is *Ticket2final OU v Wigan Athletic AFC Ltd*.[13] Ticket2final (T2F) sold options to sports fans which enabled those fans to buy a ticket to particular future sporting events. T2F entered into a three-year agreement with Wigan, pursuant to which Wigan would, in return for an annual fee, provide T2F with sponsorship rights, including options for up to 5,000 match tickets for each round of the Carling Cup and FA Cup, and up to 10,000 tickets for the semi-final and final of those Cups.

15.48   In 2013, Wigan reached The FA Cup final and was allocated 21,000 tickets by The FA, which the club limited to two per season ticket holder. Having 10,000 season ticket holders, only 1,000 tickets remained for T2F. T2F challenged this whereupon Wigan purported to terminate the agreement for T2F's breach of contract due to late payments. T2F subsequently learned that The FA did not permit or approve of the

12   [2011] EWHC 1980 (Comm).
13   [2015] EWHC 61b (CH).

sale of options for FA Cup tickets, meaning Wigan was unable to fulfil the ticket options. T2F therefore argued that Wigan was in breach of its obligations for the sale of options for match tickets, and that Wigan had fraudulently misrepresented that it had the necessary power and authority to perform its contractual obligations.

15.49   It was held that although Wigan's representation that it was able to perform its obligations under the agreement was false and relied upon by T2F, it was not fraudulent because at the time Wigan entered into the contract, it honestly believed that it would be able to provide the tickets promised and that the permission of The FA would not be needed to sell the options. However, Wigan had not been entitled to terminate the agreement as it had failed to comply with the contractual requirement to give written notice that the relevant sums owed by T2F had not been received. Therefore, the court found that T2F was entitled to damages for breach of contract, but that they were limited to £30,000 because the agreement expressly limited Wigan's liability to the amount of the fee received in the calendar year in which the claim arose.

15.50   Another sport sponsorship case which provides guidance, by way of analogy, on what constitutes repudiatory breach in the context of a sponsorship agreement is *Force India Formula One Team Ltd v Etihad Airways and Aldar Properties.*[14]

15.51   In that case, the Court of Appeal reversed the High Court's first instance decision and found in favour of the sponsor on the grounds that the sponsors were entitled to accept Force India's repudiatory breach of the parties' sponsorship agreement under common law, regardless of the contractual termination provisions.

15.52   The breaches in question had included Force India's failure to deliver some of the key sponsorship rights, including the carrying of logos/references to the sponsor's name in the team name and an obligation not to change the cars' livery without the sponsors' approval. The judgment also offered guidance on what constitutes 'remediable' and 'irremediable' breaches in the context of sponsorship agreement, most notably that breaches of confidentiality and changes to the team name and livery were irremediable. Particular care needs to be exercised by sponsors who are unhappy with the sponsored party's performance under the sponsorship agreement in order to mitigate the risk of the sponsor being deemed to have affirmed the contract and/or waived the right to terminate it in the event of repudiatory breaches by the sponsored party.

15.53   Another interesting case relating to an alleged failure to deliver the rights under a sponsorship agreement is *Northern & Shell Plc v Champion Children of the Year Awards Ltd.*[15] The claimant, who was publisher of OK! magazine, agreed to sponsor the Champion Children of the Year Awards. A fee of £160,000 was originally agreed on the basis that the awards were to be presented by Princess Diana and shown as a pre-Christmas BBC special on a Sunday afternoon prime time slot to an anticipated six million viewers. Princess Diana later pulled out and a reduced sponsorship fee of £90,000 was agreed given the likely reduced public interest. A clause was included in the final agreement stating that in the event the programme was not broadcast at a time and date acceptable to OK!, it shall be repaid the sponsorship fee on demand and no further sums would be due. However, whilst the original draft agreement referred to anticipated viewing figures of six million, no figures were mentioned in the final agreement.

14   [2010] EWCA Civ 1051.
15   [2001] EWCA Civ 1638.

15.54   In fact, the programme was actually broadcast on a Monday morning and only attracted 710,000 viewers. OK! was disappointed with the low viewing figures and issued proceedings seeking the return of the first £45,000 instalment of the sponsorship fee which it had paid. Champion Children subsequently counterclaimed for the remaining £45,000 of sponsorship fees due. On appeal, it was held that notwithstanding the disappointing viewing figures, OK! had received significant benefits from its sponsorship of the awards and could not reasonably avoid all payments by simply invoking the broadcasting clause, particularly given that OK! did not object to the new date and time of broadcast when notified of it. Therefore, OK!'s claim was dismissed and it was ordered to pay the remaining £45,000 owed to Champion Children under the contract.

15.55   This case highlights the need for sponsors to ensure that all key deliverables and objective thresholds/measurements should be clearly and expressly specified in the sponsorship contract.

(d)   Breach of morality/reputation provisions

15.56   As explained above, sponsorship agreements will generally contain obligations on both parties not to do or say anything (or omit to do or say anything) which brings the other party into disrepute or which otherwise damages the counter-party's reputation and/or commercial interests.

15.57   An example of such a provision being activated in the context of a football sponsorship agreement was property website Zoopla's decision in January 2014 to end its shirt sponsorship of FA Premier League club, West Bromwich Albion, as a result of the anti-Semitic 'quenelle' gestures which French international and West Bromwich Albion striker, Nicolas Anelka, performed after scoring in a FAPL match. Anelka was subsequently found guilty by a FA Regulatory Commission of a gesture which was abusive and/or indecent and/or insulting and/or improper and that the misconduct was an 'aggravated breach' in that it included a reference to ethnic origin and/or race and/or religion or belief. Anelka was subsequently banned for five matches and fined £80,000.[16]

15.58   Other high-profile footballer agreements terminated on similar grounds include the February 2016 termination by adidas of its boots sponsorship agreement with disgraced former England and Sunderland footballer, Adam Johnson, when he pleaded guilty to child sex offences; and Luis Suarez being dropped by betting website 888poker as its ambassador following his infamous bite on Italy's Giorgio Chiellini in the 2014 FIFA World Cup. In other sporting contexts, Tiger Woods lost major sponsorship deals with brands such as Tag Heuer, Gatorade, AT&T, Accenture and Gillette following allegations of infidelity, with one US study suggesting that the Tiger Woods scandal may have cost shareholders of sponsor companies up to $12 billion in losses.[17] In addition, Lance Armstrong referred to his '$75 million day' after admitting to systematic doping throughout his career.[18]

15.59   As an alternative to immediately terminating such agreements when the sponsored player or property (and by association the sponsor) are brought into

---

16   *The Football Association v Nicholas Anelka*, 25 and 26 February 2014.
17   See http://www.reuters.com/article/us-golf-woods-shareholders/tiger-woods-scandal-cost-shareholders-up-to-12-billion-idUSTRE5BS38I20091229 (accessed February 2018).
18   See http://www.cyclingnews.com/news/armstrong-usada-report-fallout-cost-dollar-75million-in-future-income/ (accessed February 2018).

public disrepute, some sponsors choose to weather the storm and not renew them. Coca-Cola chose not to renew its endorsement deal with Wayne Rooney in 2011 following allegations over his private life, and a number of 2014 FIFA World Cup sponsors, including Sony, Emirates and Castrol chose not to renew their deals in the wake of the FIFA corruption scandal, rather than terminating them.[19]

15.60   Whilst far more unusual, there are some cases where the nature of the sponsor causes a breakdown in the relationship between sponsor and sponsored party. One such example arose in 2013 when Newcastle striker, Papiss Cissé, refused to wear Newcastle's kit bearing the logo of its sponsor, the payday loans company Wonga, on the basis that it offended his Muslim faith and personal beliefs. This created a major issue for Newcastle, whose deal with Wonga was thought to be worth around £24 million, leading to the club considering selling the player. The dispute was eventually resolved amidst widespread press coverage, with the player agreeing to wear the kit. The sponsorship deal was not however renewed at the end of its term.

(e)   Breaches by the sponsored party of brand exclusivity provisions

15.61   Generally, a sponsorship agreement will provide the sponsor with some element of exclusivity, be it the exclusive sponsorship of an event, exclusive sponsorship in a particular territory or the exclusive sponsorship in relation to a certain brand sector, product or industry (eg the official soft drinks partner). The sponsored party may, therefore, run into difficulties where a conflict arises between an existing sponsor and a prospective sponsor.

15.62   These situations tend to occur where clubs sign up sponsors from similar or overlapping industries or sectors, for example an exclusive banking partner and an exclusive foreign exchange partner. Rights-holders are often tempted to tread a fine line in making such decisions, particularly in the more lucrative sponsor brand sectors such as banking and financial services, but it can be counter-productive because regardless of how skilfully the relevant sponsorship agreements have been drafted, the relationship damage which can result is often irremediable.

15.63   The authors are aware of a number of cases involving Premier League football clubs and other leading sports rights-holders where claims of breached exclusivity have been made by sponsors, though in all cases the disputes have been settled on the basis of additional alternative rights being provided and/or early termination of one of the agreements in question.

(f)   Disputes regarding renewal rights

15.64   Many sponsorship agreements will provide the sponsor with renewal rights such as extension options, exclusive negotiation periods, rights of first refusal and matching rights. Disputes in relation to the enforcement of such rights occasionally arise, typically where the rights-holders do not want to renew with a sponsor which is asserting such a right because they can obtain a bigger sponsorship deal elsewhere.

---

19   However, it should be noted that none of these sponsors have linked their decisions to the FIFA scandals.

15.65   Arguably the most high-profile renewal dispute in football played out in 2006/07 between FIFA and MasterCard. MasterCard had sponsored the FIFA World Cup for 16 years as its official electronic payments partner. However, in 2006 FIFA awarded Visa an eight-year contract to sponsor the 2010 and 2014 FIFA World Cups despite MasterCard's claim that it had a right of first refusal on future sponsorships of the tournament.

15.66   The New York courts found at first instance that MasterCard had, indeed, had a right of first refusal and ruled that FIFA had been in breach of contract, requiring FIFA to cancel its deal with Visa and instead award the contract for the 2010 and 2014 World Cups to MasterCard. The matter was subsequently appealed to the US Court of Appeal by FIFA. However, the parties settled the dispute, with FIFA reportedly paying MasterCard US$90 million, allowing FIFA to conclude its deal with Visa.[20]

15.67   Another example of such a dispute from a footballer's perspective is *Nike European Operations Netherlands BV v Rosicky*.[21] The Arsenal player, Tomas Rosicky, had entered into a two-year boot contract with Nike, with the option to extend for a further two years. After the initial two-year period was completed, the player signed a new boot deal with Puma and wore their boots in some pre-season games.

15.68   However, a dispute arose as to whether Nike had exercised an option to extend the contract, with the player maintaining that Nike had not served notice of its intention to do so on him or his agent within the required time period. Nike therefore brought an action for breach of contract against the player in the Netherlands, and sought an injunction in England to prevent him from wearing Puma boots as the player was playing for Arsenal at the time.

15.69   The High Court found that damages were not an appropriate remedy for either party. In particular, it concluded that the marketing value to Nike of having the player wear its boots could not be assessed, meaning that an injunction would be the appropriate remedy, if following the full trial, the player was found to be in breach. From the player's perspective, because the allegations that he had breached the contract affected his reputation, the damage caused to him was not best compensated in monetary terms. The court decided, therefore, that the matter turned on the balance of convenience and concluded that Nike had a sufficiently strong case to justify seeking relief and was likely to suffer more damage than the player if the status quo was not preserved until trial. Therefore, it granted an injunction in Nike's favour requiring the player to take the unusual step of wearing unmarked blacked-out boots, pending the outcome of the Dutch litigation.[22]

15.70   One other notable analogous sporting case in this area was UK Athletics' dispute with adidas in 2012 regarding renewal and matching rights following the expiry of its seven-year sponsorship agreement (subject to Dutch law and jurisdiction) to supply the official kit for Great Britain's track and field athletes.[23] UK Athletics engaged in renewal talks with adidas in the lead up to the expiry of the agreement, but these stalled. Nike subsequently submitted a sponsorship offer to UK Athletics, which in turn notified adidas of the offer in line with its existing matching rights.

20   Also see *Labatt Brewing Company Limited et al. v NHL Enterprises Canada*, L.P. 2011 ONCA 511 in relation to sponsorship of the NHL in Canada.
21   [2007] EWHC 1967 (Ch).
22   No record regarding the conclusion of the Dutch proceedings or any settlement is available.
23   C/13/545394/KG ZA 13-825 HB/MB, Court of Amsterdam.

15.71   However, adidas refused to match Nike's offer and instead claimed that, notwithstanding the absence of a signed agreement on the terms of the renewal, it considered that it had already materially agreed its renewal terms with UK Athletics, which amounted to a binding agreement under Dutch law meaning that it was not required to match Nike's offer.

15.72   adidas therefore applied to the Court of Amsterdam seeking specific performance by UK Athletics. However, the Dutch court found that because a number of key renewal terms were still to be agreed between UK Athletics and adidas, no binding agreement was in place and UK Athletics was not bound to enter into an agreement with adidas. Furthermore, the period of time for adidas to match Nike's offer had expired, meaning that UK Athletics was freely entitled to enter into a sponsorship agreement with Nike.

C   REMEDIES

15.73   The remedies typically sought in sponsorship disputes are one or more of injunctive relief, damages and specific performance.

(a)   Injunctive relief

15.74   In the context of sponsorship disputes, injunctive relief will usually be sought to prevent one party from committing, or continuing to commit an act in breach of the sponsorship agreement.

15.75   In assessing whether to grant an injunction, the court will generally apply the common law test set out in the leading case of *American Cyanamid Co (No 1) v Ethicon Ltd*,[24] namely asking itself the following four questions:

(a) Is there a serious question to be tried?
(b) Would damages be an adequate remedy?
(c) Would the applicant's cross-undertaking in damages provide adequate protection for the respondent if the court was to grant interim injunctive relief which, following trial, proves to have been wrongly granted?
(d) Are there any special factors from the merits of the case tipping the balance of convenience in the favour of either party (where factors remain evenly balanced, it being prudent to preserve the status quo)?

15.76   In *Nike v Rosicky*,[25] it was held that there was a serious question to be tried and that damages would not be an adequate remedy.

15.77   In assessing the balance of convenience, it was found that whilst granting the injunction would result in the player being unable to wear Puma goods and consequently would cause the postponement of Puma's advertising campaign containing the player, refusal to grant the injunction would result in a change of sponsor and publicity for Puma, which would cause more damage to Nike.

15.78   Therefore, the balance of convenience was in favour of granting the injunction, particularly given that the injunction would only be for a short period of time pending the outcome of the parallel Dutch proceedings.

---

24   [1975] UKHL 1.
25   *Nike European Operations Netherlands BV v Rosicky* [2007] EWHC 1967 (Ch).

(b)   Damages

15.79   The general purpose of an award of damages for breach of contract is to compensate the injured party for loss, rather than to punish the wrongdoer. The general rule is that damages should place the claimant in the same position as if the contract had been performed. Contract damages are, therefore, essentially compensatory, measuring the loss caused by the breach and they will generally be assessed as at the date of the breach of contract.

15.80   In the context of a sponsorship agreement, this will usually involve the sponsorship fee being repaid to the sponsor where the sponsorship rights have not been provided, as per *Ticket2final v Wigan Athletic*.[26] However, additional complexity arises in assessing damages where some, but not all, of the sponsorship rights have been provided. This may lead to a situation as in *Northern & Shell Plc v Champion Children*[27] where the court is required to assess whether the sponsorship benefits expected by the sponsor have been achieved. If no loss has been suffered, it would follow that no damages are payable.

15.81   Alternatively, where a sponsor is in breach of contract, usually because it has failed to pay the agreed sponsorship fee, damages will normally be assessed by reference to the fee payable for the remainder of the term on the contract. Again, see *Northern & Shell Plc v Champion Children*[28] where the sponsor was required to pay the outstanding sponsorship fees owed under the contract.

15.82   The sponsorship agreement will also confirm whether there are any contractual limits on liability which cap the level of damages which could be awarded for breach of contract, and separately whether an aggrieved party is entitled to liquidated damages (provided that they amount to a genuine pre-estimate of loss, failing which it will be deemed an unenforceable penalty clause).

15.83   Where the breach is founded upon misrepresentation, damages may also be awarded to compensate for losses flowing from the contract (provided that they are not too remote), rather than to put the claimant in the position it would have been in if the misrepresentation not been made.[29]

(c)   Specific performance

15.84   An order for specific performance compels a party to perform his positive contractual obligations, that is, to do what he promised to do. Specific performance will only be granted at the court's discretion where there is a valid, enforceable contract and damages would not be an adequate remedy.

15.85   In a sponsorship context, specific performance will normally be sought in relation to the enforcement of renewal rights such as extension options, rights of first refusal and matching rights, as in the *adidas v UK Athletics* and *Nike* case.

15.86   Damages can be claimed in addition to or as an alternative to specific performance. However, where the claimant could adequately be compensated by an award of damages for the breach of contract, the courts are unlikely to order specific performance.

---

26   *Ticket2final OU v Wigan Athletic AFC Ltd* [2015] EWHC 61b (CH).
27   *Northern & Shell Plc v Champion Children of the Year Awards Ltd* [2001] EWCA Civ 1638.
28   Ibid.
29   See *Spice Girls v Aprilia World Service BV* [2002] EWCA Civ 15.

CHAPTER 16

Financial Regulation and Financial Fair Play

Nick De Marco QC and **Tom Richards** (Blackstone Chambers)
and **Victoria Wakefield** (Brick Court Chambers)

A   INTRODUCTION

16.1   Financial regulation has been an integral part of football for many years. It can take many forms, justified for various reasons, most of which are beyond the scope of this chapter. For example, it might be directed at transparency and accountability, or at eliminating conflicts of interest or other challenges to the integrity of the sport. The rules prohibiting third party investments in football,[1] and those regulating intermediaries,[2] or those setting out who is a fit and proper person to be a football club owner or director,[3] considered elsewhere in this book, can all be viewed as types of financial regulation.

16.2   This chapter considers one particular, controversial, form of financial regulation – the rules regulating the amount of debt a football club is permitted to have. These rules have become known as Financial Fair Play (FFP) rules after the UEFA model that was the first to apply them. They essentially limit the amount of debt a club is permitted to have in a particular league or competition by reference to that club's income, and require the payment of debts as they fall due. They are principally directed at preventing the type of overspending and poor financial management that can (and has) led to some clubs becoming insolvent, and the negative consequences of bad debt.

16.3   There is a widely held misconception about FFP rules. By and large they are not directed at ensuring competitive balance between football clubs, although there are arguments about whether such competitive balance is strengthened or undermined by them. On the contrary, their express purpose is largely to promote financial stability (though again there are arguments about whether they come closer to achieving or undermining this purpose). They are supposed to stop clubs overspending, but overspending in relation to the spending club's revenue. A Paris Saint Germain, Real Madrid or Manchester United is able to spend significantly more on its player budget than a FC Toulouse, Girona or AFC Bournemouth.

---

1   See Chapter 11, Third Party Investment.
2   See Chapter 12, Football Intermediaries, Regualtion and Legal Disputes.
3   See Chapter 21, Ownership Issues and the Fit and Proper Person Test.

278 Financial Regulation and Financial Fair Play

16.4   The FFP model, adopted by English and European football, is very different from the salary cap model adopted in some other sports. Despite being the home of free market economics, salary caps are common across sport in the USA – they operate in the National Football League, National Hockey League and Major League Soccer, whilst a 'soft cap' and 'luxury tax' is operated by the National Basketball Association. Salary caps operate at the top level of both types of rugby in England: the Aviva Premiership in rugby union and the Super League in rugby league. Salary caps generally limit the total amount a competing club can spend on players' salaries in a given competition to an equal amount. They are justified on grounds both of competitive balance (not allowing richer clubs to have an advantage by spending more) as well as financial stability (preventing clubs overspending by reference to a league norm).

16.5   FFP rules, on the other hand, limit the amount a club can spend (or rather its debt) with reference to that club's revenue. A richer club can spend more than a poorer club. FFP rules are generally justified only as promoting financial stability – they are supposed to prevent a club amassing greater debt than it can manage, thus threatening insolvency. They are often criticised, however, for (amongst other things) hindering legitimate competition and thus also competitive balance. Whereas in the past an investor could invest more in a smaller club to help it compete with a bigger club, FFP limits the amount an investor can invest to catch up, increasing the gulf between the established bigger clubs and those who have not caught up. Clubs like Manchester City and Chelsea were fortunate enough to have wealthy investors help them catch up with the likes of Manchester United, Liverpool and Arsenal before FFP rules properly kicked in, but it will be more difficult in the future, the critics argue, for other clubs to catch up in the same way. The same arguments apply to clubs at Championship level competing for promotion to the Premier League, or those entering UEFA competitions wishing to compete with the likes of Barcelona or Juventus.

16.6   The risks of insolvency in football are nevertheless real. Changes to insolvency law, in particular heralded by the UK Insolvency Act 1986, made it easier for football clubs to write off bad debts by a period of administration. Between 1992 and 2008 as many as 40 of England's 92 football clubs were involved in insolvency proceedings, some more than once.[4] Various measures were taken by the football regulators in England to avert this, from punishing clubs that enter administration with points deductions to requiring prospective club owners to provide proof that that they are able to finance the club's obligations before being allowed to acquire a club. Nevertheless, after UEFA introduced FFP rules for its European competitions, the Football League, then the Premier League, decided to bring in their own versions of FFP.

16.7   The result is that there are three different versions of FFP operating at the highest level in English football. The UEFA FFP rules apply to any club entering a UEFA competition (such as the Champions League or Europa Cup). Many of those clubs shall also be subject to the Premier League's own FFP Rules. Then there are the Championship FFP Rules, perhaps the most controversial of them all, which have already gone through a significant change since they were introduced in 2012. Clubs in League One and Two are subject to yet further different rules.

---

4   *Soccernomics*, Simon Kuper and Stefan Szymanski, HarperSport (2012).

16.8   This chapter considers each of the different sets of rules applying in English football, some of the cases where European clubs have been subject to fines or other sanctions as a result of breaching FFP requirements, and the competition law objections to FFP.

B   SUMMARY OF THE DIFFERENT FFP RULES

(a)   The UEFA Club Licensing and Financial Fair Play Regulations

16.9   The UEFA Club Licensing and Financial Fair Player Regulations ('the UEFA FFP Regulations') were first introduced in 2011. The current version of the UEFA FFP Regulations came into force in 2015.[5] Following a two-year transitional period, since 2013 clubs competing in UEFA competitions have been assessed against 'break-even requirements', which require them to keep any spending above what the club earns within certain limits. The limits are assessed over a three-year period, that period representing a typical football business cycle (for example an average length of a player contract). The UEFA FPP Regulations also impose enhanced obligations on clubs to prove that they have no 'overdue payables' towards other clubs, in respect of employees, or to social or tax authorities.[6]

16.10   Clubs are permitted to spend up to €5 million more than they earn over the three-year assessment period, but they may exceed this level up to a certain further limit if the additional spending is covered by a contribution or payment from the club owners or a related party.[7] The limits were €45 million for the initial assessment periods in 2013/14 and 2014/15, and are €30 million for assessment periods 2015/16, 2016/17 and 2017/18. To promote investment in stadia, training facilities, youth development and women's football, costs in those areas have been excluded from this break-even calculation.

16.11   A 'related party' is a person or entity that is related to the club, attention being directed to the substance of the relationship and not merely the legal form. It includes a party where a close family member of the club owners has some control or influence over the party, or where those who control the club and party are part of the same group of companies, or are both influenced by the same government, or are engaged in a joint venture.[8] This is important because income received from a related party shall be subject to the limits set out above, unless the income is in the form of a transaction at 'fair value'. Thus, where a related party is a sponsor of a club, for example, and a fair value for its sponsorship is considered to be €1 million, if the related party actually sponsors the club in the sum of €10 million the additional €9 million will be subject to the investment limits in the Regulations.[9]

16.12   The UEFA FFP Regulations provide the enforcement bodies with a wide discretion in enforcing penalties against those clubs who exceed the limits, including the ability to impose a warning, fine or, ultimately, suspension from the relevant competition. Section C of this chapter considers the various disputes between UEFA

---

5   The UEFA FFP Regulations 2015 are available online in full at: http://www.uefa.com/MultimediaFiles/ Download/Tech/uefaorg/General/02/26/28/41/2262841_DOWNLOAD.pdf (accessed March 2018).
6   See Articles 65–66bis of the UEFA FPP Regulations 2015.
7   See Article 61 of the UEFA FFP Regulations 2015.
8   See Annex X, section F to the UEFA FFP Regulations 2015.
9   See Annex X, section B(1)(k) to the UEFA FFP Regulations 2015.

and clubs that have already taken place under the UEFA FFP Regulations and the sanctions imposed.

16.13   The stated justification for the UEFA FFP Regulations (and thus what the legality of those rules must be assessed against) is stated in Article 2, sub-paragraph (2) which provides that they aim to achieve financial fair play in UEFA club competitions and in particular:

(a) to improve the economic and financial capability of the clubs, increasing their transparency and credibility;
(b) to place the necessary importance on the protection of creditors and to ensure that clubs settle their liabilities with employees, social/tax authorities and other clubs punctually;
(c) to introduce more discipline and rationality in club football finances;
(d) to encourage clubs to operate on the basis of their own revenues;
(e) to encourage responsible spending for the long-term benefit of football;
(f) to protect the long-term viability and sustainability of European club football.

16.14   UEFA has assumed its FFP Regulations are in accordance with EU law, including competition law, not least because of a *'joint statement'* released by the European Commission and UEFA on 21 March 2012,[10] setting out the objectives of the FFP Regulations and asserting that they pursue legitimate objectives and are consistent with the aims and objectives of European Union policy in the field of State Aid. Significantly the joint statement refers to the principle behind EU policy on State Aid being that undertakings should be able to compete 'on a level playing field', and apply this to the FFP Regulations.

16.15   The only real test of the legality of the UEFA FFP Regulations to have taken place so far was in a decision of the Court of Arbitration in Sport (CAS) in *UEFA v Galatasaray*.[11] The case is discussed in more detail in section D of this chapter. In short, the CAS found that the UEFA FFP Regulations constituted a 'decision by an association of undertakings',[12] that 'may affect trade between Member States',[13] but that there was no breach of competition law – in part it appears because the club had not adduced any evidence to show the Regulations constituted a restriction 'by effect'.[14]

(b)   The Premier League Profitability and Sustainability Rules

16.16   The Premier League Profitability and Sustainability Rules ('the PL FFP Rules') were announced in February 2013 and introduced for the 2013/14 season. The PL FFP Rules can be found in the Premier League Handbook.[15] Like the UEFA FFP Regulations they have a three-year monitoring period.[16] The upper loss threshold is £105 million over the three-year period (an average of £35 million per season in

---

10   See   http://www.uefa.com/MultimediaFiles/Download/uefaorg/EuropeanUnion/01/77/21/58/ 1772158_DOWNLOAD.pdf (accessed March 2018).
11   CAS 2016/A/4492 *UEFA v Galatasaray.*
12   Paragraphs 57–60.
13   Paragraph 61 of the Award.
14   Paragraphs 73–80 of the Award.
15   The Premier League Handbook can be accessed for free on the website: https://www.premierleague. com/publications (accessed March 2018). In the 2017–2018 handbook the PL FFP Rules can be found within Section E, Clubs – Finance, pp 113–124.
16   See Rules E.56–E.57 of the PL FFP Rules.

the Premier League, reduced to £22 million for each period within the three-year reporting period that the club is in the Championship).[17]

16.17   If the club is in breach (ie its losses exceed £105 million over the three years) it shall be reported to an independent Football Disciplinary Commission which has the discretion to apply a range of various sanctions.[18]

16.18   In assessing whether a club has breached the upper loss threshold, the PL FFP Rules apply similar concepts to those found in the UEFA FFP Regulations as to 'Related Party Transactions' and 'Fair Market Value' transactions.[19]

16.19   The PL FFP Rules are more flexible than those of UEFA, and far more flexible than those of the Football League Championship. A Premier League club can sustain losses of three times the amount for a club subject to the UEFA FFP Regulations; indeed it can lose in only one year three times what the club subject to the UEFA Regulations is permitted throughout the whole three years, so long as the Premier League club has no losses in years two and three. The gulf between these limits and the limits in the Championship are greater still, in particular when one considers the very strict limits originally applied under the 2012 Championship FFP Rules (see below), allowing for roughly £8 million losses and equity contributions in one year. Whilst the disparity in different league rules can be explained by the fact that clubs in different leagues have different levels of income and expenditure, that misses the point that the leagues themselves are not separate or isolated entities. Some Premier League clubs will be at the same time competing in UEFA competitions and all Premier League clubs are, in some ways, competing to be subject to them in any given period. Every year three Premier League clubs will be relegated and subject to Championship Rules and three Championship clubs will be promoted and subject to Premier League Rules – in a three-year period it is possible that nearly half the members of the Premier League will have changed, or those clubs that go up and down be subject to different sets of rules in the same period. This is one reason why the Football League's Championship FFP Rules have since been adjusted to be more compatible with those in the Premier League.

(c)   The Football League Championship FFP Rules

16.20   The Football League Championship FFP Rules ('the Championship FFP Rules') have been subject to two important iterations. First, the 2012 Championship FFP Rules were brought in before the Premier League brought in its rules, and without consultation with the Premier League or its member clubs, some of which subsequently became subject to them following relegation. The 2012 Championship FFP Rules set the most stringent of spending limits as well as a requirement that certain clubs be subject to a fixed, non-discretionary, automatic fine that could run into tens of millions of pounds.

16.21   Following considerable pressure from the Premier League, and its member clubs, as well as disquiet from a number of Championship clubs, the Football League made various substantial changes to its FFP Rules in November 2014, introducing the Championship Profitability and Sustainability Rules for later seasons. We consider both sets of rules below.

---

17   Rules E.59 and E.60 of the PL FFP Rules.
18   Rule E.59 of the PL FFP Rules, along with section W of those Rules (discipline).
19   See the PL's Guidance on the PL FFP Rules at p 124 of the Premier League Handbook (2017–2018).

(i) The 2012 Championship FFP Rules

16.22   The stated aim of the 2012 Championship FFP Rules is the promotion of financial stability (as opposed to any notion of competitive balance).[20] Each Championship club was required to meet a 'fair play requirement' for each reporting period, based on its 'fair play result' plus 'permitted allowances'. The fair play requirement has to be positive.[21] In contrast to the UEFA and Premier League regulations, the reporting period was only one year. The permitted allowances in any one year were the aggregate of the 'acceptable deviation' and 'contributions from equity participants and/or related parties'.[22]

16.23   The maximum acceptable deviation for each football season was £4 million for seasons 2011/12 and 2012/13; £3 million for 2013/14 and 2014/15; and £2 million for season 2015/16.[23] The maximum amount of contributions from equity participants and/or related parties was £8 million for 2011/12; £6 million for 2012/13; £5 million for 2013/14; and £3 million for 2014/15 and 2015/16.[24]

16.24   Thus, a Championship club that exceeded an aggregate 'overspend' of £10 million in 2012/13, £8 million in 2013/14 or £6 million in 2014/15 would be in breach of the rules. These limits were not only significantly lower than those the Premier League introduced shortly afterwards (or those applied by UEFA), but also clubs were restricted by the fact that the monitoring period was only one year. For example, if there had been a three-year monitoring period a club could have made losses of £24 million over the three years, and it would not matter if as much as £16 million was made in any one year. This was particularly significant for relegated clubs that will often still have two years or more to run on much higher Premier League player contracts and will take time, usually longer than one season, to adjust their spending to Championship levels.

16.25   A Championship club that failed to meet the Fair Play Requirement was subject to an automatic registration embargo, preventing it from registering any new player or new contract for an existing player other than on a 'one in one out basis' where the club's squad was 24 or fewer players and the cost of the player coming in was no more than 75% of the equivalent cost of the player going out.[25] A Championship club that was relegated from the Championship that failed to meet the fair play requirement remained bound by the rules but was not subject to a registration embargo.[26]

16.26   Most controversially, a Championship club promoted to the Premier League that failed to meet the fair play requirement was subject to an automatic fine calculated on the basis of the amount by which the club failed to fulfil the fair play requirement ('the excess'), as follows:[27]

(a) 1% of the excess between £1 and £100,000;
(b) 20% of the excess between £100,001 and £500,000;
(c) 40% of the excess between £500,001 and £1,000,000;

---

20 See Regulation 18 of the Football League Regulations.
21 Regulation 1.1–1.2 of the 2012 Championship FFP Rules.
22 Regulation 5.1 of the 2012 Championship FFP Rules.
23 Regulation 5.2 of the 2012 Championship FFP Rules.
24 Regulation 5.2 of the 2012 Championship FFP Rules.
25 Regulation 6.1 of the 2012 Championship FFP Rules.
26 Regulation 7 of the 2012 Championship FFP Rules.
27 Regulation 10 of the 2012 Championship FFP Rules.

(d)   60% of the excess between £1,000,001 and £5,000,000;

(e)   80% of the excess between £5,000,001 and £10,000,000;

(f)   100% of the excess over £10,000,000.

16.27   This system of calculation is capable of staggering results. A club that overspent by £100,000 in the 2013/14 season would be fined £1,000 (1% of the overspend); if the overspend was £1 million it would be fined £281,000 (28%); if the overspend was £11 million, the fine would be £7,681,000 (70%), and if the overspend was £52 million, the fine would be £48,681,000 (94%). Not only did the rules provide that the higher the overspend, the more the club would have to pay, but also the higher the overspend the more disproportionate the penalty, as not only the amount, but the *proportion* of the amount, significantly increased. In addition to this controversial formula, the 2012 Championship FFP Rules provided that there was no discretion as to this penalty – it would be automatically applied, by way of a mathematical formula, to any promoted club in breach. This was another important feature considered in the *QPR* case (see para **16.79** below).

(ii)   The Championship Profitability and Sustainability Rules

16.28   Following considerable disquiet about the more controversial elements of the 2012 Championship FFP Rules, particularly expressed by Premier League clubs, in November 2014 the Football League voted to bring in the new Championship Profitability and Sustainability Rules from the 2016/17 season onwards.[28]

16.29   The key material differences are that clubs are monitored over a three-year period, as opposed to a one-year period;[29] the maximum acceptable deviation (or 'lower loss threshold') over three years is £15 million;[30] the permitted allowances (or 'upper loss threshold') is £39m over three years; a club is only regarded as being in breach of the Championship Profitability and Sustainability Rules if its aggregated adjusted earnings before tax across the three-year period is in excess of the upper loss threshold;[31] and there is flexibility in terms of sanction for breach. No automatic fine or embargo applies, but instead an independent Disciplinary Commission shall determine the sanction on a case-by-case basis, with a range of sanctions available to it.

(d)   The League One and League Two Salary Cost Management Protocols (SCMP)

16.30   The League One Salary Cost Management Protocol (SCMP) was introduced by the Football League in the 2012/13 season. The scheme is quite different to the various FFP models considered above because, whilst spending by clubs on player salaries was capped at 60% of the club's turnover and 100% of its 'Football Fortune' income,[32] Football Fortune income included competition winnings, cash and equity injections and accumulated profit.[33] Under the SCMP,

---

28   Amendments were made to the 2012 FFP Rules in respect of the season 2015/16, in particular the Acceptable Deviation was increased from £2 million to £5 million and the contributions from equity participants was increased from £3 million to £8 million.

29   See, eg Regulation 1.1.12 of The Championship Profitability and Sustainability Rules.

30   Regulation 3.1 of The Championship Profitability and Sustainability Rules.

31   Regulation 2.9 of The Championship Profitability and Sustainability Rules.

32   See Regulations 1.2.1 and 1.2.2 of the SCMP.

33   See paras 2.6–2.7 of the Definitions section to the SCMP.

there is no limit on the amount a club can invest in players' salaries so long as its owners and investors provided the cash or equity for that investment.

16.31   The Football League also brought in the League Two Salary Cost Management Protocol applying a similar approach with a slightly lower cap on spending (55% of turnover) but the same provision (100%) in relation to Football Fortune income.

(e)   FFP rules in other European leagues

16.32   Other European leagues have also brought in FFP rules. Since around 2014 the German Bundesliga has its own FFP Rules and in Spain, La Liga operates an FFP model based on the UEFA FFP Regulations. The Italian FA have said they shall bring in FFP Rules for Serie A clubs commencing in the 2018/19 season. In France, financial regulation in football has a long history. The focus of the French DNCG (National Direction for Management Control) regulations, however, is not overspending but solvency – whether clubs and their owners can service their debts. The various different systems of FPP schemes across European leagues outside of England and UEFA are, however, beyond the scope of the discussion in this chapter, and those practising in those jurisdictions should check the relevant primary sources.

C   UEFA FFP DISPUTES

16.33   The UEFA FFP Regulations involved the creation of a 'Club Financial Control Body' (CFCB), split into an 'investigatory chamber' and an 'adjudicatory chamber' ('the CFCB AC') which replaces the UEFA Control and Disciplinary Body (CDB).[34] An appeal from the CFCB AC lies to the CAS.[35] A developing body of case law from the CFCB AC and the CAS provides helpful guidance on the interpretation and application of the UEFA FFP Regulations, and may be of some assistance by analogy when considering other FFP schemes.[36]

16.34   The decisions of the CFCB AC involve disputes between UEFA and clubs rather than between clubs, but UEFA may open an investigation into a club at another club's request.[37] While most of the case law is concerned with breaches of the rules on 'overdue payables' rather than breach of the 'break-even' rules, many of the principles in the case law will be equally applicable to both sets of rules. We leave questions of the compliance with EU competition law of the whole scheme of FPP regulation for section D below.

(a)   Applicable law

16.35   It has been held that the law applicable to a dispute under the UEFA FFP Regulations for the purposes of the choice of law rules in the CAS Code is

---

34   UEFA FFP Regulations 2015, Article 53; AC-05/2014 *Bursaspor*, para 40.
35   Procedural rules governing the UEFA Club Financial Control Body 2015, Article 34.
36   Decisions of the CFCB AC are available on UEFA's website, at http://www.uefa.com/insideuefa/disciplinary/club-financial-controlling-body/cases/index.html (accessed March 2018). References in this chapter to proceedings before the AC in the form AC-[year/no.] are to the AC's final decision in those proceedings, unless otherwise indicated.
37   Eg AC-04/2015 *SC Braga*, para 7.

the Regulations themselves[38] supplemented by Swiss law (the law of UEFA's domicile).[39] Treating the UEFA FFP Regulations as a system of law, equivalent to (say) Swiss law or the law of England and Wales, may seem unusual. The idea is that the Regulations should be given an autonomous and uniform interpretation, rather than interpretation by reference to national laws, so as to ensure that clubs are treated equally irrespective of their domicile; recourse to national law will only be permitted where it is necessary for the application of the Regulations and does not undermine their purpose.[40] Thus for the purpose of identifying whether a debt is overdue it is immaterial whether enforcement proceedings could be taken against the debtor under national law.[41] Identifying whether there is a debt at all, by contrast, will necessarily involve consideration of the relevant national law.[42]

16.36   As a result of the application of Swiss law, mandatory rules of foreign law are also applicable where certain conditions are met; thus rules of EU competition law and free movement must be taken into account.[43]

(b)   Purpose of the UEFA FFP Regulations

16.37   In interpreting and applying the UEFA FFP Regulations, in relation to both breach and sanction, CAS and the CFCB AC make frequent reference to the Regulations' purpose. The Regulations:

> 'aim to protect the integrity and smooth running of the UEFA club competitions and to achieve financial fair play in the UEFA club competitions, in particular by improving the economic and financial capability of the clubs, increasing the transparency and credibility of the clubs, protecting creditors, encouraging the clubs to operate on the basis of their own revenues (i.e. to "break-even") and protecting the longterm viability and sustainability of European football'.[44]

The break-even requirement is the cornerstone of the rules,[45] but the overdue payables rules are also said to be aimed, by securing protection for creditors, at 'the protection of the long-term viability and sustainability of European football'.[46]

(c)   Importance of timely and accurate disclosure and submission of monitoring information

16.38   While the CFCB will not ignore any evidence of breach of the UEFA FFP Regulations that is brought to its attention,[47] the obligations on clubs to give disclosure and submit monitoring information are considered essential to the FFP

---

38   CAS 2013/A/3067 *Málaga CF SAD v UEFA*, para 9.4.
39   CAS 2014/A/3533 *FC Metallurg v UEFA*, para 35; see also CAS 2016/A/4692 *Kardemir Karabükspor v UEFA*, para 5.3 and CAS 2-16/A/4492 *Galatasaray v UEFA*, para 40.
40   CAS 2013/A/3067 *Málaga CF SAD v UEFA*, paras 9.4–9.7.
41   Ibid, para. 9.5.
42   Ibid, para. 9.4.
43   CAS 2-16/A/4492 *Galatasaray v UEFA*, paras 41–45.
44   AC-01/2016 *Galatasaray*, para 98; AC-03/2015 *FC CSKA AD*, para 42.
45   AC-02/2015 *Dynamo Moscow*, para 77.
46   CAS 2013/A/3453 *FC Petrolul Ploiesti v UEFA*, para 79; AC-04/2014 *CFR 1907 Cluj*, para 35; AC-05/2014 *Bursaspor*, para 44; AC-04/2014 *CFR 1907 Cluj*, para 37; AC-09/2015 *Targu Mures*, para 41; AC-08/2015 *Botosani*, para 35; AC-05/2015 *Inter Baku*, para 34; AC-04/2016 *FK Partizan*, para 42.
47   AC-01/2014 *FK Crvena Zvezda*, para 54.

regime.[48] It is vital that submissions by clubs are on time and are accurate.[49] A failure to make a submission altogether will lead to the conclusion that the club is in breach not only of its monitoring obligations but of the substantive rules.[50] Clubs which provide misleading information can expect to be heavily criticised and sanctioned accordingly.[51]

(d)   The importance of evidence

16.39   The CFCB AC will evaluate evidence, including expert evidence, in order to determine whether a club has breached the FFP rules[52] and whether any defence, eg of force majeure is made out.[53] Evidence to support a club's position is vital: mere assertion by way of argument will not suffice.[54]

(e)   The concept of 'overdue payables'

16.40   The concept, or in the words of the UEFA FFP Regulations the 'notion', of 'overdue payables' is defined by Annex VIII to the Regulations. Paragraph 1 of Annex VIII provides that '[p]ayables are considered as overdue if they are not paid according to the agreed terms'. Despite the reference to 'agreed terms', the concept of 'payables' is not restricted to contractual debts but includes all kinds of obligations to pay, such as tax liabilities arising under a foreign statute.[55] As noted at para **16.35** above, it has been held that recourse to national law should be had only to the extent necessary to apply the Regulations and not otherwise, and that 'overdue' has an autonomous meaning specific to the Regulations. Presumably, however, the interpretation of the 'terms' of an obligation is governed, like the question whether there is a debt at all, by the law governing the obligation in question.

16.41   Paragraph 2 of Annex VIII sets out five situations in which a payable is not considered as overdue (despite not having been paid according to the agreed terms). These are that the club: (i) has paid the amount in full; (ii) has concluded a deferral agreement in writing in respect of the debt; (iii) has brought a claim or other proceedings contesting liability (unless the decision-making bodies conclude that such a claim has been made solely to 'buy time'); (iv) has challenged a claim or other proceedings have been brought against it in respect of the payable; or (v) in the case of training compensation and solidarity contributions, can demonstrate that it has taken all reasonable measures to identify and pay the creditor club(s). These exceptions have been restrictively interpreted in the case law.

---

48   CAS 2012/A/2702 *Györi ETO FC v UEFA*, para 115; AC-06/2014 *Panevézio Futbolo Klubas Ekranas*, para 41; AC-06/2015 *FC Astra*, para 55.
49   AC-06/2014 *Panevézio Futbolo Klubas Ekranas*, para 41; AC-09/2012, *FK Vojvodina Novi Sad*, para 32; AC-04/2013 *PAS Giannina*, para 51; AC-01/2014 *FK Crvena Zvezda*, paras 123, 138; AC-01/2015 *Pallohonka Oy*, para 53.
50   AC-06/2014 *Panevézio Futbolo Klubas Ekranas*, para 42.
51   CAS 2012/A/2821 *Bursaspor v UEFA*, para 115; CAS 2012/A/2702 *Gyori ETO v UEFA*, para 146; AC-01/2014 *FK Crvena Zvezda*, para 140.
52   Eg AC-02/2015 *Dynamo Moscow*, where the CFCB AC considered rival expert evidence on the true value of a sponsorship agreement with a related party, although in that case it was held that the club had on any view breached the 'break-even' requirement.
53   See para **16.47** below.
54   AC-09/2015 *Targu Mures*, para 44; AC-01/2016 *Galatasaray*, para 61.
55   CAS 2013/A/3067 *Málaga CF SAD v UEFA*, para 9.6.

16.42   A payable will remain overdue within the meaning of the UEFA FFP Regulations notwithstanding an oral agreement to defer the debt.[56] Deferral agreements must be in writing, and while Annex VIII does not stipulate a signed agreement or any other particular form of writing, it has been held that 'a clear expression of the will of the creditor' is required.[57] This has the curious effect that a debt arising under (say) an oral contract governed by English law will be treated as a 'payable' for the purposes of the FFP Regulations but will be incapable of being rescheduled for those purposes except in writing. On the other hand, it would appear that 'a clear expression of the will of the creditor' in writing that the debt should be deferred (eg an email to that effect) would be sufficient to prevent the payable from being treated as overdue even if, as a matter of the national law governing the debt, the debt had not been rescheduled (eg because of a 'no-variation' clause in the original agreement).[58]

16.43   The failure by a creditor to render an invoice does not mean that the sum is not payable,[59] unless (perhaps) the debt as a matter of the applicable national law only arises upon presentation of an invoice.

16.44   The fact that an alleged debt is disputed does not mean that it will not be treated as an overdue payable: only if proceedings within the meaning of para 2(c) or (d) of Annex VIII have been commenced in respect of the debt, prior to the relevant assessment deadline, will an exception apply.[60] Oddly, therefore, the commencement of legal proceedings by its creditor is likely to put a club in a better position than it would be in otherwise: the commencement of proceedings will permit the club to 'challenge' the debt for the purposes of para 2(d). The extent to which it is open to a club to contend that a disputed debt should not be treated as a payable in the first place has not been specifically addressed in the case law.

16.45   The CFCB AC is critical of unjustified attempts to classify overdue payables as deferred or in dispute and may treat them as an attempt to avoid scrutiny.[61]

(f)   Defences

16.46   There are many more examples in the case law of unsuccessful defences than of successful ones. A club's poor financial situation cannot be used as justification for breaching the rules,[62] nor even can insolvency.[63] Relegation is no excuse as the risk of relegation should always be taken into account in a club's financial planning decisions.[64] A club's lack of skilled personnel and resources is irrelevant,[65] as is the fact that problems were caused under previous management,[66]

---

56   AC-01/2014 *FK Crvena Zvezda*, para 70.
57   CAS 2013/A/3067 *Málaga CF SAD v UEFA*, paras 9.8 and 9.9.
58   So much would follow from the decision in CAS 2013/A/3067 *Málaga CF SAD v UEFA*.
59   AC-01/2014 *FK Crvena Zvezda*, para 92.
60   Ibid, paras 100 and 116.
61   Ibid, para 138.
62   CAS 2006/A/110 *PAOK FC v UEFA*, para 43; CAS 2014/A/3533 *FC Metallurg v UEFA*, para 59; AC-06/2014 *Panevézio Futbolo Klubas Ekranas*, para 47; AC-01/2014 *FK Crvena Zvezda*, para 141; AC-05/2015 *Inter Baku*, para 37.
63   AC-03/2015 *FC CSKA AD*, paras 45 and 51.
64   CAS 2016/A/4692 *Kardemir Karabükspor*, para 7.18.
65   AC-06/2014 *Panevézio Futbolo Klubas Ekranas*, para 47; AC-01/2015 *Pallohonka Oy*, para 54; AC-03/2015 *FC CSKA AD*, para 51.
66   AC-03/2012 *HNK Hajduk Split*, para 40; AC-03/2013 *Panathinaikos FC*, para 88; AC-05/2014 *Bursaspor*, para 36.

or by the ill health of employees.[67] 'Solidarity' with other clubs or the status of a club within its home nation,[68] the fact that a club's national market may generate lower revenues than other national markets,[69] and the fact that revenue generation may be made more difficult by restrictions on foreign players[70] have all been rejected as defences. Indeed, not only have all of these factors been found to be no defence on the question of breach; they have been held to be incapable of amounting to mitigation on the question of sanction. The principle of equal treatment is typically prayed in aid in support of this strict approach: since most clubs comply, it is unfair to make exceptions to some.[71]

16.47   'Force majeure', defined by para (1)(f) of Annex XI to the UEFA FFP Regulations as 'extraordinary events or circumstances beyond the control of the club', will provide a defence. However, the concept of force majeure must be narrowly interpreted:[72] it 'implies an an objective, rather than a personal, impediment, beyond the control of the "obliged party" that is unforeseeable, that cannot be resisted, and that renders the performance of the obligation impossible',[73] which represents a 'high benchmark'.[74] A club invoking force majeure must provide specific evidence of the event or circumstance which made compliance with the obligation in question impossible;[75] this is a significant evidential burden.[76] A similar strict approach is taken where clubs rely upon paras 1(f) ('Major and unforeseen changes in the economic environment') and 1(g) ('Operating in a structurally inefficient market') of Annex XI.[77]

16.48   In one case, the Syrian refugee crisis, a match-fixing scandal, terrorist attacks and a general economic downturn were all held to lack the necessary causal effect, even though the CFCB AC accepted that on the facts they may well have had a general detrimental impact on the club's revenues.[78] In another case, a club successfully invoked a force majeure defence to an allegation of breach of the overdue payables rules by reference to the political situation in the Ukraine in 2014 and the problems it caused for those seeking to make foreign currency transfers;[79] but when the same club sought to run the same argument 18 months later the CFCB AC had much less sympathy and did not accept that the test for force majeure remained satisfied.[80]

---

67   AC-01/2014, *FK Crvena Zvezda*, para 141; AC-05/2014 *Bursaspor*, para 36.
68   AC-01/2014 *FK Crvena Zvezda*, para 141.
69   AC-02/2015 *Dynamo Moscow*, para 68.
70   Ibid, para 71.
71   CAS 2008/A/1579 *Fubalski Zemun v UEFA*, para 4.5; AC-06/2014 *Panevézio Futbolo Klubas Ekranas*, paras 43 and 47; AC-01/2015 *Pallohonka Oy*, para 54.
72   CAS 2006/A/110, *PAOK FC v UEFA*, para 41; AC-06/2014 *Panevézio Futbolo Klubas Ekranas*, para 48.
73   Ibid.
74   AC-02/2014 *FC Dnipro*, para 47; AC-01/2016 *Galatasaray*, para 63.
75   CAS 2008/A/1621 *Iraqi Football Association v FIFA & Qatar Football Association*, para 22; AC-06/2014 *Panevézio Futbolo Klubas Ekranas*, para 49; CAS 2014/A/3533 *FC Metallurg*, para 62; AC-02/2014 *FC Dnipro*, para 47.
76   In CAS 2016/A/4492 *Galatasaray*, para 107, the CAS held that what was required was 'comprehensive and substantial data and evidence specific to [the club's] situation, the quantitative impact of such factors on its accounts and how they would have prevented it from complying'.
77   AC-01/2016 *Galatasaray*, paras 78, 80 and 82, upheld as CA 2-16/A/4492.
78   AC-01/2016 *Galatasaray*, para 59.
79   AC-02/2014 *FC Dnipro*, para 50.
80   AC-07/2015 *FC Dnipro*, paras 41–44.

(g) Sanction

16.49   Possible sanctions for breach of the UEFA FFP Regulations range from reprimand to disqualification from competition or withdrawal of a title.[81] The CFCB AC does not have a standard menu of sanctions, but a wide discretion.[82] In practice, the sanctions imposed by the CFCB AC have ranged from small fines in less serious cases[83] to exclusion from the next UEFA competition for which the club would otherwise qualify in a period of years.[84] Sanctions may be combined:[85] so exclusion may be accompanied by a fine[86] or other measures, such as a cap on player spending.[87] The largest fines extracted from clubs have been seen not in decisions of the CFCB AC but in settlement agreements, where clubs have agreed to pay voluntary fines for breach of the break-even rules of as much as €60 million (with €40 million returnable to the club in the event of compliance) as part of the settlement.[88]

16.50   Sanctions must be proportionate,[89] although CAS will only overturn a sanction as disproportionate if it is shown to be evidently and grossly disproportionate to the breach.[90] The CFCB AC must also act consistently with decisions on similar facts,[91] but a sanction is not rendered disproportionate merely because a different sanction has been imposed in a different case.[92] The relevant factors involved will very greatly between clubs, which makes comparison between cases difficult.[93] Moreover, the FFP regime is a developing area; the type and seriousness of sanctions required to achieve compliance may change over time.[94] There is thus no 'rigid benchmark'.[95]

16.51   A common form of sanction in overdue payables cases is to provide for a conditional sanction which will be wholly or partially lifted in the event that the club can prove that the overdue sums have been paid within a short period, the rationale being that clubs 'should be given a chance to achieve financial stability'.[96] Unless the club is able to prove compliance within the necessary deadline the sanction will become effective.[97]

---

81   Article 29(1) of the Procedural rules governing the UEFA Club Financial Control Body 2015.
82   CAS 2012/A/2821 *Bursaspor v UEFA*, para 143; CAS 2012/A/2702 *Győri ETO FC v UEFA*, para 160; AC-01/2014 *FK Crvena Zvezda*, paras 130 and 131; AC-01/2016 *Galatasaray*, paras 106 and 107; AC-02/2016 *Kerdemir Karabükspor*, paras 54 and 55.
83   Eg AC-08/2015 *Botosani*, where a fine of €15,000 was imposed.
84   Eg AC-02/2015 *Dynamo Moscow* (exclusion from the next competition in a four-year period).
85   Article 29(3) of the Procedural rules governing the UEFA Club Financial Control Body 2015; AC-02/2015 *Dynamo Moscow* para 53.
86   Eg AC-06/2014 *Panevézio Futbolo Klubas Ekranas* (exclusion plus €15,000 fine).
87   Such a cap was upheld in CAS 2016/A/4492 *Galatasaray* together with an exclusion from the next competition in a two-year period.
88   Both Manchester City and Paris Saint Germain agreed to such a fine in settlement agreements dated 16 May 2014.
89   CAS 2012/A/2821 *Bursaspor v UEFA*, para 144; AC-06/2014 *Panevézio Futbolo Klubas Ekranas*, para 58.
90   CAS 2016/A/4692, *Kerdemir Karabükspor*, para 7.32.
91   CAS 2012/A/2821 *Bursaspor*, para 144; AC-01/2014 *FK Crvena Zvezda*, para 130.
92   CAS 2012/A/284 *Beşiktaş JK v UEFA*, para 127; AC-02/2016 *Kerdemir Karabükspor*, para 56.
93   AC-01/2015 *Galatasaray*, para 105; AC-02/2016 *Kardemir Karabükspor*, para 53; CAS 2016/A/4692 *Kardemir Karabükspor v UEFA*, paras 7.35 to 7.37.
94   AC-01/2014 *FK Crvena Zvezda*, para 132; AC-01/2016 *Galatasaray*, para 110.
95   AC-01/2015 *Galatasaray*, para 105; AC-02/2016 *Kardemir Karabükspor*, para 53.
96   AC-03/2014 *FC Astra*, para 43.2; AC-05/2014 *Bursaspor*, para 47; AC-04/2014 *CFR 1907 Cluj*, para 40.
97   Order dated 31 March 2015 in AC-04/2014 *CFR 1907 Cluj*; Order dated 24 August 2015 in AC-01/2015 *Pallohonka Oy*; Order dated 31 March 2016 in AC-09/2015 *Targu Mures*; Order dated 31 March 2016 in AC-05/2015 *Inter Baku*; Order dated 31 March 2016 in AC-07/2015 *FC Dnipro*.

16.52   Suspended penalties are another common form of sanction. Where a suspended penalty has been imposed, and a further breach is committed within the period of the suspension, the imposition of the penalty becomes automatic and mandatory, rather than a matter for the CFCB AC's discretion.[98] When a suspended penalty of exclusion is activated, the exclusion runs from the date the suspended penalty was originally imposed rather than the date of activation, unless the penalty expressly provides otherwise.[99]

16.53   Generally speaking, relevant factors include the reasons why the club is in breach, whether it has remedied the breach, and whether it is in a position to ensure that it complies with the rules in future.[100] In an overdue payables case, the CFCB AC will consider whether they have increased between monitoring dates[101] and what efforts have been made to reduce them;[102] what payments have been made and when, and their relative size;[103] whether there is an explanation for the sums overdue and whether the situation can reasonably be expected to improve;[104] and the overall context of the financial state of affairs of the club.[105]

16.54   Sanctions must be adequate to act as a deterrent to the club in question.[106] A sanction's deterrent effect on other clubs is also relevant: thus in one case the sanction of exclusion from UEFA competitions was imposed even though the club in question, as an 'amateur lower-division club in Bulgaria' following its insolvency, was most unlikely to qualify for such competitions.[107]

16.55   Yet the purpose of sanctions is not simply to ensure compliance with the rules. It is also to respect the principle of equal treatment and to protect the integrity of UEFA's competitions by ensuring that all clubs are subject to the same requirements.[108] This is a particular concern in the case of breach of the break-even requirement, which is liable to have a direct impact upon a club's competiveness.[109] For this reason the CFCB AC will be reluctant to order anything other than immediate exclusion where a suspended sanction would permit a club in serious breach of the rules to participate in a UEFA competition[110]; where a club has already done so while in breach, the CFCB AC is likely to require the club to disgorge the benefit by way of a fine.[111] It should be noted, however, that even a breach of the rules on overdue payables can justify immediate exclusion.[112]

16.56   Unsurprisingly, previous breaches will be taken into account,[113] including breaches under the previous CDB regime.[114] Unlike the position under the UEFA

---

98   AC-05/2014 *Bursaspor*, paras 43 and 45; CAS 2014/A/387 *Bursaspor v UEFA*, para 81.
99   CAS 2014/A/3870 *Bursaspor v UEFA*, para 84.
100 AC-01/2015 *Galatasaray,* para 105; AC-02/2016 *Kardemir Karabükspor*, para 53; AC-02/2015 *Dynamo Moscow*, para 63.
101 AC-04/2014 *CFR 1907 Cluj*, paras 32 and 33.
102 AC-08/2015 *Botosani*, para 38.
103 AC-04/2014 *CFR 1907 Cluj*, para 34.
104 Ibid, para 38.
105 AC-01/2014 *FK Crvena Zvezda*, para 133.
106 AC-04/2015 *SC Braga*, para 46 (where a €20,000 fine was imposed, being 10% of the overdue payable, which had been paid by the time of the CFCB AC's decision).
107 AC-03/2015 *FC CSKA AD*, paras 53 and 54.
108 AC-02/2015 *Dynamo Moscow*, para 80.
109 AC-02/2015 *Dynamo Moscow*, paras 79 and 80; AC-01/2016 *Galatasaray*, paras 100 to 102.
110 AC-02/2015, *Dynamo Moscow*, para 82.
111 This appears to be the basis of the voluntary fines in many settlement decisions, including those in the Manchester City and Paris Saint Germain cases (see n 88 above).
112 AC-06/2014 *Panevézio Futbolo Klubas Ekranas*, para 54.
113 AC-01/2014 *FK Crvena Zvezda*, para 142; AC-06/2015 *FC Astra*, para 57.
114 AC-05/2014 *Bursaspor*, para 40.

Disciplinary Regulations (where only previous offences in a three-year period are relevant), the CFCB AC's consideration of recidivism is unrestricted in time.[115] If, however, previous breaches have been taken into account as such as an aggravating factor in a prior decision on sanction, they will not be taken into account yet again.[116] A history of recidivism is likely to lead the CFCB AC to conclude that a stronger sanction is required in order to act as an adequate deterrent.[117] The CFCB AC takes a particularly dim view of breaches of settlement agreements; in such a case the club has already been given a 'second chance' by the settlement agreement.[118] Other aggravating factors include disregard of the rules and the provision of inaccurate information.[119]

D FFP AND COMPETITION LAW

16.57   In this section, we consider the application of competition law to FFP. We start by setting out the basic principles governing the application of competition law in the sporting context in general. We then turn to how competition law applies to FFP rules in particular, including by reference to some of the competition law challenges to FFP rules that have been, and are being, brought.

(a) The application of competition law in the sporting context

16.58   The relevant competition law provisions in the Treaty on the Functioning of the European Union are Article 101 (which prohibits agreements and concerted practices with the object or effect of the prevention, restriction or distortion of competition) and Article 102 (which prohibits abuse of a dominant position). There are domestic equivalents in Chapter I and II of the Competition Act 1998. For a fuller exploration of competition law (which falls outside the scope of the present chapter), readers are advised to consult the specialist works on the subject.

16.59   There are two principal sources which will inevitably be relied upon in any competition law challenge in the sporting context: C-519/04 P: *Meca-Medina & Majcen v Commission of the European Communities*;[120] and the Commission Staff Working Document, 'The EU and Sport: Background and Context – Accompanying document to the White Paper on Sport' ('the SWD').[121]

(i) Meca-Medina

16.60   The *Meca-Medina* case concerned a challenge to anti-doping rules adopted by the International Olympic Committee (IOC) and implemented by the International Swimming Federation. The applicants failed doping tests and were subject to four years' suspension (reduced to two years by the CAS). They complained to the European Commission, alleging that the rules were anti-competitive (and also incompatible with the rules on freedom to provide services).

115 AC-04/2016 *FK Partizan*, paras 49–53.
116 Ibid, paras 55–60.
117 Ibid, para 60.
118 AC-03/2015 *FC CSKA AD*, para 44; AC-02/2016 *Kardemir Karabükspor*, para 59.
119 AC-01/2014 *FK Crvena Zvezda*, para 134; see further para **16.38** above.
120 [2006] ECR I-6991.
121 COM(2007) 391 final.

They claimed that the threshold limit was a concerted practice between the IOC and the laboratories accredited by it, and the limit was scientifically unfounded and could lead to exclusion of innocent or merely negligent athletes. They further claimed that the anti-competitive nature of the limit was strengthened by the mechanism of strict liability and the sports arbitration system. The Commission rejected this complaint.

16.61   The applicants challenged the Commission decision before the Court of First Instance (as it then was). That challenge was rejected on the basis that purely sporting rules have nothing to do with economic activity, and so fall outside the rules on free movement. The CFI held that such rules would therefore also have nothing to do with the economic relationships of competition, with the result that they would also fall outside the scope of the competition rules. Since the prohibition of doping is based on purely sporting considerations, the relevant rules and practices fell outside the scope of Articles 81 (now Article 101) and 82 (now Article 102).

16.62   The applicants appealed to the Court of Justice. On the relevant law, the Court departed from the CFI, holding that:

- The mere fact that a rule is purely sporting in nature does not have the effect of removing from the scope of the Treaty the person engaging in the activity governed by that rule or the body which has laid it down (para 27).
- If the sporting activity in question falls within the scope of the Treaty, the conditions for engaging in it are then subject to all the obligations which result from the various provisions of the Treaty. It follows that the rules which govern that activity must satisfy the requirements of those provisions, which, in particular, seek to ensure (inter alia) competition (para 28).
- Where engagement in the activity must be assessed in the light of the Treaty provisions relating to competition, it will be necessary to determine, given the specific requirements of Articles 81 (now Article 101) and 82 (now Article 102), whether the rules which govern that activity emanate from an undertaking, whether the latter restricts competition or abuses its dominant position, and whether that restriction or that abuse affects trade between Member States (para 30).
- Even if rules do not constitute restrictions on freedom of movement because they concern questions of purely sporting interest and, as such, have nothing to do with economic activity, that fact means neither that the sporting activity in question necessarily falls outside the scope of Articles 81 (now Article 101) and 82 (now Article 102) nor that the rules do not satisfy the specific requirements of those articles (para 31).
- For the purposes of application of Article 101(1) to a particular case, account must first of all be taken of the overall context in which the decision of the association of undertaking was taken or produces its effects and, more specifically, of its objectives. It has then to be considered whether the consequential effects restrictive of competition are inherent in the pursuit of those objectives and are proportionate to them (para 42).

16.63   The Court then applied that legal approach to the facts of *Meca-Medina*. First, it held that, as regards the overall context in which the rules were adopted, they served legitimate objectives of (*inter alia*) combatting doping in order for sport to be conducted fairly (para 43). Some form of limitation on athletes' freedom of action was inherent in the pursuit of such a legitimate objective, and in 'the organisation and proper conduct of competitive sport' (para 45). It went on to find that:

> 'It must be acknowledged that the penal nature of the anti-doping rules at issue and the magnitude of the penalties applicable if they are breached are capable of producing adverse effects on competition because they could, if penalties were ultimately to prove unjustified, result in an athlete's unwarranted exclusion from sporting events, and thus in impairment of the conditions under which the activity at issue is engaged in. It follows that, in order not to be covered by the prohibition laid down in Article 81(1) EC [now 101(1)], the restrictions thus imposed by those rules must be limited to what is necessary to ensure the proper conduct of competitive sport ...' (para 47).

16.64   The Court of Justice concluded that the restrictions imposed by the threshold did not go beyond what was necessary in order to ensure that sporting events take place and function properly (para 54). Since the applicants had not pleaded that the penalties were excessive, 'it has not been established that the anti-doping rules at issue are disproportionate' (para 55).

(ii) The SWD

16.65   The SWD deals with the application of competition law to sport in section 3.4, and then in more detail in Annex I, section 2. It summarises the Court in *Meca Medina* as having:

> 'held that the qualification of a rule as "purely sporting" is not sufficient to remove the athlete or the sport association adopting the rule in question from the scope of EC competition rules. The Court insisted, on the contrary, that whenever the sporting activity in question constitutes an economic activity and thus falls within the scope of the EC Treaty, the conditions for engaging in it then are subject to obligations resulting from the various provisions of the Treaty including the competition rules. The Court spelled out the need to determine, on a case-by-case basis and irrespective of the nature of the rule, whether the specific requirements of Articles 81 EC or 82 EC are met' (3.4(a)).

It then set out the proper methodology when applying competition law to sporting rules (3.4(b); Annex I, para 2.1.2), as follows:

> 'Step 1. Is the sports association that adopted the rule to be considered an undertaking or an association of undertakings?
>
> (a) The sports association is an 'undertaking' to the extent it carries out an "economic activity" itself (e.g., the selling of broadcasting rights).
> (b) The sports association is an 'association of undertakings' if its members carry out an economic activity. In this respect, the question will become relevant to what extent the sport in which the members (usually clubs/teams or athletes) are active can be considered an economic activity and to what extent the members exercise economic activity. In the absence of "economic activity", Articles 81 and 82 EC [now Articles 101 and 102] do not apply.
>
> Step 2. Does the rule in question restrict competition within the meaning of Article [101(1)] or constitute an abuse of a dominant position under Article [102]? This will depend, in application of the principles established under the *Wouters* judgment, on the following factors:
>
> (a) the overall context in which the rule was adopted or produces its effects, and its objectives;
> (b) whether the restrictions caused by the rule are inherent in the pursuit of the objectives; and
> (c) whether the rule is proportionate in light of the objective pursued?

Step 3. Is trade between Member States affected?

Step 4. Does the rule fulfil the conditions of Article [101(3)]?'

(iii) Commentary

16.66   In a nutshell, we now know that competition law *does* apply to sporting organisational rules and we have an authoritative methodology to follow when assessing that application. However, as anyone arguing a competition law case in the sports field will quickly realise, there are some gaps in the established methodology. The authors note two of those holes here.

16.67   First, how do the steps laid down above accommodate the demonstration of a restriction of competition by object or effect? *Meca-Medina* does not contain any recognisable assessment of restriction by object or effect. Instead, in para 47 it simply says that the rules may 'result in an athlete's unwarranted exclusion from sporting events, and thus in impairment of the conditions under which the activity at issue is engaged in' and so breach Article 101(1) unless justified. That is an extremely anaemic version of a conventional effects (or object) assessment. It may well be the case that this is appropriate and was the intention of the Court. However, a defendant would surely say that, if rules are to be found to be in breach of Article 101(1) unless justified, surely they must meet the conventional Article 101(1) requirements.

16.68   Secondly, what about the degree of deference to be accorded to the relevant rule-making body? In particular, when it comes to proportionality, is the question whether the court/arbitral panel takes the view that the rule is proportionate in light of the objective pursued? Or is it the question for the court/arbitral panel in fact whether the body which made the rule could reasonably have taken the view that the rule was proportionate in light of the objection pursued? And, if so, how much margin of discretion should be accorded to the rule-making body? On this question, it may be instructive to have regard to *London Welsh RFC v RFU* (20 June 2012) in which an arbitral panel (James Dingemans QC (as he then was), Ian Mill QC and Tim Ward QC) held that the relevant rule (requiring a RFU club to have primacy of tenure over its stadium in order to be promoted) was of a 'hybrid' nature, ie partly commercial and partly sporting (para 47). The parties had agreed that, the more commercial the rule, the less deference should be accorded to the rule-maker. However, the Panel still found that the RFU was entitled to a 'substantial margin of appreciation' in formulating and applying the primacy of tenure rule (para 48). The authors respectfully suggest that this approach might be open to challenge. Moreover, even if according such a substantial margin of appreciation to the rule-maker's assessment is correct, the corollary must be that the subjective decision-making of the rule-making body is relevant in a way which would not be the case if proportionality were to be answered objectively. Thus, for example, a failure on the part of the rule-making body properly to ask itself whether a rule was proportionate might become relevant.

(b) The application of competition law to FFP rules in particular

16.69   There have been three principal challenges to FFP rules: Case C-299/15: *Striani v UEFA* (Order 16 July 2015); *Galatasaray v UEFA* (CAS 2016/A/4492); and Queen's Park Rangers' challenge to the 2012 Championship FFP Rules.

(i) Striani

16.70 This case concerned a challenge brought in the Belgian courts against the UEFA FFP Rules by Daniele Striani, a Belgian player-agent. The Belgian court used the mechanism in Article 267 of the Treaty on the Functioning of the European Union to refer questions to the Court of Justice for a preliminary ruling. In particular, the Belgian court asked the Court of Justice to rule on whether the UEFA FPP rules were compatible with Articles 101 and 102 (and various free movement provisions). The Court of Justice rejected the challenge as 'manifestly inadmissible'. However, this was on grounds which were specific to the way the challenge had been brought (in particular, that the Belgian Court had already held that it did not have jurisdiction to rule on the merits of the case and so determination of the questions was not necessary, and also that the Belgian Court had failed to provide the necessary information to allow the case to be decided). It would therefore be wrong to view this decision as a substantive rejection of the challenge.

(ii) Galatasaray

16.71 Following Galatasaray's breach of the break-even requirement in the UEFA FFP Regulations, it entered into a settlement agreement requiring it (i) to be break-even compliant at the latest in the monitoring period 2015/16, and (ii) to have aggregate employee benefit expenses of no more than €90 million in the reporting period 2015 (para 8). Galatasaray breached both those requirements: its break-even deficit was €134.2 million and its employee expenses were €95.5 million (para 9). The Investigatory Chamber referred the case to the Adjudicatory Chamber (para 11), which received written submissions and held a hearing (para 12), following which it imposed: a ban from the next UEFA competition into which it would otherwise qualify in the next two seasons; and an aggregate player salary cap of €65 million in each of the next two reporting periods (para 13).

16.72 Galatasaray challenged the decision of the Adjudicatory Chamber before the CAS. In particular, it argued that the relevant UEFA FFP rules were in breach of Article 101. The competition law analysis is contained in paras 55–80 of the CAS' Arbitral Award.

16.73 The first interesting aspect of this Award is that it does not follow the *Meca-Medina*/SWD methodology. Instead, having considered the 'first condition' of whether the rules are a 'decision by an association of undertakings' (paras 57–60) and the 'second condition' of whether the rules 'may affect trade between Member States' (para 61), the CAS's attention turned to the 'third condition' of whether they 'have as their object or effect the prevention, restriction or distortion of competition' (paras 62–80).

16.74 In the section of the Award concerned with the object or effect of the rules, the CAS held that the rules were not a restriction 'by object' (paras 62–72); nor were they a restriction 'by effect (paras 73–80). It is only in the last few paragraphs of that section that a *Meca-Medina* analysis is conducted, ie that the context, objective and proportionality of the rules is taken into account (and even here this is by reference to Case C-309/99 *Wouters* rather than by reference to *Meca-Medina*).

16.75 The second interesting aspect is that the CAS held that Galatasaray had failed to provide:

'any detailed economic analysis or empirical evidence of the impact of the [rules] and its break-even requirement on competition and the market; the Appellant failed to provide a precise definition of the relevant market, product(s) or service(s) concerned and to assess them; it also failed to provide a sound assessment, based on evidence, of the actual effects of the [rules] on such market, product(s) and service(s) … The Panel also notes that, whilst [it] had indicated in its Appeal Brief that it reserved its right to present for oral testimony two professors of economics … to address economic issues raised by the case, it did not submit any expert witness affidavits and did not ask that they, or any other expert, be present at the hearing' (para 74).

The authors suggest that the CAS's expectations mark a clear departure from the low test for a restriction indicated in *Meca-Medina* (in which the mere exclusion of an athlete from a sport was enough to require justification).

16.76 The third interesting point is that the CAS particularly emphasised the various ways in which the UEFA FFP Regulations are not 'blunt instruments' and are, instead, flexible (para 70; para 79). The authors suggest that this may be contrasted with other FFP Rules.

16.77 The fourth, and final, interesting point is that, in the authors' respectful opinion, much of the CAS's substantive reasoning is weak. For example, the CAS says that the rules:

'produce the effect that competition is not distorted by 'overspending' … In other words, their effect is to prevent a distortion of competition. Further, they do not limit the amount of salaries for the players: clubs are free to pay as much as they wish, provided those salaries are covered by revenues. In addition, they do not "ossificate" the structure of market (large dominant clubs have always existed and will always exist) …' (para 76).

With all respect to the CAS, the authors suggest that each of these three points is bad. First, the use of 'distortion' to refer to the freedom to invest in clubs is to confuse sporting competition with economic competition. Secondly, of course the rules impose some kind of limit on salaries, since the clubs cannot spend more than their revenues. And thirdly, the statement 'large dominant clubs have always existed and will always exist' is a counsel of despair which fails to acknowledge the role that investment has in challenging that incumbency.

16.78 Accordingly, in the authors' respectful view, the *Galatasaray* decision is unlikely to be the final word on this subject.

(iii) QPR

16.79 All of the authors of this chapter have been, at various times, counsel to Queens Park Rangers in its challenge to the 2012 Championship FFP Rules. That challenge is ongoing and is subject to confidentiality obligations. Accordingly, for present purposes the authors can do no more than recite the press release dated 24 October 2017:

'An Arbitral Panel has dismissed Queens Park Rangers' claim that the English Football League's 2012 Financial Fair Play Rules were unlawful under Competition Law, and also found that the fine levied by the EFL on the Club was not disproportionate … QPR has indicated that it intends to appeal the decision.'

There shall no doubt be further discussion of this important case when it is finally concluded.

CHAPTER 17

Personal Injury

Alistair McHenry (Walker Morris)

A   INTRODUCTION

17.1   There is a sense that football and the law are uncomfortable bedfellows, that football has always preferred to deal with things 'in house', so it is no surprise that in the area of personal injury recourse to the courts has been so infrequent. When courts have been required to adjudicate, they have been hesitant in doing so, treading carefully, perhaps mindful of intervening in a world which is heavily self-regulated. Such caution is apparent in the courts' use of the type of language with which football is so familiar: 'part and parcel of the game', the 'general run of play' and the 'heat of the battle' are all terms which have been used readily by judges. They not only serve to give football the reassuring familiarity it craves when taken outside of its own confines, but the phrases actually strike to the heart of when judicial intervention has been, and will continue to be, necessary.

17.2   For instance, it is now well established that it will only be when a player does something demonstrably outside the 'part and parcel' of the game that they will be fixed with any sort of civil liability. And it is normal for the courts to give considered allowance and respect for football's heat of the battle. So it can be seen that the legal threshold for liability to arise outside the game and inside the courts will be high. As we shall see, the occasions when the threshold has been reached have been few and far between, constituting what can neatly be described as 'football crimes' (a term used by Mrs Justice Hallett when giving judgment in one of the leading cases in the area).[1] It is those football crimes with which the law in this chapter is primarily concerned.

---

1   *Pitcher v Huddersfield Town Football Club* – HQ0005953 - QBD Transcript, 17 July 2001 (Hallet J).

B   ASSAULT/TRESPASS TO THE PERSON

17.3   One of the most infamous and high-profile fouls ever committed in the professional game was by Manchester United's Roy Keane on Manchester City's Alf-Inge Haaland in a Manchester derby in 2001. It is a horrible foul to watch, made more reprehensible following the release of Keane's autobiography in which he appeared to suggest that the foul was both intentional and pre-meditated. The ingredient of intent is one which can elevate a foul committed during the course of a football match to a claim actionable in assault and battery. Keane's admission of intent was about as clear (and succinct) as it gets – 'The ball was there (I think). Take that you cunt.'[2]– but no claim ever materialised in the courts, almost certainly due to Haaland's eventual retirement being due to an injury to his *left* knee (Keane had clattered his *right*) and thus falling down for a lack of causation.

17.4   Even with the requirement of intent publicly satisfied, Haaland's problem proving a specific causal link between the foul and his retirement is symptomatic of the general evidential difficulties would-be claimant footballers face when trying to establish that a foul is outside the normal 'rough and tumble' of the game. On this case, at least, we will never know; it certainly would have been interesting to watch the fireworks in court had Keane's foul been the direct cause of Haaland's immediate retirement, and Haaland had returned fire on Keane by lodging a claim for assault.[3]

17.5   There is another practical consideration which makes a successful claim of assault in football very unlikely. In *Elliott v Saunders and Liverpool Football Club*,[4] Paul Elliott's career was ended when Dean Saunders' overzealous tackle severed Elliott's cruciate ligaments in a Premier League match in September 1992 between Liverpool and Chelsea. Elliott brought claims for *both* assault and negligence, but eventually dropped the assault claim when it transpired Liverpool's insurance policy would only pay out for negligent acts, rather than deliberate ones (this case is discussed further below in the context of negligence, the head of claim Elliott did continue with). As an aside, it is worth noting Saunders' public comments at the conclusion of the case; they are telling of Saunders' ingrained belief that football should steer clear of the courts and probably reflect what the majority of footballers think – that to bring such cases is not in the spirit of the game: 'All I can say is we should never have been here in the first place'.[5] Saunders' comments are significant because they introduce a recurring theme which has impacted on the way the law in this area has developed.

C   NEGLIGENCE AND DUTY OF CARE

17.6   The main distinction between an action in assault and one in negligence is intent. Without the evidential burden of proving that a player set out to cause injury to another, actions in negligence are far more likely to succeed than actions in assault. It is worth noting that in *Watson and Bradford City v Gray and Huddersfield Town*,[6] Hooper J remarked that 'the witnesses were at one saying that professional

---

2   R Keane and E Dunphy, *Keane: The Autobiography* (London: Michael Joseph, 2002).
3   For a fuller analysis of this incident, the reader is referred to Mark James, 'The Trouble with Roy Keane' (2002) 1(3) Entertainment Law 72–92.
4   Unreported, QB Transcript, 10 June 1994.
5   See http://www.independent.co.uk/news/uk/injured-footballer-loses-pounds-1m-damages-case-better-insurance-for-players-urged-as-defender-whose-1421737.html (accessed March 2018).
6   1997 – W – no.97.

footballers do not set out to break someone's leg'. For anyone who has played the game, as a general starting point, this must surely be right and therefore claims of negligence – in which claimants do not need to show intent – is very much where the case law is focused.

17.7   The key to the principle of negligence, long established, is that the law demands you take reasonable care to avoid injuring your neighbour. Put onto the football pitch, that translates to a player having a duty to take reasonable care to avoid injuring another player in the context of the game. In his essay, 'A Duty of Care in Sport: What it Actually Means', William Norris QC points out that 'what makes sport special from a legal point of view is that all parties realise it involves risk and that, where there is a duty, the standard of care must allow for the particular and special circumstances in which harm may arise'.[7] Whilst the courts have always recognised that sporting context, specifically the 'particular and special' circumstances in which harm may arise, their judgments have led to some unmistakably grey areas. As Norris points out, this imprecision is echoed in Baroness Grey-Thompson's 'deliberately broad' definition in her April 2017 review 'Duty of Care in Sport'. The ambiguity of what players are actually consenting to is not helped by the hovering presence of the common law doctrine '*volenti non fit injuria*' – literally, 'to a willing person, injury is not done', which provides a defence to any claim brought for injury. However, the doctrine is not-overly helpful in the context of football (or sport generally) because a duty of care can never be fully extinguished. Whilst footballers would themselves undoubtedly consider getting injured as being what they might call an occupational hazard,[8] legally players can only ever consent to a reasonable amount of risk and harm. Inevitably, therefore, the definition of the duty of care owed between footballers has developed without the '*volenti*' concept being paid much heed.[9]

D   DEFINING THE DUTY

17.8   In the 1985 case of *Condon v Basi*,[10] a tackle which the match referee described as 'reckless and dangerous ... made in an excitable manner without thought of the consequences' so convinced Sir John Donaldson presiding that he did not feel obliged to seek to define the duty of care owed by players to each other. He was satisfied that Basi's tackle showed a 'reckless disregard' for Condon's safety which fell 'far below the standards which might reasonably be expected of anyone pursuing the game'. So, whilst this was a landmark case which paved the way for the principle of establishing liability for bad tackles in football, the duty of care owed as between players at this time remained in sore need of further definition.

17.9   That clarification arrived emphatically in the 2001 horse racing case of *Caldwell v Maguire & Fitzgerald*,[11] where the concept of reckless disregard was overlooked, and in its place it was established that negligence would need to be 'something more serious' than mere errors of judgment, oversights, lapses, or momentary carelessness by sporting participants. Judge LJ reminded us that each case would be decided on its own facts, and that negligence could not be resolved 'in a vacuum'. This was a progressive and important development because, as Mark

---

7   (2017) 3 JPI Law 154–167.
8   See Laurence Toczek, 'A Case of Foul Play' (2002) 152 NLJ 868.
9   The concept of contributory negligence is in any event to be preferred. See for instance Bruce Gardiner, 'Liability for Sporting Injuries' (2008) 1 JPI Law 16–25.
10   [1985] 1 WLR 866.
11   [2001] EWCA Civ 1054.

James and Fiona Deeley point out in their essay 'The Standard of Care in Sports Negligence Cases',[12] the courts would now have to accept that they needed to 'pay closer attention to the way that sport is actually played; not just by its rules but according to an unwritten code of playing culture'. The concept of a 'playing culture' was one which ensured that the inherent dangers of the sport were being taken into account, whilst preserving the common logic that participants should be bound by the same legal duty to take reasonable care as is everyone else away from the sporting environment. The James/Deeley essay concludes by saying that only those challenges that are 'clearly unacceptable and beyond the playing culture of the sport will be considered to be unlawful'.

17.10 As an aside, the concept of an 'acceptable playing culture' raises interesting questions in situations where there is no substantive physical harm suffered. Incidents such as racism, or biting, both of which the Barcelona player Luis Suarez has been found guilty by the football authorities, would certainly fall outside what is considered 'acceptable' playing culture and, so it follows, would potentially fall to be actionable as civil claims (presumably as assault/trespass to the person). Whether the victims of this kind of abuse (themselves high-profile, high earning international players) would have either the need or inclination to pursue these offences through the courts is another matter altogether. This is even more the case when you consider that football as a matter of course hands out its own football-specific punishments (and did so emphatically in both Suarez incidents). It seems that for something to even get close to the courts, a breach of football rules is the absolute minimum requirement.[13] Although, it should be noted that judging the severity of the breach is a task not made easy by the inconsistent range of punishments regularly and haphazardly handed out by footballing authorities.

E   THE MAIN FOOTBALL CASES

(a)   *Elliott v Saunders & Liverpool FC*[14]

17.11 In the verdict in *Elliott* in 1994, discussed above, Elliott failed to establish that Saunders had breached his duty of care and therefore Elliott's claim in negligence failed. In his unreported but oft-cited judgment, Drake J was keen to stress that liability in negligence actions for football injuries would depend on the facts and circumstances of each case. Here, he was not convinced that Saunders' tackle on Elliott was anything more than an instinctive misjudgement made in the heat of the game. His reticence to find against a top player was clearly evident:

> 'It is easy enough for the armchair video watcher to replay the incident frame by frame and then decide how the player should ideally have reacted to the situation, but in the real world, that is to say in the agony of the moment in the heat of the game, the player has no more than literally a fraction of one second in which to make a decision. What might be considered a mistake or error of judgment on replaying a video frame by frame may be no more than the ordinary reaction of even a skilled player. Even the very best players will not always do what in retrospect seems to have been the ideal thing to have done.'[15]

12   (2002) 1(1) Entertainment Law 104–108.
13   See, for instance, Tim Kevan, 'Sports Injury Cases: Footballers, Referees and Schools' (2001) 2 JPI Law 138–148.
14   Unreported, 10 June 1994.
15   QB Transcript, 10 June 1994 but quoted in *McCord v Cornforth & Swansea City* QB Transcript, 19 December 1996.

17.12   It is interesting that the judge refers here to 'the very best players'. It suggests he may have held a degree of trepidation about fixing liability on such an elite player in a high-profile match between two Premier League teams. Saunders was at the time a Wales international, Liverpool's most expensive signing and had, the previous close-season, been the subject of the-then record transfer fee as between English clubs. A finding against him, and his club Liverpool by way of vicarious liability, would surely have set a dangerous precedent.

(b)   McCord v Cornforth & Swansea City[16]

17.13   In the 1996 case of *McCord*, McCord was successful in claiming damages from Swansea due to a career-ending tackle by the Swansea captain John Cornforth. In terms of a successful negligence claim arising from a football injury in the professional game, this was a breakthrough victory. When the (lengthy) judgment is analysed, it feels like a surprising conclusion and contains several troubling aspects. First, Ian Kennedy J recorded that the victim McCord said he 'would not blame [Cornforth] for going for the ball' when visiting him in hospital and, moreover, that it was just 'one of those things'. Secondly, the judge noted that Cornforth had himself the previous season suffered a serious injury, and would therefore have been mindful of that when tackling McCord. Thirdly, the judge took into account evidence from a number of eye witnesses, much of it unsurprisingly conflicting. Fourthly, he considered the lack of protests from players on the pitch at the time of the foul an 'important consideration', and even sympathised with Cornforth that it was 'not the best executed piece of play'. Even the three words 'piece of play' seem to belie that this incident may in reality have simply been 'part and parcel' of the game (and therefore not actionable in negligence). And finally, it seems the judge was persuaded by the evidence of one on-looker who described the tackle as one of which 'no professional would be proud', fixating on this objective view, and concluding that Cornforth's tackle was 'unmistakably inconsistent with his taking reasonable care towards the plaintiff'. The finding went against *Elliott*, lowering the threshold of liability, and shifting the goalposts to a position where would-be personal injury claimants suddenly had a much clearer sight of goal.

(c)   Watson & Bradford v Gray & Huddersfield Town[17]

17.14   The case of *Watson* in 1997 soon followed the decision in *McCord* with predictable results. The Bradford City player Gordon Watson was successful in claiming damages for negligence from Kevin Gray and his club Huddersfield Town. Like McCord, Hooper J's judgment relies heavily on eye witness evidence, and contains much painstaking analysis. One witness, the former player and television pundit Chris Kamara, described Gray's foul on Watson as 'unacceptable as between professional footballers', inadvertently foreshadowing the 'acceptable playing culture' established later by the horse racing case of *Caldwell*. The case was notable for Hooper J describing Gray's tackle as being 'diabolical, appalling, quite unacceptable', quite stark language even for the hyperbolic rhetoric common to the game.

16   QB Transcript, 19 December 1996 and reported in (1997) *The Times*, 11 February.
17   (1998) *The Times*, 26 November.

17.15   The judge determined Gray's liability by asking whether, at the time of the incident, a reasonable professional player would have known that there was significant risk of significant injury to his opposite number. In applying his test, he adjudged that Gray would have known that his challenge on Watson carried with it a significant risk of serious injury – a concept evidently akin to foreseeability. The judge decided this despite noting that there was 'considerable evidence' Gray was going for the ball and, moreover, was entitled to do so. Unhelpfully, at a different place in the judgment the judge also describes Gray's tackle as 'negligent and a serious lapse of judgment deserving of punishment under the rules of the game'. This has the unfortunate effect of muddling the concept of negligence with the concept of a momentary judgment-lapse punishable inside the game – exactly the type of thing which *Caldwell* clarified would *not* be actionable in negligence. This confusing of definitions used by the courts is indicative of the grey areas being produced by the case law at the time, heightening the need for clarity which the judges in the case of *Caldwell* felt compelled to provide.

(d)   *Pitcher v Huddersfield Town*[18]

17.16   When viewed against the background of the mixed messages coming out of the *McCord* and *Watson* cases, it is perhaps less surprising that the next case to come to the courts ended with a different outcome. In the 2001 case of *Pitcher*, the player brought a claim in negligence against Huddersfield after his career was ended by a tackle by Huddersfield player Paul Reid. The circumstances of the foul were interesting, not least because Reid had allegedly harried Pitcher throughout the game and not even a free-kick (never mind a yellow or red card) was given for the foul at the time. The judge concluded that he was not prepared to say that the tackle was 'anything more than an error of judgment' and that there could be no finding of negligence in circumstances where Reid had only failed 'to pull up, change direction or change his mind and bring his foot down in 0.2 of a second'. The judge considered that this was the sort of foul which occurs 'up and down the country every Saturday'. Whilst this case was, like its predecessors, taken on its own facts, it is hard to avoid the feeling that the finding in this case had the effect of redressing the balance somewhat, following the awards of damages in *Watson* and *McCord*, reverting to the more forgiving allowances given by the High Court in *Saunders*, and seemingly slowing the momentum of establishing negligence in football.

(e)   Case study: *Hallows v White & Ashton United*

17.17   Just when it seemed the tables had turned back in favour of the defendants, then came another finding of negligence in football. Whilst researching this chapter the author spoke to Danny White, a former semi-professional footballer who has lived and suffered through one of these very cases. White, now working in academy football, has re-played the incident in his head so many times that he still has a crystal clear memory of his tackle on Altrincham striker Marcus Hallows (briefly of Stockport County and Bolton Wanderers) – almost 13 years later. In March 2005 White was playing for non-league Ashton United against Altrincham in the Conference North. White remembers that play was relatively pedestrian in the second half when Altrincham's Colin Little received the ball, accelerated down the wing, and slid the ball across to striker Hallows in the area for a shot on Ashton's goal.

18   [2001] All ER (D) 223 (Jul).

17.18   As a defender, White's only concerns were to prevent the shot on goal and to avoid giving away a penalty. As Hallows went to shoot, White went for the tackle and the block. In doing his job as a defender White was successful; he made contact with the ball, deflecting it from the trajectory from which it had left Hallows' foot, and so causing the Ashton goalkeeper to change direction with his dive. Unfortunately, White's unstoppable momentum caused his knees to connect with Hallows' standing leg and caused serious injury – Hallows suffered an open fracture of the shin. Hallows was in obvious agony, and White could see immediately the damage his tackle had caused, moving away carefully and waving his arms to draw attention to the referee to stop play. It did not look to anyone else at the time that anything was seriously wrong; there were no appeals by Altrincham players, no penalty was given by the referee, and play continued with the Ashton right back starting a counter-attack following the save by the Ashton goalkeeper. Months after the tackle, Hallows brought a claim in negligence against White and Ashton United for £32,500 for compensation for loss of earnings. He was successful in Manchester County Court. White and Ashton appealed to the High Court but, as no point of law was disputed, the verdict of the lower court stood.

17.19   White has strong views of the incident and is still disappointed with how the case unfolded in court. His hopes were not high when the judge opened the case by declaring that he was 'not experienced in association football', a term so rarely used to describe the sport that it might legitimately have been preferable had he used the term 'soccer'. White also harbours concerns about the type of evidence relied on by the court. There were two expert witnesses, one for each party. Gary Mabbutt, the former Tottenham Hotspur and England player, appeared as an expert for Hallows, whilst Jeff Winter, the former Premier League referee, appeared on behalf of White. Although both are respected figures in the game, neither had been present at the match, making their presence and relevance as witnesses seem somewhat arbitrary. It is a situation which is consistent with the inherent subjectivity of football and affirms the view that, perhaps even more so than in other legal situations, there will be two sides to every football story. It certainly does not feel like a sufficiently secure way of making findings of liability which can have a drastic effect on people's lives. Some of Mabbutt's analysis was as follows:

> 'From my many years of watching and playing games of football, and close analysis of the photographs, there was no prospect of Danny White making a fair challenge for the ball … Danny White should have known that this was the case and that he should have waited to try and get any rebound from a possible save by the goalkeeper.'

17.20   Mabbutt's analysis here reveals two fairly extraordinary things. First, there was no video evidence and so the non-present witnesses were being asked to make judgments based on still photographs; and secondly, by saying White should have 'waited to try to get any rebound' he is essentially saying White should have foregone his primary duty as a defender, made no attempt to prevent the shot on goal, and should instead have waited for the second phase of play – that is, assuming the goalkeeper palmed it away, and that the ball had not already ended up in the back of Ashton's net. Mabbutt's opinion is predicated on him believing White did not hold a reasonable belief he could get to the ball. But White is adamant he did. He did not hesitate for one moment in deciding to not make the tackle, and at no point did White sense that there would be a significant risk of Hallows being seriously injured. It certainly did not cross his mind that it would ever end up in court. It is plain that no central defender playing at that level could hope to have a successful career by holding back or contemplating legal liability when opposing strikers are about to shoot at goal.

17.21   Jeff Winter's analysis was as follows:

'This particular incident as seen by the photographs is a tackle made by a defender on an opponent within the penalty area. It is an incident made in isolation and therefore in the absence of other players in close proximity. The action shown in the sequence of photographs must be considered in context of a fast-moving game of football.'

17.22   HH Judge Armitage QC preferred the evidence of Gary Mabbutt over Jeff Winter and found White to be guilty, distinguishing the case from *Pitcher*:

'It was wholly improbable that it took [White] less than one second to make his leap. This is five times the length of time which deterred the judge for a finding of negligence in Pitcher's case. In my judgment this was a tackle which has been demonstrated to have arrived so late that it is reasonable to conclude that it was doomed from the start. The decision is mine, but I take comfort from Mr Mabbutt's opinion, with which I agree. Applying the fast moving split-second test, is [sic] quite clear from the photographs that the ball had departed before Mr White was in contention and that he probably never did intersect its line of flight even after the event ... In my judgment the timing of the challenge and the method adopted were such that it was reasonably foreseeable to a player of Mr White's skill that a collision was likely in circumstances where serious injury would result. The challenge was negligent.'

17.23   This feels more a case of Mabbutt v Winter, than Hallows v White. It would surely have been preferable to have relied on the evidence of the referee and linesmen (such evidence which, for reasons unknown, was not available to the court when judgment was given). It also raises concerns, explored elsewhere in this chapter, that courts can be too easily swayed by the calibre or 'star' quality of witnesses participants at court can bring along to court with them.

17.24   Mention was made by Hallows' barrister during the case that White had not signed a 'get well' card sent by Ashton United; in fact White was not in training at that time the card was circulated for signature, having been given time off following the incident, and so did not have the opportunity of signing it. This only added to the sense of unfairness felt by White.

17.25   At the conclusion of the case, Ashton's chairman David Aspinall said:

'A dangerous precedent may have been set by this verdict, which Ashton United always felt was deeply flawed and everyone at Hurst Cross urges fellow clubs who may, one day, find themselves in a similar situation to take every possible action to protect their assets against potential claims in the future.'[19]

17.26   All these years later, White is adamant his tackle was a legitimate attempt to block the ball and that he detected no more risk of serious injury than any other tackle he made during his career. By his own admission, White was a hard player – but a fair one. His honesty came across well during conversation, and it genuinely feels like he has been the victim of a decision which could so easily have gone the way of the Pitcher/Saunders cases, rather than the McCord/Watson cases.

17.27   White strongly agreed with the author's suggestion that his was a case which would have been better dealt within the game, rather than the courts. He was

---

19 As quoted in the article http://www.manchestereveningnews.co.uk/news/greater-manchester-news/soccer-club-faces-ruin-after-890849, (accessed March 2018) where a still photo of the incident is available.

very clear: footballers know best when a tackle is a good or a bad one. He feels that the judge's analogy of his tackle to him making an error of judgment in crossing a road and 'falling under the Claimant's front offside wheel', just goes to prove the point. It does seem a bizarre analogy, hardly appropriate for a tackle in a fast paced semi-professional football match. The verdict in Manchester County Court made White, only 24 at the time, fall out of love with the game, becoming afraid to tackle and scarred by the anguish suffered by his family during the trial. Delving into the specifics of this case, it feels inescapable that these are more often than not cases where the outcome really could go either way. It feels all too much like the toss of a coin, without strong enough evidence on either side. The guidance provided by the case law feels uncertain and therefore inadequate. Its regrettable consequence is that it can leave unfortunate and long-suffering victims on both sides of the courtroom.

(f) *Collett v Smith and Middlesbrough*[20]

17.28   In this case the player and his club Middlesbrough admitted liability for a foul by Gary Smith which ended the promising career of the Manchester United reserve Ben Collett, and so does not take us any further in terms of what sort of tackle attracts a finding of negligence. However, it is unquestionably the leading case in terms of quantifying what damages can be payable in the event of a career being ended by a negligent tackle. The court had to answer the question of what Collett would likely have earned based on what level he would have reached (there being a significant pay gap between, for example, the Premier League and the Championship). The court relied on what it called the 'golden opinions' of witnesses such as Sir Alex Ferguson and Gary Neville to quantify an award of damages commensurate with a career predicted to be played at a Championship team consistently playing in the upper echelons of the Championship or lower reaches of the Premier League. It feels like a generous award, one which *The Independent* called 'The £4.3m career that never was'.[21] There had been a similarly generous outcome for Watson, who in 1997 was awarded nearly £1 million – a considerable amount for a player then plying his trade in the second tier of English football.

17.29   The amount of subjectivity in football dictates that it is always going to be fairly easy to procure favourable opinions which support one side or the other. What will be less easy to procure, for the majority of footballers, is the 'golden' element of the 'golden opinions' with which to support a claim for damages. Allied to the astonishing increase in the value of players' contracts, and the ever-increasing financial might of Premier League clubs, the *Collett* case will almost certainly encourage new claims to be brought. But it will be interesting to see how the courts will treat claims by less prominent players, playing at less fashionable clubs, who are not fortunate enough to have access to the calibre of witnesses relied on by Collett at Manchester United. Without that support, awarding damages would feel even more like the proverbial finger in the air exercise than it already does.

F VICARIOUS LIABILITY

17.30   In all the above cases, the clubs of the offending players were named as co-defendants (or sole defendant in *Pitcher*) under the vicarious liability principle.

---

20   [2009] EWCA Civ 583.
21   See http://www.independent.co.uk/news/uk/home-news/the-16343million-football-career-that-never-was-891508.html (accessed March 2018).

It is well established that clubs/players fall under the traditional employer/employee relationship. This is logical, uncontroversial and could not sensibly be otherwise, as most fouls would of course be seen as having occurred in the player's ordinary employment with their club. The principle is best illustrated in the case of *Gravil v Carroll*[22] where a rugby player's club was found vicariously liable in circumstances where Gravil was punched by Carroll after the whistle had blown. The Court of Appeal found that the tort had a close connection to the player's employment, despite being outside of the laws of the game, and that the clear breach of contract between the punching player and his club actually served to highlight the close connection of the player's tort and his employment, rather than weaken it.

17.31　Where the vicarious liability principle is properly tested in football is where players go off on 'frolics of their own', and commit acts falling squarely outside doing their jobs as footballers. Two incidents which spring immediately to mind as falling into this category would be Eric Cantona's 'kung-fu' kick attack on a supporter after being sent off at a match against Crystal Palace at Selhurst Park in 1995, or Liverpool's Jamie Carragher throwing a coin (back) into the crowd at a match against Arsenal at Highbury in 2002.[23] It would be unfair for clubs to be vicariously liable for incidents as far removed from the game as those.

G SPECTATORS

17.32　Where spectators are concerned, it would seem logical that by attending matches they have consented to a risk of reasonably foreseeable events, such as that of a wayward Cristiano Ronaldo shot breaking the arm of an 11-year-old supporter in the crowd at a pre-season friendly between Bournemouth and Real Madrid,[24] but could not be taken to have consented to the Cantona and Carragher incidents (mentioned above), clearly unforeseeable on any view.[25] It would no doubt have been straightforward to make out claims of negligence against Cantona (deliberate intention to injure) and Carragher (reckless disregard as to spectator's safety). Neither case reached the courts, however, hinting once again that potential litigations have a habit of disappearing down football's deep pockets.

H REGULATORY BODIES

17.33　An extension of the applicability of the principle of vicarious liability is where claims are considered by participants against governing or regulatory bodies. The leading case in the area is *Watson v British Boxing Board of Control*,[26] in which the boxer Michael Watson successfully sued BBBC in negligence for not having appropriate medical equipment sufficiently proximate to the ring in which he had suffered several blows to the head from opponent Chris Eubank. Watson suffered brain damage in the time it took for him to be transferred to the hospital, the delay and absence of appropriate emergency treatment leading to his irreparable brain damage. Whilst the incidents share no common features other than for their seriousness, the provision of appropriate medical equipment makes for a worrying analogy with the

---

22　[2008] EWCA Civ 689.
23　See https://www.theguardian.com/football/2002/jan/28/newsstory.sport1 (accessed March 2018).
24　See http://www.bbc.co.uk/news/uk-england-dorset-23443565 (accessed March 2018).
25　See, for instance, the cases of *Murray v Harringay* [1951] 2 KB 529 and *Woolridge v Sumner* [1963] 2 QB 43.
26　[2001] QB 1134.

terrifying incident of footballer Fabrice Muamba, the Bolton player who suffered a heart attack in an FA Cup game against Tottenham Hotspur in 2012. Heart attacks during football matches are certainly not unheard of, and therefore Muamba's collapse served as a stark warning to the regulatory bodies such as the Premier League, FA and UEFA, to ensure the provision of defibrillators, and any other appropriate emergency medical equipment, at all grounds hosting their matches.[27]

17.34   If the Muamba incident was not enough warning to Tottenham and The FA, then the tragic case of Radwan Hamed certainly will have been.[28] In 2015, Tottenham (70%) and The FA's regional cardiologist (30%) were found liable to pay damages to Hamed amounting to over £7 million, after Hamed suffered irreparable brain damage following a heart attack stemming from a heart condition which had gone negligently undetected until his debut as a Spurs youth team player. The case gives further support for better provision at grounds for appropriate medical equipment, as well as greater encouragement (should it be needed) for regulatory bodies to have more rigorous heart screening processes for young players before they enter the professional game. It is unknown whether the Professional Footballers' Association, who had helped fund the screening process The FA had in place for youth team players at the time of Hamed's case, evaded blame entirely.[29]

I INTERNATIONAL DUTY

17.35   There is always a collective outbreak of concern around Premier League clubs at those times of the season when their players trot off around the globe to play for their countries. Injuries on international duty are common and news of them must be dreaded by clubs, fuelling the time-honoured 'club versus country' conflict. Whilst it is clear that this conflict has some traction in law, it is less clear where potential claims lie and against whom. It is right that whilst players are in their custody, countries assume a duty of care for those players, which means they are not immune from civil action for harm suffered on international duty. But when Dean Ashton's career was ended by a Shaun Wright-Phillips tackle during an England training session in 2006, it was reported that Ashton had threatened to bring litigation not only against the FA, but also against Wright-Phillips and *his* club Chelsea. Instinctively it feels that to have included Chelsea (whilst their player was under the care of The FA) would be extending the range of the vicarious liability principle too far. In any event, Ashton's case settled out of court and the terms of the settlement went undisclosed.[30]

17.36   For the loss of Ashton, West Ham sued The FA for compensation in an amount reported to be around £6.8 million.[31] Again the case did not reach the courts, but West Ham owner David Sullivan provided a telling insight into how The FA and its insurers went about defending the case, as well as offering some familiar views about the place of litigation in football. Sullivan told *The Guardian*:

> 'Their insurance company are trying to argue that because [Ashton] played
> 30 games after the injury, even though he retired as a result of the injury, they're

---

27   Muamba has since campaigned for the provision of more defibrillators in public places.
28   [2015] EWHC 298 (QB).
29   See https://www.theguardian.com/football/2015/feb/16/tottenham-apprentice-payout-brain-damage (accessed March 2018).
30   See http://news.bbc.co.uk/sport1/hi/football/teams/w/west_ham_utd/9385690.stm (accessed March 2018).
31   See https://www.theguardian.com/football/2011/feb/23/west-ham-compensation-dean-ashton (accessed March 2018).

not liable. But it's not like he retired because of anything else other than the ankle, which was smashed to bits because of Wright-Phillips. It was an accident and these things happen, but the FA should pick up the bill … We will have to issue a writ shortly, but it's the last thing I want to do because I don't believe people in football should be suing each other.'

17.37   It seems certain The FA's insurers paid out a significant sum to West Ham under the vicarious liability principle, although any award would have to have been reduced to have taken account of West Ham's somewhat surprising decision to give Ashton a new five-year contract in the intervening period between the tackle by Wright-Phillips and Ashton's eventual retirement.[32]

17.38   The concept of unlawful interference with a contract, where a club claims damages for a negligent player 'interfering' in the contract held between the injured player and his club, may have arisen in *Ashton* but was never adjudicated upon. A claim for unlawful interference was rejected by the court in the (footballer) *Watson* case, and so may be in need of revisiting in the future. It would be interesting to see if the principle could be relied upon in the event that, say, an opposing player specifically targets an extremely valuable player, such as Lionel Messi, fouling him negligently with the consequence of ending his playing contract with Barcelona. A successful claim for unlawful interference must surely follow if intent can be proven, which would be easier to show if the offending foul is part of an obvious strategy of targeting a team's star player. Whatever its possibilities, a claim for interference in a contract would be a highly technical argument, difficult to prove evidentially, not saying anything about the near-impossible task of trying to quantify loss of a player of Messi's stature. It is likely that negligence will remain the preferred route.

17.39   Another case which settled confidentially involved Newcastle's Michael Owen when he was injured playing for England in the 2006 World Cup. Although it involved no tackle by an opposing player, Newcastle brought an action against FIFA (whose World Cup it was) and The FA (whose team Owen was playing in). The claim for damages would have been wide-ranging and could easily have encompassed any or all of the following: (i) recompense for Owen's Newcastle wages whilst injured; (ii) the cost of having to buy a replacement player (Obafemi Martins, a £10 million signing from Inter Milan); (iii) the loss of revenue from Newcastle having an inferior team and consequently finishing lower in the league; and (iv) the cost of Owen's medical bills. It can be seen that the scope for damages has the potential to be huge, even more so if running a claim for loss of additional income flowing from, say, Champions League qualification or promotion to the Premier League. When the case settled, Newcastle publicly celebrated a win which 'taking into account that [Owen's] wages have now been paid in full and the compensation we have received … will amount to around £10m'.[33]

17.40   The issue of compensation in wages is one which has recurred regularly. When Steven Gerrard was injured playing for England in a friendly match against France in 2010, an FA spokesman said 'Liverpool do not need to pursue us for compensation as our insurers will cover the wages for Liverpool as this was clearly a legitimate injury'. This is troubling in several ways, not least because it opens up a debate about what might constitute a 'legitimate' injury. It also marks a contrast with

---

32   See   https://www.theguardian.com/football/2011/feb/23/west-ham-compensation-dean-ashton (accessed March 2018).

33   As reported in *The Guardian*, https://www.theguardian.com/football/2007/jun/26/newsstory.sport8 (accessed March 2018).

England's opponents that night, France, who themselves did not have an equivalent insurance scheme in place which provided for compensation to clubs. Furthermore, it seems to sit very uncomfortably with the common thread running through this area of law that liability should only arise in situations which are outside the normal confines of the game. This was undeniably an 'ordinary' injury, with no suggestion or evidence of malpractice from an opposing player.

17.41   Liverpool were initially furious that Gerrard had suffered the injury coming, as it did, after the point in the match which it had been agreed between Liverpool and The FA that the player would be substituted.[34] It demonstrates that international bodies can be exposed legally in circumstances where they go against a club's wishes, or do not heed the warnings of clubs about the playing or training demands which are placed on certain players, especially those injury-prone players whose regimes are bespoke or need special management. Such situations would seem to open the door wide to claims against national associations for running the international game without reasonable regard to the players it relies on.[35]

17.42   The FIFA Club Protection Programme was introduced in 2012 to compensate clubs for having a player injured on international duty. Whilst this has helped solve the problem of poorer national associations not being able to afford the insurance premiums required to pay compensation, it will only help clubs so far because players of that calibre will more often than not be earning astronomical wages which far exceed the thresholds set out in the countries' insurance policies. Moreover, the Programme only covers a player's wages and would not cover the wider reaching damages in situations such as a player's career being ended, the loss of an enormous transfer fee, or where a club misses out on lucrative Champions League qualification. The limitations of such a scheme would surely have been exposed to a far greater degree if the case of *Charleroi v FIFA*, in which a Belgian club (supported by G14) sued FIFA for losses they attributed to having their star player injured in an international friendly, and so claimed they lost their national league as a direct result, had got to be adjudicated. Whilst the case undoubtedly played a part in bringing about the compensation scheme which now exists, ultimately it had no influence on the scope of what a club's losses may potentially total. The scheme was probably the least FIFA could have done to relieve the pressure of the increasing weight of clubs' comparative financial superiority. Perhaps mindful of the limitations of those policies, it is now the norm for clubs to take out their own insurance against injuries suffered by their players on international duty.

J   THE FUTURE

17.43   There are several ways one could imagine the area of personal injury litigation in football developing. As well as increased figures and increased insurance premiums, increased awareness of the dangers of concussion (which has led to the recent implementation of the Premier League's Concussion Protocol) will no doubt come into more prominence in the cases that do make it to the courts.[36]

---

34   *The Guardian* reports that several tweets published after the game by club physio Darren Burgess were deleted, https://www.theguardian.com/football/2010/nov/19/steven-gerrard-injury-england-compensation (accessed March 2018).

35   See Mark James, 'The Trouble with Roy Keane' (2002) 1(3) *Entertainment Law* 72–92.

36   See the Guardian's Daniel Taylor's article 'Football is heading for trouble over brain injuries caused by the ball' at https://www.theguardian.com/football/blog/2017/sep/30/football-heading-brain-injuries-ball-kevin-doyle (accessed March 2018).

Similarly, the development of technology used in matches would ensure the capture of contemporaneous views of the referee, players and supporters for particularly serious injuries suffered, thus improving the quality of the evidence being relied on a later date and lessening the arbitrary reliance on 'golden' opinions in court of people not even present at the game.[37] On the other hand, the increased exposure that comes with greater technology probably means that we will become less likely to see the sort of tackles seen in the cases discussed above (at the highest level of the game, at least).

17.44   The simple, recurring problem remains that in practice not many cases will ever reach the courts. There are various reasons for that: the 'notoriously unreliable'[38] (or often unwilling) witnesses that footballers can make; the evident desire to settle differences before things reach the public forum of the courts;[39] a reluctance for public or judicial scrutiny about the way in which the game is played; the increased wealth in the game, which makes settlements easier and far more convenient. So, whilst it might feel like the area of personal injury area is ripe for more and more cases, the probability is that we will not see more cases at all, but what we will see is simply a higher number of out-of-court settlements, with ever-higher figures banded about by the media.

17.45   It is unclear why all the cases discussed above have been decided in the courts, rather than the various arbitration routes offered by the Premier League and FA Rules. There may be a number of different explanations; those advising would-be claimants might be more attracted by the eye-watering claims that are public knowledge as a result of the court cases; or they simply might not be aware of the existence of the routes provided by the game's internal laws. A more worrying possibility, based on what we have seen, is that claimants might consider they have a better chance of securing a favourable decision away from the confines of the game, by someone who might never have played the game and might be less forgiving of an isolated incident, rather than an arbitration where the case would be decided by a panel of football-savvy arbitrators (often comprising former players). It is more likely the visibility (such as it is) of the publicly available case law, as opposed to arbitrations whose outcomes remain private, simply provide a clearer path forward. It would be interesting to see whether the courts' jurisdiction will ever be challenged in this way. The question of jurisdiction was never raised by those advising Danny White, for instance, though he wishes it had been.

K   CONCLUSION

17.46   In fact the game's inherent dislike of heading for the courts probably suits judges very well. As it was said by HH Judge David Griffith-Jones QC and Nicholas Randall QC in 'Civil Liability Arising out of Participation in Sport, 'all too often, litigation between contestants involves a reflection and repetition of the adversarial on the pitch contest'.[40] This leads, inevitably, to a kind of 'two sides to every story' mentality in sport generally and certainly in football. This is borne out not only by the way one incident can be perceived in different ways by two different onlookers,

---

37   See Mark James's discussion of the Australian case of *Rodgers v Bugden and Canterbury-Bankstown* [1993] ATR 81-246 for a different slant on what type of damages could be claimed.

38   *Pitcher v Huddersfield Town* [2001] All ER (D) 223 (Jul).

39   See *The Independent*'s reporting of a John Fashanu tackle on John O Neill – 14 October 1994 or *The Guardian*'s reporting of a tackle by Kevin Muscat on Matt Holmes – 24 February 2004.

40   Lewis and Taylor, *Sport: Law and Practice*, 3rd Edition (Bloomsbury, 2014), p 1653.

but also by the way the same incident can actually result in two very different outcomes. As it was said in *McCord*: 'Incidents which involve no infringement can have dreadful consequences just as the worst foul may cause no harm at all.'[41] That inherent uncertainty is part of the unscripted drama of the game, part of its attraction, and neatly encapsulates the eternal difficulty of applying the rule of law to the game of football.

41   QB Transcript, 19 December 1996 and reported in (1997) *The Times*, 11 February.

CHAPTER 18

Broadcasting

Rhodri Thompson QC and **Anita Davies** (Matrix Chambers)

A IMPORTANCE OF FOOTBALL BROADCASTING RIGHTS

18.1   Throughout Europe, live coverage of major football competitions is one of the most popular forms of television broadcasting, attracting consistently large audiences, including high-value viewers who are in general hard to reach both by public service and commercial broadcasters. As such, broadcasters are willing to pay very substantial sums to the organisers of such competitions, particularly where rights are obtained on an exclusive basis.

18.2   Prior to the launch of major pay-TV platforms, the rights to major national and international football competitions were held either by the national free-to-air broadcasters individually or collectively through the European Broadcasting Union. However, those rights have for many years been used commercially as key drivers to attract new viewers and to establish commercial TV platforms in competition with traditional free-to-air services. Rights-owners have sought to maximise value by selling attractive bundles of rights on an exclusive basis both geographically and in terms of content and delivery platform. Where technology (notably satellite broadcasts) would allow services to be received in distinct jurisdictions, contractual and technical restrictions have been used to maximise value by selling rights to individual broadcasters on a national basis.

18.3   These economic developments have in turn raised significant legal issues concerning possible adverse impacts on competition and the cross-border supply of services, where exclusive rights are packaged and sold on a collective basis and to national broadcasters supplying encrypted services. The two key parameters of competition, the duration and scope of exclusivity, have been scrutinised carefully by regulators seeking so far as possible to compel sports organisers to 'unbundle' their rights to enable a degree of competition to emerge without undermining the value of the rights themselves. As with other forms of intellectual property, this has required the authorities to strike a difficult balance between enabling a degree of competition to emerge while preserving incentives to invest for the benefit of the consumer.

18.4   The commercial analysis of these issues is further complicated by the fact that sport itself is recognised as a social good that is entitled to a degree of special treatment under EU law. The European Commission recognises sport as 'a growing social and economic phenomenon that makes an important contribution to the

European Union's strategic objectives of solidarity and prosperity'.[1] One perceived benefit of the escalation of the value of football broadcasting rights has been to provide a source of revenue for investment in sporting infrastructure and in grass roots promotion of training for young footballers and 'trickle down' effects from the higher to the lower leagues and competitions within the UK and other EU Member States.

18.5   Moreover, the FA Cup Final (and the Scottish FA Cup Final in Scotland), the FIFA World Cup Finals and the UEFA European Football Championship Finals, are exempted from the full force of competition by inclusion in a statutory category of 'listed events', on the basis that this narrowly defined category of events (other examples have traditionally included national institutions such as the Grand National, the Derby Race, the Wimbledon finals and the Rugby Union and Rugby League World Cup Finals) constitutes an important common element of the British way of life that should be made available to the great majority of the population.

18.6   Nonetheless, while EU law accepts the 'specificity' of sport – including the setting and application of sporting rules, the autonomy and diversity of sport organisations, and the organisation of sport on a national basis – the case law of the Court of Justice of the EU (CJEU) has not granted a general exemption from the application of EU law.[2] Sporting rules remain subject to important aspects of EU law, such as the prohibition of discrimination on grounds of nationality, provisions regarding citizenship of the Union and equality between men and women in employment. In particular, both competition law and the internal market provisions apply to sport insofar as it constitutes an economic activity: see paras **18.11–18.28** below.[3]

18.7   Likewise, while the 'listed events' legislation remains in place, it is increasingly open to challenge as the transfer to digital broadcasting and the ready availability of commercially funded television to increasing numbers of viewers makes it more difficult to justify the restriction on market forces inherent in this regime: see paras **18.35–18.52** below. Technological changes in digital broadcasting have also led to significant developments in copyright law: see paras **18.53–18.68** below.

B   COMPETITION LAW AND THE COLLECTIVE SELLING OF RIGHTS

18.8   The application of the competition provisions of the Treaty on the Functioning of the European Union (2007) (TFEU) to the selling of media rights of sporting events takes into account a number of specific characteristics in this area. Sports media rights are frequently sold collectively by a sporting association on

---

1   European Commission White Paper on Sport, Brussels 11.07.2007 COM(2007) 391 final.
2   In Joined Cases T-528, 542, 543 & 546/93: *Métropole télévision SA and others v Commission* [1996] ECR II-649; Joined Cases T185, 216, 299 & 300/00: *Métropole télévision SA (M6) and others v Commission* [2002] ECR II-3805, the General Court overruled two decisions of the Commission that exempted the 'Eurovision' system (which allowed members of the European Broadcasting system to negotiate collectively to acquire sports broadcasting rights) from the general prohibition of anti-competitive agreements.
3   Case 36/74: *Walrave v Union Cycliste Internationale* [1974] ECR 1405, para 4; Case C-176/96: *Jyri Lehtonen and Castors Canada Dry Namur-Braine ASBL v Federation Royale Belge des societies de basketball ASBL* [2000] ECR 2681, paras 32–33.

behalf of individual clubs (as opposed to clubs marketing the rights individually). Key examples are UEFA, which controls the selling of broadcasting rights for the UEFA Champions League and Europa League, and the Premier League, which sells the rights to broadcast Premier League matches.

18.9   While joint selling of media rights raises competition concerns, the Commission has accepted it under certain conditions, setting out its key principles in the cases of *UEFA, Bundesliga* and the *Football Association Premier League (FA Premier League)*.[4] In the *UEFA* case, the Commission found that, whilst the joint selling arrangements did restrict competition, consumers received a fair share of the resulting benefit. UEFA was thus eligible for an exemption under Article 101(3), provided that deferred highlights and new media rights could be exploited in parallel by both UEFA and individual clubs. In the *Bundesliga* and *FA Premier League* cases the Commission opened investigations but then, following negotiation, accepted commitments on the part of both associations in order to remedy any competition concerns.

18.10   Overall, the Commission has accepted that, subject to certain conditions, collective selling can be important for the redistribution of income and can be a tool for achieving greater solidarity within sports.

18.11   Football associations (and their members) engage in economic activities including ticket sales, player transfers and the conduct of advertising and broadcasting agreements. Therefore they fall to be considered as undertakings or associations of undertakings for the purposes of Article 101(1) TFEU, which prohibits agreements, concerted practices and decisions of associations of undertakings whose object or effect is an appreciable restriction of competition within the EU. Likewise, they fall potentially within the analogous Chapter 1 Prohibition contained in the Competition Act 1998 ('the 1998 Act') in respect of the UK.

18.12   There are however conditions within Article 101(3) (and the 1998 Act), which, if satisfied, exempt certain arrangements, where they promote significant efficiencies of benefit to consumers and where the arrangements in question are indispensable to such benefits and do not eliminate all competition in the relevant market. In addition, where proportionate restrictions are proved to be necessary to the achievement of a pro-competitive objective (for example, ancillary restraints of trade in a pro-competitive transaction), then it may be possible to exclude such restrictions from the scope of UK and EU competition law altogether.

18.13   For the purposes of market definition, the Commission has defined the acquisition of TV rights for football as a specific relevant product market. In *UEFA*,[5] the Commission considered the relevant markets to be:

(a) the upstream markets for the sale and acquisition of free-TV, pay-TV and pay-per-view rights;
(b) the downstream markets on which TV broadcasters compete for advertising revenue depending on audience rates, and for pay-TV/pay-per-view subscribers;

4   Case COMP/C-2.38.173 *Joint Selling of the Commercial Rights of the UEFA Champions League*, 23 July 2003, [2003] OJ L291/25; Case COMP/C-2/37.214 *Joint selling of the media rights to the German Bundesliga* 27 May 2005, [2005] OJ L134/46; Case COMP/C-2/38.173 *Joint Selling of media rights to the FA Premier League*, 22 March 2006 [2008] OJ C7/8–18.
5   *Joint Selling of the Commercial Rights of the UEFA Champions League* (see n 4 above).

(c) the upstream markets for wireless/3G/UMTS rights, internet rights and video-on-demand rights, which are emerging new media markets at both the upstream and downstream levels that parallel the development of the markets in the pay-TV sector;

(d) the markets for the other commercial rights namely sponsorship, suppliership and licensing.[6]

18.14   The Commission concluded that the acquisition of TV broadcast rights for football matches played throughout the year constituted a specific product market:

> 'In the present case, the Commission also considers that the relevant product market can appropriately be defined as the market for the acquisition of TV broadcasting rights of football events played regularly throughout every year. This definition would in practice mainly include national first and second division and cup events as well as the UEFA Champions League and UEFA Cup. The TV rights of football events create a particular brand image for a TV channel and allow the broadcaster to reach a particular audience at the retail level that cannot be reached by other programmes. In pay-TV football is a main driver of the sale of subscriptions. As regards free TV, football attracts a particular consumer demographic and hence advertising, which cannot be attracted with other types of programming.'

18.15   Joint selling agreements, where clubs assign the selling of their media rights to an association, which generally sell off the rights collectively to one or a very limited number of broadcasters, are considered restrictions on competition for the purposes of Article 101 TFEU as they prevent individual clubs competing in the sale of media rights.[7]

18.16   In particular the Commission has been concerned with issues of foreclosure and output restrictions. Where a joint selling entity sells all media rights on an exclusive basis to one single operator in a certain downstream market, the effect is to foreclose competition from other retailers. In the *FA Premier League* case the Commission noted that:

> 'One example of such a foreclosure problem is in the exclusive sale of large packages of media rights. The FAPL has so far sold exclusive live TV rights in packages that were comparatively large in relation to that which would be sold by an individual club and to the demand from many broadcasters in these markets. This is likely to create barriers to entry on downstream markets in the United Kingdom leading to access foreclosure in these markets. Advertising-funded TV and pay-TV are the most commercially important of the markets affected by the arrangements.'

18.17   Similarly, anti-competitive output restrictions can result from joint selling entities withholding certain parts of the jointly sold media rights from the market, in order to maximise revenues from the restrictive and collective sale. This may restrict competition and limit consumer choice if valuable rights remain unsold.

18.18   In *UEFA*, the Commission found that:

> 'UEFA's joint selling arrangement therefore restricts competition in the upstream markets not only between football clubs but also between UEFA and the football clubs in supplying commercial rights to interested buyers. In addition, the notified joint selling arrangement has an impact on the downstream broadcasting markets as football events are an important element of TV broadcasters' competition for advertisers or for subscribers for pay-TV and pay-per-view services. Such an arrangement has as its effect the restriction of competition.'[8]

6   Ibid, para 56.
7   Ibid, para 114.
8   Ibid, para 116.

18.19   However, the Commission also found that joint selling arrangements had significant benefits in providing a single point of sale:

(a) Broadcasters could acquire rights packages from the original rights holders though a single outlet, reducing transaction complexity, costs and financial risks.
(b) There are specific advantages of a single point of sale in the context of an international competition where the difficulties in selling packages of rights owned by individual or groups of clubs are greater and where the efficiencies of joint selling may be high.
(c) Joint selling allows the creation of packages allowing media operators to provide coverage to consumers of the league as a whole and over the course of an entire season.
(d) Football clubs benefit from the sale of the commercial rights via a single point of sale/joint selling agency.
(e) Branding of output creates efficiencies as it helps in getting media products wider recognition and distribution.[9]

18.20   In order to balance these conflicting considerations, the Commission has applied, or accepted as commitments, a number of standard remedies in addressing competition concerns in sports broadcasting. In *Bundesliga*, commitments were offered that divided rights into separate packages for internet, TV and mobile broadcasting. The rights were to be disposed of by a public tendering process and rights contracts were not to exceed three years.[10] Similarly, in the *FA Premier League* case commitments were offered to divide rights into packages for mobile, internet and radio, in addition to a no single buyer rule for TV rights.[11]

18.21   The common remedies and commitments applied to curb competition concerns include:

(a) *Tendering* – requiring the joint sales body on the upstream market to organise a competitive bidding process under non-discriminatory and transparent terms.
(b) *Limits on duration* – requiring the collective selling entity to limit the duration of the exclusive rights offered in vertical contracts to no more than three seasons.[12]
(c) *Unbundling* – requiring the joint selling entity to unbundle the media rights in separate packages, thereby limiting the scope of the exclusivity. The European Commission may require a reasonable amount of different and independently valid rights packages; no combination of big and small packages; earmarked packages for special markets/platforms; blind selling.
(d) *No unused rights* – rights that are not sold by the joint selling entity within a certain timespan shall fall back to the individual clubs. The club is then at liberty to sell the rights to any interested buyer.
(e) *No single buyer obligation* – the joint selling body cannot accept a single buyer for all or a certain type of rights (eg live rights or both live and principal highlights rights). This is in order to prevent all packages of valuable rights being sold to a dominant player in one of the downstream markets.
(f) *Limitation of exploitation platform* – this remedy was imposed in the *SkyItalia* case.[13] In that case Newscorp and Telepiu had merged, meaning that the merged entity combined a portfolio of exclusive rights contracts related to premium content, including key sports events. Third parties would thereby be foreclosed

9   Ibid, section 7.1.1.
10   *Joint selling of the media rights to the German Bundesliga* (see n 4 above).
11   *Joint Selling of media rights to the FA Premier League* (see n 4 above).
12   In *UEFA* and *Bundesliga* contracts were limited to three years. In *SkyItalia*, agreements were limited to two years: Case No COMP/M.2876 *Newscorp/Telepiu*, Commission Decision 2 April 2003.
13   Case No COMP/M.2876 – *Newscorp/Telepiu*, Commission Decision of 2 April 2003.

from accessing premium content needed to establish a competing pay-TV offer downstream. The Commission limited the scope of the exclusive football rights to be exploited by SkyItalia to Direct to Home (through a satellite) transmission. This would allow operators competing in other means of transmission (for example cable, internet and mobile) to have access to premium sports content.

18.22 These considerations have also been relevant to competition for broadcasting rights in the UK, where rights costs have continued to spiral upwards as broadcasters and other communications providers compete for exclusive rights. In February 2015 the Premier League sold television rights to its games for a record £5.136 billion, an increase of 71% compared to 2012. Sky paid £4.2 billion for five of the seven TV packages while BT paid £960 million for the other two packages.[14]

18.23 As the UK communications regulator, Ofcom has repeatedly considered the conditions governing the sale of exclusive rights to broadcast Premier League matches.[15] The rivalry between a number of broadcasters, in particular Sky, BT and Virgin Media has led to attempts to open up the market for Premier League broadcasts. In November 2014 Ofcom launched an investigation into the broadcasting of Premiership matches, after Virgin Media lodged a complaint arguing that the Premier League should make all 380 matches live on TV. Virgin Media argued that by making just 41% of matches available – in contrast to other countries such as Germany and leagues such as the NBA which make all games available – the Premier League was keeping prices artificially high and restricting choice to consumers.[16]

18.24 In January 2015, Virgin Media made an application requesting that Ofcom issue an 'interim measures direction', pursuant to s 35 of the Competition Act 1998, to require the Premier League to suspend the forthcoming auction of audiovisual rights to broadcast live Premier League matches, until Ofcom had reached the next stage of its process in March 2015. Ofcom rejected the application, on the basis that there would be a significant gap, of around 17 months, between the auction and the start of the 2016/17 season when broadcasting of the relevant matches would commence. In the event that Ofcom's investigation concluded that there was an infringement, Ofcom had the necessary powers to require the Premier League and Premier League clubs to make changes to arrangements for the broadcasting of matches within the time available before the start of the relevant season.

18.25 Following two years of investigation, Ofcom announced that it was closing its investigation in August 2016.[17] Ofcom justified the closing of the investigation on the basis of:

(a) The Premier League's decision to increase the number of matches available for live broadcast in the UK to a minimum of 190 per season from the start of the 2019/20 season; this would be an increase of at least 22 matches per season over the number sold for live broadcast in the Premier League's auction in 2015.

(b) The inclusion of a 'no single buyer' rule at the next auction, so that more than one broadcaster must be awarded rights. At least 42 matches per season have to be reserved for a second buyer, of which a minimum of 30 will be available for broadcast at the weekend.

---

14 See http://www.bbc.co.uk/news/business-31379128 (accessed March 2018).
15 The issue had also been considered regularly by the UK competition authorities under the Competition Act 1998 and its predecessor legislation, the Restrictive Trade Practices Act 1976.
16 See http://media.ofcom.org.uk/news/2014/premier-league/ (accessed March 2018).
17 See http://media.ofcom.org.uk/news/2016/premier-league-football-rights/ (accessed March 2018).

18.26   Ofcom also took into account the results of consumer research it carried out to understand the preferences of match-going fans and those watching on TV in relation to Premier League matches. There was no clear consensus amongst fans as to whether Saturday 15.00 matches should be broadcast live. Ofcom accepted that the broadcasting arrangements struck a reasonable balance between the potential benefits of releasing more matches for live broadcast, and the disruption caused by games being rescheduled to be broadcast outside the 'closed period' of 14.45 and 17.15 on a Saturday.[18]

18.27   Other European countries have also sought to liberalise the market for the broadcasting of live matches. In April 2016 the German Federal Cartel Office (Bundeskartellamt) accepted commitments from the German Football League Association (GFLA) and the German Football League (DFL), after it had voiced concerns that competition for innovation could be restricted if there was only one rights-holder in the market for live games from the first and second divisions of the league. The commitments ensure that between 30 and 102 attractive Bundesliga matches (of a total of 306 games), together with extensive possibilities for highlights coverage, are purchased by an alternative bidder. The Bundeskartellamt did not call for a stricter 'no single buyer' rule due to the relatively strong position of free-to-air TV in Germany and the early broadcasting slot of (near) real time highlights coverage, which the current broadcasting model maintained. The authority also took into account that live sport coverage on the internet was still in the development stage.[19]

18.28   Also in April 2016 the Italian competition authority found that the two competing broadcasters Mediaset Premium and Sky Italia had allocated the 2015–18 live rights amongst each other, thereby preventing the market entry of other competitors. The authority also found that Lega Calcio (which manages Serie A games), and their Swiss-based advisers Infront Italy engaged in a negotiation with the bidders, aimed at altering the outcome of the tender. The competition authority fined Mediaset €51 million, Sky Italia €4 million, Lega €1.9 million and Infront Italy €9 million.[20]

C   EU LAW ON THE FREEDOM TO SUPPLY FOOTBALL BROADCASTING SERVICES

18.29   Broadcasting within the territory of the EU gives rise to a number of complex issues of copyright law and has been the subject of specific legislation intended to establish rules for cross-border broadcasting within the internal market. Those issues are not specific to football broadcasting and fall outside the scope of this work – however, the general Treaty rules on the free movement of services within the EU internal market are of significance for the broadcasting of football, as the leading cases of *Football Association Premier League Ltd et al v QC Leisure* and *Murphy v Media Protection Services Ltd* demonstrate.[21]

18   The press release issued by Ofcom announcing the close of the investigation suggested that resources and administrative priorities may have also played a part in deciding to close the investigation.
19   See   http://www.bundeskartellamt.de/SharedDocs/Meldung/EN/Pressemitteilungen/2016/11_04_2016_DFL%20Abschluss.html (accessed March 2018).
20   See http://www.agcm.it/en/newsroom/press-releases/2290-a-66-million-euro-fine-imposed-on-sky,-mediaset-premium,-lega-and-infront-by-the-italian-competition-authority.html (accessed March 2018).
21   Joined Cases C-403/08 and C-429/08: *Football Association Premier League Ltd v QC Leisure* and *Karen Murphy v Media Protection Services Ltd* [2011] ECR I-9083, ECLI:EU:C:2011:631 ('*FAPL*').

18.30   Those cases concerned the satellite transmission of football matches and the unauthorised use of decoders that enabled transmissions in one Member State to be received and viewed in another Member State, including on a commercial basis. The essence of the dispute in respect of the free movement of services within the internal market was whether national rules enabling the rights-owner to control such broadcasts, on the basis that they were in breach of contract and/or contrary to public policy, constituted an unlawful restriction on rights protected by EU law.

18.31   The CJEU found that to be the case, distinguishing earlier case law in which rights-holders had been found entitled to restrict broadcasts on a geographic basis in reliance on their national intellectual property rights. The Court's reasoning was that it was a clear restriction on the free movement of broadcasting services for contractual restrictions imposed by broadcasters in one Member State to be upheld and enforced in another Member State.[22] As such, there was a substantial onus on those seeking to justify such restrictions to show that it 'serves overriding reasons in the public interest, is suitable for securing the attainment of the public interest objective which it pursues and does not go beyond what is necessary in order to attain it'.[23]

18.32   The CJEU found that, although the rights of the organisers of sporting events were not strictly speaking intellectual property rights protected by national rules on copyright,[24] they were in principle entitled to protection under national law, even where they gave rise to restrictions on the free movement of services.[25] The issue therefore turned on whether the restriction at issue was proportionate to the legitimate protection of the rights of rights-holders, given its restrictive impact on cross-border services.[26]

18.33   On this issue, the CJEU considered the principal justifications in turn and rejected each of them:

(a)   The Court did not consider that the right to obtain remuneration for the exploitation of the relevant right could justify absolute territorial protection – the protected right was to obtain 'reasonable remuneration in relation to the economic value of the service provided', not 'the opportunity to demand the highest possible remuneration'; the Court considered that the rights-holder could demand remuneration that 'takes account of the actual audience and the potential audience both in the Member State of broadcast and in any other Member State in which the broadcasts including the protected subject-matter are received'.[27]

(b)   The Court distinguished the earlier case law upholding the owner of intellectual property rights to control the broadcasting on a geographical basis, on the basis that, unlike in the earlier case, the restrictions at issue concerned the reception rather than the broadcasting of the material on a geographical basis; the Court also noted the development of EU secondary legislation 'intended to ensure the transition from national markets to a single programme production and distribution market'.[28]

(c)   The Court was equally unimpressed by the argument that the restrictions could be justified by a desire to protect live attendances at FA Premier League matches,

---

22   *FA Premier League*, paras 85–89.
23   Ibid, para 93.
24   Ibid, paras 96–99.
25   Ibid, paras 100–104.
26   Ibid, paras 93 and 105.
27   Ibid, paras 107–117.
28   Ibid, paras 118–121.

on the basis that the rights owner could control the broadcasting of matches directly if it wished to achieve that objective.[29]

(d) Finally, the Court dismissed as essentially irrelevant the fact that the decoders had been obtained using a false identity and a false address, and that decoders intended for private use were being used on a commercial basis. The Court considered that such issues could be addressed either by private actions for breach of contract or breach of copyright but did not justify restrictions on the freedom to provide cross border services.

18.34   Overall, therefore, the CJEU has made it clear that the strong integrationist policy that underlies the four EU freedoms applies with full force to cross-border transmissions of football broadcasts, notwithstanding the implications for the commercial value of exclusive broadcasting rights sold on a territorial basis if such rights can be undermined to at least a limited degree by avoidance activities operating at the margins of commercial legality.

D   LISTED EVENTS

18.35   A listed events policy has been in place in the UK in a variety of forms since the 1950s. The first 'list' was a voluntary agreement drawn up in 1956 between the BBC and the Independent Broadcasting Authority. The agreement provided that neither party would seek exclusive broadcast rights for a list of major sporting events. Since that point the number of 'listed events' has evolved, and is now overseen by Article 14(1) of the Audiovisual Media Services Directive ('the AVMS Directive'),[30] which states that:

> 'Each Member State may take measures in accordance with Union law to ensure that broadcasters under its jurisdiction do not broadcast on an exclusive basis events which are regarded by that Member State as being of major importance for society in such a way as to deprive a substantial proportion of the public in that Member State of the possibility of following such events by live coverage or deferred coverage on free television.'

18.36   The current regime is set out in Part IV of the Broadcasting Act 1996 ('the 1996 Act'), as amended by the Television Broadcasting Regulations 2000[31] and Communications Act 2003, which restricts the acquisition by television programme providers of exclusive rights to the whole, or any part of live television coverage of 'listed events', without the prior consent of Ofcom.[32]

18.37   Listed events are defined by s 97 of the 1996 Act as 'a sporting or other event of national interest which is for the time being included in a list drawn up by the Secretary of State for the purposes of this Part'. In drawing up the list the Secretary of State for Digital, Culture, Media and Sport is required to consult the BBC, the Welsh Authority, the Commission and for relevant events the person from whom the rights to televise that event may be acquired.

18.38   The events are divided into two categories, A and B. For Category A events full live coverage must be offered to the free-to-air channels that are received by at least 95% of the UK population. Section 97 of the Digital Economy Act 2017 gives

29   Ibid, paras 122–124.
30   Directive 2010/13/EU.
31   SI 2000/54.
32   Broadcasting Act 1996, s 101.

the Secretary of State the power to amend the percentage figure in the qualifying criteria. This is designed to 'future-proof' the listed events regime as the number of television sets decrease and the devices people use to watch sport changes.

18.39 So far as football broadcasting is concerned, the FIFA World Cup Finals and the European Football Championship, as well as the FA Cup Final (and Scottish FA Cup Final for coverage in Scotland) are all contained in the Category A list.[33] Category B events may have live coverage on subscription television provided that secondary coverage is offered to free-to-air broadcasters.[34]

18.40 For the purpose of the live broadcasting of listed events the 1996 Act defines two categories of television programme services: those television programme services and EEA satellite services which for the time being satisfy the qualifying conditions ('the first category'); and all other television programme services and EEA satellite services ('the second category').[35] The qualifying conditions are defined as (i) that the service is provided without any consideration being required for reception of the service; and (ii) that the service is received by at least 95% of the population of the UK.[36] The current services meeting the qualifying conditions as set out in the Television Broadcasting Regulations 2000 are Channel 3 (ITV), Channel 4, BBC 1, BBC 2 and Channel 5.[37]

18.41 Any contract for televising live coverage of a listed event which is entered into by a broadcaster must state that the rights are available for showing the event on a service falling within only one of the two categories.[38] A broadcaster providing a service in either category ('the first service') is prohibited from showing exclusively live coverage of the whole or any part of a Category A event without the previous consent of Ofcom unless a broadcaster providing a service in the other category ('the second service') has acquired the right to show live coverage of the event or the same part of the event. The area served by the second service must consist of or include the whole, or substantially the whole, of the area served by the first service. The first and second services may be provided by licensees in the same ownership, but between them they must include a broadcaster in each of the two categories.

18.42 Under s 104(1)(b) of the 1996 Act, Ofcom is required to provide guidance as to the matters it will take into account in determining whether to grant its consent to a broadcaster providing a service in one category (the first service) to provide exclusive live coverage of an event (or part of an event) where no broadcaster providing a service in the other category (the second service) has acquired the same rights, or where the area for which the second service is to be provided does not consist of or include the whole, or substantially the whole, of the area for which the first service is provided.

---

33   The other current Category A list events are: the Olympic Games; the Grand National; the Derby; the Wimbledon finals; the Rugby League Challenge Cup final; and the Rugby Union World Cup final.
34   The current Category B list comprises: Cricket Tests in England; Wimbledon up to finals; all other Rugby Union World Cup matches; Six Nations Rugby matches involving the home countries; the Commonwealth Games; the World Athletics Championships; the Cricket World Cup final, semi-finals and matches involving home countries; the Ryder Cup Golf tournament; and the Open Golf Championship.
35   Broadcasting Act 1996, s 98.
36   Ibid, s 98(2).
37   OFCOM Code on Sports and Other Listed and Designated Events, Annex 2. http://stakeholders.ofcom.org.uk/binaries/broadcast/other-codes/ofcom_code_on_sport.pdf (accessed March 2018).
38   Broadcasting Act 1996, s 101.

18.43   According to Ofcom's most recent guidance (July 2014), in deciding whether to give its consent it may be sufficient for Ofcom to establish that the availability of the rights was generally known and no broadcaster providing a service in the other category had expressed an interest in their acquisition to the rights-holder, or had not bid for the rights. However, Ofcom will wish to be satisfied that broadcasters have had a genuine opportunity to acquire the rights on fair and reasonable terms and, in reaching a view, will take account of some or all of the following criteria:

(a)   any invitation to express interest, whether in the form of public advertisement or closed tender, in the acquisition of the rights must have been communicated openly and simultaneously to broadcasters providing services in both categories;

(b)   at the beginning of any negotiation the documentation and/or marketing literature must set out in all material respects the process for negotiating and acquiring the rights and all material terms and conditions, including what rights were available;

(c)   if the rights to the listed event were included in a package of rights, the package must not have been more attractive to broadcasters providing services in one of the two categories. Preferably, the rights should be capable of being purchased independently of other rights, eg to highlights, delayed transmissions, other events;

(d)   the conditions or costs attached to the acquisition of the rights (for example, production costs) must have been clearly stated and must not be preferential to one category of service;

(e)   the price sought for the rights must have been fair, reasonable and non-discriminatory as between the two categories of programme service.[39]

18.44   Section 104 of the 1996 Act requires Ofcom to specify the circumstances in which the coverage of listed events generally, or of a particular listed event, is, or is not, to be treated as 'live'. According to Ofcom's most recent guidance Ofcom suggests that 'live television coverage of most sports events, including those taking place in different time zones, should be defined as coverage which is simultaneous with the event'.[40] However, Ofcom may also take into account the following factors when defining 'live coverage' for the purposes of broadcasting events:

(a)   the restrictions on live coverage will apply while the event concerned is in progress;

(b)   if the event involves separate games or matches, the restrictions will apply while each game or match is in progress;

(c)   in the case of a single event which is scheduled to last over several days, the restrictions will apply to each day's play, while it is in progress;

(d)   in the case of an event which consists of defined separate parts which overlap in time (eg the Olympic Games or the FIFA World Cup Finals) and cannot therefore be televised simultaneously in full, the restrictions will apply to each match or competition as if it was a single event;

(e)   for Group B events, Ofcom will give its consent to exclusive live coverage of an event by a broadcaster providing a service in one category (the first service) if adequate provision has been made for secondary coverage by a broadcaster providing a service in the other category (the second service). The minimum which Ofcom will consider to be adequate is where the second service has acquired rights for the provision of edited highlights or delayed coverage amounting to at least 10% of the scheduled duration of the event (or the play in

39   OFCOM Code on Sports and Other Listed and Designated Events, para 1.14.
40   Ibid, para 1.13.

the event taking place on any day), subject to a minimum of 30 minutes for an event (or the play in the event on any day) lasting an hour or more, whichever is the greater.[41]

18.45   Under the 1996 Act, Ofcom has powers to impose a financial penalty on licensees if the restriction on broadcasting live coverage of listed events has not been observed, if Ofcom has been given false information or if material information has been withheld.[42] According to Ofcom's guidance, given the long lead times which are generally available for offering, selling and acquiring the rights, Ofcom believes that there are very few circumstances in which it would be reasonable for a broadcaster to proceed with exclusive coverage without Ofcom's consent. A broadcaster who proceeds to broadcast a listed event live without Ofcom's consent and not in compliance with s 101(1) will need to convince Ofcom that for legitimate reasons the period between the rights becoming available and the event taking place was too short for this consent to be obtained or that he believed he had complied but that belief was based on false information. In the latter situation, however, Ofcom will need to be convinced that the broadcaster had taken all reasonable steps to satisfy himself that another broadcaster providing a service in the other category had acquired the rights.[43]

18.46   Certain requirements are also placed on broadcasters by Article 14 of the Audiovisual Media Services Directive, as applied in the Television Broadcasting Regulations 2000. The requirements are designed to ensure that broadcasters under the jurisdiction of the UK and broadcasting to other EEA states do not circumvent the rules on listed (or 'designated') events which apply in those states. Designated events are defined by s 101A of the 1996 Act, and in essence are those events that a state has designated in accordance with Article 14(1) of the AVMS Directive as being of major importance to its society.[44] UK broadcasters must seek Ofcom's approval to broadcast designated events where a substantial proportion of the public in that EEA State is deprived of the possibility of following that event by live or deferred coverage on free television as determined by that state.[45]

18.47   In December 2008, the Labour government announced that a review of listed events would be carried out by an independent advisory panel.[46] The panel reported in November 2009 and supported the continued protection of some major sporting events.[47] However, it recommended that there should be a single list of live events, with some current events de-listed. A consultation document on the panel's report was published in December 2009 and proposed a single list based on the criteria of:

> 'an event must have a special national resonance and not simply a significance to those who ordinarily follow the sport concerned. Such an event is likely to fall into one or both of the following categories: it is a pre-eminent national or international event in sport; it involves the national team or national representatives in the sport concerned. It should also be likely to command a large television audience.'[48]

---

41   Ibid, para 1.18.
42   Broadcasting Act 1996, s 102.
43   OFCOM Code on Sports and Other Listed and Designated Events, para 1.22.
44   The current UK list of designated events is listed as Annex 3 of the current Ofcom guidance on listed events, but it is a broadcaster's responsibility to check whether an event is designated or not. At present the UK only lists sporting events, but non-sporting events could also be listed: Austria lists the Vienna Opera Ball, Belgium lists the Queen Elisabeth Music Competition, and Italy lists the San Remo Music Festival.
45   OFCOM Code on Sports and Other Listed and Designated Events, para 1.25.
46   Archived DCMS website, *Free-to-air listed events review* [dated 7 April 2010].
47   *Review of free-to-air listed events*, Report of the Independent Advisory Panel, November 2009.
48   Ibid, para 124.

18.48   The consultation proposed a single list of events consisting of: the Summer Olympic Games; the FIFA World Cup Finals Tournament; the UEFA European Football Championship Finals Tournament; the Grand National; the FA Cup Final (in England, Wales and Northern Ireland only); the Scottish FA Cup (in Scotland only); home and away qualification matches in the FIFA World Cup and UEFA European Football Championships (listed in the Home Nation to which they relate); the Wimbledon All England Lawn Tennis Championship (listed in its entirety); the Open Golf Championship; the Cricket Home Ashes Test matches between England and Australia; the Rugby Union World Cup Tournament; Wales matches in the Six Nations Rugby Championship (in Wales only).

18.49   In 2010 the Coalition government stated that it would not make any decision on future events until after the digital switchover. However, the government's December 2015 Sports Strategy stated that it did not intend to reopen discussion on listed events but stated the following policy:

> 'Rather than being told by government what to show and what not to show on free-to-air television, it is for NGBs [national governing bodies] and other rights holders to strike the right balance between reaching a wide audience and using their rights to generate as much revenue as possible. However, one of the two fundamental principles of the SRA's [Sport and Recreation Alliance] Voluntary Code of Conduct on the Broadcasting of Major Sporting Events is that, wherever possible, all major events under the control of signatories to the code receive free-to-air television coverage in the UK. We would like to see more organisations sign up to this part of the code and ensure that live sport can have the widest reach possible and fulfil its inspirational potential.'[49]

18.50   The Voluntary Code referenced in the strategy is that of the Sport and Recreation Alliance. The Voluntary Code of Conduct for Rights Owners outlines the ongoing commitment of the UK's leading sports bodies to two general principles:

(a) *Accessibility* – Ensuring that, wherever possible, all major events under their control receive free-to-air television coverage in the UK (live, recorded or highlights).

(b) *Reinvestment* – Ensuring a minimum of 30% of their net UK broadcasting revenue is put back into grassroots development within their sport.[50]

18.51   The current position, in the UK at least, appears to be that it is not regarded as a political priority for the listed events regime to be dismantled. However, the regime continues to be a target of criticism – for example, the Sport Rights Owners Coalition responded to the May 2015 EU consultation on the AVMS Directive,[51] arguing that the listed events regime was no longer necessary, given that pay-TV penetration was over 60% in 20 EU states and over 90% in nine EU countries.[52] In addition, the growing costs of sports rights and growing pressure upon public

49   HM Government, *Sporting Future: A New Strategy for an Active Nation*, December 2015, p 41.
50   See   http://www.sportandrecreation.org.uk/policy/campaigns-initiatives/broadcasting-of-major-sporting-events-the-vol (accessed March 2018). The FA is a signatory to the Code whereas the Premier League is a signatory to the Accessibility principle. The other full signatories to the Code are the England and Wales Cricket Board, the Lawn Tennis Association/All England Lawn Tennis and Croquet Club (joint), the Royal & Ancient, the Rugby Football League and the Rugby Football Union. Two other bodies are signatories to the Accessibility Principle: the European Tour and UK Athletics.
51   See   https://ec.europa.eu/digital-single-market/en/news/public-consultation-directive-201013eu-audiovisual-media-services-avmsd-media-framework-21st (accessed March 2018).
52   See   https://ec.europa.eu/digital-single-market/en/news/contributions-received-european-level-representative-associations-avmsd-public-consultation (accessed March 2018).

service broadcasters to compete with commercial broadcasters to secure rights has continued.[53] The BBC has also partnered with other public service broadcasters in order to maintain certain rights.[54]

18.52   So far as football coverage is concerned, the principal club competitions are no longer covered by the regime (with the exception of the FA Cup final), so that highlights coverage is likely in practice to be the only broadcasting available to viewers on a free-to-air basis. Commercial competition for exclusive live rights packages will remain fierce for the foreseeable future, as operators on a range of commercial platforms compete for exclusive rights, but the major international tournaments seem likely to remain protected for as long as such a regime exists at all.

E   COPYRIGHT LAW AND BROADCASTING

18.53   The advent of digital broadcasting and technical advances have led to significant litigation developments as broadcasters, rights holders and courts seek to keep pace with technical innovation. This is particularly apparent in the field of UK copyright law. In terms of broadcasting two types of copyright are generally relevant, namely (i) television broadcasts of sports matches staged under the auspices of a particular sporting organisation, such as the Football Association Premier League (FAPL), the Rugby Football Union or the England and Wales Cricket Board, and (ii) films made during the course of the production of the broadcasts, in particular by recording broadcast footage for the purposes of action replays. It is the exploitation of such copyright that is sold to various broadcasters. Ensuring such rights are protected has involved the holders of such rights bringing actions for copyright infringement against persons illegally exploiting them.

18.54   The primary piece of UK legislation is the Copyright, Designs and Patents Act 1988 ('the 1988 Act'). The 1988 Act includes the following provisions:

'**Copyright and copyright works**

1.(1)   Copyright is a property right which subsists in accordance with this Part in the following descriptions of work –

...

(b)   sound recordings, films or broadcasts, and

...'

'**The acts restricted by copyright in a work**

16.(1)   The owner of the copyright in a work has, in accordance with the following provisions of this Chapter, the exclusive right to do the following acts in the United Kingdom –

(a)   to copy the work (see section 17);

...

(d)   to communicate the work to the public (see section 20);

...

---

53   In February 2015 the BBC lost the live coverage of the Open Golf Championship to Sky: http://www.radiotimes.com/news/2015-02-03/sky-sports-wins-rights-from-bbc-to-show-golfs-open-championship (accessed March 2018); and terminated its contract with Formula One ahead of schedule in December 2015: http://www.bbc.co.uk/news/uk-35149963 (accessed March 2018).

54   In July 2015 BBC and ITV announced a six-year deal to provide live coverage of the Six Nations, with ITV offering England, Ireland and Italy home matches and the BBC Wales and Scotland matches. http://www.bbc.co.uk/sport/rugby-union/33369443 (accessed March 2018). In June 2015 the BBC lost control of the rights to the Olympic Games from 2022 onwards after the US broadcaster Discovery, owner of Eurosport, signed a £920 million exclusive pan-European deal with the International Olympic Committee. However, the listed events legislation will ensure that there will be sub-licensing of rights for free-to-air coverage.

(3)   References in this Part to the doing of an act restricted by the copyright in a work are to the doing of it –
(a)   in relation to the work as a whole or any substantial part of it ...
(b)   either directly or indirectly;
and it is immaterial whether any intervening acts themselves infringe copyright.

(4)   This Chapter has effect subject to –
(a)   the provisions of Chapter III (acts permitted in relation to copyright works)
...'

'Infringement of copyright by copying

17.(1) The copying of the work is an act restricted by the copyright in every description of copyright work; and references in this Part to copying and copies shall be construed as follows.

(2)   Copying in relation to a literary, dramatic, musical or artistic work means reproducing the work in any material form. This includes storing the work in any medium by electronic means.
...

(6)   Copying in relation to any description of work includes the making of copies which are transient or are incidental to some other use of the work.'

'Infringement by communication to the public

20.(1) The communication to the public of the work is an act restricted by the copyright in –
...
(b)   a sound recording or film, or
(c)   a broadcast.

(2)   References in this Part to communication to the public are to communication to the public by electronic transmission, and in relation to a work include –
(a)   the broadcasting of the work;
(b)   the making available to the public of the work by electronic transmission in such a way that members of the public may access it from a place and at a time individually chosen by them.'

'Criticism, review, quotation and news reporting

30. ...

(2)   Fair dealing with a work (other than a photograph) for the purpose of reporting current events does not infringe any copyright in the work provided that (subject to subsection (3)) it is accompanied by a sufficient acknowledgement.

(3)   No acknowledgement is required in connection with the reporting of current events by means of a sound recording, film or broadcast where this would be impossible for reasons of practicality or otherwise.'

18.55   One increasingly significant challenge has been managing the changing way in which consumers watch sports broadcasts; rather than watch matches on television, consumers increasingly watch sports on computers and mobile devices via streaming services. The increase of live streaming has led to the development of 'blocking injunctions'. In March 2017, *The Football Association Premier League Ltd v British Telecommunications Plc*,[55] saw the grant of the first 'blocking injunction', which allowed FAPL to prevent matches in the UK being streamed without the consent of FAPL (or its licensees) on the internet.

18.56   The injunction application was made by FAPL against the six main retail Internet service providers (ISPs) in the UK. FAPL sought an injunction, supported by a number of other sports rights-holders including the BBC, PGA European Tour, The Professional Darts Corporation Ltd and the Rugby Football Union, against the ISPs pursuant to s 97A of the 1988 Act,[56] requiring the defendants to take measures to block, or at least impede, access by their customers to streaming servers delivering infringing live streams of Premier League footage to UK consumers.

18.57   Section 97A of the 1988 Act empowers the High Court 'to grant an injunction against a service provider, where that service provider has actual knowledge of another person using their service to infringe copyright'. Five of the defendants, BT, EE, Sky, Virgin and Plusnet also supported the application for the injunction. BT and Sky are two of the exclusive rights holders for Premier League broadcasting. The other ISPs included broadcasting of Premier League games as part of their service packages.

18.58   FAPL had previously succeeded in obtaining a blocking order against a website known as FirstRow Sports in *Football Association Premier League Ltd v British Sky Broadcasting Ltd*.[57] The May 2017 application differed in that it was directed at streaming servers rather than a website. In the 2017 judgment Arnold J noted that the problem of individuals illegally streaming matches had been exacerbated by technological changes and developments in the manner in which individuals watch matches. He noted that (i) consumers were increasingly turning to set-top boxes, media players and mobile device apps to access infringing streams, rather than web browsers running on computers, which meant traditional blocking orders that targeted websites no longer prevented the majority of infringements (because these devices do not rely upon access to a specific website in order to enable consumers to access infringing material, such devices instead connect directly to streaming servers via their IP addresses); (ii) the skill and effort required to find and use such devices and apps to access infringing content had fallen dramatically (devices such as set-top boxes and media players are easy to connect to domestic televisions and software to access suitable streams had become much easier to find and install); (iii) it was now possible to access a large number of high-quality infringing streams of footage of each Premier League match; (iv) a significantly higher proportion of UK consumers believed that it is lawful to access unauthorised streams using such devices and software than believed it lawful to access unauthorised content via file-sharing websites; (v) the streaming servers used to make available infringing streams to the public increasingly had been moved to offshore hosting providers who do not cooperate with rights-holders' requests to take down infringing content either at all or in a timely manner.[58] Arnold J went on to describe streaming servers as 'the crucial link in the chain' by which an unauthorised copy of footage of a Premier League match is transmitted to the consumer.

18.59   The order was granted against a list of 'target servers' identified by FAPL. The order had a number of unusual features. First, the order was a 'live' blocking order, which only had effect at the times when live Premier League match footage is being broadcast. Secondly, the order provided for the list of Target Servers to be 're-set' each match week during the Premier League season. This allowed for new

---

56   The Copyright, Designs and Patents Act 1988 implements Article 8(3) of European Parliament and
      Council Directive 2001/29/EC of 22 May 2001 on the harmonisation of certain aspects of copyright
      and related rights in the information society.
57   [2013] EWHC 2058 (Ch), [2013] ECDR 14.
58   *The Football Association Premier League Ltd v British Telecommunications Plc* [2017] EWHC 480,
      paras 10–15.

servers to be identified by FAPL and notified to the defendants for blocking each week, and ensured that old servers were not blocked after the end of a week unless they continue to be observed as sources of infringing footage. The order applied only for the period 18 March 2017 until 22 May 2017, ie the end of the 2016/17 Premier League season. The short period of the order was designed as a test period, with a view to FAPL applying for a similar order to cover the entirety of the 2017/18 season.[59]

18.60 In weighing up the comparative importance of, and the justifications for interfering with, FAPL's copyrights on the one hand and the defendants' freedom to carry on business and Internet users' freedom to impart or receive information on the other hand, Arnold J found that FAPL had a legitimate interest in curtailing copyright infringement, as did its licensees BT and Sky. Moreover, there was a public interest in combatting infringements of its rights given FAPL's role in supporting sport in the UK and given the substantial contributions made by FAPL and its licensees to the UK economy. As for the freedom of internet users to impart or receive information, this plainly does not extend to a right to engage in copyright infringement. Arnold J also found that granting such an order was likely to lead to a decrease in illegal streaming and also help to educate UK consumers that accessing infringing streams is not a lawful or reliable way to access Premier League content.[60]

18.61 In July 2017 FAPL announced that following the 'test run' of the order granted in March until the end of the 2017 season, a live blocking injunction would be in place for the whole of the 2017/18 season.[61]

18.62 Another example of the developing area of litigation arising out of technological developments was the case of Fanatix, a sports clips company, in the case *England and Wales Cricket Board Ltd v Tixdaq Ltd*.[62] Fanatix launched an app and website allowing fans to upload and share, on a near-live basis, eight-second clips of sports broadcast footage. Users could search for their favourite sport or team and view the latest action for free. The case arose after frequent near-live highlights of the Ashes series were copied and shared through the app. The rights-holders, the England and Wales Cricket Board (ECB) and its broadcaster partner, Sky, brought proceedings against Fanatix, arguing that their copyright was being infringed.

18.63 Fanatix relied on s 30 of the 1988 Act, which provides a 'fair dealing' defence to a copyright infringement claim where the purpose of copying material is 'reporting current events'. Fanatix argued that users could only post eight-second clips, with commentary and attribution, viewable for 24 hours, and that it amounted to 'citizen journalism' comparable to broadcasters showing goals on the evening news.

18.64 Arnold J made a series of findings. First, the claimants contended that each eight-second clip constituted a substantial part of one (or more) of the claimants' copyright works. Arnold J found that quantitatively, eight seconds is not a large proportion of a broadcast or film lasting two hours or more. Qualitatively, however, it was clear that most of the clips uploaded constituted highlights of the matches such as wickets taken, appeals refused and centuries scored. Thus each clip substantially exploited the claimants' investment in producing the relevant broadcast and/or film.[63]

59   Ibid, paras 24–27.
60   Ibid, paras 44–47.
61   See https://www.premierleague.com/news/442401 (accessed March 2018).
62   [2016] EWHC 575.
63   *England and Wales Cricket Board Ltd v Tixdaq Ltd*, para 95.

18.65   In assessing the scope of the 'fair dealing' defence, Arnold J disagreed with the defendant's submissions. He agreed that 'citizen journalism' can qualify as reporting current events. If a member of the public captures images and/or sound of a newsworthy event using their mobile phone and uploads it to a social media site like Twitter, then that may well qualify as reporting current events even if it is accompanied by relatively little in the way of commentary. However, evidence showed that the predominant purpose of Fanatix was sharing sports clips, not informing users about current events. In particular Mr Justice Arnold referred to a marketing presentation for Fanatix that listed the aims of the app as:

> 'By connecting sports fans from around the world and enabling them to capture and share their favourite sports moments, Fanatix is disrupting the global sports "clips" marketplace and creating a single brand that users can access from any territory in the world in order to discover and share the key moments from the sports that matter most to them.'

18.66   Mr Justice Arnold therefore found that the clips were reproduced and communicated to the public for the purposes of (i) sharing the clips with other users and (ii) facilitating debate amongst users about the sporting events depicted. Of those two purposes, the first was the primary or predominant purpose. Users added comments to the clips they were uploading, they did not create a report to which they added clips. Equally, the clips were presented to viewers accompanied by the comments, rather than reports being presented to viewers illustrated by clips, therefore the purpose of the app was not for the purpose of reporting current events.[64]

18.67   Nor was its dealing fair in any event: presenting extensive sports clips on a near-live basis was disproportionate and reduced the attractiveness of the rights-holders' packages by competing with their normal commercial exploitation of their copyright.

18.68   The rise of blocking injunctions and the *Fanatix* case illustrate the challenges faced by rights-holders in protecting rights as both the means by which sports are broadcast to consumers, and the way in which consumers watch sports broadcasts changes. Given the pace of technological development and the tendency of software entrepreneurs to take pride in being 'disruptors' of traditional markets, it is likely that this area of litigation will continue to expand.

F   THE FUTURE

18.69   As noted at the start of this chapter, the broadcasting of premium sports, and in particular football, has been a principal driver of commercial television since the advent of commercial satellite and cable broadcasting in the 1990s – these technological changes disrupted the traditional links between sports and public service broadcasters that had existed for many years and led to the commercial issues that have driven each of the legal issues discussed above: the application of the competition rules to sport and broadcasting; the free movement of broadcasting services within the EU; the challenge to the protection of public or free to air broadcasting of major sporting events by 'listing' provisions; and the use of copyright in sports recordings to protect the value of investment in the filming of sporting events.

18.70   The pace of technological change shows no sign of abating – on the contrary, just as the advent of satellite and cable television disrupted traditional

---

64   Ibid, paras 106–156.

terrestrial broadcasters and opened up new economic possibilities, including the convergence of broadcasting and telecommunications, it now seems inevitable that the internet giants that have challenged traditional retail distribution of goods and services, including broadcasting and film, will challenge the established commercial broadcasters for exclusive or unbundled rights; and the ability to distribute films by and to mobile devices will create new possibilities for the live recording and distribution of sporting events.

18.71   Finally, there are also major economic and political developments that will provide further stimulus for legal challenges. These possibilities have not featured in this chapter, but two issues are obviously worthy of mention:

(a)   One discrete but significant aspect of the UK withdrawal from the EU, whether in March 2019 or at some later date, will be to allow for the possibility of divergence between UK and EU law in each of the areas discussed in this chapter. While it seems unlikely that the UK will rapidly diverge from the EU in the principles of competition law or intellectual property protection applicable to broadcasting rights, it is much less certain that principles of free movement of services or the status of national sporting events will develop in the same way in the UK domestic context and in the wider EU.

(b)   It is well known that the major emerging economies, notably Brazil, China and India, have massive potential as audiences for sporting events, including in particular the major European club competitions and leagues, including the FA Premier League. Whether in combination with technological change or as a separate source of economic and political uncertainty, the history of commercial broadcasting since 1990 suggests that such a major economic upheaval will in due course lead to further novel and challenging legal questions.

CHAPTER 19

Stadia, Hillsborough, Health & Safety and Policing

Michael J Beloff QC, **Shane Sibbel** and **George Molyneaux** (Blackstone Chambers)

A   INTRODUCTION

19.1   The law relating to football stadia encompasses a statutory regime, backed by criminal sanctions, as well as certain obligations in tort. The statutory regime aims to protect health and safety at football matches, against a historical background of several tragic incidents, most obviously the Hillsborough disaster. There has also been repeated litigation over the circumstances in which the football club, rather than the police force, ought to pay for police services provided on football match days.

B   STADIA, HILLSBOROUGH AND HEALTH & SAFETY

(a)   Statutory control of sports grounds

19.2   The Safety of Sports Grounds Act 1975 ('the 1975 Act') makes provision for safety at sports grounds which have been designated by the Secretary of State. Any sports ground which the Secretary of State considers to have accommodation for more than 10,000 spectators may be so designated.[1] In the case of football grounds, the minimum capacity for a designation order is 5,000 spectators.[2] This lower threshold reflects the particular concerns which arise in relation to safety at football grounds, following a number of disasters at such grounds. The 1975 Act was itself enacted in order to implement the recommendations of the Wheatley Report,[3] following the deaths of 66 spectators (and more than 200 injuries) at Ibrox Park in Glasgow in 1971.

19.3   Any sports ground designated under the 1975 Act requires a safety certificate (s 1(1) of the 1975 Act), which is issued by the local authority. The certificate may be general or specific to certain occasions. It will contain such terms and conditions as the local authority considers 'necessary or expedient to secure reasonable safety at the sports ground' when it is in use for the specified activity or activities (s 2(1) of the 1975 Act).

---

1   The Safety of Sports Grounds (Designation) Order 2015 (SI 2015/661) provides (at Schs 1 and 2 to the Order) the current list of sports grounds so designated.
2   Pursuant to the Safety of Sports Grounds (Accommodation of Spectators) Order 1996 (SI 1996/499). For these purposes 'football grounds' mean those used by clubs in either the FA Premier League, or the English Football League: see article 3 of the Order.
3   See the Report of the Inquiry into Crowd Safety at Sports Grounds ('the Wheatley Report') (1972) London; HMSO; Cmnd 4952.

19.4   It is a criminal offence to admit spectators into a designated sports ground in the absence of a valid and applicable safety certificate (see s 12(1)(a)–(c) of the 1975 Act). It is likewise a criminal offence to contravene any term or condition of a safety certificate (s 12(1)(d) of the 1975 Act).

19.5   On an application for a safety certificate, the local authority has a duty to determine whether the applicant is a person likely to prevent contravention of the terms and conditions of a certificate (a 'qualified person') (s 3(1) of the 1975 Act) and may only issue a safety certificate to such a person. Once granted, a safety certificate can thereafter be amended, transferred or replaced on an application under s 4 of the 1975 Act.

19.6   Safety certificates are only as good as the terms and conditions therein. The Sports Grounds Safety Authority is the UK government's expert body on safety at sports grounds. Its core statutory functions are set out in the Football Spectators Act 1989 and the Sports Ground Safety Authority Act 2011. The Authority provides advice to local authorities and others via the 'Green Guide',[4] which sets out detailed guidance as to planning, stewarding, structures, installations and components, circulation, barriers, spectator accommodation, fire safety, communications, electrical and mechanical services, and medical and first aid provision for spectators.

19.7   Responsibility for enforcing the statutory regime (apart from its criminal provisions) rests with local authorities. Under s 10B of the 1975 Act, local authorities are obliged to arrange for the periodical inspection of all designated sports grounds in their area (where periodical means at least once every 12 months), using their powers under s 11 of the 1975 Act. Local authorities also have the power, under s 10 of the 1975 Act, to serve a 'prohibition notice' where they are of the opinion that:

> 'the admission of spectators to a sports ground or any part of a sports ground involves or will involve a risk to them so serious that, until steps have been taken to reduce it to a reasonable level, admission of spectators to the ground or that part of the ground ought to be prohibited or restricted.'

The notice may prohibit or restrict the admission of spectators, and include directions as to the steps which must be taken to reduce the risk.

19.8   Statutory rights of appeal exist in respect of a local authority's decision to refuse an application for a safety certificate, or to refuse to amend or replace a safety certificate, as well as in respect of a decision to issue a prohibition notice: see ss 5 and 10A of the 1975 Act, and regulation 5 of the Safety of Sports Grounds Regulations 1987.[5] Such rights are only enjoyed by the relevant applicant, and certain interested parties (as defined in ss 5 and 10), including the police. Section 13 of the 1975 Act moreover makes clear that no civil action may be brought for breach of the statutory duties owed under the Act.

19.9   Where a sports grounds is not designated under the 1975 Act, a safety certificate for one or more of its stands may still be required under Part III of the Fire Safety and Safety of Places of Sports Act 1987 ('the 1987 Act'), where the relevant stand provides covered accommodation for 500 or more spectators. Part III

---

4   Guide to Safety at Sports Grounds, Fifth Edition (2008): available for download at http://www. safetyatsportsgrounds.org.uk/publications/green-guide (accessed March 2018). The sixth edition of the Guide was due to be published shortly after the time of writing, and should be available from the SGSA website.
5   SI 1987/1941.

of the 1987 Act provides for a similar system of certification, inspection and statutory appeals in that regard.

(b)   The Hillsborough disaster

19.10   The regime established under the 1975 Act did not prevent the disaster which struck Hillsborough Stadium in Sheffield on 15 April 1989, at an FA Cup semi-final between Liverpool and Nottingham Forest. Hillsborough was a neutral venue, and like many stadia of its time a mix of seated areas and modified standing terraces. A crush occurred within two pens of the Leppings Lane terrace, resulting in the deaths of 96 people and the injury of hundreds more.

19.11   In the words of the Lord Chief Justice, many years later:[6]

> 'within a very short time it was being peddled about that this disaster was one more consequence of the kind of hooliganism which had manifested itself at and around football matches during the 1980s … the disaster was attributed to the drunken misbehaviour of the fans, and the Liverpool fans in particular. Yet in August 1989, in a Report which the then Prime Minister, Margaret Thatcher described as "devastating criticism of the police", Taylor LJ stated in quite unequivocal terms that: "the main reason for the disaster was the failure of police control".
>
> … That should have been that. Unfortunately, the culpability of the police was not acknowledged, and indeed a campaign was mounted to undermine confidence in Taylor LJ's conclusions. These were developed at the inquest which took place in the winter of 1990/1991 and continued thereafter. Notwithstanding its falsity the tendency to blame the fans was disappointingly tenacious and it lingered on for many years.'

19.12   The campaign for justice by the families of the Hillsborough victims has taken over a quarter of a century. The observations of the Lord Chief Justice above were made in the course of a decision of the Divisional Court in 2012 to quash the original inquests into the deaths of those victims. Those inquests had taken place between 19 April 1989 and 26 March 1991. They had returned verdicts of accidental killing in each case. Following a review of over 450,000 pages of relevant documentation between February 2010 and September 2012, the Hillsborough Independent Panel produced its report into the disaster on 12 September 2012.[7] It was largely on the basis of the findings in that report that the Divisional Court quashed the original inquests.

19.13   Fresh inquests began on 31 March 2014. The jury delivered its verdict on 26 April 2016. It found that there had been unlawful killing in each of the 96 cases, and that the match commander was responsible for their manslaughter by gross negligence. Amongst the problems identified were a failure to prevent congestion, a failure to close the nearest exit tunnel before a late influx of fans, not delaying kick off, a slow and inadequate emergency response, and a failure to respond to previous 'near misses' at the stadium. On 28 June 2017 the Crown Prosecution Service announced its decision to charge six former police officers in relation to the deaths. The criminal proceedings are ongoing as at the time of this publication.

---

6   *Her Majesty's Attorney General v Her Majesty's Coroner of South Yorkshire* [2012] EWHC 3783 (Admin), at para 3.
7   See http://hillsborough.independent.gov.uk/report/ (accessed March 2018).

19.14   The legal consequences of the disaster included the Football Spectators Act 1989 (enacted on 16 November 1989), which established the Football Licensing Authority (whose functions are now performed by the Sports Grounds Safety Authority: see para **19.6** above). The Taylor Report included a series of recommendations which continue to inform the safety guidance issued by that authority.

19.15   More controversially, the civil claims which followed the disaster resulted in a significant narrowing by the courts of the circumstances in which a duty of care will be owed in the tort of negligence, for fear of the 'floodgates', and in particular in relation to psychiatric injury.[8] Most notorious, perhaps, is Lord Keith of Kinkel's holding in *Alcock* at para 398 that the 'mere fact' of the relationship between brothers was insufficient to establish the 'particularly close ties of love or affection' required in order for the police to be liable for psychiatric injury.

(c)   Civil liability

19.16   What *Alcock* does establish, in the context of football stadia, is that the duty of care in negligence will be owed to all those to whom physical harm was reasonably foreseeable, as well as (within certain very narrow limits) those to whom psychiatric injury was foreseeable.

19.17   Beyond the tort of negligence, the Occupiers' Liability Act 1957 ('the 1957 Act') imposes a duty of care on 'occupiers' of premises towards 'visitors' thereto. The duty is to take such care as in all the circumstances of the case is reasonable to see that the visitor will be reasonably safe in using the premises for the purposes for which he is invited or permitted to be there (s 2(1)). Warning will not automatically suffice (see s 2(4)).

19.18   The duty is owed not only by those in physical occupation of the premises but also by those with control over the premises: ss 1(2) and 2(6) of the 1957 Act. A 'visitor' includes anyone who comes lawfully onto the premises, though s 1(3) of the Occupiers' Liability Act 1984 imposes limited duties in respect of certain dangers to trespassers: see *Tomlinson v Congleton BC*.[9]

19.19   In *Cunningham v Reading Football Club Ltd*,[10] a match took place between Bristol and Reading, at which 'large numbers of hooligans purporting to support the Bristol City side showed even before the game started that they were mainly interested in fighting with and doing violence to supporters of the Reading team', as part of which 'a very large number of missiles were thrown', which included 'a considerable number of pieces of concrete, of sizes varying from the small to that of a cricket ball and in some cases even larger and heavier lumps'. The club was held liable in negligence and under s 2 of the 1957 Act in claims by injured police officers, where the club had known of the risk of such conduct by the fans and was found to have taken insufficient steps to repair the grounds and prevent such missiles being available.

---

8   See in particular *Alcock v Chief Constable of South Yorkshire* [1992] AC 310 (HL) and *White v Chief Constable of South Yorkshire* [1999] 2 AC 455.
9   [2004] 1 AC 46 (HL).
10   (1991) 157 LG Rev 481.

C CHARGES FOR POLICING

(a) Introduction

19.20   The need (or perceived need) for substantial policing operations if football matches are to be held safely and without disorder raises a policy issue of who should cover the cost of such policing. On one view, clubs should pay for all match-related policing: organisations which, for commercial gain, choose to stage events that increase the risk of disorder should arguably foot the bill for managing that risk.[11] On the opposite view, all match-related policing should be funded by the state, given that such policing can be regarded as an aspect of the police's public duty to prevent crime and maintain order, and that clubs contribute to the cost of the police through rates and taxation. That opposite view can be buttressed by arguments based on the need for the law to be consistent. Given that criminals are not charged for the cost of their detection and arrest, why should a club be billed when (at most) its matches merely increase the risk of public order problems? And, if clubs are to be charged when they put on events that may be associated with disorder, why not persons who organise political demonstrations?

19.21   Whatever may be the merits of these rival views, the current law is based on s 25(1) of the Police Act 1996, the interpretation of which is the focus of the relevant jurisprudence. Section 25(1) provides:

> 'The chief officer of police of a police force may provide, at the request of any person, special police services at any premises or in any locality in the police area for which the force is maintained, subject to the payment to the local policing body of charges on such scales as may be determined by that body.'

19.22   The provision of 'special police services' (SPS) is a matter of discretion, not duty. There is limited authority on the circumstances in which a request for SPS may be declined.[12] It is, however, clear from s 25(1) that the police may charge when they provide SPS in response to a 'request'. The key issues are thus: first, what qualifies as 'special police services', an expression for which there is no statutory definition; and secondly, what constitutes a 'request'.[13]

19.23   As to the first, the most recent authority on the extent to which the police can charge for football-related policing is *Ipswich Town Football Club Company Ltd v Chief Constable of Suffolk Constabulary* (*'Ipswich'*).[14] In broad terms, the position in light of *Ipswich* is that a club is likely to be liable for policing costs if: (i) the policing was provided on the club's private land, eg inside a stadium;[15] (ii) the policing had been expressly or impliedly requested by the club; and (iii) the request was made otherwise than in response to an actual or imminent crime or emergency.

11   Certain judges have expressed sympathy for this view, while emphasising that it does not represent the law: *Yorkshire Police Authority v Reading Festival Ltd* [2006] EWCA Civ 524, [2006] 1 WLR 2005, para 72; *Ipswich Town Football Club Company Ltd v Chief Constable of Suffolk Constabulary* [2017] EWCA Civ 1484, [2017] 4 WLR 195, para 67.
12   The authors are aware of one case in which a club applied for an injunction to require a police force to provide SPS; the application was settled on the day of the hearing.
13   There is also some authority on quantum, which indicates that it is for the policing body to set the scale of charges, and that charges may take account of indirect costs and overheads: *Leeds United Football Club Ltd v Chief Constable of West Yorkshire* [2012] EWHC 2113 (QB), [2013] LLR 380, at [58].
14   [2017] EWCA Civ 1484, [2017] 4 WLR 195.
15   There is a potential ambiguity in respect of land that is privately owned but accessible to the public: see paragraph 19.30 below.

The scope for argument about the meaning of the statutory expression 'special police services' has not been entirely eliminated and a survey of the pre-existing law shows how judges have not always agreed about it.

(b)   The meaning of 'special police services'

19.24   Section 25(1) of the Police Act 1996 replaced a substantially identical provision in s 15 of the Police Act 1964, which was in turn a codification of the common law, as expressed in *Glasbrook Brothers Ltd v Glamorgan County Council*.[16] In *Glasbrook*, the House of Lords held that police authorities could not lawfully charge for the performance of their duty: 'to take all steps which appear to them to be necessary for keeping the peace, for preventing crime, or for protecting property from criminal injury', but that 'where individuals desire that services of a special kind which, though not within the obligations of a police authority, can most effectively be rendered by them, should be performed by members of the police force, the police authorities may ... "lend" the services of constables for that purpose in consideration of payment'.[17] In *Glasbrook*, a colliery manager requested that police officers provide a garrison at the colliery during a miners' strike. The police authority concluded that the colliery could be adequately protected by a mobile force, but agreed to provide a garrison in return for payment. The majority of the House of Lords held that the police authority could enforce the payment agreed, since the provision of the garrison went beyond what was necessary for the authority to discharge its duties. The distinction drawn was between the provision of services that were 'necessary', and those which were a 'superfluity'.[18] The police could charge for the latter, but not the former.

19.25   The first case to address the meaning of SPS in the context of football was *Harris v Sheffield United Football Club Ltd* ('*Harris*'),[19] which focused on whether the police could charge for routine policing inside the club's stadium. It was argued for the club that they could not. The Court of Appeal rejected that argument. Neill LJ (with whom Kerr LJ agreed) declined to lay down any general definition of SPS, but suggested that four factors should be taken into account.[20] First, Neill LJ said that policing on private (as opposed to public) land would *prima facie* constitute SPS, given that the police do not generally have access to private premises. Secondly, police attendance to deal with actual or imminent violence or an emergency would not be SPS. Thirdly, regard should be had to the nature of the event for which police attendance was requested; relevant matters could include the extent to which the event had a public character, and whether it formed part of a series. Fourthly, Neill LJ suggested that it was relevant to consider whether the policing sought could be provided without diverting officers from other duties and/or calling up off-duty officers. In light of these factors, Neill LJ concluded that the provision of officers inside the stadium (when no violence or emergency was imminent) constituted SPS, for which the police could charge.[21]

---

16   [1925] AC 270.
17   Ibid, at 277–278.
18   Ibid, at 281.
19   [1988] 1 QB 77.
20   Balcombe LJ reached a similar conclusion, if for somewhat different reasons.
21   *Harris*, at 91D–93A. In *Ipswich*, Leading Counsel for the club reserved the right to contend, should the case go to the Supreme Court, that *Harris* was wrongly decided and that the application of *Glasbrook* (properly interpreted) would oblige the police to provide policing in the stadium without charge: *Ipswich*, para 33, footnote 9. See also *Leeds United Football Club Ltd v Chief Constable of West Yorkshire Police* [2013] EWCA Civ 115, [2014] QB 168, paras 15, 28–29.

19.26   The meaning of SPS was considered further, albeit not in the context of football, in *West Yorkshire Police Authority v Reading Festival Ltd* (*'Reading Festival'*).[22] In that case, the police authority sought to charge for the cost of deploying officers in the vicinity of a music festival. The Court of Appeal decided the case on the basis that the festival's organiser had not requested the policing provided. The Court did, however, go on to consider *obiter* whether the policing constituted SPS. The Court had regard to the four factors identified in *Harris*, and concluded that the policing was not SPS, primarily on the grounds that officers were not deployed on private property.[23]

19.27   In *Chief Constable of the Greater Manchester Police v Wigan Athletic AFC Ltd*,[24] Mann J held at first instance that the Chief Constable could charge for policing provided on certain privately-owned (but publicly accessible) land surrounding a stadium, notwithstanding that the club itself did not have an ownership interest in that land. On appeal, the club successfully argued that it had not requested the services provided (see para **19.34** below). There was no appeal on whether the services would have qualified as SPS, but in *Leeds United Football Club Ltd v Chief Constable of West Yorkshire Police* (*'Leeds'*)[25] the Court of Appeal said that Mann J's conclusion on that issue carried little weight.[26]

19.28   *Leeds* is a counterpart to *Harris*. While the focus in *Harris* was on policing inside the stadium, the focus in *Leeds* was on policing outside it. The club conceded that policing provided on land that it owned or controlled, including areas to which the public had unrestricted access, was SPS.[27] The dispute focused on public highways and car parks owned by third parties.[28] Lord Dyson MR (with whom Moore-Bick and McCombe LJJ agreed) said that the four factors identified by Neill LJ in *Harris* were 'in varying degrees useful pointers' as to whether policing constituted SPS.[29] As to Neill LJ's first factor, Lord Dyson said that, where services are provided in order to promote the maintenance of law and order, the question of whether they are provided on private or public land is 'plainly of central importance'.[30] Lord Dyson treated Neill LJ's second factor as essentially a qualification of the first: policing in any location would be unlikely to constitute SPS if it was in response to actual or imminent violence, but on public land even preventative policing would be unlikely to constitute SPS.[31] On the third and fourth factors, Lord Dyson appeared to regard as relevant the fact that professional football matches are 'essentially public events', but questioned whether much weight should be placed on the extent of the burden on

22   [2006] EWCA Civ 524, [2006] 1 WLR 2005.
23   *Reading Festival*, paras 58–73.
24   [2007] EWHC 3095 (Ch), [2008] LLR 423.
25   [2013] EWCA Civ 115, [2014] QB 168.
26   Ibid, para 21.
27   The ambit of the concession is not wholly clear from the judgments, which do not define precisely what was meant by 'control' in this context. 'Control' would most obviously cover a situation (as in *Wigan*) where a club had no proprietary interest in its stadium, and occupied it by virtue of a licence. It is, however, apparent that the concession covered some land to which the public had unrestricted access but that land was private and not publicly owned land (as distinct from the situation in *Ipswich* for example): see the first instance judgment, *Leeds United Football Club Ltd v Chief Constable of West Yorkshire* [2012] EWHC 2113 (QB), [2013] LLR 380, para 38. There are some remarks on the concept of 'control' at paras 44–45.
28   *Leeds United Football Club Ltd v Chief Constable of West Yorkshire* [2012] EWHC 2113 (QB), [2013] LLR 380, paras 18, 33, 38, 44.
29   Ibid, para 29.
30   Ibid, para 30. Lord Dyson noted that the provision on public land of such services as a road escort (ie services other than to maintain law and order) may constitute SPS.
31   Ibid, paras 30, 37.

police resources.[32] Lord Dyson also played down the utility of any test based on who benefited from policing.[33] In light of these considerations, the Court of Appeal held that the policing of the disputed areas (ie land that the club did not own or control) did not constitute SPS.

19.29   In *Ipswich*, the dispute concerned policing of parts of the public highway which were closed to traffic (pursuant to an order of the local authority) on match days, and on which the club placed temporary kiosks to sell programmes. The club failed at first instance, but was successful on appeal. Gloster LJ (with whom Gross LJ agreed, and Lord Briggs substantially agreed) quoted extensively from *Leeds*, and concluded that it was not possible to distinguish the two cases on their facts. She emphasised the importance of 'whether the place where police provide public order services is private or public land', and noted that such *de facto* control as the club exercised over the streets in question did not cause them to cease to be public land. Further, Gloster LJ pointed out that there are principled justifications for giving 'special importance' to the distinction between public and private land. In particular, police access to private premises is restricted by law, and (as noted at para **19.17** above) the occupiers of private land owe legal duties in respect of the safety of persons coming onto that land.[34] If an occupier wishes to use police officers to assist in the discharge of such duties, there is a principled basis for requiring the occupier to pay, not least because the alternative would presumably be for the occupier to provide (and pay for) a greater number of stewards.

19.30   All three judgments in *Ipswich* emphasise the importance of certainty and predictability, and identify the distinction between public land and private land as the most workable basis on which to demarcate whether match-related policing constitutes SPS.[35] There remains, however, some potential uncertainty about the meanings of 'public' and 'private'. In *Ipswich*, the distinction is expressed primarily in terms of proprietary rights – ie is the land privately owned?[36] In *Leeds*, however, Lord Dyson referred to policing in 'places to which members of the public have recourse' and 'public places'.[37] He thus appeared to define 'public land' primarily in terms of accessibility, rather than ownership. This is consistent with the outcome in *Leeds*; policing requested by the club on land owned by third parties but accessible to the public, such as car parks, was held not to be SPS. *Leeds* did not decide that policing on publicly-accessible club-owned land was SPS – the club conceded the point. The club's concession would imply that non-emergency policing on a third party's car park would also be SPS, if requested by the car park owner. The result of *Leeds*, however, is that the same car park policing is not SPS if requested by the club. This is arguably anomalous, particularly if the club requests car park policing with the express or implied consent of the car park owner. As such, there may be scope for clubs to question whether Leeds United's concession went further than it needed to. *Ipswich* may therefore not be the final word on what constitutes SPS, despite the quest for predictability in the judgments, and the Supreme Court's refusal of an application by the police for permission to appeal.

---

32   Ibid, paras 31, 38.
33   Ibid, paras 32–33, 44. A 'benefit' test had been floated in *Reading Festival*.
34   *Ipswich*, para 38.
35   Ibid, paras 58, 65, 72.
36   Ibid, paras 44, 58.
37   *Leeds*, paras 36, 43.

(c) The meaning of 'request'

19.31   A policing body can only charge for SPS if the services in question were provided in response to a request. Where a club expressly asks the police to provide certain services and those services are then provided, the identification of a request is straightforward. Problems arise where (i) the police provide services without an express request; or (ii) a club requests certain services, and the police provide services which do not match those requested.

19.32   The issue of the provision of SPS otherwise than in response to an express request was considered in *Harris*. On the facts, the Court of Appeal held that a request was to be implied, since it was common ground that the club could not have continued to hold matches if police officers had ceased to attend the stadium. The Court of Appeal noted that this implied request may have been made without enthusiasm, but held that it was sufficient to enable the police authority to charge for the SPS provided.[38]

19.33   The issue of a mismatch between a request and the services provided arose in *Reading Festival* and *Chief Constable of Greater Manchester Police v Wigan Athletic AFC Ltd* (*'Wigan'*).[39] In *Reading Festival*, it appears that the festival organisers indicated that they wanted (and would be willing to pay for) policing on the event site itself, but expressly said that they would not pay for officers deployed offsite (except for certain officers managing traffic). The police refused to station officers at the site, but mounted an extensive operation in surrounding areas. The Court of Appeal held that there was no implied request for the services provided: the services were not necessary for the festival to go ahead, and the organisers had said that they were unwilling to pay for them.[40]

19.34   In *Wigan*, the Chief Constable had historically provided certain levels of policing, and the club had paid for that policing. Following the club's promotion to a higher league, the Chief Constable proposed to increase the level of policing, and to impose accordingly higher charges. The club said that it refused to accept the proposals, but the Chief Constable provided policing as he had proposed. The club paid at the level that it had done previously, and the Chief Constable sought to recover the cost of the additional policing. The Court of Appeal said that it was not necessary for there to be an exact match between a request and the services provided, but that no request for the additional policing could be implied, since the club had said it did not want it.[41]

19.35   Wigan AFC's certificate under the Safety of Sports Grounds Act 1975 required it to secure the presence at matches of such number of police officers as the Chief Constable deemed necessary.[42] This raises the issue of what the club could have done, had the Chief Constable refused to supply officers unless the club paid the sums demanded. In such a scenario, it would in principle be possible to challenge by way of judicial review a Chief Constable's assessment of the level of policing required.[43]

---

38   *Harris*, at 93A–D.
39   [2008] EWCA Civ 1449, [2009] 1 WLR 1580.
40   *Reading Festival*, especially paras 34–57.
41   *Wigan*, paras 15–35.
42   Ibid, para 1.
43   Ibid, para 57.

(d)   Restitutionary claims

19.36   Where a club has made payments in respect of services for which the police could not lawfully charge, the club can bring a claim for restitution of the sums by which the police have been unjustly enriched. In *Ipswich Town Football Club Company Ltd v Chief Constable of Suffolk Constabulary*,[44] Green J held that such a claim could be made on either of two bases, namely: (i) on the principle in *Woolwich Equitable Building Society v Inland Revenue Commissioners*,[45] under which a public body can be obliged to refund sums paid in response to ultra vires demands; and/or (ii) that the payments had been made in the mistaken belief that the policing body was lawfully entitled to demand them.

19.37   In a *Woolwich* claim, the normal six-year limitation period applies, but the defendant cannot rely on the defences of change of position or *quantum meruit*. In a claim premised on a mistake, such defences are available, but the start of the limitation period is postponed until the claimant has discovered the mistake or could by reasonable diligence have discovered it. Green J held that, given that the legality of charging for match-related policing had been an issue of legal controversy since *Harris*, Ipswich Town FC's mistake could with reasonable diligence have been discovered by at least 1988.[46] The postponement of limitation in mistake claims is therefore unlikely to assist clubs in practice. *Woolwich*-based claims will, given the absence of defences, probably be more advantageous.

19.38   In *Wigan*, the Chief Constable sought to recover the cost of the additional policing on the basis that it was a benefit that the club had freely accepted, and by which the club had thus been unjustly enriched. The majority of the Court of Appeal rejected this argument, holding that (i) there was no evidence that the additional officers had been of benefit to the club; (ii) the club had not freely accepted any benefit, since it could not have rejected the additional services without also rejecting the services that it did want; and (iii) for the same reason, the retention of any benefit was not unjust. The majority also suggested that, if a policing body is not entitled to payment under s 25 of the Police Act 1996, to allow a restitutionary claim by the police might illegitimately undermine the statutory scheme for when police charging is permissible.[47]

(e)   Conclusion

19.39   *Ipswich* has considerably clarified the law, notwithstanding the possible ambiguity regarding policing on land that is privately owned but publicly accessible. The judgments emphasise the need for, and seek to promote, predictability. Gross LJ did, however, express unease about the policy ramifications of requiring the police to foot the bill for policing on public land, where the need for that policing arises from the staging of an event on a commercial basis. Both he and Gloster LJ canvassed the possibility that Parliament might change the law.[48] It remains to be seen whether Parliament will do so.

---

44   [2017] EWHC 375 (QB).
45   [1993] AC 70.
46   *Ipswich Town Football Club Company Ltd v Chief Constable of Suffolk Constabulary* [2017] EWHC 375 (QB), para 109.
47   *Wigan*, paras 36–51, 53–57.
48   *Ipswich*, paras 58, 67–68.

CHAPTER 20

Ticketing

Nick Bitel, **Zane Shihab** and **James Thorndyke** (Kerman & Co)

A INTRODUCTION

20.1 This chapter is concerned with the law of ticketing in football and considers the legal remedies that may be available in the civil law to football clubs or institutions responsible for issuing tickets to football matches played in England and Wales. Also considered are the statutory provisions that make it an offence for unauthorised persons to sell or otherwise dispose of tickets in England and Wales.

20.2 However, before a detailed discussion of such topics, it is important to consider how the court interprets the definition of a 'ticket' and reflect why and how ticketing law has developed in this jurisdiction.

B WHAT IS A TICKET?

20.3 In the case of the *RFU v Viagogo*,[1] Tugendhat J provided a succinct definition of a ticket which he described as being:

> 'Permission to the public to enter premises … It does not have to be in writing, but it often is. If it is in writing, then it is usually printed on a permanent medium.

> The permission and the physical medium are distinct. The permission may be revoked or expire even if the physical medium cannot be retrieved from the holder by the owner of the premises.'

20.4 In *Winter Garden Theatre v Millennium Productions*,[2] Viscount Simon described a ticket as a contractual licence of which the ticket is the physical embodiment.

---

1   *Rugby Football Union v Viagogo Ltd* [2011] EWHC 764 (QB).
2   *Winter Garden Theatre v Millennium Productions* [1947] AC 173 at 189 per Viscount Simon.

C   PREVENTING UNLAWFUL ACCESS TO A VENUE

20.5   Venue owners must rely on three distinct but synergistic areas of law to control access to a sporting venue.

20.6   The first of these is property law; the event organiser will either be the landowner (as is the case with the majority of the higher-tier football league clubs) or have a lease or licence to use the venue to stage the event (for example, in 2016 the Premier League club Tottenham Hotspur entered into a licence with Wembley National Stadium Limited to stage its league and cup games at Wembley for the 2017/18 season).[3]

20.7   Secondly, venue owners use the law of contract to enable them to impose strict stipulations that act to govern an individual's access to the venue. To state the obvious, this usually manifests itself in the form of written ticket terms and conditions (which are discussed in more detail below).

20.8   Lastly, the tort of trespass (again, examined further below) can be utilised to exclude anyone who either enters the venue without permission or contravenes the aforementioned terms and conditions.

20.9   Generally, these tenets have developed due to two connected legal principles: English law's lack of recognition of an existence of proprietary rights in a sports event and the resistance to calls for a general tort of unfair competition.

D   PROPRIETARY RIGHTS IN A SPORTS EVENT

20.10   Broadly speaking, in England, the rights that arise in sporting events arise under copyright law and its associated rights (for example, performers' rights). However, for the following reasons, English copyright law does not recognise sport as a dramatic work in which copyright subsists.

20.11   A 'dramatic work' under the Copyright Designs and Patents Act 1988 (CDPA 1988) is one that is capable of being performed and 'includes a work of dance or mime'.[4]

20.12   The CDPA 1988 defines 'performance' as '(a) a dramatic performance (which includes dance and mime), (b) a musical performance, (c) a reading or recitation of a literary work, or (d) a performance of a variety act or any similar presentation, which is, or so far as it is, a live performance given by one or more individuals'.[5]

20.13   The Court of Appeal has stated that the term 'dramatic work' must be given its natural and ordinary meaning; in other words, a 'work of action, with or without words or music, which was capable of performance'.[6]

20.14   In 2008, the Premier League brought a high-profile case against a number of UK pub landlords who were using non-UK satellite decoder cards and boxes

---

3   See http://www.wembleystadium.com/Press/Press-Releases/2016/5/Spurs-are-on-their-way-to-Wembley.aspx (accessed March 2018).
4   CDPA 1988, s 3 (Literary, dramatic and musical works).
5   Ibid, s 180(2) (Rights conferred on performers and persons having recording rights).
6   *Norowzian v Arks Ltd (No 2)* [2000] FSR 363.

(obtained from the Premier League's exclusive licensees in other territories) to enable the viewing of Premier League matches in their UK pubs. This was later referred to the European Court of Justice[7] which, inter alia, concluded that sporting events and, in particular, football matches, could not be classified as works as they are not the 'author's own intellectual creations' classifiable as copyright works under the Copyright Directive.[8]

20.15   Whilst there is an argument that choreographed sports (ie those created by intellect and capable of being re-performed) should be protected by copyright as a dramatic work (for example, who could argue that Nadia Comaneci's first perfect 10 on the bars at the 1976 Olympics in Montreal was not dramatic), it is clear that a non-choreographed sporting event, such as a football match, does not fit into the definition of a 'dramatic work' (although some may argue that the histrionics that grace football pitches up and down the country are often worthy of Oscars).

E   THE TORT OF UNFAIR COMPETITION

20.16   The tort of unfair competition is designed to protect traders in their dealings with one another and is recognised in many jurisdictions outside of England and Wales. For example, competition contrary to honest practices in commercial matters amounts to an act of unfair competition under the Paris Convention which states that the 'countries of the union are bound to assure to nationals of such countries effective protection against unfair competition'.[9]

20.17   With respect specifically to access to a venue, the key case remains *Victoria Park Racing v Taylor.*[10] The claimant owned and operated a racecourse in Sydney. One of the defendants owned property adjacent to the claimant's land and permitted the other defendant to erect a scaffold tower which overlooked the racecourse. The defendants transmitted race commentary from that vantage point leading to, it was alleged, a fall in attendance at the races. As a result, the claimant argued that it had a quasi-property right in the races (due to the money and other resources invested therein) and that the defendants had unjustly interfered with this right.

20.18   The case was dismissed by a majority of three to two on the rationale that the:

> 'court has not been referred to any authority in English law which supports the general contention that if a person chooses to organise an entertainment ... which other persons are able to see he has a right to obtain an order that they shall not describe to anybody what they see ... A "spectacle" cannot be "owned" in the ordinary sense of the word'.[11]

20.19   In the 2007 House of Lords *Douglas v Hello!,*[12] Hollywood actors Michael Douglas and Catherine Zeta-Jones had sold the exclusive rights to OK! Magazine to

---

7   Joined Cases C-403/08 and C-429/08: *Football Association Premier League Ltd v QC Leisure; Karen Murphy v Media Protection Services Ltd.*
8   Copyright Directive 2001/29/EC.
9   Article 10bis of the 1883 Paris Convention. The UK is a contracting party to the Paris Convention but purports to comply with this requirement through a combination of passing-off, malicious falsehood and various criminal provisions.
10   *Victoria Park Racing and Recreation Grounds Co Ltd v Taylor* (1938) 58 CLR 479.
11   *Victoria Park Racing and Recreation Grounds Co Ltd v Taylor* (1938) 58 CLR 479, at 496.
12   *Douglas v Hello!* [2007] UKHL 21.

cover their wedding, leading to OK! bringing a claim against Hello! Magazine for publishing photographs surreptitiously taken at the event. Many legal commentators initially believed that this case represented a departure from the position reached in *Victoria Park Racing v Taylor* by implying a new proprietary right in an event. However, Lord Hoffmann made it clear that the decision was instead made on the basis that Douglas and Zeta-Jones controlled access to the venue, had imposed strict terms on the attendees to the event (being that the event was confidential and that no photographs should be taken; the equivalent of ticket terms and conditions that are seen at all major sporting events) and that Hello! had breached such terms.

20.20   Thus, *Victoria Park Racing v Taylor* remains sound legal precedent and highlights English law's lack of recognition of an existence of proprietary rights in a sports event. Further, even the dissenting minority in that case were not minded to recognise a general law of unfair competition.

20.21   Consequently, the issuance of tickets and the strict enforcement of the ticket terms and conditions attached thereto has provided the most effective method to prevent unauthorised attendance at events. Clearly this is important to clubs and leagues for a myriad of reasons, including:

(a) allowing clubs to control public order (discussed further below);
(b) the protection of valuable commercial income streams such as:
   (i)   the exclusive rights granted to official sponsors. By using tickets in their promotions, a third party could attempt to associate itself directly or indirectly with a major event to benefit from the goodwill and prestige of such event, without having to pay for that privilege as an official sponsor would do;[13]
   (ii) the sale of premium packages. Clearly the value of these would be significantly reduced if unofficial third parties were permitted to bundle tickets with travel and hospitality; and
   (iii) broadcasting rights;[14] and
(c) the perception that too much corporate hospitality can damage the atmosphere at a game and hence the need to control the pirate hospitality.[15]

F   THE STATUTORY PROVISIONS

20.22   Before we consider the civil law remedies available to football clubs to enable them to regulate the distribution and transfer of tickets to football matches played in England and Wales and thus the ability to control access to the same, it is important to understand that football is distinct from other sports in that legislation has been enacted to make it a criminal offence to deal in and/or dispose of tickets to football matches without having any authority to do so.

20.23   Since the 1980s (and following the Heysel disaster, in which a 'charge' by Liverpool fans towards Juventus supporters prior to the start of the 1985 European Cup Final at the Heysel Stadium in Belgium caused a wall to collapse, resulting in 39 deaths), substantial efforts have been made in the UK to bring the problem of

---

13 See Chapter 15, Sponsorship and Commercial Rights, for further discussion on ambush marketing.
14 See Chapter 18, Broadcasting, for a detailed discussion on broadcasting rights.
15 See http://www.dailymail.co.uk/sport/rugbyunion/article-2954832/Twickenham-not-produce-atmosphere-sporting-venues-fans-best-behaved.html (accessed March 2018).

football hooliganism under control. Furthermore, in his report on the Hillsborough Stadium disaster,[16] Lord Justice Taylor made it clear that he was concerned that touting outside a ground on the day of a match encouraged fans without tickets to arrive at the ground in the hope of getting in. This led to disorder outside the ground and, by undermining the arrangement for segregating rival groups of fans, led to disorder inside the ground as well. He recommended that the activity of ticket touts at grounds on the day of a match should be made unlawful.

20.24   Public order dictates that the control of the distribution of tickets is an essential part of the management of the venue. Control over the terms of a ticket allows an event organiser to impose segregation of fans inside a venue and limit the number of fans attending a match.

20.25   Section 166 of the Criminal Justice and Public Order Act 1994 (CJPOA 1994) made it a criminal offence to sell a ticket to a designated football match to another person, unless authorised to do so.[17] The penalty for being engaged in the trading of tickets to a football match in breach of the CJPOA is a fine not exceeding level 5 on the standard scale,[18] currently set at £5,000. Furthermore, any offence under s 166 of the CJPOA 1994 carries with it the risk of a football banning order under the Football Spectators Act 1989.[19]

20.26   While effective at preventing street touts from operating outside of a venue, the CJPOA 1994 proved to be limited in scope as touts found ways and means to effectively circumvent its provisions. For example, resellers found that by offering an item of nominal value at an inflated price with the inclusion of a 'free' match ticket or by offering tickets in exchange for other goods or services, the onward transfer of the ticket was not caught by the CJPOA 1994.

20.27   To counter this, the Violent Crime Reduction Act 2006, amended the provisions of CJPOA 1994, s 166 by extending the scope to include, among other things, prohibitions preventing the disposal or otherwise of a ticket (as opposed to merely the sale of a ticket) and thus sought to stop: (i) offering to sell a ticket; (ii) exposing a ticket for sale; (iii) making a ticket available for sale by another; (iv) advertising that a ticket is available for purchase; and (v) giving a ticket to a person who pays or agrees to pay for some other goods or services or offering to do so.[20]

20.28   The Ticket Touting (Designation of Football Matches) Order 2007, widened the definition of football matches covered by the aforementioned legislation to include: (i) any match involving one or more teams who are members of the Premier League, the Football League or the Conference; (ii) every match in England or Wales in which an international team or a club side from outside of England and Wales will play; (iii) every match outside of England and Wales in which a national team representing England and Wales will play; (iv) every match in the UEFA Champions League and UEFA Cup; (v) every match in the UEFA European Championship; and (vi) every match in the FIFA World Cup and FIFA World Club Championship.[21]

---

16   See http://hillsborough.independent.gov.uk/repository/docs/HOM000028060001.pdf (accessed March 2018), paras 273–279.
17   CJPOA 1994, s 166(1), (2).
18   Ibid, s 166(3).
19   Football Spectators Act 1989, s 14A.
20   Violent Crime Reduction Act 2006, s 53.
21   Ticket Touting (Designation of Football Matches) Order 2007 (SI 2007/790).

20.29   Notwithstanding the statutory legislation in place, ticket touting remains big business. In an era where touting on the secondary market is dominated by the buying and selling of tickets online, including through ticket exchange websites, the authors are of the firm opinion that the existing legislation still does not go far enough.

20.30   Section 166A of the CJPOA 1994 created a liability for information service providers (including auction and ticket exchange websites) in the event that they: (i) knew that tickets were being sold illegally at the time the tickets were advertised; or (ii) became aware that tickets were being sold illegally but did not take immediate steps to remove the advertisements.

20.31   In *Rugby Football Union v Viagogo Limited*,[22] the Court of Appeal granted a Norwich Pharmacal Order against Viagogo requiring it to provide the RFU with the names and addresses of all individuals who had sold tickets on its website during the Autumn International matches played at Twickenham stadium in 2010 and the following Six Nations matches played at the same venue in 2011 to enable the RFU to take action against those individuals.

20.32   However, s 166A of the CJPOA 1994 states that any service provider established outside of the UK who provides information society services shall not be guilty of an offence under the CJPOA 1994, s 166. For example, ticket sales made outside of England and Wales are not, as it stands, covered by the existing legislation. This means that a company incorporated in, for instance, Sweden can sell tickets to a football match in England and Wales (provided the sale takes place outside of England and Wales) without the authority of the football club which owns or otherwise controls access to the host stadium, in the knowledge that they are unlikely to be caught by the provisions of the CJPOA 1994.

G   THE CIVIL LAW

20.33   To mitigate, therefore, against the limitations of the criminal law, football clubs may wish to rely on various civil law remedies to prevent the unauthorised sale or resale of tickets to matches at venues owned or operated by them, provided that those clubs have in place strict terms and conditions that govern the sale and distribution of match tickets.

20.34   The case of *RFU v Viagogo* sets out a number of relevant causes of action in this regard including breach of contract, inducement to breach of contract, trespass, joint liability to trespass and conversion.

(a)   Breach of contract/inducement to breach of contract

20.35   Provided that a football club's ticket terms and conditions contain an express provision banning an original purchaser of a ticket from selling on that ticket to a third party (unless such sale is made to a third party authorised by the football club), any sale of a ticket in contravention of that football club's conditions can be the basis for an action for breach of contract against the original purchaser.

20.36   In order to aid any claim for breach of contract, it will be important for the football club to demonstrate that the original purchaser has accepted or otherwise

---

22   *The Rugby Football Union v Viagogo* [2011] EWCA Civ 1585.

affirmed the football club's terms and conditions. This is usually implemented online when a purchaser seeks to purchase a ticket (for example, a tick box accepting such terms prior to completion of purchase), or through a script recited by a telephone attendant of the club if a purchase is made through a telephone booking service.

20.37   In the event that the original purchaser succeeds in selling on a ticket to a third party or if he or she chooses to advertise a ticket on a third party's ticket exchange website, it may also be possible to take action against that third party for breach of contract if they seek to sell on that ticket either on behalf of the original purchaser or itself (having purchased the ticket from the original purchaser). For example, a claim against an online third-party ticket exchange company may exist if such third party encourages the original purchaser of a ticket to list their tickets on their ticketing platform. In entering into the agreement with an original purchaser to provide them with a facility to sell their tickets, the third party is, in effect, procuring the original purchaser to breach their contract with the football club.

20.38   To intentionally procure a breach of contract is an actionable tort. In *OBG v Allan*,[23] the House of Lords restated the elements of the cause of action for inducement of breach of contract. The elements were summarised usefully by the Court of Appeal in *Meretz Investments v ACP Limited*.[24] In summary:

(a) Inducing breach of contract is a tort of ancillary liability.
(b) The essential elements of the tort are: (i) knowledge of the contract; (ii) intention to induce a breach of contract; and (iii) breach of contract.
(c) In order to be liable, a person must know that his action will result in a breach of contract. It is not enough that the defendant obstructed a person in the performance of a contract. The defendant's conduct must have in fact caused a breach of contract.
(d) The defendant need not have a desire to injure the claimant.
(e) If a party genuinely believes facts, which if true show there was no breach of contract, he is not liable.
(f) Knowledge of the contract is required, but this may include 'shut eye' knowledge, that is knowledge that would have been obtained had not a decision been made not to enquire as to the existence of a relevant fact.
(g) If a person intends to cause a breach of contract, it does not matter that he intended thereby to achieve another purpose or would have preferred not to induce a breach.
(h) To foresee that a breach of contract will occur is not the same as intending it. The intention would not be present simply because of a muddle-headed or illogical belief.

20.39   A breach of contract claim in the manner set out above entitles the football club to seek damages. Those damages (in the case of a claim for procuring a breach of contract) may come in the form of the costs of operating a system for detecting and minimising unauthorised resales.

(b) Trespass/joint liability for trespass

20.40   Provided that a football club's terms and conditions state that upon any sale of a ticket in breach of its terms, that ticket will stand as null and void, it is arguable that an end-user of the ticket will be a trespasser as and when they enter the stadium.

---

23   *OBG Limited v Allan* [2008] 1 AC 1.
24   *Meretz Investments NV v ACP Limited* [2007] EWCA Civ 1303 per Arden LJ at para 114.

20.41   It is also arguable that the seller of the ticket will have incited or encouraged the end-user to commit trespass so as to make that seller jointly liable for such trespass.[25]

(c)   Conversion

20.42   *Clerk & Lindsell on Torts* states that:

> 'Anyone who without authority receives or takes possession of another's goods with the intention of asserting some right or dominion over them, or deals with them in a manner inconsistent with the right of the true owner is prima facie guilty of conversion; provided there is an intention on the part of the person so dealing with them to negative the right of the true owner or to assert a right inconsistent therewith […].'[26]

20.43   Provided, therefore, that the football club's ticket terms and conditions state that ownership of the ticket remains the property of that club at all times, any person intending to sell or otherwise transfer a ticket in breach of the club's terms may be guilty of the act of conversion entitling the club to an immediate right to possession of the same from the wrongdoer.[27]

(d)   Passing-off and misrepresentation

20.44   Finally, it may also be possible (depending on the circumstances of the specific case) for a football club to take action on the basis that the offender has misrepresented an association with the event. In the case of *Professional Golfing Associaition v Evans*,[28] the court decided that the defendant's services that were offered under the description 'Ryder Cup Hospitality' misrepresented to the public that the hospitality services were associated with the event organiser (being the PGA Limited) or its authorised hospitality agent.

H   TICKETS SOLD IN BREACH OF THE TERMS – INJUNCTIVE RELIEF

20.45   If a football club discovers that its tickets are being sold in a manner that is inconsistent with its terms and conditions of sale, the club may wish to take action through the court in order to protect its position and prevent the ongoing sale and or disposal of its tickets to third parties.

20.46   The first consideration, once a club has resolved to take action, is to decide whether the matter is sufficiently urgent enough to seek injunctive relief on an interim basis either with or without notice to the offender. This will involve a consideration of the well-known principles set out in the case of *American Cyanamid v Ethicon*[29] which would require the club to consider and take advice on: (i) whether it can establish a serious issue to be tried on the merits of their substantive claim; (ii) whether, and what, damages would be an adequate remedy for the club if the interim relief were to be refused or for the offender if the relief were to be

---

25   *Clerk & Lindsell on Torts*, 21st Edition (Sweet & Maxwell), para 4-04: 'All persons in trespass who aid or counsel, direct, or join, are joint trespassers.'
26   Ibid, para 17-09.
27   Torts (Interference with Goods) Act 1977, s 4.
28   (25 July 1989, unreported).
29   [1975] AC 396.

granted; and (iii) if and to the extent that the matter is not clearly resolved with reference to the above issues, whether the balance of convenience favours granting or refusing the club's interim injunctive relief sought.

20.47 If the matter is sufficiently urgent enough to seek interim relief without notice to the offender (ie the club has reasonable grounds to suspect that an offender may frustrate service of an injunction order until after a forthcoming match has been played) then the club is best advised to pursue its application without notice to the offender.

20.48 If the circumstances do not warrant urgency and/or a without notice application, then the club should follow the Practice Direction – Pre-Action Conduct and Protocols which appear at Section C of the Civil Procedure Rules of Court. This would entail writing to the offender setting out the basis of its claim and seeking undertakings, the effect of which would be to restrain him or her from undertaking any further activity that infringes the club's rights over the distribution and disposal of its tickets.

20.49 If the club is unable to resolve matters with the offender through any Protocol correspondence, the club will need to then consider the prospect of issuing court proceedings. Those proceedings ought to seek a permanent injunction restraining the defendant from infringing its rights in the manner set out above. The proceedings should also include a claim for damages to compensate it for the losses flowing from the above infringements and/or an account of profits that the defendant has made by means of the infringements.

I COMPETITION LAW CONSIDERATIONS

20.50 The Treaty on the Functioning of the European Union (TFEU), provides the foundation for EU competition law. The EU competition provisions are deliberately mirrored at a domestic level by the Chapter I and II prohibitions in the Competition Act 1998 (CA 1998) and the practical difference in application between them is simply their geographical scope. We should therefore not expect any swift, significant departures from the European competition regime after the withdrawal of the UK from the EU.

20.51 The EU competition provisions are not triggered at all unless there is an actual or potential effect on trade between Member States. In contrast, there must be an equivalent effect on competition within the UK for the CA 1998, Chapter I or Chapter II prohibitions to be engaged.

20.52 The provisions of TFEU that are relevant here are Articles 101 and 102. Article 101 states:

'1. The following shall be prohibited as incompatible with the internal market: all agreements between undertakings, decisions by associations of undertakings and concerted practices which may affect trade between Member States and which have as their object or effect the prevention, restriction or distortion of competition within the internal market, and in particular those which:
   (a) directly or indirectly fix purchase or selling prices or any other trading conditions;
   (b) limit or control production, markets, technical development, or investment;
   (c) share markets or sources of supply;
   (d) apply dissimilar conditions to equivalent transactions with other trading parties, thereby placing them at a competitive disadvantage;

(e) make the conclusion of contracts subject to acceptance by the other parties of supplementary obligations which, by their nature or according to commercial usage, have no connection with the subject of such contracts.

2. Any agreements or decisions prohibited pursuant to this Article shall be automatically void.

3. The provisions of paragraph 1 may, however, be declared inapplicable in the case of:

- any agreement or category of agreements between undertakings,
- any decision or category of decisions by associations of undertakings,
- any concerted practice or category of concerted practices,

which contributes to improving the production or distribution of goods or to promoting technical or economic progress, while allowing consumers a fair share of the resulting benefit, and which does not:

(a) impose on the undertakings concerned restrictions which are not to the attainment of these objectives;

(b) afford such undertakings the possibility of eliminating competition in respect of a substantial part of the products in question.'

20.53 Thus, in short, Article 101 TFEU and the CA 1998, Chapter I prohibition render unlawful agreements or concerted practices between undertakings which restrict competition in the relevant market and which do not benefit from the exemption criteria set out in those provisions. These provisions essentially target bilateral or multi-lateral anti-competitive activity. Article 102 TFEU provides:

'Any abuse by one or more undertakings of a dominant position within the internal market or in a substantial part of it shall be prohibited as incompatible with the internal market in so far as it may affect trade between Member States.

Such abuse may, in particular, consist in:

(a) directly or indirectly imposing unfair purchase or selling prices or other unfair trading conditions;

(b) limiting production, markets or technical development to the prejudice of consumers;

(c) applying dissimilar conditions to equivalent transactions with other trading parties, thereby placing them at a competitive disadvantage;

(d) making the conclusion of contracts subject to acceptance by the other parties of supplementary obligations which, by their nature or according to commercial usage, have no connection with the subject of such contracts.'

20.54 Therefore, Article 102 TFEU and the CA 1998, Chapter II prohibition make unlawful any abuse of a dominant position by an undertaking in the relevant market. Anti-competitive behaviour by a dominant undertaking will be abusive unless it is able to provide objective justification for its conduct. The prohibition primarily targets unilateral conduct.

20.55 There have been numerous ticket related anti-trust cases concerning exclusive distribution rights and exclusive national sales territories.[30] These cases are

---

30 For example, see *World Cup 1990 Package Tours: Pauwels Travel Bvba v FIFA Local Organising Committee Italia '90*, Commission decision of 27 October 1992, OJ L326, 12/11/92, p 31, [1994] 5 CMLR 253. This concerned the exclusive worldwide distribution of package tours combined with tickets for the 1990 World Cup thus preventing the possibility of alternative sources of supply. Here, the World Cup Organising Committee appointed a sole travel agency as the worldwide exclusive supplier of venue entrance tickets for the purpose of including them within package tours. The result of this was that other travel agents could only obtain tickets from the exclusive agent. The Commission found that the exclusive distribution system infringed Article 81 EC (now Article 101 TFEU) as it restricted competition between EU tour operators and travel agencies on the market for the sale of package tours to the 1990 World Cup.

not discussed further here as this chapter focuses instead on the use of tickets as a method of controlling access to a venue as opposed to the legality of the arrangements between an event organiser and its sales agents.

20.56   Conversely, there have been relatively few competition law cases that have concentrated on the enforcement of ticket terms and conditions.

20.57   Secondary market ticket resellers often aver that after they have purchased a ticket they should have free rein to do as they wish with said ticket, including selling it on for a profit. Therefore, they argue, any non-transferability clause in the ticket terms and conditions should be void under TFEU and CA 1998.

20.58   Taking 2018 FIFA World Cup tickets as an example, if the Commission construed the market narrowly and limited it to the market for tickets for the 2018 FIFA World Cup (as opposed to a wider definition, such as tickets to any sporting event in 2018)[31] it is not a stretch to believe that the Commission may consider that artificial restraints (such as non-transferability clauses) subvert the laws of supply and demand under:

(a) Article 101 TFEU and CA 1998, Chapter I: Whilst tickets for the 2018 FIFA World Cup are available to purchase by the members of the general public directly from FIFA,[32] the governing body has also appointed exclusive official hospitality rights-holders from whom customers may purchase ticket-inclusive official hospitality packages.[33] This therefore amounts to an agreement between undertakings and the question would be whether this affects trade between Member States and restricts competition within the market; and/or

(b) Article 102, TFEU and CA 1998, Chapter II: Sports Associations such as FIFA will be considered to have a practical monopoly in international football and will thus be considered to be dominant in the market if the market is defined narrowly in this way. FIFA would plainly be dominant in the market for tickets to the 2018 World Cup, as the concept of dominance is typically applied to the supplier in the relevant market, not the buyer. A market share in excess of 50% gives rise to a presumption of dominance[34] and, if the market is defined narrowly (as above), FIFA would possess a 100% market share. With FIFA dominant in the market, the question then arises as to whether the proposed agreement with FIFA would constitute an abuse of its dominant position.[35] It might be said that FIFA would be using its market power to disadvantage other tour operators.

---

31   Ibid. Whilst the case did not carry out a detailed analysis of the market definition, it is likely that (based on the fact that the Commission came to the conclusion that elite football, in a broadcasting context, is a market of its own) the Commission would have determined that the popularity of football World Cup tickets is such that tickets to no other event are an adequate replacement (and they are therefore non-substitutional).
32   See http://www.fifa.com/worldcup/organisation/ticketing/legal/unauthorized-ticket-sales.html (accessed March 2018).
33   See https://hospitality.fifa.com/hospitality2018 (accessed March 2018).
34   Case 62/86: *Akzo Chemie BV v Commission* [1991] ECR I-3359, paras 58–62.
35   Case 85/76: *Hoffmann-La Roche v Commission* [1979] ERC 461, [1979] 3 CMLR 211, para 91. This case provided the classic description of abuse as follows: 'The concept of abuse is an objective concept relating to the behaviour of an undertaking in a dominant position which is such as to influence the structure of a market where, as a result of the very presence of the undertaking in question, the degree of competition is weakened and which, through recourse to methods different from those which condition normal competition in products or services on the basis of the transactions of commercial operators, has the effect of hindering the maintenance of the degree of competition still existing in the market or the growth of that competition.'

20.59   On the face of it, therefore, the prevention of the resale of tickets could be an abuse under Article 101 TFEU and CA 1998, Chapter I and/or Article 102 TFEU and CA 1998, Chapter II. If that is the case then the burden would be on FIFA to justify the rationale behind blocking this secondary market.

20.60   This very issue was discussed by the Culture, Media and Sport Committee.[36] Here it was argued (specifically in relation to The Championships, Wimbledon) that the terms and conditions of tickets prohibiting transfer and onward sale are justifiable for the following reasons:

- 'Tickets are issued at a price which, knowingly, is less than a full market price.
- The non-transferability condition is clearly drawn to the attention of any applicant in the public ballot or other purchaser.
- Adequate arrangements exist for a full refund of the ticket price (up to the eve of the day in question) if the individual is unable to attend.
- [The] ticket terms and conditions have been reviewed and approved by Trading Standards and our ticket distribution policy and allied terms and conditions have been cleared by the OFT of allegations of anti-competitive behaviour.
- In addition to police measures to enforce street trading and public nuisance laws in and around Wimbledon, [they] take extensive legal and administrative measures to ensure that (as far as possible) these ticket conditions are enforced – particularly against suspected "professional touts".'

20.61   This approach was successfully argued in a case again involving The Championships, Wimbledon[37] where the UK Office of Fair Trading (OFT) rejected a complaint from a corporate hospitality provider that the exclusive appointment by the organiser of two official agents to supply hospitality packages (including tickets) restricted competition in the market to supply packages of hospitality services and admission tickets to The Championships, Wimbledon. Here the OFT concluded that the non-transferability provision in the ticket terms and conditions was a legitimate measure to ensure that a balance was struck between ordinary tennis fans and those individuals attending via corporate hospitality (or the 'prawn sandwich brigade' as Roy Keane may have put it).[38]

20.62   Thus, provided that venue owners and event organisers follow a similar rationale for restricting the resale of tickets, it is difficult to envisage how a claim from a frustrated ticket reseller could be successful under the current competition framework in the UK or Europe.

---

36   See House of Commons, Culture, Media and Sport Committee on Ticket Touting, Second Report of Session 2007–2008.

37   OFT press release no. 20/93, 3 March 1993. The OFT also asserted that the providers of corporate hospitality were clearly not limited to providers of Wimbledon tickets as the customer could substitute such hospitality packages for other high-profile sporting or non-sporting events. Therefore, the hospitality packages were interchangeable leading to a finding that there was no monopoly or restriction of competition to an appreciable extent.

38   See http://news.bbc.co.uk/sport1/hi/football/champions_league/1014868.stm (accessed March 2018).

CHAPTER 21

Ownership Issues and the Fit and Proper Person test

Tim Owen QC and **Andrew Smith** (Matrix Chambers)

A   INTRODUCTION

21.1   Anyone aspiring to own or to become an officer or director of a football club in the Premier League, Football League, National League, Southern Football League, Isthmian Football League, Northern Premier League or Women's Super League must be able to pass what has become known as the Owners' and Directors' Test ('the ODT') but which is more widely, but inaccurately, called the 'fit and proper person' test.[1] The Premier League and English Football League (EFL) administer the ODT for the clubs in their respective leagues, with The FA administering their own ODT for member clubs of the other leagues listed above. The criteria applied under the three discrete tests are essentially the same albeit expressed in frustratingly different terms in separate Rules and Regulations. The bottom line is that the ODT is intended to set a higher standard of conduct than is normally applied to company directors and to affect a broader class of person involved in the running of a football club than merely Board members. As The FA's Policy on Financial Regulation states, the aim of the ODT is 'to meet standards greater than that required under law so as to protect the reputation and image of the game'. The Football League advances a similar justification, stating that 'the intention behind [the ODT] is to protect the image and integrity of the League and its competitions, the well-being of the Clubs and the interests of all the stakeholders in those Clubs by preventing anyone who is subject to a disqualifying condition being involved in or influencing the management or administration of a Club'.

21.2   It is fair to say that not all observers of the game would agree that the ODT – or certainly the approach to enforcing it – has achieved this aim. The aim of this chapter is to summarise what the rules require and to whom they apply, to explain criticisms of the test and its application, as well as examining examples of individuals

---

1   The idea of introducing a fit and proper person test for directors of football clubs was first proposed in a report published in 1999 by the Football Task Force. The Football League and Premier League introduced such a test in 2004 and The FA soon followed in 2005 with the introduction of a test applicable to the Football Conference (now called the National League), the Southern Football League, the Isthmian Football League and the Northern Premier League. The test now also applies to the Women's Super League.

who have fallen foul of its impact and the potential avenues for challenging an adverse regulatory ruling.

B   ELEMENTS OF THE OWNERS' AND DIRECTORS' TEST

21.3   Under all three versions of the ODT, persons seeking to control, manage or own a football club must be able to demonstrate that they are not subject to either a 'Disqualifying Condition' (FA[2] and Football League)[3] or a 'Disqualifying Event' (Premier League)[4]. Such disqualifying conditions or events broadly fall into two categories: (i) offences or requirements under the law of the land; and (ii) what can be called football specific requirements. As will be seen they cover a multitude of sins and include events or actions abroad as well as within England and Wales.

(a)   Behaviour contrary to law: previous criminal convictions

21.4   In terms of the criminal law, the Premier League's version of the ODT is the most succinct. It identifies (see Section F.1.5 of the Rules) as a disqualifying event any situation in which a person has a conviction (which is not a spent conviction pursuant to the Rehabilitation of Offenders Act 1974) by a court of the UK or a competent court of foreign jurisdiction:

(a)   in respect of which an un-suspended sentence of at least 12 months' imprisonment was imposed;

(b)   in respect of any offence involving any act which could reasonably be considered to be dishonest (and for the avoidance of doubt, irrespective of the actual sentence imposed); or

(c)   in respect of an offence set out in Appendix 1 (Schedule of Offences)[5] or a directly analogous offence in a foreign jurisdiction (and, for the avoidance of doubt, irrespective of the actual sentence imposed).

21.5   Section F.1.6 of the Premier League Rules provides in addition that a person will also be disqualified if, in the reasonable opinion of the Board of the Premier League, he has engaged in conduct outside the UK that would constitute an offence of the sort described in (b) and (c) above if such conduct had taken place in the UK, whether or not such conduct resulted in a conviction.

21.6   The FA's test (applicable to the National League, Southern Football League, Isthmian Football League, Northern Premier League and Women's Super League) approaches the relevance of past criminal convictions by identifying as a disqualifying condition any unspent conviction involving:

(a)   an offence involving a dishonest act;

(b)   corruption;

---

2   See the Regulations for the Owners' and Directors' Test for Clubs Competing in The National League, The Southern Football League Limited, The Isthmian Football League Limited, The Northern Premier League Limited and The FA Women's Super League, made pursuant to Rule J1(F) of the Association.
3   See the EFL Regulations, Appendix 3.
4   Premier League Rules, Section F, Owners' and Directors' Test.
5   The offences cited are a curious mix – dishonestly receiving a programme broadcast from within the UK with intent to avoid payment (contrary to the Copyright, Designs and Patents Act 1988, s 297); admitting spectators to watch a football match at unlicensed premises (contrary to the Football Spectators Act 1989, s 9); persons subject to a banning order (Football Spectators Act 2000, Sch 1) and ticket touting (contrary to the Criminal Justice and Public Order Act 1994, s 166).

(c) perverting the course of justice;

(d) committing a serious breach of any requirement under the Companies Act 1985 or 2006 or any statutory modification or re-enactment thereof;

(e) dishonestly receiving a programme broadcast from within the UK with intent to avoid payment under s 298 of the Copyright, Designs and Patents Act 1988;

(f) admitting spectators to watch a football match at unlicensed premises under s 9 of the Football Spectators Act 1989;

(g) ticket touting under s 166 of the Criminal Justice and Public Order Act 1994;

(h) conspiracy to commit any of the offences set out in paras (a) to (g) above;

(i) any conviction for a like offence to any of the above offences by a competent court having jurisdiction outside England and Wales.

21.7   The EFL test (as set out in Appendix 3 of the EFL Regulations) adopts an almost identical list of offences as the basis of its disqualifying conditions but, like the Premier League, also includes having an unspent conviction by a court of competent jurisdiction anywhere in the world that results in an un-suspended sentence of at least 12 months' imprisonment.[6] It should be noted that only The FA requires applicants to confirm that they are not currently subject to criminal proceedings for any of the listed offences.[7]

(b) Behaviour contrary to law: non-criminal matters

21.8   The ODT does not of course displace the ordinary law of the land insofar as it applies to company directors. Accordingly, anyone disqualified from being a director of a UK company pursuant to the Company Directors Disqualification Act 1986 is disqualified from being a director of a football club. Disqualification orders are made in relation to various forms of misconduct related to companies including, of course, criminal conduct. In addition, persons who are the subject of a suspension or ban or other form of disqualification issued by another sporting or professional body (such as the Law Society, the Solicitors' Regulation Authority, the Bar Council or other equivalent body in other jurisdictions) are equally disqualified from owning or managing a football club. Finally, anyone subject to an individual voluntary arrangement (under Part V of the Insolvency Act 1986), bankruptcy order, interim bankruptcy order or a bankruptcy restriction order, a debt relief order, an administration order, an enforcement restriction order or a debt management scheme or any equivalent provision in any other jurisdiction which has a substantially similar effect will also be disqualified under the various versions of the ODT.

(c) Football specific disqualifying conditions

21.9   In addition to ordinary law-based disqualifications, the various versions of the ODT include further reasons for disqualification based on purely football related matters, including:

(a) being directly or indirectly involved in the management or administration of the affairs of another club (as specified by the respective rules);

---

6   Or a suspended jail sentence which is subsequently activated for a period of at least 12 months for whatever reason: see Appendix 3, Rule 1.1(h) of the EFL Regulations.

7   It was the absence of such a requirement that enabled Thaksin Shinawatra to take over the ownership of Manchester City despite an active criminal investigation in Thailand into allegations of fraud and corruption.

(b) having been an officer of two or more clubs that have entered into an insolvency event, or having been an officer of one club that has had two separate insolvency events;[8]

(c) Being an officer of a club that has been expelled, either during their tenure or within 30 days following their resignation as an officer, from the Premier League, Football League, National League, Isthmian League, Northern Premier League, Southern Football League or Women's Super League;

(d) Being found to have breached rules relating to football betting or bribery offences.

(e) In the case of the Premier League and the Football League (but not The FA), any person who fails to provide all relevant information or provides false, misleading or inaccurate information in connection with the assessment of their compliance with the ODT.

C HOW IS THE ODT ADMINISTERED IN PRACTICE?

21.10   Although differing in their details, all versions of the ODT contain objective criteria which require a simple Yes/No answer to a series of questions or statements. This box ticking exercise thus involves no exercise of subjective assessment of an individual's personal qualities and fitness to hold the position they seek. At the commencement of each new season all clubs must submit a list of relevant individuals to the relevant regulatory authority accompanied by a declaration that none of the individuals is subject to a disqualifying condition/event. Any director seeking to take up office after the season has started must submit a separate declaration before s/he assumes office. Any change of circumstances after a declaration has been submitted must be reported.

21.11   It is important to note that the ODT does not exclusively apply to club owners and members of the club's Board. The FA's Guide to the ODT, published in August 2013, summarised the scope of the ODT by stating that it applies

> 'to any person that is defined as an Officer of a club and includes any person operating the powers that are usually associated with those of (a) a director of a company incorporated under the Companies Act; (b) direct or indirect control over a Club including a shareholding of 30% or more; (c) an officer of an Industrial & Provident Society; or (d) a Chairman, Secretary or Treasurer of a Club that is an unincorporated association.'

As previously stated, the ODT supplements rather than displaces existing legal duties and obligations (including fiduciary duties) contained, for example, in the Companies Act 2006. The impact of such duties/responsibilities is outside the scope of this chapter but must obviously be borne in mind by any person contemplating buying, controlling or directing a regulated club.

D CRITICISMS OF THE ODT

21.12   It is fair to say that the ODT has been the subject of sustained criticism almost since its inception and at the time of writing the Football League is in the

---

8   Under Premier League Rules (Sections F.1.9 and F.1.10) and Appendix 3 of the EFL Regulations, the disqualifying condition includes the requirement that in relation to the insolvency events, a points deduction was imposed. Moreover under all versions of the ODT a person shall effectively be deemed to have been a director of a club which has suffered a relevant insolvency event if such event occurred in the 30 days immediately following his having resigned as a director of that club.

process of reviewing its ODT in the wake of a series of controversial episodes involving clubs across the various divisions of the League.[9] According to press reports,[10] the League's Chief Executive, Sean Harvey, said in July 2017 that the terms upon which individuals are considered fit and proper to take ownership of a club were being reviewed with a report due to be circulated to clubs in September 2017. Harvey explained that the general view was that it was necessary to look at the pre-acquisition test to see if it should and could be expanded. He also hinted that the League would review the fact that the ODT does not consider what happens to a club after it has been bought, including factors such as whether staff are paid or players' bonuses are paid as promised. In the event that the League opts for a major change to its ODT it might reasonably be assumed that pressure would increase on the Premier League and The FA to review their tests also. It is sometimes said that the problem with football is that under the ODT, football club owners can be deemed fit and proper but utterly useless at the day-to-day management of what is inevitably a complex and unusual business.[11]

21.13 At the heart of the criticism of the ODT is that insofar as it excludes spent convictions, pending charges (as well as allegations under active investigation), basic financial competence and the substance of claims to significant financial means, it is too narrow, too objective and thus too weak, with insufficient allowance made for examining, on a more subjective basis, the true character, suitability and competence of would be owners, directors and officers of English football clubs. Concern about the inadequacy of the ODT was expressed in strong terms by the Culture, Media and Sport Select Committee in its 2011 *Report on Football Governance*. In suggesting the need for changes to the ownership model, the Committee observed that:

> 'The governance challenge ... is to create an environment where clubs are protected from over-ambitious or otherwise incompetent or duplicitous owners exploiting their football club, and good owners are encouraged to stay in the game. Much of the evidence we have received however has suggested first that the current English model has made ownership issues more problematic and second that the measures to address the increased challenge have been inadequate.'[12]

21.14 The Select Committee Report made the point that the measures taken by the football authorities in the 1980s and 1990s to encourage the commercialisation of the game had certainly had some positive effects, citing by way of example the removal of restrictions on paying full time directors, which enabled clubs to recruit professionals who helped to increase turnover and thus boost funds for stadium improvements. But they also pointed to the downside in that these same reforms also increased the opportunities for bad owners to exploit clubs. They cited the views of one supporter who identified one consequence of the changes as a shift in the ownership model away from the traditional best practice of 'the philanthropic local businessman supporter'. It is undoubtedly the case that the past 20 years has

---

9   Leyton Orient was relegated from Division Two in 2017 after 112 years of continuous League membership amidst intense criticism of the ownership skills of Francesco Beccheti. Fan protests were also maintained against the owners of Coventry City, Nottingham Forest, Charlton Athletic, Blackburn Rovers and Blackpool. Indeed, Blackpool's internal strife was recently laid bare by the High Court in *VB Football Assets v Blackpool Football Club (Properties) Ltd* [2017] EWHC 2767 (Ch).

10 See for example 'Football League to run rule over fit and proper persons' test for club owners', Paul McInnes, *The Guardian*, 13 July 2017.

11 See for example, Martin Samuel, 'Football club owners can be fit and proper but they can still be useless' *Daily Mail*, 16 April 2017 and Henry Winter, 'FA has lost its moral courage over club ownership. It's time for change' *The Times*, 4 September 2017.

12 Culture, Media and Sport Select Committee, *Report on Football Governance* (2011), para 161.

witnessed a dramatic shift in the ownership of UK (mainly English) football clubs. Where previously clubs were owned by local business people, they are now bought and sold by a new type of entrepreneur from both the UK and abroad. As the Select Committee commented, 'in many cases owners have been proved to be short-termist, seeking swift improvements in team performance through debt-funded investment, often mortgaging the ground and/or future ticket revenue in pursuit of success'.[13]

21.15   The *Report on Football Governance* focused on the woes of Portsmouth FC as an example of how weak ownership rules could lead to disaster:

> 'We asked both the Premier League and the Football League about the governance rules for owning a football club in their competitions. In the case of the Premier League we were particularly concerned that, as recently as 2010, the (foreign) ownership of Portsmouth could change hands four times on its way into administration. Indeed a number of submissions had highlighted the example of Portsmouth as proof that the Premier League sets too low a threshold for ownership. For Patrick Collins:
>
>> "If you had fit and proper people running football clubs, there would be fewer bankruptcies and administrations. The one that is always picked out is Portsmouth, of course. They had four different owners last year. One was a fantasist who made lots of promises that were quite baseless. Another, much more intriguingly, did not actually exist."
>
> Football supporter and retired lecturer in business ethics, John Bentley, also asked: "How could the FA and Premier League bodies approve a person to be a fit and proper person to be the owner of Portsmouth FC when they never even met him or interviewed him to inspect his financial assets?". Pompey Supporters Trust lamented that once an owner has passed relatively weak criteria, "there are very few rules preventing him from doing what they like". As an example of how weak the criteria were, they pointed to their own case where the owner who put Portsmouth into administration was then allowed to buy it out of administration.'[14]

21.16   The Select Committee concluded that The FA, the Premier League and the Football League had all spent too long 'behind the curve on ownership matters' and that between them they had allowed some startlingly poor business practices to occur and tolerated an unacceptably low level of transparency. This in turn had led to insolvencies, too many clubs losing their grounds to property developers and contributed to high levels of indebtedness throughout the League pyramid. The Committee was not convinced that the football authorities had focused sufficiently on the link between the fit and proper owner test and the sustainability of English football's uniquely deep pyramid structure. A key issue which they believed had been overlooked was the need for regular monitoring, given that the intentions of owners can change over time. They recommended that:

> 'robust ownership rules, including a strong fit and proper person test, consistently applied throughout the professional game with the FA having a strong scrutiny and oversight role, should be a key component of the licensing model we propose. The presumption should be against proposals to sell the ground unless it is in the interests of the club. There should be complete transparency around ownership and the terms of loans provided by directors to the club. In this respect there is no more blatant an example of lack of transparency than the recent ownership of Leeds United and we urge the FA to demonstrate its new resolve by conducting a thorough investigation and, if necessary, to seek the assistance of Her Majesty's Revenue and Customs.'[15]

13   Ibid, para 164.
14   Ibid, para 186.
15   Ibid, para 192.

21.17   The Select Committee's reference to Leeds United concerned the circumstances leading up to the purchase of the club by Ken Bates in May 2011 after a period during which The FA had confirmed to MPs that they did not know who the ultimate owners of the Championship club were. Bates would eventually sell the club to a Bahrain based Investment Bank, Gulf Finance House, in 2012; subsequently, in April 2014 Italian entrepreneur and the former Cagliari football club owner, Massimo Cellino, acquired a 75% shareholding in Leeds United before his company, Eleonara Sport Limited, eventually acquired 100% ownership in September 2016. Mr Cellino's period of involvement in Leeds United was hallmarked by drama at all stages and demonstrated, according to many observers of the game, just why the Select Committee's concerns about the narrowness of the ODT were fully justified. Mr Cellino had two prior criminal convictions in Italy dating back to 1996 and 2001, both of which involved allegations of dishonesty, but neither could be taken into account under the League's ODT because they were spent. Nor could the fact that Mr Cellino had been arrested in February 2013, along with the local Mayor and public works commissioner, for attempted embezzlement and fraudulent misrepresentation following an investigation into the construction of a football stadium. At the time he acquired his original 75% stake in Leeds, the English press reported Mr Cellino as being an untrustworthy character but none of the publicly available knowledge of his past was able to be taken into account in terms of assessing his fitness to own and run an English football club.

21.18   Matters changed however when, in March 2014, a Sardinian Court convicted Mr Cellino of an offence relating to non-payment of import tax in respect of a yacht, fining him €600,000 and confiscating the yacht. In light of this decision, the Football League unanimously agreed that Mr Cellino was now subject to a disqualifying condition under the League's ODT as, in their view, he had an *un*spent conviction 'for an offence involving a dishonest act' and accordingly he was prevented from buying a majority stake in the club under Appendix 3, Rule 2.1 of the League's Rules. Cellino's appeal to the Professional Conduct Committee was successful in light of the finding by the Chair of the PCC (sitting alone), Tim Kerr QC, that there was insufficient information about the Italian offence reasonably to conclude that his offence was dishonest. At the time of the appeal hearing before the PCC, the reasoned judgment of the Cagliari Court was not available and expert evidence about Italian law revealed that the relevant VAT offence might be capable of being committed on the basis of a mental element known as *dolo eventuale* which did not equate to the English law of dishonesty. Mr Kerr QC accepted this analysis and accordingly held that it would not be reasonable on the evidence before him to consider Mr Cellino's conduct to be dishonest, with the consequence that he was not subject to a disqualifying condition. He rejected the argument that because Italian law held that the presumption of innocence applies to an accused person until the exhaustion of the appeal process the League was wrong to find that he had a conviction at all. He held that so long as a foreign court's finding of guilt was 'worth the name by English standards of justice' that was sufficient for it to amount to a conviction under the ODT regardless of the continuing application of the presumption of innocence under foreign law. In relation to the judgment of the Cagliari Court, Mr Kerr QC did however state that 'if the reasoned ruling of the court in Cagliari discloses that the conduct of Mr Cellino was such that it would reasonably be considered to be dishonest, he would become subject to a disqualifying condition'.

21.19   In the wake of this ruling, the League sought and obtained a copy of the Italian court's reasoned judgment in October 2014 and, having read it, they once more concluded that Mr Cellino was subject to a disqualifying condition under the ODT and disqualified him from acting as a director or exercising any control over the club.[16] His appeal against this decision failed and accordingly Mr Cellino was disqualified from acting as a relevant person until 20 April 2015 – a period of only 79 days – the date when his Italian conviction would become spent. While it might be said that the final outcome of the Cellino saga demonstrated how effective the ODT can be when it is pursued and applied with vigour and enthusiasm by the regulatory body, the reality is that it exposed the extraordinary weakness of the test in terms of its ability to apply a broad judgment of suitability and character to persons who seek to acquire ownership of football clubs in England and Wales.

E   CHALLENGING DECISIONS UNDER THE ODT RULES

21.20   The primary route for challenging an adverse ruling of a football governing body regarding the ODT is via the appeal provisions contained in the ODT Rules themselves. With regard to the Premier League Rules, a person who has received a notice of disqualification has 21 days from the date of that notice to deliver to the Premier League Board a notice of appeal setting out full details of his/her grounds of appeal, together with a deposit of £1,000. The potential grounds of appeal are defined in Section F.15 of the Premier League Rules and may be summarised as follows:

(a) none of the disqualifying events apply;
(b) in respect of certain disqualifying events, there are 'compelling reasons' why it/ they should not lead to disqualification;
(c) it can be proven that the disqualifying event has, or will within 21 days of the notice of appeal, cease to exist;
(d) the disqualifying event is a conviction imposed between 19 August 2004 and 5 June 2009 for an offence which would not have led to disqualification as a director under the Premier League Rules as they applied during that period;
(e) the disqualifying event is a conviction which is the subject of an appeal which has not yet been determined and in all the circumstances it would be unreasonable for the individual to be disqualified as a director pending the determination of that appeal.

21.21   A notice of disqualification is not lifted or suspended whilst an appeal process is ongoing; it will only cease to have effect if and when an appeal is upheld.

21.22   An appeal under Section F of the Premier League Rules will be heard by an appeal tribunal, comprised of three panel members who are appointed by the Premier League Board. The Chairman of the panel must be legally qualified. With regard to the appeal process, Section F.17 of the Premier League Rules affords the chairman of the panel considerable discretion as to how to manage the proceedings, stating that 'The Chairman of the appeal tribunal shall have regard to the procedures governing the proceedings of Commissions and Appeal Boards set out in Section W of these Rules (Disciplinary) but, subject as aforesaid, shall have an overriding discretion as to the manner in which the appeal is conducted.'

---

16   The Italian judge described Mr Cellino's conduct as 'Macchiavellica Simulazione' which was translated to mean that Cellino adopted 'a cunning plan to evade payment of the tax due' and the PCC held that that this 'was integral to her conclusion that he was guilty of the offence'. This reasonably equated to a state of mind akin to dishonesty and thus satisfied the relevant ODT requirement for disqualification. It should be noted, however, that Mr Cellino was subsequently successful in his appeal quashing the convictions.

21.23   With regard to the appeal tribunal's powers, Section F.22 of the Premier League Rules provides as follows:

'The appeal tribunal shall have the following powers:

F.22.1.   to allow the appeal in full;

F.22.2.   to reject the appeal;

F.22.3.   if it determines that a Disqualifying Event exists, to determine that the individual concerned should not be banned for that period during which they will remain subject to it and substitute such period as it shall reasonably determine, having regard to all of the circumstances of the case;

F.22.4.   to declare that no Disqualifying Event ever existed or that any Disqualifying Event has ceased to exist;

F.22.5.   to order the deposit to be forfeited to the League or to be repaid to the appellant person or Club; and

F.22.6.   to order the appellant Person or Club to pay or contribute to the costs of the appeal including the fees and expenses of members of the appeal tribunal paid or payable under Rule F.21.'

21.24   The appeal tribunal, which may reach a unanimous or majority decision, is obliged to provide written reasons for its decision. Section F.23 of the Premier League Rules stipulates that the decision of the appeal tribunal 'shall be binding on the appellant Person and Club'.

21.25   With regard to the EFL Regulations governing appeals in respect of the ODT, the amended version (which came into force on 6 June 2015) is contained in Appendix 3, Rule 5 of the Rules and operates as follows.

21.26   The time limit for appealing against a decision that a person is subject to a disqualifying condition is shorter than that under the Premier League Rules; under the EFL Regulations an appeal, setting out the grounds on which the appeal is brought, must be filed with the company secretary within 14 days of receipt of notice of the League's decision.

21.27   The potential grounds for appeal are set out in Rule 5.2(d), which stipulates that an appeal shall only be upheld if the appellant establishes that:

'(i)   contrary to The League's decision, he is not subject to a Disqualifying Condition; or

(ii)   he is subject to a Disqualifying Condition but:

(A)   that Disqualifying Condition is a Conviction by a court outside of England and Wales, a finding of the conduct referred to in paragraph (j) of the definition of Disqualifying Condition, or a suspension or ban or other disqualification by a Sports Governing Body or professional body; and

(B)   there are compelling reasons why it should not prevent him acting as a Relevant Person.'

21.28   An appeal under Appendix 3, Rule 5 of the EFL Regulations will be heard by the League Arbitration Panel ('the LAP'), in accordance with the provisions of Section 9 of the EFL Regulations, supplemented by the provisions of Rule 5 (albeit in the event of any conflict between them, Rule 5 shall prevail).

21.29   Unlike the Premier League Rules, the EFL Regulations do permit the LAP to suspend implementation of the League's decision pending determination of the appeal, where the appellant satisfies the panel that such a delay is necessary to avoid undue prejudice.

21.30   Following the conclusion of an appeal hearing, the LAP may:

(a) uphold the appeal and set the League's decision aside;
(b) reject the appeal but, where the grounds of the appeal include grounds for a review application, consider the matter as a review application (discussed below);
(c) reject the appeal, in which case the LAP may stipulate: (i) a deadline for implementation of the League's decision; and (ii) a period within which a review application may not be made.

21.31   Appendix 3, Rules 5.4 to 5.6 of the EFL Regulations govern the process for review applications. Rule 5.4 provides as follows:

> 'Where a person does not appeal against The League's decision that he is subject to a Disqualifying Condition, or his appeal against that decision is unsuccessful, he may (subject to any Rule 5.3(c)(ii) stipulation), apply to the League Arbitration Panel for an order that his disqualification should be for a shorter period than the period during which his Disqualifying Condition subsists (a "Review Application").'

21.32   A review application will also be heard by the LAP. The sole basis on which a review application may be upheld is if the applicant satisfies the LAP that disqualifying him for the entirety of the period for which his disqualifying condition subsists would be disproportionate in light of the nature of that disqualifying condition.

21.33   The LAP powers in respect of a review application are defined in Appendix 3, Rule 5.6 of the EFL Regulations as follows:

> 'The League Arbitration Panel may:
>
> (a) uphold the Review Application and specify a shorter period of disqualification, having regard to all of the circumstances of the case; or
> (b) reject the Review Application and direct that the person shall remain disqualified for so long as the Disqualifying Condition subsists (in which case the League Arbitration Panel may also stipulate a period of time within which a subsequent Review Application shall not be made).'

21.34   With regard to The FA Regulations governing appeals in respect of the ODT, the applicable time limit for lodging an appeal is within seven days of the date of the relevant decision. The appeal process is a 'fast track' one, requiring an appeal hearing to be held by an Appeal Board within 14 days of the appeal being lodged with The FA. As is the position under the EFL Regulations, the effect of an ODT decision may be suspended pending the outcome of an appeal. The potential grounds for appeal are as follows:

(a) none of the disqualifying conditions apply;
(b) any applicable disqualifying condition has or will within 14 days of the date of the appeal being lodged with The Association cease to exist;
(c) the disqualifying condition is a conviction that is subject to an appeal which has not yet been determined and in all the circumstances it would be unreasonable for the individual to be disqualified as an officer pending the determination of that appeal; or
(d) The disqualifying condition is in respect of a conviction of a court of foreign jurisdiction; or suspension or ban by Sports Governing Body; or disqualification or striking off by a professional body and there are compelling reasons why that particular conviction, suspension or ban, disqualification or striking off should not lead to disqualification.

21.35   With regard to the appeal process, save in respect of the deadlines for lodging and hearing an appeal (as identified above), the Regulations for Football Association Appeals shall apply.

F   OTHER POTENTIAL AVENUES FOR CHALLENGING DECISIONS OF GOVERNING BODIES

21.36   The appeal mechanisms discussed above will apply in circumstances where the subject of an adverse ODT ruling wishes to challenge a decision taken under the specific provisions of the ODT Rules. However, there may be other decisions, actions or omissions of football governing bodies that affect the interests of interested persons, but which do not engage the appeal mechanisms discussed above. This may be because, for example, the ODT Rules do not apply to the particular scenario in which a dispute has arisen; a decision is taken by the governing body outwith the scope of the ODT Rules; and/or the interested party is not a proposed director or officer (or other specified person) but rather, for example, an investor with no (or no proposed) controlling influence on the running of the club.

21.37   In circumstances where there is no binding arbitration agreement between the aggrieved party and the governing body (as to which, see further Chapter 28, Arbitration in Football) and the specific ODT appeal processes are inapplicable, legal action may be pursued in the courts. As regards the nature of such claims, it is well established that a claim for judicial review will generally not be appropriate, on the basis that most sports governing bodies are private rather than public bodies (or bodies exercising public or quasi-governmental powers). For example, in *R v Jockey Club ex parte Agha Khan*,[17] Hoffmann LJ (as he then was) held:

> '… the mere fact of power, even over a substantial area of economic activity, is not enough. In a mixed economy, power may be private as well as public. Private power may affect the public interest and the livelihoods of many individuals. But that does not make it subject to the rules of public law. If control is needed, it must be found in the law of contract, the doctrine of restraint of trade, the Restrictive Trade Practices Act 1976, arts 85 and 96 of EEC Treaty and all the other instruments available in law for curbing excesses of private power.'[18]

21.38   In light of the above, most civil claims against sports governing bodies are brought on the basis that: (i) there is an express or implied contractual relationship between the aggrieved party and the governing body; and (ii) the governing body has, by acting in a particular manner, acted in breach of express or implied contractual obligations owed to the claimant.

21.39   Depending on the nature of the particular dispute under consideration, the 'instruments available in law for curbing excesses of private power' (per Hoffmann LJ in the *Aga Khan* case) may include principles of public policy, including in respect of restraint of trade; principles of competition law (ie agreements between undertakings which unjustifiably restrict competition, or the abuse of a dominant position); and principles relating to fundamental human rights.

---

17   [1993] 2 All ER 853.
18   See also, to similar effect, the decision of the High Court in *R (Mullins) v Appeal Board of the Jockey Club* [2005] EWHC 2197.

21.40   In the context of disputes relating to sports governance, the courts have, in effect, side-stepped the public/private law debate by applying judicial review type *principles* when assessing the lawfulness of governing bodies' actions. In *Bradley v Jockey Club*,[19] Richards J described the court's function, and its powers of review in such cases, as follows:

> '37 That brings me to the nature of the court's supervisory jurisdiction over such a decision. The most important point, as it seems to me, is that it is *supervisory*. The function of the court is not to take the primary decision but to ensure that the primary decision-maker has operated within lawful limits. It is a review function, very similar to that of the court on judicial review. Indeed, given the difficulties that sometimes arise in drawing the precise boundary between the two, I would consider it surprising and unsatisfactory if a private law claim in relation to the decision of a domestic body required the court to adopt a materially different approach from a judicial review claim in relation to the decision of a public body. In each case the essential concern should be with the lawfulness of the decision taken: whether the procedure was fair, whether there was any error of law, whether any exercise of judgment or discretion fell within the limits open to the decision maker, and so forth …'

21.41   In summary, therefore, courts will be willing to scrutinise a football governing body's conduct in order to determine, *inter alia*, whether:

(a) it had the authority and power, under the relevant regulatory/contractual framework, to act as it did;
(b) it abused its power;
(c) it reached a rational decision; and
(d) broadly speaking, it acted fairly as regards the process by which a decision was taken – ie in accordance with the principles of natural justice.[20]

21.42   In addition to claims for damages arising from the alleged breach(es) of contract by the governing body, a claimant may seek a declaration as regards the parties' legal rights and obligations, and/or injunctive relief. The latter remedy can be particularly important in the context of sporting disputes.

21.43   In circumstances where a complainant is unable to identify a direct contractual entitlement to sue in respect of a governing body's decision, it is possible that s/he may nevertheless be able to pursue a civil claim by invoking the supervisory jurisdiction of the court. In order to demonstrate legal standing to pursue a claim on this basis, a complainant will have to establish, *inter alia*, that the decision in question affects an important interest which they possess (this may include, for example, where an individual's right to work is at stake,[21] or where the public interest is affected). However, in *McInnes v Oslow Fane*,[22] a dispute concerning the British Boxing Board of Control and an application for a boxers' manager's licence, Sir Robert Megarry VC made the following observations:

> 'I think that the courts must be slow to allow any implied obligation to be fair to be used as a means of bringing before the courts for review honest decisions of bodies exercising jurisdiction over sporting and other activities which those bodies are far better fitted to judge than the courts. This is so even where those bodies are concerned with the means of livelihood of those who take part in those activities.

---

19   [2004] EWHC 2164 QB; upheld on appeal: [2005] EWCA Civ 117.
20   See for example *Flaherty v The National Greyhound Racing Club Limited* [2005] EWCA Civ 117.
21   In the sporting context, see for example the discussion of the High Court in *Nagle v Feilden* [1966] 2 QB 633, a case concerning a decision of the stewards of the Jockey Club to reject the claimant's application for a trainer's licence.
22   [1978] 1 WLR 1520.

The concepts of natural justice and the duty to be fair must not be allowed to discredit themselves by making unreasonable requirements and imposing undue burdens. Bodies such as the board which promote a public interest by seeking to maintain high standards in a field of activity which otherwise might easily become degraded and corrupt ought not to be hampered in their work without good cause. Such bodies should not be tempted or coerced into granting licences that otherwise they would refuse by reason of the courts having imposed on them a procedure for refusal which facilitates litigation against them.'[23]

21.44   Where the underlying facts of a disagreement between an aggrieved party and a sporting governing body are not materially in dispute, the procedure under Part 8 of the Civil Procedure Rules is likely to be appropriate for such claims.

---

23   See also, to similar effect, the observations of Sir Nicholas Browne-Wilkinson VC in *Cowley v Heatley, The Times*, 24 July 1986, a case concerning *inter alia* an athlete's claim for a declaration that she was eligible to represent England in the 1986 Commonwealth Games.

CHAPTER 22

Privacy, Defamation and Football

Gavin Millar QC and Sara Mansoori (Matrix Chambers)

A   INTRODUCTION TO PRIVACY

22.1   Since 2000 our courts have fashioned new law protecting private information out of the existing law of confidential information. This was possible because the Human Rights Act 1998 (HRA 1998) introduced Article 8 of the European Convention on Human Rights into our law. This provides:

> '1.   Everyone has the right to respect for his private and family life, his home and his correspondence.
> 2.   There shall be no interference by a public authority with the exercise of this right except such as is in accordance with the law and is necessary in a democratic society in the interests of national security, public safety or the economic well-being of the country, for the prevention of disorder or crime, for the protection of health or morals, or for the protection of the rights and freedoms of others.'

Many of the cases in the development of the new law have involved footballers and managers.

22.2   Article 8 protects many aspects of privacy. In this chapter we consider protection for private information. This is often contained in private text messages, telephone conversations, photographs and other images. The law relating to private information has two components.[1] First, the 'confidentiality component' by which any non-public information from the areas of life listed in Article 8(1) may be protected from unauthorised disclosure. Secondly, the 'intrusion component'. This protects against such disclosure even if the information has entered the public domain, by preventing the recycling of that information in a harmful way. Whereas defamation is concerned with damaging allegations that are untrue, a claim for misuse of private information can relate to any damaging disclosure, whether true or false. Damages are awarded principally to compensate for the injury to feelings and distress caused by the misuse,[2] with an element to compensate for the loss of control and autonomy in relation to the private information.[3]

---

1   See *PJS v News Group Newspapers Ltd* [2016] UKSC 26, [2016] 2 WLR 1253. This is explained further at para **22.3** below. News Group Newspapers Ltd is abbreviated below as 'NGN'.
2   See *Cooper v Turrell* [2011] EWHC 3269, para 102 involving some true and some false information.
3   See, for example, *TLT v Home Office* [2016] EWHC 2217.

B THE LEGAL TEST

22.3 There are two stages in identifying misuse of private information. First the claimant's rights under Article 8 must have been brought into play on the facts – 'engaged' in the language of human rights. The claimant must establish 'a reasonable expectation' of privacy in relation to the information in issue. Secondly, if Article 8 is engaged the court must then balance the Article 8 rights against the right of the defendant/discloser (usually the media) to freedom of expression under Article 10 of the Convention. Should the right to protect the information prevail over the right to disclose it? Or vice versa?

C THE FIRST STAGE: A REASONABLE EXPECTATION OF PRIVACY

22.4 The concept of a 'reasonable expectation' of privacy is required in order to protect the autonomy and dignity of the individual. It is a legal tool for protecting our rights to control the dissemination of information about our private lives and to preserve the esteem and respect of others.[4] The reasonable expectation is that the private nature of the information will be respected and it will not be used by others in a way that intrudes into the person's private life.[5] So even 'the repetition of known facts about an individual may amount to unjustified interference with the private lives not only of that person but also of those who are involved with him'.[6]

22.5 Whether there is a 'reasonable expectation' of privacy is an objective question. In a case involving media publication the court considers 'what a reasonable person of ordinary sensibilities would feel if she was placed in the same position as the claimant and faced with the same publicity' (see *Murray v Express Newspapers plc*).[7] In answering this question it will take account of all the circumstances of the case which may include:

(a) the attributes of the claimant;
(b) the nature of the activity in which the claimant was engaged;
(c) the place at which it was happening;
(d) the nature and purpose of the intrusion;
(e) the absence of consent and whether it was known or could be inferred;
(f) the effect on the claimant; and
(g) the circumstances in which and the purposes for which the information came into the hands of the defendant.

22.6 Where the information is leaked by a confidant the nature of the relationship is of considerable importance in deciding whether the claimant had a reasonable expectation of privacy.[8] The discloser may be under a legal obligation to keep it confidential, whether impliedly or explicitly – perhaps under a contract. Those working for a player or a club are liable to have such obligations.

22.7 The fact that the information may be known to a person's friends, team mates or other work colleagues does not mean that there cannot be a reasonable expectation that it will not appear in the media.[9]

---

4   *Campbell v Mirror Group Newspapers Ltd* [2004] 2 AC 457, para 51 per Lord Hoffmann. Mirror Group Newspapers Ltd is abbreviated below as 'MGN'.
5   *PJS v NGN*(n 1), paras 58–60.
6   *JIH v News Group Newspapers Ltd* [2011] EMLR 9, para 59 per Tugendhat J.
7   [2009] Ch 481, para 35.
8   See *Lord Browne of Madingley v Associated Newspapers Ltd* [2008] QB 103, para 26.
9   See *Ferdinand v MGN* [2011] EWHC 2454 (QB) [53], citing *Browne v Associated Newspapers Ltd* (n 8 above), para 61.

(a)   Footballers or those involved in football

22.8   A claimant's involvement in the game may be relevant to whether there is a reasonable expectation. In *A v B (Garry Flitcroft v Mirror Group Newspapers Ltd)*,[10] Flitcroft sought an interim injunction to prevent publication in a tabloid of stories about his adulterous affairs with two women. The injunction was granted by the judge but the Court of Appeal allowed an appeal. It considered it likely that, at trial, the right to publish would prevail. The court said: 'Footballers are role models for young people and undesirable behaviour on their part can set an unfortunate example.'[11]

22.9   It also said that it was not 'self-evident' that how a well-known premiership player, with a position of responsibility at his club, chooses to spend his time off the football field does not have a 'modicum' of public interest.[12] It recognised that Flitcroft was entitled to a private life but his public position required him to accept that his actions would be more closely scrutinised by the media, and that even trivial facts relating to a public figure can be of great interest to readers.[13] It accepted that he would establish at trial that his Article 8 rights were engaged. But, importantly, his public profile as a premiership footballer was regarded as a reason why he or other footballers *might* fail to cross this threshold.

22.10   These issues were addressed again by the Court of Appeal in *Campbell v MGN*.[14] Noting these observations, it nonetheless emphasised that 'the fact that an individual has achieved prominence on the public stage does not mean that his private life can be laid bare by the media'.[15]

22.11   This view was echoed in *AMC v NGN*,[16] in which Elisabeth Laing J stated that she did not consider that 'being a public figure of and by itself makes the entire history of that person's sex life public property'.[17]

22.12   While a footballer's private life may not be 'laid bare' in the media simply because of their status, involvement in elite sport is likely to be a factor limiting the width of the privacy right at the first stage of the test. In *Spelman v Express Newspapers*, Tugendhat J stated:

> '[T]hose engaged in sport at the national and international level are subject to many requirements which are not imposed on other members of the public. Matters relating to their health have to be disclosed and monitored, and they may have little if any control over the extent to which such information is disseminated. It is a condition of participating in high level sport that the participant gives up control over many aspects of private life. There is no, or at best a low, expectation of privacy if an issue of health relates to the ability of the person to participate in the very public activity of national and international sport.'[18]

---

10   [2003] QB 195.
11   *A v B (Garry Flitcroft v Mirror Group Newspapers Ltd)*, para 43(vi). The appeal court also thought an adulterous affair was different to a marital relationship and therefore 'at the outer limits of relationships which require the protection of the law': para 47. As to the 'role model' issue, see para **22.37** below regarding publicity about Rio Ferdinand when he was England captain.
12   *A v B (Garry Flitcroft v Mirror Group Newspapers Ltd)*, para 43(vi).
13   Ibid, para 11(xii).
14   *Campbell v MGN* (n 4 above).
15   [2003] QB 633, para 41.
16   *AMC v NGN* [2015] EWHC 2361.
17   [2015] EWHC 2361, para 19.
18   *Spelman v Express Newspapers* [2012] EWHC 355 (QB), para 69.

22.13   In *Spelman* the court indicated that the restricted expectation of privacy applying to professional sportspeople is not confined to those who achieve at the highest levels. They reach these by ascending from the lower levels. The restricted right may well apply to those striving to get to the top, even if they do not achieve it, or can no longer realistically expect to achieve it.[19]

(b)   Reasonable expectation of privacy: areas commonly protected

22.14   Many types of personal information may be protected under Article 8. The following are the types most likely to be protected by the courts.

(i)   Sexual information

22.15   This is invariably about one's private life. Information about sexual activity has often been held to engage Article 8.[20] It may relate to male homosexual relationships,[21] lesbian relationships[22] and extramarital affairs.[23] It also includes general information relating to sexuality, such as gender identification and sexual orientation.[24] In Rio Ferdinand's privacy case against the *Sunday Mirror* for disclosure of an extramarital relationship, Nicol J held that the information in the article 'was in principle protected by Article 8'.[25] This was so even though the woman's evidence was that they had been seen in nightclubs at the same time and the information was known to some family and friends.

22.16   Similarly personal data relating to an individual's 'sexual life' is 'sensitive personal data' under s 2 of the Data Protection Act 1998 (DPA 1998) and, if processed, attracts additional protection under that Act.

(ii)   Other information about relationships

22.17   In some circumstances there may be a reasonable expectation of privacy in relation to the bare fact that a relationship exists, quite aside from the information about the *contents or detail* of that relationship.[26] The most obvious example is a secret adulterous relationship.

22.18   In *Gulati v MGN*, assessing compensation in eight phone hacking claims, Mann J said that information obtained from voicemail interception about 'matters internal to a relationship will be treated as private'.[27] When considering the publication by *MGN* of information about Paul Gascoigne's divorce obtained in this way, Mann J held that a couple has a reasonable expectation of privacy in what passes between them; their views about financial dealings after a divorce and the

---

19   Ibid, para 70.
20   See *Mosley v NGN* [2008] EWHC 687; *PJS v NGN* (n 1 above).
21   *Barrymore v News Group Newspapers Ltd* [1997] FSR 600; *Dudgeon v UK* (1981) 4 EHRR 149.
22   *Stephens v Avery* [1988] 1 Ch 449. The relationship was protected as confidential, though it would now be considered private information.
23   See *PJS v NGN* (n 1 above).
24   See *PG and JH v UK* (2008) 46 EHRR 51.
25   *Ferdinand v MGN* (n 9 above), para 51.
26   *Browne v Associated Newspapers Ltd* (n 8 above), para 57 and *Hutcheson v NGN* [2011] EWCA Civ 808, para 26.
27   *Gulati v MGN* [2015] EWHC 1482 (Ch), para 229(iv).

implementation of arrangements;[28] and in reconciliation attempts.[29] Similarly information about private arguments between spouses whose marriage is collapsing engaged their Article 8 rights.[30] A dispute over maintenance for a child is likely to be an inherently private matter.[31]

(iii)   Medical and health information

22.19   This falls squarely within the scope of Article 8. Protection of medical data is recognised as of fundamental importance to a person's enjoyment of his or her right to respect for private and family life. It is crucial also to preserve confidence in treatment by medical professionals and in the health services in general.[32]

22.20   Unauthorised disclosure of medical information was said to be of a 'high level of seriousness' by Tugendhat J in *Cooper v Turrell*.[33] The case concerned disclosure by one director of a company to another of the claimant's health information, obtained by covertly recording a private conversation.[34] In *Gulati v MGN* the court observed that medical information is likely to be ranked highly as information expected to be private, and that it could relate to matters of mental health as well as physical health.[35]

22.21   In *Campbell v MGN* the House of Lords identified information about Naomi Campbell's Narcotics Anonymous meetings as private. The Judicial Committee recognised the explicitly private nature of the meetings, encouraging addicts to attend on an understanding of confidentiality and anonymity.[36] The extent to which information about one's state of health, including drug dependency, should be communicated to other people was plainly something which an individual was entitled to decide for themselves.

22.22   In *Gulati* it was held that Paul Gascoigne's treatment at a rehabilitation clinic fell within this category of private medical information.[37] So did articles about the actor Sadie Frost: having a collapsed lung when she was 4, leaving her with permanent weakness;[38] having sleep therapy at a clinic;[39] attending Alcoholics Anonymous;[40] and being admitted to a clinic with flu-like symptoms.[41] Information about losing weight and being treated for food rejection by a psychologist revealed her mental health state at the time and was treated as a 'health related matter'.[42]

22.23   Personal data relating to an individual's 'physical or mental health or condition' is 'sensitive personal data' under s 2 of the DPA 1998 and attracts additional

---

28   Ibid, para 578.
29   Ibid, para 587.
30   Ibid, para 674 in relation to Sadie Frost.
31   Ibid, para 592 in relation to Paul Gascoigne.
32   See *Z v Finland* (1998) 25 EHRR 371, para 95, relating to disclosure of the applicant's HIV status. Disclosure could cause harm 'by exposing him or her to opprobrium and the risk of ostracism': para 96.
33   *Cooper v Turrell* (n 2 above).
34   Ibid, para 103.
35   *Gulati v MGN* (n 27 above), para 229(i).
36   *Campbell v MGN* (n 4 above), para 95.
37   *Gulati v MGN* (n 27 above), para 574.
38   Ibid, paras 622 and 673.
39   Ibid, paras 624 and 675 where Mann J stated 'disclosure of the treatment is akin to disclosure of medial treatment in terms of privacy'.
40   Ibid, para 692.
41   Ibid, paras 632 and 683.
42   Ibid, para 668.

protection under that Act if processed. It is also protected under the Independent Press Standards Organisation (IPSO) Editors' Code of Practice which provides that 'everyone is entitled to respect for his or her private and family life, home, *health* and correspondence, including digital communications' (Clause 2(i), emphasis added). The Code provides that journalists must identify themselves and obtain permission from a responsible executive before entering non-public areas of hospitals or similar institutions to newsgather.[43] Footballers and clubs will be particularly concerned to protect information about ill health and injuries affecting fitness to play.

(iv) Financial information

22.24 In *Gulati* Mann J suggested that information about 'significant financial matters' was likely to attract a high degree of privacy.[44] Thus information about a person's debts and the consequenatial remortgaging of their property have been held 'obviously private and confidential'.[45] In *Ahuja v Politika* details about an individual's private bank transactions were also identified as private.[46] Gambling addictions and amounts spent gambling would usually be considered private and such reporting about footballers' or managers' habits would need to be justified as being in the public interest.

(v) Home

22.25 The 'home' is identified in Article 8(1) as entitled to 'respect'. It has been said that:

> '[E]ven relatively trivial details would fall within this protection because of the traditional sanctity of hearth and home. To describe a person's home, the décor, the layout, the state of cleanliness or how the occupiers behave inside it, is generally regarded as unacceptable. To convey such details, without permission, to the general public, is almost as objectionable as spying into the home with a long distance lens and publishing the resulting photographs.'[47]

David and Victoria Beckham's Article 8 rights' protection for their 'home' was recognised when they obtained an injunction to prevent the *Sunday People* from publishing unauthorised photographs of the interior of their new house.[48]

(vi) Correspondence

22.26 'Correspondence' is also mentioned in Article 8(1). In *Ferdinand v MGN* intimate text messages from Ferdinand to a woman were identified as 'correspondence' and in principle deserving of the protection of Article 8.[49] This may not be true of all digital communications however. In *Karl Oyston v The FA Ltd*, it was held that the chairman of Blackpool Football Club did not have a reasonable expectation of privacy in text messages he exchanged with a member of a supporters

---

43 See to similar effect section 8.8 in the Ofcom Broadcast Code available at https://www.ofcom.org.uk/tv-radio-and-on-demand/broadcast-codes/broadcast-code (accessed March 2018).
44 *Gulati v MGN* (n 27 above), para 229(ii).
45 Ibid, para 522.
46 *Ahuja v Politika & others* [2016] 1 WLR 1414, para 73.
47 See *McKennitt v Ash* [2005] EWHC 3003, [2006] EMLR 178 (QB), para 135 per Eady J, approved by the Court of Appeal in [2008] QB 73, para 22.
48 *Beckham v MGN* [2001] All ER (D) 307 (Jun): 23 June 2001, Stanley Burton J; 28 June 2001, Eady J.
49 *Ferdinand v MGN* (n 9 above), para 44.

group challenging his chairmanship. The tribunal took into account the abusive nature of the texts, the intention to insult and the absence of any prior relationship between sender and recipient.[50]

D THE SECOND STAGE: A BALANCING EXERCISE

22.27 The second stage looks at the disclosure or intended disclosure to others of the private information. This is an act of expression and therefore engages the rights to freedom of expression under Article 10 of the Convention of the discloser and recipients (who has a presumptive right under Article 10 to receive it). The discloser may be a source passing it to the press or a media organisation publishing or broadcasting it to the world. The rights of the discloser and recipients have to be weighed by the court in deciding what the outcome should be. Should publication be prevented or (if it has already happened) should damages be awarded? Or should free speech prevail? This requires a balance to be struck between the competing rights in play.

22.28 The House of Lords explained how this should be done in the case of *Re S (A Child)*:[51]

(a) Neither article starts with any presumed precedence over the other. At the outset of the exercise they are taken to be of equal value in principle.
(b) An 'intense focus' upon the comparative importance of the specific rights being claimed in the individual case is then required. This requires the court to value, or 'weigh', each right that is in play on the facts of the case. How private is the information and how harmful will be/was the disclosure in issue? How strong is/ was the case for disclosing the information without the consent of the claimant?
(c) The court must take into account the resulting justifications for interfering with, or 'restricting', each right in order to protect the exercise of the other right.
(d) The proportionality test must be applied. Will the outcome of the balancing, favouring one right over the other, only interfere with the other to the extent necessary to protect the right that prevails?

(a) Factors relevant to the balancing exercise

22.29 Some issues arise repeatedly when defendants seek to defend their Article 10 rights in cases involving private information. Many are likely to be relevant in football-related claims.

(i) Public interest

22.30 The press has a duty to act as a 'public watchdog'. Information that is capable of contributing to a debate of public interest in a democratic society should generally circulate freely via the press. Restrictions on press freedom to report on such matters will have to be convincingly justified. Information about corruption in football, perhaps in relation to transfers, is of legitimate public interest because

---

50 Arbitral Tribunal Decision dated 21 May 2015 (Tim Kerr QC, Desmond Browne QC and Charles Flint QC). Contrast with the FA's decision not to investigate/commence proceedings against Richard Scudamore, CEO of Premier League, in relation to sexist emails he sent to a friend which were accessed by his PA (who complained), because they were private emails.
51 [2005] 1 AC 593.

laws and regulations must be respected. The fact that it may have been obtained by journalists through subterfuge, perhaps secretly recording a confidential discussion, does not undermine its public interest value (but see **22.47** below).

22.31   The court will, however, look critically at claims that private information is of public interest. It distinguishes between matters in the 'public interest' in the legal sense and those that are merely 'of interest to the public'. Extreme examples of the latter are what the Court of Human Rights has described as press reports 'concentrating on sensational and, at times, lurid news, intended to titillate and entertain, which are aimed at satisfying the curiosity of a particular readership regarding aspects of a person's strictly private life'. These 'do not attract the robust protection of Article 10 afforded to the press'.[52] The Strasbourg court has emphasised that articles 'aimed solely at satisfying the curiosity of a particular readership regarding the details of a person's private life, however well-known that person might be, cannot be deemed to contribute to any debate of general interest to society'.[53] Indeed in *PJS v NGN Ltd* the majority of the Supreme Court went so far as to suggest that 'it may be that the mere reporting of sexual encounters of someone like the appellant, however well known to the public, with a view to criticising them does not even fall within the concept of freedom of expression under Article 10 at all'.[54]

22.32   In *Terry v Persons Unknown,* however, the claimant was trying to prevent disclosure of information about private conduct. Without characterising the conduct in issue, Tugendhat J observed that criticising the conduct (even in private) 'of other members of society as being socially harmful, or wrong' could have a public interest value.[55]

22.33   The concept of a 'debate of public interest' is very wide with no set boundaries or categories. It is not confined to the exposure and discussion of illegal conduct. Some insight can be gained from the IPSO Editors' Code of Practice which sets out a list of the types of information that are of public interest.

(ii) Public figures

22.34   There is more scope to publish the private information of public figures than there is to publish that of private individuals.[56] There is more likely to be a public interest in doing so, so this factor is connected to the previous one. In *Spelman v Express Newspapers* the claimant was a 17-year-old. He had played rugby union for a professional club and at international level in his age group. As noted above, Tugendhat J observed that it is 'a condition of participating in high level sport that the participant gives up control over many aspects of private life', adding that '[the] restriction on what might otherwise be a reasonable expectation of privacy may well apply to those who aim for the highest level, even if they do not achieve it, or can no longer expect to achieve it'. Tugendhat J went on to characterise the claimant, in the context of discussion about his sporting life, as 'a person who is to be regarded as exercising a public function'.[57]

---

52   *Mosley v UK* [2012] EMLR 1, para 114.
53   *Couderc and Hachette Filipacchi Associés v France* [2016] EMLR 19, para 100.
54   *PJS v NGN* (n 1 above), para 24.
55   *Terry v Persons Unknown* [2010] EMLR 16, para 104.
56   *Axel Springer v Germany* [2012] EMLR 15, para 89(b).
57   *Spelman v Express Newspapers* (n 18 above), paras 69–70 and 72.

22.35   Similarly, in *McClaren v NGN*, Lindblom J found that the claimant, as a former manager of the England team, was 'undoubtedly a public figure within the definition recognised by Tugendhat J in *Spelman*' and 'is clearly still a prominent public figure who has held positions of responsibility in the national game'. Accordingly he was considered to be a person from whom the public could reasonably expect a higher standard of conduct. A 'kiss and tell' story about an adulterous sexual encounter could therefore be published. The fact that the story had been set up so that a photograph could be taken of McClaren arriving at the woman's flat was 'peripheral' to the balancing exercise.[58]

(iii)   Role model

22.36   Footballers who hold (or have held) prominent positions, such as captain of the national team, have been held to be role models of whom high standards of conduct are expected both on and off the pitch. These may stem from club or team conduct rules, though not necessarily so. This is a particular example of where the role of the claimant as a public figure is important. The press may be entitled to disclose aspects of private conduct which fail to meet the high standard.[59]

22.37   This principle was applied in *Ferdinand v MGN*. Nicol J said that the captaincy of the England team, for a substantial body of the public, would come comfortably within the category of positions where higher standards of conduct can rightly be expected[60] and that there were 'many who would indeed see the captain, at least, of the England football team as a role model'. The judge noted that Ferdinand had chosen to accept the role, that carried with it an expectation of high standards. The judge observed that 'in the views of many the captain was expected to maintain those standards off, as well as on, the pitch'.[61]

22.38   In *McClaren v NGN* Steve McClaren was refused an interim injunction to prevent publication of the article about his sexual encounter, because he was considered to be a role model.[62] He was married at the time with three children aged 24, 20 and 15.

22.39   In *AMC v NGN*,[63] however, a 'prominent and successful professional sportsman' obtained an interim injunction to prevent the *Sun on Sunday* from publishing details about a short-lived sexual relationship between himself and a woman a few years before. At the time the claimant had a girlfriend, who by the time of the hearing was his wife. Elisabeth Laing J considered AMC was 'a role model for sportsmen and aspiring sportsmen' and that scrutiny of his conduct away from sport ought to bear a reasonable relationship with the fact that he is a sportsman. But she held that 'a discreetly conducted affair, before he was married, some years ago, is not obviously inconsistent with his public role, even if its conduct involved the breach of team rules'.[64]

---

58   [2012] EWHC 2466 (QB), para 34. But see *AMC v NGN* at para **22.39** below.
59   See para **22.8** above.
60   Nicol J was citing Buxton LJ who in *McKennitt v Ash* [2008] QB 73, para 65 identified those of whom such conduct could be expected as including 'headmasters and clergyman, who according to taste may be joined by politicians, senior civil servants, surgeons and journalists'.
61   *Ferdinand v MGN* (n 9 above), paras 88–90.
62   *McClaren v NGN* (n 58 above), para 34.
63   *AMC v NGN* (n 16 above).
64   *AMC v NGN*, para 20.

(iv)   Correcting a false image

22.40   Correcting a false public image is one facet of the public interest. This has been raised by media defendants in cases brought by sportsmen, particularly those who trade on a wholesome public image. In *Campbell v MGN* the claimant 'supermodel' had publicly denied taking illegal drugs or being an addict. In her claim for infringement of privacy she accepted that these statements were untrue and that the newspaper had the right to set the record straight.[65] Her complaint was about the *additional* private matters that were reported, being a photograph and details of her attendance at Narcotics Anonymous. These went beyond what was justifiable as a correction of the false image.

22.41   There can be much evidence and argument about whether there was a false image and what it was. In *Ferdinand v MGN* the judge found that the claimant had sought the image of someone who had 'belatedly matured', but that this was a false image as far as relationships with women were concerned.[66]

22.42   In *AMC v NGN*,[67] however, Elisabeth Laing J rejected an argument that the disclosures were necessary to correct a false image of AMC as a 'clean-living family man', which the newspaper claimed AMC had used to attract sponsorship and advertising revenue. She found that there was not a misleading or untruthful image to correct.[68]

22.43   The Court of Appeal reached the same conclusion in *PJS v NGN*, concerning information about an extramarital affair. The court found that the claimant had projected an image of commitment to a spouse. But since 'commitment may not entail monogamy', there was nothing to correction through disclosure of the appellant's occasional sexual encounters with others.[69]

(v)   Plurality of opinion and the right to criticise

22.44   Article 10(1) of the Convention gives rights to 'hold opinions' and to 'impart ... ideas', as well as to 'receive and impart information'. The press may argue it needs to reveal aspects of the private conduct of a public figure in order to crticise their conduct. Depending on the facts, this can be worthwhile argument. In *Terry v Persons Unknown*,[70] John Terry's application for an injunction preventing disclosure of details about a sexual relationship failed. Tugendhat J emphasised the importance of public discussion and the freedom to criticise in a 'plural society'.[71] His observations were described as 'powerful' by the Court of Appeal in *Hutcheson (formerly known as KGM) v NGN*.[72]

22.45   But in *AMC v NGN*,[73] the court rejected the newspaper's argument that it was entitled to criticise AMC as a hypocrite. This criticism would have been based on information about him having broken team rules by having a woman staying with him in a hotel and deceiving his then girlfriend and his manager.

---

65   *Campbell v MGN* (n 4 above), para 24.
66   *Ferdinand v MGN* (n 9 above), para 93.
67   *AMC v NGN* (n 16 above).
68   *AMC v NGN*, paras 19, 24–26.
69   [2016] EMLR 17, para 52.
70   *Terry v Persons Unknown* (n 55 above).
71   *Terry v Persons Unknown*, paras 101 and 104.
72   *Hutcheson (formerly known as KGM) v NGN* [2012] EMLR 2, para 29.
73   *AMC v NGN* (n 16 above).

(b)   Others factors relied upon by defendants

22.46   Other arguments that may be relied upon by defendants include that the information is already in the public domain or that there has been consent or a waiver of privacy rights. Footballers who have 'courted the media' or publicised their private lives (perhaps through social media as many are wont to do these days) are likely to be faced with this line of argument.

(c)   Other factors relied upon by claimants

22.47   First, a court will consider the impact on family life and children. Publicity can be harmful to other members of a claimant's family, particularly children, and can damage family relationships. Evidence of this will be considered when weighing the Article 8 rights at stake.[74] In *PJS v NGN* the Court of Appeal discharged an injunction after the protected information was circulated widely on the internet.[75] But the Supreme Court reinstated the injunction.[76] One reason was the appeal court's failure properly to consider the impact that publication of the protected information in newspapers in this jurisdiction would have on PJS's children. Lady Hale emphasised that children have independent privacy interests that require consideration and noted that HRA 1998, s 12(4)(b) requires courts to have regard to 'any relevant privacy code'.[77] The IPSO Editors' Code states that that editors must demonstrate an exceptional public interest to override the normally paramount interests of children. Secondly, a court will consider the source of the information and whether 'the important public interest in the observation of obligations of confidence [is] outweighed by sufficiently significant matters of public interest in favour of publication'.[78]

E   PRE-PUBLICATION PRIVACY INJUNCTIONS

(a)   Summary

22.48   There is no legal obligation on media organisations to pre-notify the subject of a report containing private information, nor on the State to require this.[79] But media organisations usually do so as a matter of good practice, so that the claimant can respond on the record. This also enables the claimant to consider applying for an interim injunction order to prevent publication (a 'prior restraint' order). A pre-publication ruling on the two-stage test may avoid the risk of lengthy and expensive litigation later on. Sometimes, as in *Terry v Persons Unknown*[80] the injunction is sought because the claimant discovers an unknown source has offered the private information to the newspapers.

22.49   The application is heard by a judge, usually with both sides present. Evidence is given by witness statement, not orally. If the judge decides that the applicant is likely to obtain a final injunction at trial, the interim injunction is usually

---

74   See too *K v NGN* [2011] 1 WLR 1827, para 17 per Ward LJ.
75   *PJS v NGN* (n 69 above).
76   See *PJS v NGN* (n 1 above).
77   *PJS v NGN* (n 1 above), para 72.
78   *Brevan Howard Asset Management LLP v Reuters Ltd* [2017] EWCA Civ 950, para 75.
79   *Mosley v United Kingdom* (n 52 above).
80   *Terry v Persons Unknown* (n 55 above).

granted. As these applications are often made to prevent imminent publication there may not be time for the parties to file detailed (or indeed any) witness statements at the first hearing. So there may be a holding injunction, preventing publication for a few days, and a 'return' date for a further hearing at which the court recives more evidence and detailed legal argument.[81]

(b)   The test under section 12 of the Human Rights Act

22.50   HRA 1998, s 12 applies to this sort of interim injunction application. Section 12(3) provides that a prior restraint order should not be granted unless the applicant 'is likely to establish that publication should not be allowed' at the full trial of the claim. There is some flexibility in the application of these words to the facts but the court will be exceedingly slow to make interim restraint orders where the applicant has not satisfied the court that he will probably ('more likely than not') succeed at the trial.[82]

22.51   HRA 1998, s 12(4)(a)(i) recognises that where the information is already in the public domain this may shift the balance towards allowing publication. But it does not preclude a court, when deciding whether to grant or lift injunctive relief, from having regard to both:

'a)   the nature of the journalistic material involved and the medium in which it is, or is to be, expressed, and

b)   the extent to which it is already available in that medium and the extent to which steps are being or can be taken to remove or limit access to any other publication in that or any other medium.'[83]

(c)   The two-stage test

22.52   In essence, therefore, the judge deciding the interim injuction application is predicting the likely outcome of the application of the two-stage test at the trial – where the claimant will seek a permanent injuction as a final remedy. All the principles discussed above may be considered. The task can be a difficult one. Conflicts of evidence in witness statements are left to be resolved at trial. The judge may have to anticipate what further evidence there is likely be at trial.

(d)   Impact of disclosures despite the existence of interim injunction

22.53   An interim injunction can be continued, even where the material is published abroad and/or on the internet so that it can no longer be said to be 'secret' or confidential. The Supreme Court did this in *PJS v NGN*. The injuction against the tabloid was continued even though the story (including the claimant's identity), which had been published outside the jurisdiction, was circulating widely on the internet and so was being dicussed in this jurisdiction. The court considered that the intrusion and distress involved in 'unrestricted publication by the English media in

---

81   Note that CPR, PD 25A, para 5.1 states that unless the court orders otherwise, the order *must* provide for a return date if the application was made without notice (emphasis added).
82   See *Cream Holdings Ltd v Banerjee* [2005] 1 AC 253, para 22 per Lord Nicholls.
83   See *PJS v NGN* (n 1 above), para 34.

hard copy as well as on their own internet sites' was qualitatively different from the more limited intrusion/distress caused by the publicity to date.[84]

22.54   This may be important for premiership players with global profiles. In *CTB v NGN* a famous footballer sought to prevent disclosure of information about a sexual relationship. In the five or so weeks after the injunction and anonymised ruling in his favour, information circulated on Twitter and the internet generally indicating the identity of the footballer as the claimant. But Eady J refused the newspaper's application to lift the injunction on the basis that the information was now in the public domain.[85] A second application took place late on the same day after the footballer had been named in Parliament by an MP. This time Tugendhat J refused to discharge the injunction, saying its purpose was not to protect a secret but to prevent intrusion or harassment for which it was still an effective remedy.

(e)   The procedure

22.55   An application should not be made unless there is a sufficient threat that Article 8 rights are going to be infringed. There is useful Practice Guidance on Interim Non-Disclosure Orders which contains a Model Order and an Explanatory Note that can be served with the application.[86]

22.56   The application papers should be served on the publisher and any non-parties who have an interest in the information which is to be protected by the injunction. Failure to pre-notify interested parties can only be justified, on clear and cogent evidence, by compelling reasons. One reason would be a real prospect of a pre-notified person publishing online before the application can be heard.[87] It is assumed, however, that mainstream media organisations will hold off publication once served. Another is where there is convincing evidence that the respondent is blackmailing the applicant.[88] If an application is made without notice the applicant is under a duty to disclose all relevant evidence to the court (even if it is unhelpful to the applicant's case) and to draw the court's attention to all the important factual, legal and procedural aspects of the case.

F   DEFAMATION: THE CAUSE OF ACTION

22.57   The basis of a claim in defamation is a statement:

(a)   published by the defendant to a third party or parties;
(b)   refering to the claimant; and
(c)   carrying a meaning which is defamatory of the claimant (an 'imputation'), in that:

  (i)   it substantially affects in an adverse manner the attitude of other people towards the claimant, or has a tendency to do so; and
  (ii)   has caused, or is likely to cause, serious harm to the reputation of the claimant.

---

84   *PJS v NGN* (n 1 above), para 35.
85   *CTB v NGN* [2011] EWHC 1326 (QB) and 1334 (QB).
86   [2012] 1 WLR 1003.
87   *RST v UVW* [2009] EWHC 24, paras 7 and 13.
88   *ASG v GSA* [2009] EWCA Civ 1574, para 3; *DFT v TFD* [2010] EWHC 2335 (QB), para 7.

22.58   Requirements (a)–(c)(i) derive from the common law. Broadly a defamatory statement is one that alleges some form of discreditable conduct on the part of the claimant. The requirement of 'serious harm' (or 'serious financial loss' in the case of a body that trades for profit) derives from s 1(a) and (b) of the Defamation Act 2013 (DA 2013) (as to which see para **22.66** below).

(a)   Publication

22.59   The claimant may also need to prove the extent of the publication (for example the viewing figures for a TV show) and how this caused serious harm to the claimant's reputation. 'Publication' here requires that one or more people actually read, viewed or listened to the material. Where the defamatory material is communicated through the mass media, publication will usually be inferred at recognised circulation/audience levels. The extent of readership on the internet can be harder to prove, especially on social media or small websites.

22.60   The limitation period in defamation is one year.[89] Each instance of communication of the defamatory statement to an individual reader, viewer or listener is, technically, a distinct 'publication' giving rise to a fresh cause of action. DA 2013, s 8, however, establishes a 'single publication rule'. If a person republishes the same or substantially the same defamatory statement, the cause of action is deemed to have accrued on the date of first publication. So the one year starts to run from that date. The rule does not apply if the manner of re-publication is materially different, for example in terms of prominence or in relation to the extent of the publication.

22.61   Anyone who has authorised or knowingly taken part in making and communicating a defamatory statement is responsible in law for its publication. There is a defence under DA 2013, s 5 for website operators sued for defamatory statements posted on their websites.[90]

22.62   A statement is published in the location where it is read, heard, viewed or downloaded by the third party. Thus a Spanish or Italian football magazine available online or in print in this jurisdiction is 'published' to its readers in the UK. As mentioned above, however, the claimant must prove readership in the UK.

(b)   Reference to the claimant

22.63   The general rule is that the published material must be such that a reasonable person who knows the claimant would understand it as referring to her or him.[91] The test is objective. The defendant's intention is not relevant. So, anonymising a defamatory allegation may not protect against a claim. It would be no use anonymising a goalkeeper, for example, said to have been bribed to concede a goal in a particular 1–0 defeat.

---

89   Limitation Act 1980, s 4A. Section 32A of the Act gives the court a discretion to exclude this short time limit if it appears that it would be 'equitable' to allow an action to proceed having regard to the prejudice that such a decision would cause to each of the parties.

90   See too Sch 1 to the Defamation (Operators of Websites) Regulations 2013 (SI 2013/3028). In essence, the operator must ask the poster to consent to removal of the statement or provide contact details which can be provided to the complainant.

91   See eg *Barron, Healey and Champion v Collins* [2015] EWHC 1125, para 45.

22.64   There is also reference to the claimant, however, where particular readers had knowledge of extrinsic matters (not in the published material) which would have led them to identify the claimant. Such extrinsic facts must be pleaded as they are part of the claim.[92] For example if an article says that an unnamed player at a particular club sexually assaulted a woman at a nightclub, they might plead identification by those who knew he held a party at the club on that night.

(c)   Defamatory statements

22.65   Claimants must establish that the published material complained of is defamatory of them, specifically that it would tend to lower them in the estimation of right-thinking members of society generally or would be likely to affect a person adversely in the estimation of reasonable people generally.[93]

22.66   DA 2013, s 1(1) provides that a statement is not defamatory, however, unless its publication has caused or is likely to cause 'serious harm' to the reputation of the claimant. Section 1(2) provides that harm to the reputation of a body that trades for profit is not 'serious harm' unless it has caused or is likely to cause the body serious financial loss. In *Lauchaux v Independent Print Ltd*[94] the Court of Appeal held that 'likely to cause' in DA 2013, s 1 means 'a tendency to cause'. It confirmed that s 1 raises the bar for bringing a defamation claim but that where a publication bears a serious defamatory meaning an inference of serious reputational harm should ordinarily be drawn.

22.67   Examples of defamatory statements include allegations of: hypocrisy;[95] habitual drunkenness;[96] use of hard drugs;[97] fraudulent and corrupt behaviour;[98] match-fixing;[99] having sex with a prostitute;[100] selfishly disrupting a committed family relationship;[101] motivation by vanity or self-delusion;[102] taking performance enhancing drugs in sport;[103] being an incompetent football coach;[104] favouritism in refereeing matches;[105] being a professional footballer incapable of using his right foot to kick a ball;[106] and being a jockey who rode horses unfairly and dishonestly.[107] Even a statement that someone was hideously ugly was held to be defamatory as it held the claimant up to ridicule.[108]

---

92   *Bruce v Oldham Press Ltd* [1936] 1 KB 697; *Budu v BBC* [2010] EWHC 616 (QB), para 40.
93   *Skuse v Granada Television Limited* [1996] EMLR 278 per Sir Thomas Bingham MR.
94   [2017] EWCA Civ 1334. Note permission to appeal to the UKSC was granted on 21 March 2018.
95   *Mawdsley v Guardian Newspapers* [2002] EWHC 1780.
96   *Alexander v Jenkins* [1892] 1 QB 797 at 804.
97   *Niall Horan v Express Newspapers* [2015] EWHC 3550.
98   *Oyston v Ragozzino* [2015] EWHC 3232 (QB). Statements were made by a Blackpool football club fan against Karl Oyston, the Chairman of Blackpool football club. The club was also a claimant.
99   *Bruce Grobbelaar v News Group Newspapers* [2002] UKHL 40, [2002] 1 WLR 3024; *Chris Cairns v Modi* [2013] 1 WLR 1015.
100 *Dwek v Macmillan Publishers Ltd* [2000] EMLR 284 CA.
101 *Danny Simpson v MGN* [2016] EMLR 26.
102 *Branson v Bower* [2002] QB 737.
103 *Lance Armstrong v Times Newspapers Ltd* [2006] EWHC 1614 (QB).
104 *Hoeppner v Dunkirk Printing* 227 NYAD 130 (1929).
105 *Harrigan v Jones* [2001] NSWSC 623.
106 *Fullam v Associated Newspapers Ltd* [1955–56] IR Jur Rep 45.
107 *Wood v Earl of Durham* (1888) 21 QBD 501.
108 *Steven Berkoff v Julie Burchill and Times Newspapers Ltd* [1996] 4 All ER 139.

22.68   By contrast in the Australian case of *Boyd v Mirror Newspapers* it was held that it was not defamatory to say of a footballer that he was too fat to play except insofar as it was capable of meaning that he was ridiculous or that the condition was his fault.[109] Nor was an allegation, in the autobiography of a former chairman of Crystal Palace, that a business partner had been sacked. This was because no reasonable person would infer from such a statement that the sacking was the fault of the business partner (who was the claimant).[110]

22.69   It is also possible to establish a particular defamatory meaning by pointing to extrinsic facts known by some readers of the material, known as an 'innuendo meaning'. In *Johnson v MGN Limited*[111] Glen Johnson said the article meant that he missed a Boxing Day game for Portsmouth, not because of a claimed injury, but because he had agreed to join Liverpool. He also argued successfully that it meant that he had breached Clause 6 of Rule K of the Premier League Rules prohibiting unauthorised approaches by a contracted player to another club.[112] Clause 6 of Rule K was not discussed in the article but Johnson's case was that it would have been known to readers of the article who were involved with professional football.

G   DEFENCES

22.70   DA 2013 replaced corresponding common law defences with statutory defences of: truth (s 2); honest opinion (s 3); and publication on a matter of public interest (s 4) for publications after 1 January 2014. It also created a defence for operators of websites on which defamatory material is posted by others (s 5) and new rules restricting the scope for defamation claims against defendants who are not domiciled in the EU (known as 'libel tourism') (s 9).

(a) Truth

22.71   This defence replaces the common law defence of 'justification'.[113] It applies to factual defamatory statements. Section 2(1) makes it a defence to show that the imputation conveyed by the statement complained of is 'substantially true'. This gives statutory form to the common law principle, identified in *Chase v NGN*[114] that the defendant does not have to prove that 'every word … published' was true. Establishing the 'essential' or 'substantial' truth of the libel's sting is enough.

22.72   DA 2013, s 2(2) and (3) replace s 5 of the Defamation Act 1952. They concern publications containing two or more distinct imputations. The defendant may fail to prove all of them to be substantially true. But the truth defence can still succeed if, considering those that *are* substantially true, the false imputations do not seriously harm the claimant's reputation. For example, if an allegation that a manager corruptly takes 'bungs' on transfers is proved true but a charge of betting on his own teams games is not, the falsity of the latter would not harm his reputation.

---

109 [1980] 2 NSWLR 449.
110 *Briggs v Simon Jordan and others* [2013] EWHC 3205 (QB), para 17 per Tugendhat J.
111 [2009] EWHC 1481 (QB).
112 This is now reflected in Rule C, Clauses 1 and 2 relating to players with and without written contacts.
113 Section 2(4) abolishes the defence of 'justification'.
114 [2003] EMLR 218.

(b) Honest opinion

22.73 This s 3 defence replaces the common law defence of fair comment.[115] The defendant must show that: the defamatory statement was an expression of opinion not a factual allegegation; the published material indicated, 'whether in general or specific terms, the basis of the opinion'; and an 'honest person' could have held that opinion.[116]

(c) Publication on matter of public interest

22.74 The s 4 defence replaces the common law defence known as *Reynolds* privilege.[117] It can succeed without proving the truth of a factual imputation.[118] It applies to statements of both fact and opinion and protects statements that are published as part of a discussion in the public interest. Under s 4 a defendant needs to show that:

(a) the statement complained of was, or formed part of, a statement on a matter of public interest; and
(b) the defendant (ie its journalists in the case of a media organisation) reasonably believed that publishing the statement complained of was in the public interest.

The latter usually requires the defendant to show appropriate steps were taken to verify damaging factual imputations.

22.75 The Act does not attempt to define 'the public interest'. As with misuse of private information it is for the judge to assess whether the statement was in the public interest in all the circumstances. In determining whether it was reasonable for the defendant to believe that publishing the statement complained of was in the public interest, the court must make such allowance for editorial judgment as it considers appropriate.[119] In *Yeo v Times Newspapers* the judge had 'no hesitation' in finding that the newspaper article was on a matter of public interest, namely current legitimate concerns about standards of behaviour in Parliament in relation to lobbying by commercial organisations.[120] Many aspects of professional football raise issues of legitimate public interest given the imperative of having a fair and well-regulated sport. For this reason many properly sourced articles about corruption at FIFA, match-fixing, ticket-touting and bribery of referees and other officials have not attracted libel claims. The same is true of some material about breaches of regulatory rules imposed on managers and players.

22.76 DA 2013, s 4(3) recognises that the statement complained of was, or may have formed part of, an accurate and impartial account of a dispute to which the claimant was a party. This is sometimes called 'reportage' journalism. In such cases, when it is deciding whether it was reasonable to believe that publication was in the

---

115 Section 3(8) abolishes the defence of fair comment and repeals s 6 of the Defamation Act 1952.
116 See further s(3)(s).
117 Named after the case in which the defence was identified, *Reynolds v Times Newspapers Limited* [2001] 2 AC 127. The Act's explanatory notes suggest preceding *Reynolds* case law would be a helpful guide to interpreting the new statutory defence.
118 In *Yeo v Times Newspapers* [2015] EWHC 3375 (QB), Warby J stated that it should be 'less challenging' to show that the articles represented responsible journalism on a matter of public interest than to prove that they were true (para 128).
119 Section 4(4).
120 [2015] EWHC 3375 (QB), para 129.

public interest, the court can disregard any omission of the defendant to take steps to verify the truth of the imputation conveyed by it.[121] This is because the allegation is part of the dispute and is not made by the publisher.

(d) Qualified privilege

22.77 This is a common law defence which protects defamatory statements made on a 'privileged occasion'. This is 'an occasion where the person making the communication has an interest or a duty – legal, social, or moral – to make it to the person to whom it is made, and the person to whom it is so made has a corresponding interest or duty to receive it. This reciprocity is essential'.[122] This defence exists to protect communications which are for the 'common convenience and welfare of society'.[123] An example would be alleging to FA safeguarding officials that a club coach is sexually abusing young players.

22.78 Various publications have qualified privilege by statute. The main provision is s 15 of the Defamation Act 1996. Examples include fair and accurate reporting of proceedings at a press conference held anywhere in the world for the discussion of a matter of public interest;[124] and a fair and accurate copy of, extract from or summary of a notice or other matter issued for the information of the public by or on behalf of an international organisation or international conference.[125]

(e) Malice

22.79 In contrast to the defence of absolute privilege (see paras **22.80–22.82** below), the defence of qualified privilege fails if the claimant proves that the statement was made maliciously.[126] The claimant must show the statement was made knowing it is untrue or recklessly, not caring whether or not it is true. Alternatively the claimant can show that the motive for the statement was simply to damage the claimant so that the defendant was not acting in pursuance of the duty or interest protected by privilege. The improper motive must have been the dominant one if there was more than one motive. Here malice can be proved even though the defendant (wrongly) believed the statement complained of to be true, though if this is the case the court would be slow to draw the inference that the dominant motive was an improper one.

(f) Absolute privilege

22.80 A libel claim about a statement protected by absolute privilege will be struck out. Absolute privilege can be conferred by statute or common law and protects the maker of the statement from being sued, even if the untrue and defamatory statement has been made maliciously.

---

121 DA 2013, s 4(3).
122 *Adam v Ward* [1917] AC 309 at 334 per Lord Atkinson.
123 *Toogood v Spyring* (1834) 1 CM&R 181 at 193.
124 DA 2013, s 7(5).
125 DA 2013, s 7(4), amending s 9(1)(c) of the Defamation Act 1996.
126 *Horrocks v Lowe* [1975] AC 135 HL. The passage that is often cited is Lord Diplock's at 149–151.

22.81   Examples include statements made in Parliamentary proceedings and statements made in or in connection with judicial proceedings or other proceedings having judicial characteristics.[127]

22.82   In the case of *Makudi v Triesman*,[128] a Thai member of the FIFA Executive brought a libel claim against Lord Triesman, Chairman of The FA, in relation to The FA's 2018 World Cup bid. The defendant had given evidence to the Culture, Media and Sports Select Committee alleging that the claimant had offered to arrange an England-Thailand football match in return for TV broadcasting rights in the UK. The defendant was later interviewed in an FA investigation into his allegations. He went no further than what he had said to the Select Committee, at one point stating that there was nothing he could add to the evidence that he had already given to Parliament. The claimant sued over these statements made outside of Parliament. The Court of Appeal held that absolute Parliamentary privilege could apply to such statements and that, generally, such cases will possess these two characteristics:

(1)   a public interest in repeating what was said in Parliament which the speaker is seeking, reasonably, to pursue;
(2)   so close a nexus between the occasions of his speaking, in and then out of, Parliament that the prospect of his obligation to speak on the second occasion (or the expectation or promise that he would do so) is reasonably foreseeable at the time of the first and his purpose in speaking on both occasions is the same or very closely related.[129]

Applying this test the Court of Appeal held that Lord Treisman's remarks were protected by the privilege.

(g)   Actions against a person not domiciled in the UK or another Member State

22.83   DA 2013, s 9 is concerned with 'libel tourism', where a claimant tries to bring a libel claim in the courts of England and Wales even though the defamatory material was primarily published in other jurisdictions. It provides that a court does not have jurisdiction to hear and determine an action against a person not domiciled in the UK or another EU or EFTA state unless it is satisfied that, of all the places in which the statement complained of has been published, England and Wales is clearly the most appropriate place in which to bring an action.

22.84   The explanatory notes to the section indicate that the court should consider the overall global picture to determine the most appropriate forum for it to be heard. The aim is to ensure the courts cannot accept jurisdiction simply because the claimant limits their claim to damage occurring through publication in the UK or EU.

22.85   This section raises potential difficulties for individuals, such as some sportsmen and women, who work around the world and are well known abroad as well as in the UK. In *Ahuja v Politika*[130] Tugendhat J held that the claimant, an international businessman resident in England, would need to present evidence of his

---

127   Further information about these categories can be found in *Duncan & Neill on Defamation*, 4th Edition (Lexis Nexis 2015), Chapter 16 and *Gatley on Libel and Slander*, 12th Edition (Sweet & Maxwell, 2013), Chapter 13.
128   [2014] 1 QB 839.
129   Ibid, para 25.
130   [2016] 1 WLR 1414.

links with all the jurisdictions where the defamatory statement had been published and in which he spends a significant part of his time and in which he owns properties.[131]

H   REMEDIES

(a)   Damages

22.86   Libel damages have three elements, they should compensate the claimant for the damage to their reputation; vindicate their good name; and take account of the distress, hurt and humiliation which the defamatory publication has caused.[132] The gravity of the allegation is the most important factor in assessing damages, although the scope and extent of the publication are also highly relevant, as is the effect that the allegation has had on the claimant.

22.87   The law recognises that defamatory allegations are likely to be repeated once put into circulation. As Bingham LJ observed:

> 'the law would part company with the realities of life if it held that the damage caused by publication of a libel began and ended with publication to the original publishee. Defamatory statements are objectionable not least because of their propensity to percolate through underground channels and contaminate hidden springs.'[133]

22.88   The current 'ceiling' on libel awards, identified by the courts by reference to the amounts awarded for pain, suffering and loss of amenity in personal injury claims, is about £300,000. Awards at that level are reserved for the gravest of allegations, for example of terrorism or murder.[134]

22.89   *Cairns v Modi*[135] was about a tweet to 65 publishees. It made an allegation of match-fixing against the claimant New Zealand cricketer. The Court of Appeal held that the 'percolation' phenomenon referred to above was a legitimate factor to be taken into account in the assessment of damages.[136] It upheld the judge's award to the claimant of £75,000 damages with a further £15,000 in aggravation of the damage through the way the claimant had conducted the trial.

22.90   Karl Oyston, the Chairman of Blackpool football club, was awarded £30,000 in his successful libel claim against Stephen Reed, a Blackpool Football club fan opposed to his chairmanship. The defendant made various allegations against Mr Oyston including that he had committed a deliberate and aggravated contempt of court and that he brandished a shotgun in order to intimidate the defendant.[137]

(b)   Injunction

22.91   If there is a risk that a defendant will continue to publish the statements complained of unless restrained, then the court can grant an injunction as a final

---

131   Ibid, para [40].
132   *John v MGN* [1997] EB 586 CA, para 607.
133   *Slipper v BBC* [1991] 1 QB 283 at 300.
134   For a useful table setting out awards of damages see *Duncan & Neill on Defamation*, 4th Edition (Lexis Nexis 2015), Appendix 7.
135   [2013] 1 WLR 1015.
136   *Cairns v Modi*, para 27.
137   [2016] EWHC 1067 (QB).

remedy. This is usually framed to prevent the defendant from making the same or any similar allegation defamatory of the claimant as complained about in the action.[138]

(c)   Orders to remove statements or cease distribution

22.92   DA 2013, s 13 provides that where a court gives judgment for the claimant in an action for defamation the court may order (i) the operator of a website on which the defamatory statement is posted to remove the statement, or (ii) any person who was not the author, editor or publisher of the defamatory statement to stop distributing, selling or exhibiting material containing the statement.

(d)   Statements in open court

22.93   If a libel claims settles it is possible for the parties jointly, or the claimant unilaterally, to make a 'Statement in Open Court'. This provides an opportunity to correct the false and defamatory statement in a public forum and to record the apology or regret usually expressed by the defendants. Such statements are often reported in the media and therefore can assist in a claimant obtaining vindication and repairing the damage to their reputations.[139]

---

138 Note an injunction was granted in *Oyston v Reed* [2016] EWHC 1067 (QB). This appears to have also included a harassment injunction which, on the face of the judgment, seems to be remarkably wide in its terms (see para 34).

139 For examples of Statements in Open Court involving footballers see: *Michael Owen v Express Newspapers Plc* before Eady J on 3 June 2009; *Christiano Ronaldo v Telegraph Media Group Ltd* before Eady J on 8 November 2010; *Lord Triesman v UTV Media*; Statement in Open Court before Eady J on 7 December 2010; and *O'Neill v 365 Media Group plc*; before Eady J on 23 April 2008.

CHAPTER 23

Discipline

Jim Sturman QC and **Alice Bricogne** (2 Bedford Row)
and **Nick De Marco QC** (Blackstone Chambers)

A INTRODUCTION

23.1   The powers and obligations of football governing bodies to regulate football by means of imposing discipline on their participants represent one of the most important aspects of football generally, and for lawyers practising within the football industry in particular.

23.2   Discipline in football covers the wide panoply of the sport. It covers everything from the Laws of the Game, including sanctions for violent misconduct on the field by players, doping, match-fixing and betting on the one hand to such matters as the regulation of intermediaries, third party investment in players, and the financial spending of clubs on the other.

23.3   What might resemble purely commercial or employment arrangements in other industries are often, in football, strictly governed by regulation backed by stringent disciplinary sanctions in football. A club (and its directors) may find itself facing serious disciplinary sanction because of the nature of the lender it has borrowed money from,[1] or as a result of allowing its investors to invest more in the squad than rules provide.[2] A player might find himself banned from playing football and thus earning a living for a significant period of time because he bet on another football match or matches, even if there is no suspicion of match-fixing involved,[3] or he might be fined and banned for a shorter period for something he said on Twitter.[4] If a club offers employment to a player in contract with another club who unlawfully walks out of his contract the new club may be fined and banned from signing new players under FIFA rules,[5] and it might be banned from signing academy/youth

---

1   See, eg *The Football League v Watford Association Football Club and Mr Laurence Bassini*, Football Disciplinary Commission (Ch Alexander Milne QC), 18 March 2013.
2   See, eg *Queens Park Rangers FC v the Football League*, Football Disciplinary Commission, 2017 (Ch Lord Collins), Award confidential at time of publication.
3   See, eg *The FA v Joeseph Barton*, FA Appeal Board (Ch David Casement QC), 25 July 2017 reducing Mr Barton's ban from playing football from 18 months to 13 months.
4   See, eg *The FA v Andre Gray*, FA Regulatory Commission (Ch David Casement QC), 22 September 2016.
5   FIFA Regulations on the Status and Transfer of Players, Article 17(4); see, eg DRC 9 November 2004, no 11417, *Majewski v New Panionios*.

players because it approached other young players in breach of various regulations.[6] Intermediaries (formerly football agents) may be banned from carrying out their activity because they have become involved in a breach of the rules, and players and clubs may also be sanctioned for involvement with rule breaches.[7] Clubs might face points deduction, relegation or even expulsion from the competition in which they play as a result of serious disciplinary breaches.[8]

23.4   The substantive rules forming the basis for disciplinary action in many of the most important cases are considered elsewhere in this book.[9] This chapter focuses principally on the procedural elements of discipline in football. Discipline in English football is largely governed by The FA, and thus most of this chapter (section D) considers the detail of The FA's disciplinary rules. Having considered the importance of fairness generally (in section B), section C of this chapter considers more generally the disciplinary procedures of other football regulators, such as the Premier League, the Football League and international bodies such as FIFA and UEFA.

B   THE IMPORTANCE OF FAIRNESS

(a)   The legal requirement

23.5   As a starting point, it is necessary to emphasise the importance of fairness in football disciplinary proceedings. Many football disciplinary tribunals have wide and far reaching powers to sanction participants. Ultimately, they can (and often do) prevent a player or intermediary from earning his or her living and they can cause a club to face serious financial hardship or a points deduction and relegation (or both). As such, it is imperative that football disciplinary tribunals act within the law and act fairly.

23.6   The courts, or arbitral tribunals sitting in place of the courts, exercise a supervisory jurisdiction over football disciplinary bodies. In English law the modern basis for this can be derived from the seminal decision of Richards J in *Bradley v The Jockey Club*.[10] In short, whilst sports governing bodies (such as The FA or the various league bodies) are not public bodies for the purposes of the court's judicial review jurisdiction, their monopolistic control over sport and especially their powers to affect an individual's right to work mean they must be subject to a supervisory

---

6   See, eg *FAPL v Liverpool FC*, 3 April 2017; CAS 2014/A/3813 *RFEF v FIFA* (concerning transfers of youth players to Barcelona).
7   See, eg *The FA v Phil Smith & Wycombe Wanderers FC (Sanctions decision)*, FA Regulatory Commission (Ch Craig Moore), 23 May 2014; and appeal decision in *Phil Smith v The FA*, FA Appeal Board (Ch Richard Smith QC), 11 July 2014; and *The FA v Kleinman, Levack, Rahnama & Brighton & Hove Albion FC*, FA Regulatory Commission (Ch David Casement QC), 16 February 2015; and the appeal decision in *Kleinman & Levack v The FA* FA Appeal Board (Ch Nicholas Stewart QC) 21 April 2015.
8   In 2007 the Football League imposed a 15-point deduction on Leeds United FC in relation to breaches of its insolvency rules. The points deduction was imposed as a condition for permitting the club to continue to participate in the league (https://www.theguardian.com/football/2007/aug/09/newsstory.leedsunited (accessed March 2018)). Luton Town FC faced a 30-point deduction by the Football league in 2008 for breaching insolvency rules and other financial misconduct (http://news.bbc.co.uk/sport1/hi/football/teams/l/luton_town/7500435.stm (accessed March 2018)).
9   See, in general, Chapters: 10, Academies and Youth Issues; 11, Third Party Investment; 12, Football Intermediaries, Regulation and Legal Disputes; 16, Financial Regulation and Financial Fair Play; 24, Doping; and 25, Corruption and Match-fixing.
10   [2004] EWHC 2164 QB; approved by the Court of Appeal in [2005] EWCA Civ 1056.

standard equivalent to that applied by the courts to public bodies. They must act lawfully (including in accordance with their own rules), fairly in a procedural sense and in accordance with the principles of natural justice; they must act rationally and their disciplinary decisions must be proportionate. Whether the courts' (or arbitral tribunals') basis for review of the decision of a football disciplinary tribunal is based on a claim in contract (ie a claim that the body has breached its rules) or on the wider restraint of trade jurisdiction even where no contract exists, the available grounds of review are the same.[11]

23.7   Similarly, decisions of international bodies, such as UEFA, will be subject to review under principles of European law (including competition law) or, in the case of FIFA, Swiss law, including, for example, the principle of proportionality.[12]

23.8   It is important for participants and those representing them in disciplinary proceedings before football bodies to recall that whatever those bodies say about their own powers or procedures, or the fact that there can be no further appeal from their decisions, they must still act lawfully and in accordance with the principles of fairness. If they fail to do so a court or tribunal may (in the right case) intervene to quash their decision.

23.9   In English football a challenge to a decision of a football disciplinary panel will usually be by way of an application under Rule K of The FA Rules to an independent arbitral tribunal to quash the decision of a football disciplinary or appeal panel under the arbitral tribunal's *Bradley* jurisdiction (see para **23.6** above). The FA, and other football regulators, have accepted that a Rule K tribunal has such a jurisdiction in various cases, and Rule K arbitral panels have exercised it.[13]

(b)   Procedural problems with football disciplinary proceedings

23.10   The supervisory jurisdiction over football disciplinary proceedings is even more significant when one considers some of the potential weaknesses that exist in football disciplinary rules and procedures. The FA's disciplinary proceedings, in particular, have come under criticism in the past by some participants and those who represent them.

23.11   For example (at the time of writing and for many years), as explained in more detail in section D below, The FA has a two-tier disciplinary procedure. A Regulatory Commission (often chaired by a lawyer) and an Appeal Board. However, the persons who constitute these disciplinary tribunals are drawn from a small pool of people appointed by The FA. Members of that pool may one day be appointed to a first instance Regulatory Commission and another day to an appellate Appeal Board, so members of the same small group regularly review each other's decisions.

---

11   For a more lengthy discussion of the *Bradley* decision and courts' supervisory powers of review see, Lewis, Taylor, De Marco and Segan, *Challenging Sports Governing Bodies* (Bloomsbury, 2016), Chapter 7.

12   See, Chapter 29, International Disputes and the CAS.

13   For example, in *West Ham United v The FA*, FA Rule K Tribunal (sole arbitrator, Nicholas Stewart QC) 7 February 2014, concerning a challenge to the legality of a final decision relating to the player, Andy Carroll's, red card appeal, The FA accepted that the interim Rule K panel was entitled to exercise a supervisory jurisdiction. The interim panel declined to grant an injunction against The FA, but accepted its supervisory role. In *Hull City Tigers FC v The FA*, 23 February 2015, the Rule K arbitral panel (Ch Sir Stanley Burnton QC) quashed a decision of The FA's highest body, The FA Council (concerning the club's proposed name change) on grounds of bias/procedural fairness.

The FA decides who shall sit on any given Regulatory Commission often without input from the participant. In practice participants are given notice that they can object to a person who has been nominated if there are grounds to do so, a club might therefore object to a panel member sitting for a second time against a club facing a charge of failing to control its players, or an individual participant may have good cause to object to a panel member. Such objections as there are have to be put in writing. Those who sit on the tribunals are remunerated by The FA, again with no consultation with the participant about who is selected or how much they shall be paid (even though the participant is often ordered to pay the costs).

23.12   More controversially, The FA has frequently included members of its own leading body, The FA Council, on its tribunals, including leading and active members of various other FA committees. It is easy to see how such a practice could be argued to be unlawful considering the general principle that a person shall not be judge in his own cause, and the application of that principle to regulatory proceedings by the Court of Appeal in *R (Kaur) v Institute of Legal Executives*.[14]

23.13   With the growing commercialisation of football, where the decisions of disciplinary tribunals have greater economic impact, old fashioned attitudes to discipline in football – assuming the governing body is always right – face increasing scrutiny, and lawyers acting in the field need to be familiar with the various routes by which flawed procedures and other instances of unfairness can be challenged. Bringing an effective challenge will often be difficult, however, not least considering the inequality of arms that often exists between the participant on the one hand and the regulator on the other, the deference many courts have tended to afford the regulator in the past and the costs and delay such challenges may cause.

C   LEAGUE AND INTERNATIONAL DISCIPLINARY PROCEDURES

23.14   The FA is the principal body responsible for dealing with misconduct in English football and most of this chapter is devoted to discussion of its disciplinary processes. In some cases, however, the Premier League, the Football League or lower leagues have jurisdiction over disciplinary matters. In cases where there is concurrent jurisdiction between The FA and the relevant league, rules exist to determine which body should conduct the disciplinary process.

23.15   In international football, subject to certain exceptions, disciplinary power lies with the body organising the match or competition. Both FIFA and UEFA also have a general disciplinary jurisdiction over serious misconduct (whether or not it occurs in an international competition) in cases where national football authorities have failed to act.

---

14   [2011] EWCA Civ 1168 (appearance of bias where member of ILEX Council sat on ILEX's disciplinary tribunal). In *Cellino v The FA*, FA Appeal Board (January 2017) a member of The FA Council sat on an FA Appeal Board that upheld a substantial sanction against former Leeds United Chairman, Massimo Cellino. Mr Cellino brought a challenge to the decision of the Appeal Board by way of FA Rule K on grounds, amongst others, that the Appeal Board was not independent due to the membership of an FA Council Member on it. The FA compromised the arbitral challenge and agreed to a fresh Appeal Board considering the appeal without a member of The FA Council on it, strongly indicating The FA recognised the vulnerability of its previous practice of allowing Council Members to sit on supposed independent Regulatory Commissions and Appeal Boards; see: '*The FA v Cellino – Behind the Headlines*', Nick De Marco, Blackstone Chambers Sports Law Bulletin, 6 November 2017: https://www.sportslawbulletin.org/fa-v-cellino-behind-headlines (accessed March 2018).

23.16 In some cases, a set of facts will give rise both to a disciplinary issue and to a dispute between two or more participants in the game. Depending on which body has jurisdiction in the case, it may be that an aggrieved participant has standing to seek a remedy as part of the disciplinary process.

(a) English football

23.17 The FA is the ultimate regulator of all Association Football in England,[15] whether that football is played by professionals in the Premier League or the various leagues in the Football League, or in lower leagues such as the National League or in many of the Sunday leagues played in parks across the country by amateur players. However, in addition, each of those various leagues have their own rules and (most often) disciplinary proceedings.

(b) Division of jurisdiction between The FA and the leagues

23.18 An incident of misconduct may give rise to breaches of league rules as well as FA rules. A pitch invasion which stops play, for example, may lead to a breach of league rules requiring clubs to fulfil fixture obligations[16] and a breach of FA rules requiring clubs to maintain order at matches.[17] The Rules of The FA require participants to adhere to the rules and regulations of affiliated leagues and make breaches of such rules a form of misconduct actionable within The FA's disciplinary processes.[18] The rules of the Premier League and the Football League also require member clubs to adhere to the Rules of The FA and the Laws of the Game, but do not expressly provide that breaches of the same will be actionable within the leagues' disciplinary processes.[19]

23.19 It follows that an incident of misconduct may be actionable both by The FA and by the relevant league, either because it discloses a breach of both relevant sets of rules or because it amounts to a breach of league rules, which is *per se* capable of giving rise to FA disciplinary proceedings. In such cases, whether The FA or the league will act depends on the nature of the misconduct and which league is involved.

23.20 Disciplinary measures for breaches of the Laws of the Game are dealt with by The FA rather than by the relevant league. For clubs in competitions at county level and below, breaches of the Laws of the Game will be dealt with on behalf of The FA by the relevant Affiliated Association which has authority over the player's club in relation to the match concerned. The FA therefore deals with breaches of the Laws of the Game by players for clubs in the Premier League, the Football League,

---

15 Similar functions are performed in other parts of the UK by the Scottish Football Association, the Football Association of Wales and the Irish Football Association. For football played in England at county level and below, The FA's functions are delegated to the relevant county and affiliated associations.
16 Premier League Rules, Rule L.15; Football League Regulations, Regulation 31.
17 Rules of the FA, Rule E21.
18 Rules of the FA, Rule E1.
19 Rule B.15 of the Premier League Rules states that membership of the league constitutes an agreement between the league and club and between each club 'to be bound by and comply with' the Rules of The FA. Premier League Rule W.1 gives the Board power to enquire into breaches of 'these Rules' (ie the Premier League Rules). The equivalent Football League Regulations are 3.1 and 80.2.

The National League, the Isthmian League, the Northern Premier League and the Southern League.[20]

23.21 Other misconduct which gives rise to a breach of the Premier League or Football League rules will generally be dealt with by The FA unless The FA agrees with the league in question that the league should act.[21] If the misconduct gives rise to a breach of the rules of any other league, the general rule is that the league should deal with it unless The FA (or the relevant Affiliated Association) decides that it will act.

23.22 Disciplinary processes under the auspices of the Premier League or the Football League are thus rarer than those conducted by The FA. Recently, disciplinary cases heard at league level have dealt with rules relating to 'tapping up',[22] third party ownership,[23] ownership and management of clubs,[24] coaching standards,[25] approaches to academy players,[26] failure to fulfil fixture obligations,[27] and the fielding of ineligible players.[28] Although the rules appear to be calculated to ensure that a given set of facts does not give rise to a multiplicity of disciplinary proceedings, there is no express rule that proceedings may not be held separately at FA and league level.[29] In practice the leagues and The FA ensure that only one set of proceedings in relation to the same facts are ever pursued.

(c) League disciplinary proceedings

23.23 Premier League disciplinary matters are dealt with in the first instance by the Board of the Premier League, which has the power to issue a reprimand, impose a fixed penalty or other sanction where the rules so provide, exercise its

---

20 Rules of the FA, Rules G1, G7 and G8.
21 Rules of the FA, Rule G3.
22 *FAPL v Ashley Cole, Chelsea FC and Jose Mourinho*, 1 June 2005.
23 *FAPL v West Ham United*, FAPL Disciplinary Commission, 27 April 2007; *The Football League v Watford Football Club and Mr Laurence Bassini*, Football Disciplinary Commission (Ch Alexander Milne QC), 18 March 2013; but such proceedings may also be brought by The FA where the breach is of one of its Rules regarding third party investment: see *The FA v Queens Park Rangers & Gianni Paladini*, FA Regulatory Commission (Ch Craig Moore), 20 May 2011.
24 *The Football League v Massimo Cellino*, Board of the Football League, 24 March 2014; Professional Conduct Committee (Tim Kerr QC sitting alone), 5 April 2014; Board of the Football League, 1 December 2014; Professional Conduct Committee (Tim Kerr QC sitting alone), 19 January 2015, and Board of the Football League, 19 October 2015; *The Football League v Reading*, Football Disciplinary Commission, 30 March 2015.
25 *The Football League v Accrington Stanley*, Football Disciplinary Commission, 20 January 2014.
26 *FAPL v Liverpool FC*, 3 April 2017.
27 *The Football League v Blackpool FC*, Football Disciplinary Commission, 2 September 2015.
28 *The Football League v Mansfield Town*, Football Disciplinary Commission, 23 February 2015; *The Football League v Cambridge United*, Football Disciplinary Commission, 23 February 2016; *The Football League v Bury*, Football Disciplinary Commission, 1 July 2016; *The Football League v Accrington Stanley*, Football Disciplinary Commission, 15 August 2016; *The Football League v Shrewsbury Town*, Football Disciplinary Commission, 22 December 2016.
29 See, for example, *The FA v Blackpool FC*, FA Regulatory Commission (Ch David Casement QC), 13 July 2015 and 29 July 2015; FA Appeal Board (Ch Richard Smith QC), 11 September 2015 where The FA imposed a fine and a suspended spectators' ban in relation to the same pitch invasion incident as gave rise to *The Football League v Blackpool FC*, Football Disciplinary Commission, 2 September 2015, where the Football League imposed a points deduction. See also *The FA v Jonathan Barnett*, FA Disciplinary Commission, 26 September 2006, in which an agent was fined and banned by The FA for his role in the Ashley Cole 'tapping up' affair, where the Premier League had acted against the club, player and manager (*FAPL v Ashley Cole, Chelsea FC and Jose Mourinho*, 1 June 2005). The Premier League had no jurisdiction against an agent (and still does not), hence there were separate proceedings against Mr Barnett before The FA.

summary jurisdiction, appoint a Commission to deal with the matter or refer the matter to The FA.[30] The Board's summary jurisdiction can be exercised in relation to any breach of the Premier League Rules, except where a fixed penalty is provided. Under the Board's summary jurisdiction, the sanction imposed cannot exceed a fine of £25,000.[31] A Commission has wide-ranging powers of sanction including the imposition of an unlimited fine, the suspension of players, managers and officials, a points deduction, recommending a match be replayed, recommending the expulsion of a club, ordering the payment of compensation, cancelling or refusing a player's registration, ordering a party to pay costs or making any other order.[32] An appeal lies to a Premier League Appeal Board from a decision of a Commission or a decision of the Board to impose a fixed penalty.[33]

23.24　Where disciplinary matters fall within the jurisdiction of the Football League, it may impose a fixed penalty (for certain strict liability offences), appoint a Disciplinary Commission to deal with the matter or refer the matter to The FA.[34] A Disciplinary Commission of the Football League has wide-ranging powers of sanction.[35] An appeal lies from a final decision of a Disciplinary Commission to the League Arbitration Panel.[36]

23.25　The Board of the National League has the power to apply and enforce the league's rules.[37] In the first instance, any 'protest, claim or complaint' relating to the rules will be heard and determined by the Board or a sub-committee thereof.[38] An appeal lies from decisions of the Board to The FA.[39]

(d)　International football

23.26　As set out in chapter 3, football's international structure has FIFA at its top and then various international confederations, such as UEFA in Europe, the Asian Football Confederation in Asia and the Confederation of African Football in Africa, sitting above the various national federations, such as The FA in England. Each of these international confederations, as well as FIFA, has its own disciplinary rules and procedures. Whilst the discussion below focuses on UEFA, other regional confederations have similar competences.

(e)　FIFA

23.27　FIFA's Disciplinary Code[40] deals with infringements of the Laws of the Game[41] and with a range of other matters relating to the conduct of players[42] and

---

30　Premier League Rules, Rule W.3.
31　Or, in the case of a breach of the Premier League Rules by a manager, a fine or penalty as provided in a tariff agreed with the League Managers Association; see Premier League Rules W.7 and W.8.
32　Premier League Rules W.55.
33　Premier League Rules W.62 and W.63.
34　Football League Regulation 81.1.
35　Football League Regulation 88.2.
36　Football League Regulation 90.1 and 90.2.
37　National League Rule 4.2.
38　National League Rule 16.1.
39　National League Rules 4.3, 16.4.
40　(2017) available online at: https://img.fifa.com/image/upload/koyeb3cvhxnwy9yz4aa6.pdf (accessed March 2018).
41　FIFA Disciplinary Code Articles 46 and 47.
42　FIFA Disciplinary Code Articles 48, 49 and 60.

teams,[43] incitement and provocation,[44] the fielding of ineligible players,[45] unplayed or abandoned matches,[46] offensive and discriminatory behaviour,[47] threats and coercion,[48] forgery,[49] corruption,[50] and doping.[51] The Disciplinary Code also applies to a breach of any other FIFA regulations that does not fall under the jurisdiction of any other body.[52] FIFA has wide-ranging powers of sanction in relation to breaches of the Disciplinary Code.[53] FIFA can impose sanctions that apply purely to international matches, but also has the power to impose bans that apply to all football (including domestic matches).[54]

23.28   The Disciplinary Code applies to member associations and their members (in particular clubs), officials, players, match officials, agents, spectators and anyone else authorised by FIFA.[55] In general, the Disciplinary Code is applicable and enforced by FIFA in relation to any match or competition organised by FIFA.[56] National associations and other sports organisations which organise matches remain responsible for the enforcement of discipline within their own jurisdictions.[57] It is worth noting that FIFA requires national associations to adopt certain mandatory provisions of the Disciplinary Code into their own rules and regulations.[58] Where a national association or other body imposes sanctions for a serious infringement (in particular doping, match-fixing, misconduct against match officials, forgery or violations of the rules on age limits), FIFA may extend that sanction to have worldwide effect.[59]

23.29   The general rule is subject to two exceptions: first, where a friendly match is played between teams from different associations, disciplinary sanctions are the responsibility of the association to which the player in question belongs. In a friendly match, FIFA will only intervene in serious cases of misconduct.[60] Secondly, the Disciplinary Code applies and FIFA may take action if a match official is harmed or if there is a breach of FIFA's statutory objectives (particularly with regard to forgery, corruption and doping) in circumstances where the national association or other organisation with jurisdiction has failed to prosecute the infringement or failed to do so in accordance with fundamental principles of law.[61]

23.30   Breaches of the FIFA Disciplinary Code are determined in the first instance by the Disciplinary Committee.[62] An appeal lies from the Disciplinary Committee

---

43   FIFA Disciplinary Code Article 52.
44   FIFA Disciplinary Code Articles 53 and 54.
45   FIFA Disciplinary Code Article 55.
46   FIFA Disciplinary Code Article 56.
47   FIFA Disciplinary Code Articles 57 and 58.
48   FIFA Disciplinary Code Articles 59 and 60.
49   FIFA Disciplinary Code Article 61.
50   FIFA Disciplinary Code Article 62.
51   FIFA Disciplinary Code Article 63.
52   FIFA Disciplinary Code Article 2.
53   FIFA Disciplinary Code Articles 10–12.
54   See, *FIFA v Rajkovic, The Serbian FA, Twente Enschede and Chelsea FC* (10 November 2008). A one-year ban from all football was reduced to a ban purely from international football after an appeal to the FIFA Appeals Committee.
55   FIFA Disciplinary Code Article 3.
56   FIFA Disciplinary Code Article 2.
57   FIFA Disciplinary Code Article 70.1.
58   FIFA Disciplinary Code Article 146.
59   FIFA Disciplinary Code Articles 136–141.
60   FIFA Disciplinary Code Article 71.1.
61   FIFA Disciplinary Code Article 2, Article 70.2.
62   FIFA Disciplinary Code Article 76.

to the Appeal Committee.[63] From the Appeal Committee, a further appeal lies to the Court of Arbitration for Sport (CAS)[64] except in disciplinary proceedings for violations of the Laws of the Game or which result in suspensions of up to four matches or three months (other than doping decisions).[65]

(f) UEFA

23.31 UEFA's Disciplinary Regulations ('UEFA 2017 DR')[66] require adherence to the Laws of the Game, UEFA's rules and regulations (except for Financial Fair Play and other club licensing criteria which are enforced separately) and 'the principles of ethical conduct, loyalty, integrity and sportsmanship'.[67] Specific offences exist in relation to match fixing,[68] doping,[69] racism, discrimination and propaganda,[70] misconduct in the course of matches[71] and order and security.[72] UEFA has wide-ranging powers of sanction in relation to breaches of its Disciplinary Regulations.[73]

23.32 The Disciplinary Regulations apply to member associations and their officials, clubs and their officials, match officials, players and persons exercising a function for UEFA.[74] They apply to matches and competitions organised by UEFA[75] and to serious violations of UEFA's statutory objectives which have not otherwise been prosecuted appropriately by a member association.[76] UEFA may extend sanctions imposed by FIFA or a UEFA member association to UEFA competitions.[77]

23.33 Breaches of the Disciplinary Regulations are determined in the first instance by the Control, Ethics and Disciplinary Body.[78] At first instance an oral hearing is rarely granted. An appeal lies from the Control, Ethics and Disciplinary Body to the Appeal Body where an oral hearing is readily available.[79] UEFA enforces strict time limits and they need to be considered carefully by practitioners at all stages. A further appeal lies to CAS, except in matters relating to the application of a purely sporting rule or a decision through which a natural person is suspended for up to two matches or one month.[80]

23.34 The UEFA Club Licensing and Financial Fair Play Regulations are administered jointly by UEFA, member associations and in some cases national leagues. Any club which qualifies to compete in UEFA club competitions must meet

---

63   FIFA Disciplinary Code Article 79.
64   FIFA Disciplinary Code Article 74.
65   FIFA Statutes, Article 58.3.
66   (2017) available online at: http://www.uefa.com/MultimediaFiles/Download/Regulations/uefaorg/ UEFACompDisCases/02/48/23/06/2482306_DOWNLOAD.pdf (accessed March 2018).
67   UEFA 2017 DR, Article 11.
68   UEFA 2017 DR, Article 12.
69   UEFA 2017 DR, Article 13.
70   UEFA 2017 DR, Article 14.
71   UEFA 2017 DR, Article 15.
72   UEFA 2017 DR, Article 16.
73   UEFA 2017 DR, Article 6.
74   UEFA 2017 DR, Article 3.1.
75   UEFA 2017 DR, Article 2.3.
76   UEFA 2017 DR, Article 2.4.
77   UEFA 2017 DR, Article 74.
78   UEFA 2017 DR, Articles 28 and 29.
79   UEFA 2017 DR, Article 30.
80   UEFA 2017 DR, Article 54; UEFA Statutes, Articles 62 and 63.

certain requirements with respect to club finances and administration, infrastructure and youth development.[81] Licensing of clubs is the responsibility of member associations but may be delegated to the body which organises the top national league.[82] Breaches of the Club Licensing and Financial Fair Play Regulations are dealt with by the UEFA Club Financial Control Body.[83]

(g)   Discipline and the determination of disputes between parties

23.35   Some disciplinary matters will also raise issues of fairness or require the determination of rights as between different participants in the game. It may be that one party has suffered loss as a result of another party's disciplinary infraction or it may be that one party wishes to press for sporting sanctions against another, for example where a points deduction could affect league ranking, promotion or relegation.[84]

23.36   The rules of The FA, Premier League and Football League all provide that the appropriate disciplinary body may order the payment of compensation instead of or in addition to any other sanction.[85] Under the Premier League Rules, where the Commission determines that no compensation is to be awarded, the party claiming compensation may appeal to an Appeal Board but is otherwise barred from bringing any further claim against the other club of any kind for compensation or damages arising out of the incident.[86] FIFA and UEFA do not have the power to award compensation as part of their disciplinary proceedings.[87]

23.37   The FA, Premier League and Football League arbitral bodies, before which participants can raise disputes, lack express powers to impose sporting sanctions.[88] The arbitral bodies may, however, make an order relating to sanctions when The FA or league (as the case may be) is a party to proceedings.[89] FIFA, when acting as arbitral body under the Regulations on the Status and Transfer of Players, has the power to impose sporting sanctions for breaches in addition to awarding compensation or other remedies.[90]

---

81   UEFA Club Licensing and Financial Fair Play Regulations Article 14.1.
82   UEFA Club Licensing and Financial Fair Play Regulations Article 5; Annex II.
83   UEFA 2017 DR, Article 2.1; Procedural rules governing the UEFA Club Financial Control Body.
84   In *Sheffield United FC v FAPL* [2007] ISLR-SLR 77, FAPL Arbitration Panel (Ch Sir Philip Otton) Sheffield United challenged the Premier League's decision not to deduct points from West Ham United FC as a result of its breaches of the rules regarding third party ownership and the player Carlos Tevez. The panel found Sheffield United had standing to bring the claim, but found against them on the substance. However, Sheffield United went on to win damages against West Ham United in an FA Rule K arbitration [2009] ISLR 25 (Ch Lord Griffiths). See also proceedings by way of protest brought by *Parma v CSKA Moscow* in May 2005 where Parma (unsuccessfully) sought to overturn the result of the UEFA Cup Semi-Final after a flare was thrown onto the pitch allegedly 'injuring' the Parma goalkeeper.
85   FA Disciplinary Procedures Regulations, Regulations 8.5–8.7; Premier League Rules, Rule W.55.5; Football League Regulations, Regulation 88.2.5.
86   For example, a claim under FA Rule K arbitration; Premier League Rules, Rule W.29. It remains to be seen whether such restriction on a club's rights is lawful but, in any event, it should be open for the club to bring a claim under FA Rule K arbitration against the Premier League itself if there has been some illegality/procedural unfairness (etc) in the disposal of its disciplinary and/or appeal procedures in relation to the matter.
87   FIFA Disciplinary Code, Articles 10–12; UEFA Disciplinary Regulations, Article 6.
88   Rules of The FA, Rule K7; Premier League Rules, Rule X.27; Football League Regulations, Regulation 96.1.
89   All the arbitral bodies have a power to order a *party* to do or refrain from doing anything.
90   FIFA Regulations on the Status and Transfer of Players, Article 22.

D   THE FA'S RULES ON MISCONDUCT

(a)   Misconduct by participants

23.38   The FA has the power to act against any participant[91] in respect of any misconduct by bringing a charge against the offending party. Misconduct is defined by Rule E1 to mean a breach of:

(a)   the Laws of the Game;[92]
(b)   the Rules and regulations of The FA and Rules E3–28 in particular;
(c)   the statutes and regulations of UEFA;
(d)   the statutes and regulations of FIFA;
(e)   the rules or regulations of an Affiliated Association[93] or Competition;[94] and
(f)   an order, requirement, direction or instruction of The FA.[95]

23.39   An attempt or agreement to breach will count as a breach in itself,[96] and behaviour or conduct may breach more than one of the rules, regulations, statutes or laws listed above. In the latter circumstances The FA may choose to bring more than one charge against the participant.[97]

23.40   The behaviour expected of participants is set out in Rule E3(1), which stipulates that a participant must act in the best interests of the game at all times and therefore must not act in any manner which is improper; bring the game into disrepute; engage in any violent conduct; engage in serious foul play; or use threatening, abusive indecent or insulting words or behaviour.

23.41   As discussed in section C of this chapter, those representing participants should note that on occasion there is an overlap between the jurisdiction of The FA and the jurisdictions of the Premier League and English Football League to bring disciplinary cases for breaches of the rules those Leagues have in place that deal with matters such as 'tapping up' and other aspects of misconduct (see *The Premier League v Ashley Cole, Chelsea FC and Jose Mourinho*).[98]

(b)   Duty to report misconduct

23.42   All participants are under a duty to report anything that might constitute misconduct to The FA (or an Affiliated Association) immediately. This is so even

---

91   Defined at Rule A2 to mean 'an Affiliated Association, Competition, Club, Club Official, Intermediary, Player, Official, Manager, Match Official, Match Official observer, Match Official coach, Match official mentor, Management Committee Member, member or employee of a Club and all such persons who are from time to time participating in any activity sanctioned either directly or indirectly by The Association'. For The FA to establish jurisdiction it must show not only that the person charged is a participant under its Rules but also that that person has agreed to be bound by those Rules – see, eg *The FA v Sam Bethell*, FA Regulatory Commission (Ch Nicholas Stewart QC), 8 September 2008.
92   Defined in the Articles of Association to mean 'the laws of the game as settled and in force from time to time by the International Football Association Board and FIFA'.
93   Defined at Rule A2 to mean 'an association which is either a County Association or an Other Football Association'.
94   Defined at Rule A2 to mean 'any competition (whether a league or knock-out competition or otherwise) sanctioned by The Association and/or an Affiliated Association'.
95   Rule E1.
96   Rule E9.
97   Rules E1 and E2.
98   1 June 2005.

if, for example, a non-participant approaches a participant in relation to betting on football contrary to the rules.[99] However, a participant must not make a report simply for vexatious or frivolous reasons.[100]

(c)   Particular instances of misconduct

(i)   Discrimination

23.43   Carrying out any act of victimisation[101] or of discrimination, whether that be by reason of ethnic origin, colour, race, nationality, religion or belief, gender, gender reassignment, sexual orientation, disability, age, pregnancy, maternity, marital status or civil partnership, shall constitute an instance of misconduct.[102] This offence has become known as the 'aggravated offence' and where such an offence is committed during a match a mandatory minimum five-match suspension shall be imposed. If an 'aggravated' offence is committed solely in writing (often charges that relate to such offences are the result of unwise postings on social media platforms) then the minimum five-game ban is not mandatory and sentence is at the discretion of the tribunal determining the case.

23.44   A number of players have been charged for breaches of FA rules as a result of postings on social media; the charges tend to be reserved for postings that would otherwise have amounted to an 'aggravated' offence on the basis of references to colour, gender, ethnicity or sexuality, but have also encompassed accusations made by a participant of cheating on the part of another participant. Increasingly in social media cases large numbers of previous 'similar' cases are brought to the attention of the sentencing panel by counsel for The FA and it is a wise precaution to check recent decisions.

23.45   High-profile cases included proceedings against Benoit Assou Ekotto of Tottenham Hotspur for 'referencing' the 'quenelle' gesture of Nicholas Anelka (which led to a ban against Mr Assou Ekotto as well as for Mr Anelka),[103] Andre Gray of Burnley for some rather ancient social media postings made before he was a high-profile player and which were complained about after Liverpool fans took exception to his scoring for Burnley against them at Anfield.[104] The FA takes any complaint of breaches of the rules seriously, wherever and whoever makes it, and complaints by fans about the social media outpourings of the stars of opposing teams are increasingly common.

(ii)   Bribes, gifts, rewards or other matters in relation to matches

23.46   Participants must not, whether directly or indirectly, seek to influence for an improper purpose the result, progress or conduct of a football match or competition,[105] nor offer, agree to give, give, solicit, agree to accept, or accept any bribe, gift,

99   Rule E14.
100 Rule E15.
101 As defined in the Equality Act 2010.
102 Rule E4.
103 FA Regulatory Commission (Ch Peter Griffiths QC), 22 September 2013.
104 FA Regulatory Commission, 22 September 2013; and see, http://www.independent.co.uk/sport/football/premier-league/andre-gray-has-been-suspended-for-four-matches-after-being-found-guilty-of-misconduct-a7326361.html (accessed March 2018).
105 Including Matches and Competitions, as defined at Rule A2.

reward, or consideration of any nature which is, or could appear to be, related in any way to that participant (or any other person) failing to perform to the best of their ability or seeking to influence the outcome or conduct of a match or competition.[106]

23.47   If any offer etc is made to a participant, or anything occurs which seems to be related to seeking to influence the outcome or conduct of a match or competition, he must immediately report it to The FA. Similarly, if a participant comes to know of such an offer being made to another participant, he is under a duty to relay the information to The FA.[107]

(iii) Tickets

23.48   A participant is not allowed to sell or otherwise dispose of any ticket for any football match unless he has been authorised to do so by the organisers of the match.[108]

(iv) Betting

23.49   Participants (which in this context do not include the match officials, referee coaches or referee assessors described in Rule E8) are not allowed to bet, either directly or indirectly, or instruct, permit, cause or enable any other person to bet on the result, progress, conduct or any other aspect of a football match or competition or any related matter (such as for example the transfer of players, employment of managers, team selection or disciplinary matters);[109] see further Chapter 25. When defending in such cases it is important to ensure that the rules that were in force at the time of the bets are carefully considered, investigations into these offences often involve offences of some antiquity (or which cover more than one season) and the rules in this area have changed significantly over the years. It is vital to ensure those representing participants have in mind the differing rules and sanctions that may apply to offences committed in different seasons. The FA has published 'sentencing guidelines' for breaches of the betting rules, and whilst those guidelines are not slavishly followed (there is no principle of precedent in sentencing in FA disciplinary cases albeit Regulatory Commissions are increasingly referred to 'similar' cases by advocates for both The FA and the defence) they should be considered carefully when mitigating in the event that a charge results in a guilty plea or a finding of guilt after contested proceedings.

(v) Doping

23.50   All participants must comply with anti-doping regulations set by The FA and in force from time to time;[110] see further Chapter 24.

(d) Aggravating factors

23.51   A reference to any of the following, if made during the commission of a breach of the standards of behaviour required of participants as set out in

---

106 Rule E5(a) and (b).
107 Rule E6.
108 Rule E7.
109 Rule E8(1)(a).
110 Rule E25.

Rule E3(1), will be treated as an aggravating factor: ethnic origin, colour, race, nationality, religion or belief, gender, gender reassignment, sexual orientation and disability.[111]

(e)   Misconduct by others

23.52   Any individual attending or taking part in a match must observe the Rules, which must also be followed and enforced by each affiliated association, competition or club.[112] These bodies are under a duty to ensure that everyone involved in any way in a match, be that as directors, players, officials, employees, spectators etc, behaves in an orderly fashion. No disorderly behaviour will be tolerated; nor is any person allowed to encroach onto, or throw anything onto, the pitch.[113] Anyone who fails to respect these rules may be removed from the ground with such force as is necessary.[114] The FA has separate rules regulating the conduct of officials in the technical area.

23.53   Clubs must observe specific practical rules as part of their general duty, for example they must provide a private way from the playing area to the dressing room wherever this is practicable,[115] and they must post bills in their grounds threatening expulsion as the punishment for anyone engaging in insulting or improper conduct towards a match official.[116]

23.54   As far as affiliated associations, competitions or clubs are concerned, misconduct will consist of any failure to carry out its responsibilities as set out above. However, if the misconduct has been committed by spectators, a club can defend itself by showing that all events, incidents or occurrences were the result of circumstances over which it had no control or for reasons of crowd safety, or if it used all due diligence to ensure its responsibility was met. However, this defence is not available where the spectator or supporter of the club included a reference, whether express or implied, to ethnic origin, colour, race, nationality, religion or belief, gender, gender reassignment, sexual orientation or disability.[117] The amended Rule 21 presents clubs with the difficult – if not impossible – position that they face sanctions (on a vicarious liability basis) for any racist conduct by so called 'fans' on a strict liability basis, however diligent and conscientious they are in relation to education and efforts to control fans' behaviour.

(f)   Compliance

23.55   Participants must comply with any decision made under The FA's Rules and regulations,[118] and clubs must do all that is necessary to ensure that any player associated with it complies with any order or penalty imposed thereunder.[119]

---

111 Rule E3(2).
112 Rule E19.
113 Rule E20.
114 Rule E22.
115 Rule E23.
116 Rule E24.
117 Rule E21.
118 Rule E10.
119 Rule E12.

23.56 Specific FA charges can be brought for breaches of the FA Regulations on Working with Intermediaries, and indeed the Third Party Interest in Players Regulations (see Chapters 11 and 12) and although those rules are very different to the general misconduct regulations the procedures used are the same.

E THE FA'S DISCIPLINARY PROCEDURES

(a) Relevant governing procedures

23.57 In the event that a participant breaches the Laws of the Game, the breach will be dealt with by either The FA or an affiliated association in accordance with the relevant Memorandum of Disciplinary Procedures,[120] which can be found in The FA Handbook. It is important to note that the rules in relation to 'Fast Track' cases – which normally involve incidents on the field of play 'not seen' by officials during the game – provide much tighter deadlines for responses (and do not give participants the right to attend in person or to be represented at a hearing, although written submissions can be placed before The Commission deciding 'Fast Track' cases) than the times given in other cases.

23.58 If a participant breaches any of the following, he will be dealt with by The FA on the authority of the Council[121] and under the Regulations for Football Association Disciplinary Action:[122] the Rules and regulations of The FA (and Rules E3–28 in particular); the statutes and regulations of UEFA; the statutes and regulations of FIFA; the rules or regulations of an Affiliated Association or Competition; or an order, requirement, direction or instruction of The FA. If the facts would also establish a breach of the rules and regulations of either the Premier League or the Football League and the relevant league agrees with The FA that it would be appropriate for it to deal with it, the Premier League or Football League shall have jurisdiction,[123] and if the facts would also establish a breach of the rules and regulations of a Competition, and as long as The FA or Affiliated Association has not acted first, the Competition may deal with it.[124] As stated above, although both The FA and a League may each be entitled to claim jurisdiction the effect of Rule G3 is that The FA and the relevant League always agree amongst themselves as to who is the appropriate regulator to deal with a disciplinary matter that might be caught under the rules of either organisation.

(b) Powers of inquiry

23.59 The FA, on the authority of Council,[125] has the power to monitor compliance with all rules, regulations etc, the breach of which would constitute misconduct, and may inquire into any related incident, fact or matters in such manner as it sees fit.[126] In conducting such an inquiry, The FA may require any participant or other person to attend and answer questions or provide information, to take part in a recorded interview, or to produce documents or any other material either in his possession or

---

120 Rules G7 and G8.
121 Rule G2.
122 Rule G9.
123 Rule G3.
124 Rule G4.
125 Rule F6.
126 Rule F1.

obtainable by him,[127] and failure on the part of a participant to comply with any such requirement may constitute misconduct and result in a charge.[128]

23.60   It is the responsibility of each affiliated association, competition or club to ensure the compliance of its officials, directors, players, representatives or servants with any such requests.[129] The chairman of the Football Regulatory Authority may, for other inquiries, appoint a commission of inquiry, which can exercise the same powers of requesting information etc as above, which can adopt such procedures as it considers appropriate and which will report back to the chairman, who may in turn publish such report.[130]

23.61   The terms upon which The FA may share information held by it about any participant are dealt with in Rule F7.

(c)   Disciplinary powers

23.62   The power to impose a penalty or other order for misconduct, or to impose an interim or provisional suspension where misconduct has been alleged, shall be exercised on the authority of Council as it sees fit.[131]

(d)   Suspension

(i)   Suspended persons

23.63   If a participant has been suspended from carrying out any particular activity, it will be a breach of the Rules if another participant participates in that activity with him,[132] and equally it will be a breach if an affiliated association, competition or club appoints a person to a position from which that person has been suspended.[133]

(ii)   Suspension for serious criminal offences

23.64   Where a participant has been convicted of a criminal offence, Council[134] can, if it considers there to be a risk of physical harm to another participant as a result of the convicted person's continuing participation in football activity, suspend him from all or any specific participation in the game for whatever period and on whatever conditions it chooses to impose.[135]

(iii)   Interim suspension

23.65   Interim suspension orders can be imposed before or after charge, but in either case the suspension may not last beyond the date upon which either the related

---

127 Rules F2 and F5.
128 Rule F3.
129 Rule F4.
130 Rules F8–F11.
131 Rule G5.
132 Rule E11.
133 Rule E13.
134 Defined in the Articles of Association to mean 'the Council of The Association for the time being constituted in accordance with these Articles, and Member of (the) Council shall be any person for the time being appointed to and serving on (the) Council in accordance with Article 119'.
135 Rule E26.

investigation ends, or the proceedings arising from the related charge terminate.[136] The individual subject to the suspension (and/or the club with which he is associated) must be notified of it as soon as reasonably practicable.[137]

(iv) Interim suspension – before charge

23.66 A Regulatory Commission[138] can suspend a club official, club employee or player associated with a club[139] before charge if the conditions set out in Rule E16(a) are met and in accordance with the procedure set out in Rule E16(b) to (d).

23.67 The Regulatory Commission must be satisfied that the serious nature and/ or the factual circumstances of the allegation mean that the participant's continued participation in football presents a real risk that either the integrity of football would be affected, and/or the public's confidence in the integrity of football would be affected. The Commission must undertake a balancing exercise and may only suspend the participant if the risk posed is such that it outweighs the participant's interest in continued participation in football.[140]

23.68 The suspension can be for such a period and on such conditions as it sees fit.[141]

(v) Interim suspension – after charge

23.69 Any club official, club employee or player[142] who has been charged with any alleged act of misconduct or any criminal offence may be suspended by The FA[143] from all or any football activity for such period and on such terms as it sees fit provided the conditions set out in Rule E16(f) are met.

(vi) Interim suspension – periodic review

23.70 The subject of an interim suspension order can have it reviewed by a Regulatory Commission. The first review will take place after a period of not more than 21 days after the imposition of the order, that period being determined by the Regulatory Commission in the case of pre-charge suspension, or by the Chief Regulatory Officer in the case of post-charge suspension. Thereafter the subject can have the order reviewed by a Regulatory Commission after a period to be determined by the Regulatory Commission which conducts each review, but again that period cannot be more than 21 days after the previous review.[144] The manner in which the review is conducted, or in which the application by the subject of the order for the review to take place is considered, will be dictated either by any regulations brought into force by The FA or by the Regulatory Commission itself, with the guiding

136 Rule E17.
137 Rule E18.
138 Defined at Rule A2 to mean 'any regulatory commission as established from time to time whose purpose is to hear Participants' cases'.
139 Provided they are associated with a club in The FA Premier League, the Football League, the National League, Isthmian League, Northern Premier League or Southern League.
140 Rule E16(e).
141 Rule E16(a).
142 Associated with a Club in The FA Premier League, the Football League or the National League.
143 Acting by the Chief Regulatory Officer or his nominee.
144 Rule E16(g).

principle being that all procedures must ensure that the subject has a fair opportunity to make representations.[145]

(e) Appeals

23.71 A person or body subject of a decision[146] may appeal to an Appeal Board[147] only where either The FA's Rules and regulations allow for such a right of appeal, or The FA agrees to an appeal taking place.[148] If an affiliated association has already heard an appeal against a decision of a Competition, then no appeal shall lie to an Appeal Board; nor shall it lie in respect of decisions arising out of competitions of affiliated associations where the rules and regulations provide that such decisions are final.[149]

F THE REGULATIONS FOR FA DISCIPLINARY ACTION

(a) Application

23.72 As stated above, these Regulations apply to any alleged breach of the rules and regulations of The FA and Rules E3–28 in particular; the statutes and regulations of UEFA; the statutes and regulations of FIFA; the rules or regulations of an affiliated association or competition; and an order, requirement, direction or instruction of The FA.[150]

23.73 However, there are specific categories of case (incidents on the field of play which fall within Law 12, which were not seen by match officials, but caught on video; incidents of misconduct on or around the field of play (including the tunnel area), incidents outside the jurisdiction of match officials but reported to The FA and media comments) where special procedures apply.

(b) Collection of evidence

23.74 It is the duty of all participants to take all reasonable measures to assist The FA in collecting evidence, and they must furnish the latter with such evidence as is requested, unless this would contravene an obligation arising out of legal professional privilege.[151] This evidence may take the form of video or DVD evidence where the offence is on-field, in which case The FA may request that a club deliver the footage as soon as reasonably practicable after the request and no later than by 12 noon on the next working day after the request. Any failure to comply can itself constitute misconduct.[152]

---

145 Rule E16(h).
146 Rule H3.
147 Pursuant to Rule H4, the appeal shall be dealt with under the relevant regulations of The FA from time to time in force. 'Appeal Board' is defined in Rule A2 to mean 'any appeal board as established from time to time whose purpose is to hear appeals made by Participants pursuant to its terms of reference from time to time'.
148 Rule H1, a little used rule but one invoked by Tottenham Hotspur FC after Moussa Dembele was suspended for five matches on the basis the standard penalty was 'clearly insufficient' after an incident during the season 2015/16.
149 Rule H2.
150 Rule E1(b) to E1(f) and Rule G9.
151 Regulation 2.1.
152 Regulation 2.2.

(c) The charging procedure

23.75   Once the Chief Regulatory Officer has decided that a charge for misconduct ought to be brought,[153] The FA must serve on the participant concerned a written charge which must state in brief the nature of the alleged misconduct, identify the provision alleged to have been breached, and include copies of documents or other material referred to in the charge. A request for a summary of the current terms and conditions of employment of a participant may also be served.[154]

23.76   More than one instance of misconduct may be included in a single charge, provided that the charge states separately the nature of each alleged instance of misconduct and the provision supposedly breached; thus the effect will be that there is a single charge that is in fact one of several charges.[155]

23.77   The chairman of the Judicial Panel, on receipt of a copy of the charge, will appoint a Regulatory Commission. The Secretary of the Regulatory Commission will then forward to both parties a copy of the Standard Directions and/or the date of the proposed Directions Hearing,[156] the latter usually being reserved for complex and serious matters.[157]

(d) Procedure following charge

23.78   Having been served with the charge, the Rules provide that the participant charged must respond within seven days by serving a written reply which:

(a) admits or denies the misconduct detailed in the charge;
(b) states whether the participant charged would prefer the matter to be dealt with by way of written submissions (in which case the reply must include full details of any defence), or at a hearing (in which case the reply must include full details of any defence and include a fee of £100);
(c) includes a summary of the current terms and conditions of employment of a participant who is a player or manager or where the charge requests such information;[158]
(d) includes a clear explanation of the nature and extent of the participant's admission or denial of the charge(s) or any part thereof;
(e) lists witnesses upon whom the participant intends to rely together with witness statements from each witness;
(f) appends copies of any documentation, evidence, mitigation or other relevant material on which the participant intends to rely.[159]

23.79   A failure by the participant charged to comply with any of the above requirements will result in the Regulatory Commission determining the charge in such a manner and upon such evidence as it considers appropriate.[160] However, in many cases it is impossible or unfair for the participant to be expected to provide their full reply within such a short timescale, especially in complex cases where The FA may have had weeks or months to prepare its case. In such cases extensions

153 Regulation 3.1.
154 Regulation 3.2.
155 Regulation 3.4.
156 Regulation 3.3.
157 Regulation 4.1.
158 Regulation 4.4.
159 Regulation 4.5.
160 Regulation 4.6.

of time are routinely requested and granted, and those representing participants should make such requests where necessary.

(e)   Directions

23.80   Examples of directions that the Regulatory Commission may make in order to ensure the proper conduct of the proceedings include:[161]

(a)   *Disclosure*: The FA, participants, or any third party participant may be directed to disclose any documents in their possession and which are considered relevant by the Regulatory Commission.

(b)   *Time limits*: these many be extended or abridged by direction of the Regulatory Commission.

(c)   *Procedural steps*: any procedural steps set out in the Regulations can be waived if the Regulatory Commission so directs.

(d)   *Written submissions*: parties may be required to make written submissions or to submit skeleton arguments prior to the hearing.

(e)   *Preliminary issues*: the Regulatory Commission may decide that certain issues ought to be dealt with as preliminary issues or at a preliminary hearing.[162]

(f)   *Hearing*: directions may establish the date, time and place of the hearing or determine who shall attend.

(g)   *Transcript*: a direction may order that a transcript be made of proceedings.

23.81   If it deems it necessary, the Regulatory Commission may order a Directions Hearing to take place either in person, via telephone conference or video link, or by written submissions, unless directions agreed prior to the date set render one unnecessary.[163] If such a hearing does take place, a written note of any resulting decisions will be circulated by the Regulatory Commission within three days.[164]

(f)   Preliminary applications and hearings

23.82   A party to disciplinary proceedings can apply, as soon as practicable after the service of the charge and in any event within 10 working days prior to the hearing, for issues to be dealt with on a preliminary basis. Such an application may result in the Regulatory Commission deciding to dismiss the preliminary application; order that the issues raised therein be dealt with as part of the main proceedings rather than on a preliminary basis; allow or dismiss the preliminary action in full or in part; or make such further order as it considers appropriate. Any such decision will be final and binding with no further right of challenge.[165]

(g)   Determination on written submissions

23.83   A matter can be dealt with solely on written submissions if:

(a)   the participant charged denies the charge in his reply and therein expresses his wish for this option, in which case the Regulatory Commission will

---

161   Regulation 4.9.
162   For example in *The FA v Sam Bethell*, FA Regulatory Commission (Ch Nicholas Stewart QC), 8 September 2008, the Chairman made a ruling that Mr Bethell, the Chelsea groundsman, had not agreed to be bound by The FA Rules so that there was no jurisdiction to proceed with a disciplinary charge against him.
163   Regulation 4.10.
164   Regulation 4.11.
165   Regulation 4.2(a).

determine the charge in the absence of any parties and make whatever order it sees fit; or
(b) the participant charged admits the misconduct in his reply and wishes his mitigation to be considered on paper rather than following oral submissions.[166]

(h) Determination at a hearing

(i) Procedures prior to the hearing

23.84 A party who is due to appear at a hearing before a Regulatory Commission may, within seven days of the charge being issued, apply to the Judicial Panel Chairman (having given notice to all other parties) for an order that the chairman of that Regulatory Commission shall be a Specialist Panel Member who is a solicitor or barrister of seven or more years' standing. Approval must not be unreasonably withheld or delayed. The party making the application will be responsible for any additional costs incurred as a result of having such a Specialist Panel Member chairing the Regulatory Commission.[167]

23.85 The FA may, upon receipt of the reply, provide further evidence and material to the participant and the Regulatory Commission, in which case the participant then has until seven days before the hearing to provide copies of all documents upon which he intends to rely (although this should be provided at the earliest opportunity). Failure to adhere to the time limit may, at the discretion of the Regulatory Commission, result in the relevant document being disallowed from the hearing.[168]

(ii) The hearing

(A) Attendance

23.86 The parties to a hearing will be The FA and the participant charged,[169] both of whom must be in attendance. If the participant charged is an individual he must attend in person; if not, it must attend through an officer or club official (unless the Regulatory Commission orders otherwise).[170] If a participant charged does not attend and the Regulatory Commission is satisfied that there are no reasonable grounds for his absence, it may decide to proceed regardless.[171]

23.87 The FA, through the Chief Regulatory Officer, will nominate an individual to present the charge, call evidence and make submissions before the Regulatory Commission.[172] Frequently in-house legal staff at The FA 'prosecute' the cases, but in complex cases independent counsel are often instructed.

23.88 A participant may be required to attend a hearing, either at the application of one of the parties or of the Regulatory Commission's own motion; the participant may be asked to provide information, answer questions, or produce documents before or during the hearing.[173]

166 Regulation 5.
167 Regulation 4.8.
168 Regulation 4.7.
169 Regulation 6.2.
170 Regulation 6.3.
171 Regulation 6.11.
172 Regulation 6.4.
173 Regulation 6.6.

23.89 Any participant charged appearing before the Regulatory Commission may choose to be represented, legally or otherwise, provided notice and the representative's name is given at the time of the reply.[174]

(B) Adjournments

23.90 The Regulatory Commission can exercise its power to adjourn a hearing on whatever terms (be they as to period or costs etc) as it considers appropriate.[175]

(C) Evidence

23.91 Where the subject matter of a complaint before the Regulatory Commission has been the subject of previous civil (including disciplinary or regulatory) or criminal proceedings, the result and its underpinning facts will be presumed to be correct and true unless this is shown to be otherwise by clear and convincing evidence.[176]

(D) Defence witnesses

23.92 A participant charged who wishes to give evidence must do so before any other defence witness of fact, none of whom may be present until they are called to give evidence themselves.[177]

(E) Failure to comply

23.93 Any party that fails to comply with an order, requirement, direction or instruction of the Regulatory Commission may be dealt with in any way considered appropriate by the Regulatory Commission, whether that be by bringing misconduct proceedings into play or by awarding costs against the offending party.[178]

(F) Burden of proof

23.94 The burden of proof in FA proceedings is normally the civil standard of 'the balance of probability'.[179]

23.95 The Rules thereafter usually refer to 'proven or not proven' (eg pp 338, 343 of the FA Handbook) with no qualification as to the standard, save that in cases where The FA allege that 'the standard punishment is clearly insufficient' the standard is the criminal standard of 'sure'.[180]

23.96 In the season 2017/18 the new offence of 'successful deception of a match official' was introduced.[181] Although under this schedule the rule refers to whether the charge is 'proven or not proven' without qualification of the standard, both the

---

174 Regulation 6.7.
175 Regulation 6.5.
176 Regulation 6.8.
177 Regulation 6.9.
178 Regulation 6.11.
179 Rule 1.5 General Provisions relating to Inquiries, Commissions of Inquiry, Regulatory Commissions of the Association, Other Disciplinary Commissions, Appeal Boards and Safeguarding Review Panel Hearings – the 'general provisions': FA Handbook 2017–2018 season, p 322.
180 General Provisions Part 7(1)iii (Handbook 2017/18, p 365).
181 Handbook 2017/18, p 349.

rule and the guidance note published and sent to clubs before the season began refers to a 'clear' act of simulation. Under this procedure three persons (an ex-referee, an ex-player and an ex-manager) are tasked with reviewing the video and deciding whether or not they 'agree' that there is clear evidence of the successful deception of an official. If the three are unanimous a charge is issued, which is thereafter dealt with by way of written submissions. One assumes that the standard for 'clear' is also the balance of probabilities.[182]

(i) Decisions

23.97   The Regulatory Commission will convene in private and decide by at least a majority whether or not the charge of misconduct has been proved and, if so, the factual basis on which it has been proved.[183] If it decides that the charge has been proved, this decision will be communicated to the participant charged as soon as reasonably practicable (and if possible at the end of any hearing).[184] The parties will then be invited to raise matters relevant to the penalty, such as mitigation or the participant's disciplinary record.[185]

23.98   The Regulatory Commission will then retire to determine an appropriate sanction. The decision must be announced as soon as reasonably practicable and, if it is reached at a hearing at which the participant is present, immediately. However the Regulatory Commission always retains discretion as to how and when it makes its announcement.[186]

(j) Penalties

23.99   The Regulatory Commission may impose any one or more of the following penalties;[187]

(a) a reprimand;
(b) a warning;
(c) a fine;
(d) suspension from all or any specified football activity for a stated period or permanently;
(e) the closure of a ground, permanently or for a stated period;
(f) expulsion from a competition;
(g) expulsion from membership of The FA or an affiliated association;
(h) any order which may be made under the rules and regulations of a competition in which the offender participates or with which it is associated (including the deduction of points and removal from a competition at any stage of any playing season);
(i) drug rehabilitation and counselling[188] (where a participant has breached any doping control regulations);
(j) compensation orders for such amount as is considered appropriate: the claimant must have made a written claim setting out the amount claimed with detailed

---

182 See Handbook 2017/18, pp 349–351.
183 Regulation 7.1 and 7.2. Each member of the Regulatory Commission will have one vote. In the event of a deadlock, the chairman of the Regulatory Commission will have a second and casting vote.
184 Regulation 7.3.
185 Regulations 7.4 and 7.5.
186 Regulation 7.6.
187 Regulation 8.1.
188 Regulation 8.4.

reasons; the Regulatory Commission must be satisfied that the claimant has suffered loss as a result of the misconduct; and the participant must have had an opportunity of seeing the claim in advance and of making submissions to the Regulatory Commission;[189] or

(k) any further or other penalty deemed appropriate.

23.100 A penalty may be suspended (subject to Regulation 8.3(d) which states that no more than three-quarters of a suspension may be suspended, rendering applications for a suspended playing ban wholly redundant unless the player has been banned for at least four games) for a specified period on whatever conditions the Regulatory Commission deems appropriate. The Regulatory Commission must consider suspending a portion of the penalty where the participant in question has breached Rules E5, E8 or E14 and has provided assistance or information which has resulted in the discovery of a criminal offence or the breach of disciplinary rules by another relating to betting or integrity in football or sport generally.[190]

(k) Written decision

23.101 The announcement of the decision and penalty must be followed, as soon as reasonably practicable, by a written statement of the Regulatory Commission's decision, which will constitute the conclusive record of thereof. It must include:

(a) the charge and whether it was admitted or denied;
(b) the decision as to whether the misconduct was proved or not;
(c) any penalty or order imposed.[191]

23.102 The Regulatory Commission may also have to state in writing its findings of fact, the reasons behind it having found the charge proved, and the reasons for any penalty or order, if it is asked to do so by the Chief Regulatory Officer or the participant within seven days of the written statement of its decision.[192]

(l) Costs

23.103 Costs incurred in bringing or responding to a charge must be borne by the party incurring the costs, whereas costs incurred in relation to the convening of the Regulatory Commission will be paid according to any order made by the Commission. All financial orders, including costs orders, must have been paid in full before any notice of appeal will be deemed to have been lodged, unless they have been expressly set aside by the chairman pending appeal. An appeal against the quantum of costs will be heard by a single person appointed by the Sports Dispute Resolution Panel.[193]

(m) Compliance with penalties and orders

23.104 Failure to comply with a penalty or order made by the Regulatory Commission (which shall come into effect immediately at the date of the announcement of the

---

189 Regulations 8.5–8.7.
190 Regulation 8.3.
191 Regulation 9.1–9.2.
192 Regulation 9.3; see http://www.thefa.com/football-rules-governance/discipline/written-reasons (accessed March 2018).
193 Regulation 8.8.

decision, unless otherwise stated)[194] may result in the immediate suspension of the participant from all or any football activity.[195]

23.105 The participant may apply to a Regulatory Commission to suspend the effectiveness of any penalty or order pending the outcome of an appeal. The obligation to comply may be stayed by a Regulatory Commission in the following circumstances:[196]

(a) where the participant has made a written application;
(b) where the participant has made an appeal; and
(c) where the Regulatory Commission allows a stay in its absolute discretion.

(n) Time limits in exceptional circumstances

23.106 Any time limits set out in any of the procedures above to do with the processing of a charge may be amended, suspended, abridged or dispensed with by the Chief Judicial Officer (or his nominee) on the application of the Chief Regulatory Officer or a participant, if it would be impractical or unfair for the charge to be processed within the normal time limits,[197] such as where:

(a) there is a pending police investigation;
(b) the seriousness or complexity of the matter necessitates a longer period of investigation; or
(c) substantial evidence needs to be obtained from non-participants.[198]

G APPEALS

23.107 Regulation 9.4 gives participants and The FA the right to appeal a decision of a Regulatory Commission to an Appeal Board. These are conducted pursuant to the Regulations for Football Association Appeals.

(a) Commencement of appeal

23.108 An appeal is commenced when a Notice of Appeal is lodged with The FA[199] within 14 days of the notification of the decision subject to the appeal.[200] The Notice of Appeal must:[201]

(a) identify the decision being appealed;
(b) set out the ground(s) of appeal and the reasons why it would be substantially unfair not to alter the original decision;

---

194 Regulation 8.9.
195 Regulation 8.10.
196 Regulation 8.11.
197 Regulation 4.17.
198 Regulation 4.18.
199 Appeal Regulation 1.1.
200 Appeal Regulation 1.2. Pursuant to Appeal Regulation 1.3, in the case of an appeal from a decision of a Regulatory Commission, notification of the intention to appeal must be made in writing to The FA within seven days of notification of the decision, and the date of notification of the decision shall be the date of the written decision or, if applicable, the date of the written reasons for the decision. In relation to any other decision, the relevant date shall be the date on which it was first announced.
201 Appeal Regulation 1.4.

(c)   set out a statement of the facts;

(d)   be accompanied by the requisite fee;[202]

(e)   where appropriate, apply for leave to present new evidence. The nature of the new evidence, its relevance and the reason why it was not presented at the original hearing must be set out.[203]

23.109   Once commenced, an appeal cannot be withdrawn unless the Appeal Board gives its leave, and this may be subject to any order for costs deemed appropriate by the Board.[204]

(b)   The response

23.110   The respondent must serve a written reply on the appellant and Appeal Board within 21 days of the Notice of Appeal being lodged.[205] If the respondent is applying for leave to present new evidence, the nature of the new evidence, its relevance and the reason why it was not presented at the original hearing must be set out.[206]

(c)   Grounds of appeal

23.111   There are four grounds of appeal available to participants. These are that the decision-making body:[207]

(1)   failed to give the participant a fair hearing;

(2)   misinterpreted or failed to comply with the rules or regulations relevant to its decision;

(3)   came to a decision to which no reasonable such body could have come;

(4)   imposed a penalty, award, order or sanction that was excessive.

23.112   There are three grounds of appeal available to The FA. These are that the decision-making body:[208]

(1)   misinterpreted or failed to comply with the rules or regulations relevant to its decision;

(2)   came to a decision to which no reasonable such body could have come;

(3)   imposed a penalty, award, order or sanction that was so unduly lenient as to be unreasonable.

23.113   Where an appeal is brought against a decision of a Regulatory Commission by FIFA, UKAD or WADA pursuant to the Doping Regulations, any and all of the appeal grounds set out in the above two paragraphs may be relied upon.[209]

23.114   Regulation 1.7 sets out the circumstances in which a league may apply for a bond.

---

202   If the appellant is the FA, no fee will be required. The amount payable will be prescribed in the relevant Rules of the FA or Regulations. If the appeal is lodged by email or fax, the deposit must be received no later than the third day following the day upon which the fax or email was dispatched.
203   Appeal Regulation 2.6.
204   Appeal Regulation 1.8.
205   Appeal Regulation 2.4.
206   Appeal Regulation 2.6.
207   Appeal Regulation 1.6.
208   Appeal Regulation 1.5.
209   Appeal Regulation 1.6.

(d) Appeal proceedings

23.115 The appeal will be conducted in such manner, time and place as the Appeal Board chooses,[210] and will proceed by way of a review of documents only, with no oral evidence being adduced (except where leave is given for new evidence to be adduced). However, both parties will be entitled to make oral submissions. An Appeal Board is not bound by any enactment or rule of law as to the admissibility of evidence before a court of law.[211]

(i) Directions

23.116 The chairman of an Appeal Board may make directions, either of his own motion or upon the application of a party, as to:[212]

(a) time limits – extending or abridging them;
(b) adjournments – for such period and on such terms as are considered appropriate;[213]
(c) procedural steps – amending or dispensing with them;
(d) preliminary hearing – ordering that parties attend a preliminary hearing;
(e) written submissions – ordering that a party provide these;
(f) transcript – instructing that one be made of proceedings;
(g) any other matter which the chairman deems necessary for the proper conduct of the proceedings.

(ii) Appeal bundle

23.117 It is the appellant's responsibility to prepare a bundle comprising the following documents, which must be provided to the Appeal Board and the respondent at least seven days before the hearing:[214]

(a) the charge;
(b) the reply;
(c) any documents or evidence referred to at the original hearing which are relevant to the appeal;
(d) any transcript of the original hearing;
(e) notification of the decision appealed against;
(f) the notification of and any reasons given for the decision appealed against;
(g) any new evidence;
(h) the Notice of Appeal;
(i) the response.

23.118 Where the body appealed against has not given reasons for its decision, either:

(a) the appellant will request written reasons from that body which shall be provided to the Appeal Board; or
(b) the Appeal Board will require that a member of the body that made the decision attends the hearing, in which case the Appeal Board (and only the Appeal Board) may ask questions to satisfy itself as to the reasons for the decision.

---

210 Appeal Regulation 2.5. Reasonable notice must be given by the Appeal Board of the date, time and venue of the appeal.
211 Appeal Regulation 2.5.
212 Appeal Regulation 2.7.
213 Appeal Regulation 2.8.
214 Appeal Regulation 2.9.

Representations may be made by the parties to the Appeal Board who may then put questions to the member of the body that made the decision, but no direct cross-examination of that person is allowed by the parties themselves.[215]

(iii) The hearing

23.119 The Appeal Board will proceed as follows, although it has discretion to amend the standard procedure in the event that this is thought appropriate:[216]

(a) if there is to be new evidence adduced at the appeal, the party wishing to adduce it will make the application orally to the Appeal Board and the other party will be given an opportunity to respond; the Appeal Board will then decide whether or not to receive it;

(b) the appellant will address the Appeal Board, summarising its case;

(c) the appellant will present any new evidence, with the respondent and Appeal Board being able to put questions to any witness giving such evidence;

(d) the respondent will address the Appeal Board, summarising its case;

(e) the respondent will present any new evidence, with the appellant and Appeal Board being able to put questions to any witness giving such evidence;

(f) the respondent can then make closing submissions;

(g) and lastly the appellant will make closing submissions.

(iv) Attendance

23.120 The FA will be represented by an individual nominated to act on its behalf.[217] If any party fails to attend, the Appeal Board will proceed with the appeal hearing unless it is satisfied that there are reasonable grounds for the absence.[218]

(e) Decisions

23.121 Decisions, which will be made by a majority,[219] will be announced as soon as practicable and will come into effect immediately unless otherwise directed.[220] The Appeal Board may decide to follow any of the following courses of action:[221]

(a) allow the appeal;

(b) dismiss the appeal;

(c) exercise any power which the body against whose decision the appeal was made could have exercised (whether the effect is to increase or decrease any penalty, award, order or sanction originally imposed);

(d) remit the matter for re-hearing;

(e) order a deposit to be forfeited or returned;

(f) make such further or other order as it considers appropriate.

23.122 After the decision has been announced, it will be published in writing as soon as practicable. This written decision will constitute a conclusive record of the

---

215 Appeal Regulation 2.9.
216 Appeal Regulation 2.10.
217 Appeal Regulation 2.3.
218 Appeal Regulation 2.11.
219 Appeal Regulation 3.1. Each member of the Appeal Board will have one vote, unless a deadlock occurs in which case the chairman will have a second and casting vote.
220 Appeal Regulation 3.2.
221 Appeal Regulation 3.3.

decision, and will include the names of the parties, the decision appealed against, the grounds of appeal, the result of the appeal and any orders made by the Appeal Board.[222] Either party can request written reasons for the decision within three days of its announcement.[223]

23.123 The Appeal Board's decision is said to be final and binding, with no right of appeal existing unless in relation to appeals to CAS brought by FIFA or WADA under the FA Anti-Doping Regulations.[224] In exceptionally rare cases, involving clear irrationality or unfairness it might be possible to bring a challenge to an Appeal Board using the Rule K procedure.

(f) Failure to comply

23.124 If a party fails to comply with an order, requirement or instruction made by the Appeal Board, it may be punished in any way deemed appropriate by the Appeal Board; this may include being subject to an award for costs.[225]

(g) Costs

23.125 Any costs incurred in bringing or responding to an appeal will usually be borne by the party incurring the costs, although in exceptional circumstances, and upon application by a party, the Appeal Board may order that one party pays some or all of the other party's costs (not including legal costs).[226] The Appeal Board may order that any or any part of the costs incurred by itself be paid by any one party, or that they be shared between them as stipulated by the Board.[227]

222 Appeal Regulation 3.7.
223 Appeal Regulation 3.8.
224 Appeal Regulation 3.4.
225 Appeal Regulation 2.12.
226 Appeal Regulation 3.5.
227 Appeal Regulation 3.3

CHAPTER 24

Doping

James Segan and Tom Mountford (Blackstone Chambers)

A   GENERAL INTRODUCTION TO ANTI-DOPING

24.1   It is of the essence of sport that it takes place on a level playing field; that competitors participate in accordance with the rules of the game and do not secure unfair advantage; and that they are sanctioned, on or off the pitch, if they contravene the applicable rules and standards.

24.2   One of the most fundamental breaches of the applicable standards is the use of illicit performance-enhancing substances or methods which may artificially increase a competitor's performance and give an unfair competitive advantage. One of the essential aspects of the competition inherent in sport, which underlies its entertainment value, is the demonstration of the highest levels of human physical ability, skill and endurance. Where a competitor's performance reflects not only his or her abilities and training, together with the magic variable of luck, but also an additional element attributable to the use of illicit performance-enhancing substances (for example steroids) or methods (for example blood manipulation) which *artificially* increase performance, then the essence of the sporting competition is impaired or destroyed.

24.3   Equally, the distortion of the sport's level playing field by the use of such substances or methods places clean competitors at an unfair disadvantage or incentivises them also to breach the sport's anti-doping rules, compounding the unfairness to other clean competitors and raising serious implications for the health of participants.

24.4   However, what amounts to a substance or method which is *permissible* (such as training at altitude, diet, substances taken for a health reason or to increase performance where the substance is permitted) and what constitutes an *impermissible* substance or method has not always been an easy question and is still a question which generates considerable debate at the margins. It has therefore been necessary for all sports, including football, to develop a comprehensive regulatory framework defining and identifying prohibited substances and methods and providing for consistent (if not exactly uniform) consequences of contravention of those standards. As set out in more detail in the following section, the global standard that has emerged and been adopted by most sports, including football, is the World Anti-Doping Agency Code ('the WADA Code').

24.5   The prevalence of doping across different sports is a much-contested question. There is greater obvious incentive to dope in individual sporting disciplines, where illicit substances may give a very meaningful marginal improvement to an individual competitor's performance and success (measured at the level of the individual competitor). By contrast, in team sports, such as football, it is less obvious that the use of an illicit substance would affect overall team performance, even if it has performance-enhancing effects on an individual player. However, a countervailing school of thought argues that doping may be considerably underreported in such team sports on account of less frequent testing and less sophisticated testing methodologies (athletics, for example, has introduced longitudinal analysis by way of sophisticated athlete biological passports). Doping may be an attractive way for an individual player to speed recovery from injury so as to participate in a team sport, for instance.

24.6   In English football, as explained below, most of the reported doping cases concern use of illegal drugs more associated with recreational purposes than their performance-enhancing effect (such as cocaine) or substances which have been taken, at least arguably, for medical reasons (such as salbutamol in asthma inhalers). The reported decisions do not, in themselves, suggest a widespread doping problem in English football. However, the doping case law in the Court of Arbitration for Sport (CAS) reveals a far wider range of prohibited substances turning up in the samples of footballers from the wider game, and it would be naïve to assume that English football is somehow isolated from this. Furthermore, the fight against doping is constantly developing new frontiers and the past is not necessarily a sure guide to the prevalence of doping in the sport in the future (even assuming that the present system is generally successful in detecting present violations).

B   INTERNATIONAL APPROACH TO ANTI-DOPING: WADA CODE AND CAS

24.7   As with most sports, participation in the sport of football is subject to compliance with an anti-doping regime derived from a number of principal documents, most important of which is the WADA Code (and the subsidiary WADA International Standards and Models of Best Practice). It is these instruments (and the case law around them) that CAS looks to in seeking to approach issues of anti-doping which go on appeal to CAS from the decisions of relevant national, regional or international sporting disciplinary bodies tasked with upholding anti-doping rules, albeit through the lens of the specific applicable rules giving effect to the WADA Code and principles in the sport and territory in which the case has arisen.

24.8   The first WADA Code was created in 2004 and the Code is the central document harmonising anti-doping standards applicable in sports worldwide and providing for uniform anti-doping offences. An organisation can be a direct or indirect signatory: some organisations are party to the WADA Code by virtue of their membership of an association of organisations which is itself a signatory to the Code and makes compliance with the Code a requirement of membership of the association. FIFA has adopted the WADA Code and is an indirect signatory through its membership of the Association of Summer Olympic International Federations.

24.9   The current applicable version of the WADA Code is the version published on 1 January 2015 ('the 2015 Code'). The Code is only updated periodically, with the

1 January 2015 updating the 1 January 2009 version ('the 2009 Version'), which was itself the first update to the original 2004 version of the Code. The Code is divided into four main sections:

Part One	Doping Control (setting out anti-doping rules violations (ADVs) and making provision as to the banned substances and testing procedures and the disciplinary process).
Part Two	Education and Research.
Part Three	Roles and Responsibilities (setting out the roles of the relevant organisations and individual participants in sport).
Part Four	Acceptance, Compliance, Modification and Interpretation.

24.10   For an organisation to be 'code compliant' with the WADA Code, it must have accepted the principles contained in the Code and agreed to implement and comply with the Code, implemented that commitment by amending its rules and policies to include the mandatory articles and principles of the Code and be able to show enforcement of those standards.

24.11   WADA's statutes mandate that CAS is the ultimate appellate body in respect of decisions concerning doping.

24.12   The WADA Code mandates that WADA publishes an annual list of prohibited substances and methods ('the Prohibited List'). The list differentiates between substances and methods which are prohibited in and out of competition, and in particular sports. The Prohibited List is categorised as one of five WADA International Standards.

24.13   A key distinction within the WADA Code is between substances prohibited in competition only and substances which are also prohibited out of competition. The presence or use of a substance prohibited out of competition will constitute a violation whether the violation is detected in or out of competition. A substance which is only banned in competition will not constitute a violation where it is used or detected to be present outside of competition. A distinction is also drawn between prohibited substances (which will always generally constitute a violation, subject to limited available defences) and a specified substance, where the range of potential defences and the seriousness of an ADV may be lesser. The reason for this, as the comment to Article 4.2.2 of the WADA Code notes, is that:

> 'Specified Substances identified in Article 4.2.2 should not in any way be considered less important or less dangerous than other doping offences. Rather, they are simply substances which are more likely to have been consumed by an Athlete for a purpose other than the enhancement of sport performance.'

24.14   The main categories of violations under the WADA Code are as follows:

(a) *Presence* violation. This is a violation based on the detected presence of a prohibited substance or its metabolites or markers in an athlete's sample collected for the purposes of doping control and analysed for prohibited substances. This is the most common ADV.

(b) *Use* violation. This is a violation based on use, or attempted use, of a prohibited substance. This may be substantiated by evidence other than a positive sample, such as written records, testimony, confession or inferential evidence.

(c) *Evasion or Failure to Submit* violation. Evading, refusing or failing to submit to sample collection.

(d) *Whereabouts* failure. Failure without due cause to provide whereabouts information to allow for samples to be collected if a player is selected for random or targeting testing.

(e) *Tampering* violation. Tampering or attempted tampering with any part of the anti-doping control.

(f) *Possession* violation. Possessing a prohibited substance or method.

(g) *Trafficking* violation. Trafficking or attempted trafficking in any prohibited substance or method.

C   ANTI-DOPING IN ENGLISH FOOTBALL: THE FA'S RULES IMPLEMENTING THE WADA CODE

24.15   The FA's 2017/18 Anti-Doping Regulations ('the FA ADR') set out the anti-doping principles which apply to the sport. Acceptance of the FA ADR, and agreement to be bound by them, is a condition of participation in football (Regulation 3). As described in the FA ADR, the regulatory system seeks to:

(a) uphold and preserve the ethics of the sport;
(b) safeguard the physical health and mental integrity of players; and
(c) ensure that all players have an equal chance.

24.16   Regulation 3 provides for a series of responsibilities upon participants in the sport. These apply to 'players' (defined to bear the same meaning as at Rule A2 of the Rules of The FA) and 'player support personnel' (defined as 'any personnel working with, treating or assisting a Player in participating in or preparing for football matches or training sessions, including but not limited to coach, trainer, manager, agent, Intermediary … club staff, official, nutritionist, medical or paramedical personnel, or parent'). Certain obligations are common to players and player support personnel, for example the obligation to be aware of and comply with all applicable anti-doping policies, rules and regulations. Anti-doping jurisprudence continually stresses the importance of this personal responsibility to be familiar with anti-doping rules and the personal responsibility as to substances which are taken (this is another specific obligation on players, to 'Take responsibility for all substances that they ingest and for all substances and methods that they Use'). This issue often comes up in disciplinary proceedings when a player argues that he or she has simply taken a substance given to him or her by a coach or other third party and that he or she was not aware of what the substance was or believed it to be a permissible substance.

24.17   Other obligations are specific to either players or player support personnel. For example, players are subject to obligations to:

● make themselves available for (biological) sample collection at all times and provide whereabouts information as required (and are specifically required by regulation 3 to undergo drug tests as set out in the FA ADR);
● inform medical personnel of their obligation not to use prohibited substances and prohibited methods.

24.18   The FA ADR note that the list of prohibited substances and methods are definitively set out in the WADA Prohibited List and that any changes made to this by WADA will be immediately recognised by The FA. It is therefore important to check the version of the Prohibited List on the WADA website[1] or on The FA's website.[2]

---

1   See www.wada-ama.org.
2   See www.TheFA.com/anti-doping.

24.19   Certain concepts have a football-specific meaning. For example, the definition of 'in competition' in the FA ADR is 'the time period starting at midnight on the day of a match until the time of that match day that the Sample collection procedures have been completed by the Competent Officials', and 'out of competition' is any time which is not 'in competition'.

(a)   Violations under the FA ADR

24.20   The violations set out at para **24.14** above, by reference to the WADA Code, are specified in Regulation 3 (Presence), Regulation 4 (Use), Regulation 5 (Evasion), Regulation 6 (Whereabouts failure), Regulation 7 (Tampering), Regulation 8 (Possession) and Regulation 9 (Trafficking).

(i)   Presence (Regulation 3)

24.21   A presence violation is established by the testing of a player's A and/ or B sample (ie the two samples, usually urine or blood, taken during the sample collection process) and the violation is established unless the player can establish that the presence of the substance is consistent with a Therapeutic Use Exemption (TUE) that has been granted to the player. A TUE may be granted where there is a legitimate medical reason for a player to use a substance which would otherwise be a prohibited substance and the conditions set out in Schedule 5 to the FA ADR are satisfied. A TUE granted by a National Ant-Doping Organisation (NADO) in accordance with that procedure will not necessarily satisfy all TUE requirements placed on him or her by FIFA or UEFA.[3] Players bear strict responsibility for substances entering their bodies and a player's lack of intent, fault, negligence or knowledge is not a valid defence to a charge that an ADV has been committed.[4]

(ii)   Use (Regulation 4)

24.22   This prohibits a prohibited substance from entering a player's body or use of a prohibited method. Again, a player's lack of intent, fault, negligence or knowledge is not a valid defence to a charge of a use violation, and the success or failure of the use or attempted use is irrelevant.[5] However, it is necessary to show intent on the player's part to establish an *attempted* use ADV.[6] Whilst out of competition use of a substance which is only prohibited in competition is not a use violation, if the substance is detected in sample taken in competition that will still amount to a presence violation.[7]

(iii)   Evasion or failure to submit (Regulation 5)

24.23   There is a general prohibition against evasion of sample collection without any specified exceptions. By contrast, refusing or failing to submit to sample collection is a violation unless there is 'compelling justification' for the failure or refusal (Regulation 5(a)).[8]

---

3   FA ADR, Sch 5, para 1.5.
4   FA ADR, reg 3(c).
5   FA ADR, reg 4(c).
6   FA ADR, reg 4(b).
7   FA ADR, reg 4(d).
8   FA ADR, reg 5(a).

(iv) Whereabouts failure (Regulation 6)

24.24 A player who is in a Registered Testing Pool (a pool of highest priority players who are subject to focused testing in and out of competition and are required to provide, and keep updated, details of their whereabouts for the purposes of any unannounced testing) commits an ADV to have three filing failures and/or missed tests within a 12-month period.

(v) Tampering (Regulation 7)

24.25 A tampering, or attempted tampering, violation is conduct which subverts the doping control process but which is not a prohibited method. The definition of tampering is broad and includes (without limitation) intentionally interfering or attempting to interfere with a doping control official, providing fraudulent information to an anti-doping organisation or attempting to intimidate a potential witness.

(vi) Possession (Regulation 8)

24.26 A possession violation is made out where a person possesses a prohibited substance or method at a relevant time when it would be prohibited to use such a substance or method (whether in or out of competition).

(vii) Trafficking (Regulation 9)

24.27 A trafficking violation is made out where a person traffics, or attempts to traffic, in a prohibited substance or prohibited method.

(viii) Administration (Regulation 10)

24.28 An administration violation is made out where a participant administers or attempts to administer a prohibited substance or prohibited method to a player (save where a TUE applies).

(ix) Complicity (Regulation 11)

24.29 Complicity is a broadly drawn offence including assisting, encouraging, aiding, abetting, conspiring in, covering up or any other type of intentional complicity by a participant in an ADV or attempted ADV or other relevant violation by another participant.

(x) Prohibited association (Regulation 12)

24.30 This ADV is made out where a participant associated with someone who is suspended from activity in the sport by authority of an anti-doping organisation an analogous offences.

(xi) Other requirements

24.31 There are then a number of requirements[9] the breach of which will not amount to an ADV but will constitute misconduct under The FA's disciplinary rules.

---

9   FA ADR, regs 14–17.

(b) Sanctions

24.32   In relation to an admitted or established ADV, sanctions are provided for by Part 6 (first ADV) and Part 7 (multiple or subsequent ADVs) of the FA ADR. In addition, it is possible in certain limited cases to argue that a period of suspension for a presence, use or attempted use or possession violation should be eliminated on the basis of the participant charged bearing no fault or negligence.[10] No fault or negligence is strictly construed and confined to a limited class of cases such as certain categories of spiking or contamination cases. Additionally, where an ADV involves a specified substance, and the participant can establish that he or she bears no significant fault or negligence, then the penalty can be reduced as specified.[11]

24.33   A person who may have committed an ADV may be entitled to a reduction in any sanction on the basis of providing substantial assistance in discovering or establishing ADVs.[12]

D ANTI-DOPING IN ENGLISH FOOTBALL: THE FA'S SOCIAL DRUGS POLICY

24.34   Many of the most commonly consumed recreational drugs, such as cannabis or cocaine, are prohibited under the WADA Code only *in* competition. It is, in other words, not a breach of the WADA Code – or therefore the FA ADR – for a player to consume cocaine in a nightclub on a Friday night, so long as none is in his system by the time of a match on Sunday.

24.35   The FA has, however, gone further and adopted a set of Social Drugs Policy Regulations ('the SDPR'). The SDPR recognise that players 'due to their age, spare time, disposable income, etc. … are at risk of being exposed to Social Drugs while Out of Competition', with a series of negative consequences for themselves and the sport of football, including damage 'to the image and reputation of the sport'.[13] For the purposes of the SDPR, a 'Social Drug' is any drug in a familiar list of recreational drugs which includes cocaine, cannabis, amphetamines, ecstasy and the such like.[14]

24.36   The prohibitions in the SDPR upon Social Drugs are closely modelled upon the main prohibitions in the WADA Code: there are accordingly prohibitions on the presence in a sample,[15] use or attempted use,[16] possession,[17] administration or attempted administration[18] and trafficking or attempted trafficking.[19] Many of the key defined terms from the FA ADR such as 'out of competition', 'use' and such like are defined to mean the same thing in the SDPR.[20]

24.37   As regards sanctions, however, the SDPR take a very different course from the FA ADR. The focus is, at least in the first instance, upon rehabilitation by way of

10   FA ADR, Part 8, para 66.
11   FA ADR, Part 8, paras 67–69.
12   FA ADR, Part 8, para 70.
13   SDPR, reg 3.2.
14   SDPR, reg 2.1.
15   SDPR, reg 4.1.1.
16   SDPR, reg 4.1.2.
17   SDPR, regs 4.1.3 and 4.1.4.
18   SDPR, reg 4.1.5.
19   SDPR, reg 4.1.6.
20   SDPR, reg 2.3.2.

education, counselling and treatment.[21] For a first offence of presence in a sample, use or attempted use or possession, a suspension cannot exceed three months.[22] For a second offence, there is a mandatory suspension of 6–12 months,[23] with even longer suspensions for third and fourth offences.[24] More severe penalties attend in respect of the more serious offences such as trafficking and attempting trafficking, where even a first breach requires a six-month minimum suspension.[25]

24.38 A particular feature of the SDPR is that cases are ordinarily entirely confidential, subject to a discretion on the part of The FA to publish details or answer press queries.[26] This discretion does not appear regularly to be exercised: no decisions under the SDPR are available on The FA's website. The FA has maintained this position notwithstanding considerable adverse publicity in September 2011, when a Channel 4 'Dispatches' programme revealed that ex-Birmingham City striker Gary O'Connor had tested positive for cocaine during the 2009/10 season, and had received a 'secret' two-month suspension coinciding with an injury. The FA's view is that privacy is necessary for players to undergo the requisite counselling and rehabilitation.

E ANTI-DOPING CASES IN ENGLISH FOOTBALL

24.39 For the reasons explained immediately above, it is not known how many cases the FA deals with under the SDPR. Decisions finding breaches of the FA ADR are, however, published by the FA. They are, by the standards of many sports, comparatively few. The decisions which have been published fall into three broad categories, which can be taken in turn.

(a) Salbutamol cases

24.40 In *FA v Chey Dunkley*[27] and *FA v Alan Judge*,[28] The FA's Regulatory Commission considered violations of the FA ADR for the presence of salbutamol in players' in competition samples, at a concentration of over 1,000ng/ml. In *Dunkley*, the concentration was 1,500ng/ml, and in *Judge* it was 1,600ng/ml. Under the WADA Code, it was a defence for the players to prove on the balance of probabilities, if they could, that the concentrations resulted from the inhalation of no more than 1,600μg for therapeutic purposes in the 24-hour period prior to the sample being provided. In both cases, the players were asthmatics who sought to explain their positive tests by explaining that they had taken puffs on a Ventolin inhaler at or around the time of training or a match. In the *Judge* case, the Commission heard 'impressive' evidence from two experts as to whether it was necessary to adjust the findings for the effects of strenuous exercise.[29] Ultimately, however, the player's own evidence was that he had inhaled some 2,000–2,500μg in the relevant period, which the Regulatory Commission could not ignore.[30] He received a warning and

21 SDPR, regs 6.1, 8.1.1.
22 SDPR, reg 8.1.1(a).
23 SDPR, reg 8.1.1(b).
24 SDPR, reg 8.1.1(c)–(d).
25 SDPR, reg 8.3.1(a).
26 SDPR, reg 9.2.
27 FA Regulatory Commission (Ch T. Win, JP), 17 June 2015.
28 FA Regulatory Commission (Ch D. Casement QC), 8 June 2016.
29 At paras 27–32.
30 At paras 25, 35.

a reprimand and was made the subject of target testing for two years. In *Dunkley*, the player admitted the charge in view of a Pharmacokinetic Study, and again received a warning and a reprimand and was made the subject of target testing for two years.

(b)   Cocaine cases

24.41   In *FA v Livermore*[31] and *FA v Lacey*,[32] The FA's Regulatory Commission considered violations of the FA ADR for the presence of cocaine in players' in competition samples. The *Livermore* case was both high-profile and of wider significance in anti-doping. The player and his partner had suffered the tragic loss of their new born son during labour, in circumstances which could have been prevented. The devastating effect of this loss caused the player's mental health to enter a spiral of decline. Most of the details of that decline – defined in the decision as 'the Circumstances' – are redacted from the public version of that decision. But the Commission ultimately found that the ADV had 'only occurred as a result of the severe impairment of Mr Livermore's cognitive functions and judgment caused by the Circumstances for which he was in no way at fault'.[33] Circumventing the minimum sanction of 12 months' suspension, the Commission reduced it to zero, relying on the line of CAS cases confirming the availability of such a reduction in truly exceptional circumstances in which even the minimum penalty would be disproportionate.[34] The Commission directed a programme of rehabilitation and one year of target testing. In *Lacey*, the player had also been suffering from moderate depression at the time of taking cocaine, and on the night in question his 'cognitive function was impaired such … he had an inability to properly weigh up risks and the consequences of those risks'.[35] The player did not suggest that the case was in the same category as *Livermore* and the Commission recorded this to be 'realistic'.[36] The Commission imposed a 14-month suspension.[37]

(c)   Whereabouts cases

24.42   In *FA v Fleetwood Town*,[38] *FA v Manchester City*[39] and *FA v Bournemouth*,[40] three clubs were fined for repeated failures in furnishing whereabouts information as to their players, in breach of FA ADR Regulation 14. In *Fleetwood* the fine was £4,000; in *Manchester City* and *Bournemouth* the fine was £35,000. Although the Regulatory Commission made reference in *Fleetwood* to the need to set fines at a level which were a 'sufficient deterrent',[41] this factor was not mentioned in *Manchester City* and *Bournemouth*. It seems unlikely indeed that a fine of £35,000 would have any significant deterrent effect in the context of a Premier League club.

31   FA Regulatory Commission (Ch D. Casement QC), 8 September 2015.
32   FA Regulatory Commission (Ch D. Casement QC), 8 May 2017.
33   At para 14.4.
34   At paras 28–34.
35   At para 14.4.
36   At para 16.
37   At para 20.
38   FA Regulatory Commission (Ch G. Farrelly), 26 January 2017.
39   FA Regulatory Commission (Ch T. Win, JP), 17 February 2017.
40   FA Regulatory Commission (Ch G. Farrelly), 14 March 2017.
41   At para 13.

F   ANTI-DOPING CASES IN WORLD FOOTBALL: THE CAS

24.43   By contrast with the relatively small number of reported decisions in English football, football more widely has generated a significant number of anti-doping cases in the CAS.

(a)   No doctrine of precedent

24.44   A preliminary point to note is that CAS decisions must be approached carefully by common law lawyers used to applying rules of precedent. Whilst CAS decisions are often replete with citation from previous authorities, the CAS treats its 'full power to review the facts and the law'[42] as effectively requiring relatively little restraint in terms of following those earlier decisions. It is perfectly open to one CAS Panel to depart from the decision of an earlier Panel, on a point of law. As a CAS Panel recently observed, '… no doctrine of binding precedent applies to the CAS jurisprudence'.[43] There is no particular constraint on a CAS Panel from departing from an earlier Panel on an issue of law, and they regularly do.

24.45   With that caveat, a review of the football doping cases in the CAS reveals some interesting trends, of which five can be highlighted in particular.

(b)   Prohibited substances

24.46   First, the range of prohibited substances with which CAS cases are concerned is far wider than the narrow range of such substances found in the English cases. CAS cases have concerned, for example: Bromantan[44] (said to combine the properties of steroid, stimulant and masking agent); steroids such as stanozolol,[45] norandrosterone,[46] oxymesterone[47] and methyltestosterone;[48] stimulants such as fenproporex[49] and methylhexamine;[50] the protein Thymosin Beta-4;[51] the hormone clomiphene;[52] and masking agents such as furosemide.[53] This might suggest that whilst individual incentives to dope may be intuitively less powerful in a team sport such as football than in an individual sport such as cycling or athletics, the temptation is nevertheless present and in some cases very powerful.

---

42   CAS Code of Sports-Related Arbitration, 2017, Article 57.
43   *Sharapova v ITF* (CAS 2016/A/4643), 30 September 2016 at para 82.
44   *Football Association of Wales v UEFA* (CAS 2004/A/593), 6 July 2004.
45   *WADA v FMF & Alvarez* (CAS 2006/A/1149), 16 May 2007; *WADA v CBF & De Oliveira Filho* (CAS 2014/A/3842), 9 July 2015; *Ademi v UEFA* (CAS 2016/A/4676), 24 March 2017.
46   *Giovanella v FIFA* (CAS 2006/A/1155), 22 February 2007; *FIFA v Malta Football Association & C* (CAS 2008/A/1588), 9 February 2009; *WADA v FPF & Fernandes* (CAS 2012/A/2922), 10 December 2013.
47   *WADA & FIFA v Cyprus Football Association* (CAS 2009/A/1817), 26 October 2010.
48   *FIFA v Korea Football Association & Kang Soo Il* (CAS 2015/A/4215), 29 June 2016.
49   *FIFA v CBF* (CAS 2007/A/1370), 11 September 2008.
50   *Wawrzyniak v Hellenic Football Federation* (CAS 2009/A/1918), 21 January 2010; *Alegria v FIFA* (CAS 2013/A/3262), 30 September 2014.
51   *WADA v Bellchambers* (CAS 2015/A/4059), 11 January 2016.
52   *WADA v Turkish Football Federation & Kuru* (CAS 2016/A/4512), 21 November 2016.
53   *FIFA v FIGC & Schurtz* (CAS 2008/A/1495), 30 April 2009; *Rybka v UEFA* (CAS 2012/A/2759), 11 July 2012.

(c)   Policing 'home town' decisions

24.47   Secondly, the bulk of CAS doping cases in the footballing context are concerned with appeals by WADA and FIFA against final decisions of national governing bodies, and in almost all cases because the national-level decision had been, in WADA or FIFA's view, too lenient upon the player. There are some striking examples. In *Kuru*,[54] an appeal by WADA resulted in the CAS overturning the disqualification of a Turkish player for just six months (and only from 'official games') and substituting it with a four-year ban. In *Alvarez*,[55] a national-level decision dismissing a charge was replaced with a lifetime ban. In a considerable number of cases, national-level findings of 'no significant fault or negligence' were overturned in their entirety, along with the commensurate reductions in sanction.[56] In other cases, sanctions were lengthened.[57] This will of course partly reflect the fact that in many cases FIFA and WADA will be the only persons with an appeal right, after any national-level appeal has been exhausted. But the pattern, and the success rate, are remarkable.

(d)   Disputes between national associations

24.48   Thirdly, reflecting the status of the CAS as an international-level arbiter of choice, the CAS has on occasion entertained disputes in effect *between* national associations in the anti-doping context. In the *Football Association of Wales* case,[58] although the respondent was UEFA, the real target was the Russian Football Union, with the applicant association arguing that Russia should be disqualified from Euro 2004 since the team had fielded a player in a critical qualifier against Wales who later transpired to have been doping. The CAS dismissed the complaint, finding that there was no evidence that the Russian federation, or the player's club, had cooperated intentionally or negligently in the use of a banned substance by the player.

(e)   Ensuring proper governing rules and allocation of jurisdiction

24.49   Fourthly, the CAS has consistently played an important role in settling disputes as to which anti-doping rules apply, and which bodies have jurisdiction. In *WADA v FIFA*,[59] the CAS gave an advisory opinion clarifying that whilst FIFA was free as a matter of Swiss law to implement rules differing from the WADA Code, the numerous differences between FIFA's then anti-doping rules and the WADA Code could expose it to sanctions under the Olympic Charter. This case was a classic example of the utility of the CAS as a forum for the independent settlement of legal issues between two international-level governing bodies. In *Giovanella*[60] and *Malta*,[61] the CAS confirmed that FIFA had no power to intervene and review disciplinary decisions adopted by national federations in anti-doping matters: the

---

54   See n 52 above.
55   See n 45 above.
56   See eg *FIFA v FIGC & Recchi* (CAS 2008/A/1494), 30 April 2009; *Schurtz* (n 53 above); *Cyprus* (n 47 above); *De Oliveira Filho* (n 45 above); *Bellchambers* (n 51 above).
57   See eg *FIFA v Malta Football Association & R* (CAS 2008/A/1576), 9 February 2009; *FIFA v CBF & Fernandez* (CAS 2016/A/4416), 7 November 2016.
58   See n 44 above.
59   *WADA v FIFA* (CAS 2005/C/976), 21 April 2006.
60   See n 46 above.
61   See n 57 above.

proper mechanisms were either an appeal where available, or disciplinary measures against a national federation to encourage it to bring its national rules into line. In cases concerning the *CBF*[62] and *Maltese* football authorities,[63] the CAS made clear that FIFA's international-level anti-doping rules did not apply in national cases unless there was express adoption thereof.

(f) Ordinary appeals

24.50   Fifthly, the CAS has also entertained a substantial number of more 'ordinary' first or second appeals against decisions of UEFA and FIFA disciplinary bodies in anti-doping cases arising from European or international matches which fall under the direct jurisdiction of UEFA or FIFA.[64]

---

62   See n 45 above.
63   See nn 46 and 57 above.
64   See eg *Alegria* (n 59 above), which arose from a preliminary competition match of the 2014 World Cup in Brazil.

CHAPTER 25

Corruption and Match-fixing

Nick De Marco QC (Blackstone Chambers) and **Karim Bouzidi** (Clintons)

A   INTRODUCTION

25.1   The Oxford English Dictionary defines the verb 'to corrupt' as meaning (*inter alia*) 'To destroy or pervert the integrity or fidelity of (a person) in his discharge of duty; to induce to act dishonestly or unfaithfully; to make venal; to bribe'. Corruption covers a wide spectrum. In sport it can arise in various quite different forms.

25.2   First, perhaps the most obvious form, and usually the focus of those governing sport, is the corruption of players and athletes – match-fixing, or 'spot-fixing' whereby a player does not perform to his or her best abilities, or causes a particular incident to happen in a match (a throw in, or a yellow card for instance) in exchange for payment; or the corruption of a referee or match official, bribed to favour a certain outcome. This type of corruption is intrinsically linked to, and usually funded by, gambling on sport.

25.3   Secondly, there is what might be described as 'business corruption', bribery and 'kick-backs' being exchanged for favours in the course of the multifarious commercial transactions that take place in sport, and in football in particular. This form is most often linked to the highly lucrative transfer market in players.

25.4   Finally, there is the corruption of the regulators themselves – those responsible for administrating and controlling the sport taking bribes in return for granting business or sporting favours to those corrupting them. This form might also be linked with match-fixing or business corruption.

25.5   All corruption in sport is corrosive. It undermines the integrity of sport. At its best sport is supposed to be about fair play, a level playing field, an element of unpredictability. If you were to go to watch a football match with the knowledge, before the game kicked off, of who would win and what the score would be, even when the goals were scored, then much, if not all, the pleasure and excitement of watching (or playing in) the match would be lost. Match-fixing is perhaps even more destructive to sport than doping is. Both are forms of cheating, and thus threaten the integrity of sport, but whereas those who deliberately take prohibited substances with the intention of enhancing their sporting performance do so to win or over-achieve, sportsmen involved in match-fixing invariably aim to underperform, to lose, in exchange for bribes. Match-fixing is not only antithetical to the whole ethos of sport, it poses a real threat to the survival of sport. People will cease paying to watch matches they know are fixed from the outset, and sponsors and broadcasters will follow them away from the sport. Fighting corruption in sport is critical. Identifying, punishing and preventing match-fixing essential.

25.6   But it is not only match-fixing that undermines sport. Business and regulatory corruption pose equal threats. Indeed, as the recent scandal in world athletics showed, you cannot combat corruption amongst athletes in sport when those who regulate the sport are themselves corrupt – the scandal involved the most senior IAAF officials taking bribes in order to cover up certain athletes' failed doping tests. Likewise, the integrity of competitions like the FIFA World Cup are undermined by the perception that certain unlikely countries are chosen to host a competition because they were able to bribe more senior FIFA officials with more money, or more effectively, than the other bidders to host the competition were. Business corruption in football, often arising in connection with the football transfer market, undermines the confidence of the public in the way in which football is run, or the reasons players move, and raises concerns about the amount of money seemingly going out of football into the hands of third party middlemen.

25.7   Somewhat predictably the regulators, including the major football regulators such as FIFA and The FA, focus their regulations on the dangers of corruption by the players, and not of the danger of their own corruption. Business corruption is only partially regulated by the regulators, much of it is regulated by the general law and the parties themselves. So the regulations in football that concern integrity issues are principally all about policing those who participate in the sport itself, as opposed to those who control it.

25.8   Section B of this chapter will examine the recent history of corruption in football, with respect to each of the main three forms of corruption described in this introduction, as well as containing a summary of the regulations or law relevant to those forms. Sections C and D then consider more closely the main regulation football has incorporated in recent years to deal with match- and spot-fixing, including principally the universal ban on football betting directed at participants in the sport.

B   CORRUPTION IN FOOTBALL

(a)   Match-fixing and spot-fixing

25.9   It is sometimes said that match-fixing in football is less of a problem than in other sports because of the fact football is a team game. The argument goes that it takes a number of players, playing in collaboration with each other, for a team to perform and a result to follow, and that result depends also on how the other players in the other team perform. Thus, on the face of it, it is easier to corrupt a tennis match between two people than a football match between two teams of 11 and substitutes.

25.10   This is true, but only to a certain extent. First, individuals can be corrupted and the corruption of one person may have a decisive effect on the outcome – consider the corruption of a referee or a goalkeeper, or the team's penalty taker, or the manager who selects the team and decides the substitutes. The possibility of one person having a decisive outcome is even more easy to contrive when one considers 'spot-fixing' – where an individual is corrupted to cause a certain outcome at a certain moment in the match for example – such as a throw in on the 32nd minute, a yellow card in the first half, or being substituted during the second half. Because of the increasing sophistication and proliferation of sports betting, the public can now bet on just about any event occurring during a match, and match officials or spectators are far less likely to be suspicious about a throw in on the 32nd minute of a match than they are an unlikely result.

25.11 Secondly, the corruption of a number of players in the same team has occurred in football with greater frequency than might be expected. It often arises in circumstances that might not appear as morally culpable to those corrupted as others – for example the last match of the season for a lower league team, the result of which shall have no effect at all on that team's final place in the league, or that of its rival. In such a match the attitude of the players may well be quite relaxed, unless it is a local derby or 'grudge match', even the fans might have little interest in the outcome of the result. The corrupter may be able to persuade a few players on either (or both) teams to try and achieve a draw as the outcome of the match in exchange for some payment. What is the real harm to anyone, the corrupter will ask, and especially if the players are on low salaries and see an opportunity to earn more money for something that might not offend their own moral compass or have any effect on their team, then the temptation may be there.

(b)   Examples of match-fixing scandals in football

25.12 A consideration of some of the known recent examples of corruption in football assists in understanding the problem, though those involved in the industry know all too well that these examples most likely represent a fraction of the problem. Match-fixing in football is notoriously difficult to identify or prove.

25.13 The live transmission of football internationally makes it an easy target for illegal bookmakers. In the late 1990s a number of Asian businessmen and an English football ground stadium officer were jailed for their role in a scandal involving switching off the stadium floodlights at Crystal Palace's home ground to abandon games when a certain score had been reached. Bets had been placed in Asia that a match would result in a draw, and when the teams were drawing the lights would be turned off causing the match to be abandoned and the bets paid out. It was believed that at least three English Premier League games were affected by the scandal.[1]

25.14 In 2003, a number of players from both Accrington Stanley and Bury ended up being charged by The FA in relation to the last game of the League 2 season between those two clubs. The FA was alerted by reports of highly unusual betting activity surrounding the game in different parts of the country. As the summary of FA betting cases in section D of this chapter shows, The FA was ultimately unable to prove match-fixing, but was left with a lingering suspicion, not least as players from both rival teams had attended the same bookmaker together to place their bets.[2]

25.15 In 2005, the German referee Robert Hoyzer was convicted and sentenced to more than two years in prison for his part in accepting money to fix matches. He was found guilty of fixing multiple matches in the German second and third

1   'The floodlights went out and an Asian betting syndicate raked in a fortune' The Independent, 30 August 2010: http://www.independent.co.uk/news/uk/crime/the-floodlights-went-out-ndash-and-an-asian-betting-syndicate-raked-in-a-fortune-2066133.html (accessed March 2018).

2   See *The FA v Mangan*, FA Regulatory Commission (Ch Mr N Stewart QC) 23 July 2009, see further paras **25,129**, **25.144–25.145** and **25.148**, below.

divisions, as well as cup matches involving Bundesliga clubs in what was reported to be a €2 million betting scam. It was reported that he was paid €67,000 to arrange the matches, which involved awarding controversial penalties and red cards across 23 separate matches.[3]

25.16   In 2006 a major match-fixing scandal rocked the highest level of Italian football. '*Calciopoli*' as it became known, involved match-fixing of the games of a number of Italy's top football clubs including the league champions Juventus, Milan, Fiorentina, and Lazio. Telephone interceptions showed relations between team managers and referee organisations, and suggested matches were fixed by the selection of favourable referees for certain teams. A number of clubs were punished including by large points' deductions; Juventus, Fiorentina and Lazio were all relegated. Around 20 leading individuals in Italian football, including club owners, were banned from football for lengthy periods and some were imprisoned for their role in the scandal.[4]

25.17   Betting may also be on 'friendly games', so they are not averse to match-fixing. In 2010, when Bahrain beat Togo 3-0 in an international friendly, it transpired that the entire Togo national team was fake, masquerading as the national team. Togo's former national coach, Tchanile Bana, was suspended for three years for his role in organising the fake Togo team.[5]

25.18   In one game in the Italian third division between Cremona and Paganese in 2010, the Cremona goalkeeper, Marco Paolini, was found to have spiked his own team mates' water bottles. Paolini was a heavy gambler who ended up promising to fix matches to pay off his debts. When he could not recruit his fellow team mates to the scam he resorted to drugging them. He was imprisoned for five years. It was reported that the Singaporean illegal bookmaker, Dan Tan, was behind this and many other fixing scams in Italy.[6]

25.19   In 2013, a Europol investigation identified 380 football matches in Europe they suspected had been fixed.[7] An organised crime syndicate based in Asia was allegedly involved with fixing taking place via networks in 15 countries across Europe, including World Cup and European Championship qualifiers, two Champions League ties and 'several top football matches in European leagues'. It was alleged that €16 million was placed on the matches and €8 million made in betting profits. As many as 425 match officials, club officials, players and criminals were suspected of being involved. Payments of €2 million were suspected of being made in bribes. A UEFA Champions League match played in England was one of those suspected of being fixed, but it was not identified by Europol. A Danish paper, *Ekstra Bladet*, reported it as having been Liverpool's 1-0 win over Debrecen – the Hungarian team's goalkeeper had been banned for two years by UEFA (upheld by the Court of

3   'Two years in jail for match-fixing German referee' *The Guardian*, 18 November 2005: https://www.theguardian.com/football/2005/nov/18/newsstory.sport4 (accessed March 2018).

4   *2006 Italian football scandal,* Wikipedia: https://en.wikipedia.org/wiki/2006_Italian_football_scandal (accessed March 2018).

5   'Togo wants the truth about Bahrain scam' *Reuters*, 21 September 2010: http://uk.reuters.com/article/uk-bahrain-togo-soccer/togo-wants-the-truth-about-bahrain-scam-idUKTRE68K4KU20100921; 'The matches that sparked the doubts', *Daily Telegraph*, 6 May 2011: http://www.telegraph.co.uk/sport/football/8496779/The-matches-that-sparked-the-doubts.html (both accessed March 2018).

6   'Dan Tan: the man who fixed football' *The Independent*, 29 March 2013.

7   'Europol: investigators identify 380 fixed football matches' *The Guardian*, 4 February 2013: https://www.theguardian.com/football/2013/feb/04/europol-investigation-football-matchfixing (accessed March 2018).

Arbitration for Sprot (CAS)) for failing to report an approach from match-fixers in relation to another match.[8]

25.20   Match-fixing often takes place in the lower leagues where players earn less (or sometime no) money and may be more easily corrupted. In 2015, the former Premier league football player, Delroy Facey, was jailed for two-and-a-half years for his role in a conspiracy to corrupt a number of lower league players in the Football Conference on behalf of Singaporean and Indian fixers who were also jailed. Facey had sent *WhatsApp* messages to players, such as a player from Hyde FC, which read: 'Check this out. Four goals in a game – two in either half – and you guys can get 2k each, win, lose or draw. You guys can't win for shit so you might as well make some peas.'[9]

(c)   The response of the regulators

25.21   One of the most dramatic responses to match-fixing in football was a recent decision by FIFA to order that the World Cup qualifying match between South Africa and Senegal must be replayed. South Africa won the initial match 2-1 in November 2016 following a controversial penalty for a non-existent handball, awarded to them by referee Joseph Lamptey. FIFA found the referee guilty of unlawfully influencing match results and banned him for life. The ban was upheld by CAS in September 2017,[10] and FIFA announced the match would be replayed.[11]

25.22   Where there is proof of actual match-fixing (or spot-fixing), lifetime bans are likely to be applied by the regulators (and have previously been upheld by the CAS), as they were recently by UEFA against two Maltese under-21 players for the offences of 'having acted in a manner that is likely to exert an unlawful or undue influence on the course and/or result of a match or competition with a view to gaining an advantage for himself or a third party' in relation to two UEFA European Under-21 Championship 2017 matches played in March 2016 by Malta against Montenegro (on 23 March) and the Czech Republic (on 29 March).[12]

25.23   Apart from the various individual investigations and sanctions, the regulators' response to match-fixing in football has been to prohibit players (and others involved in football) from betting on football. Not only are footballers obviously prohibited from any involvement in fixing matches, or events in matches, or sharing inside

8   'Liverpool's 2009 Champions League match against Debrecen allegedly fixed by Hungarian side's goalkeeper', *Daily Telegraph*, 4 February 2013: http://www.telegraph.co.uk/sport/football/teams/liverpool/9848809/Liverpools-2009-Champions-League-match-against-Debrecen-allegedly-fixed-by-Hungarian-sides-goalkeeper.html (accessed March 2018).

9   'Ex-Premier League footballer jailed for part in match-fixing plot', *The Guardian*, 29 April 2015: https://www.theguardian.com/football/2015/apr/29/ex-premier-league-footballer-delroy-facey-jailed-match-fixing-plot (accessed March 2018).

10   CAS 2017/A/5173, *Joseph Odartei Lamptey v FIFA* http://resources.fifa.com/mm/document/affederation/footballgovernance/02/92/63/65/cas2017-a-5173josephodarteilampteyv.fifa_neutral.pdf (accessed March 2018).

11   'South Africa v Senegal World Cup qualifier to be replayed after referee ban', The *Guardian*, 6 September 2017: https://www.theguardian.com/football/2017/sep/06/south-africa-senegal-world-cup-qualifier-replayed (accessed March 2018).

12   See, 'UEFA bans six Malta under-21 players for match-fixing offences', Tuesday 9 January 2018, https://www.uefa.com/insideuefa/protecting-the-game/integrity/news/newsid=2529210.html#/ (accessed March 2018). In addition to the two players banned for life (Emanuel Briffa and Kyle Cesare), four more players were banned for between one and two years for the offences of 'not immediately and voluntarily informing UEFA if approached in connection with activities aimed at influencing in an unlawful or undue manner the course and/or result of a match or competition.'

information, or receiving bribes in exchange for underperforming in some way, but they are prohibited from placing any bet on any football match anywhere in any competition anywhere in the world. Section C of this chapter considers those various regulations and section D the leading betting cases that have been held under them in English football.

25.24   Whilst a complete ban on football betting may be an understandable response to a difficult problem, there are obvious inconsistencies in the football regulators' approach. In the 2016/17 football season, Premier League clubs earned over £225 million from sponsorship alone. Half of all Premier Clubs had gambling companies as their main front-of-shirt sponsor. Players of those 10 teams were required by contract to promote betting on sport, by simply wearing their shirts, at the same time as being told that it is a strict offence for them to do what they were promoting.

25.25   The FA itself was until recently sponsored by the betting industry. In June 2017, The FA announced it was ending its sponsorship deal with Ladbrokes, citing concerns about 'integrity and trust' in football. There is a contradiction between football's increasing financial dependency on betting on the one hand and its outright ban on anyone involved in football betting on the sport on the other. Nobody would seriously imagine runners in athletics being paid to promote performance enhancing drugs on the one hand and being banned from using them on the other. Indeed, the contradiction is so acute that in August 2017 the *New York Times* reported that The FA had told it that it had a set of unpublished rules whereby it allowed those involved in running betting companies to own and operate football clubs whilst their companies took and placed bets on football, even though those who work for football clubs are banned from even betting on football.[13] Football's dependence on betting, to the extent it is prepared to shape its rules to suit the needs of the betting companies, raises at least as many concerns about integrity as players innocently betting on a football match.

(d)   Business corruption

25.26   In September 2016 the *Daily Telegraph* ran a series of front page stories about alleged corruption in English football. The 'investigation' under the name 'Football for Sale' started with revelations that England's then manager, Sam Allardyce, had negotiated a '£400,000 deal and offered advice to businessmen on how to "get around" FA rules on player transfers'.[14] The paper promised further scandalous exposés about the extent of corruption in English football, but it turned out to be a damp squib. QPR's then manager, Jimmy Floyd Hasselbaink was enticed into requesting a fee of £55,000 to speak to football agents and Leeds United then Chairman, Massimo Cellino, explained to his entrappers that whilst they could not purchase a share in football players, if they invested in the club they could have a return on profit from player sales. Apart, perhaps, from the unfortunate assistant head coach of Barnsley, Tommy Wright, set up by the *Daily Telegraph* with a £5,000 'bung' to agree to place players in the team, none of this revealed any breaches of the

13   'England Bans Betting in Soccer, but Not for "The Lizard"' *New York Times*, 11 August 2017: https://www.nytimes.com/2017/08/11/business/britain-bans-betting-in-soccer-but-not-for-the-lizard.html (accessed March 2018).
14   'Exclusive investigation: England manager Sam Allardyce for sale', *Daily Telegraph*, 27 September 2016: http://www.telegraph.co.uk/news/2016/09/26/exclusive-investigation-england-manager-sam-allardyce-for-sale (accessed March 2018).

FA Rules, let alone the criminal law. Wright lost his job, as did Allardyce, the latter more as a result of The FA's embarrassment then any rule breaches. To date, nobody identified in the feature has been charged with breaking any rule.

25.27   Ten years earlier the BBC put on a similar sting. BBC's *Panorama* broadcast a programme under the salacious title 'Undercover: Football's Dirty Secrets'. It featured allegations about rule breaking and 'bungs' involving (amongst others) the then Bolton Wanderers manager, Sam Allardyce, and then Portsmouth manager Harry Redknapp. A centrepiece of the programme was a secret film recording of football agent Charles Collymore caught on camera saying 'There's managers out there who take bungs all day long. I would say to you comfortably there's six to eight managers we could definitely approach and they'd be up for this no problem.' Apart from a failed FA charge against Mr Collymore, who appeared to have been a scapegoat for The FA's embasssment at the claims, no action followed.[15]

25.28   The *Daily Telegraph*'s story was much more hot air and hype than substance. Yet the interest in the story reflects a growing disquiet about perceived corruption in football amongst the public, the press, and also politicians. If you asked many people working in the football industry about the story they would express surprise, not at what the media uncovered but rather the fact that so little of what is known to go on was actually exposed. The more serious allegations of corruption, some of which have been made in public, remain largely uninvestigated.

(e)   The reality of corruption in football

25.29   Business corruption in football is prolific. By 'corruption' here we mean anything from the obvious bribe to persuade a club to engage a player or a player to sign with an agent, to deliberate and concealed breaches of the rules so that a club, player or agent may achieve some financial or sporting other advantage, such as occurred in respect to the Tevez affair discussed elsewhere.[16] Corruption in this sense is not necessarily criminal activity (though it may be), it might not even create civil liability (but it usually will), it may involve a dishonest breach of the regulators' rules in order to obtain some advantage (which can often be referred to as simple 'cheating' and might be lawful conduct at civil law) or, as a result for example of de-regulation, may not even breach the relevant regulations.

25.30   Corruption in football has, and in many cases continues, to operate on many levels, but it mostly centres on the lucrative and highly specialised transfer market of football players. Previously allegations of corruption in football focused on football managers receiving cash payments for signing players from particular agents. Whilst that no doubt continues at some levels it is less widespread today than it was years ago. Football clubs, particularly at the top level, have moved away from allowing managers to conduct their most important and risky financial business. The advent of the modern football Chief Executive or Director of Football in large part reflects the fact that football clubs understand the need to act more as professional businesses than they did in the past; owners who plough millions of pounds into the clubs expect some kind of checks and balances on spending.

15   'FA unable to prove charges against agent Charles Collymore', *The Guardian*, 2 May 2009: https://www.theguardian.com/football/2009/may/02/collymore-cleared-fa-commission (accessed March 2018).
16   For a discussion on the Tevez case, see chapter 11, Third Party Investment, paras **11.85–11.87** and **11.111–11.112**.

25.31 Yet if anything there has been an increase in arrangements in breach of the rules, including the payment of bribes, in the transfer market. As even greater amounts of money pour into football the competition between the top clubs for the best players increases. What in most other businesses might appear to be unorthodox payments, to or from intermediaries, or to families of players, often undeclared and in breach of the FA Rules, are not uncommon, even at the highest level. There is a widespread perception that sometimes the only way to secure the signing of a player is to engage in the same type of conduct that everybody else seems to be engaged in, otherwise the club or agent will miss out on a player to their competitors.

(f) The failure and retreat of regulation

25.32 Football regulators such as The FA do not have the resources to investigate and charge every suspicious transfer or payment. The problem has been made worse by FIFA. In particular, the decision to scrap the licensing of football agents and replace it with a far lighter touch regulation of 'intermediaries' from 2015 led to an increase in precisely the type of corrupt payments (often to young players' families), 'tapping up' and 'poaching' that many predicted.

25.33 After The FA's agents license was first abolished in 2015, the number of intermediaries registered with The FA started at just over 770. In only two years that has increased to over 1,700 individual registered intermediaries and over 160 registered intermediary companies.[17] Yet the number of football players, clubs and transfers remained more or less the same in those two years. Many more intermediaries were chasing the same deals as two years previously, and most of the new intermediaries had not received any training and had never been subject to a licensing regime; many of them will not have started out with their own clients. In addition, when The FA replaced its Football Agents Regulations with the Regulations on Working with Intermediaries, it decided to scrap the prohibitions on agents 'tapping up' or 'poaching' (approaching players under contract to a club in an attempt to induce them to leave the club and join another, or under a contract with another intermediary, inducing them to breach it and sign with the new intermediary).[18] This activity was prohibited by the old FA Football Agents Regulations.

25.34 The consequence of this de-regulation led to a 'privatisation of regulation' – it was left to the parties to enforce their rights against each other with little recourse to regulation. With many more intermediaries as there were previously agents, and most of the new intermediaries having few or no clients, the inevitable increase in attempts to poach players from existing intermediaries was aggravated by the fact that there was no longer the deterrent of action by the regulator against the poaching intermediary. The intermediary who has his client poached only had one recourse, to privately sue the new intermediary for inducement to breach contract. There was a dramatic and predictable escalation in the number of disputes and FA Rule K arbitrations between intermediaries, and between intermediaries and players, and in private contractual disputes between players, clubs and intermediaries before FIFA

---

17   See   http://www.thefa.com/football-rules-governance/policies/intermediaries/fa-registered-intermediaries-list (accessed March 2018).

18   But note, perhaps having realised this led to an inevitable increase in the disputes between players and Intermediaries, The FA decided to bring back in a prohibition on 'tapping up' in its revisions to its Intermediaries Regulations in August 2017 – see, chapter 12, The Regulation of Intermediaries, paras **12.25–12.26**.

and/or the CAS in the years following the de-regulatory moves. It remains to be seen whether The FA's decision to re-prohibit poaching will stem this tide.

25.35   In addition to de-regulating agency activity FIFA decided, also from 2015, to bring in a worldwide prohibition on Third Party Investment (TPI) in football players. Previously third party influence was banned, but many parts of the world allowed third parties to invest in the future transfer value of a player thus allowing poorer clubs to borrow money and arguably players from poorer countries or backgrounds to be promoted on a bigger stage. But whatever the arguments about TPI (and there are strong ones on both sides),[19] FIFA prohibited TPI outright rather than setting up a transparent system of regulation of it. The inevitable consequence of these twin moves (de-regulating agents and banning TPI) has been to drive practices underground and outside a regulatory framework. Some investors still see the opportunities of investment in the potentially lucrative risk of a player's future transfer value, and certain players, agents or clubs still have a need for investment of this kind. Because FIFA has retreated from regulating the activity, it is now conducted in a more concealed fashion than it was previously. It is perhaps no surprise that the *Daily Telegraph*'s sting was largely based on a pretend scheme to 'get around' the ban on TPI.

(g)   The privatisation of regulation

25.36   The increasing sums of money pouring into football and revolving around football transfers on the one hand, and the failure and retreat of regulation on the other, has led to a 'privatisation' of regulation. The parties themselves must enforce contracts as against each other, rather than seek redress from the regulator, for the loss caused to them by various forms of corruption, fraud or cheating.

25.37   The bellweather case for this dynamic in the UK was the *Tevez* case. West Ham United acquired the Argentinian player, Carlos Tevez's registration in circumstances where a third party maintained an interest and influence over the player in breach of the Premier League's rules, and West Ham was fined for its breach by the Premier League.[20] Sheffield United then brought arbitral proceedings against the Premier League arguing that West Ham ought to have been subject to a points' deduction by the regulator for its rule breach – had it been so West Ham would have been relegated instead of Sheffield United. The Arbitral panel failed to overturn the decision not to impose a points' sanction instead of a fine for this breach.[21]

25.38   Sheffield United then changed tack and brought a private claim (in FA Rule K arbitration) for breach of contract against West Ham. After establishing that the Premier League rules constituted a contract not only between each club and the regulator but between each club with each other, and that West Ham's breach of the relevant rule caused Sheffield United loss, in that it would not have been relegated had West Ham not benefited (in points) from its breach, Sheffield United succeeded in securing many millions of pounds in compensation from West Ham for breach of the contractual obligation that it owed Sheffield United to comply with the rules.[22]

---

19   See further, chapter 11, Third Party Investment.
20   *FAPL v West Ham United*, FAPL Disciplinary Commission, 27 April 2007.
21   *Sheffield United v Premier League* [2007] ISLR, SLR-77, Premier League Rule S Arbitration (Ch Sir Philip Otton); and see West Ham's failure to overturn the decision of the arbitrators in the Commercial Court: *Sheffield United v Premier League*, 13 July 2007 Smith J Comm Ct.
22   *Sheffield United v West Ham*, FA Rule K arbitration (Ch Lord Griffiths) 18 September 2008.

25.39   The case remains the high-water mark for participants wishing to secure compensation for losses suffered as a result of rule or contract breaches by others, but it is also significant because it reflected, or perhaps heralded, a new response to breaches, cheating and corruption generally by participants no longer confident that they can achieve a remedy via normal regulatory means. Football is big business, and clubs, players and agents are less likely to rely on the unpredictable discretion of an under-resourced regulator to effectively regulate the sport.

25.40   Ten years on private remedies for corruption and breach are far more common than complaints to the regulator. Disputes concerning the transfer of players and payments to agents, especially, are far more frequently determined now by claims for damages (and sometimes other relief such as injunctive relief) between participants, whether in the courts, before FIFA or the CAS, or in FA Rule K or league arbitration.[23]

25.41   Because these disputes are largely determined in arbitration, and arbitrations are generally confidential (though many of the decisions in disputes of this kind before the FIFA Dispute Resolution Chamber or the CAS are published), there are fewer precedents that can be relied on or referred to than is desirable, but there are nevertheless a number of cases and sources of law that should help practitioners and participants involved in disputes of this kind.

(h)   Causes of action and defences

25.42   Any English law cause of action that can be brought in the civil courts can naturally be brought by way of arbitration. Whilst the majority of claims in football arbitration remain claims for breach of contract, we are increasingly seeing more complex claims including allegations of fraud, conspiracy and inducement by third parties to breach contract.

25.43   The Court of Appeal decision in *Anthony McGill v The Sports and Entertainment Media Group (SEM)*[24] is a useful indication of the way the law approaches agreements that do not comply with the regulations. McGill claimed he had reached an oral contract to act as agent for the player in a transfer to Bolton Wanderers FC, but that SEM and Bolton induced a breach of the contract. SEM had entered into an agency agreement with Bolton to find the player and received commission from Bolton. McGill brought various claims (including inducement to breach contract and conspiracy) against both the agency SEM and Bolton. The defendants argued, amongst other things, that McGill had not reached a valid contract with the player as there was only an oral contract that he would act as agent – there was no executed written Representation Contract (that would have to be lodged with The FA) that would have entitled McGill to act as agent in the deal and receive fees. At first instance, the judge accepted that there had been an oral contract but dismissed the claim, holding that McGill had not demonstrated that the player would have entered into a written contract with him had it not been for the defendants' unlawful conduct. The Court of Appeal held that whilst the judge had been entitled to find on the balance of probabilities that the player would not have entered into a written contract with McGill, that was not the end of the matter. McGill was entitled to an award of damages on the basis of loss of his opportunity to earn a fee under a written agency agreement when the player's transfer to Bolton was completed.

---

23   See, generally, chapter 28, Arbitration.
24   [2016] EWCA Civ 1063, [2017] 1 WLR 989.

The correct approach was not (only) whether the player would or would not have signed a contract, but what percentage chance was there that he would have. As the judge had been entitled to find the player would not have signed, the percentage could not be more than 50%, but the case was remitted to the judge to determine what percentage chance there was that the player would have signed with McGill, and for that to then inform the damages to McGill.

25.44   Another important Court of Appeal football case that remains relevant to many disputes where corruption is alleged in relation to player transfers and agents is *Imageview Management Ltd v Jack*.[25] A football agent owes fiduciary duties to his client and the non-disclosure of a conflict of interest between the agent's own interest and those of his player client was a breach of the agent's duty of good faith to his client. In the circumstances, the agent forfeited his right to the commission he was otherwise contractually entitled to, and the fee he earned in breach of the duty was a secret profit, recoverable by the player, subject to the possibility of an equitable allowance. *Imageview* is not only relevant to allegations of secret profits (not unusual in football), but to any breach of fiduciary duty – the principle being that if a fiduciary (such as a football intermediary) acts dishonestly he will forfeit his right to fees by the principal (subject to that being inequitable).[26]

25.45   Business corruption in football remains a considerable issue. The 'battleground' has shifted somewhat from the conventional perspective of regulator on the one hand and wrongdoer on the other, to one where participants seek their own remedies against other participants.

(i)   Corruption of the regulators

25.46   In May 2015, the FBI arrested a number of FIFA officials, linked to widespread corruption and money laundering, that subsequently brought the long-awaited downfall of President Blatter and plunged FIFA, and in turn many regional football bodies including UEFA, into crisis. Later, in November 2015, French police investigated the former International Association of Athletics Federation (IAAF) president Lamine Diack, along with the institution's legal director and anti-doping director, relating to allegations that substantial bribes were accepted to conceal the positive doping test results of athletes. These two major crises, which reached the very top of two of the largest and most important international sports federations, posed a serious question: how can sport be serious about tackling corruption and cheating by individual athletes when the regulators themselves have been engaged in corruption and rigging on an industrial and criminal scale?

25.47   Football and FIFA provide a prime example. Nearly every informed observer knew, or should have known, that the institution had been corrupt for years. The evidence was there, but it was largely ignored or concealed. Andrew Jennings' book, *The Dirty Game: Uncovering the Scandal of FIFA*[27] revealed the scale of corruption throughout the institution that 'governs' world football. The heads of FIFA operated a system whereby hundreds of millions of dollars were paid in bribes to sports administrators, where money laundering was conducted on such a scale it shocked the organised crime unit of the FBI, and whereby nearly every

---

25   [2009] EWCA Civ 63, [2009] 2 All ER 666.
26   For a recent restatement of this principle see *Jeremy Hosking v Marathon Asset Management LLP* [2016] EWHC 2418 (Ch), [2017] 2 WLR 746.
27   Jennings, *The Dirty Game: Uncovering the Scandal at FIFA* (Century Press 2015).

World Cup bid that most football fans can remember was connected with corrupt payments made either through states or with funds coming from multinational corporations.

25.48   The 20 May 2015 New York Court indictment, in *The USA v Jeffrey Webb*[28] listed 47 counts of racketeering, wire fraud conspiracy, money laundering, preparation of fraudulent tax returns and obstruction of justice charges against a number of senior FIFA officials. This was just the tip of the iceberg. One telling passage from the indictment explained:[29]

> 'The corruption of the enterprise became endemic. Certain defendants and co-conspirators rose to power, unlawfully amassed significant personal fortunes by defrauding the organizations they were chosen to serve, and were exposed and then either expelled from those organizations or forced to resign. Other defendants and co-conspirators came to power in the wake of scandal, promising reform. Rather than repair the harm done to the sport and its institutions, however, these defendants and co-conspirators quickly engaged in the same unlawful practices that had enriched their predecessors.'

25.49   The last big FIFA corruption scandal before this one dated back to the operations of Swiss-based sports marketing company International Sport and Leisure (ISL), set up by former Adidas boss, Horst Dassler. The ISL became closely associated with FIFA, the International Olympic Committee (IOC) and the IAAF and paid tens of millions of dollars in bribes to senior sports administrators for corporate rights for its large multinational clients. The commercialisation of sport has brought billions of pounds of broadcasting and sponsorship revenue to sports where the administrators have the power to award contracts out to their friends (or often family). In turn, those same administrators, desperate to hang on to their position of power which allowed them to embezzle so much, would often need more corporate money to pay in bribes so other federations and administrators would vote for them to stay in charge. So the systematic corporate funded corruption of world football through Swiss companies and banks became established.

25.50   There was suggestion too that World Cup matches could have been fixed as a result of pressures from corrupt officials – from the Germany v Austria fixture in the 1982 World Cup[30] to Italy's surprising and controversial defeat by South Korea during the 2002 World Cup, where FIFA officials were allegedly concerned about host nation South Korea being knocked out too early and disgraced former FIFA Vice President Jack Warner is said to have picked the referee who went on to make a number of highly unusual decisions.[31] In any event, corruption appears to be at the heart of the decisions to stage big international competitions in certain countries in football.

25.51   The FIFA and IAAF scandals raise serious questions about whether sport is fit to govern itself. When the same people are involved in the administration and regulation of sport, including in determining which nations get to host events or which sponsors are associated with those events, inevitable conflicts of interest arise. To paraphrase Juvenal, who regulates the regulators? There is often nobody a player

28   See http://www.justice.gov/opa/file/450211/download (accessed March 2018).
29   Paragraph 75.
30   See the chronology in http://www.latinospost.com/articles/62672/20150528/fifa-corruption-scandal-timeline---bribery-and-racketeering-precede-sepp-blatter-presidency.htm (accessed March 2018).
31   http://www.eurosport.co.uk/football/south-korea-results-from-2002-world-cup-now-under-scrutiny_sto4758133/story.shtml (accessed March 2018) and see chapter 8 of Jennings, *The Dirty Game*.

or club can turn to complain about corruption or bias by the regulator. If there is the complaint may end up determined by the same hand-picked bodies which owe their existence to the regulator. It is no surprise that the recent exposures of corruption in sport have come not from inside the sport itself but from outside – whether by investigative journalists working with whistle-blowers or by foreign police forces taking action when the level of corruption became so significant as to constitute serious criminal offences.

25.52   Arguably the problem is institutional. Without proper independent scrutiny of sport, where the regulator is separate from those who administer the funds and the contracts and has real power over them, corruption scandals are likely to continue.

25.53   Until such time that effective and independent sports regulators come into existence the courts will inevitably become more involved in scrutinising the decision of sports governing bodies. Not only from the *Bradley*-type review standard that essentially limits the court's intervention to dealing with unreasonable, procedurally unfair or unlawful decisions;[32] but also by further developing the 'restraint of trade' or contractual bases for that review to exercise a more searching scrutiny into the administration of sport itself. In addition, we are more likely to see the intervention of elements of the criminal law, including the UK Bribery Act.[33] Just as the regulators' failure to regulate business corruption in football has led to a privatisation of that regulation – by parties enforcing their rights themselves – so also the regulators failure of self-regulation is likely to lead to a greater intervention by the courts. The historical judicial reluctance to interfere in the decisions of sports governing bodies may have to be relaxed.

C   CRIMINAL PROVISIONS AND RULES AND REGULATIONS FOR MATCH-FIXING AND BETTING

25.54   There is no legal (statutory or common law) definition of match-fixing. The Council of Europe Convention on the Manipulation of Sports Competitions refers to 'Manipulation of sports competitions' as being 'an intentional arrangement, act or omission aimed at an improper alteration of the result or the course of a sports competition in order to remove all or part of the unpredictable nature of the aforementioned sports competition with a view to obtaining an undue advantage for oneself or for others'.[34] As described in the sections above, it is conduct liable to fall within the ambit of both the criminal law and sports regulation.

(a)   Criminal law

25.55   In this jurisdiction, instances of match-fixing may be prosecuted under the Gambling Act 2005, s 42; Bribery Act 2010, ss 1 and 2; Criminal Law Act 1977, s 1; and the Fraud Act 2006. One of the most recent and successful prosecutions for match-fixing was the case of *R v Majeed (Mazhar)*[35] concerned with spot-fixing

---

32   *Bradley v Jockey Club* [2004] EWHC 2164; see further para **23.6** above.
33   For example, s 2 of the Bribery Act 2010 creates an offence where a person 'requests, agrees to receive or accepts a financial or other advantage as a reward for the improper performance' of a relevant function or activity.
34   See https://www.coe.int/en/web/conventions/full-list/-/conventions/rms/09000016801cdd7e (accessed March 2018).
35   [2012] EWCA Crim 1186.

in cricket. In that case the prosecution relied upon, *inter alia*, the Prevention of Corruption Act 1906, s 1. That statutory provision has been repealed and replaced by the Bribery Act 2010, ss 1 and 2.

25.56   There has been much criticism of the inadequacy of current criminal provisions to deal with match-fixing. By way of example, Alldrige[36] speculates that a prosecution in *Majeed* applying the Bribery Act 2010, following the repeal of the Prevention of Corruption Act 1906, might have been complicated by the requirement that the person performing the function or activity the subject of the bribe is 'expected to perform it in good faith'.[37] He suggests that such an expectation would arise from a fiduciary relationship or a contract with an obligation of utmost good faith, which is not present in all cases involving match-fixing. In the authors' view there is merit in that proposition given that, whilst it is likely that a jury would have little difficulty in finding that there exists an expectation of good faith on the part of a footballer playing for his country, the same might not apply to a disaffected footballer, badly treated by his club, and playing under protest. It is noteworthy in this regard, however, that the current UEFA Disciplinary Regulations ('the UEFA 2017 DR') discussed at paras 25.73 ff below, impose upon those bound (excluding players) a fiduciary duty towards UEFA.[38]

25.57   A further and/or alternative basis for prosecution for match-fixing may be found in the Gambling Act 2005, s 42. These provisions, however, have also been criticised for being inadequate. This is in part because of the limited deterrence effect of the maximum two year imprisonment[39] which the statute provides for, and in part because of the lack of specific reference in the legislation to match-fixing and spot-fixing, which, it has been argued, makes its application in these precise circumstances more problematic.[40]

25.58   That criticism has been levelled by many with an interest in these matters. Attempts were made to include provisions in the Gambling Act 2005 specifically aimed at match-fixing through the tabling of amendments[41] to the Gambling (Licensing and Advertising) Act 2014. These amendments themselves reflected the substantial amendments to the Gambling Act, s 42, proposed in a wide ranging Governance of Sports Bill sponsored by Lord Moynihan.[42] As well as providing for extensive detail about the types of conduct which would amount to 'cheating at gambling', and the persons whose conduct would be engaged by the relevant provisions, the amendments also proposed an increase in the maximum imprisonment from two to ten years.

25.59   The then Department of Media, Culture and Sport expressed the view, in response to criticism from the Sport Betting Group (SBG), that the Gambling Act 2005 s 42 was deliberately wide in order to extend its applicability. It stated in correspondence with the SBG that 'If it explicitly focused only upon match-fixing we may then lose its applicability to other circumstances'.[43] The authors venture to

---

36   P Alldridge, 'R. Majeed: corruption – conspiracy to give corrupt payments – accepting corrupt payments' (2012) 12 Crim LR 965–967.
37   Bribery Act 2010, s 3(3).
38   UEFA 2017 DR Title 1, Substantive Law, III Ethical provisions, Article 17(4).
39   Gambling Act 2005, s 42(4)(a).
40   Leanne O'Leary, 'Match-fixing' Westlaw Latest Update (8 May 2015), Westlaw UK.
41   Hansard, HL Vol 752, Part 122, cols 1318–1328 (4 March 2014).
42   *Governance of Sport Bill* HL Bill 20 (2014).
43   Kevin Carpenter, 'Tackling match-fixing: a look at the UK's new Anti-Corruption Plan' (13 February 2015), Law in Sport.

say that such an argument does not bear scrutiny when an amendment by addition rather than replacement could easily ensure both wide and precise applicability. It is difficult not to reach the conclusion that, in the age of austerity, government considers it preferable to pass the responsibility for governance and enforcement of sports to the relevant governing bodies, rather than seeking to extend the applicability of criminal legislation and with it the obligation of detection and enforcement.

(b)   Match-fixing and betting regulations

25.60   Match-fixing and betting regulations in respect of football have evolved over time and are to be found principally within the codes, rules and regulations of FIFA, the various football confederations, and national governing bodies. It is interesting to note, however, that as late as 2009, UEFA did not have specific match-fixing prohibitions and it was forced to rely principally upon the obligation not to bring football into disrepute in order to discipline a football club, its President and its captain suspected of fixing a Champion League match.[44] This section considers, therefore, the rules and regulations of, and their enforcement by, FIFA, UEFA and The FA. Provisions concerned with betting also exist within the Premier League Rules and English Football League Regulations, and these will also be briefly considered.

25.61   In broad terms, the approach taken by football governing bodies to combat match-fixing has been three-pronged. In addition to specific prohibitions on match-fixing, they have also introduced offences of failing to report approaches to fix matches, and bans on betting on football (even where there is no ability to influence the outcome of, or occurrence in, a match; or possession of insider knowledge). The latter has expanded from a ban on betting on matches in leagues and competitions in which the person placing the bet is or has been involved, to the present worldwide blanket ban on betting on football.

25.62   The rationale for the first two is difficult to question, although it is hoped that the football authorities exercise their discretion in cases of failure to report where there is clear evidence of duress and fear for one's own and one's family's life. The merit of a worldwide blanket ban on football is however, it is respectfully suggested, less easy to justify and may even be counter-productive, given that it is likely to drive the conduct underground where it is more difficult to detect and address, and potentially into the arms of unregulated and unscrupulous bookmakers where the individual concerned may become susceptible to blackmail.

(i)   FIFA regulatory provisions

25.63   FIFA has three principal regulatory codes concerned with integrity which have specific provisions dealing with corruption, match-fixing and betting: the FIFA Disciplinary Code 2017 edition ('the Disciplinary Code'); the FIFA Code of Ethics ('the Code of Ethics'); and the FIFA Code of Conduct 2017 ('the Code of Conduct'). The Disciplinary Code applies to every match and competition organised by FIFA, as well breaches of its statutory objectives particularly with regards to forgery, corruption and doping. It also applies to breaches of FIFA regulations not subject to the jurisdiction of other bodies. It is largely concerned with infringements and disciplinary matters directly related to matches and competitions.[45] In contrast the Code of Ethics is concerned with issues of integrity and ethics outside of the field of play.[46] The third code, the Code of Conduct, is a document setting out FIFA's 5 key values of 'Fair Play', 'Team Spirit', 'Diversity & Sustainability' and 'Innovation' which expressly include the 11 core principles of behaviour and conduct of the 2012 FIFA Code of Conduct. It applies to 'FIFA team members' which is said to include the Secretary General, the Deputy Secretary General, all other employees of FIFA, all freelancers and volunteers, and all employees and all members of executive bodies of FIFA's consolidated subsidiaries (the latter two catogories to the extent permitted by applicable laws).

(A) The Disciplinary Code

25.64   The main provisions concerned with match-fixing are to be found in First Title, Substantive Law, Chapter II of the FIFA Disciplinary Code.
Section 6, Article 62 deals with corruption generally and states as follows:

'1. Anyone who offers, promises or grants an unjustified advantage to a body of FIFA, a match official, a player or an official on behalf of himself or a third party in an attempt to incite it or him to violate the regulations of FIFA will be sanctioned: a) with a fine of at least CHF 10,000, b) with a ban on taking part in any football-related activity, and c) with a ban on entering any stadium.
2. Passive corruption (soliciting, being promised or accepting an unjustified advantage) will be sanctioned in the same manner.
3. In serious cases and in the case of repetition, sanction 1b) may be pronounced for life.'

Section 10, Article 69 addresses the unlawful influencing of match results and states as follows:

'1. Anyone who conspires to influence the result of a match in a manner contrary to sporting ethics shall be sanctioned with a match suspension or a ban on taking part in any football-related activity as well as a fine of at least CHF 15,000. In serious cases, a lifetime ban on taking part in any football-related activity shall be imposed.
2. In the case of a player or official unlawfully influencing the result of a match in accordance with par. 1, the club or association to which the player or official belongs may be fined. Serious offences may be sanctioned with expulsion from a competition, relegation to a lower division, a points deduction and the return of awards.'

25.65   An important provision which serves to potentially extend sanctions imposed by national associations and confederations so as to have worldwide effect is to be found in Second Title, Organisation and Procedure, Chapter II of the FIFA Disciplinary Code. Section 4, Subsection 3, Article 136 states as follows:

'1. If the infringement is serious, in particular but not limited to doping (cf. art. 63), unlawfully influencing match results (cf. art. 69), misconduct against match officials (cf. art. 49), forgery and falsification (cf. art. 61) or violation of the rules governing age limits (cf. art. 68 a), the associations, confederations, and other organising sports bodies shall request FIFA to extend the sanctions they have imposed so as to have worldwide effect.

---

45 The Disciplinary Code, Preliminary Title, Article 2.
46 The Code of Ethics, I. Scope of Application, Article 1 – Scope of Applicability.

2.   …
3.   The request shall be submitted in writing and enclose a certified copy matching the decision. It shall show the name and address of the person who has been sanctioned and that of the club and the association concerned.
4.   If the judicial bodies of FIFA discover that associations, confederations and other sports organisations have not requested a decision to be extended to have worldwide effect, these bodies may themselves pass a decision.'

25.66   Clearly, Article 62 is of wider applicability but there is no reason why disciplinary action in respect of match-fixing would not be brought for infringement of both Article 62 and 69. Indeed in the case of historic match-fixing allegations, the absence of any limitation period for infringements of Article 62[47] may mean that such cases will need to brought under those provisions. Article 69, on the face of it, appears to fall within 'other infringements' to which a limitation period of 10 years applies.[48] The reason for the difference in the limitation period is not clear and it is not reflected in the UEFA rules and regulations which are addressed below.

25.67   The burden of proof as with all cases of disciplinary infringements under the Disciplinary Code (excluding doping violations) lies with FIFA.[49] The FIFA Disciplinary Code is silent on the standard of proof but most commonly adopts that which is used by the Court of Arbitration for Sports (CAS), namely 'comfortable satisfaction'.

(B)   The Code of Ethics

25.68   The Code of Ethics is said to apply to all officials, players, as well as match and players' agents. The definition of 'Persons covered'[50] lacks the precision of the definition in the Disciplinary Code but it is presumed to cover the same individuals and entities.

25.69   The provisions of the Code of Ethics reflect the three-pronged approach described above. Article 13 'General rules of conduct' obliges those bound by the Code of Ethics to 'show commitment to an ethical attitude' and 'not to abuse their position in any way, especially to take advantage of their position for private aims or gains'. Article 18 'Duty of disclosure, cooperation and reporting' requires any potential breach of the Code of Ethics to be reported immediately. Article 25 'Integrity of matches and competitions' provides for a blanket ban on betting on football matches and also forbids those bound by the code 'from having stakes, either actively or passively, in companies, concerns, organisations, etc. that promote, broker, arrange or conduct' betting and gambling connected with football matches.

25.70   As with the Disciplinary Code the burden of proof lies with FIFA, or its Ethics Committee to be precise. The standard of proof is judged and decided on the basis of the members of the Ethics Committee's personal convictions.[51] How that operates as a matter of practice is unclear but the ultimate appeal body is CAS which applies the 'comfortable satisfaction' standard referred to above.

---

47   The Disciplinary Code, Chapter I, Section 6, Article 42(3).
48   The Disciplinary Code, Chapter I, Section 6, Article 42(1).
49   The Disciplinary Code, Chapter II, Section 1, Subsection 3, Article 99.
50   The Code of Ethics, I. Scope of Application, Article 2 – Persons covered.
51   The Code of Ethics, Chapter II: Procedure, Section 1: Procedural rules, Subsection 2: Proof, Article 51 – Standard of Proof.

(C)　The Code of Conduct

25.71　As well as expressing a zero tolerance approach to corruption and bribery, the Code of Conduct reiterates the strict blanket prohibition (direct or indirect) on betting, gambling, lotteries or similar transactions related to football matches and connects it expressly with 'manipulation' and 'integrity'. Three of the 11 core principles found in the 2012 FIFA Code of Conduct are also directly concerned with match-fixing and betting: 3.1 'Integrity and ethical behaviour'; 3.10 'Zero tolerance of bribery and corruption'; and 3.11 'No betting or manipulation'. The Code of Conduct has force as a set of directives under article 15, paragraph 6 of the FIFA Governance Regulations.

(ii)　UEFA regulatory provisions

25.72　UEFA has arguably the most comprehensive set of rules concerned with match-fixing and betting. It must be said that it faces a perfect cocktail of circumstances when it comes to the potential for match-fixing. The Champions League and Europa League matches it is responsible for organising involve teams, certainly at the early stages of the competitions, that share many of the characteristics of the lower league teams referred to above (and with it the same susceptibility to match-fixing) pitted against higher profile teams. In consequence, the pools of bets are larger, and the available betting markets more varied, making them an attractive proposition for criminals, particularly as the detection of suspicious betting patterns may be more difficult.

25.73　UEFA's match-fixing and betting regulations are set out in the UEFA 2017 DR. The UEFA 2017 DR apply to every match and competition organised by UEFA and to any serious violations of UEFA's statutory objectives (unless appropriately dealt with by a UEFA member association).[52] They cover member associations and their officials, clubs and their officials, match officials, players, and UEFA functionaries and elected representatives.[53]

25.74　UEFA 2017 DR make the member association or club responsible, and subject to disciplinary proceedings, for the action of its members, players, officials and functionaries, even in the absence of negligence or fault on the part of the club or member association,[54] and they stipulate that proceedings must not be abandoned notwithstanding the fact that the individual or entity the subject of the proceedings may no longer fall under its jurisdiction.[55]

25.75　The operative provisions potentially applicable to match-fixing are wide ranging and detailed. They include general provisions against: active and passive bribery[56] and/or corruption;[57] offering and accepting gifts or other benefits which might be considered liable to influence the recipient's behaviour;[58] using confidential

52　UEFA 2017 DR, Preliminary Title, Article 2(3) & (4)- Scope of material application.
53　UEFA 2017 DR, Preliminary Title, Article 3(1) – Scope of personal application.
54　UEFA 2017 DR, Title I – Substantive Law, I – General provisions, Article 8 – Responsibility.
55　UEFA 2017 DR, Preliminary Title, Article 4 – Scope of temporal application (2).
56　UEFA 2017 DR, Title I – Substantive Law, II – Offences, Article 11.2 – General principles of conduct.
57　UEFA 2017 DR, Title I – Substantive Law, III – Ethical provisions, Article 21 – Bribery and corruption.
58　UEFA 2017 DR, Title I – Substantive Law, III – Ethical provisions, Article 20 – Offering and accepting gifts and other benefits.

information in order to obtain or attempt to obtain a personal advantage or for an illegitimate purpose;[59] and bringing football and UEFA into disrepute.[60] The UEFA 2017 DR also require principles of loyalty, integrity, sportsmanship, and complete honesty to be observed and obliges all those bound by the regulations to report unethical conduct to UEFA without delay.[61] They also include specific provisions under Article 12 'Integrity of matches and competitions and match-fixing' which make it an offence not only to engage directly and indirectly in match-fixing[62] but also to fail to immediately and voluntarily inform UEFA of any such approach or awareness of such conduct.[63]

25.76   Whilst it is not suggested that the UEFA 2017 DR are not capable of addressing instances of spot-fixing, not least given the use of far more general provisions to deal with match-fixing in the *Pobeda* case (see para **25.99** below), unlike The FA match-fixing provisions discussed below which deal expressly with an 'occurrence'[64] in a match or competition, the UEFA 2017 DR refer only to 'the course and/or result of a match or competition'.[65]

25.77   The seriousness with which UEFA appears to treat match-fixing is also reflected in the absence of any statute of limitations,[66] or time limits for enforcement,[67] for offences involving match-fixing, bribery and corruption. Further, the period during which recidivism, being the repetition of an offence of a similar nature, is considered an aggravating feature, is significantly longer for match-fixing and corruption, 10 years against one to three years for all other offences[68]. The standard of proof is expressly stated to be 'comfortable satisfaction'.[69]

(iii)   The English Football Association regulatory provisions

25.78   The Football Association Rules and Regulations (Season 2017–2018) ('the FA Rules') which address match-fixing and betting follow the same familiar pattern of prohibitions and requirements as those described above. They include specific prohibitions on match-fixing and an express requirement to report any approach associated with match-fixing, as well as a blanket worldwide prohibition on betting on football. It is to be noted that the rules covering the ban on betting are more complicated and detailed than those concerned with match-fixing.

---

59   UEFA 2017 DR, Title I – Substantive Law, III – Ethical provisions, Article 18 – Use of confidential information and abuse of position.
60   UEFA 2017 DR, Title I – Substantive Law, II – Offences, Article 11.2(d) – General principles of conduct.
61   UEFA 2017 DR, Title I – Substantive Law, III – Ethical provisions, Article 17 – Ethical provisions: scope, UEFA's competence and general principles.
62   UEFA 2017 DR, Title I – Substantive Law, II – Offences, Article 12.2(a)–(c) – Integrity of matches and competitions and match-fixing.
63   UEFA 2017 DR, Title I – Substantive Law, II – Offences, Article 12.2(d) & (e) – Integrity of matches and competitions and match-fixing.
64   FA Rules, Rule E5(a).
65   UEFA 2017 DR, Title I – Substantive Law, II – Offences, Article 12 – Integrity of matches and competitions and match fixing.
66   UEFA 2017 DR, Title I – Substantive Law, I – General provisions, Article 10 – Statute of limitation (2).
67   UEFA 2017 DR, Title III – Special Provisions, IX – Enforcement, Article 72 – Time limits on enforcement of decisions.
68   UEFA 2017 DR, Title I – Substantive Law, IV – Other provisions, Article 25 – Recidivism.
69   UEFA 2017 DR, Title I – Substantive Law, IV – Other provisions, Article 24 – Evaluation of evidence and standard of proof.

25.79 The FA Rules deal with issues of conduct in Rule E. Rule E empowers The FA to take action against a 'participant' for breaches of a wide range of laws, rules, regulations, and statutes of not only The FA, but also UEFA and FIFA[70]. 'Participant' has a very wide definition, namely any:

> 'Affiliated Association, Competition, Club, Club Official, Intermediary, Player, Official, Manager, Match Official, Match Official observer, Match Official coach, Match Official mentor, Management Committee Member, member or employee of a Club and all such persons who are from time to time participating in any activity sanctioned either directly or indirectly by The Association.'[71].

The standard of proof applied in disciplinary case (excluding doping cases) is the civil standard of the balance of probability.[72]

(A) Match-fixing

25.80 Match-fixing is dealt with under the heading 'Integrity Matters in Relation to Matches and Competitions' under Rule E5 and E6. Rule E5(a) prohibits seeking 'to influence for an improper purpose the result, progress, conduct or any other aspect of, or occurrence in, a football match or competition'. The application of Rule E5 extends, therefore, beyond pure match-fixing for illegitimate betting purposes to the type of incident referred to in para **25.50** above, which, whether intentional or not, was likely to be driven by two teams wishing to ensure passage to the next round of a competition, to the detriment of a third, rather than betting. Rule E5(b) specifically addresses match-fixing for betting purposes. It provides that:

> 'A Participant shall not, directly or indirectly, offer, agree to give, give, solicit, agree to accept or accept any bribe, gift or reward or consideration of any nature which is, or could appear to be related in any way to that Participant, or any other, failing to perform to the best of their ability, or to that Participant or any other person (whether a Participant or not), directly or indirectly, seeking to influence for an improper purpose, the result, progress, conduct or any other aspect of, or occurrence in, a football match or competition.'

25.81 The reporting requirement is encapsulated in Rule E6. The requirement to report is, however, expressly linked to the offer to the participant of 'any offer made to him or any Participant of any bribe, gift, or reward or consideration of any offer' which arguably means that it will not apply to all breaches of Rule E5(a).

25.82 Football matches covered by Rule E5 and E6 include any football match or competition defined as such in Rule A2, meaning 'any football match sanctioned by The Association and /or an Affiliated Association' and 'any competition (whether a league or knock-out competition or otherwise) sanctioned by The Association and/ or an Affiliated Association', as well as any other football match or competition including those sanctioned by UEFA, FIFA or any other association, federation or governing body.[73]

(B) Betting

25.83 The provisions against betting are lengthy and on the face of it appear to be complicated when compared to those in respect of match-fixing. This is in part due

---

70   FA Rules, Rule E1(c) and (d).
71   FA Rules, Rule A2.
72   FA Rules, Disciplinary Regulations – General Provisions – Rule 1.5.
73   FA Rules – Rule E1(c) and (d).

to the fact that different provisions apply depending on the level of football that the participant is involved in. Rule E8(2) applies to persons whose status as a participant is solely as a result of their involvement at a club below Step 4 in the National League System (9th tier and below) and Steps 3 to 7 inclusive of the Women's Football Pyramid (3rd tier and below), as well as match official, referee coach and referee assessor operating at Level 4 or below. Rule E8(1) applies to all other participants but expressly not those subject to Rule E8(1). Rule E8(3) applies to all participants. Football matches covered by Rule E8 are the same as those covered under Rule E5 described in para **25.79** above.

25.84   Rule E8(1) prohibits participants from betting on:

'the result, progress, or any other aspect of, or occurrence in a football match or competition; or any other matter concerning or related to football anywhere in the world, including for example and without limitation, the transfer of players, employment of managers, team selection, or disciplinary matters'.

The prohibition is engaged whether or not the participant had any ability to influence the outcome or occurrence or any connection with (however remote), or knowledge of, the team or match with which the bet was concerned. There is no restriction on the level of football match to which the prohibition applies. In principle a bet placed by a physiotherapist employed by a non-league club on a lower league match in Bolivia would amount to a breach of Rule E8(1), although the sanction to be applied will not be as severe as one which may be perceived to be raising questions about the integrity of the game.

25.85   Rule E8(2)(a) adopts a more restrictive approach to what it deems to be a breach of the FA Rules. Participants (with the restricted meaning described at para **25.82** above) are prohibited from betting on:

'(i) the result, progress, conduct or any other aspect of, or occurrence in, a football match or competition: (A) in which the Participant is participating, or has participated in that season; or (B) in which the Participant has any influence, either direct or indirect; or (ii) any other matter concerning or related to any Club participating in any league Competition, as defined in Rule A2, that the Participant is participating in or has participated in during that season, including, for example and without limitation, the transfer of players, employment of managers, team selection or disciplinary matters.'

25.86   Given that participants include all employees and officials of football clubs, and given the condition of participation which attaches to Rule E8(2), Rule E8(2) makes it clear that:

'all Employees and Officials of a Club are deemed to participate in every football match played by that Club while they are so employed or acting as a Club Official; all Players registered with a Club are deemed to participate in every football match played by that Club while they are so registered.'

In principle this prohibits a catering employee of a national league club from placing a bet on The FA Cup final even after his or her employer has been knocked out of the competition.

25.87   Additional provisions include Rule E8(2)(b), which prohibits betting on any football match played at under 18 level or below (the reason for that prohibition, without some additional requirement of a connection with the youth match in issue, is unclear) and Rule E8(2)(c), which prohibits the *use* of any information which is not publicly available, and obtained as a result of the participant's position within football, for betting purposes.

25.88   Rule E8(1) and Rule E8(2) have identical provisions which make supplying information to a third party, obtained as a result of the participant's position within football, which is not publicly available, and which is used for betting purposes, a breach of the FA Rules. In both cases it is a defence for a participant charged under these rules to:

> 'establish, on the balance of probability, that the Participant provided any such information in circumstances where he did not know, and could not reasonably have known, that the information provided would be used by the other person for or in relation to betting.'

25.89   Rule E8(3) prohibits a participant acting in an individual and personal capacity from advertising or promoting any betting activity which would amount to a breach of Rule E8 insofar as it is applicable to that individual. It might be said that there is a degree of hypocrisy in that rule given the current level of sponsorship of football by betting companies.

(C)   Reporting

25.90   In addition to the reporting requirement in Rule E6, the FA Rules also provide for a self-standing reporting provision in Rule 14 under the heading 'Reporting Misconduct' which makes express reference to approaches made to a participant 'in relation to betting on football contrary to FA Rules'.

(D)   Disciplinary procedures, penalties and sanctions

25.91   The Disciplinary Regulations of the FA Rules set out how proceedings for breaches of Rule E are to be conducted although those regulations state expressly that 'procedural and technical considerations must take second place to the paramount object of being just and fair to all parties'.[74]

25.92   The Disciplinary Regulations deal, *inter alia*, with the collection of evidence, directions, determination of the charge and penalty, and costs.

25.93   The Regulatory Commission has the power to impose a wide range of sanctions from a reprimand and/or warning as to future conduct to a lifetime ban, fine and costs. In determining the appropriate sanction, the Regulatory Commission has an unfettered discretion but the starting point is the 'Sanction Guidelines' issued by the Football Regulation Authority. The table is set out below:[75]

---

74   FA Rules, Disciplinary Regulations, General Provisions, Rule 1.1.
75   An important note to the Guidelines table states:

> '*A suspension equivalent to betting on own team may be appropriate where a Participant has recently been on loan at the Club bet on.

> The guidelines are not intended to override the discretion of Regulatory Commissions to impose such sanctions as they consider appropriate having regard to the particular facts and circumstances of a case. However, in the interests of consistency it is anticipated that the guidelines will be applied unless the applicable case has some particular characteristic(s) which justifies a greater or lesser sanction outside the guidelines.

> The assessment of the seriousness of the offence will need to take account of the factors set out above [ie in the sanctions table]. A key aspect is whether the offence creates the perception that the result or any other element of the match may have been affected by the bet, for example because the Participant has bet against himself or his club or on the contrivance

SANCTION GUIDELINES – BETTING CASES CHARGED UNDER FA RULE E8(b)

	Bet placed on any aspect of any football match anywhere in the world, but not involving Participant's Club competitions.	Bet placed on Participant's competition but not involving his Club (including spot bet).	Bet placed on own team to win	Bet placed on own team to lose.	Bet placed on particular occurrence(s) not involving the player who bet (spot bet).	Bet placed on particular occurrence(s) involving the player who bet (spot bet).
Financial Entry Point – Any fine to include, as a minimum, any financial gain made from the bet(s)	Warning/Fine	Fine	Fine	Fine	Fine	Fine
Sports sanction range	Suspension n/a	Suspension n/a where Participant has no connection with the Club bet on*	0–6 months to be determined by factors below	6 months – life to be determined by factors below	0–12 months	6 months – life
Factors to be considered in relation to any increase/ decrease from entry point	Factors to be considered when determining appropriate sanctions will include the following: • Overall perception of impact of bet(s) on fixture/game integrity; • Player played or did not play; • Number of Bets; • Size of Bets; • Fact and circumstances surrounding pattern of betting; • Actual stake and amount possible to win; • Personal Circumstances; • Previous record – (any previous breach of betting Rules will be considered as a highly aggravating factor); • Experience of the participant; • Assistance to the process and acceptance of the charge.					

25.94   It is to be noted that the range of sporting sanctions in respect of a 'spot bet' placed by the player responsible for the occurrence is the same as for a player betting against his team to lose even where the player had no involvement in, confidential information about, or ability to influence the match in issue. It seems surprising given that one offence involves an intentional and improper attempt to take advantage of an ability not only to influence, but to determine, an 'occurrence', and the other is a 'strict liability' offence demonstrating a degree of disloyalty.

25.95   The provisions relating to the determination of penalties in respect of breaches of Rule E5, E8 and E14 are also designed to tackle match-fixing by encouraging the provision of information by those found to be in breach of those rules. Clause 8.3(b) and (c) of the Disciplinary Regulations stipulates that:

'(b) The Regulatory Commission must consider suspending a portion of the penalty to be imposed in any case where a Participant –
   (i) has committed a breach of Rule E5, E8 or E14 of the Rules of The Association; and,
   (ii) has provided assistance and/or information to The Association, UEFA, FIFA, any other national football association, a law enforcement agency or professional disciplinary body; and,

> of a particular occurrence within the match. Such conduct will be a serious aggravating factor in all cases. A further serious aggravating factor will be where the Participant played or was involved in the match on which the bet was made.
>
> Betting offences are separate and distinct from charges under FA Rule E5 which concerns match-fixing. It should be noted that save in exceptional circumstances a Participant found to have engaged in fixing the outcome or conduct of a match would be subject to a lifetime ban from the game. Where it can be proved that a bet has actually affected a result or occurrence within the match then such conduct will be specifically charged rather than treating the incident as a betting offence.'

(iii) the assistance and/or information provided results in the discovery or establishment of a criminal offence or the breach of disciplinary rules by another person relating to betting or integrity (not including anti-doping, in respect of which the Anti-Doping Programme Regulations shall apply) in football or sport generally.

(c) If in any such case the Regulatory Commission, in its discretion, considers it to be appropriate to suspend a portion of the penalty to be imposed, the extent to which the otherwise applicable penalty may be suspended will be based on the significance of the assistance provided by the Participant to the effort to eliminate corruption from sport.'

(iv)   English Premier League regulatory provisions

25.96   Presumably as a result of the wide jurisdiction and ambit of the UEFA 2017 DR and the FA Rules, the Premier League addresses the issue of betting and match-fixing only in the briefest terms in the Premier League Rules. Rule J.6 which is to be found in the Club: Finance and Governance part of the Rules provides as follows:

> 'No Club, Official or Player may, in connection with betting on an event in, or on the result of, a League Match or a match in a competition which forms part of the Games Programmes or Professional Development Leagues (as those terms are defined in the Youth Development Rules): offer or receive a payment or any form of inducement to or from any Club or the Official or Player of any Club; or receive or seek to receive any payment or other form of inducement from any Person.'

(v)   Owners and directors

25.97   In addition to the applicability of the rules and regulations set out above to owners and directors of football clubs by virtue of the scope of the application of those rules and regulations, the rules against betting and match-fixing also feature in the owners' and directors' test prescribed by The FA,[76] the Premier League[77] and the English Football League.[78]

D   SUMMARY OF REGULATORY CASES

25.98   This section will consider in more detail three important international cases involving match-fixing prosecuted by UEFA and FIFA respectively and determined on a final basis by CAS, namely *Pobeda Oriekhov*[79] and *Lamptey*.[80] Additionally, and given the increasing number of gambling related cases in this jurisdiction, the authors consider that there is significant value to practitioners in including an analysis of gambling cases dealt with under the FA Rules.

---

76   FA Rules, Owners' and Directors Test – The Declaration (vii).
77   Premier League Rules, Clubs: Finance and Governance, Section F: Owners' and Directors Test F.1.14.
78   EFL Regulations, Appendix 3, 1 Interpretation, 1.1(e).
79   CAS 2010/A/2172 *Mr Oleg Oriekhov v UEFA*.
80   See http://www.fifa.com/worldcup/news/y=2017/m=3/news=match-official-banned-for-life-due-to-match-manipulation-2876513.html (accessed March 2018).

(a)   International cases

(i)   UEFA

(A)   Pobeda

25.99   FK Pobeda – Prilep ('Pobeda'), a football club affiliated to the Football Federation of Macedonia, Aleksandar Zabrcanec, its President, and Nikolce Zdraveski, its captain ('the defendants'), had charges of match-fixing brought against them by UEFA in respect of the first qualifying round of the UEFA Champions League 2004/05 in which Pobeda participated.

25.100   Following a UEFA Disciplinary Inspector report which concluded that the club, Mr Zabrcanec, and Mr Zdraveski had acted in breaches of the principles of integrity and sportsmanship set out in Article 5 of the 2004 edition of the UEFA Disciplinary Regulations ('the UEFA 2004 DR'), the UEFA Control and Disciplinary Body held a hearing, suspended Pobeda from competing in any UEFA competition for eight years and banned Mr Zabrcanec and Mr Zdraveski from exercising any football-related activities for life.

25.101   The defendants lodged an appeal against the decision of the UEFA Control and Disciplinary Body with the UEFA Appeals Body ('the UEFA Appeals Body'). The UEFA Appeals Body reviewed the case *de novo* and it upheld the decision resulting in the defendants filing an appeal with CAS.

25.102   By registering for the 2004/05 UEFA Champions Leagues qualifying rounds, Pobeda had submitted to the 2004 edition of the UEFA Statutes ('the 2004 Statutes') and UEFA 2004 DR but because of the principle of *lex mitior*, the UEFA Control and Disciplinary Body and in turn the UEFA Appeals Body applied the 2008 edition of the Disciplinary Regulations ('the UEFA 2008 DR') where the UEFA 2008 DR were more favourable to the defendants. The CAS Panel in turn adopted the same approach.

25.103   As explained above, because there were no provisions in the 2004 Statutes and the UEFA 2004 DR referring specifically to 'match-fixing', the charges against the defendants were brought under Article 52 of the 2004 Statutes, and Articles 5 and 8 of the UEFA 2004 DR.

25.104   Article 52 of the 2004 Statutes provides that 'disciplinary measures may be imposed for unsportsmanlike conduct, violations of the Laws of the Game, and contravention of UEFA's Statutes, regulations, decisions and directives as shall be in force from time to time'.

25.105   Article 5, para 1 of the UEFA 2004 DR provides that 'Member associations, clubs, as well as their players, officials and members shall conduct themselves according to the principles of loyalty, integrity and sportsmanship', and Article 5, para 2 of the UEFA 2004 DR sets out specific examples of breaches of these principles which did not, however, specifically include match-fixing or match manipulation.

25.106   Article 8 of the UEFA 2004 DR, para 1 provides that 'Unsporting conduct, breaches of the Laws of the Game, as well as infringements of UEFA's Statutes, regulations, decisions and directives, are penalised by means of disciplinary measures' and para 2 that 'Disciplinary measures provided for may be taken against members associations, clubs and individuals for offences before, during or after the match'.

25.107   As to Pobeda's liability for the alleged actions of its president and captain, Article 11 of the UEFA 2004 DR provides that disciplinary measures could be taken against clubs if 'a team, player, official or member is in breach of Article 5' of the UEFA 2004 DR. As such the CAS Panel found that:

> 'The mere fact that the president of Pobeda is found guilty of fixing matches is, according to article 11 2004 DR, sufficient to also sanction the Club as such. The objective of this provision can only be reached by a rigorous application of the sanctions provided under article 14 2004 DR.'[81]

25.108   The disciplinary measures that could be imposed against clubs were set out in Article 14 of the UEFA 2004 DR and those against individuals set out in Article 15 of the UEFA 2004 DR.

25.109   The CAS Panel found, relying primarily on expert evidence in relation to betting patterns which indicated that there was ten times the amount usually wagered on this kind of match, that the games between Pobeda and Pyunik had been manipulated. Applying the standard of proof of 'comfortable satisfaction' it deemed that Mr Zabrcanec had actively participated in fixing the matches. It was not, however, satisfied with the evidence against the Mr Zdraveski and set aside the sanctions imposed on him.

25.110   On the basis that match-fixing is 'one of the worst possible infringements of the integrity of sports',[82] the CAS Panel considered that the life ban imposed on Mr. Zabrcanec was an 'adequate sanction and not disproportionate'. The CAS Panel also considered that the sanction imposed on Pobeda was correct on the basis that sanctions should 'not only prevent individuals from manipulating games, but also encourage the other members of the club to take action when they become aware of such manipulations'.[83]

(B)   Oriekhov

25.111   Mr Oleg Oriekhov was a UEFA Category 2 Referee appointed to officiate a group stage match between FC Basel 1893 and PFC CSKA Sofia in the 2009/10 UEFA Europa League.

25.112   In the context of a criminal investigation into possible fraud related to match-fixing and illegal gambling, conducted by the Public Prosecutor of Bochum, Germany, several suspects were put under surveillance and their telephone conversations were intercepted. Mr Oriekhov was implicated in those conversations.

25.113   In light of evidence gathered as part of that investigation and in accordance with Article 32*bis* of the 2008 edition of the UEFA Disciplinary Regulations ('the UEFA 2008 DR'), the Chairman of the UEFA Control and Disciplinary Body provisionally suspended Mr Oriekhov from all refereeing activities. The decision was confirmed on a permanent basis by the UEFA Control and Disciplinary Body and a request made to FIFA to give the ban worldwide effect. The request was duly granted by the Chairman of the FIFA Disciplinary Committee, but subject to the outcome of any appeal.

81   CAS 2009/A/1920 *FK Pobeda, Aleksandar Zabrcanec, Nicolce Zdraverskiv/UEFA*, para 117.
82   Ibid, para 115.
83   Ibid, para 116.

25.114   Mr Oriekhov appealed to the UEFA Appeals Body which found that there was enough evidence of repeated contacts between Mr Oriekhov and the criminals responsible for betting fraud. The UEFA Appeals Body found that Mr Oriekhov had, by not immediately reporting to UEFA that he had been approached to participate in match-fixing, breached his duty to disclose such illicit approaches, and breached principles of conduct under UEFA 2008 DR. It considered the offence committed by the appellant to be extremely serious and, in consequence, imposed a life ban, a decision which Mr Oriekhov appealed to CAS.

25.115   Because the match in issue had taken place in 2009 the relevant rules were those set out in the UEFA General Terms and Conditions for Referees, Edition 2003 and the UEFA 2008 DR.

25.116   The charges against Mr Oriekhov were brought pursuant to the following regulatory provisions:

- Article 13 of the UEFA General Terms and Conditions for Referees, which provides as follows:

  'Respect of the rules

  Referees undertake to apply and respect the applicable Laws of the Game published by FIFA, any related decisions, any and all UEFA's rules, regulations and statutes as well as any and all instructions or circulars issued by the UEFA Referees Committee or UEFA Administration.

  Any breach by Referees and/or national associations of the current General Terms and Conditions as well as any breach of the UEFA statutes, regulations, directives, decisions, instructions or circulars letters could entail the instigation of proceedings by the Disciplinary authorities of UEFA.'

- Article 5 of the UEFA 2008 DR which notably now included specific match-fixing and match manipulation:

  'Principles of conduct

  Member associations, clubs, as well as their players, officials and members, shall conduct themselves according to the principles of loyalty, integrity and sportsmanship.

  For example, a breach of these principles is committed by anyone:

  a)   who engages in or attempts to engage in active or passive bribery and/or corruption; …
  d)   whose conduct brings the sport of football, and UEFA in particular, into disrepute; …
  j)   who acts in a way that is likely to exert an influence on the progress and/or the result of a match by means of behaviour in breach of the statutory objectives of UEFA with a view to gaining an undue advantage for himself or a third party; …
  l)   who participates directly or indirectly in betting or similar activities relating to UEFA competition matches, or who has a direct or indirect financial interest in such activities.'

- Article 6 of the General Terms and Conditions for Referees:

  'Referees undertake to behave in a professional and appropriate manner before, during and after their appointment.

  Referees also undertake not to accept any gifts worth more than CHF 200 (or of an equivalent value) from bodies and/or persons directly and/or indirectly connected with the UEFA matches for which they have been appointed. Match souvenirs such as pennants and replica team shirts are acceptable. Under no circumstances are Referees allowed to keep the match ball(s).

Any Referee who is the target or considered to be the target of attempted bribery shall notify UEFA immediately.

…

Referees shall not take part in any betting activities concerning UEFA matches.'

25.117 Based on the above provisions and the available evidence, the CAS Panel considered it unnecessary to make a finding on the issue of whether Mr Oriekhov had manipulated the match or actually accepted or received money. It was sufficient, and the CAS Panel considered it proven to its comfortable satisfaction, that there had been repeated and undisclosed contact between Mr Oriekhov and the criminals responsible for the match-fixing and betting fraud.

25.118 In terms of sanction, the CAS Panel applied Articles 8, 11, 15 and 17 of the UEFA 2008 DR. Despite making no finding as to Mr Oriekhov's active participation in the match-fixing, indeed even though the CAS Panel proceeded expressly on the basis that he had not so participated, it found that the life ban from any football-related activities was the correct and proportionate sanction in all the circumstances. In support of that finding, the CAS Panel referred, *inter alia*, to sporting regulators being under an obligation to 'demonstrate zero-tolerance against all kinds of corruption and to impose sanctions sufficient to serve as an effective deterrent to people who might otherwise be tempted through greed or fear to consider involvement in such criminal activities'[84]; the 'great and widely publicized damage to the image of UEFA and of football in general'[85] that the allegation of match-fixing had caused; and 'the importance of the UEFA Europa League, of the level of this competition, and of the sporting and financial interests at stake'.[86]

25.119 The outcome of those two important CAS sanctioned UEFA decisions are in line with other decisions made by UEFA. The table below[87] sets out some of the significant cases prosecuted by UEFA.

Case	Decision	Year
FK Pobeda	Club: 8-year ban from UEFA competitions President: life ban	2009
Tomislav Setka	One year and six months' suspension	2010
Novo Panic	Life ban	2010
Oleg Oriekhov	Life ban	2010
Vukasin Poleksic	One year and six months' suspension	2010
Olympiacos Volou FC	One year of ineligibility in UEFA competitions	2011
SK Sigma Olomouc	One year of ineligibility in UEFA competitions	2012
Kevin Sammut	Life ban reduced to 10 years by CAS	2012
Fenerbahce SK	Two years of ineligibility in UEFA competitions	2013
Besiktas JK	One year of ineligibility in UEFA competitions	2013
FC Metalist Kharkiv	One year of ineligibility in UEFA competitions	2013

(continued)

84 CAS 2010/A/2172 *Mr Oleg Oriekhov v UEFA*, para 80.
85 Ibid, para 83.
86 Ibid, para 82.
87 See http://www.uefa.com/insideuefa/protecting-the-game/integrity/news/newsid=1950012.html? redirectFromOrg=true#/ (accessed March 2018).

Case	Decision	Year
Vasile Mungiu	Life ban	2013
Andranik Arsenyan & Hovhannes Avagyan	Life ban	2013
Eskisehirspor	One year of ineligibility in UEFA competitions	2014
Sivasspor	One year of ineligibility in UEFA competitions	2014
KF Skenderbeu	One year of ineligibility in UEFA competitions	2016

(ii)   FIFA

Lamptey

25.120   Mr Joseph Lamptey was an experienced Ghanaian FIFA referee who had previously officiated at both the 2015 Africa Cup of Nations and 2016 Rio Olympics. He was selected to referee a World Cup qualifier between Senegal and South Africa on 12 November 2016. During that match, he awarded a penalty to South Africa for a handball which was duly converted, contributing to a 2-1 win for South Africa. Replays showed the ball had hit the Senegal player on the knee.

25.121   The FIFA Disciplinary Committee brought charges against Mr Lamptey under Section 10, Article 69 of the FIFA Disciplinary Code and found him guilty. According to FIFA this was based on reports of irregular betting activities from a number of international companies engaged in monitoring betting, and what FIFA described as a 'sporting analysis of the match'.[88] He was sanctioned with a lifetime ban from taking part in any kind of football-related activity (administrative, sport or any other) at national and international level.[89] CAS, to whom Mr Lamptey appealed, upheld both the finding and the sanction, finding that 'it is essential ... for sporting regulators to demonstrate zero-tolerance of all kinds of activities intended to influence the result of a match in a manner contrary to sporting ethics and to impose sanctions sufficient to serve as an effective deterrent to people who might otherwise be tempted to consider involvement in such activities',[90] and that therefore a life ban from any football-related activities was a proportionate sanction.[91] Unusually, FIFA ordered a replay of the match having found that neither the Senegal nor the South Africa member associations were involved in the manipulation of the match.[92]

(b)   FA cases

25.122   The FA cases set out below will be of particular interest to practitioners in this field. Whilst Regulatory Commissions which deal with breaches of betting offences under Rule E8 ('the Betting Rules') are not bound, as a matter of law and precedent, by previous decisions of other Regulatory Commissions, the principles of natural

---

88   See http://www.fifa.com/worldcup/news/y=2017/m=9/news=south-africa-vs-senegal-world-cup-qualifier-to-be-replayed-in-november-2907241.html (accessed March 2018).
89   See http://www.fifa.com/worldcup/news/y=2017/m=3/news=match-official-banned-for-life-due-to-match-manipulation-2876513.html (accessed March 2018).
90   CAS 2017/A/5173 *Joseph Odartei Lamptey v FIFA*, para 93.
91   Ibid, para 94.
92   See http://www.fifa.com/worldcup/news/y=2017/m=9/news=south-africa-vs-senegal-world-cup-qualifier-to-be-replayed-in-november-2907241.html.

justice, fairness, consistency and proportionality which they are bound to follow, require that those subject to proceedings should not be sanctioned substantially more harshly for committing the same, or similar offences, as others.

25.123   The very wide range in the recommended sanctions for particular conduct provided by the Sanction Guidelines – by way of example the recommended sanction under the Sanction Guidelines for a participant betting against his own team ranges from 6 months to life – makes an understanding of other cases all the more important.

(i)   The role and relevance of perception

25.124   As explained in the notes to the Sanction Guidelines central to the question of appropriate sanction for a breach of the Betting Rules is the issue of perception and the distinction to be drawn between breaches of the Betting Rules and match-fixing. The notes to the Sanction Guidelines state:

> 'Betting offences are separate and distinct from charges under FA Rule E5 which concerns match-fixing. It should be noted that save in exceptional circumstances a Participant found to have engaged in fixing the outcome or conduct of a match would be subject to a lifetime ban from the game.'[93]

25.125   Proving match-fixing is notoriously difficult, but it is precisely because it is so difficult to prove, that The FA has brought in the Betting Rules as strict liability offences without any need for evidence of an intention to influence a match. The Betting Rules are intended to protect the integrity of football, and the public confidence in the integrity of football, so their overriding focus is on perception:

> 'would a reasonable person, with knowledge of the bets and circumstances of the bets, conclude that the integrity of football has been compromised? Would the public think the bets mean a player may have influenced the result or used inside information for reward?'

25.126   An important point about the meaning of perception in this regard is that, like the 'reasonable bystander' test, it does not relate to the perception of an ill-informed person reading a newspaper headline or a tweet in a hurry. It means what the reasonable observer, possessed with all the facts and knowledge the Regulatory Commission is in possession of, would perceive. Would that observer still be suspicious that there may be 'something more' to the betting than simply a breach of the rules?

25.127   According to The FA, between the 2007/08–2016/17 seasons 59 betting cases were considered by its Regulatory Commissions.[94] In between a third and half of all previous betting cases there was no sporting sanction at all. Where there have been sporting sanctions, 14 were for suspensions of three months or less (many for only one month, some sanctions being suspended such that there was no immediate sanction), a further ten were for between three and six months, and less than a third of all cases were for over six months.

25.128   The case summaries set out below relate to many of the more serious cases.

---

93   See n 75, above.
94   Based in information released by The FA at the beginning of 2017 in the course of proceedings in which the authors were acting.

FA v Mangan (2009)[95]

25.129   The participant, a football player, had made a number of relatively large bets on his own team to win. The Regulatory Commission found that he had given a knowingly false explanation and untrue story to try and avoid the charges.[96] No credit was given for later admissions that he was bound to make, not least as the Regulatory Commission found that he had given 'blatantly dishonest evidence'.[97] The case involved what was deemed to be highly 'suspicious' conduct because, whilst the player bet on his own team and did not play in the match, he went to the betting shop and placed those bets with two friends who played for the opposing team in one of the matches.[98] The player was banned for five months and fined £2,000.

FA v Heys (2013)[99]

25.130   The participant admitted 735 breaches of the Betting Rules. He had held the roles of Administrator, Chief Executive and then Managing Director of the Club Accrington Stanley FC. He placed 231 bets on his own team; 33 of the bets were for Accrington Stanley to lose. He did not play in the matches but he was 'in a position to know non-public information' about the matches and held a position of influence at the club.[100] The Regulatory Commission was particularly troubled by the large number of bets on his own team (231).[101] He was suspended from football activity for a period of 21 months and fined £1,000.[102] The sanction was upheld by an Appeal Panel.

FA v Blackstock (2014)[103]

25.131   The participant, a football player, had made a number of bets (655) contrary to the Betting Rules in the previous five to six years. Some of the bets involved his own team in three matches, although he did not play in those matches.[104] The overall stake was £105,196.62.[105] The FA submitted that as the participant had bet seven bets on his win team to win, a sporting sanction should be involved.[106] The Regulatory Commission decided that the starting point was to consider the entry point as a zero-month suspension,[107] and then took the following matters into account:

(a)   there was no impact on the result of the matches or the integrity of the game;[108]

(b)   the participant had not played in the matches he bet on;[109]

(c)   657 bets in six years was not a particularly large number to deviate from entry point;[110]

---

95   Regulatory Commission (Ch Mr N Stewart QC) 23 July 2009.
96   Para 17.
97   Para 21.
98   Paras 25–26.
99   Regulatory Commission (Ch Mr M Armstrong) 22 August 2013.
100 Para 28.
101 Para 29.
102 Para 41.
103 Regulatory Commission (Ch Mr T Win, JP) 2 May 2014.
104 Paras 5–6.
105 Para 34.9.
106 Para 41.
107 Para 62.
108 Para 64.
109 Para 65.
110 Para 66.

(d) the size of the individual bets were not significant;[111]
(e) there was no evidence of '*insider information*';[112]
(f) the total stake, of over £100,000 was a large stake;[113]
(g) the Regulatory Commission took into account that many of the bets were placed when the participant was bored and depressed as a result of injury;[114]
(h) the participant was genuinely remorseful and seeking help.[115]

Taking into account all the various factors, the Regulatory Commission decided a suspension of three months was appropriate but suspended that suspension in its entirety until 31 March 2016, to be automatically invoked upon a proven breach of the betting rules during that period. He was also fined £60,000, reflecting the gain made on the prohibited bets.[116]

FA v Lewis Smith (2016)[117]

25.132 This was a particularly long period of suspension for a participant, a football player, totalling just short of 17 months, and a fine of £22,865. The specific factors that meant it was so long were that the participant had:

(a) made a number of bets on his own team to win and one on his own team to lose in a period of just over a year;[118]
(b) played in those games where he bet on his own team, including where he bet on his team to lose;
(c) was an 'unimpressive and unreliable witness';[119]
(d) the scale of the betting activity was 'prolific';[120]
(e) the record of success was 'remarkable' (which goes to perception, see para **25.125** above) – in betting over £4,586.50 he achieved a total return of £22,863.67, a profit of £18,277.17.[121] For every £1 he bet he made nearly £5;
(f) there was a discernable pattern of placing larger bets on matches in which his team played and on betting activity flagged as suspicious by betting operators;[122]
(g) others associated with the participant placed identical bets on identical outcomes in certain matches. The Regulatory Commission concluded this was because he provided information to others and his suggestion that the identical bets were co-incidental was fanciful.[123]

FA v Demichelis (2016)[124]

25.133 The participant, a football player, was charged with respect to 29 bets placed in a short period. He did not participate in any of the matches in which the bets were placed. The stake was £9,254.57 and the profit was £2,058.17. The participant was subject to a fine of £20,000 and ordered to repay the profit from the bets. There

111 Para 67.
112 Para 68.
113 Para 70.
114 Para 75.
115 Para 76.
116 Para 93.
117 Regulatory Commission (Ch Mr C Moore) 9 March 2016.
118 Paras 2.1–2.3.
119 Para 3.6(i).
120 Para 4.1(iii).
121 Para 2.3(vii) and para 4.1(v).
122 Para 4.1(vi).
123 Para 4.1(vii).
124 Regulatory Commission (Ch Mr B Jones) 20 May 2016.

was no sporting sanction. The following matters (amongst others) were specifically regarded as mitigating by the Regulatory Commission:

(a) the participant was contrite;[125]
(b) he had made an immediate and most frank admission and cooperated with the investigation;[126]
(c) he never sought to blame anyone else;[127]
(d) the bets were all made in his own name with no attempt to disguise his identity;[128]
(e) there was no suggestion that he made use of inside information and there was not even a suspicion of match-fixing, which was confirmed by The FA. The integrity of the game was not in jeopardy.[129]

FA v Pilkington (2016)[130]

25.134 The charges related to 831 bets in breach of the rules and also a charge of providing inside information which was admitted. The participant played in six matches in which he placed 16 bets for his own team to lose.[131] He also gave inside information about players being rested to a relative who then placed bets on the matches (staking £200 and winning £875).[132] He was banned for four years, with the final 12 months suspended.

Leadbetter v FA (2016)[133]

25.135 The reasons for the decision of the Regulatory Commission are not available, but the Appeal Board upheld a sanction of 12 months. Without the reasons for the decision it is impossible to consider all of the factors that led to the suspension being for as long as 12 months. However, it appears one significant factor was that the participant bet against his own team and played in both of the games in which he made those bets (coming on as a substitute in both of them): the Appeal Board seems to have reached the view this meant that he was intended to influence the game and so there was a particular issue as to the confidence fans have in the integrity of football.[134]

FA v Bunyard (2016)[135]

25.136 Mr Bunyard was the manager of Frome Town FC. He was charged with 98 breaches of the Betting Rules *and* of passing on inside information. Three bets were on Frome to lose, and in one match to lose by more than 1.5 goals – in that match Frome lost 2-0. Bunyard staked £800 and made a return of £1,600.[136] The Regulatory Commission suspended Bunyard for four complete football seasons, with the last year's ban suspended. The Regulatory Commission considered the Sanction Guidelines and emphasised that a 'key aspect is whether the offence

---

125 Para 16.
126 Para 17.
127 Para 19.
128 Para 21.
129 Para 25.
130 Regulatory Commission (Ch Mr WTE Thomson) 25 July 2016.
131 Para 16(b).
132 Para 12.
133 Appeal Board (Ch Mr N Stewart QC) 27 September 2016.
134 Para 11.
135 Regulatory Commission (Ch Mr C Moore) 14 November 2016.
136 Para 1.2.

creates the perception that the result of any other element of the match may have been affected by the bet'.[137] In determining sanction the Regulatory Commission had particular regard to the following facts:

(a) Forty-five bets were placed by Bunyard on the team he was managing to lose. This was an 'extremely serious aggravating factor'. In 'the eyes of an objective bystander, such betting activity by the manager of a team creates a very serious adverse perception regarding the genuineness of the outcome of the matches in question, and undermines the integrity of the game.'[138]
(b) Bunyard's bet against Frome to lose by more than 1.5 goals in the match they lost 2-0 was the most serious of his activity. The bet generated a profit of £1,436.02.[139] The fact he was the manager meant he played an 'extremely important role, and is capable of influencing the outcome of matches'.[140]
(c) As manager, given his superior knowledge (eg of which players would be playing etc) this was a 'serious case of insider dealing' and a 'serious aggravating factor'.[141]
(d) The Regulatory Commission compared the sanction for Bunyard to that of the player, Pilkington (four-year ban) and a chief executive, Heys (two-year ban). The Regulatory Commission found the aggravating factors meant Bunyard's activity was more serious than Pilkington's. The Regulatory Commission went on to stress the following points as relevant to the question of perception of betting activity:[142] whereas a player in a game has a direct involvement in the match, it is as one of 22 players – a manager indirectly influences outcomes but his sphere of influence is potentially greater than one player. Heys was in a more administrative role, with less ability to influence matches.

FA v Barton (2017)[143]

25.137 Mr Barton, a football player, was charged with 1,260 bets on football in breach of the Betting Rules over a 10-year period ending in September 2016. His bets were part of a wider, and much larger, pattern of betting on all sports. Only a tiny fraction of the bets subject to the charges were on his own team; he did not play in, and was not in the squad for, any of the matches that he bet on his team to lose, and those bets were amongst the oldest in the 10-year period.

25.138 The Regulatory Commission accepted that Mr Barton had no influence on any of the games he bet on and that there was nothing suspicious about any of the bets he placed; he actually did more poorly whenever he bet on his own team.[144] Mr Barton's bets were placed openly, using his own name and account. Despite all of this, in April 2017 the Regulatory Commission imposed an 18-month ban, one of the longest suspensions against a player under the Betting Rules, banning Mr Barton from all footballing activity for a period of 18 months.

25.139 Mr Barton appealed the 18 month ban, *inter alia*, on the basis that the sanction was excessive and out of all proportion to previous decisions by other

---

137 Para 2.5.
138 Para 3.24(i)(a).
139 Para 3.24(i)(b).
140 Para 3.24(ii)(a).
141 Para 3.24(v)(b).
142 Para 3.25
143 Regulatory Commission (Ch Mr C Quinlan QC) 21 April 2017; Appeal Board (Ch Mr D Casement QC) 25 July, 2017
144 Appeal Board, para 139.

FA Regulatory Commissions (players who had been banned for 12 months or longer had not only bet against their own team, they had also played in the games (and thus may have influenced them)), had used inside information, or had highly suspicious returns on their bets.

25.140   The Appeal Board did not accept Mr Barton's arguments about the sanction being excessive compared to other FA cases, finding at para 34 that previous cases are not binding and each case turns on its own facts. Considering the Sanctioning Guidelines allowed for a wide discretion in sanction where a player bets against his own team, from six months to life, the Regulatory Commission had been entitled to take into account the number of bets and other factors in imposing an 18-month ban. However, the Regulatory Commission had unreasonably rejected part of the expert evidence called by Mr Barton, namely that his addiction, as opposed to anything suspicious, explained much of Mr Barton's betting behaviour, including the number and frequency of his bets.[145] It was an important mitigating factor.[146]

25.141   In the circumstances, the Appeal Board found the Regulatory Commission's rejection of part of the expert evidence to be unreasonable and they exercised their discretion to reduce the sanction from 18 months to just over 13 months.[147]

(ii)   General principles emerging from the cases

25.142   In considering the cases above a clear pattern emerges. As one would expect, where the betting breaches lead to a perception, or in the more serious cases, a real suspicion, that a player or manager might have either influenced the outcome of a match or had inside information that assisted in making a bet, then the sanction shall be far more serious than when these aggravating factors are not present.

25.143   The Sanction Guidelines are a rough and ready reflection of this legitimate and reasonable approach. It will usually be the case that a player betting on his own team commits a more serious breach than when he bets on another team, and that betting on his team to lose is more serious than betting on his team to win. The various guidelines reflect this.

25.144   But what the cases also show is that there is no 'one size fits all' guideline for betting in different circumstances. In *Mangan*, betting offences were arguably more serious than those of a player who bet on his team to lose rather than win, and his sanction (five-month ban) reflected that. That is because there was some 'highly suspicious' betting activity – Mr Mangan going with friends from an opposing team when placing bets on the match between their teams. In addition his sanction was longer because he was deemed to have given 'blatantly dishonest evidence'.

25.145   The suspicion that may have arisen in the *Mangan* case shows why it is not always right that a participant who bets on his own team to lose shall be sanctioned for longer than a participant who bets on his own team to win. That may well be the general approach but the following three examples of things that may (and do) arise show it will not always be the case.

25.146   Consider first player A who has (or is perceived to have) special access to inside information, maybe because he is captain, or a player manager, or for

145 Appeal Board, para 39.
146 Appeal Board, para 42.
147 Appeal Board, para 43.

any other reason, and he makes a number of bets on matches for his team to win, whether or not he plays in those matches. The odds are good for player A, he bets large stakes, and wins a good profit. But there is no actual evidence of use of inside information. On the other hand, player B, with no special information, places one bet on his team to lose in a game in which he does not play and has no influence. Surely most Regulatory Commissions will regard player A's breach as more serious than player B's, precisely because of the perceptions or suspicions that are likely to arise, and thus the effect of these on the integrity of football (the protection of which is of course the main objective of the Betting Rules).

25.147 Or player A, with influence on a game because he plays in it, makes bets on his team to win against the odds, and it does win, with player A playing an important role and making a substantial betting profit. Player B bets on his team to lose in a match most people would expect the team to lose. He does not play and has no influence. The odds are not particularly attractive. Again, player A's activity is likely to be treated more seriously, even though player A bet on his team to win, player B to lose.

25.148 And of course, as the situation in *Mangan* gets close to, betting on your own team to win in connection with others from an opposing team causes considerable concerns. If there is a perception that player A, who bets on his own team to win, may in some way be acting in combination with players B and C who play for the opposing team, then the perceptions and suspicions that may arise threaten the integrity of football even more. The perception that players from both opposing teams may have some a combined interest in a particular result is even worse than the perception that a single player in one team has an interest in that team losing.

25.149 In the authors' opinion, it is in the interests of upholding the integrity of sport, including protecting it from match-fixing and the perception of match-fixing, for sanctions to be effective, fair and proportionate. In general, actual match-fixing should often result in a life time ban. But simple betting on football where there is no evidence of fixing or use of inside information at all, on the other hand, ought not to attract lengthy bans from sport, for example bans for as long as, or longer than, six months – in particular considering the very short working lifetime most professional footballers have. Where the type of betting, or the results of bets, cause a reasonable suspicion of fixing or the use of inside information, then sanctions will often be (quite properly) longer than six months (as they were in *Bunyard*). Simply punishing a player with a very long ban because of the number of bets he placed, even when there was no suspicion of anything untoward at all (as for example the original Regulatory Commission did in the *Barton* case with its 18-month ban) is not proportionate and only serves to undermine the integrity of the rules generally.

CHAPTER 26

Players' Representation, the PFA and FIFPro

Nick Cusack (Assistant Chief Executive, PFA)

A   THE PROFESSIONAL FOOTBALLERS' ASSOCIATION

26.1   The Professional Footballers' Association (PFA) has been in existence for over 100 years making it the oldest sporting union. In that time, the game has seen huge changes and the PFA has been instrumental in ensuring that the players' voice has been heard. Unlike other industries the union has a seat at the top table and its influence has led to its members being amongst the best supported and protected sports people in the world.

26.2   This was not always the case as can be seen with the PFA's fight for recognition in the first decade of its existence and other important battles to reform the retain and transfer system and abolish the maximum wage in the 1960s. The PFA and its current Chief Executive Gordon Taylor OBE also played a pivotal role in restructuring and professionalising the international footballer's union FIFPro.[1] This organisation changed the footballing landscape through its support of Jean Marc Bosman, whose legal victory[2] heralded the biggest change in football regulations to date ensuring free movement of players at the end of their contract.

26.3   In terms of the PFA's progression to what it is today, probably the most significant development has been the enormous growth in revenues emanating from television subscription. The creation of the Premier League in the 1990s and the exponential growth in TV monies in subsequent Premier League broadcasting deals has enabled the union to expand and develop a role in every aspect of the modern game. The solidarity of the players (the PFA in union terms is unique as it has 100% membership across all the professional leagues in England) as well as the strong leadership at the helm of the organisation has created the environment where collective bargaining can take place.

26.4   A favourable environment is important, but relationships between key personnel can make an enormous difference and it is a combination of these two elements that has seen the game at the highest level in England dominate the world stage. Unions need more than a good case and reasoned argument to get a good deal

---

1   FIFPro is the name for the Fédération Internationale des Associations de Footballeurs Professionnels (the International Federation of Professional Footballers).
2   See Case C-415/93: *Union Royale Belge des Sociétés de Football Association (ASBL) v Bosman* [1996] All ER (EC) 97.

for their members. They also need power and this comes from the players sticking together and the employers recognising that in this industry substitution of the existing workforce is not a viable option.

26.5   In English football, the money flowing into the game via television is at a level where the union's demands and the employer's ability and desire to meet these demands can be accommodated.

26.6   Put all these things together and you have an industry that has gone from strength to strength with union members unusually but properly getting a good proportion of the spoils. There is a school of thought that this success would have taken place without the top players being unionised. However, when you look overseas at many leagues where there is an imbalance in the power between club and player with the attendant adverse consequences, the case for the 'English model' is a good one.

26.7   The key relationship in English football is the one between Gordon Taylor OBE and the Premier League Chief Executive Richard Scudamore. For nearly 20 years under their stewardship, agreements have been signed between the two organisations that have ensured continuity and stability within our national sport. The collective bargaining agreement that is in place facilitates a close working relationship in many areas such as in football in the community work and player care. However, the PFA, unlike many other unions in other countries is not subservient to the Federation or League and fights its corner robustly when necessary.

26.8   This independence has been built into the architecture of the regulations with checks and balances in place, with the intention being that no organisation can become too dominant and unresponsive. To this end the Professional Football Negotiating & Consultative Committee (PFNCC) was initiated in the 1990s, evolving from the Professional Football Negotiating Committee (PFNC) which was set up in the late 1970s and early 1980s after the Commission on Industrial Relations Enquiry into Professional Football. This Committee meets on a regular basis with equal representation from the PFA, Premier League, English Football League (EFL) and the Football Association ('The FA') under an independent chairman. This body discusses all matters affecting the game in England and importantly any changes to a player's terms and conditions cannot come into force without the union's agreement.

26.9   What is clear in English football is that the union has established itself as a partner with the other footballing bodies in administering the game. This position of influence has greatly benefited the players and has led to the PFA being able to offer support and assistance in a wide range of areas that can be accessed by them throughout their playing career and beyond as a life member.

26.10   This includes funding for education and re-training, financial support towards post-career medical care and operations, and financial help and debt advice in times of need. The PFA has also made provision around player welfare with a nationwide network of counsellors and a 24-hour helpline for players to utilise.

26.11   Most players have a desire to stay involved in the game after their career finishes and with this in mind, the PFA provides funding for several bespoke degree courses at various universities up and down the country. These include physiotherapy, sports science and sports journalism but in addition to these specific disciplines, members may receive funding for all manner of courses from medicine and law to plumbing and construction.

26.12   In addition to the PFA's education provision, the coaching department of the PFA also provides FA and UEFA accredited courses and programmes for players who want to pursue a career in management and coaching after they hang up their boots.

26.13   One of the most important aspects of the PFA's work is around equality and diversity. The union has done pioneering work to challenge and counter discrimination in all its forms and along with organisations like Kick It Out and Show Racism the Red Card has done much to change the landscape in football. Back in the late 1970s and 1980s, when there were appalling levels of abuse directed at black players, it was the union that stood up and demanded action whilst others in the game were nowhere near as forthright. There is still much to do and of concern at present is the low number of black, Asian and minority ethnic (BAME) managers and coaches in the game. The PFA continues to campaign strongly on this matter and is pressing the football authorities to work with the PFA to make greater and faster progress in this area.

26.14   The union was also instrumental in setting up the Football in the Community programme in the 1980s which was an initiative to formalise the strong bonds between local people and their football club and an answer to the severe problems of health and safety, crowd control and hooliganism in that decade. This has grown from strength to strength and in 2016 was responsible for PFA members making more than 40,000 player appearances in support of club initiatives in health, education, social inclusion and equalities.

26.15   As can be seen from what has been outlined, what is on offer to PFA members far exceeds what is available from other trade unions and is in addition to all the normal benefits and support that come with a conventional union membership. In this regard, there is the Delegate Liaison Department that looks after players' day-to-day problems and disputes and provides members with advice and representation.

26.16   This includes support at FA hearings for breaches of betting or doping rules or any other FA charges as well as at internal club disciplinary hearings. If disputes cannot be settled between a player and their club, then there is a mechanism set out in the contract by which the player has the right of appeal to an independent tribunal under the auspices of the League in which they play. In addition, rules and regulations affecting players are agreed with the PFA together with recommended sanctions and fines.

26.17   The PFA will provide advice and representation and if necessary will instruct external lawyers if the case is very serious and/or complex.

26.18   The fact that the PFA has the resources to bring in expertise when required is important and is fundamental in ensuring that clubs do not have a financial advantage if cases cannot be settled. Many players' unions in other countries as well as other sporting unions often rely on donations from the Federation or League to support them which does call into question their independence. The PFA has always argued that the union should receive a share of football's wealth as of right and has fought hard over the years to ensure that this is recognised via its collective bargaining agreements. That has given the PFA the independent means to be able to always act in the best interests of the players and fight their corner whoever is challenging them.

26.19   In terms of further support for players in the workplace, the PFA has negotiated a standard contract with the Premier League and EFL that covers all

92 professional clubs. The PFA has also negotiated a standard contract in the women's game covering the Women's Super League (WSL) with the FA. These contracts are detailed and govern all aspects of a players' working life, setting out clearly the obligations of clubs and players during their employment relationship.

26.20 They deal with all the key areas that can affect a player during their employment at their respective club. Whether it be related to medical provision or disciplinary matters it is set out in the contract. The rules relating to transfers and registrations as well as the regulations under The FA's jurisdiction are also laid down in the various rule books which have been the subject of consultation and agreed upon by the various footballing bodies, including the union. Only very rarely do cases go outside of football to the law courts or employment tribunals.

26.21 This is good for the game as everyone knows where they stand and how things work. There is enough scope in the contract and the regulations to encourage resolution of disputes which is important, as disagreements and unresolved grievances in football can quickly have a significant impact on team spirit and morale.

26.22 However, as alluded to previously, there is an independent dispute resolution mechanism in place to deal with the relatively few cases that do not get resolved before this final stage.

26.23 The role of PFA Executives is also very important in ensuring that the many and varied problems and issues that inevitably materialise between players and clubs are dealt with sensibly. In a working environment that involves constant assessment and appraisal, with players having to deal with being in the team one minute and out of favour the next, tensions are bound to arise. The fact that PFA Executives have all been professional players and have experienced all the highs and lows that are typical in a football career enables them to advise players accordingly and work with the clubs to ensure fair outcomes from disputes.

26.24 Sometimes players may need to be advised that their behaviour or actions are not what they should be and, in these circumstances, PFA Executives are best placed to do this. Of course, the PFA are working for the players and this should never be overlooked, but it is also important to have good relationships with key personnel at clubs so that any problems can be dealt with effectively and expeditiously. There are occasions when a sanction is necessary and it is in these circumstances that those links with the Chief Executive and Chairman play their part in ensuring that disciplinary measures are proportionate and leave both player and club with an opportunity to move forward.

26.25 One of the biggest changes in the English game in recent years is the influx of players from Europe and the rest of the world. The union has welcomed this development and is proud to have such a diverse and multi-national membership. Many saw this change as a potential source of weakness for the union as commentators argued that overseas players being relatively transient would not see the benefits of joining the union. This has proved to be a false premise with every player that has come to these shores thus far becoming a member of the PFA and being very supportive of their union.

26.26 What has become apparent is that these players want to play in England not just because of the competition and salaries but also because contracts are protected and the union looks after their interests. This contrasts with their experiences playing in other countries where a contract often does not get honoured and loss of form or injury can see them face adverse consequences.

26.27   Favourable provisions in the contract such as no diminution in pay when injured, severance pay and medical treatment guaranteed even after their contract has expired have resulted from the union negotiating these terms on the players' behalf. Payment of a year's salary if the player has to retire through injury is another term of the contract in England that is not common in other countries. These elements, together with a non-contributory pension scheme and all the other unrivalled benefits of PFA membership has meant that players whatever their nationality or length of stay support the union and, far from weakening our ranks, the influx of overseas players has strengthened the union and helped in so many positive ways.

26.28   These ingredients as well as the power dynamic in the English game provide for a level of stability that hopefully will see football continue to prosper going forward. Indeed, this state of affairs confounds the view that for a business or industry to be successful, management knows best and should be left to take all the major decisions unfettered by interference from the workforce. This could be described as the typical industrial relations model in Britain today. English football demonstrates that a partnership between employer and employee with neither being subservient to the other can be very successful and is a template perhaps for government and other industries to look at and try to emulate.

26.29   In summary, the PFA has been successful as an organisation because the top players have been prepared to support their fellow professionals in the lower leagues. The monies received by football from television revenues largely come from Premier League matches and it is the collective bargaining agreement between the PFA and the Premier League that ostensibly enables the union to look after all its 5,000 current and 50,000 former members. This involves a redistribution to support players who suffer injuries or do not have the financial resources of players playing in the top divisions. This solidarity is important and ensures that good terms and conditions are available across the board and cannot be chipped away at even at the highest level.

26.30   In terms of moving forward, perhaps one of the biggest challenges football faces over the coming years is the potential impact of Brexit. Currently, the PFA has hundreds of members that are EU nationals who, like their counterparts in other UK industries and businesses, face an uncertain future.

26.31   As there are so many other important economic and social issues that are up in the air following the 'Leave' vote, sport has not really featured thus far in the negotiations with the EU. This needs to change and our industry needs to initiate this.

26.32   Football's answer to dealing with players coming from outside the EU has been to develop a work permit system that only sanctions the signing of players who meet the specific criteria in respect of international appearances made. The number of international games a player must have played over the last two years is linked to the countries' FIFA rankings.

26.33   If EU players were subject to the same requirements, then 75% of EU players currently playing in the Premier League would not be eligible and only three of the 161 EU players playing in the Championship would meet the criteria.

26.34   It is possible that this current regime will be changed or that special rules will come into force for EU players, including protection for those already here, but very little has been discussed in relation to these important matters within the game, and with government, and the clock is most definitely ticking. The PFA's priority is to protect our current EU members so that they have certainty in relation to their existing contracts and the ability to sign new contracts in the future.

26.35   Many questions surrounding this area need to be considered and addressed and all the footballing bodies need to develop an agreed position to be put on the agenda as part of the government's negotiations with Brussels. Failure to do this could replicate what is feared in many other industries and result in a cliff-edge Brexit that will be very damaging for our sport.

B   THE PFA STRUCTURE

26.36   The PFA's main offices are in Manchester and London but it also has a presence at the National Football Centre at St George's Park in Staffordshire. In terms of day-to-day working, the PFA is run by the full-time officers of the union with Gordon Taylor OBE at the helm as Chief Executive. Gordon Taylor has been in charge since 1981 and has been the main driver in the PFA's growth and development to date. From a staff of five back then to more than 60 today, the PFA has departments covering such wide-ranging areas as equality and diversity, player welfare, coaching, community and social responsibility, education, commercial as well as undertaking core union work via the Delegate Liaison Department.

26.37   Although key personnel are in the main ex-players, the structure of the PFA reflects the need to have input and direction from current players with the PFA Management Committee having an important role to play in decision making and flagging up topical issues and concerns direct from the dressing room. This Committee elects a Chairman, meets every few months and is made up of a cross section of senior players nominated by their fellow professionals from across the men's and women's game.

26.38   There is also a Board of Trustees responsible for the PFA's Charity Fund (education, hardship, welfare, equalities, corporate social responsibility etc) made up from the Chief Executive, Financial Director and experienced ex-professionals and ex-chairmen.

26.39   A further link with the executive are the PFA delegates of which there is one at every professional club. In union terms, these are the 'shop stewards' who are usually the captain of the team or a senior player who is respected and highly thought of at the club. This individual links up with the staff in the Delegate Liaison Department to flag up issues and obtain support and assistance for any player that needs it. Many delegates go on to join the Management Committee as their knowledge and awareness of the union grows and a number subsequently have gone on to be full-time officers when their career has come to an end. This structure is important as it empowers players and gives them a pathway to getting involved with the union and having a big say in what it does and how it is done.

26.40   When this path is taken, as the author of this chapter did, there is a real insight into the great work that the PFA does to support players in so many areas during and after their careers. Working at the PFA is a privilege and much more than just a job. Having been a player and experienced the very real challenges in the profession gives a genuine passion for the job and a drive to work hard to guide and help players so that perhaps they will not make the mistakes that are easily made in what is at times such a tough working environment.

C   FIFPro

26.41   FIFPro is the worldwide organisation for all professional footballers representing more than 65,000 players in total with 60 national players' associations as members. Funding primarily comes from players' image rights, which in particular emanate from electronic games and picture cards.

26.42   The organisation was set up in 1965–66 with England (Cliff Lloyd), Scotland, France, Holland, Belgium, Italy and Spain being the founding members. In the early 1990s Theo Van Seggelen as Secretary and Gordon Taylor as President were the architects responsible for growing FIFPro worldwide, taking in all the continents to match FIFA. What followed was support for *Bosman*, the international transfer system and representation on the Boards at both FIFA and UEFA.

26.43   FIFPro, like the PFA, is built on solidarity but in a slightly different but related way. Here the big countries, who tend to have the most established and most powerful unions, support and help to fund the smaller unions that are trying to grow and develop. This approach has enabled the smaller unions from countries where money is in short supply to have their voice heard and issues raised. This can then be brought to the attention of FIFA and UEFA and other governing bodies through FIFPro's representation on the various committees and structures of these bodies.

26.44   FIFPro, in line with the PFA, has had to fight hard to establish itself and gain recognition from its main counterparts.

26.45   This has come about with the help of the European Commission who have been instrumental in ensuring that the representatives of the federations and the clubs engage with the representatives of the players in key areas. Good examples of this are the reform of the international transfer system back in 2001 and the implementation of the initiative to bring about social dialogue in European professional football in 2003. The latter has led to regular set meetings between FIFPro, UEFA, the national football leagues and the Commission which have brought about reform and change in several key areas and has firmly entrenched FIFPro as a major player in shaping world football.

26.46   Clear evidence of FIFPro's influence is its representation on the FIFA Stakeholders Committee, FIFA Players Status Committee, FIFA Dispute Resolution Chamber (DRC) as well as the UEFA Strategy Council. Senior FIFPro representatives also meet regularly and have good working relationships with both the FIFA and UEFA Presidents ensuring that player related issues are addressed and prioritised.

26.47   Further recognition for FIFPro has come about with the incorporation of the FIFPro World Players XI into the wider FIFA Awards.

26.48   The most significant development since *Bosman* has been FIFPro's challenge to the current transfer system. The FIFPro complaint was lodged at the European Commission in Brussels in September 2015.

26.49   The main points of the challenge are based around competition law which states that the Regulations on the Status and Transfer of Players limit competition because of the restrictions they place on freedom of contract.

26.50   It also highlights an imbalance under Article 17(2) whereby a club breaching a contract is treated much more favourably than a player under the same circumstance. That is, if a player breached a contract the club could be entitled to the full value of the contract plus a replacement value whereas a club in breach would only be liable to pay a balance of the existing contract after mitigation.

26.51   In practice, this has meant that clubs which are either late paying their players, or which do not pay their players at all, could safely expect to save money in that the onus was on the player to mitigate his loss, whereas this restriction does not apply to clubs.

26.52   At the time of writing negotiations are taking place between the major stakeholders to try and reach an agreement within football without recourse to the courts and all parties are optimistic that a positive resolution can be achieved.

D   FIFPro STRUCTURE

26.53   FIFPro has its headquarters in Amsterdam and is led, on a day-to-day basis, by its General Secretary, Theo Van Seggelen. The organisation is overseen by the FIFPro Board consisting of 11 members. This key decision-making body has input from the four geographical divisions, Europe, Americas, Africa and Asia/Oceania.

26.54   Key figures in the organisation are Gordon Taylor OBE who is Honorary President, Phillipe Piat from France who is the President, Luis Rubiales from Spain who is Vice-President and Bobby Barnes from England who is President of Division Europe. These individuals and other Board members work closely with the General Secretary and his staff to formulate policy and conduct the business of the organisation.

CHAPTER 27

Mediation

Edwin Glasgow QC (39 Essex Chambers) and Peter Stockwell (Solicitor/Mediator)

A INTRODUCTION

27.1   Mediation is a process by which a neutral person facilitates negotiations between parties to a dispute in an effort to reach a mutually acceptable resolution. In the world of football, it may be useful to think of the process as being one in which a totally independent but skilled and knowledgeable person works with parties who are in disagreement in an attempt to enable them to find a solution and settle their differences, which can arise is so many different ways in relation to the game, ideally before those differences develop into a dispute which in turn could develop into full blown litigation.[1]

27.2   The principal advantages of mediation, which we examine below, make it particularly appropriate for the resolving of differences in football disputes; they are that it is:

(a) consensual and voluntary;
(b) confidential and without prejudice;
(c) flexible and constructive;
(d) informal;
(e) quick; and
(f) cost effective.

27.3   Mediation is proven to be successful. It is estimated that in 2016 there were approximately 10,000 civil and commercial cases[2] referred to mediation. The Centre for Effective Dispute Resolution (CEDR) undertakes a biannual audit and in its last report (May 2016) found a constant overall success rate of 86%. The proportion of mediations that settled on the day was 67% but a further 19% settled shortly after the mediation.

---

1   In this chapter references to litigation in the generality includes arbitration, the formal and binding process whereby an individual or panel decide the outcome of a dispute by reference to governing law.
2   CEDR – The Seventh Mediation Audit.

B HISTORY OF MEDIATION

27.4 Although mediation can be traced back to pre-Roman times, the use of the process in the UK in everyday circumstances is comparatively recent. Mediation as it is practised currently was developed in the United States in the late 1970s as an alternative to the traditional legal system and emerged under the label of 'ADR'. There are a number of variations of what the A in ADR stands for but it is probably best known as Alternative Dispute Resolution, a term that encompasses arbitration, mediation, adjudication and conciliation – all being alternatives to litigation in a court.

27.5 ADR crossed the Atlantic to the UK in the late 1980s. Its introduction can be dated to the creation in 1990 of two organisations, CEDR and the ADR group, to promote ADR and to provide training for mediators.

27.6 There are now many organisations involved in the promotion of mediation, the provision of mediation services generally and training and accrediting mediators, all of which confirms the significant growth in mediations since 1995. There is every reason to believe that this growth in the use of mediation will continue, albeit probably at a less rapid rate.

27.7 The popularity and growth of mediation is almost certainly due to: (i) disenchantment on the part of those involved in litigation, and now arbitration, with the length of time it can take to obtain a decision and the costs involved; and (ii) the recognition by the courts that mediation is a preferred route and the encouragement the courts provide to parties to attempt mediation in the context of the litigation process.

27.8 Mediation is the world of sport generally first began to take off in the UK with the establishment of the Sports Dispute Resolution Panel in 1997 which was set up in the wake of the litigation which financially ruined Diane Modahl and doomed the British Athletics Federation to administration. SDRP was renamed Sport Resolutions UK in 2008 and among the many services it provides it set up the only sport specialist panel of mediators with experience in a wide range of sports including football.

C RELATIONSHIP BETWEEN MEDIATION AND THE COURTS

27.9 The Commercial Court, a division of the High Court, openly acknowledged the potential value of ADR in 1993 but it was not until 1999 that its use found its way into the Civil Procedure Rules (CPR); the rules of procedure governing all civil litigation. There had been widespread concern about the working of the civil justice system in practice, and in 1994 a Committee under the chairmanship of the then Master of the Rolls, Lord Woolf, was formed to carry out a wide ranging review of civil court procedures. Lord Woolf's Committee published a Report entitled Access to Justice in 1996.

27.10 It came as no surprise to anyone that in his Report, Lord Woolf concluded that the then current system of civil justice was too slow, too expensive, too complex and too inaccessible. Serious reform was necessary to enable the courts to deal justly with cases and the recommendations made in the Report were substantially accepted and implemented through the CPR which came into effect in 1999. Far reaching and sweeping changes to the way that civil claims were brought and pursued were introduced.

27.11   Most relevant of these changes to mediation was the introduction of the overriding objective of 'enabling the court to deal with cases justly and at proportionate cost'. The CPR provides for the achievement of this objective by active case management[3] and it is in relation to this that ADR is specifically referred to.

27.12   The CPR does not provide any direct power enabling the court to compel the parties to attempt ADR although it has been argued that in effect the CPR gave the courts that power. It is now accepted that it is by the exercise of discretionary powers in relation to costs that the courts are able to influence the use of ADR. Costs sanctions can be a very powerful tool and parties to litigation would only very rarely decline to follow a direction from the court to engage in ADR for fear of the potentially adverse use of the courts' wide discretion as to costs.

27.13   Following the introduction of the CPR, the role of ADR in litigation was tested in a number of cases that came before the courts and in *Halsey v Milton Keynes NHS Trust*[4] the Court of Appeal expressly held that the courts had no power to require parties to enter into an ADR process. Despite some learned and authoritative observations that *Halsey* was wrong, and that two members of the Court of Appeal who decided *Halsey*[5] have since suggested that it should be revisited, the Court of Appeal has recently endorsed the decision and the conclusion that the court lacks an express power to order ADR.[6]

27.14   This is not the place for a detailed discussion on the matters that influence the court when exercising a discretion as to who will pay the costs on conclusion of a case. The following factors, however, are most likely to feature in that process: the extent to which other settlement methods have been attempted; whether costs of ADR would have been disproportionately high; whether any delay in using ADR would have been materially prejudicial; and whether ADR had a reasonable prospect of success.

27.15   There can be no doubt that the CPR has been a significant factor in the increase of cases being referred to mediation and the decrease in the number of cases going to trial and it is now difficult to envisage a case reaching the trial stage without the possibility of mediation having been at the very least considered seriously by the parties and their advisors.

D   BENEFITS OF MEDIATION

27.16   We now examine why mediation, and its hallmark qualities listed above, is so well suited to the resolution of sporting disagreements of all kinds – and why mediations in the world of football have proved to be so successful.

(a)   Consensual and voluntary process

27.17   One of the fundamental elements of the mediation process is that it can only take place with the consent of all parties to the disagreement or dispute in question.

---

3   CPR, r 1.4(1).
4   [2004] 2 All ER 58.
5   Ward LJ and Lord Dyson.
6   *PGF II SA v OMFS Company 1 Ltd* [2014] 1 WLR 1386.

Whilst some parties to mediation are less enthusiastic than others, the process is, and can only be, voluntary. As we have seen the courts do not have power to force parties to engage in any form of ADR and no one can be made to mediate if they refuse to participate in the process. It has, however, been the experience of those who have handled disputes and disagreements in football that those who participate in the game, and those who are commercially engaged in it, need little persuasion that litigation should be regarded as the last resort. Indeed, it is notoriously true that many of the cases in which courts have had to decide whether or not it is in the public interest or otherwise appropriate that the media should know about cases have been those which have in some way involved football.

27.18   Crucially it is no part of the mediation process to determine the issues and differences between the parties. On the contrary, the mediator(s) will not volunteer a view on the likely outcome although the parties will quite often be encouraged to undertake some 'reality testing'. No decision will be made in relation to the underlying dispute and the outcome will be either successful with a settlement agreed and signed up to by the parties, or unsuccessful, in which event the case will continue as if nothing had happened.

(b)   Confidential and without prejudice

27.19   Another fundamental element of mediation is that it is confidential and without prejudice to the rights of the parties. Whilst a court might be informed of the fact that mediation has been attempted, nothing that is said or done by the parties or the mediator during the course of the mediation will be revealed to any third party or the court. The mediation agreement (see section G below) will specifically provide that the process is 'without prejudice' and confidential. Further, since mediation is commonly used to settle litigation, whether underway or threatened, the process must be 'without prejudice' and the courts have shown a willingness to accept and support the confidentiality of the process.

27.20   As with a willingness to engage in the consensual process without being compelled to do so, those in football who find themselves involved in disagreements or disputes will usually need no persuasion that it is at least worth an attempt at resolving their differences in private and away from the glare of media spotlight, which not infrequently aggravates, and in some instances has actually been seen to cause, issues precisely because it is 'the beautiful game' which provides so much 'copy' for journalists and media reporters. Commercial disputes over players' contracts, transfer fees or agents' commissions are likely to be singularly ill-suited to litigation in open court.

27.21   While it is right to say that arbitration should, in principle, also be a confidential process, glances at the sporting press illustrate the extent to which that principle is sometimes more honoured in the breach. Additionally, the losing party can challenge the arbitrators' 'confidential' award in open court on a point of law opening the whole case to public scrutiny.[7]

---

7   The case of *Pulis v Crystal Palace FC* [2016] EWHC 2999 (Comm) is a recent and vivid example of both leakage (see *Evening Standard*, 17 March 2016) and an appeal (see *Daily Telegraph*, 28 November 2016).

(c)   Flexible and constructive

27.22   It should be emphasised that in mediation it is the parties who are in control of their own processes. The mediator will guide the process but it is the parties who remain in control of the outcome. This is, of course, quite contrary to the role of the courts. The whole litigation process is geared to a conclusion in which the judge finds for one party or the other, and sometimes even delivers a judgment with which neither party is wholly content. The 'rulings' and findings are largely outside the control of either party and must, subject to any question of appeal, be accepted. In a mediation, there can and will only be a settlement if all parties are in agreement as to the terms.

27.23   There is virtually no limit on the type of situations that can be the subject of mediation. Whilst the majority of mediations take place in the context of impending or threatened litigation, it often makes more sense, particularly if there is a desire to avoid any publicity, to attempt to settle a dispute by mediation before proceedings are actually commenced.

27.24   It is not even necessary for there to be a 'dispute' which is yet capable of being litigated to enable the mediation process to be initiated. Take for example the situation where a football club doctor cannot 'get on' with the head of physiotherapy with whom he needs to work on a daily basis. The relationship has become so bad that one of them will have to leave or be moved. Neither of them, nor indeed the club, want that outcome. It may be possible with a skilled mediator for them to be able to re-create a viable working relationship. That is not a scenario that could be litigated, because it is unlikely that either party would have had a cause of action and, even if they had, it is difficult to envisage a remedy/order which could have provided a practical, let alone constructive, solution.

27.25   There is no restriction on possible outcomes that can be achieved by mediation. If a dispute is litigated, the court will rule on which party is to succeed and apply the law and legal remedies available to it. There will be a winner and loser. In mediation, however, we have already seen that no decision about the merits of the claim itself will be made, and it is open to the parties to come to any arrangement that might be agreed between them.

27.26   Particularly in football-related cases, mediators who can encourage the parties to think constructively, and not about their 'rights' or the other party's 'wrongs', are not infrequently successful in restoring sporting relationships between players and team members, both with one another and with agents, and/or managers. A significant number of settlements that are arrived at as a result of mediation include terms that no court has the power to impose. The restoration of working relationships is not infrequently the goal of the competent mediator, although the most successful examples of this, within the experience of the authors, are by definition those which never became exposed to the glare of publicity.

(d)   Informality

27.27   Unlike the court process which is very rigidly structured, there is no set format for a mediation. There are no rules governing the process of mediation other than those agreed by the parties with the mediator. Whilst there has been developed what might be regarded as standard procedures for a mediation, no two cases are ever identical and the process permits the formulation of whatever procedures are most likely to succeed in any set of circumstances. The format needs to be flexible in order to meet developments and, in stark contrast to the legal process, as informal as circumstances permit.

27.28 It is sometimes the case that a party to litigation really wants their day in court. Mediation does not deprive the party of their right to have their day in court or, far more likely in football, in arbitration if it remains the intractable stance of that party. If that is so, then whilst the process is of course not really comparable, parties can be encouraged to treat the mediation as their 'day in court' – or at least as a day when they are able to put forward their case in circumstances far less daunting than a court room.

27.29 We have already seen that there is a high percentage success rate of cases referred to mediation. Even if not successful on the day, a good mediator will follow up by making contact with the parties to ascertain if there were thoughts on how the mediation had developed and whether there were areas that might fruitfully be addressed further with or without the further involvement of the mediator.

(e) Speed

27.30 As it is the parties, not the court, who control the process, the speed at which a mediation is conducted is entirely in the hands of the parties. Very often a mediation can be completed in a matter of days after an agreement to mediate has been reached.

(f) Cost-effectiveness

27.31 A settlement achieved as a result of mediation will always be very significantly more cost effective than litigating to trial. That is not to say that the mediation, when properly prepared for, is necessarily a 'cheap' exercise but compared with the costs incurred in the course of litigation, each party is most definitely going to be financially much better off. It is a matter for agreement, but ordinarily the costs of the mediation will initially be shared between the parties with a proviso that if it is unsuccessful the costs of the mediation will be treated as costs of the proceedings and therefore at the discretion of the court. If the mediation succeeds, the costs will form part of the agreed terms of settlement, but the most usual outcome is that both parties are so pleased to put the dispute behind them that they are willing to share the relatively modest costs that have been incurred.

E THE MEDIATOR

27.32 No formal qualifications are required of a mediator but it is a highly responsible role and considerable skills are needed. A number of organisations provide training and a recognised accreditation will be required before a mediator will be listed and available for appointment through a recognised panel. Further, mediators are rightly required to undertake continuing professional education and mediate a minimum number of cases each year to remain on recognised lists for appointment.

27.33 Mediators come from a wide range of professions and specialisms. There are some types of dispute that benefit from a specialist subject mediator but the majority of cases do not require any specific subject expertise other than the personal skills of the mediator. The mediator must understand the issues between the parties but generally mediations are dealt with on a fairly broad basis and success does not depend on an examination of the minutiae.

27.34   It is for the parties to agree the choice of mediator. There is sometimes some tactical manoeuvring before an agreed appointment is made and a number of factors may come into play and will be considered by those advising the parties.

(a) The role of the mediator

27.35   The key attributes for a success mediator are set out below.

(i) Neutrality

27.36   If the mediator is going to facilitate meaningful and productive discussions, she or he will have to gain and maintain the confidence of the parties in a short space of time and demonstrate transparent and genuine neutrality from the outset.

(ii) Managing the process and framework of the day

27.37   Whilst it is ultimately for the parties to agree how the mediation should proceed, they will look to the mediator to give firm guidance on the management of the day.

(iii) Being a buffer to absorb feelings and frustrations

27.38   Emotions frequently run high and skilled mediators will often seek to redirect feelings of anger or frustration towards themselves so as to prevent emotion or anger being exchanged between the parties.

(iv) Taking a fresh look at a stale problem

27.39   The mediator comes completely new to a case which may well have been boiling up or stagnating for years. Shining a light from a new direction can be advantageous when it comes to steering parties towards new goals.

(v) Helping parties take a broader view and explore creative solutions

27.40   It is totally understandable for parties (and even some lawyers) to a dispute to get too close to it and thus become entrenched in the views they genuinely hold about their case and about the case of the other party. Good mediators get parties to look for a wider perspective and suggest possible solutions that may never have been contemplated.

(vi) Listening and encouraging focus on the real issues

27.41   It is only by understanding the point of view of the parties that the mediator may be able to suggest a different focus that itself might lead to viewing the case and possible settlement very differently.

(vii) Providing 'reality testing'

27.42 To encourage the parties and their advisors objectively to test the reality of their position is one of the most important functions of the mediator.

(viii) What the mediator will not do

27.43 Having looked at some of the things a mediator will do, there are a number of things a mediator will not do. It is no part of the mediators function to provide legal advice. An equally important 'no go' area is advice or even expressing a view on the merits of a particular settlement proposal. Of course, the mediator can steer parties towards a settlement, that is the whole purpose, but the mediator should not offer an opinion directly as to whether any settlement proposal is good or otherwise.

F THE ROLE OF LAWYERS IN MEDIATION

27.44 Some people say that there is no role for lawyers in the mediation process particularly in relation to disagreements that are not yet, and may never be, the subject of litigation. At the other end of the scale, parties who have become entrenched in litigation over a long period of time will want to have their lawyers involved. Experience shows that lawyers, adopting a constructive approach, can make a real contribution to the process. Conversely, passionate advocating of one case and disparaging of the other is never condusive to settlement.

27.45 There are obvious and potentially significant benefits to an early consideration of mediation as a possible means of resolving the dispute before it becomes litigious. The problem with this is that generally parties are not able to assess the strengths and weaknesses of the case before the litigation has gone some way down the expensive road that it will travel. Nevertheless, the client should at the very least be made aware of the mediation process and its benefits at the outset.

27.46 It is the lawyer's job to ensure that the mediator is not just experienced and 'good' but appropriately skilled and experienced for a football dispute.

27.47 The lawyer will advise on who should attend the mediation session. It must include a decision-maker, someone who is authorised to sign up to a settlement if acceptable terms are agreed. If the dispute is largely technical, the process can be enhanced by the presence of experts. On the other hand, the presence of large numbers of lawyers never helps. One of the most important skills of the competent mediator, is the ability to compensate for any perception, real or imagined, of 'inequality of arms'. Football disputes are frequently between wealthy clubs and comparatively less wealthy individuals.

27.48 The mediator will have agreed a timetable with the parties or their lawyers who will prepare a mediation bundle for the mediator's use. The lawyers will also be invited to submit 'position papers' setting out the key points on behalf of their clients. This is an important part of the process as it is a summary of the position and an indication of the views of each party to a settlement. But it is essential to bear in mind that position papers should set out the parties' position – not pleadings which assert legal rights.

27.49   Realism features highly in the mediation process. We have already seen that reality testing forms an important tool for the mediator. The lawyers, too, need to be realistic in their assessment of what litigation can or might achieve compared to a negotiated settlement. Often, one of the most significant issues to be settled is who will pay the costs; it is inevitable that any settlement will need to deal with the costs issue bearing in mind that in litigation the loser of the case will generally have to bear their own costs and pay the costs of the winner. It is not uncommon for the total of these costs to exceed what is at stake and consequently the lawyers must have full details available at the mediation so that this element of the case can be dealt with in any settlement.

27.50   On the day of the mediation, there is likely to be a good deal of 'down time' when the mediator is absent talking to the other party. The lawyers should use this time to be supportive and creative. Encouraging a positive outlook and adopting or raising and discussing creative ideas for settlement is a very useful way of spending what may be quite lengthy periods of apparent inactivity. Although underlying litigation cannot be ignored, the lawyers can really help by encouraging a constructive approach to the discussions and avoid taking entrenched positions that might make a 'climb down' embarrassing to the point of making an otherwise acceptable settlement unattainable.

27.51   Just as mediation is an entirely different process to litigation; so too is the approach necessary to make a success of it. If lawyers are to participate constructively in the mediation, it needs a change in the traditional mindset of the litigator, if only for the day.

G   THE MEDIATION AGREEMENT

27.52   The mediator will prepare the mediation agreement and get the parties to sign up to it. There is no standard form for this agreement but there are certain provisions that will usually be included – and which will be essential in sporting cases.

27.53   There should be a clause by which the parties agree to negotiate in good faith. While such an 'obligation' is impossible to enforce, it is useful to set the tone for mediation by expressly recording it and to emphasise that the parties are entering the process voluntarily with, at the very least, a stated intention to engage fully with the process. There should also always be a requirement, which tends to get overlooked, for the attendance of someone with authority to settle on behalf of each party. One of the real benefits of mediation is that, if a settlement is achieved, it will be recorded in a written and signed agreement and is binding from that moment onwards. If the real decision-maker is not present settlement is always more difficult to achieve. Football is noted for having some 'larger than life' characters, who often hold the purse strings. Some can be 'too important to waste time in boring meetings'. That can be a very serious mistake and needs to be avoided.

27.54   The agreement will also confirm the mediator's obligations so that everyone can see what they are, and will set out the fees and the time for payment to be made.

27.55   We have already seen that the parties will prepare a mediation bundle and position papers. They may wish to introduce other documents into the process and, consistent with the principle that the process is 'without prejudice', the mediation agreement will typically expressly provide that no material produced for the mediation will be admissible in any proceedings.

27.56 There will be a specific provision and acknowledgement in the agreement by all parties that they will maintain the confidentiality of the mediation and the information introduced into the process whether oral or written. Usually, the agreement will include an acknowledgement by the parties that any settlement that might be negotiated will not be binding unless and until it is reduced to writing and signed by the parties.

27.57 During the course of the mediation the mediator is likely to be entrusted with confidential information by the parties and there will be an understandable concern that he could be required to divulge that information if no settlement is agreed. For this reason, the mediation agreement will usually include a specific provision to the effect that the mediator will not be required to give evidence or be a witness in relation to anything that has taken place during the mediation process, thereby giving the parties additional reassurance as to the confidentiality of the mediation. Quite apart from any specific provisions in the mediation agreement, the legal concepts of confidentiality and privilege are both relevant to any subsequent attempt by a party to introduce evidence about what transpired in the mediation process or to compel the mediator to give evidence. It appears from the limited number of cases[8] where such attempts have been made that the courts seem willing to uphold the principles of confidentiality and privilege of the mediation process. There is, however, an overriding discretion for the court to apply the 'interests of justice' test which, while acknowledged in what many regard as the surprising decision in *Farm Assist Ltd (In liquidation) v DEFRA (No 2)*,[9] has yet to lead to any mediator being actually compelled to give evidence. The court will admit evidence of the mediation process if called upon to determine whether a settlement was achieved or not.[10] With those points in mind it is impossible to guarantee that total confidentiality can be maintained in every case. It also, of course, goes without saying that no principle of confidentiality in any dispute resolution process can or indeed should prevent disclosure of criminal conduct, whether in relation to money laundering within the meaning of the Proceeds of Crime Act 2002 or under the general principles of criminal law and professional ethics.

27.58 Confidentiality is, however, often really important in high-profile football cases and will also need to be stressed by the mediator at the start of the meeting; unless parties have total confidence that no aspect of the negotiation is going to be leaked to the media, settlement may be impossible to reach – on that ground alone.

27.59 The mediator will wish to incorporate a provision allowing him a complete discretion as to the termination of the mediation. The mediator cannot be obliged to continue the mediation indefinitely and the most obvious situation leading to the termination of the process is the assessment by the mediator that the process is completely deadlocked. An indication that the mediator is about to reach that conclusion can sometimes provoke further movement.

27.60 These are just a few of the more important provisions routinely included in the mediation agreement.

---

8   See, eg *Cumbria Waste Management Ltd v Baines* [2008] EWHC 786 (QB).
9   [2009] EWHC 1102 (TCC).
10   *Brown v Rice* [2007] EWHC 625 (Ch).

H   PRACTICAL ELEMENTS OF A MEDIATION

27.61   The nature of the process is such that there is no set precedent as to how a mediation is conducted. Each mediation will differ according to the particular circumstances but there are some elements that will generally form part of the process. We have already emphasised the informality and flexibility of the process and this will be apparent from the outset. On appointment, the mediator will make preliminary contact with the parties or their advisors. There will be discussions about timing, venue and procedures. The mediator will want to use this contact to develop a relationship and gain the confidence of the participants.

27.62   A timetable will have been agreed for preparation and delivery of position papers and mediator's bundles. The mediator will have prepared for the day and be fully conversant with the issues that will need to be addressed.

27.63   A mediation might typically involve five phases:

(a) *The opening phase*. This might simply be the mediator meeting and greeting the parties and their representatives and outlining his thoughts on how the day might be used.

(b) *The exploration phase*. The mediator will meet privately with the parties, establishing how they see the process and assessing the really important issues.

(c) *An initial joint meeting*. Usually called the 'first plenary session', this might be the first time the principals have ever met and great skill is needed in chairing these meetings, particularly if feelings are running high and there has been a history of aggressive litigation. It is usually the opportunity for the introduction and development of position papers.

(d) *The bargaining phase*. The parties having set out their positions, the mediator will often follow the joint meeting with private sessions with each party to understand what they really need to achieve by way of settlement. The need for confidence in the mediator is probably now at its highest as he may well invite the parties to reveal what they want on the basis that he will not disclose it to the other side. The mediator may well be in the position of knowing what each side will accept and he can steer the discussions accordingly. Further joint meetings may follow but the process will remain entirely flexible to cater for any developments, some of which may not have been foreseen by the parties or the mediator.

(e) *The concluding phase*. This includes the preparation and signing of a settlement agreement. At this point the attendance of lawyers can be most valuable as they can negotiate the detail of the settlement, draft the agreement and advise their clients on the terms.

27.64   A settlement represents the optimum outcome but if the mediation concludes without agreement, the mediator will not give up if there have been signs that a settlement might be possible. After a few days, perhaps, the mediator may contact the parties to ascertain if they see any prospect of a settlement after the mediation experience. In this way, the mediator may still be able to broker a deal or the parties may see benefits in resuming the mediation on a specific basis.

27.65   In the mediation of some football disputes, these phases may well be taken much more shortly – but there will always be a need for some real structure to the process if it is to be effective.

CHAPTER 28

Arbitration in Football

Ian Mill QC (Blackstone Chambers), **Andrew Smith** (Matrix Chambers)
and **Richard Bush** (Bird & Bird LLP)

A   INTRODUCTION

28.1   The role of arbitration as the primary dispute resolution mechanism within football is enshrined within the FIFA Statutes (which are the foundation of the laws for world football).[1]

28.2   Article 59 of the FIFA Statutes states:

'59 Obligations relating to dispute resolution

1   The confederations, member associations and leagues shall agree to recognise CAS as an independent judicial authority and to ensure that their members, affiliated players and officials comply with the decisions passed by CAS. The same obligation shall apply to intermediaries and licensed match agents.

2   Recourse to ordinary courts of law is prohibited unless specifically provided for in the FIFA regulations. Recourse to ordinary courts of law for all types of provisional measures is also prohibited.

3   The associations shall insert a clause in their statutes or regulations, stipulating that it is prohibited to take disputes in the association or disputes affecting leagues, members of leagues, clubs, members of clubs, players, officials and other association officials to ordinary courts of law, unless the FIFA regulations or binding legal provisions specifically provide for or stipulate recourse to ordinary courts of law. Instead of recourse to ordinary courts of law, provision shall be made for arbitration. Such disputes shall be taken to an independent and duly constituted arbitration tribunal recognised under the rules of the association or confederation or to CAS.

The associations shall also ensure that this stipulation is implemented in the association, if necessary by imposing a binding obligation on its members. The associations shall impose sanctions on any party that fails to respect this obligation and ensure that any appeal against such sanctions shall likewise be strictly submitted to arbitration, and not to ordinary courts of law.'

28.3   Of particular note, Article 59 therefore:

(a) serves to recognise the Court of Arbitration for Sport (CAS) as the international 'supreme court' of football;

(b) precludes (save in very limited circumstances) recourse to ordinary courts of law; and

---

1   See FIFA Statutes, Articles 57–59.

(c) dictates that national associations ensure disputes are resolved by way of arbitration.[2]

28.4   There are clear advantages to football in having a uniform approach to dispute resolution – at least in relation to issues that affect the sport globally – because it enables consistency of approach across the worldwide game. This consistency would be impossible to achieve, or at least be greatly eroded, if disputes were instead subject to the courts of FIFA's 211 member associations (and the inconsistent approaches that would inevitably follow).[3] Precluding recourse to ordinary courts of law also serves to ensure that legal disputes can be resolved within the sport (and therefore outside of the full public glare).

28.5   In England, Article 59 is respected by virtue of FA Rule K, which is an arbitration agreement contained within The FA's Rules. Further, the rules of the Premier League and English Football League (EFL) also have a number of arbitration provisions applicable to certain disputes arising between participants in those leagues.

28.6   This chapter is concerned with arbitration in the context of professional English football. It details a number of considerations that apply to domestic arbitration generally (ie arbitration governed by the Arbitration Act 1996), before considering specific arbitration provisions contained within the rules and regulations of The FA, Premier League, and EFL. The chapter concludes with brief consideration of some international dispute resolution procedures, including the procedures of FIFA and UEFA decision-making bodies and the CAS.

B   DOMESTIC ARBITRATION UNDER THE ARBITRATION ACT 1996

(a)   What is arbitration?

28.7   Under English law, arbitration is governed by the Arbitration Act 1996. The Arbitration Act 1996 contains no statutory definition of arbitration, although it does set out the following general principles:[4]

(a) the object of arbitration is to obtain the fair resolution of disputes by an impartial tribunal without unnecessary delay or expense;[5]

---

2   See also FIFA Statutes, Article 15.f, concerning member associations' statutes, 'all relevant stakeholders must agree to recognise the jurisdiction and authority of CAS and give priority to arbitration as a means of dispute resolution'.

3   As noted by Professor John G Ruggie in an independent report commissioned by FIFA, '[Precluding recourse to national courts] is a complex issue, especially as it relates to human rights—which include the right to effective remedy as well as the right to a fair trial. Leaving all disputes to be settled in the domestic courts of 209 member associations would wreak havoc on common standards and consistency of application, and quite possibly undermine the game itself. Moreover, an arbitration system may be able to resolve many issues more quickly than courts and may be preferable on other grounds as well, including for players victimized by their own clubs or national associations.' See 'FOR THE GAME FOR THE WORLD.' FIFA and Human Rights. Corporate Responsibility Initiative Report No 68 (Cambridge, MA: Harvard Kennedy School, 2016), at p 26.

4   Arbitration Act 1996, s 1. The lack of statutory definition of the term 'arbitration' is intentional, because it was not considered by the drafters of the Act to serve a useful purpose. See *Report on the Arbitration Bill,* Departmental Advisory Committee on Arbitration Law, para 18 (February 1996).

5   This objective is supported by Arbitration Act 1996, s 33(1) which places a general duty on tribunals to (i) act fairly and impartially as between the parties, giving each party a reasonable opportunity of putting his case and dealing with that of his opponent, and (ii) adopt procedures suitable to the circumstances of the particular case, avoiding unnecessary delay or expense, so as to provide a fair

(b) parties to arbitration should be free to agree how their disputes are resolved, subject only to such safeguards as are necessary in the public interest; and

(c) the court should not intervene except where necessary (ie to the extent provided by the Arbitration Act 1996).

28.8 In the absence of a statutory definition, case law provides us with the following description of arbitration:

> '[T]he hallmark of the arbitration process is that it is a procedure to determine the legal rights and obligations of the parties judicially, with binding effect, which is enforceable in law, thus reflecting in private proceedings the role of a civil court of law.'[6]

28.9 In essence then, arbitration is an alternative to litigation before the courts, enabling parties to achieve a binding resolution to their disputes.

(b) Key features of arbitration compared to litigation

28.10 Arbitration is often said to have a number of advantages and disadvantages when compared to litigation in the courts. However, thinking of it in that way is not always helpful, because depending on the circumstances of any particular case the features of arbitration may be either advantageous or disadvantageous, or largely neutral, when compared to litigation (and vice-versa). Further, in the context of football and rules that provide for mandatory arbitration, it will seldom be a matter of choice in any event.

28.11 Key features of arbitration are as follows:

(a) *Speed and flexibility.* Arbitral tribunals can usually readily adapt procedures in order to suit the particular needs of a dispute (including in relation to important matters such as disclosure and evidence), and parties can generally influence procedure far more than is possible in litigation. Largely as a result of this flexibility, arbitration is often faster than litigation (and, at least historically, it was also typically said to be cheaper).[7] There are however no guarantees that arbitration will in fact progress quicker than litigation (or be cheaper) – much

---

means for the resolution of the matters falling to be determined. Similarly, Arbitration Act 1996, s 40(1) places a general duty on the parties to an arbitration to do all things necessary for the proper and expeditious conduct of the arbitral proceedings.

6   *O'Callaghan v Coral Racing Ltd*, The Times, 26 November 1998, per Hirst LJ at p 7. The reference to 'judicial' determination implies that the arbitral tribunal will decide the dispute in accordance with principles of fairness, equating to natural justice. See *Russell on Arbitration* 24th Edition (Sweet & Maxwell, 2015), para 1-002, and *England and Wales Cricket Board Limited v Danish Kaneria* [2013] EWHC 1074 (Comm), per Cooke J at para 27.

7   In terms of typical timescales, the Standard Directions under FA Rule K4 (for example) envisage that the hearing will take place within 119 days (17 weeks) following the appointment of a Tribunal chairman (which should itself take no longer than 28 days under FA Rule K2). If one were to assume that a 'standard' Rule K arbitration can be heard within that timescale, those Standard Directions compare favourably with the average time taken for multi and fast track claims in litigation, which (as of September 2017) take some 56.5 weeks (see Civil justice statistics quarterly: July to September 2017 (provisional) (Ministry of Justice, 7 December 2017), available at https://www.gov.uk/government/uploads/system/uploads/attachment_data/file/665073/civil-justice-statistics-quarterly-july-sept-2017.pdf (accessed March 2018)). However, it must also be noted that over the last few years amendments have been made to the Civil Procedural Rules to enable litigation to become more flexible and costs conscious. For example, the 'Jackson reforms' in 2013 introduced, amongst various other things, costs budgeting requirements and various options in relation to disclosure (which appear at CPR, r 3.12 *et seq* and CPR, r 31.5(7) respectively).

will depend on such things as the nature and complexity of the case, the conduct of the parties to the arbitration, and the robustness of the arbitral tribunal in terms of procedure.

(b) *Choice of arbitrator(s) and specialist knowledge.* In litigation, judges will be selected for individual cases by court officials. In arbitration, the parties are often free to choose how many arbitrators they wish to make up the tribunal, and also appoint some or all of those arbitrators.[8] Tribunals appointed to determine disputes in football can (and often do) therefore include members who have specialist knowledge, such as sports law practitioners or experienced participants from the game (for example, former players, managers and agents/ intermediaries), meaning that there is little or no need to educate them in relation to footballing matters that pertain to a dispute (whereas there would be no guarantee that a judge would have any such knowledge). The appointment of specialist members should also help ensure some level of consistency in terms of the approach taken by arbitral tribunals in respect to contentious issues.[9] The ability to choose arbitrators can also help ensure that matters progress swiftly (if the parties are aware that tribunal members are available and willing to hear the dispute). There is, however, some risk that specialist tribunal members might have preconceptions in terms of industry practice (that may or may not be conducive to a party's case), and it is occasionally suggested that the quality of decision-making by specialist arbitrators can be lower (compared to judicial reasoning).[10]

(c) *Confidentiality.* Litigation is typically conducted publicly. This not only applies to the trial itself, which members of the public may attend, but also to various documents produced during the course of litigation,[11] and of course the final judgment. Arbitrations, on the other hand, are typically private affairs.[12] This can be particularly attractive to parties involved in football disputes, because such disputes will often carry significant public and media attention.[13] The primary disadvantage arising from confidentiality – assuming it extends to the final award[14] – is that it may result in inconsistent decision-making (because of a lack of readily available precedents). There is, for example, a danger that terms of FA standard representation contracts may be interpreted differently by different tribunals.

(d) *Third parties and res judicata.* It follows from the private and confidential nature of arbitration proceedings that issues decided in arbitral awards are generally

---

8   Under the rules of some arbitration organisations which regulate procedures for arbitrations under its auspices (such as Sports Resolutions and the London Court of International Arbitration (LCIA)), the chairperson of a panel of three arbitrators, or a sole arbitrator, will be selected by that organisation. Typically, he or she will be legally qualified.

9   To some extent, this can help to mitigate the difficulties that arise in obtaining decisions in previous arbitrations to use by way of precedents (see below).

10 The likelihood of this can however be mitigated by having a legally qualified chairperson.

11 See CPR, rr 5.4C and 5.4D.

12 In general terms, the parties to arbitration, and the tribunal, are under implied duties to maintain the confidentiality of the hearing, documents generated and disclosed during the arbitral proceedings, and the award. See *Dolling-Baker v Merrett* [1990] 1 WLR 1205, at 1213. Those duties may also be express under the terms of the applicable arbitration agreement.

13 This confidentiality can however be lost if a party seeks to challenge an arbitral award in the courts under the Arbitration Act 1996 (in that respect, see generally paras **28.40** and **28.41** below). For example, in *Tony Pulis v Crystal Palace (CPFC Limited)* [2016] EWHC 2999 (Comm), Mr Pulis (former manager of Crystal Palace) sought to challenge an award of a Premier League Managers' Arbitration Tribunal. Consequently, much of the detail of the arbitration was brought into the public domain.

14 Which will not always be the case – for example, FA Rule K11(c) envisages that 'Unless otherwise agreed between the parties, where the Association is party to an arbitration, the Award shall be made public, subject to appropriate redaction to protect third party confidentiality'.

only binding on the parties to the arbitration, and not third parties[15] (although of course this does not mean that they cannot be persuasive). Unlike in litigation, it is also not generally possible to join third parties to arbitration, unless all relevant parties consent.[16] These issues can serve significantly to complicate multi-party disputes.

(e) *Finality*. Arbitration agreements often prescribe that awards are to be 'final and binding' and, for arbitrations governed by the Arbitration Act 1996, there are very limited avenues of challenge or appeal.[17] Whether or not a party perceives this as an advantage or disadvantage is likely to depend on the outcome of the arbitration, but generally it ensures that disputes are resolved with a higher degree of finality than a first instance judgment in litigation.

(c) Distinguishing arbitration from other forms of proceedings

28.12 The rules and regulations of each of English football's professional governing bodies – The FA, Premier League, and the EFL – refer various forms of disputes to a variety of decision-making panels.

28.13 Some of these panels are expressly stated to be arbitral in nature, with arbitral tribunals established to resolve disputes between parties, including FA Rule K arbitration, arbitration pursuant to Sections X ('Arbitration') and Y ('Managers' Arbitration Tribunal') of the Premier League Rules, and Section 9 ('Arbitration') of the EFL Regulations. These tribunals often – though not by any means exclusively – deal with disputes between participants (as opposed to between participants and The FA or one of the Leagues).

28.14 Other forms of proceedings are, however, more squarely concerned with disciplinary matters (ie prosecution by the relevant governing body of participants for alleged breaches of rules and regulations). In the case of The FA and the Premier League, their disciplinary panels do *not* purport to be arbitral – indeed, in the case of The FA, it is expressly stated that: 'It should be borne in mind that [The FA's various disciplinary bodies] are not courts of law and are disciplinary, rather than arbitral, bodies.'[18] However, as set out below, just because a panel is stated to be

---

15 There are limited exceptions to this rule, such as where a third party agrees to be bound by an arbitral award, or seeks to rely on it to demonstrate that subsequent proceedings are an abuse of process. As to the effect of an arbitral award, see generally *Russell on Arbitration* 24th Edition (Sweet & Maxwell, 2015), para 6-176 *et seq*. In the context of football arbitration, this principle was applied by the Tribunal in *Fulham Football Club v West Ham United Football Club* (2011) International Sports Law Review 1, SLR 1-7 (at para 10), 'Arbitration is, in contrast to litigation, a consensual private affair between the particular parties to a particular arbitration agreement in which the arbitrators are appointed to decide the particular dispute which has arisen between the parties to that arbitration. It follows that the award made in such proceedings remains private to those parties and may not subsequently be used in other proceedings without the parties' consent'. In that case Fulham FC unsuccessfully sought to admit into evidence an arbitral award in the related arbitration between Sheffield United and West Ham United (concerning what became commonly known as the 'Carlos Tevez affair').

16 For example, West Ham United was refused permission in 2012 to intervene in the FA Rule K arbitration between Leyton Orient and the Premier League, concerning the latter's grant of permission to West Ham to move ground to the Olympic Stadium.

17 See paras **28.40** and **28.41** below.

18 See para 1.1 of The FA's General Provisions Relating to Inquiries, Commissions of Inquiry, Regulatory Commissions of the Association, Other Disciplinary Commissions, Appeal Boards and Safeguarding Review Panel Hearings (the 'General Provisions') at p 322 of The FA Handbook 2017–2018. This wording was first introduced in the 2013–2014 FA Handbook (following the judgment in *England and Wales Cricket Board Limited v Danish Kaneria*, cited below).

'disciplinary' does not also mean it cannot also be 'arbitral'. Indeed, the EFL's disciplinary proceedings are explicitly so.[19]

28.15   Whether or not proceedings constitute arbitration under English law has potentially significant legal consequences. In the event that such proceedings do constitute arbitration, then they are subject to the supportive powers and challenge provisions of the Arbitration Act 1996,[20] whereas if they do not they may be challenged in accordance with the grounds for court review arising out of a sport's governing body's control of the sport.[21] In practice, little may turn on the distinction when considering matters of procedural fairness, because both contain important procedural safeguards (and both have high bars to overcome to mount successful challenges), but only arbitrations can benefit from the supportive powers of the English courts provided by the Arbitration Act 1996 (see paras **28.30** *et seq* below). In *England and Wales Cricket Board Limited v Danish Kaneria*,[22] the ECB successfully sought a witness summons under s 43 of the Arbitration Act 1996 (which of course would not have been open to it if its internal proceedings were not arbitral).[23] In his judgment, Cooke J emphasised that the question of whether proceedings are arbitral is one of substance, not labelling; and set out (at paras 31–41 of his judgment) 10 relevant factors when determining the correct classification of proceedings (adopting in part the analysis set out in Mustill & Boyd):[24]

(1) It is a characteristic of arbitration that the parties should have a proper opportunity to present their case.
(2) It is a fundamental requirement of an arbitration that the arbitrators do not receive unilateral communications from the parties and disclose all communications with one party to the other party.
(3) The hallmarks of an arbitral process are the provision of proper and proportionate procedures for the provision and for the receipt of evidence.
(4) The agreement pursuant to which the process is, or is to be, carried on ('the procedural agreement') must contemplate that the tribunal which carries on the process will make a decision which is binding on the parties to the procedural agreement.
(5) The procedural agreement must contemplate that the process will be carried on between those persons whose substantive rights are determined by the tribunal.
(6) The jurisdiction of the tribunal to carry on the process and to decide the rights of the parties must derive either from the consent of the parties, or from an order of the court or from a statute, the terms of which make it clear that the process is to be an arbitration.

19   See Section 8, Regulation 86.6 of the EFL Regulations.
20   Save to the extent the non-mandatory provisions of the Arbitration Act 1996 are excluded (see paras **28.23** et seq below).
21   *Bradley v Jockey Club* [2004] EWHC 2164 QB, [2004] All ER (D) 11 (1 October 2004, Richards J) upheld on appeal [2005] EWCA Civ 1056, (2005) Times, 14 July (12 June 2005, Lord Phillips MR, Buxton LJ, Scott Baker LJ). In short, a sports governing body is required (along with any decision-making panels constituted by it) (i) to act lawfully and in accordance with its rules, (ii) to act fairly in a procedural sense, (iii) to take into account only relevant considerations, (iv) to instruct itself properly as to the facts, (v) not to act contrary to a legitimate expectation, and (vi) not to act unreasonably, irrationally, arbitrarily, or capriciously. See Lewis, Taylor, De Marco and Segan, *Challenging Sports Governing Bodies* (Bloomsbury Professional, 2016), Chapter 7.
22   [2013] EWHC 1074 (Comm).
23   See paras **28.38** and **28.39** below.
24   *Mustill & Boyd on Commercial Arbitration* 2nd Edition (LexisNexis, 2001), p 41.

(7) The tribunal must be chosen, either by the parties, or by a method to which they have consented.
(8) The procedural agreement must contemplate that the tribunal will determine the rights of the parties in an impartial manner, with the tribunal owing an equal obligation of fairness towards both sides.
(9) The agreement of the parties to refer their disputes to the decision of the tribunal must be intended to be enforceable in law.
(10) The procedural agreement must contemplate a process whereby the tribunal will make a decision upon a dispute which has already been formulated at the time when the tribunal is appointed.

28.16   Historically, it was largely assumed that disciplinary processes established under the rules of sports governing bodies would not be arbitral, particularly where (as was often the case) panels were formed of a committee of members of the sport's governing body (leading to the conclusion that such panels would not be regarded as sufficiently 'judicial' or 'impartial' to qualify as arbitral). However, for some time now there has been a move towards sports governing bodies actively choosing to make their disciplinary proceedings qualify as arbitral. Examples at the time of writing include disciplinary proceedings under the rules and regulations of the Rugby Football Union, the England and Wales Cricket Board (appeal proceedings only), the Lawn Tennis Association, the Rugby Football League, and the National Anti-Doping Panel.

28.17   As above, however, The FA's disciplinary proceedings are expressly stated not to be arbitral and, whilst it is a question of substance not labelling, in the authors' view it is unlikely that The FA's disciplinary proceedings would be classified as arbitral. This is principally because of the operation of The FA's 'Judicial Panel', which is 'established by [The FA] Council as the group of individuals from which Regulatory Commissions and Appeal Boards will be drawn by the Judicial Panel Chairman or his nominee, to hear cases or appeals in connection with disciplinary and other regulatory processes of The Association'.[25]

28.18   First, it can be seen from this definition that the Judicial Panel (whilst it includes independent members) is not an independent body as such (rather, it is established by The FA Council). Secondly, although in any given case the first instance and appeal panels will be made up of different individuals, Judicial Panel members can and often have reviewed each other's decisions. Thirdly, the Judicial Panel membership includes a number of members of The FA Council itself. Considering all these things, it would seem that the panels appointed under The FA's disciplinary procedures are unlikely to be sufficiently 'impartial' to satisfy the requirements for an arbitral tribunal.[26]

---

25   Paragraph 3.1 of the Terms of Reference for the Composition and Operation of the Judicial Panel, at p 50 of The FA Handbook 2017–2018.
26   The appointment of FA Council Members to the Judicial Panel is potentially vulnerable to challenge, and does not appear to sit comfortably alongside the decision in *R (Kaur) v Institute of Legal Executives Appeal Tribunal* [2011] EWCA Civ 1168, in which an ILEX appeal tribunal decision was quashed because the tribunal included an ILEX Council Member. Interestingly, in *Cellino v FA*, FA Rule K Arbitral Tribunal award dated 2 October 2017, it is documented that The FA compromised an apparent bias issue in respect of a leading member of The FA Council sitting on an FA Appeal Board (leading to the FA Rule K Arbitral Tribunal sitting as a *de novo* Appeal Board).

(d)   Arbitration agreements

(i)   *Agreement in writing*

28.19   Pursuant to s 5 of the Arbitration Act 1996, for any dispute to be referred to arbitration, there must be an agreement in writing to that effect. As to whether such an agreement can be said to exist, s 5(2)–(6) of the Arbitration Act 1996 provides as follows:

> '(2)   There is an agreement in writing –
>   (a)   if the agreement is made in writing (whether or not it is signed by the parties),
>   (b)   if the agreement is made by exchange of communications in writing, or
>   (c)   if the agreement is evidenced in writing.
> (3)   Where parties agree otherwise than in writing by reference to terms which are in writing, they make an agreement in writing.
> (4)   An agreement is evidenced in writing if an agreement made otherwise than in writing is recorded by one of the parties, or by a third party, with the authority of the parties to the agreement.
> (5)   An exchange of written submissions in arbitral or legal proceedings in which the existence of an agreement otherwise than in writing is alleged by one party against another party and not denied by the other party in his response constitutes as between those parties an agreement in writing to the effect alleged.
> (6)   References in this Part to anything being written or in writing include its being recorded by any means.'

28.20   In the context of arbitration in English football, arbitration agreements are most likely to be contained within the rules and regulations of The FA, the Premier League or the EFL, also in contracts between various participants (such as player contracts[27] and representation contracts[28]).[29] Whilst most disputes within football (however they arise) will typically fall to be determined by some form or other of procedural rules established by one of the governing bodies, ad hoc arbitration agreements outside of those frameworks may also be a consideration.

28.21   Any arbitration agreement should ideally set out its scope in clear terms, both as regards who is bound by it, and which disputes (or types of disputes) it covers.[30] There are, however, certain disputes that are not capable of being resolved by arbitration (and so, in that respect, an arbitration agreement cannot be valid

---

27   For example, clause 17 of the Premier League standard player contract states '17. Arbitration Any dispute between the Club and the Player not provided for in clauses 9, 10, 11,12 and Schedule 1 hereof shall be referred to arbitration in accordance with the League Rules or (but only if mutually agreed by the Club and the Player) in accordance with the FA Rules.' See Premier League Handbook Season 2017–18, at p 332.

28   For example, clause 6 of the FA Standard Representation Contract between an Intermediary and a Player, available on The FA's website at http://www.thefa.com/football-rules-governance/policies/ intermediaries/representation-contracts (accessed March 2018), states: 'Any dispute between the parties arising out of or in connection with the Contract, including but not limited to any question regarding its existence, validity or termination, shall be referred to and finally resolved by arbitration under Rule K of the Rules of The FA (as amended from time to time).'

29   For completeness, pursuant to s 7 of the Arbitration Act 1996, an arbitration clause in a larger agreement is treated as a separate agreement, so it is not automatically invalidated by the invalidity of the main agreement (so, for example, Rule K would not be invalidated if The FA Rules – or perhaps more realistically any other part of The FA Rules – were found to be invalid).

30   Of particular note in respect to arbitration in English football, two recent cases, *Wilfried Bony v Kacou* [2017] EWHC 2146 (Ch) and *Davies v Nottingham Forest FC* [2017] EWHC 2095, have cast some doubt over the scope of FA Rule K, and are discussed further below at para **28.46** *et seq*.

in respect of such disputes).[31] Insofar as they are of foreseeable relevance to arbitration in football, they include:

(a) criminal matters, which are reserved to the courts;[32]
(b) disputes for which access to the courts is an inalienable right, most notably employees' rights to enforce statutory rights in the employment tribunal, under the Employment Rights Act 1996 and Equality Act 2010;[33] and
(c) insolvency proceedings, which are governed by the Insolvency Act 1986.

28.22   In the event that there is a dispute about the validity or scope of an arbitration agreement, then it is a matter that (subject to agreement to the contrary) falls within the jurisdiction of the appointed arbitral tribunal.[34]

(ii)   Mandatory and non-mandatory provisions of the Arbitration Act 1996

28.23   It is a principle of the Arbitration Act 1996 that the parties to arbitration should be free to agree how their disputes are resolved, subject only to such safeguards as are necessary in the public interest. This is reflected in the existence of 'non-mandatory' and 'mandatory' provisions of the Act.[35] In other words, the parties are free to opt out of certain provisions of the Act (and can instead make their own arrangements by agreement), but cannot opt out of certain provisions that constitute necessary safeguards.

28.24   The mandatory provisions of the Act are contained in its Schedule 1, and include (but are not limited to) important matters such as the power of the court to remove an arbitrator (s 24), the general duties of the tribunal and the parties (ss 33 and 40), securing the attendance of witnesses (s 43), and challenges to arbitral awards on the grounds of substantive jurisdiction and serious irregularity (ss 67 and 68).

(iii)   Consent

28.25   In all cases, an agreement to arbitrate will not be constituted unless there is consent by and between the parties to that agreement.[36] The question has upon occasion arisen in the context of arbitration agreements mandated by the rules of sport governing bodies as to whether participants have provided effective consent; particularly so in the case of individuals, if the 'take it or leave it' choice is between participation and non-participation in a particular sport, competition or event. However, as a matter of English arbitration law as it applies to football, the position appears to be relatively settled, with little if any scope to challenge the validity of

---

31   See, generally, *Russell on Arbitration* 24th Edition (Sweet & Maxwell, 2015), paras 2-080 *et seq.*
32   However, a tribunal may make findings of fact that would constitute a criminal offence, for example fraud.
33   This means that, notwithstanding mandatory arbitration provisions in football, an aggrieved player or manager may legitimately elect to sue his club in respect of certain matters in the employment tribunal – this occurred, for example, in the cases of *McCammon v Gillingham FC*, UKEAT/0559/12/ DM; UKEAT/0560/12/DM and *Gutierrez v Newcastle United FC*, unreported 14 April 2016 (ET).
34   See Arbitration Act 1996, ss 30–32.
35   See Arbitration Act 1996, s 4. Where an arbitration agreement is silent on a non-mandatory matter covered by the Arbitration Act 1996, the relevant provision of the Arbitration Act 1996 applies. Arbitration Act 1996, s 4(2) provides that, while the parties can make their own arrangements by agreement, the non-mandatory provisions lay down rules 'which apply in the absence of such agreement'.
36   As above, Arbitration Act 1996, s 1 states that the parties to arbitration should be free to *agree* how their disputes are resolved.

such arbitration clauses based on a lack of consent (consent in the context of the CAS and international arbitration is considered at paras **28.110** *et seq.* below).

28.26   In *Stretford v FA*, a prominent English football agent, Paul Stretford, faced disciplinary charges brought by The FA. Mr Stretford brought litigation against The FA and sought to challenge The FA's disciplinary process alleging (amongst other things) that it lacked independence and breached his human rights under Article 6 of the European Convention on Human Rights. The FA sought a stay of the litigation on the basis that Rule K arbitration applied to the dispute. Mr Stretford disputed the validity of the Rule K arbitration agreement on the ground that he never agreed to it, or that it would be a breach of his Article 6 rights to enforce it. Mr Stretford was unsuccessful, both at first instance[37] and on appeal.[38]

28.27   As to the first argument (in relation to which permission to appeal was not given), the Chancellor of the High Court found that Mr Stretford was bound by FA Rule K as a result of a course of dealings under FA Rules:[39]

> 'Given that Rule K applies to all parties alike and in the way such clauses conventionally operate I do not consider that it required any particular or special notice to be given by The FA to Mr Stretford. But even if it did I conclude that such notice was given. Mr Stretford knew that he was obliged to observe the Rules. The Rules were published by The FA at least once a year in its handbook and were available at all times through its website ... I am not prepared to go further and conclude that The FA had to make Mr Stretford sit down and read it in order to bring Rule K fairly and reasonably to his attention ...'

28.28   As to the second argument, the Chancellor concluded that Mr Stretford's agreement to Rule K amounted to an informed waiver of his Article 6 rights, which was valid in the absence of duress, undue influence, fraud, mistake or misrepresentation. This conclusion was upheld by the Court of Appeal. Sir Anthony Clarke MR held:[40]

> 'An arbitration clause has become standard in the rules of sporting organisations like the FA. The rules regulate the relationship between the parties, which is a private law relationship governed by contract ... Clauses like Rule K have to be agreed to by anyone, like Mr Stretford, who wishes to have a players' licence, but it does not follow that the arbitration agreement contained in them was required by law or compulsory. To strike down clauses of this kind because they were incompatible with art 6 [ECHR] on that basis would have a far-reaching and, in our opinion, undesirable effect on the use of arbitration in the context of sport generally.'

28.29   So, the impact of the *Stretford* litigation on arbitration in sport is twofold: first, it will be very difficult for a participant to argue that he/she is not contractually bound by the arbitration agreement (because the dispute will almost inevitably arise out of his/her participation, and so he/she will – expressly or by implication – have agreed to be bound by the arbitration agreement) and, secondly, such an arbitration agreement will almost inevitably result in an effective waiver of Article 6 rights (absent duress, undue influence, fraud, mistake or misrepresentation).

(e)   Court supervision

28.30   In keeping with the principle that the court should not intervene except where necessary, the role of the English courts in respect to arbitration is predominantly

---

37   *Stretford v Football Association Ltd* [2006] EWHC 479 (Ch).
38   *Paul Stretford v The Football Association Ltd* [2007] EWCA Civ 238.
39   Above n 37, at para 26.
40   Above n 38, at para 49.

supportive, not supervisory. The court's statutory powers in relation to arbitrations are set out in various sections of Part I of the Arbitration Act 1996, and some key powers are set out below.

28.31 Arbitration claims (ie claims that seek to trigger the court's powers in relation to arbitration) are principally governed by Part 62 of the Civil Procedure Rules and various Court Guides (ie the Admiralty and Commercial Court Guide, the Technology and Construction Court Guide, and Mercantile Court Guides). Depending on the section of the Arbitration Act 1996 that an applicant seeks to invoke, considerations relevant to the application will include such things as (i) whether all available recourse in the arbitration process has been exhausted,[41] (ii) whether the applicant has waived his/her/its right to make certain objections to the process,[42] and (iii) any time limit for making the application.[43]

(i) Upholding the arbitration agreement

28.32 Where there is a binding arbitration agreement between parties to a dispute, the English courts will seek to support that agreement. Therefore, in the event that litigation is brought before the English courts in breach of the arbitration agreement, the court will stay its proceedings in deference to the arbitration agreement. Where court proceedings are commenced outside the jurisdiction in breach of the arbitration agreement, the courts have the power to grant anti-suit injunctions (similarly, although less commonly, the courts may also grant anti-arbitration injunctions where arbitral proceedings have been commenced in breach of an arbitration agreement ie in the wrong arbitral forum).

28.33 The court's power to stay proceedings derives, principally,[44] from s 9(1) and (4) of the Arbitration Act 1996, which state:

'(1) A party to an arbitration agreement against whom legal proceedings are brought (whether by way of claim or counterclaim) in respect of a matter which under the agreement is to be referred to arbitration may (upon notice to the other parties to the proceedings) apply to the court in which the proceedings have been brought to stay the proceedings so far as they concern that matter …

(4) On an application under this section the court shall grant a stay unless satisfied that the arbitration agreement is null and void, inoperative, or incapable of being performed.'

28.34 Applications to stay proceedings must be made to the court in which the proceedings have been commenced.[45] The application will be rejected if the relevant dispute(s) are not subject to an obligation to arbitrate ie where there is no such agreement or it is null and void, inoperative or incapable of being performed.

---

41   For example, under Arbitration Act 1996, s 24(2), 'If there is an arbitral or other institution or person vested by the parties with power to remove an arbitrator, the court shall not exercise its power of removal unless satisfied that the applicant has first exhausted any available recourse to that institution or person.'

42   Arbitration Act 1996, s 73 sets out the grounds on which a party may lose its right to object.

43   For example, under Arbitration Act 1996, s 70(3), 'Any application or appeal must be brought within 28 days of the date of the award or, if there has been any arbitral process of appeal or review, of the date when the applicant or appellant was notified of the result of that process.'

44   The court may also, exceptionally, stay proceedings under its powers of inherent jurisdiction. See Senior Courts Act 1981, s 49(3) and *Reichold Norway ASA v Goldman Sachs International* [1999] EWCA Civ 1703.

45   For a detailed analysis of the legal principles relating to a stay of legal proceedings, in favour of arbitration, see the Court of Appeal's judgment in *Fulham Football Club (1987) Ltd v Richards* [2011] EWCA Civ 238.

An applicant may also risk the court rejecting its application if that party has taken a substantive step in the court proceedings (which is something of a trap for the unwary – stay applications must be made promptly).[46]

28.35   Applications for anti-suit or anti-arbitration injunctions are made pursuant to s 37 of the Senior Courts Act 1981. An example of a case in the footballing context where such an injunction was sought and granted is *Sheffield United Football Club Plc v West Ham United Football Club Plc*,[47] in which West Ham sought to appeal a decision by a Rule K tribunal to CAS (despite FA Rule K stating that such arbitration is final and binding).

28.36   In the case of litigation issued in breach of an arbitration agreement contained within the rules of a sporting body, the court's ability to uphold the agreement could be further supported – at least in theory – by disciplinary action by the body in question. For example, a party who issued litigation in breach of Rule K would commit misconduct under FA Rule E1(b) (breach of FA rules).

(ii)   Removal of an arbitrator

28.37   Section 24(1) of the Arbitration Act 1996 sets out four grounds on which a party may apply, having exhausted any avenues of recourse available in the arbitration,[48] to remove an arbitrator, namely that:[49]

(a)   circumstances exist that give rise to justifiable doubts as to his impartiality;
(b)   he does not possess the qualifications required by the arbitration agreement;
(c)   he is physically or mentally incapable of conducting the proceedings or there are justifiable doubts as to his capacity to do so;
(d)   he has refused or failed:
    (i)   properly to conduct the proceedings, or
    (ii)   to use all reasonable despatch in conducting the proceedings or making an award, and that substantial injustice has been or will be caused to the applicant.

(iii)   Powers of the court in relation to arbitral proceedings

28.38   Sections 42 to 45 of the Arbitration Act 1996 contain a number of provisions that enable the court to support the progress of an arbitration:

(a)   s 42 enables the court to make an order requiring a party to comply with a peremptory order made by the arbitral tribunal;

46   Arbitration Act 1996, s 9(3).
47   [2009] 1 Lloyds Rep 167.
48   Arbitration Act 1996, s 24(2).
49   The authors are aware of one case in the sporting context that considered the application of s 24, being *Paul Smith & Jamie McDonnell v British Boxing Board of Control Ltd, Frank Warren & Dennis Hobson* (QB, Liverpool DR, Mercantile Court 13 April 2015, unreported), available at https://www. lawtel.com/UK/FullText/AC0146050QBD(Liverpool).pdf. In that case the British Boxing Board of Control was arbitrating a dispute that concerned the validity of its own rules. Two boxers sought to argue that this raised justifiable doubts as to impartiality under s 24(1) of the Arbitration Act 1996. The challenge failed, *inter alia*, because they had consented to the arbitral proceedings. However, *Smith and McDonnell* is nonetheless notable to the extent it applied *Sierra Fishing company v Hasan Said Farran* [2015] EWHC 140 (Comm), which confirmed that the test under s 24(1)(a) is the same as the common law test of bias. That test was established in *Porter v Magill* [2002] AC 357 (at para 103), and it is whether 'the fair minded and informed observer, having considered the facts, would conclude that there was a real possibility that the tribunal was biased'. In applying that test to

(b) s 43 enables the court to use the same court procedures as are available in relation to legal proceedings to secure the attendance of a witness in order to give oral testimony or to produce documents or other material evidence;[50]

(c) s 44 enables the court to exercise a number of powers in support of an arbitration, including the taking of the evidence of witnesses, the preservation of evidence, orders relating to property, the sale of goods, and the granting of interim injunctions or the appointment of a receiver;

(d) s 45 enables the court to determine preliminary points of law which substantially affects the rights of one or more parties.

28.39   Of the above, only s 43 is a mandatory provision. The others may be, and often are, excluded by agreement.

(iv) Challenges to the award

28.40   Under the Arbitration Act 1996, an application may be made to the court to challenge an arbitral award on three grounds:

(a) s 67: the tribunal did not have substantive jurisdiction;[51]

(b) s 68: there has been a serious irregularity affecting the tribunal, the proceedings or the award, that has caused or will cause substantial injustice to the applicant;[52] and

(c) s 69: appeal on a question of law arising out of the award.

28.41   Sections 67 and 68 are mandatory provisions of the Arbitration Act 1996, whereas the operation of s 69 may be – and often is – excluded by agreement. The main advantage of excluding s 69 is that doing so significantly increases the prospect of awards being final and binding, whereas the main disadvantage is of course that there is no scope to appeal arbitral awards that are flawed as a matter of law. The parties can consent to an appeal on the basis of s 69, whereas leave of the court is otherwise required for any appeal under ss 67, 68 and 69.[53]

C ARBITRATION IN ENGLISH FOOTBALL

28.42   As explained below, the rules and processes that govern football-related arbitration in England depend on the identity of the participants and the nature of the dispute. The main forms of arbitration in the domestic context are:

(a) arbitration under Rule K of the FA Rules;

(b) arbitration under Sections X, Y and Z of the FA Premier League Rules; and

(c) arbitration under Section 9 of the EFL Regulations.

---

the facts of *Smith and McDonnell*, HHJ Bird noted that the arbitration process needed to be looked at in its entirety, and there was an appeal process conducted by Appeal Stewards, which he described as an 'independent experienced quasi-judicial body'.

50   As above, the ECB sought a witness summons under Arbitration Act 1996, s 43 in *England and Wales Cricket Board Limited v Danish Kaneria*.

51   Pursuant to Arbitration Act 1996, s 72(1), a tribunal will not have substantive jurisdiction if (i) there is no valid arbitration agreement, (ii) the tribunal was not properly constituted, or (iii) the matters submitted to arbitration are not in accordance with the arbitration agreement.

52   Challenges under Arbitration Act 1996, s 68 face a very high threshold for success. For example, in *Tony Pulis v Crystal Palace (CPFC Limited)* [2016] EWHC 2999 (Comm), at para 53, the court emphasised that its s 68 jurisdiction was 'designed as a long-stop available only in extreme cases where the Tribunal has gone so wrong in its conduct of the arbitration that justice calls out for it to be corrected' (a position derived from *Lesotho Highlands Development Authority v Impreglio SpA* [2006] 1 AC 221).

53   See Arbitration Act 1996, ss 67(4), 68(4) and 69(2).

(a)   Arbitration under Rule K of The FA Rules

(i)   *What type of disputes are to be referred to Rule K arbitration?*

28.43   Rule K1(a) of the FA Rules provides that, subject to a limited number of specific exceptions (discussed below), *any* dispute or difference between any two or more 'participants' 'including but not limited to a dispute arising out of or in connection with' the following (non-exhaustive) matters 'shall be referred to and finally resolved by arbitration under these Rules':

(a)   the Rules and regulations of The Association which are in force from time to time;
(b)   the rules and regulations of an affiliated association or competition which are in force from time to time;
(c)   the statutes and regulations of FIFA and UEFA which are in force from time to time; and
(d)   the Laws of the Game.

28.44   It can be seen, therefore, that a vast array of football-related disputes between participants (as broadly defined – see immediately below) may fall within the scope of the Rule K arbitration provisions. Common types of dispute that are referred to Rule K arbitration are disputes between clubs and intermediaries regarding transfer-related commission entitlements, and disputes between players and intermediaries in connection with representation contracts.

(ii)   *Who is a participant for the purpose of Rule K?*

28.45   The concept of 'participant' is a very broad one under the FA Rules, meaning:

> 'Affiliated Association, Competition, Club, Club Official, Intermediary, Player, Official, Manager, Match Official, Match Official observer, Match Official coach, Match Official mentor, Management Committee Member, member or employee of a Club and all such persons who are from time to time participating in any activity sanctioned either directly or indirectly by The Association.'[54]

(iii)   *The applicability of Rule K arbitration – Davies and Bony*

28.46   Whilst the scope of Rule K is drafted very broadly, the question of the applicability of Rule K to parties in football disputes has been considered in two recent High Court decisions, *Davies v Nottingham Forest FC*[55] and *Wilfried Bony v Kacou.*[56]

28.47   In *Davies,* a dispute arose between the club and its former manager, Billy Davies. Mr Davies sought to sue for damages in the civil court but the club objected, contending that the court had no jurisdiction and applying for a stay under s 9 of the Arbitration Act 1996 to have the matter resolved by way of arbitration under Rule K of the FA Rules. The relevant employment contract did not contain any express arbitration agreement. In the circumstances, Mr Davies contended that he was not bound by any arbitration agreement and that he had the right to pursue his claim in the civil court.

---

54   FA Rules, Rule A.2.
55   [2017] EWHC 2095.
56   [2017] EWHC 2146 (Ch).

28.48   The Manchester District Registry of the High Court found in favour of Nottingham Forest and made an order staying the court proceedings and referring the claim to arbitration. It did so on the following basis. First, the judge analysed the relevant regulatory framework and concluded that the FA Rules 'are intended to lay down a mechanism to decide and settle any differences which arise between a club and its manager'.

28.49   Having regard to this regulatory framework, the judge noted that as between Mr Davies and The FA on the one hand, and the club and The FA on the other, both were bound by the FA Rules. In this factual matrix, the judge posed the question; 'if the Club has an agreement with The FA that "any dispute or difference between any two or more Participants ... shall be referred to and finally resolved by arbitration under these Rules", and Mr Davies has the same agreement with The FA, are the Club and Mr Davies parties to an arbitration agreement?' The judge answered this question in the affirmative., basing his decision on the decision of the House of Lords in *The Satanita*[57] (a dispute between owners of yachts, one of which was damaged in a race) in which Lord Herschell observed:

> 'the effect of their entering for the race and undertaking to be bound by these rules
> to the knowledge of each other, is sufficient, I think, where those rules indicate
> a liability on the part of the one to the other, to create a contractual obligation to
> discharge that liability.'

28.50   A different conclusion was reached by the same District Registry of the High Court (albeit by a different judge) in *Bony*. In this case, the former Swansea and Manchester City striker claimant issued a civil court claim, seeking substantial damages on the basis that the defendants (including his former agents) had received secret and unlawful commissions. An application on behalf of the first to fourth (out of five) defendants to stay those proceedings, on the basis that the dispute should instead be determined by arbitration under Rule K of the FA Rules, was rejected by the county court and, on appeal, by the High Court. This conclusion was reached on the basis that the claimant had failed to demonstrate the existence of a valid arbitration agreement between him and the first to fourth defendants.

28.51   The claimant submitted that, on the particular facts of the case, there was no proper basis for implying an arbitration agreement that he and any of the four defendants would submit their disputes to arbitration under Rule K of the FA Rules (or otherwise). It followed, in the claimant's submission, that he was entitled to pursue his claim in the civil courts.

28.52   As in *Davies*, the judge considered *The Satanita*, but concluded that it ought to be distinguished on its facts. The judge concluded that it was not necessary to imply an agreement to arbitrate between the claimant and any of the four defendants.

28.53   In the circumstances, he therefore concluded that the claimant was entitled to proceed with his claim in the civil courts, and there was no obligation to stay the proceedings in favour of a Rule K arbitration.

28.54   It has been suggested that these two judgments of the same District Registry of the High Court, handed down within weeks of one another in the summer of 2017,

---

57   [1897] AC 59.

are irreconcilable – both in terms of their outcomes *and* their analysis of the law in this context. In the authors' view that is not necessarily so, albeit the conflicting outcomes in these two cases are likely to increase the scope for, and the number of, jurisdictional challenges in football-related disputes.

28.55   A detailed analysis of these two cases, and how they are likely to be treated going forward, is beyond the scope of this chapter. However, the authors anticipate that, in circumstances where the parties to a football-related dispute:

(a) are each (or all) authorised participants within the meaning of the relevant Rules; and
(b) can each be shown to have expressly or impliedly agreed to be bound by the same set of Rules, including the written arbitration provisions which form an integral part of those Rules,

it is likely that arbitral tribunals will be willing to accept jurisdiction to determine such disputes, and that courts will be inclined to stay civil litigation in favour of arbitration. In the authors' view, this would accord with the overarching regulatory regime which, as explained in the introductory section of this chapter, enshrines the importance of arbitration in the context of football-related disputes.

(iv)   When will Rule K not be the appropriate route for dispute resolution?

28.56   Arbitration under Rule K will not necessarily be the first or appropriate mechanism for resolving a dispute between two or more participants. First of all, Rule K1(b) provides that:

> 'No arbitration shall be commenced under these Rules unless and until the party or parties wishing to commence an arbitration under these Rules … has exhausted all applicable rights of appeal pursuant to the Rules and regulations of The Association.'

27.57   In addition, Rule K1(c) is what may be described a 'deferred jurisdiction' clause; it provides that 'any dispute or difference which falls to be resolved pursuant to any rules from time to time in force of any Affiliated Association or Competition' shall be resolved pursuant to *those* rules, rather than Rule K. Such rules would include those of the FA Premier League and the EFL.

(v)   How does the nature of the dispute affect the arbitral panel's powers in Rule K proceedings?

28.58   Rule K1(d) is what may be described as a 'limited jurisdiction' clause; it provides that Rule K1(a):

> 'shall not operate to provide an appeal against the decision of a Regulatory Commission or an Appeal Board under the Rules and shall operate only as the forum and procedure for a challenge to the validity of such decision under English law on the ground of ultra vires (including error of law), irrationality or procedural unfairness, with the Tribunal exercising a supervisory jurisdiction.'

This is significant, as it means that arbitration proceedings under Rule K1(a) will not amount to a substantive appeal on the merits, or a full re-hearing of a case determined by a Regulatory Commission or Appeal Board, but rather will constitute a judicial review-type process in such cases, with relatively narrow scope for interfering with the decision under challenge.[58]

---

58   See above, n 21.

(vi)   Commencing an arbitration under Rule K

28.59   Rule K2(a) sets out the procedure for commencing an arbitration – put simply, by serving a written Notice of Arbitration which complies with the various requirements specified therein. The claimant may, if it wishes, serve detailed Points of Claim at the same time as submitting the Notice of Arbitration. This commonly occurs in circumstances where the parties have already engaged in detailed pre-action correspondence and can serve to speed up the arbitral process.

(vii)   Responding to a claim under Rule K

28.60   The requirements for the respondent's response are set out in Rule K2(b). Whilst it is under no obligation to do so, in circumstances where the notice of arbitration was accompanied by the claimant's points of claim, the respondent may serve its points of defence at the same time as submitting the response to the notice of arbitration. Again, this can serve to speed up the arbitral process.

(viii)   Appointing the arbitrator(s)

28.61   The process by which an arbitrator or arbitrators is/are to be nominated and appointed is detailed in Rules K2(c) and (d) and Rule K3. In broad summary:

(a)   where the parties agree that the matter should be determined by a sole arbitrator, they should seek to agree the identity of that arbitrator between themselves;

(b)   if they cannot agree the identity of the sole arbitrator within 14 days of service of the response(s), the sole arbitrator shall be appointed by:
–   the Chairman of the Football Regulatory Authority (FRA) or his nominee, in a dispute to which The FA is not a party; or
–   the President of the Chartered Institute of Arbitrators shall appoint the sole arbitrator, in a dispute to which The FA is a party;

(c)   where a respondent fails to serve a response to a notice of arbitration and the claimant consents to the appointment of a single arbitrator, this will be done by the FRA or his nominee, or the President of the Chartered Institute of Arbitrators (depending on whether The FA is a party to the dispute, as noted above);

(d)   in all other cases, the dispute will be resolved by a panel of three arbitrators;

(e)   in such cases, the parties are required to notify each other (in the notice of arbitration and response respectively) of the identity of their appointed arbitrator, who must have confirmed his/her willingness and availability to accept the appointment;

(f)   the parties should then, within 14 days of service of the response(s), agree to the appointment of a third arbitrator who shall act as the Chairman of the Tribunal; and

(g)   where the parties cannot agree on the appointment of the chairman, he/she will be appointed by the FRA or his nominee, or the President of the Chartered Institute of Arbitrators (depending on whether The FA is a party to the dispute, as noted above).

28.62   Unsurprisingly, the Rules require that 'each arbitrator must be, and remain, impartial and independent of all the parties to the arbitration at all times' (Rule K3(d)). It is also a condition that each arbitrator must be resident in England.

(ix)   Challenging the appointment of an arbitrator(s)

28.63   Rules K3(d)(i) specifies the basis on which a party may challenge the appointment of an arbitrator, providing that: 'Any arbitrator may be challenged if circumstances exist that give rise to justifiable doubts as to the arbitrator's impartiality or independence.' As regards the procedure for lodging such a challenge, it must be submitted, with reasons: (i) within 14 days after notification of the appointment of the challenged arbitrator; or (ii) if later, within 14 days from the date when the party making the challenge is informed of the facts and circumstances upon which the challenge is based. The notice of challenge must be sent to the other party/parties to the dispute; the challenged arbitrator, the other members of the Tribunal, and The FA or the President of the Chartered Institute of Arbitrators (in circumstances where the challenged arbitrator was appointed by them).

28.64   If the other party/parties agree to the challenge, or the challenged arbitrator decides to withdraw, then a replacement arbitrator will be appointed on the basis set out above. If this does not happen, then the challenge will be decided by the FRA or his nominee, or the President of the Chartered Institute of Arbitrators (depending on whether The FA is a party to the dispute, as noted above).

(x)   Procedural rules, the Tribunal's general powers and the obligations of the parties

28.65   Rule K4 lays down various procedural rules, including the applicable time limits for completing different stages of the proceedings and the potential consequences of failing to comply with the Rules and/or the directions of the Tribunal. The Standard Directions for a Rule K arbitration (which may be varied by the agreement of the parties or at the discretion of the Tribunal), running from the date on which the Tribunal is fully constituted, are as follows:

(a)   within 21 days, the claimant(s) shall serve its (their) points of claim;
(b)   within 42 days, the respondent(s) shall serve its (their) points of defence;
(c)   within 70 days, the parties shall exchange statements of the witnesses they will rely upon;
(d)   within 98 days, the parties shall exchange and serve on the tribunal their written submissions; and
(e)   within 119 days, the hearing shall take place.

28.66   With regard to the possible sanctions for non-compliance with an order or direction of the Tribunal, Rule K4(g) provides that the Tribunal shall have the power, upon application by any party or of its own motion:

(a)   to debar that party from further participation, in whole or in part, in the arbitration; and/or
(b)   to proceed with the arbitration and deliver its award; and/or
(c)   to make such other order as it sees fit.

28.67   Rule K5 sets out the Tribunal's 'General Powers'. There is a long list of general powers, followed by a 'catch-all' provision at (xvii), which provides the power to 'give such other lawful directions as [the Tribunal] shall deem necessary to ensure the expeditious, economical, just and final determination of the dispute'. Rule K5 must, however, be read in conjunction with the 'limited jurisdiction' clause contained in Rule K1(d) (discussed at para **28.58** above).

28.68   Rule K6 imposes a general obligation on the parties to cooperate with each other and the Tribunal, such as is necessary to ensure a 'proper and expeditious conduct of the arbitration'.

28.69   Rule K13 sets down the presumptions for deemed service of documents and Rule K14 confirms that:

(a) English law is the governing law;
(b) the seat of the arbitration shall be England & Wales (unless otherwise agreed between the parties and the Association); and
(c) the arbitration shall be conducted in the English language.

(xi)   Interim applications

28.70   Rule K8 governs the procedure for making an application for interim relief. It begins by stating, in unequivocal terms, that s 44 of the Arbitration Act 1996 (which details the court's powers exercisable in support of arbitral proceedings – including the power to grant interim injunctions) has no application to arbitrations conducted under Rule K.[59] An application for interim relief may be made before or after the Tribunal has been fully constituted. In the former scenario, the procedures detailed in Rule K8(c) shall apply – in essence, Sports Resolutions (UK) will promptly appoint a single arbitrator (who shall be a barrister or solicitor of seven years' or more standing) to hear the application (and referred to as the 'interim tribunal').

28.71   The tribunal or interim tribunal hearing the interim application shall have the powers specified under Rule K5 (General Powers) and Rule K7 (Remedies). One particularly important remedy in this context is the power to 'order a party to do or refrain from doing anything' – in essence, granting an injunction.

28.72   One example of an interim relief application under Rule K8 is *West Ham United FC v The FA*. In this case, following the sending off of striker Andy Carroll in a match against Swansea City (on the ground of violent conduct), West Ham lodged a complaint of 'wrongful dismissal' with an FA Regulatory Commission. By a 2:1 majority, West Ham's complaint was rejected. The effect of this decision was that the player was banned from playing in the club's next three matches, all within about two weeks of the decision. Whilst there is no right under the FA Rules to appeal such a decision, West Ham argued that the Regulatory Commission had applied the wrong test and committed a serious procedural failure by failing to afford the player and club an oral hearing. In the circumstances, West Ham submitted that it was entitled to bring a Rule K arbitration against The FA. Given that the sanction of the Regulatory Commission would have immediate ramifications for the player and the club, West Ham lodged an application for interim relief, requesting that the three-match suspension be stayed pending the outcome of its Rule K challenge. An interim hearing was convened within 24 hours of the application being lodged and the day before the first match of the player's pending suspension.

28.73   The interim tribunal approached West Ham's application in the same way that courts ordinarily approach applications for interim injunctive relief – in essence, by considering whether there was a serious issue to be tried, whether damages were an adequate remedy, and the balance of convenience. Whilst the interim tribunal

---

59   Its application is excluded by Rule K1(e).

accepted that West Ham would suffer significant harm from being deprived of a key player for three matches (and therefore significant prejudice, in the event that the challenged decision turned out to have been wrongly made), it rejected the application for interim relief on the basis that there was no serious prospect that the fully constituted tribunal (to be appointed under FA Rule K in due course) would set aside the decision of The FA Regulatory Commission – in short, there was no 'serious issue to be tried'. In light of the interim tribunal's decision, West Ham were ordered to pay the costs of the interim tribunal and The FA's costs incurred in connection with the interim relief application (pursuant to the interim tribunal's powers specified in Rule K8(vi)–(ix)).

(xii)   Provisional awards

28.74   Rule K9 affords the Tribunal the power to make provisional awards during the proceedings – for example, in respect of costs or a payment on account of the claim.

(xiii)   What is the scope for court intervention in a Rule K arbitration?

28.75   Rule K1(e) is an 'exclusion clause', which provides that the parties to a Rule K arbitration agree to exclude the following provisions of the Arbitration Act 1996:

(a) s 44 – the court's powers exercisable in support of arbitral proceedings (for example powers in respect of evidence, interim injunctions etc) – see above;
(b) s 45 – the court's power to determine a preliminary point of law arising in the course of the arbitral proceedings; and
(c) s 69 – the court's power to consider an appeal against an arbitration award on a point of law.

28.76   Accordingly, by virtue of Rule K1(e), the scope for court intervention in respect of a Rule K arbitration process is particularly limited. With regard to the scope for court intervention in respect of a Rule K final award, see the discussion of Rule K10 below.

(xiv)   Remedies

28.77   With regard to the suite of remedy options at the Tribunal's disposal, Rule K7 provides that the Tribunal shall have the power to do any of the following:

(a) make a declaration as to any matter to be determined in the proceedings;
(b) order the payment of a sum of money;
(c) award simple or compound interest;
(d) order a party to do or refrain from doing anything;
(e) order specific performance of a contract (other than a contract relating to land);
(f) order the rectification, setting aside or cancellation of a deed or other document.

(xv)   The final award

28.78   Rule K10 concerns the making of the final award. It specifies, *inter alia*, that the Tribunal's decision shall be made in writing and, unless all parties otherwise agree in writing, that the Tribunal shall state the reasons for its decision. Where a dispute is resolved by a panel of more than one arbitrator, a majority decision on any issue will suffice; failing a majority decision, the chairman of the Tribunal shall decide that issue.

28.79   Rule K10 further emphasises that any right of appeal against the Tribunal's decision will be strictly confined to the grounds of appeal specified in ss 67 and 68 of the Arbitration Act 1996, namely challenging the Tribunal's substantive jurisdiction (s 67) or challenging the Tribunal's award on the grounds of serious irregularity affecting the Tribunal (s 68). As explained above, the rights of appeal under ss 67 and 68 of the Arbitration Act 1996 are mandatory provisions and parties cannot contract out of them. The threshold for mounting a successful appeal under either of these provisions is, however, a high one; and the leave of the court is required before any appeal will be permitted to proceed (see paras **28.40** and **28.41** above).

(xvi)   Confidentiality

28.80   Rule K11 is a confidentiality provision. The starting point is that the existence and content of the proceedings shall remain confidential as between the parties, unless disclosure is necessary to comply with a legal duty, to protect or pursue a legal right or to enforce an award, or unless the parties have given their prior written consent to disclosure. Another exception to the general rule applies where The FA is a party to the proceedings. In such cases, the general rule is that the award shall be made public, but subject to appropriate redaction to protect third party confidentiality. This presumption in favour of publication may be displaced by the agreement of the parties. Although there is no system of binding precedent in the Rule K arbitration process, the confidentiality of arbitral awards can present a significant impediment for practitioners wishing to advise clients on how arbitration tribunals have tended to approach the same or similar issues in previous cases. One consequence of a party seeking to challenge an award through court process is that the veneer of confidentiality may well be removed. So, in the case of *Pulis v Crystal Palace FC*,[60] Sir Michael Burton decided to deliver his judgment in open court following Mr Pulis's failed s 68 challenge to a previously confidential arbitral award.

(xvii)   Costs

28.81   Rule K12 confers upon the Tribunal the power, but not the obligation, to make a costs award 'against one or more of the parties as it considers appropriate.'

(b)   Arbitration under the FA Premier League Rules

28.82   Section X of the Premier League Rules contains detailed provisions relating to arbitration. Rule X.3 identifies three categories of disputes under the Rules, namely:

(a)   'Disciplinary Disputes' – ie disputes arising from decisions of Commissions or Appeal Boards made pursuant to Rules W.1 to W.83;
(b)   'Board Disputes' – ie disputes arising from the exercise of the Premier League Board's discretion; and
(c)   'other disputes arising from these Rules or otherwise'.

60   Above, n 52.

504 *Arbitration in Football*

28.83   Rule X.2 is formulated in the following terms:

'Membership of the [FA Premier] League shall constitute an agreement in writing between the League and Clubs and between each Club for the purposes of section 5 of the [Arbitration] Act [1996] in the following terms:

X.2.1.   to submit all disputes which arise between them (including in the case of a Relegated Club any dispute between it and a Club or the League, the cause of action of which arose while the Relegated Club was a member of the League), whether arising out of these Rules or otherwise, to final and binding arbitration in accordance with the provisions of the Act and this Section of these Rules;

X.2.2.   that the seat of each such arbitration shall be in England and Wales;

X.2.3.   that the issues in each such arbitration shall be decided in accordance with English law; and

X.2.4.   that no other system or mode of arbitration will be invoked to resolve any such dispute.'

28.84   Rules X.4 and X.5 expressly limit the grounds on which an arbitration tribunal may review a decision of a Disciplinary Commission or Appeal Board, or disputes arising from the exercise of the Premier League Board's discretion. As is the position under Rule K1(d) of the FA Rules, the nature and standard of review in such disputes is similar to that of judicial review, with the Tribunal exercising a supervisory jurisdiction: Rules X.4 permit challenges on grounds of *ultra vires*, irrationality, perversity, error of law and/or serious procedural unfairness.[61]

28.85   With regard to the issue of standing, Rule X.6 provides that 'A Person who is not a party to a Disciplinary Dispute or a Board Dispute may not invoke these arbitration provisions in respect of such a dispute, unless that party can show that they are sufficiently affected by the outcome of the dispute that it is right and proper for them to have standing before the tribunal.'

28.86   The procedures for commencing an arbitration under Section X of the Premier League Rules, appointing an arbitrator(s) and replacing an arbitrator are laid down in Rules X.7–X.16. The Tribunal's general (and wide-ranging) powers are set out in Rule X.21. Rule X.23 specifically confers on the Tribunal the power to make peremptory orders against a party, in the event of non-compliance with a direction of the Tribunal.

28.87   In terms of remedies, Rule X.27 lists the Tribunal's powers as follows:

'The tribunal shall have power to:

X.27.1. determine any question of law or fact arising in the course of the arbitration;

X.27.2. determine any question as to its own jurisdiction;

X.27.3. make a declaration as to any matter to be determined in the proceedings;

X.27.4. order the payment of a sum of money;

X.27.5. award simple or compound interest;

X.27.6. order a party to do or refrain from doing anything;

X.27.7. order specific performance of a contract (other than a contract relating to land);

X.27.8. order the rectification, setting aside or cancellation of a deed or other document.'

28.88   The Tribunal is required to provide its decision in writing, with reasons for its determination (Rule X.32). Rule X.28 states that where the case is determined by a panel of arbitrators, a majority decision will be binding on all panel members;

---

61   See above, n 21.

the Rules expressly preclude a dissenting panel member from producing a dissenting judgment.

28.89   Again, the scope for challenging a decision of the arbitration tribunal in the courts is very limited; Rule X.38 provides that:

> 'Subject to the provisions of Sections 67 to 71 of the [Arbitration] Act [1996], the award shall be final and binding on the parties and there shall be no right of appeal. There shall be no right of appeal on a point of law under Section 69 of the Act …'

28.90   The stipulation that such decisions are 'final and binding' has been interpreted to preclude any further right of appeal to the CAS. In *Ashley Cole v FAPL*,[62] the former England left-back was originally fined £100,000 for his role in the 'tapping up' dispute arising out of his transfer from Arsenal to Chelsea. This fine was reduced on appeal to £75,000, but Cole remained dissatisfied with the outcome and sought to appeal to the CAS. In a preliminary ruling, the CAS concluded that it did not have jurisdiction to hear the dispute and declined to consider the substantive merits of the appeal.

28.91   With regard to disputes between players and their clubs, clause 17 of the standard Premier League Contract (Form 19) provides as follows:

> 'Any dispute between the Club and the Player not provided for in clauses 9, 10, 11, 12 and Schedule 1 hereof shall be referred to arbitration in accordance with the League Rules or (but only if mutually agreed by the Club and the Player) in accordance with the FA Rules.'

28.92   Clauses 9 to 12 of the Premier League Contract, and Schedule 1 thereto (Parts 1 and 2), contain specific provisions regarding the applicable processes and procedures for player grievances, disciplinary action and contract terminations. A player or club who is unhappy with the outcome of an internal disciplinary process or contract termination may refer that matter on appeal to the Board of the Premier League (in accordance with Rule T.28 or T.27, as applicable), and the Board also has jurisdiction under Rule T.31 to consider 'Any dispute or difference between a Club and a Player not otherwise expressly provided for in these Rules.' Rule T.36 provides that a party who is aggrieved with a decision of the Board, taken pursuant to Rule T.30 or T.31, has the right to appeal to the Premier League Appeals Committee (PLAC).

28.93   Section Z of the Premier League Rules includes detailed provisions relating to the jurisdiction of the PLAC, the composition of such committees, and the format and conduct of PLAC proceedings. Among other matters, it is a requirement that PLAC proceedings be conducted in private (Rule Z.18); the PLAC has the 'power to summon any Person to attend the hearing of the proceedings to give evidence and to produce documents' (Rule Z.13); the Chairman has 'an overriding discretion as to the manner in which the hearing of the proceedings shall be conducted' (Rule Z.16); the PLAC is obliged to confirm its decision in writing (with reasons) (Rules Z.20 and Z.21); and the decision of the PLAC 'shall be final and binding' on the parties (Rule Z.22).

28.94   With regard to disputes between Premier League managers and their clubs, Rule P.12 of the Premier League Rules provides as follows:

> 'Any dispute arising between the parties to a Manager's contract with a Club shall be dealt with under the procedures set out in Section Y of these Rules (Managers' Arbitration Tribunal).'

---

62   CAS 2005/A/952.

28.95   Section Y of the Premier League Rules contains some provisions which are specific to the arbitration process for Premier League managerial disputes, albeit Rule Y.21 provides that 'The provisions of Rules X.28 to X.41 inclusive ... shall apply to proceedings of the [Managers' Arbitration] Tribunal.' With regard to the potential remedies in managerial disputes before the Managers' Arbitration Tribunal, Rule Y.20 provides as follows:

> 'Except for the power to order specific performance of a contract, the Tribunal shall have the powers set out in Rule X.27 together with the following additional powers:
>
> Y.20.1. to order the cancellation of the registration of the Manager's contract of employment;
> Y.20.2. to order that the deposit [of £5,000, payable by the party requesting the arbitration] be forfeited by or returned to the party paying it;
> Y.20.3. to make such other order as it thinks fit.'

(c)   Arbitration under Section 9 of the EFL Regulations

28.96   Section 9 of the EFL Regulations is comprised of the arbitration rules for disputes involving EFL clubs. Regulation 91.2 specifies the type of disputes which fall to be resolved under section 9 of the EFL Regulations, providing as follows:

> '91.2   The following disputes fall to be resolved under this Section of the Regulations:
> 91.2.1   disputes arising from a decision of The League or the Board ('Board Disputes');
> 91.2.2   Disciplinary Appeals;
> 91.2.3   'Force Majeure' appeals pursuant to Regulation 12.3 (Sporting Sanction Appeal);
> 91.2.4   applications pursuant to Rule 5 of Appendix 3 (Appeal Application and/or Review Applications under the Owners' and Directors' Test);
> 91.2.5   other disputes between The League and Clubs and between each Club arising from these Regulations or otherwise ("Other Disputes"), unless such disputes were dealt with by way of the following proceedings:
> (a) a Player Related Dispute Commission (or subsequent appeal to the League Appeals Committee (if any)); or
> (b) proceedings before the Professional Football Compensation Committee;
>
> as the decisions of those bodies themselves are deemed to be final with no subsequent right of appeal or challenge.'

28.97   The jurisdiction of the League Arbitration Panel, in terms of its ability to review decisions in a supervisory/judicial review type capacity, or to hear and determine cases on a *de novo* or first instance basis, depends on the nature of the dispute before it, as specified in Regulations 91.3 to 91.6.

28.98   In terms of standing, Regulation 92 confirms that a person who is not a party to a dispute may only invoke the provisions of Section 9 of the EFL Regulations if they 'are sufficiently affected by the outcome of the dispute that it is right and proper for them to have standing before the League Arbitration Panel.'

28.99   Regulation 93 identifies the requirements for commencing an arbitration before the League Arbitration Panel, and Regulation 94 details the rules applicable to the appointment of arbitrators. With regard to the conduct of the proceedings, the procedural rules are set out in Appendix 2 to the EFL Regulations (subject to the proviso that in the event of any conflict between those rules and Section 9 of the EFL Regulations, section 9 shall prevail). The Panel's award is required to be in writing, accompanied by reasons for its decision (Regulation 98.3). Where the case is determined by three arbitrators (which will be the composition of the panel, unless the parties have agreed to the appointment of a sole arbitrator), a majority decision will be binding on all panel members. As is the position under the Premier League Rules, the EFL Regulations expressly preclude a dissenting panel member from producing a dissenting judgment (Regulation 97.1).

28.100 With regard to remedies, the League Arbitration Panel's powers correspond with the potential remedies listed in Rule X.27 of the Premier League Rules (see paragraph 28.87 above). Finally, the scope for appealing a decision of the League Arbitration Panel is again very limited; Regulation 99 provides as follows:

> '99.1   Subject to the provisions of Sections 67 and 68 of the Arbitration Act, the award shall be final and binding and there shall be no right of appeal or further arbitration and the parties exclude irrevocably any right to any other form of appeal, review or recourse in or by a court, judicial authority or other arbitral body, in so far as such waiver may validly be made.
>
> 99.2   For the avoidance of doubt, the exclusion extends to any rights that would otherwise arise under:
> 99.2.1   Sections 44, 45 and 69 of the Arbitration Act; or
> 99.2.2   Rule K of the Football Association Rules (or any replacement provisions of substantially similar effect).'

(d) Alternative dispute resolution

28.101 Whilst not a form of arbitration, it is worth noting that the Independent Football Ombudsman (IFO) provides another form of alternative dispute resolution in the football context. The IFO focuses principally on complaints involving consumer issues – ie where an individual, group of individuals or an organisation feels aggrieved about the goods or services received from a football provider (for example, disputes about tickets or a club's facilities), and the provider has failed to resolve the issue to their satisfaction. If a complaint to the IFO is wholly or partially upheld, the IFO will make recommendations deemed appropriate in the circumstances. Such recommendations are non-binding, but the football authorities have stated that they and their member clubs would normally expect to implement IFO findings. If the respondent to a successful complaint considers that it cannot implement any recommendation of the IFO, it should publish the reasoning behind such a decision and any proposed alternative resolution to the complaint.

D INTERNATIONAL FOOTBALL ARBITRATION

(a) FIFA and UEFA bodies

(i) The judicial bodies of FIFA

28.102 Article 52(1) of the FIFA Statutes identifies FIFA's three 'judicial bodies' as the Disciplinary Committee, the Ethics Committee and the Appeal Committee. The function of the Disciplinary Committee is governed by the FIFA Disciplinary Code, whilst the function of the Ethics Committee is governed by the FIFA Code of Ethics. Pursuant to Article 55(2) of the FIFA Statutes, the Appeal Committee is responsible for hearing appeals against decisions from the Disciplinary Committee and the Ethics Committee that are not declared final by the relevant FIFA regulations. Decisions from the Appeal Committee may be appealed to the CAS.

(ii)   The FIFA Dispute Resolution Chamber and the Players' Status Committee

28.103   Separate from the judicial bodies identified above, the FIFA Dispute Resolution Chamber (DRC) is competent for adjudicating upon employment-related disputes between clubs and players that have an international dimension (including in respect of overdue payables), as well as disputes between clubs related to training compensation and the solidarity mechanism. In terms of the composition of DRC panels in individual disputes, decisions are generally made by a panel of five members, comprised of two player representatives, two club representatives and one chairman.

28.104   The Players' Status Committee (PSC) is responsible for determining the status of players for various FIFA competitions – for example, whether a player satisfies the eligibility criteria to represent a particular country in an international fixture. The most recent set of rules governing the procedures of the PSC and the DRC came into force on 1 January 2017 and are comprised of 21 Articles. A party who is dissatisfied with a decision of the DRC or the PSC may appeal to the CAS.

(iii)   The UEFA Control, Ethics and Disciplinary Body and the UEFA Appeals Body

28.105   The UEFA Control, Ethics and Disciplinary Body has the power to impose bans, fines and other disciplinary sanctions on players, managers and/or clubs who contravene the applicable UEFA rules and regulations. A party who is dissatisfied with the outcome of that process may appeal to the UEFA Appeals Body. If a party is dissatisfied with that decision, there is then a further right of appeal to the CAS. The UEFA rules of procedure are contained within the UEFA Disciplinary Regulations, which are to be read in conjunction with the UEFA Statues.

(b)   The CAS

(i)   The role of the CAS

28.106   In July 2001, the FIFA Congress decided to create an arbitration tribunal for football, and initially opted to establish an entirely independent arbitration tribunal with its own infrastructure and administration – to be known as the 'International Chamber for Football Arbitration'. However, the FIFA administration was unable to deliver such a tribunal (citing the time-consuming nature of the exercise and the limited time available for it) and in September 2002 the FIFA Executive Committee acknowledged that the project was not possible. In need of an alternative solution, FIFA entered into discussion with the International Council of Arbitration for Sport (ICAS) in relation to a possible alternative, which ultimately resulted in an agreement in December 2002 whereby the CAS was granted jurisdiction to settle football-related legal disputes.[63]

---

63   See letter from FIFA to National Associations dated 10 December 2002, titled 'Arbitration Tribunal for Football (TAF) – Court of Arbitration for Sport (CAS)', available at https://resources.fifa.com/mm/document/affederation/administration/tas_827_en_63.pdf (accessed March 2018), and FIFA media release dated 12 December 2002, titled 'Court of Arbitration for Sport (CAS) to settle football-related legal disputes', available at http://www.fifa.com/about-fifa/news/y=2002/m=12/news=court-arbitration-for-sport-cas-settle-football-related-legal-disputes-87198.html (accessed March 2018).

28.107 The current (April 2016) FIFA Statutes recognise the CAS as competent to (i) resolve disputes between participants,[64] and (ii) act as the final appeal body in relation to decisions passed by confederations, member associations or leagues (such as those of the FIFA and UEFA bodies addressed immediately above).[65] The CAS is therefore the 'supreme court' of football and as such has a central role in the development of the law relating to football and seeking to ensure consistency of approach across the worldwide game.

28.108 However, the CAS cannot hear cases until any internal remedies have been exhausted and it is also not competent to hear any appeal cases arising from (i) violations of the Laws of the Game, or (ii) suspensions of up to four matches or up to three months (with the exception of anti-doping decisions). Further, under the FIFA Statutes, tribunals recognised by an association or confederation can (to the exclusion of the CAS) determine (i) disputes between participants, and (ii) appeals from disciplinary/regulatory decisions. Most notably in the context of this chapter, this is the case in relation to FA Rule K tribunals, which are competent to determine both (i) disputes between participants in English football, and (ii) legal challenges to the decisions of FA Appeal Boards (again, with the exception of anti-doping decisions).[66]

28.109 The role and procedures of the CAS is considered in depth in Chapter 29, International Disputes and the CAS.

(ii) Challenges to CAS arbitration (the Pechstein litigation)

28.110 As already noted in this chapter, an agreement to arbitrate will not be constituted unless there is consent by and between the parties to that agreement. However, where arbitration is mandated by the rules of a sport governing body, there is a question as to whether participants (and particularly individual participants) can be said to have provided effective consent.

28.111 This was the fundamental question in the long-running *Pechstein* litigation, which may be summarised briefly as follows. Claudia Pechstein is a highly decorated German speedskater (with multiple Olympic and World titles to her name) who was banned for two years by the International Skating Union (ISU) after a blood test showed unusually high levels of red blood cells, indicative of doping. Ms Pechstein challenged the ban before the CAS but was unsuccessful.[67] She then twice challenged the CAS Award before the Swiss Federal Tribunal (the CAS having its arbitral seat in Switzerland), but again she was unsuccessful.[68]

28.112 Ms Pechstein also issued a claim in the German courts ie her home courts, suing the ISU and the German Skating Federation for damages. At first instance, the local Court of Munich found both that (i) the arbitration clause in Ms Pechstein's

64 FIFA Statutes, Article 57.
65 FIFA Statutes, Article 58.
66 Appeals relating to anti-doping decisions under The FA's Anti-Doping Regulations may be appealed to CAS by FIFA and WADA (see Regulations 76–78 of The FA's Anti-Doping Regulations, at pp 249–250 of The FA Handbook 2017–2018).
67 CAS 2009/A/1912 *Claudia Pechstein v International Skating Union*; CAS 2009/A/1913 *Deutsche Eisschnelllauf Gemeinschaft eV v International Skating Union*, Court of Arbitration for Sport, 25 November 2009.
68 *Claudia Pechstein v International Skating Union*, 4A_612/2009, First Civil Law Court, 10 February 2010, *Claudia Pechstein v International Skating Union (ISU)*, 4A_144/2010, First Civil Law Court, 28 September 2010.

licence with the ISU and German Skating Federation was void, owing to the fact that it had been forced upon her – ie because if she wanted to compete, she had no option but to agree to the arbitration clause, and (ii) CAS arbitration did not satisfy all the requirements of Article 6 of the European Convention on Human Rights (the right to a fair and public hearing within a reasonable time by an independent and impartial tribunal established by law) owing to the way in which arbitrators were appointed and institutional bias in favour of sports federations. However, the court found that Ms Pechstein was nonetheless bound by the CAS Award, owing to the fact that she had never raised any objection to the arbitration process (including the competence and impartiality of the panel) at the time, and the court was precluded from reconsidering the decision pursuant to the *res judicata* doctrine.

28.113   Ms Pechstein then appealed her claim to the Munich Higher Regional Court, which concluded that owing to the particular nature of international sports competitions and the disputes arising therefrom, there was nothing unlawful *per se* about sports federations requiring athletes to sign, as a condition of eligibility to compete in its competitions, an agreement to refer disputes to arbitration. However, it also concluded that the CAS Award amounted to a violation of German anti-trust/ competition law, which prohibits the abuse of a dominant position (or monopoly) in a particular market. It was therefore unenforceable as being contrary to German public policy.

28.114   The Munich Higher Regional Court's conclusion on anti-trust/competition law was based – among other points – on the following:

(a) whilst there was no identification of actual bias on the part of the Arbitral Panel appointed to hear Ms Pechstein's appeal before the CAS, the composition and structure of the ICAS – the body which is responsible for establishing the approved list of CAS arbitrators – was weighted heavily in favour of sports federations, which in turn fundamentally undermined the neutrality of the CAS itself;

(b) the resulting structural imbalance (for which there was no rational justification and which was not ameliorated by the fact that many representatives of governing bodies are former athletes) gave rise to a risk that the arbitrators appointed to determine individual disputes at the CAS would (or may) have a tendency to favour the governing bodies, rather than acting in a wholly neutral, objective and independent manner;

(c) further, there was a lack of transparency in the method of appointing the Chairman of a CAS panel, which again gave rise to legitimate concerns regarding the objectivity and impartiality of CAS panels (in general); and

(d) having regard to the above points, an exclusive arbitration clause in favour of the CAS would not, under normal circumstances in a competitive market, be freely entered into by participants such as Ms Pechstein.

28.115   However, the Munich Higher Regional Court's decision was then itself overturned by way of appeal to the German Federal Tribunal,[69] which held (in summary) that:

(a) the CAS is a genuine court of arbitration within the meaning of the applicable German Code on Civil Procedure – in particular, it is an 'independent' and 'neutral' tribunal;

(b) whilst the ISU's effective monopoly on organising and allowing athletes' participation in its competitions does constitute a dominant position, for the

69   German Federal Court of Justice, judgement of 7 June 2016 – KZR 6/15.

purpose of applicable anti-trust/competition law, the imposition of a requirement that athletes agree to submit to arbitration, as a condition of participating in its competitions (in accordance with the World Anti-Doping Code), did not constitute an abuse of that dominant position vis-à-vis Ms Pechstein;

(c) as a general principle, there were sufficient guarantees in the CAS rules to protect the rights of athletes (including Ms Pechstein);

(d) there was no evidence of any actual bias or partiality in the CAS proceedings involving Ms Pechstein; and

(e) there is common interest between governing bodies and athletes in the fight against doping.

28.116 The ultimate result of the Pechstein litigation – assuming there are no further twists and turns – no doubt came as a very significant relief to the ICAS, the CAS, and sport governing bodies generally. However, regardless of the fact that Ms Pechstein was ultimately unsuccessful, her case provoked much discussion and has served to intensify the scrutiny of the way in which the CAS and the ICAS (and by extension domestic tribunals) are structured and operate, and potential areas of reform.

28.117 Once the German Federal Tribunal's decision was known, the CAS responded by publishing a statement in which it stated that, whilst the decision was a 'ratification of the current CAS system', the CAS would 'continue to listen and analyse the requests and suggestions of its users, as well as of judges and legal experts in order to continue its development, to improve and evolve with changes in international sport and best practices in international arbitration law with appropriate reforms.'[70] FIFPro – the worldwide representative body for professional footballers (which has expressed concerns about the CAS since the CAS's creation and supported Ms Pechstein in her legal battle) – responded to the decision by calling on the CAS and other sport stakeholders to work with player and athlete unions to ensure a proper structural representation and absolute impartiality of its tribunals and administrations.[71]

28.118 The applicability of competition law principles to sports federations and their governing rules and regulations was recently reaffirmed by the European Commission, which concluded that ISU Eligibility rules imposing severe penalties on athletes participating in speed skating competitions *not* authorised by the ISU are in breach of EU antitrust law.[72] Interestingly, whilst the Commission did not conclude that the Appeals Arbitration rules (which grant exclusive jurisdiction to the CAS regarding appeals against eligibility decisions affecting skaters and officials) constituted a breach of the athletes' right to a fair hearing, when viewed in combination with the Eligibility rules, they did "reinforce the restriction of their commercial freedom and the foreclosure of ISU's potential competitors."[73] In the

---

70 See 'Statement of the Court of Arbitration for Sport (CAS) on the decision made by the German Federal Tribunal (Bundesgerichtschof) in the case between Claudia Pechstein and the International Skating Union', dated 7 June 2016 available at http://www.tas-cas.org/fileadmin/user_upload/ Media_Release_Pechstein_07.06.16_English_.pdf. As to suggestions in relation to reform of the CAS system, see De Marco, N., 'Compelled Consent – Pechstein & the Dichotomy and Future of Sports Arbitration', dated 4 July 2016, available at https://www.blackstonechambers.com/news/ analysis-compelled_consent_/.

71 See FIFpro statement, 'Despite decision, Pechstein must trigger reform', dated 7 June 2016, available at https://www.fifpro.org/news/despite-decision-pechstein-must-trigger-reform/en/.

72 Case AT.40208, dated 8 December 2017 and published on 23 March 2017, available at http:// ec.europa.eu/competition/antitrust/cases/dec_docs/40208/40208_1384_5.pdf.

73 See above, n 71, at paragraph 286.

Commission's view, "The hurdles that the Appeals Arbitration rules impose on athletes in obtaining effective judicial protection against potentially anti-competitive ineligibility decisions of the ISU reinforce the restriction of their commercial freedom and the foreclosure of third party organisers of speed skating events since those rules protect potentially anti-competitive decisions issued under the Eligibility rules by curtailing the reach of Union and EEA competition law to those decisions."[74]

28.119 The legal issues surrounding 'compelled consent' have historically been – and in all likelihood will continue to be – fertile ground for legal challenge (by athletes/players in particular). Whilst such challenges are perhaps to an extent inevitable (given the high stakes for the individuals involved), the risks of such challenges being successful can be mitigated by governing body and arbitration service providers actively monitoring their arbitration processes to ensure that they conform to prevailing best practice. There is no necessary tension between the desirability of having a universal approach to dispute resolution in sport through arbitration on the one hand, and ensuring that athletes are treated with fairness on the other.

---

74 See above, n 71, at paragraph 6.

CHAPTER 29

International Disputes and the CAS

Mark Hovell (Mills & Reeve)

A INTRODUCTION

29.1   The *Bosman*[1] decision changed football in a way that no other case before it or since has. Many see that decision as the start of player rights or the start of the modern transfer system, but it also set football down the Alternative Dispute Resolution path that has led it to the doors of the Court of Arbitration for Sport (CAS).

29.2   One of the key principles of the agreement that was eventually reached between FIFA, UEFA, FIFPro and the European Commission in March 2001 was 'to provide for an appropriate dispute resolution system inside the football structures, without prejudice to the right of any player or club to seek redress before a civil court for employment related disputes'.[2]

29.3   FIFA took this agreement and codified it within the FIFA Statutes at Article 68.2: 'recourse to ordinary courts of law is prohibited unless specifically provided for in the FIFA Regulations'.

29.4   Additionally at Article 4.2 of the same Statutes: 'FIFA shall provide the necessary institutional means to resolve any dispute that may arise between Members, Confederations, clubs Officials and players.'

29.5   This all resulted in FIFA establishing its own internal chambers to resolve disputes between those bodies. In 2002 it created its Dispute Resolution Chamber (DRC), the Players' Status Committee (PSC) with both bodies also having single judges ('Single Judge' or 'DRC judge') as well.

29.6   At the end of 2002, FIFA recognised the CAS as the appeal body for decisions from the DRC, the PSC or the Single Judges.[3]

---

1   See Case C-415/93: *Union Royale Belge des Sociétés de Football Association ASBL v Jean-Marc Bosman, Royal Club Liégeois SA v Jean-Marc Bosman and Others and Union des Associations Européennes de Football (UEFA) v Jean-Marc Bosman* [1995] ECR I-4921.
2   See Joint Statement by Commissioners Monti, Reding and Diamantopoulou and Presidents of Fifa Blatter and of Uefa Johansson [2001] European Commission Press Release IP/01/209.
3   See FIFA Circular No 827 dated 10 December 2002.

29.7   It was recognised that an independent and impartial appeal body was required, and one that was sports-specific. Arbitration was favoured over the court system, as it is perceived to be cheaper, faster and sector-specific.

29.8   In furtherance of the principle agreed with the European Commission, FIFA were looking for football disputes to be judged by experts and for the judging body to produce a line of jurisprudence which would create consistent practices within football going forward.

29.9   The CAS was already long established and whilst FIFA had considered establishing its own football court of appeal, it eventually decided to utilise the services of the CAS. FIFA did express some concerns that CAS would require more football sector arbitrators. As a result a number of new arbitrators joined the CAS closed list in 2002 as the footballing stakeholders such as the confederations, the federations and FIFPro all nominated arbitrators with that football-specific experience and the CAS established its 'football list'.

29.10   In the 15 or so years following, the CAS has dealt with thousands of football disputes and, as the game continues to grow, there are no signs of the workload reducing.

B   BRIEF HISTORY OF THE CAS

29.11   The CAS had been long established by the time FIFA determined to amend its Statutes and Regulations and to direct appeals from its internal legal chambers to the CAS.

29.12   A Court of Arbitration was first considered by the International Olympic Committee (IOC) President Juan Antonio Samaranch in the early 1980s. His idea was to create a sports-specific arbitration centre. The IOC established a taskforce in 1982 to prepare the constitution of what would eventually be the Court of Arbitration for Sport headed by the IOC member, HE Judge Kéba Mbaye, himself a judge at the International Court of Justice in The Hague. In its early days the CAS was not the mandatory home for international sports disputes, rather an arbitral institution that was available to settle international disputes if the parties wished to submit their disputes to that body. It was seen as a limb of the IOC, however, and the IOC bore all the operating costs for the court.

29.13   As the CAS developed its members were appointed by the IOC, International Federations and the National Olympic Committees. The IOC President had the ability to choose a quarter of the members from outside of those three groups too.

29.14   By the 1990s, the CAS published its first Guide to Arbitration and encouraged international federations to give jurisdiction to the CAS to settle its disputes. The CAS was still heavily reliant on the IOC and this did lead some to question its independence. Over the years there have been a succession of cases where the CAS's independence has been challenged, starting with Elmar Gundel's appeal to the Swiss Federal Tribunal (SFT). Mr Gundel was appealing the outcome of an Award rendered by the CAS in 1992[4] and he claimed that the CAS did not meet the conditions of impartiality and independence which were required for any arbitration body.

---

4   See CAS 92/A/63 *Elmar Gundel v FEI*.

29.15 In 1993 the SFT handed down its rulings[5] recognising the CAS as a 'true court of arbitration'. The SFT noted that the CAS was independent of the FEI (the respondent to Mr Gundel); however, it also made reference to the fact that the CAS was almost totally funded by the IOC and should the IOC be a party to any proceedings before it then perhaps the outcome of its decision would be different.

29.16 The CAS reacted to this decision by making certain reforms in 1994. The largest one was the creation of the International Council of Arbitration for Sport (the ICAS) which was established to govern the operations and finances of the CAS. At the same time the CAS was split into two divisions which still exist today, the Ordinary Arbitration Division and the Appeals Arbitration Division. In 1994 the CAS produced the 'Code of Sports-related Arbitration' ('the CAS Code') which despite having being modified a number of times over the years, is still at the heart of the CAS and governs the procedures before it.

29.17 The next major challenge to the independence of this restructured CAS was not until 2013 when Larissa Lazutina and Olga Danilova took their appeal against the CAS award that disqualified them from the Salt Lake City Olympic Winter Games to the SFT.

29.18 The SFT looked at the creation of ICAS and the restructuring of the CAS and concluded that the CAS was not 'the vassal of the IOC' and was sufficiently independent of it.

29.19 In the present day ICAS remains the supreme body of the CAS. It is tasked with safeguarding the independence of the CAS. The ICAS is composed of 20 individuals who are all experts in issues of arbitration and sports law. A number are former athletes themselves.

29.20 The ICAS is responsible for any changes to the CAS Code and two of its members sit as the respective presidents of the Ordinary and Appeals Divisions of the CAS. ICAS is also responsible for appointing the CAS arbitrators and approving the finances of the CAS.

29.21 The members of ICAS are nominated by the IOC, the Association of National Olympic Committees, the International Federations and the athletes' representative bodies. In rough terms two-thirds of the ICAS funding comes from the IOC, the International Federations and the National Olympic Committees. The CAS itself receives funding from ICAS but additionally is no longer totally free to the parties, as is detailed below.

29.22 The latest significant challenge to the independence of the CAS was brought by Claudia Pechstein[6] through the German courts. While a large part of that case focused on the 'forced' arbitration (the practice of including an arbitration clause on the entry form to major games such as the Olympics, whereby any athlete that wishes to compete has to submit any disputes to the CAS) it also considered the structure of ICAS and the CAS again, focusing on the independence and impartiality of the CAS. Pechstein's original case dated back to 2009 and the German appeal courts considered that there had been significant changes to the CAS rules and its structure since that date (predominantly the development of ICAS), which the original decision of the Oberlandesgericht in Munich had not taken into account.

---

5 See Recueil Officiel des Arrêts du Tribunal Fédéral Suisse ATF 119 II 271.
6 See Bundesgerichtshof KZR 6/15 *Deutsche Eisschnelllauf-Gemeinschaft eV & International Skating Union (ISU) v Claudia Pechstein.*

29.23   The CAS has evolved considerably over the first few decades of its existence and these changes will undoubtedly continue as the number of referrals to it every year and its influence on *Lex Sportiva* continue to grow. Indeed the CAS is no longer a one-site arbitration centre in Lausanne (although the majority of the cases are still heard there, at the Château de Béthusy); it now has decentralised offices in Sydney and New York and alternative hearing centres in Shanghai, Abu Dhabi and Kuala Lumpur. Indeed there have been a number of cases in South America, Central America, Africa and other parts of the world where it has made more economic sense for the arbitrators to travel to a hearing at a location which is more convenient for the parties concerned. It truly is a global court of arbitration.

29.24   Additionally the CAS has established 'ad hoc' divisions for major games such as the Olympics (since 1996) and the Commonwealth Games (since 1998). In football, the CAS ad hoc divisions have been established for the UEFA Championships since 2002 and at the FIFA World Cups since 2006.

29.25   The number of cases coming to the CAS has averaged at around 500 for the last few years, with it having dealt with over 5,000 matters by 2016, roughly 80% of which went through the Appeals Division.[7]

29.26   Approximately half of all cases since 2002 have been football-related and heard largely by the 'football list' arbitrators. Football disputes thus dominate the workings of the CAS far more than any other world sport.

29.27   Assisting the Secretary General, Mr Matthieu Reeb, are 12 legally qualified counsels who work with the arbitrators on each of the cases or carry out the scientific research at the CAS. The CAS has developed into one of the biggest and busiest arbitration centres in the world.

C   INTERNATIONAL SPECTRUM: WHO LITIGATES AT THE CAS

29.28   Article R27 of the CAS Code stipulates that the CAS procedural rules apply only when the parties have agreed to refer a sports-related dispute to the CAS. Such reference may arise from an arbitration clause contained in a contract or regulations or by reason of a later arbitration agreement. It is therefore important to understand the dispute mechanisms that exist within the various statutes and regulations in football.

29.29   Within FIFA, the relevant statute is Article 58.1 of the FIFA Statutes which says 'appeals against final decisions passed by FIFA's legal bodies and against decisions passed by confederations, member associations or leagues shall be lodged with CAS within 21 days of notification of the decision in question'. What constitutes a decision is often debated (whether a letter from a Governing Body suffices), as is whether decisions arising from the 'Laws of the Game' or the 'field of play' are appealable or not. It should be noted that the 21-day deadline to file the statement of appeal is not extendable.

29.30   Parties that are not happy with the decision of FIFA's DRC or PSC or indeed a Single Judge, or that are not happy with decisions that have come from the confederations or those national associations that allow it, can then appeal the decision to the CAS.

---

7   See http://www.tas-cas.org/fileadmin/user_upload/CAS_statistics_2016_.pdf (accessed March 2018).

29.31   Before looking at the CAS itself in more detail, it is important to understand how first instance decisions are made.

D   FIFA AND THE CONFEDERATIONS: APPEALS PROCEDURES

29.32   With over 80% of the matters coming before the CAS being in the Appeals Division, it is no surprise that this trend is replicated in football matters. The CAS deals with some appeals from dispute resolution chambers at a national level, some from the confederations (usually arising from their own competitions – so for example appeals coming from UEFA are usually around either the European Championships, the Champions League, the Europa League or breaches of other general regulations such as Anti-Doping Regulations or the Financial Fair Play Regulations and the like) but the majority come from appeals from decisions of FIFA itself. These can be matters where FIFA has adjudicated on disputes between players and clubs, clubs and clubs, players, clubs and agents (in the past) whether it is in relation to contracts of employment, the transfers or loan system, solidarity payments, training compensation, the transfer of minors, the release of players for national teams, players passports, overdue payables, match-fixing, crowd violence, racism, governance, etc. The list goes on. Since 1 April 2015, when FIFA amended its Regulations on Working with Intermediaries, the CAS no longer has jurisdiction for disputes regarding players or clubs against agents. Instead these types of disputes are dealt with domestically or by ordinary arbitration, straight to the CAS.

29.33   FIFA has produced various statutes and regulations over the years, but perhaps the most common one to feature at the Court of Arbitration is the Regulations for the Status and Transfer of Players (FIFA RSTP).

29.34   In line with the accord made with the EU, FIFA does recognise the ability of a player or indeed a club to take its employment-related disputes to the civil courts but otherwise anticipates that it will have jurisdiction for many of these disputes. Depending on the nature of the dispute it will direct the parties to either the DRC or the PSC or indeed to one of the Single Judges. These bodies are different from a CAS Panel in that the members of the PSC or DRC are appointed by the associations, the leagues, the clubs and the players' associations. In a player versus club dispute, for example, an equal number of player representatives and club representatives would sit on the Panel. A chairman from the Executive Committee of FIFA is the final member of the Panel. They do not need to be lawyers and indeed many are not. It is extremely rare for there to be an oral hearing; the disputes are normally dealt with on the papers alone and the operative part of the decision will be issued to the parties first and reasons will be issued only if any of the parties ask for the grounds of the decision to be issued (this must be done within 10 days to comply with FIFA's procedural rules).[8] If the parties do not ask for the grounded decision then the procedure before FIFA becomes final and binding, but is also cost free.

E   DOMESTIC DISPUTES AND JURISDICTION CHALLENGES

29.35   FIFA's competence relates to disputes with an international dimension meaning that the parties are from different countries or member associations. This

---

8   See CAS 2008/A/1708 which demonstrates that if this 10 day window is missed then the operative award will be final and binding upon the parties and the right of appeal to CAS will be lost.

does not mean that decisions from national or domestic bodies cannot be appealed to the CAS, but the route must be within the national association's own regulations or statues. Many national associations have an appeal route to CAS, but many others do not. Indeed in English football there is no appeal from The FA or the leagues to the CAS (save for in doping cases where FIFA or WADA can appeal domestic decisions to the CAS). This was tested in the *Ashley Cole* case[9] which determined that:

> 'In order for the CAS to have jurisdiction to rule on an appeal, article R47 of the Code requires that a direct reference to the CAS be contained in the statutes or regulations of the body whose decision is being appealed against'.

29.36   Additionally, FIFA does not always have competence over disputes that have an international dimension. Pursuant to Article 22b of the FIFA RSTP, if an 'independent arbitration tribunal guaranteeing fair proceedings and respect of the principle of equal representation of players and clubs has been established at a national level' then that independent arbitration tribunal may well seize jurisdiction of an employment-related dispute between a club and a player.

29.37   FIFA has issued some guidance[10] as to what it means by 'fair proceedings'. Effectively the tribunal would have to be independent and impartial, it would also need to respect the principles of a fair hearing and of equal treatment and allow the parties the right to contentious proceedings.

29.38   There have been a number of cases concerning this over the years with the leading case being the *Ashley Cole* case.[11] Players that are playing in a foreign country often prefer to have their disputes heard by FIFA, with an appeal to the CAS. They often perceive that the domestic system may favour the clubs. They may be in a system that has no appeal to the CAS. The *Cole* case does not preclude an overseas player playing in England from looking to take his dispute to FIFA, but he would need to convince FIFA that the leagues or The FA do not offer fair proceedings or that the domestic bodies are not independent.

F   CAS PROCEDURES

(a) Appeals

29.39   The vast majority of disputes that come before the CAS come before the Appeals Division. Typically this means that there has been a first instance decision from a dispute resolution chamber of a sport's governing body, international federation or domestic governing body.

29.40   Perhaps the most important lesson to learn for anybody coming to the CAS is that the time limit to appeal (ie to file the statement of appeal with the CAS Court Office), which is typically found in the statutes or regulations of the body that has issued the first instance decision, is to be respected. Pursuant to Article R32 of the CAS Code, no extensions can be granted. It is obviously therefore very important to make sure that the correct number of days are taken into account. If there is a 21-day limit and that expires on a bank holiday or non-working day then it is the next working day that counts. Many a CAS case has ended before it has even begun when a party has missed the initial deadline.

---

9   See CAS 2005/A/952 *Ashley Cole v Football Association Premier League (FAPL)*.
10   See FIFA Circular No 1010 dated 20 December 2005.
11   See CAS 2005/A/952 *Ashley Cole v Football Association Premier League (FAPL)*.

29.41   It is also important for a party that anticipates being a respondent but is not entirely happy with the underlying decision either to consider whether or not it wishes to appeal that decision. If that party is broadly in acceptance with the first instance decision then it may wait to see whether its opponent decides to appeal the decision or not and then it would be the respondent. However, respondents are not able to include counterclaims in their answer[12] and if that party feels that it would want to challenge the underlying decision itself, then it must bring its own appeal too. For example, there may be a breach of contract case between a player and a club where the player is in breach and the club claims €1 million before FIFA but are only awarded €750,000. This may be a sum they can live with; however, if the player is going to take the club through an appeal they may well want to claim the €1 million again before CAS. Unless they issue their own separate appeal (which will likely be consolidated with the player's appeal, pursuant to Article R42 of the CAS Code) then they will be left claiming up to the amount that was awarded by FIFA and no more.

29.42   The CAS Code sets out at Article R48 what is required to comprise the Statement of Appeal. As well as proof of payment of the CAS filing fee[13] and a copy of the statute or regulations that provide the route to the CAS, an appellant is expected to clearly identify the respondent (the full name and address are required) and to provide a copy of the appealed decision.

29.43   The choice of arbitrator is also to be made at this initial stage when the statement of appeal goes to the CAS. The arbitrator must be selected from the closed list which is maintained by the CAS. There are approximately 350 arbitrators from 90 different countries all of whom are legally qualified and either involved in sport or the field of arbitration. They are appointed for four-year terms and, unlike the representatives at the DRC and the PSC, they are wholly independent of the stakeholders that may have nominated them. For example, stakeholders like the European Club Association, FIFPro etc will all be able to nominate suitably qualified arbitrators to ICAS but each arbitrator, regardless of how they have come to CAS, will be required to sign a statement confirming their independence of the parties and their willingness to deal with every case subjectively and impartially. The arbitrator is to disclose any relevant information that he or she wishes to bring to the parties' attention and this transparency has improved in recent years.

29.44   It is possible to find a CV or resumé for most of the arbitrators on line and indeed many will have written academic articles and will have sat on previous cases which the parties are able to find and review.

29.45   The respondent has its opportunity to nominate an arbitrator from the list within the following 10 days, pursuant to Article R53 of the CAS Code. If there are multiple appellants or multiple respondents then they will be asked to agree on their nomination. The President of the Appeals Division of the CAS will appoint the President to any CAS Panel. In some instances (usually cost-related) a sole arbitrator may be appointed. This will again be done by the President of the Appeals Division.

29.46   Arbitrators can be challenged pursuant to Article 34 of the CAS Code; however, grounds such as sharing a nationality with one of the parties are unlikely to result in a successful challenge. There have, however, been cases where a perceived

---

12   Article R39 of the CAS Code changed in 2013, removing the ability for respondents to counterclaim.
13   CHF 1,000.

conflict of interest is sufficient to successfully challenge an arbitrator. For example if one of the parties uses a barrister and that barrister appoints a CAS arbitrator who is also from their chambers, then that may well be seen as a conflict of interest.[14] Much as in common law countries we are familiar with judges and barristers from the same chambers being involved in the same matter; internationally, however, many parties struggle to see the difference between barristers and solicitors and would just see two lawyers from the same business entity (a barristers' chambers) and would perceive that there would be the potential for conflict of interest.

29.47   The closed list has led to criticism from time to time where parties would like to be able to select arbitrators outside of that list; however, the aims of the CAS are to bring specialist arbitrators forward for the parties to work with and nominate and to ensure a consistent line of jurisprudence. The closed list has developed somewhat from the early days of CAS when there were only around 60 arbitrators from which to select. There is now approximately six times that number and as the CAS continues to grow the number of arbitrators will likely increase too. The list is reviewed every four years and arbitrators have been removed from the list where ICAS deems it appropriate.

29.48   Finally at the statement of appeal stage, the appellant needs to select in which language it wishes the arbitration to be conducted in accordance with Article R29 of the CAS Code. The official languages of the CAS are French and English but if the parties agree on a different language then that can be the language of the arbitration. There have been cases in Spanish, German and Italian over the years.

29.49   Just after this initial stage the CAS finance director will propose an advance of costs for the parties to share. However, it is quite common now for the respondent to decline to pay its share of the cost leaving the appellant with the decision to either pay the other half of the advance of cost or have its appeal deemed withdrawn in accordance with Article R64.2 of the CAS Code. In reality most appellants pay both shares of the advance of costs and then have to wait for the final outcome to see if the CAS Panel makes a final order which enables them to reclaim some or all of those costs.

29.50   The CAS Code does enable the parties to request provisional and conservatory measures even before the Panel is formed. The most common type of provisional and conservatory measures is for the stay of execution of the first instance decision.

29.51   Ten days after the filing of the appeal, the appellant must file its Appeal Brief with the CAS Court Office. It is in the Brief that the final prayers for relief are made, along with the detailed legal arguments and any evidence adduced. This extends as far as witnesses. Whilst many appellants include signed witness statements at this stage, the CAS Code[15] only requires a short summary of what the witness is anticipated to say. Again, this is a fixed deadline which can only be extended with the agreement of the other parties.

29.52   The respondent then has 20 days (although this time is often allowed to run from the date when the advance of costs has been fully paid) to file its answer.

---

14   See Mavromati and Reeb, *The Code of the Court of Arbitration for Sport: Commentary, Cases and Materials*, 1st Edition (Wolters Kluwer, 2015), pp 169–180.
15   See Article R51 of the CAS Code.

Article R55 of the CAS Code lists the required contents for this defence. In addition to the prayers for relief and arguments, all its evidence must also be included.

29.53 So far as written proceedings go, this can be it. The parties are not allowed to supplement their submissions, alter their prayers for relief or bring new evidence, or even bring such things as written skeleton arguments unless the President of the Panel allows, based on exceptional circumstances.[16]

29.54 The dispute can be dealt with on the papers if the parties want or if the Panel deems itself sufficiently able to dispense with the need for a hearing. There can, of course, be disagreement between the parties. One may want a day in court, the other may want to avoid the expense.

29.55 Any decisions, whether at a hearing or on the papers, require a majority of the arbitrators; however, if all three are in disagreement, the President of the Panel can sign the award alone. The decision is communicated to the parties in the form of a detailed written award. The aim is to complete this within three months of the CAS file being delivered to the Panel.

29.56 The procedure can be expedited (pursuant to Article R44.4 of the CAS Code, but only with the agreement of the parties) and in some instances the Panel will issue an operative award (the bare decision) in advance of the detailed grounds.

(b) Ordinary arbitration

29.57 The Ordinary Division is a little different from the Appeals Division. It tends to deal with contractual disputes and there are rarely the same time limits to commence the arbitration as seen in the Appeals Division. Again the contract or the regulations that have allowed for ordinary arbitration need to be referred to on a case-by-case basis.

29.58 The procedure is also a little different in that there is a request for arbitration and in this the claimant must, pursuant to Article R38 of the CAS Code, set out its prayers for relief, a summary of its legal arguments, include a copy of the arbitration agreement and nominate its arbitrator. Again this must be from the closed list.

29.59 In the response to the request for arbitration the respondent must set out briefly the grounds for its defence, set out its prayers for relief (noting that pursuant to Article R39 of the CAS Code counterclaims are allowed) and raise any jurisdictional challenges. Finally, it will get to appoint its arbitrator from the list.

29.60 Rather than the President of the Ordinary Arbitration Division appointing the President of the Panel, the two arbitrators themselves will agree on the appointment of the president and the parties will be notified. If the parties have agreed to refer the matter to a sole arbitrator, but cannot agree on who to nominate, then the President of the Ordinary Arbitration Division can step in and make the nomination.

29.61 There then will follow a further round of submissions before the parties will follow a similar process to that in appeal disputes of dealing with such matters as disclosure, witness evidence, the hearing etc.

---

16   See Article R56 of the CAS Code.

(c)   The next steps

29.62   Articles R40 through to R46 deal with the procedural steps that the arbitration will follow, largely regardless as to whether it is an Appeal or an ordinary arbitration. Matters such as disclosure, joinder, conciliation and the like are all covered by the CAS Code.

29.63   Over the years the entire CAS procedure has been examined and tested in many cases. Helpfully, the Secretary General at the CAS and a former legal counsel wrote *The Code of the Court of Arbitration for Sport: Commentary, Cases and Materials*.[17] Any practitioner coming to the CAS would be well advised to refer to this book.

(d)   Ad hoc procedures

29.64   As noted above, both UEFA and FIFA have utilised the Ad Hoc Division services of the CAS in recent years at the World Cups and the European Championships. The number of cases that the Ad Hoc Division have had to deal with has been significantly fewer than the Olympic Games and as such typically the games organisers do not ask that a group of arbitrators are present at the games, but rather are on standby and available to fly in to deal with any disputes.

29.65   However a decentralised CAS Court Office will be in the country of the competiton. In addition, the Ad Hoc Division has its own rules which are separate from the CAS Code. Perhaps the most important difference is that any Panel would seek to render a decision within 48 hours of first being charged with an appeal. Clearly legal disputes are a threat to the smooth running of a competition, especially a competition that is televised right across the world. The idea of the Ad Hoc Division is to make quick decisions to enable any appeal to be dealt with fairly and completely, but to ensure that the competition is not unduly interrupted.

29.66   This certainly demonstrates one of the key benefits of arbitration as opposed to the civil courts. The sheer speed with which effective decision-making can take place is incredibly impressive.

(e)   Mediation

29.67   The CAS runs a mediation service and will direct all parties to this when the CAS Court Office initiates correspondence with them following the commencement of an arbitration.

29.68   Any mediation is governed by a separate set of rules, the CAS Mediation Rules. As with all mediation, it is a non-binding and informal procedure, where the parties attempt to negotiate in good faith with each other, with the assistance of a CAS mediator. Again there is a closed list from which to select, with a specialist football list.

29.69   A successful settlement may result in the arbitration being withdrawn or the parties requesting that the settlement forms part of a Consent Award, which the arbitrators can produce.

---

17   See Mavromati and Reeb, *The Code of the Court of Arbitration for Sport: Commentary, Cases and Materials* (1st edn, Wolters Kluwer, 2015).

(f)   Pre-claim considerations

29.70   Having explained how and when a statement of appeal should be submitted, it will be noted that any appellant has to work extremely quickly to satisfy all the requirements under the CAS Code. That said, after a decision is made and before a statement of appeal is submitted, there are a number of key considerations that a potential appellant or claimant would be well advised to consider.

29.71   First, does the appellant have standing to bring an appeal?; and secondly who would be the appropriate respondent to bring such an appeal against? Whilst this may seem obvious, it is not always as clear as it looks. An interesting example of having the standing to sue was seen in the *Suarez* biting case.[18] In that case, the Spanish player Suarez bit the Italian player Chiellini during the World Cup in Brazil in 2014. The full extent of the incident was not seen by the referee and as such this opened the door for FIFA to charge the player under its regulations for a number of disciplinary matters. This was not a typical field of play incident. Suarez ended up receiving a four-month ban from all footballing activities which he duly appealed to the CAS. In the intervening time between the FIFA decision and the appeal being made to the CAS, the player moved from Liverpool FC to FC Barcelona. As such Barcelona had not been a party to the original FIFA decision but nevertheless the CAS Panel said it had standing to appeal that decision as it was now sufficiently affected by the decision; being Suarez's employer it would face the loss of the use of his services if the FIFA ban was to be upheld by a CAS Panel.

29.72   A far more common consideration is whether the parties that are being brought in as respondents actually have standing to be sued. There are many academic articles on the standing to be sued[19] which should be considered. An example of when this becomes relevant would be when there is a breach of contract case between a player and a club where the player walks out on his first club only to sign with another club. If FIFA were to decide that the player had just cause to walk out on that contract then the old club would have no entitlement to damages nor would the player or the new club face the risk of any sporting sanctions. The old club may not be happy with that decision and may then bring an appeal to CAS. It is not uncommon for the appellant in such instances to not only ask for a finding that the player did not have just cause but also to ask for compensation;[20] and then to ask for the new club to be joint and severally liable[21] to pay such compensation and finally to ask that both the player and the new club are issued with sporting sanctions (for the player between four to six months out of the game and for the new club a two transfer window ban).[22]

29.73   In such a case there are both 'horizontal' and 'vertical' disputes at play. The horizontal dispute is the dispute between a club and a fellow club and a player,

---

18   See CAS 2014/A/3665 *Luis Suarez v FIFA*; CAS 2014/A/3666 *FC Barcelona v FIFA*; and CAS 2014/A/3667 *Uruguayan Football Association v FIFA*.

19   Haas, 'Standing to Appeal and Standing to be Sued' (2016) Association of Swiss Lawyers and the CAS joint conference; Valloni and Pachmann, *Sportrecht: in a nutshell* (Dike, 2012) 11; Fenners, *Der Ausschluss der staatlichen Gerichtsbarkeit im organisierten Sport* (Schulthess, 2006), p 213; Heini, Portmann and Seemann, *Grundriss des Vereinsrechts* (Helbing Lichtenhahn, 2009), p 228; Schütz, *Decision-Making and Appeals against Resolutions of (Sports) Associations* (Helbing Lichtenhahn Verlag, 2016), p 307; Bernasconi and Huber, *Die Anfechtung von Vereinsbeschlüssen: Zur Frage der Gültigkeit statutarischer Fristbestimmungen* (SpuRt, 2004), p 268; Mavromati and Reeb, *The Code of the Court of Arbitration for Sport: Commentary, Cases and Materials* (Wolters Kluwer, 2015), p 68.

20   See FIFA Regulations on the Status and Transfer of Players (RSTP), Article 17.1.

21   RSTP, Article 17.2.

22   RSTP, Article 17.4.

based on the breach of contract claim. The vertical dispute would be between FIFA itself and that player and the new club, based on FIFA's ability to discipline clubs and players that breach contracts within the protected period. If the appellant has requested the CAS Panel to consider all of the factors ie the horizontal and the vertical disputes with its prayers for relief, then it must bring FIFA into the case as well as the player and the new club.[23]

29.74   Equally critical is that the CAS actually has jurisdiction to deal with the appeal. As has been mentioned above, the CAS does not automatically have jurisdiction of every single international dispute in football. In addition to there being an actual right within the statutory regulations or some contract that contained the arbitration clause that is necessary to give CAS jurisdiction, it is also critically important to note that for appeals under Article R47 of the CAS Code that all internal avenues have been exhausted before coming to the CAS.[24]

29.75   Every single case that comes to the CAS requires the Panel to consider whether it has jurisdiction to hear the claims and whether or not such claims are admissible. Again there have been numerous academic papers on the same which should be considered by any potential appellant or claimant coming to the CAS.[25] It is not uncommon for a party to request that the Panel determines any jurisdictional issues before it considers the merits of a claim.

29.76   Finally, it is important that any appellant coming to the CAS states its position on the applicable law. For appeal cases, Article R58 of the CAS Code says a Panel is to apply the regulations of the body that has given the first instance body and subsidiarily the law chosen by the parties. This, in itself, is often debated by scholars and practitioners: is the law in a contract between them any chosen law or is it Swiss law, as the governing body (usually FIFA) has its seat in Switzerland, as does the CAS, to where the parties have agreed to take their dispute? In football, it is a little clearer, as the FIFA Statutes themselves refer to the application of the Regulations of FIFA being the applicable law and if there is any lacuna or gap in such ones then Swiss law would apply, subsidiarily.

29.77   It is important that the parties recognise that Swiss law is likely to dictate procedural and substantive law issues. So for example if there was a penalty clause in a contract or liquidated damages clause then whilst common lawyers may be expecting it to be struck out if it is not a genuine pre-estimate of damages, Swiss law applies,[26] then the Panel will simply reduce the penalty so it is no longer excessive.

29.78   However, if a contract is subject to a law of a particular country (so for example Russian employment law) then that may well be taken into account by the Panel when interpreting any clause within the contract. Again this whole area has been the subject of many an academic paper.

---

23   See CAS 2007/A/1329 *Chiapas FC v Criciuma Esporte Clube*; CAS 2007/A/1330 *Chiapas FC v R*; CAS 2014/A/3489 *Sociedade Esportiva Palmeiras v David F. and Panathinaikos FC*; and CAS 2014/A/3490 *Panathinaikos FC v Sociedade Esportiva Palmeiras, David F. and FIFA*; also CAS 2014/A/3690 *Wisla Kraków SA v Tsvetan Genkov*.

24   See CAS 2004/A/748 *Russian Olympic Committee & Viatcheslav Ekimov v International Olympic Committee, United States Olympic Committee & Tyler Hamilton*; also CAS 2008/A/1705 *Grasshopper v Alianza Lima*.

25   Fumagalli, 'Review of CAS jurisprudence regarding jurisdiction and admissibility' (2016) CAS Bulletin.

26   See Article 163(3) of the Swiss Code of Obligations.

29.79 In summary before any claim is brought to the CAS it is absolutely imperative that the lawyers fully consider all these issues and fully consider whether or not they have the necessary expertise to advise on them all. These days many international law firms will work collaboratively with Swiss lawyers where Swiss law is going to be an important factor in the case at hand.

29.80 Arbitration is supposed to provide a quicker resolution than the courts, but time may well be of the essence for some cases. Expediting a procedure can result in a decision in a number of days. For example, where a confederation has an important draw to make for its cup competitions and there is a dispute between it and a club it has perhaps expelled, that issue needs resolving quickly.[27]

29.81 However, if both parties do not agree to expedite,[28] then that process is not available. The party that wanted the expedited procedure can still nominate an arbitrator that is able to work quickly, can ask the CAS to do so too, can request that any hearing is made by a certain date and can ask for an operative award, but none of that would stop the other party from filing at the last minute and looking to generally slow down the process.

29.82 As mentioned above, the CAS Code does allow for requests for provisional and conservatory measures to be considered from an early stage.[29] Even if the Panel has not been constituted, the President of the relevant CAS Division is empowered to grant these. The most common request will be for a stay of the appealed decision (although this is not appropriate when the decision is purely financial). Any party making such a request has to satisfy the Panel on three issues – that it will suffer irreparable harm should the request not be granted, that there is a likelihood that it will ultimately be successful on the merits when heard by the Panel, and that its interests outweigh the respondent's.

(g) Up to the hearing

29.83 It is anticipated that the majority of the evidence that the appellant wishes to rely upon should be included in the appeal brief. Indeed, only in exceptional circumstances[30] is it possible for later evidence to be adduced. Evidence also includes witness evidence, albeit there is no actual requirement for witness statements unless the Panel orders the same. Rather the Code requires a summary of what a witness is likely to say.[31] This can be rather surprising to a common law lawyer who would anticipate detailed witness statements to be submitted duly signed by the witness. With only a brief summary attached to the appeal brief, the appellant does have the ability to surprise the respondent a little bit at any hearing with what a witness may say in detail under examination. The same is of course true for respondents, as they may only include a brief summary for their witnesses in their answer.

29.84 Expert evidence is becoming more and more common at the CAS: sometimes forensic experts dealing with matters such as forgeries and deleted emails

---

27 See CAS 2013/A/3256 *Fenerbahçe Spor Kulübü v UEFA*; CAS 2016/A/4492 *Galatasaray v UEFA*.
28 See Articles R44.4 and R52 of the CAS Code.
29 See Article R37 of the CAS Code.
30 See Article R44.1 of the CAS Code.
31 See Article R44.1 of the CAS Code.

and the like; often now financial experts such as accountants for financial fair play cases. Clearly with doping cases the use of medical experts has been longstanding. With the importance of Swiss law in many cases, parties often bring either an expert witness specialising in Swiss law or, more usually, collaborate with a Swiss lawyer in their legal team.

29.85   It is not uncommon for a party to make disclosure requests within their submissions and the Panel have to give these due consideration in accordance with article R44.3 of the CAS Code. The nature of arbitral proceedings tends to be quicker and therefore a full-blown disclosure exercise such as one may see before common law courts is not the usual practice at the CAS. Certainly any 'fishing exercise' will see the disclosure request denied.

29.86   What is becoming more common these days is the use of a *Redfern* schedule by CAS Panels which involves the arbitrators asking the appellant and the respondent certain questions in writing. On the appellant's side it is for a description of what documents they are seeking, why each is likely to exist and how its existence is known about, then to explain the relevance of each document. That information is provided to the respondent, who is then asked whether the documents exist and whether they are in the respondent's possession; then to produce the document or give the reasons why it will not. Thereafter the Panel will decide whether or not to order disclosure.

29.87   What is important to note is that the CAS Panel pursuant to Article R57 of the CAS Code have *de novo* powers. This means the Panel has 'full power to review the facts and the law' so that they can hear the case afresh or send the matter back to the first instance body if they so wish. This is important for the parties, as the first instance procedure (such as at FIFA) may have been on the papers alone.

29.88   These powers are not without limits. If in the Appeals Division something new is being requested before CAS that was not requested at first instance it is unlikely that the CAS Panel will entertain such a request.[32] However, if the claim remains the same but the amount increases or decreases, then it is likely that the appellant's prayers for relief will be accepted.

29.89   Of late there has been a number of Article R57.3 of the CAS Code cases where evidence has been brought before the CAS Panel that was not brought before the first instance body. The CAS Panel does have the discretion to disregard such evidence if it sees fit, but there tends to be a requirement of bad faith by the party bringing the evidence only on appeal for the Panel to exercise this discretion.[33]

29.90   The Panel can order, in appeal cases, a second round of submissions, otherwise, pursuant to Article R56 of the CAS Code, nothing more is expected after the answer has been filed. If a disclosure exercise does reveal additional issues that need addressing, then the Panel may well allow a second round. Where the parties agree that no hearing is necessary, the Panel may direct a second round of submissions and ask the parties to address some specific points on which it requires to hear them. The respondent has the last word, pursuant to Article R44.2.1 of the CAS Code.

---

32   See CAS 2012/A/2874 *Grzegorz Rasiak v AEL Limassol.*
33   See CAS 2013/A/3237 *Bratislav Ristic v FK Olimpic Sarajevo.*

(h)   The hearing

29.91   As detailed above, the hearing will normally take place in Lausanne, Switzerland. Cost and time constraints may result in witnesses, experts, even the parties and/or their attorneys appearing by video conferencing. The Panel will always prefer to see all these people face-to-face; however, the arbitrators are experienced in running hearings with the aid of technology.

29.92   On the date of the hearing, it is not unusual for parties to try and bring last minute evidence before the Panel. If the other party objects then the Panel must see evidence of exceptional circumstances to allow such late filings on to the CAS file.[34] However, the CAS Code only extends to the filing of late evidence, not the production of jurisprudence on the day. Frequent visitors to the CAS will have access to more CAS jurisprudence than a practitioner who is a first-time visitor. Many Panels these days are wary of one party taking advantage of the other by swamping it with CAS jurisprudence on the day of the hearing and often request that the parties exchange jurisprudence they intend to rely on in advance, usually when the order of procedure is to be signed and returned.

29.93   The hearing itself is normally held at the CAS offices, the Château de Béthusy in Lausanne. However with the number of cases increasing at the level it is currently at (circa 500 cases a year) on some days the CAS Court is full and CAS cases have to be heard in the business centres at various hotels around Lausanne.

29.94   The hearings are recorded and copies of the audio recording are available to the parties. They are rarely public hearings but a detailed award is prepared by the Panel at the end of each hearing and delivered to the parties. Typically these can range from 20 to 100 pages depending on the complexity of the matter and the issues under consideration. The aim of the Panel is to issue its written decision within three months of it receiving the pleadings (so usually the CAS court file is transmitted to the Panel upon receipt of the respondent's answer). In ordinary arbitrations the procedure tends to be a little longer, more like six months.

(i)   Costs

29.95   Aside from appeals against disciplinary sanctions of international sports governing bodies where the procedure is cost free pursuant to Article R65 of the CAS Code, all the procedures at CAS do require an advance of costs to be made by the parties. Depending on the complexity of the case, the amount at stake in financial matters, the number of arbitrators, where they are from, where the hearing will be, how many arbitrators there are, and the like, the advance can be for tens of thousands of Swiss Francs.

29.96   As detailed above, tactically, quite often respondents refuse to pay their share of the advance of costs leaving the claimant or appellant having to advance all these funds. In addition the parties will often use counsel, may well have to travel out to Switzerland and have the expense of staying there for a night or so.

29.97   The prevailing party will normally see its opponent be ordered to pay the costs of the arbitration (the fees of the CAS itself and the fees and expenses of the arbitrators) but CAS Panels only tend to award the prevailing party a token sum

---

34   See Article R44.1 of the CAS Code.

towards their own legal and other expenses (often in the region of CHF 3,000 to 5,000). This of course can give some comfort to a party going into these proceedings that they will not be landed with huge adverse costs where their opponent goes to a large legal firm which turns up to the hearing with three or four lawyers. But on the other side, it means that either win or lose a party will have to pay the vast majority of their own legal costs and other expenses.

29.98   One of the attractions of arbitration as opposed to the court route is that it is supposed to be cheaper. The costs can vary dramatically if the parties consider a number of tactics. It is possible for the parties to agree or to request the Divisional President to appoint a sole arbitrator which can reduce the arbitration costs. It is also possible for the parties to ask if their witnesses and experts (and sometimes even their counsel and themselves) can be heard by the video conferencing. This can of course reduce the potential travel expenses quite significantly. There is also a legal aid system now potentially available for individual applicants.[35] The legal aid can cover the arbitration costs and even make a small contribution towards legal counsel for the appellant or, indeed, find it *pro bono* counsel. There can still be some travel expenses and the like but between these different tactics it is possible in the right circumstances to make the proceedings far more accessible.

(j)   Appeals to the SFT

29.99   As with all litigation, there will be winners and losers. If the CAS decision goes against a party, then it can appeal, but on limited grounds.

29.100   As the CAS has its seat in Switzerland any appeals are governed by Article 190(2) of the Swiss Federal Statute on Private International law.[36] However the grounds for this are extremely limited. There have to be issues regarding the constitution of the CAS Panel; or if the Panel held that it had or did not have jurisdiction by mistake; or if the Panel ruled upon matters that were beyond the claims that the parties actually included in their prayers for relief or if the Panel failed to rule on such claims; if the equality of the parties or their rights to be heard in adversarial proceedings were not respected; or, finally, if any award issued was incompatible with Swiss public policy. Findings of fact and the like are not overturned or necessarily reviewed.

29.101   Over the years the Court of Arbitration has become perhaps almost the best 'client' for the SFT with over 130 cases being referred there by 2016. Only nine appeals have been successful and two were partially upheld.[37]

(k)   Enforcement

29.102   Like most arbitral awards, decisions of CAS Panels can be enforced in national courts using the New York Convention. However, in football, the decisions will be enforced by the national associations, as FIFA has directed all its members to recognise CAS decisions.

29.103   Indeed, FIFA itself tends to enforce such decisions through its Disciplinary Committee. The CAS itself lacks any power to enforce its own decisions.

---

35   See http://www.tas-cas.org/en/arbitration/legal-aid.html (accessed March 2018).
36   See Article 190(2) of the Swiss Federal Statute on Private International Law.
37   See http://www.swissarbitrationdecisions.com/ (accessed March 2018).

G   CAS JURISPRUDENCE

(a)   No binding precedents

29.104   Another important difference from common law principles is that CAS Panels are not bound by decisions of a previous Panel in a previous case. Whilst there is not any principle of binding legal precedents, CAS Panels certainly try to produce consistent jurisprudence and on the whole where they do not follow a previous Panel's decision on similar grounds, then the Panel tends to say why they have not done so.

29.105   Perhaps the best example of this, and indeed the jurisprudence often most relevant to a number of football disputes, relates to breach of contract cases between football players and clubs. This is governed by Article 17 of the FIFA RSTP and CAS Panels have found various different ways of arriving at how to compensate a party who has breached a contract with just cause or who has been injured by the other party breaching a contract without just cause.

(b)   Article 17: *Matuzalem, Webster* and *De Sanctis*

29.106   On the face of it, the issues in Article 17 cases are limited. The concept of what constitutes 'just cause' for the purposes of FIFA RSTP, Article 17 is considered in Chapter 6, Contracts – Players (at paras **6.62–6.67**). In brief, the issues shall be: who breached the contract, did they have just cause and if not, what compensation is due and should sanctions be issued. However, the question of how to calculate compensation for the breach of a playing contract by a player without just cause has been the basis of many legal conferences and academic papers over the years.

29.107   The relevant provision of the FIFA RSTP in this regard is Article 17 para 1, which reads as follows:

> '**Article 17 Consequences of terminating a contract without just cause**
>
> The following provisions apply if a contract is terminated without just cause:
>
> In all cases, the party in breach shall pay compensation. Subject to the provisions of article 20 and Annexe 4 in relation to training compensation, and unless otherwise provided for in the contract, compensation for breach shall be calculated with due consideration for the law of the country concerned, the specificity of sport, and any other objective criteria. These criteria shall include, in particular, the remuneration and other benefits due to the player under the existing contract and/or the new contract, the time remaining on the existing contract up to a maximum of five years, the fees and expenses paid or incurred by the Former Club (amortised over the term of the contract) and whether the contractual breach falls within a protected period.'

29.108   In broad terms there are three methods that have been applied. All three seek to put the injured party back in the position it would have, but for the breach. This is the 'positive interest' principle, as per Swiss law. All three methods compensate the breach in slightly different ways. To examine these, it helps to consider a typical example. Player 1 terminates his contract with Club A (which paid €500,000 a year and had two years left to run) without just cause and then joins Club B, signing a five-year contract on €1 million per year. If player 1 was worth €5 million in the transfer market at the time of the breach with a new club, then what compensation is Club A entitled to?

29.109   The first method of calculation is that from the *Webster* case.[38] This is often referred to as the 'residual value' method, in that the balance of the remuneration of player 1 from the contract with Club A should be the basis of compensation for Club A. So, in the above example, two years at €500,000, totals €1 million. If club A had paid €10 million to transfer player 1 from his previous club and had signed him on a five-year contract, then the unamortised transfer fee would be due too, but we shall assume there was no transfer fee paid. The Panel in *Webster* also determined that any lost transfer value was not claimable by club A.

29.110   The second method was first seen in the *Matuzalem* case.[39] The Panel took the view that the injured club should be put back in the position it would have been if not for the breach of contract. However, as player 1 had left Club A and could not be forced to go back, Club A's loss needed to be assessed in the light of bringing in a replacement player. Club A had not, however, brought a new player in.

29.111   As such, a virtual replacement player needed to be found for Club A. If player 1 is worth €5 million at the time of the breach to sign a five-year contract with Club B, then the transfer fee for his virtual replacement would be €5 million too. If his salary at the Club B is €1 million per year, then this is what Club A would have to pay the virtual replacement player. If there were two years left on the old contract, then the cost (or value of the services) of the virtual replacement player would be two times €1 million; for the transfer fee to acquire him, add two times €1 million to pay his salary, but deduct what Club A saves by not having to pay the salary of player 1 (€1 million over two years), giving compensation of €3 million.

29.112   The third method (the 'actual replacement' method) was applied by the Panel in the *De Sanctis* case.[40] In that case the old club reacted immediately after the breach by stopping another young player's transfer to a third club and bringing in an experienced free agent, with the strategy of starting with the older player, but eventually replacing him with the younger player, in that same position (goalkeeper).

29.113   Adding those facts to the example, Club A was ready to transfer player 2 for €1 million, but stopped that transfer and lost the potential fee; giving player 2 a new contract that was improved by €500,000 a year; and also bringing player 3 and also paying him €500,000 per year.

29.114   The Panel awarded Club A the lost transfer fee and the salary of player 3, the increased salary for player 2, but deducted the saving of player 1's salary, for the two years that the contract with player 1 had to run: in total €2 million.

29.115   As can be seen, the compensation varied between €1 million and 3 million, depending on which method was followed. However, each Panel was applying the criteria in Article 17.1 of the FIFA RSTP and applying the positive interest. The differences are largely due to the wide-ranging wording in that Article and the various

---

38   See CAS 2007/A/1298 *Wigan Athletic FC v Heart of Midlothian*; CAS 2007/A/1299 *Heart of Midlothian v Webster & Wigan Athletic FC*; and CAS 2007/A/1300 *Webster v Heart of Midlothian*.
39   See CAS 2008/A/1519 *FC Shakhtar Donetsk (Ukraine) v Mr. Matuzalem Francelino da Silva (Brazil) & Real Zaragoza SAD (Spain) & FIFA*; and CAS 2008/A/1520 *Mr Matuzalem Francelino da Silva (Brazil) & Real Zaragoza SAD (Spain) v FC Shakhtar Donetsk (Ukraine) & FIFA*.
40   See CAS 2010/A/2145 *Sevilla FC SAD v Udinese Calcio SpA*; CAS 2010/A/2146 *Morgan de Sanctis v Udinese Calcio SpA*; and CAS 2010/A/2147 *Udinese Calcio SpA v Morgan de Sanctis & Sevilla FC*.

criteria contained therein. The CAS Panel in *Matuzalem* considered how to deal with this non-exclusive list of criteria:[41]

> 'The fact that the judging authority when establishing the amount of compensation due has a considerable scope of discretion has been accepted both in doctrine and jurisprudence. Already for this reason, this Panel does not feel itself bound by the alleged existence of an internal 'list' established, apparently – on the basis of what the parties have exposed during the hearing – by some members of the FIFA DRC in order to help the DRC to set some fix, standard amounts when compensation is due. First, it has remained undisputed among the parties that such a "list" is not part of any official FIFA rule or regulation and that it does not have any binding nature. Furthermore, should the DRC have applied in the past such "list", secretly or openly, to establish the amount of compensation in the meaning of art. 17 para. 1 of the FIFA Regulations, this would have been in deviation of the clear mandate given to the judging authority by art. 17 para. 1 FIFA Regulation itself, i.e. to establish on a case-by-case basis the prejudice suffered by a party in case of an unjustified breach or termination of contract, with due consideration of all elements of the case including all the non-exclusive criteria mentioned in art. 17 para. 1 of the FIFA Regulations.'

29.116   Unless the parties have decided to include some form of liquidated damages clause in the contract, there are many factors the Panel has to consider under Article 17, such as the law of the country concerned, the specificity of sport and any other objective criteria. That latter factor is not limited, but includes the salaries under the old and new player contracts, the time left on the old contract, the unamortised transfer and other fees paid for the player by the old club and whether the breach occurred within the protected period or not.

29.117   There is no reference to replacement costs, lost transfer fees or lost opportunities in Article 17 itself, but CAS Panels (in cases such as *Matuzalem*, *Al-Hadary* and *Sion*, to name a few)[42] have determined that this is within 'any other objective criteria', as referred to in Article 17. For lost transfer fees, these are not ruled out in those cases (as they were by the CAS Panel in *Webster*), but a 'logical nexus' is required.

29.118   Typically, players prefer the *Webster* method and clubs the *Matuzalem* method, with the *De Sanctis* method giving perhaps the most accurate calculation, but only ever being applicable when the facts allow. However, it is unlikely that Panels will feel constrained to follow one method over another.

29.119   Consider if player 1 had played the first season for Club A without issue, but a new manager came in who only played him as a reserve, perhaps in the odd cup game for the next two seasons. He wanted to go out on loan, but no club wanted him at that level of wages. Club A could not transfer him either. The wages were an issue. The best offer was another club that would take him on loan, but only pay 50% of the wages. After the third season, player 1 had had enough and walked out on Club A. There was no argument that this was a termination by player 1 without just cause.

29.120   Following the *Webster* method, the compensation would be his wages for the last two years of his old contract ie €1 million. However, following the positive interest method, the virtual replacement would be the fee to bring in a replacement

---

41   See CAS 2008/A/1519 *FC Shakhtar Donetsk (Ukraine) v Mr Matuzalem Francelino da Silva (Brazil) & Real Zaragoza SAD (Spain) & FIFA*; and CAS 2008/A/1520 *Mr Matuzalem Francelino da Silva (Brazil) & Real Zaragoza SAD (Spain) v FC Shakhtar Donetsk (Ukraine) & FIFA*, para 87.

42   See CAS 2009/A/1880 *FC Sion v Fédération Internationale de Football Association (FIFA) & Al-Ahly Sporting Club*; and CAS 2009/A/1881 *Essam El-Hadary v Fédération Internationale de Football Association (FIFA) & Al-Ahly Sporting Club*.

(as Club A tried, but could not sell him, so he had no transfer value); the virtual replacement's wages would be €250,000 a year (what the other club were willing to pay); yet Club A would save €1 million in wages. In total, why would any compensation be payable to Club A? With these facts, player 1 would prefer the *Matuzalem* method.

29.121   Ultimately, each case should be dealt with on its own merits (as the CAS Panel in *Matuzalem* noted, 'on a case-by-case' basis) and each CAS Panel should be free to find the appropriate method, always applying Article 17 of the FIFA RSTP, to find the correct solution for that case, but should always provide reasoning as to which criteria they place the most emphasis on, in order to preserve the line of CAS jurisprudence.[43]

(c)   Availability of CAS cases

29.122   Pursuant to Article R43 of the CAS Code the entire CAS procedure has to remain confidential. However the final award in appeal cases will be made available unless both parties agree that it should be kept confidential, pursuant to Article R59 of the CAS Code. In ordinary arbitrations the situation is somewhat different these will always remain confidential pursuant to Article R43 of the CAS Code, unless the parties agree to make it public.

29.123   As such, it is important to realise that not all CAS awards are to be published. Of those that are not confidential, a proportion of them are published (or summarised in a CAS press release) and the CAS does maintain its online database[44] with a large number of awards.

29.124   In addition the CAS has produced a number of digests of CAS Awards in the past[45] and produces a CAS Bulletin three times a year which identifies the recent key cases and often features academic articles on matters such as admissibility, jurisdiction, applicable law and the like.

29.125   Perhaps the most welcome publication in recent years has been the Commentary produced by Matthieu Reeb and Despina Mavromati, referred to above. This is an extremely detailed piece of work which looks at every procedural aspect involved in taking a case to the CAS with many, many useful citations of the leading cases.

29.126   Finally, it should be noted that the CAS hosts (on its own or with other bodies), or its arbitrators speak at, numerous seminars and conferences around the world each year, which further enables practitioners to familiarise themselves with the jurisprudence of the CAS.

29.127   The fact that not all non-confidential awards are on the database can give an advantage to more experienced practitioners who have looked at their own databases

---

43   See Siekmann, *Introduction to International and European Sports Law* (TMC Asser Press, 2012), pp 269–312; de Wenger, 'De Sanctis and the Article 17: the last of the saga?' (2011) International Sports Law Journal; Czarnota, 'FIFA Transfer Rules and Unilateral Termination Without "Just Cause"' (2013) Berkeley Journal of Entertainment and Sports Law.

44   See http://jurisprudence.tas-cas.org (accessed March 2018).

45   See Reeb, *Digest of CAS Awards 1986–1998* (Kluwer Law International, 1998); Reeb, *Digest of CAS Awards 1998–2000* (Kluwer Law International, 2001); and Reeb, *Digest of CAS Awards 2001–2003* (Kluwer Law International, 2004).

over the years and who are frequently attendees at the CAS. Indeed, bodies such as FIFA, whose internal Chambers' decisions are often at the heart of an appeal, receive all the awards, so have an extensive library of its own. However, if Panels direct that there is an exchange of jurisprudence that is to be used in any hearing and in advance of the hearing, then the element of surprise can be taken away and the parties are on a fairer footing.

H CONCLUSION

29.128 The way sport is continuing to grow, one can only see the workload of the CAS increasing.

29.129 There are plans to either extend the current facilities in Lausanne or to move to new premises which would accommodate additional hearing rooms and the additional counsel and staff that will be required to keep a pace with the number of referrals each year.

29.130 There will doubtless be challenges regarding the structure and independence of the CAS, as we see periodically, but another role of ICAS is to consider improvements to the CAS. Some[46] suggest that the future might be the establishment of domestic CAS's in every country, leaving the CAS to act as the final appeal court, acting with the power of a review, rather than with *de novo* powers.

29.131 This may take some implementation. In England we see Sport Resolutions, which is funded by the government and relatively independent of the sports; however, it is limited to assisting footballing bodies in the selection of some Panel members for The FA and the leagues. By and large in England football disputes are dealt with by the football governing bodies (The FA, the Premier League, the English Football League etc) or by way of private arbitration held under the Rules of The FA (see further, Chapter 28, Arbitration in Football, section C, Arbitration in English Football, paras **28.42–28.101**).

29.132 The CAS has come a long way in 30 years, but it feels like the journey is far from over.

---

46 Besson, McAuliffe and Rigozzi, 'International Sports Arbitration' (2016) European, Middle Eastern and African Arbitration Rev.

Index